FINANCIAL ACCOUNTING

FINANCIAL ACCOUNTING

Second Edition

Michael Jones
University of Bristol

WILEY

Registered office
John Wiley & Sons Ltd, The Atrium, Southern Gate, Chichester, West Sussex, PO19 8SQ, United Kingdom

For details of our global editorial offices, for customer services and for information about how to apply for permission to reuse the copyright material in this book please see our website at www.wiley.com.

Library of Congress Cataloging-in-Publication Data
Jones, Michael, 1953-
Financial accounting / Michael Jones, University of Bristol. — Second edition.
pages cm
Includes index.
ISBN 978-1-119-97715-5 (pbk.)—ISBN 978-1-118-89619-8 1. Accounting. I. Title.
HF5636.J66 2014
657—dc23

2014003209

ISBN 978-1-119-97715-5 (pbk)
ISBN 978-1-118-89619-8 (ebk)
ISBN 978-1-118-89617-4 (ebk)

A catalogue record for this book is available from the British Library.

Set in 10/12pt SabonLTStd-Roman by Thomson Digital, India
Printed and bound in Great Britain by Bell & Bain Ltd, Glasgow

I would like to dedicate this book to the following

people who have made my life richer:

- *My father, Donald, who died in 2003*
- *My mother*
- *My daughter, Katherine*
- *Tony Brinn (in memoriam)*
- *All my friends in Hereford, Cardiff and elsewhere*
- *All my colleagues*
- *And, finally, my past students!*

Contents

About the Author

Michael Jones has taught accounting to both specialists and non-specialists for 33 years, first at Hereford Technical College, then at Portsmouth Polytechnic (now University) and currently at the School of Economics, Finance and Management, University of Bristol. He has taught accounting at all levels from GCSE level, to final-year degree courses, to MBA and MSc courses as well as supervising accounting PhDs. He has published over 140 articles in both professional and academic journals. These articles cover a wide range of topics such as financial accounting, the history of accounting, social and environmental accounting and international accounting. He has also published *Accounting* 3rd edition, *Creative Accounting, Fraud and International Accounting Scandals* and *Management Accounting*, all published by John Wiley and Sons Ltd. The author's main research interest is in financial communication. He was formerly Professor of Financial Reporting at Cardiff Business School and Director of its Financial Reporting and Business Communication Unit. He is currently Professor of Financial Reporting at the School of Economics, Finance and Management, University of Bristol (Head of Department 2009–2014). He is Chair of the British Accounting and Finance Association's Financial Accounting and Reporting Special Interest Group and was Joint Editor of the *British Accounting Review* (2009–2013).

About the Author

About the Book

Background

Accounting is a key aspect of business. All those who work for, or deal with, businesses need to understand accounting. Essentially, understanding accounting is a prerequisite for understanding business. This book aims to introduce students to accounting and provide them with the necessary understanding of the theory and practice of financial and management accounting. The book, therefore, is aimed primarily at students studying accounting for the first time and seeks to be as understandable and readable as possible.

The Market

This book is intended as a primary text for students studying accounting for the first time: either those following an undergraduate degree in a business school or non-business studies students studying an accounting course. Thus, this includes students on both accounting and non-accounting degrees as well as MBA students and MSc students. The book therefore covers, for example, accountants, business, engineers, physicists, hotel and catering, social studies and media-study students. The text aims to produce a self-contained, introductory, one-year course covering the major aspects of accounting. However, it is also designed so that students can progress to more advanced follow-up courses in financial accounting. The text is thus well suited as an introduction for mainstream accounting graduates or MBA and MSc students as a basic text. In particular, MBA and MSc students should find the chapters on creative accounting and international accounting beneficial. The book should be particularly useful in reinforcing the fundamental theory and practice of introductory accounting.

Scope

The book sets down my acquired wisdom (such as it is) over 33 years and interweaves context and technique. It aims to introduce the topic of accounting to students in a student-friendly way. Not only are certain chapters devoted solely to context, but the key to each particular topic is seen as developing the student's understanding of the underlying concepts. This is a novel approach for this type of book.

The book is divided into 14 chapters within two sections. Section A deals with the context and techniques of basic financial accounting and reporting. Then Section B looks at the context of financial accounting and reporting.

Section A: Financial Accounting: The Techniques

In the first section, after introducing the context and background to accounting, the mechanics of financial accounting are explored; for example, bookkeeping and the preparation of financial statements (such as the income statement and statement of financial position). This section is presented using a tried and tested example, which starts from the accounting equation. An income statement and statement of financial position are then prepared. The section continues by explaining the adjustments to financial statements, different enterprises' financial statements, the statement of cash flows statement and the interpretation of accounts.

Section B: Financial Accounting: The Context

The focus in this section is on exploring some wider aspects of external financial reporting. It begins by contextualising financial reporting by looking at the regulatory framework, measurement systems and the annual report. This is followed by an introductory overview of creative accounting and international accounting. This part of the book allows students to appreciate how accounting is rooted in a wider social and international context. Particularly novel is the inclusion of the regulatory framework, corporate governance, international accounting and creative accounting. This material is included to give students a wider appreciation of accounting than is traditionally presented.

Coverage

The issues of double-entry bookkeeping, partnerships, manufacturing accounts, computers, internationalism and the public sector are tricky ones for an introductory text. I include double-entry bookkeeping, but I have tried to introduce a no-frills approach and focus on the essentials. This is because I strongly believe that double-entry bookkeeping is a fundamental stepping stone to understanding accounting. *The book is so designed that it is possible to miss out the detailed explanation of double-entry bookkeeping, but still follow the rest of the textbook*. This book, after much consideration, focuses on three types of business enterprise: sole traders, partnerships and limited companies. These three enterprises comprise the vast bulk of UK businesses. Indeed, according to the Office of National Statistics (2009), in the UK, 59% of enterprises are companies, 24% sole traders and 13% partnerships. The sole trader is the simplest business enterprise. The earlier chapters in Section A, therefore, focus primarily on the sole trader to explain the basics. However, later chapters in Section A are more concerned with companies. A distinction is made throughout the book between the requirements of listed and non-listed companies.

Manufacturing accounts are excluded because I consider them unnecessarily complex for students studying accounting for the first time and also because of their diminishing importance within the UK economy. Indeed, in 2009, only 5% of UK businesses were in production (Office for National Statistics, 2009). The impact of computers on accounting is covered in the text where appropriate. I consider that the widespread use of computers makes it even more important than before to understand the basics of accounting. Although the primary audience for this textbook is likely to be the UK, I have, where possible, attempted to 'internationalise' it. In fact, I have taught international accounting for 16 years. A synthesis of international accounting is thus provided in Chapter 14. However, I have also tried to integrate other international aspects into the book; for instance, drawing on the International Accounting Standards Board's Statement of Principles. Throughout the book, I use IFRS terminology and format. A decision was taken at an early stage to focus on the private sector rather than the public sector. So when the terms company, firm, enterprise and organisation are used, sometimes interchangeably, generally they refer to private sector organisations. There is some coverage of public sector issues, but in general, students interested in this area should refer to a more specialised public sector textbook.

Special Features

A particular effort has been made to make accounting as accessible as possible to students. There are thus several special features in this book which, taken together, distinguish it from other introductory textbooks.

Blend of Theory and Practice

I believe that the key to accounting is understanding. As a result, the text stresses the underlying concepts of accounting and the context within which accounting operates. The book, therefore, blends practice and theory. Worked examples are supplemented by explanation. In addition, the context of accounting is explored. The aim is to contextualise accounting within a wider framework.

Novel Material

There has been a conscious attempt to introduce into the book topics not usually taught at this level; for example, the regulatory framework, corporate governance, creative accounting and international accounting. The regulatory framework is introduced to give students the context within which accounting is based. Corporate governance aims to set accounting within the wider relationship between directors and shareholders. Creative accounting, I have found, is an extremely popular subject with students and demonstrates that accounting is an art rather than a science. It is particularly topical, given the collapse of the US company Enron and other recent accounting scandals such as WorldCom, Xerox and Parmalat. Creative accounting also enables the behavioural aspects of accounting to be explored. International accounting allows students to contextualise UK accounting within a wider international setting. This is increasingly important with the growth in international trade.

Interpretation

I appreciate the need for students to evaluate and interpret material. There is thus a comprehensive chapter on the interpretation of accounts. Equally important, the book strives to emphasise why particular techniques are important.

Readable and Understandable Presentation

Much of my research has been into readable and understandable presentation. At all times, I have strived to achieve this. In particular, I have tried to present complicated materials in a simple way.

Innovative Presentation

I am very keen to focus on effective presentation. This book, therefore, includes many presentational features which aim to enliven the text. Quotations, extracts from newspapers and journals (real-world views), and extracts from annual reports (company cameras) convey the day-to-day relevance of accounting. I also attempt to use realistic examples. This has not, however, always been easy or practical given the introductory nature of the material. In addition, I have attempted to inject some wit and humour into the text through the use of, among other things, cartoons and soundbites. The cartoons, in particular, are designed to present a sideways, irreverent look at accounting which, hopefully, students will find not only entertaining, but also thought-provoking. Finally, I have frequently used boxes and diagrams to simplify and clarify material. Throughout the text there are reflective questions (pauses for thought). These are designed as places where students may pause briefly in their reading of the text to reflect on a particular aspect of accounting or to test their knowledge.

End-of-Chapter Questions and Answers

There are numerous questions and answers at the end of each chapter which test the student's knowledge. These comprise both numerical and discussion questions. The discussion questions are designed for group discussion between lecturer and students. At the end of the book an outline is provided to, at least, the first discussion question of each chapter. This answer provides some outline points for discussion and allows the students to gauge the level and depth of the answers required. However, it should not be taken as exhaustive or prescriptive. The other discussion answers are to be found on the lecturers' area of the website. The answers to the numerical questions are divided roughly in two. Half of the answers are provided at the back of the book for students to practise the techniques and to test themselves. These questions are indicated by the number being in blue. The other numerical answers are to be found on the lecturers' area of the website. A further testbank is also available to lecturers on the website: **www.wiley.com/college/jones**.

Companion Websites

In addition to the supplementary questions, there are Powerpoint slides available on the lecturers' website (visit **www.wiley.com/college/jones**). On the students' website, there are 140 multiple-choice questions (ten for each chapter) as well as 14 additional questions with answers (one for each chapter). The website also houses an impressive range of interactive concept modules that engage students, helping them to master key accounting concepts.

Overall Effect

Taken together, I believe that the blend of theory and practice, focus on readable and understandable presentation, novel material, interpretative stance and innovative presentation make this a distinctive and useful introductory textbook. Hopefully, readers will find it useful and interesting! I have done my best. Enjoy!

Second Edition

The second edition has been extensively updated for new developments in accounting and to better reflect the nature of the book. In particular, it has been comprehensively updated to use IFRS terminology and formats throughout. The main changes are outlined below.

New Developments

Since first publication, the book has been updated to reflect new developments in accounting such as the creation of the new UK Accounting Standards Setting Regime, the creation of limited liability partnerships, the change of certain accounting standards and the evolving nature of the annual report.

International Financial Reporting Standards (IFRS)

The adoption of IFRS by European listed companies from 1st January 2005 has been fully reflected in this book. The book clearly distinguishes between listed companies that follow IFRS and non-listed companies that do not. Following discussions and feedback with UK and international scholars, IFRS terminology is now used consistently throughout this book for sole traders, partnerships and companies. Therefore, for example, as a rule, after much reflection, the term Income Statement replaces Profit and Loss Account, the Statement of Financial Position replaces Balance Sheet and Statement of Cash Flows replaces Cash Flow Statement. In addition, for the elements of the financial statements I also use IFRS terminology, such as revenue for sales, inventory for stock, and trade receivables and trade payables for debtors and creditors, respectively. This new terminology and the new formats have been used consistently throughout the book, including in the management accounting sections for consistency and ease of understanding. This has necessitated a comprehensive rewriting of the book. This has necessitated extensive changes to Chapter 7 on partnerships and limited companies, Chapter 8 on statement of cash flows and Chapter 9 on interpretation of accounts as well as Chapter 14 on international accounting. The updating of the book for IFRS has also enabled the book to be more international in outlook; examples of foreign companies such as Christian Dior, Nokia and Volkswagen have been used.

Updating of Features

Key features of the book such as Real-World Views, Soundbites and Company Cameras have, wherever possible, been updated. Hopefully, these changes have improved the book!

Mike Jones
April 2014

Acknowledgements

In many ways writing a textbook of this nature is a team effort. Throughout the time it has taken to write this book, I have consistently sought the help and advice of others in order to improve it. I am, therefore, extremely grateful to a great number of academic staff and students (no affiliation below) whose comments have helped me to improve this book. I list below colleagues who have commented on earlier versions of my textbooks. I then give a special mention to the individuals who have commented extensively on this edition. The errors, of course, remain mine.

Malcolm Anderson (Cardiff Business School)
Tony Brinn (Cardiff Business School, RIP)
Alex Brown
Peter Chidgey (BDO Binder, Hamlyn)
Mark Clatworthy (Cardiff Business School)
Alpa Dhanani (Cardiff Business School)
Mahmoud Ezzamel (Cardiff Business School)
Charlotte Gladstone-Miller (Portsmouth Business School)
Paul Gordon (Heriot Watt University)
Tony Hines (Portsmouth Business School)
Deborah Holywell
Carolyn Isaaks (Nottingham Trent University)
Tuomas Korppoo
Margaret Lamb (Warwick Business School)
Andrew Lennard (Accounting Standards Board)
Les Lumsdon (Manchester Metropolitan University)
Claire Lutwyche
Louise Macniven (Cardiff Business School)
Neil Marriott (University of Glamorgan/University of Winchester)
Howard Mellett (Cardiff Business School)
Joanne Mitchell
Peter Morgan (Cardiff Business School)
Barry Morse (Cardiff Business School)
Simon Norton (Cardiff Business School)
Phillip O'Regan (Limerick University)
David Parker (Portsmouth Business School)
Roger Pegum (Liverpool John Moores University)
Maurice Pendlebury (Cardiff Business School)
Elaine Porter (Bournemouth University)
Neil Robson (University of the West of England)
Julia Smith (Cardiff Business School)
Aris Solomon (University of Exeter)
Jill Solomon (Cardiff Business School/Kings College, London)

Ricky Tutin (University of Bristol)
Tony Whitford (University of Westminster)
Jason Xiao (Cardiff Business School)

On this edition I would like to thank, in particular:

Matt Bamber (University of Bristol)
Elizabetta Barone (Kings College London/Henley Business School)
Gin Chong (Prairie View/A&M University)
Christopher Coles (Glasgow University)
Wayne Fiddler (University of Huddersfield)
Ioannis Tsalavoutas (University of Stirling)
Richard Tutin (University of Bristol)
Tony Wall (University of Ulster)

This book is hopefully enlivened by many extracts from books, newspapers and annual reports. This material should not be reproduced, copied or transmitted unless written permission is obtained from the original copyright owner. I am, therefore, grateful to all those who kindly granted the publisher permission to reproduce the copyright material. Accordingly, every effort has been made to trace the original copyrighter owners. Thanks to Deloitte, GlaxoSmithKline, Stagecoach Group, News and Media, and I am also grateful to ACCA, Elsevier, CIMA (Chartered Institute of Management Accountants), Fame Database, IASB, IFRS Foundation, John Wiley & Sons Ltd, the *New Scientist*, the Office for National Statistics, Oxford University Press and Pearson.

I should also like to thank Steve Hardman and his team at John Wiley, particularly Juliet Booker, Sarah Booth and Georgia King, for their help and support. Finally, last but certainly not least, I should like to thank Jan Richards for her patience and hard work in turning my generally illegible scribbling into the final manuscript.

Chapter 1

Introduction to accounting

'One way to cheat death is to become an accountant, it seems. The Norfolk accountancy firm W.R. Kewley announces on its website that it was "originally established in 1982 with 2 partners, one of whom died in 1993. After a short break he re-established in 1997, offering a personal service throughout." He was, feedback presumes, dead only for tax purposes.'

New Scientist, 1 April 2000, vol. 166, no. 2232, p. 96. © Reed Business Information Ltd, England. Reproduced by Permission. http:www.newscientist.com/article/mg16622327.100-feedback.html.

Learning Outcomes

After completing this chapter you should be able to:

- Explain the nature and importance of accounting.
- Outline the context which shapes accounting.
- Identify the main users of accounting and discuss their information needs.
- Distinguish between the different types of accountancy and accountant.

Go online to discover the extra features for this chapter at **www.wiley.com/college/jones**

Chapter Summary

- Accounting is the provision of financial information to managers or owners so that they can make business decisions.
- Accounting measures, monitors and controls business activities.
- Financial accounting supplies financial information to external users.
- Users of accounting information include shareholders and managers.
- Accounting theory and practice are affected by history, country, technology and organisation.
- Auditing, bookkeeping, financial accounting, financial management, insolvency, management accounting, taxation and management consultancy are all branches of accountancy.
- Accountants may be members of professional bodies, such as the Institute of Chartered Accountants in England and Wales.
- Although very useful, accounting has several limitations such as its historic nature and its failure to measure the non-financial aspects of business.

Introduction

The key to understanding business is to understand accounting. Accounting is central to the operation of modern business. Accounting enables businesses to keep track of their money. If businesses cannot make enough profit or generate enough cash, they will go bankrupt. Often accounting is called the 'language of business'. It provides a means of effective and understandable business communication. If you understand the language, you will, therefore, understand business. However, like many languages, accounting needs to be learnt. The aim of this book is to teach the language of accounting.

Nature of Accounting

At its simplest, accounting is all about recording, preparing and interpreting business transactions. Accounting provides a key source of information about a business to those who need it, such as managers or owners. This information allows managers to monitor, plan and control the activities of a business. This enables managers to answer key questions such as:

- How much profit have we made?
- Have we enough cash to pay our employees' wages?
- What level of dividends can we pay to our shareholders?
- Should we expand our product range?

PAUSE FOR THOUGHT 1.1

Some Accounting Questions

You are trying to assess the performance of your business, Superco. What are the main accounting questions you would ask?

The principal questions would relate to revenue (sales), assets and profit. They might be:

- How much profit am I making?
- What are the net assets?
- What is the cash flow?
- How much debt do I have?
- What are the prospects for the future?
- What is my revenue?

In small businesses, managers and owners will often be the same people. However, in larger businesses, such as public limited companies, managers and owners will not be the same. Managers will run the companies on behalf of the owners. In such cases, accounting information serves a particularly useful role. Managers supply the owners with financial information in the form of an income statement, a statement of financial position and a statement of cash flows. This enables the owners to see how well the business is performing. In companies, the owners of a business are called the shareholders.

Essentially, therefore, accounting is all about providing financial information to managers and owners so that they can make business decisions (see Definition 1.1). The formal definition (given below), although dating from 1966, has stood the test well as a comprehensive definition of accounting.

DEFINITION 1.1

Accounting

Working definition
The provision of information to managers and owners so that they can make business decisions.

Formal definition
'The process of identifying, measuring and communicating economic information to permit informed judgments and decisions by users of the information.'

Source: American Accounting Association (1966), *Statement of Basic Accounting Theory*, p. 1.

Importance of Accounting

Accounting is essential to the running of any business or organisation. Organisations as diverse as Microsoft, Barclays Bank, General Electric Company, Volkswagen, The Royal Society for the Protection of Birds (RSPB) and Manchester United football club all need to keep a close check on their finances.

At its simplest, money makes the world go round and accounting keeps track of the money. Businesses depend on cash and profit. If businesses do not make enough cash or earn enough profit, they will get into financial difficulties, perhaps even go bankrupt. Accounting provides the framework by which cash and profit can be monitored, planned and controlled. It is useful not only to monitor the activities of a business, but also to plan for the future.

Unless you can understand accounting, you will never understand business. This does not mean everybody has to be an expert accountant. However, it is necessary to know the language of accounting and to be able to interpret accounting numbers. In some respects, there is a similarity between learning to drive a car and learning about accounting. When you are learning to drive a car, you do not need to be a car mechanic. However, you have to understand the car's instruments, such as a speedometer or fuel gauge. Similarly, with accounting, you do not have to be a professional accountant. However, you do need to understand the basic terminology such as income, expenses, profit, assets, liabilities, equity and cash flow.

PAUSE FOR THOUGHT 1.2

Manchester United

What information might the board of directors of Manchester United find useful?

Manchester United is both a football club and a thriving business. Indeed, the two go hand in hand. Playing success generates financial success, and financial success generates playing success. Key issues for Manchester United might be:

- How much in gate receipts will we get from our league matches, cup matches and European fixtures?
- How much can we afford to pay our players?
- How much cash have we available to buy rising new stars and how much will our fading old stars bring us?
- How much will we get from television rights and commercial sponsorship?
- How much do we need to finance new capital expenditure, such as building a new stadium?

Financial Accounting and Management Accounting

There is a basic distinction between financial accounting and management accounting. Financial accounting is concerned with information on a business's performance and is targeted primarily at those outside the business (such as shareholders). However, it is also used internally by managers. By contrast, management accounting is internal to a business and used solely by managers. A brief overview is provided in Figure 1.1.

Figure 1.1 Overview of Financial and Management Accounting

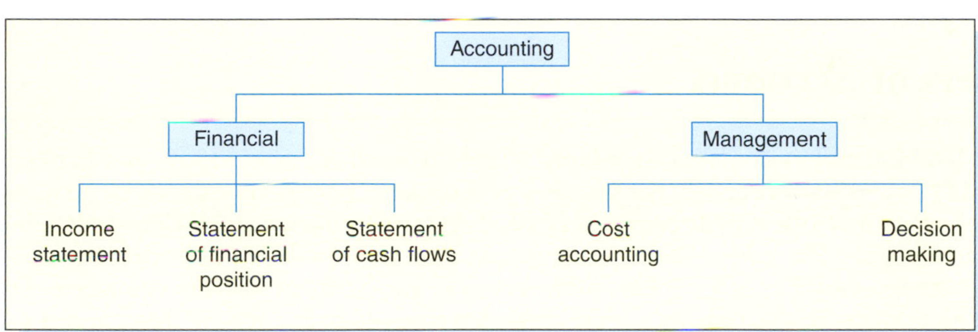

Financial Accounting

Financial accounting is the provision of financial information on a business's recent financial performance targeted at external users, such as shareholders. However, internal users, such as management, may also find it useful. It is required by law. Essentially, it is backward-looking, dealing with past events. Transactions are initially recorded using double-entry bookkeeping (see Chapter 3). Three major financial statements can then be prepared: the income statement, the statement of financial position and the statement of cash flows (see Chapters 4–8). In this book, I primarily use these three terms. They are the terms used by the International Accounting Standards Board (IASB) in International Financial Reporting Standards (IFRS). IFRS are widely used worldwide, for example, by listed companies in Europe (see Chapter 14 for more details). However, there are also often national reporting rules. In the UK, for example, Generally Accepted Accounting Principles (GAAP) are often used by UK non-listed companies. Alternative terminology is used as follows: income statement (alternative: profit and loss account), statement of financial position (alternative: balance sheet) and statement of cash flows (alternative: cash flow statement). These standards are then interpreted using ratios (see Chapter 9) by users such as shareholders and analysts.

SOUNDBITE 1.1

Investment Analysts

'Over-paid, under-qualified and inappropriately influential. That seems to be the conventional view of that rampaging beast, the city analyst.'

Source: Damian Wild, *Accountancy Age*, 21 October 2004, p. 14.

Users of Accounts

The International Accounting Standards Board (covered in more detail in Chapters 10 and 14) now takes a relatively narrow view of the users of accounts, identifying only investors, lenders and other creditors in its 2010 conceptual framework. However, there are in fact many more.The users of accounting information may broadly be divided into insiders and outsiders (see Figure 1.2). The insiders are the management and the employees. However, employees are also outsiders in the sense that they often do not have direct access to the financial information. The primary user groups are management and shareholders. Shareholders or investors are often advised by professional financial analysts who work for stockbrokers or big city investment houses. These financial analysts help to determine the share prices of companies quoted on the stock exchange. However, sometimes, they are viewed with mistrust (see Real-World View 1.1).

Figure 1.2 Main Users of Accounting Information

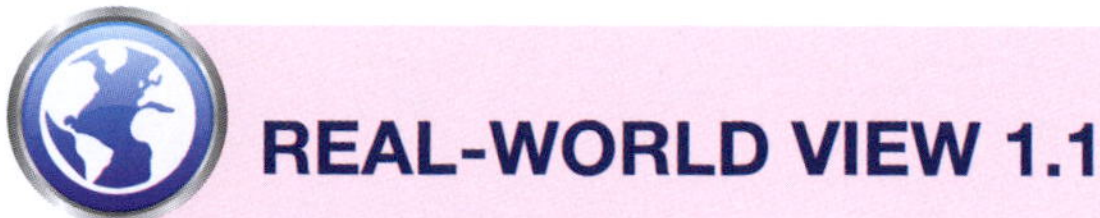

REAL-WORLD VIEW 1.1

Financial Analysts

Working with analysts is a little like being a member of the Magic Circle or the freemasons – those who know how to perform these masterful sleights of hand or arcane rituals are forbidden from ever revealing them to outsiders. Of course, the alternative is that I can't reveal them because I don't understand them myself – I'll let you decide.

Source: James Montier, Showbiz values come to the City, *The Guardian*, 15 January 2000, p. 5. Guardian Newspapers Ltd 2000. Reproduced by permission of James Montier.

The influence of other users (or stakeholders) is growing in importance. Suppliers, customers and lenders have a closer relationship to the company than the government and tax authorities, or the public. These users all need accounting information to help them make business decisions. Usually, the main information requirements concern a company's profits, cash flow, assets and debt (see Figure 1.3).

Figure 1.3 User Information Requirements

User Group	*Possible Information Requirements*
Internal Users	
1. Management	Information for costing, decision making, planning and control.
2. Employees and employee organisations (Trade Unions)	Information about job security and for collective bargaining.
External Users	
1. Shareholders (current and potential)	Information for buying and selling shares.
2. Analysts advisers (brokers, dealers)	Information for buying and selling shares.
3. Lenders (bank, creditors)	Information about assets and the company's cash position.
4. Business contacts	
i. Competitors	i. Information about revenue and profits so they can judge market share.
ii. Suppliers	ii. Information about the company's cash position, to assess whether they will be paid and how long it will take.
iii. Customers	iii. Information about the long-term prospects and survival of the business.
5. Government and agencies (such as tax authorities or government statistical departments)	Information to enable governmental planning. Information primarily on profits to use as a basis for calculating tax.
6. Public (e.g., individual citizens, local communities, educational groups or non-governmental organisations such as Greenpeace)	Information about the social and environmental impact of corporate activities.

Shareholders, for example, require information so that they can decide whether to buy, hold or sell their shares. The information needs of each group differ slightly and, indeed, may conflict (see Pause for Thought 1.3).

PAUSE FOR THOUGHT 1.3

Conflicting Interests of User Groups

Can you think of an example where the interests of users might actually conflict?

A good example would be in the payment of dividends to shareholders. The higher the dividend, the less money is kept in the company to pay employees or suppliers. Another, more subtle, example is the interests of shareholders and analyst advisers. Shareholders own shares. However, they rely on the advice of analyst advisers such as stockbrokers. Their interests may superficially seem the same (e.g., selling underperforming shares and buying good performers). However, the analyst advisers live by the commission they make. It is in their interests to advise shareholders to buy and sell shares. Unfortunately, it costs money to buy and sell shares; therefore, this may not always be in the potential shareholders' best interests. Shareholders' and employees' interests may also conflict in certain circumstances. For instance, in companies with low profits there may not be sufficient money to pay both generous dividends and generous bonuses.

Accounting Context

It is important to realise that accounting is more than just a mere technical subject. Although it is true that at the heart of accounting there are many techniques. For example, as we will see in Chapter 3, double-entry bookkeeping is essential when preparing financial statements. However, accounting is also determined by the context in which it operates. Accounting changes as society changes. Accounting in medieval England and accounting today, for example, are very different. Similarly, there are major differences between accounting in Germany and in the United Kingdom. We can see the importance of context if we look briefly at the effects of history, country, technology and organisation (see Figure 1.4).

Figure 1.4 Importance of Accounting Context

Historical factors

Country factors

Nature of accounting

Organisational factors

Technological factors

History

Accounting is an integral part of human society. Early societies had accounting systems which, although appearing primitive to us today, served their needs adequately. The Incas in South America, for example, used knotted ropes, called quipus, for accounting. In medieval England notched sticks called tally sticks were used to record transactions.

PAUSE FOR THOUGHT 1.4

The Term 'Accounting'

Why is accounting so called?

It is believed that accounting derives from the old thirteenth-century word *aconter*, to count. At its simplest, therefore, accounting means counting. This makes sense as the earliest accountants would have counted sheep or pigs!

Gradually, over time, human society became more sophisticated. A form of accounting called double-entry bookkeeping (every transaction is recorded twice) arose. Emerging from Italy in the fifteenth century, at the same time that Columbus discovered America, double-entry bookkeeping is now the standard way by which accounting transactions are recorded throughout the world.

International Accounting

Double-entry bookkeeping, the income statement (the profit and loss account) and the statement of financial position (balance sheet) are now routine in most major countries. The International Accounting Standards Board (IASB) is also making great efforts to harmonise the disclosure and measurement practices of listed companies worldwide and publishes International Financial Reporting Standards (IFRS). However, there is still great diversity in the broader context in which accounting is carried out. These differences are explained more fully in Chapter 14.

Accounting in the UK, for example, is very different from accounting in France, despite the fact that both countries are members of the European Union. Listed companies in both France and the UK, however, do have to follow IFRS. However, for non-listed companies and other enterprises, the situation is

SOUNDBITE 1.2

'We now operate in a global marketplace, and this is driving the need for universal professional standards and the global qualifications that can deliver them.'

Source: Chris Ward, One World, One Revision, *Accountancy Age*, 11 April 2005, p. 16.

very different. The UK traditionally has been proud of a flexible and self-regulated accounting system largely free of government control. By contrast, the French system has traditionally been very standardised and largely governmentally controlled. In general, as Soundbite 1.2 shows, accounting plays an important role globally.

There are also clear differences between the UK and the US. For example, in the UK, there are Companies Acts, which apply to all UK companies whereas in the US only companies quoted on the stock exchange (i.e., listed companies) are subject to detailed and comprehensive Federal regulations. Also, US listed companies, unlike those in the UK, do not have to comply with IFRS. Unlisted companies are subject only to state regulations, which vary from state to state.

Technology

A rapid change which has affected accounting is computerisation. Up until the advent of computers, accounting was done manually. This was labour-intensive work. Each transaction was entered into the books twice using double-entry bookkeeping. The accounts were then prepared by hand. Similarly, costing, budgeting and decision making were all carried out manually.

Today, almost all businesses use computers. However, they must be used with caution. For the computer, GIGO rules. If you put garbage in, you get garbage out. To avoid GIGO, one needs to understand accounting. In fact, computerisation probably makes it more, rather than less, important to understand the basics.

Organisations

The nature of accounting will vary from business to business. It will depend on the structure of the business and the nature of the business activity.

Structure

If we take the accounts of the three types of business enterprise with which this book deals, a sole trader's accounts will normally be a lot simpler than those of either a partnership or a company. Sole traders, generally run by one person, are smaller, less complicated businesses (for example, a small butcher's shop). Partnerships run by two or more people are multi-owned businesses typically larger in size than sole traders. The sole traders' and partnerships' accounts will normally be less complicated than company accounts as they are prepared for the benefit of active owner-managers rather than for owners who do not actually run the business. Companies are owned by shareholders who own shares in them while managers run the business.

Nature of the Business

Every organisation is different. Consequently, every organisation's accounts will differ in certain respects. For example, property companies will own predominantly more land and buildings than non-property companies. Manufacturing companies will have more inventory than non-manufacturing companies.

It is clear from Figure 1.5 that the nature of revenue or sales varies from business to business. In some businesses, a service is provided (e.g., bank, football club, insurance company and plumber).

Company Snapshot 1.1 shows the sales revenue (sometimes termed turnover) of Manchester United plc, mainly gate receipts, television and merchandising, which is generated by entertaining its customers.

Figure 1.5 Nature of the Revenue

Business	***Nature of Main Revenue***
Bank	Interest received
Football club	Gate receipts
Insurance company	Premiums received
Manufacturing company	Sales of goods to retailers
Plumber	Sales of services and other goods
Shop	Sales of goods to customers

COMPANY SNAPSHOT 1.1

Turnover [i.e., revenue or sales]

Turnover, all of which arises from the Group's principal activity, can be analysed into its main components as follows:

	Year ended 30 June 2010 £'000	Year ended 30 June 2009 £'000
Match Day	100,164	108,799
Media	104,814	99,735
Commercial	81,438	69,942
	286,416	278,476

Turnover, all of which originates in the United Kingdom, can be analysed by destination as follows:

	Year ended 30 June 2010 £'000	Year ended 30 June 2009 £'000
United Kingdom	283,552	272,021
Rest of world – tour income	2,864	6,455
	286,416	278,476

Media income from European cup competitions is distributed by the Football Association and is therefore classified as being of United Kingdom origin and destination.

The Group's activities are managed as one business and, as such, the operating expenses are not separately identifiable to any particular segment. As a result, no segmental analysis of operating performance or net assets is provided.

Source: Manchester United Ltd, *Annual Report and Financial Statements for the Year Ended 30 June 2010*, p. 21.

In other businesses, the sale is more tangible as goods change hands (for example, manufacturing companies and shops).

Overall, within the UK economy, services are becoming relatively more important and manufacturing industry is declining. In particular, there is an increase in information technology and knowledge-based industries. This trend is set to continue.

Types of Accountancy

We need to distinguish between the types of accountancy and the types of accountant. Accountancy refers to the process, while accountant refers to the person. In other words, accountancy is what accountants do! In this book, we primarily focus on bookkeeping and financial accounting. However, accountants perform other roles such as management accounting, auditing, financial management, insolvency, fraud detection, taxation and management consultancy. All of these are briefly covered below. Auditors charge management audit and consultancy fees. For example, KPMG, a firm of auditors, charged HSBC Holdings £24.5 million in 2008 for auditing and £17.2 million for consultancy services. Audit fees are shown for the banking system in the UK in 2008 in Real-World View1.2.

REAL-WORLD VIEW 1.2

Audit Fees

According to *Accountancy's* most recent survey of auditors' fees, the Big Four made £36.4m in non-audit fees and £90.6m in audit fees from their FTSE 100 banking clients last year.

Bank	Auditor	Audit fee (£m)	Related fee (£m)	Other services (£m)
Barclays	PwC	25.0	4.0	15.0
HBOS	KPMG	8.0	1.0	2.4
HSBC	KPMG	24.5	9.8	7.4
Lloyds TSB	PwC	9.3	3.8	1.5
RBS	Deloitte	17.0	4.9	9.3
StanChart	KPMG	6.8	1.5	0.8

Source: Emily Beattie, Don't Bank on it, *Accountancy Magazine*, June 2009, p. 17. Copyright Wolters Kluwer (UK) Ltd.

Auditing

Auditing is carried out by teams of staff headed by qualified accountants who are independent of the business. Essentially, auditors check that the financial statements, prepared by management, give a true and fair view of the accounts. The auditors do not comment on the efficiency of a company and an audit will not necessarily detect fraud or misstatements as the auditors cannot check every single company transaction. Auditing is normally associated with company accounts. However, the tax authorities or the bank may request an audit of the accounts of sole traders or partnerships. For companies, auditors issue an auditors' report annually to shareholders. Company Snapshot 10.1 in Chapter 10 provides an auditors' report for J. Sainsbury plc. An auditors' report is issued after a thorough examination by the auditors of the accounting records and systems of the company.

Bookkeeping

Bookkeeping is the preparation of the basic accounts (bookkeeping is dealt with in more depth in Chapter 3). It involves entering monetary transactions into the books of account. A trial balance is then extracted, and an income statement and statement of financial position are prepared. Nowadays, most companies use computer packages for the basic bookkeeping function, which is often performed by non-qualified accountants.

Financial Accounting

Financial accounting is a wider term than bookkeeping. It deals not only with the mechanistic bookkeeping process, but also with the preparation and interpretation of the financial accounts. For companies, financial accounting also includes the preparation of the annual report (a document sent annually to shareholders, comprising both financial and non-financial information). In orientation, financial accounting is primarily outward-looking and aimed at providing information for external users. However, monthly financial accounts are often prepared and used internally within a business. Within a company, financial accounting is usually carried out by a company's employees. Smaller businesses, such as sole traders, may use professionally qualified independent accountants.

Financial Management

An area of growing importance for accountants is financial management. Some aspects of financial management fall under the general heading of management accounting. Financial management, as its name suggests, is about managing the sources of finance of an organisation. It may, therefore, involve managing the working capital (i.e., short-term assets and liabilities) of a company or finding the cheapest form of borrowing. There is often a separate department of a company called the financial management or treasury department.

Insolvency

One of the main reasons for the rise to prominence of professional accountants in the UK was to wind up failed businesses. This is still part of a professional accountant's role. Professional accounting firms are often called in to manage the affairs of failed businesses, in particular to pay creditors (trade payables or banks) who are owed money by the business.

Management Accounting

Management accounting covers the internal accounting of an organisation. There are several different areas of management accounting: costing, budgeting, standard costing, short-term decision making, strategic management accounting and capital investment appraisal.

Essentially, these activities aim to monitor, control and plan the financial activities of organisations. Management uses such information for decisions such as determining a product's selling price or setting the sales budget.

Fraud Detection

Accountants who detect fraud are often called forensic accountants. The frauds they investigate may be personal or corporate and often involve large amounts of money. Real-World View 1.3 shows an interesting example.

REAL-WORLD VIEW 1.3

Forensic Accounting

Case Study: Lust, Lies and the Law

I was once involved in a divorce case, acting on behalf of the wife. We believed her husband was withholding information about assets, and had not disclosed all of his income (wives tend to remember being told these things). We had to get hold of evidence.

We knew that the husband kept a large number of documents in his garage so, accompanied by the local police, the solicitor and I conducted a 6am visit to his house.

The husband's new girlfriend opened the door. Minutes later, she was replaced by a man carrying a shotgun, which he thrust in my face. Luckily, the local sergeant was quite relaxed and talked the man round by assuring him it wasn't worth killing me as I was, after all, 'only a bean counter'. I found out later that the gun wasn't loaded – it didn't make much difference. The husband had originally made an offer of £1m, but the documents we seized proved that he held a lot of assets in Switzerland. He increased the offer to £2.5m, and eventually paid out a total of £3m.

The final ironic twist in the saga was that he dropped his girlfriend and had an inappropriate affair with his solicitor.

The shotgun man was charged with threatening behaviour with a dangerous weapon. In the long term, it all made me more determined to fight for justice.

Steven Redhead is a member of the ICAEW forensic group, interviewed by Ruth Banks.

Source: Ruth Banks, CSI Accountancy, *Accountancy Magazine*, June 2010, p. 106. Copyright Wolters Kluwer (UK) Ltd.

Taxation

Taxation is a complicated area. Professional accountants advise businesses on a whole range of tax issues. Much of this involves tax planning (i.e., minimising the amount of tax that organisations have to pay by taking full advantage of the often complex tax regulations). Thus, for example, Lisa O'Carroll (*Guardian*, 14 October 2011) commented that it had been calculated that over a three-year period, Google had 'saved $3.1 bn in tax revenues

SOUNDBITE 1.3

Management Consultancy

'[Definition of management consultancy] Telling a company what it should already know.'

The Economist (12 September 1987)

Source: The Wiley Book of Business Quotations (1998), p. 359.

using a subsidiary located in Bermuda where the corporate tax rate is zero'. A Google spokesperson told the *Guardian* 'We have an obligation to our shareholders to set up a tax-efficient structure, and our present structure is compliant with the tax rules in all the countries where we operate.' This tax avoidance which operates within the law should be distinguished from tax evasion which is illegal. Professional accountants may also help individuals with a scourge of modern life, the preparation of their annual income tax assessment.

Management Consultancy

Management consultancy is a lucrative source of income for accountants (see Real-World View 1.4). However, as Soundbite 1.3 shows, management consultants are often viewed cynically. Management consultancy embraces a whole range of activities such as special efficiency audits, feasibility studies and tax advice. Many professional accounting firms now make more money from management consultancy than from auditing. Examples of management consultancy are investigating the feasibility of a new football stadium or the costing of a local authority's school meals proposals.

REAL-WORLD VIEW 1.4

Management Consultancy

To be fair, many of these issues were problems of success. The accountancy industry had kick-started phenomenal growth and change in the management consultancy services it offered its client base. It was natural to sell those services to its existing clients who eagerly purchased the IT, strategy and financial management consultancy on top of the bog-standard audit and tax services. Suddenly audit became the poor relation, both in terms of excitement and financial return. Audit became a commodity and we all know what happens then – the product becomes devalued and the price goes down.

Source: Peter Williams, How the Brits started the Rot, *Accountancy Age*, 11 November 2004, p. 28.

Types of Accountant

There are several types of accountant. In the UK, for example, the most high-profile are those belonging to the six professionally qualified bodies. In addition to these accountancy bodies, there are other accounting associations in the UK, the most important of which is probably the Association of Accounting Technicians. The web addresses for these institutes are listed at the end of the chapter.

Professionally Qualified Accountants

Chartered Accountants

Six institutions of professionally qualified accountants currently operate in the UK (see Figure 1.6). All jealously guard their independence and the many attempts to merge have all failed (see Real-World View 1.5). 'It's like proposing that Manchester United and Manchester City merge, suggests one indignant ICAEW member, illustrating the strength of feeling' (Michelle Perry, *Accountancy Age*, 22 July 2004, p. 6).

Figure 1.6 Main UK Professional Accountancy Bodies

Body	*Main Activities*
Institute of Chartered Accountants in England and Wales (ICAEW)	Generally auditing, financial accounting, management consultancy, insolvency and tax advice. However, many work in industry.
Chartered Accountants Ireland (CAI)	Similar to ICAEW.
Institute of Chartered Accountants of Scotland (ICAS)	Similar to ICAEW.
Association of Chartered Certified Accountants (ACCA)	Auditing, financial accounting, insolvency, management consultancy and tax advice. Many train or work in industry.
Chartered Institute of Management Accountants (CIMA)	Management accounting.
Chartered Institute of Public Finance and Accounting (CIPFA)	Accounting within the public sector and privatised industries.

REAL-WORLD VIEW 1.5

Professional Accountancy Bodies

There have been several attempts to persuade the UK's accountancy bodies to merge over the past few years, all without much success. Six accountancy bodies is rather a lot and the government understandably gets exasperated from time to time by six (and sometimes seven) different responses to a consultation paper. But the bodies' members have consistently refused merger initiatives, always citing differing training requirements as a major consideration – and not without justification.

Source: Elizabeth Mackay, Big Five Pressure Gets Results, *Accountancy Age*, 9 March 2000, p. 18.

There are three institutes of chartered accountants: the Institute of Chartered Accountants in England and Wales (ICAEW), the Chartered Accountants Ireland (CAI) and the Institute of Chartered Accountants of Scotland (ICAS). The largest of these three is the ICAEW. Its members were once mainly financial accountants and auditors, but now take part in a whole range of activities. Many leave the professional partnerships with which they train to join business organisations. In fact, qualifying as a chartered accountant is often seen as a route into a business career.

Association of Chartered Certified Accountants (ACCA)

The ACCA's members are not so easy to pigeonhole as the other professionally qualified accountants. They work both in public practice as auditors and as financial accountants. They also have an enormous number of overseas students. Many certified accountants train for their qualification in industry and never work in public practice. The ACCA qualification is very popular overseas.

Chartered Institute of Management Accountants (CIMA)

This is an important body whose members generally train and work in industry. They are found in almost every industry, ranging, for example, from coal mining to computing. They mainly perform the management accounting function.

Chartered Institute of Public Finance and Accountancy (CIPFA)

This institute is smaller than the ICAEW, ACCA or CIMA. It is also much more specialised with its members typically working in the public sector or the newly privatised industries, such as Railtrack. CIPFA members perform a wide range of financial activities within these organisations, such as budgeting in local government.

Second-Tier Bodies

The main second-tier body in the UK is the Association of Accounting Technicians. This body was set up by the major professional accountancy bodies. Accounting technicians help professional accountants, often doing the more routine bookkeeping and costing activities. Many accounting technicians go on to qualify as professional accountants. The different accountancy bodies, therefore, all perform different functions. Some work in companies, some in professional accountancy practices, some in the public sector. This diversity is highlighted in an original way in Real-World View 1.6.

REAL-WORLD VIEW 1.6

A Sideways Look at the Accounting Profession

Thus, to take parallels from the religious world, we have:

- **the lay priest:** the accountant working for a company;
- **the mendicant priest:** the professional accountant in a partnership;
- **the monastic priest:** the banker, who, while not strictly an accountant, serves much the same ends in a separate and semi-isolated unit;
- **the father confessor:** the auditing accountant to whom everything is (officially) revealed, and who then grants absolution.

Source: Graham Cleverly (1971), *Managers and Magic*, Longman Group Ltd, London, p. 47.

Limitations of Accounting

Accounting, therefore, measures business transactions in numerical terms. It thus provides useful information for managers and other users of accounts. It is, however, important to appreciate certain limitations of accounting. First, accounting tends to measure the cost of past expenditures rather than the current value of assets. There have been attempts to introduce 'fair value' or 'market prices' in some cases. However, this then brings in a great deal of subjectivity into accounting. This is dealt with in more detail in Chapter 11. Second, traditional accounting does not capture non-financial aspects of business. Thus, if an industry pollutes the air or the water, this is not recorded in the conventional accounts. Nor does traditional accounting measure the human resources of a business or its knowledge and skills base. The accounts can, thus, only give a partial picture of a business's activities.

SOUNDBITE 1.4

Limitations of Traditional Accounts

'Non-financial items like business opportunities, management strategies and risks have a big effect on company performance and need to be reflected in company reports.'

Mike Starr, Chairman of American Institute of Certified Public Accountants. Committee on Enhanced Business Reporting.

Source: Nicholas Neveling, Consortium Urges Reporting Reforms, *Accountancy Age*, 17 February 2005, p. 11.

Conclusion

Accounting is a key business activity. It provides information about a business so that managers or owners (for example, shareholders) can make business decisions. Accounting provides the framework by which cash and profit can be monitored and controlled. A basic distinction is between financial accounting (accounting targeted primarily at those outside the business, but also useful to managers) and management accounting (providing information solely to managers).

Accounting changes as society changes. In particular, it is contingent upon history, country, technology and the nature and type of the organisation. There are at least eight groups which use accounting information, the main ones being managers and shareholders. These user groups require information about, amongst other things, profits, cash flow, assets and debts. There are several types of accountancy and accountant. The types of accountancy include auditing, bookkeeping, financial accounting, financial management, insolvency, management accounting, taxation and management consultancy. The six UK professional accountancy bodies are the Association of Chartered Certified Accountants, the Chartered Institute of Management Accountants, the Chartered Institute of Public Finance and Accountancy, and the Institute of Chartered Accountants in England and Wales, the Institute of Chartered Accountants in Ireland and the Institute of Chartered Accountants of Scotland. Although very useful, accounting has certain limitations; for example, its historic nature and its failure to measure non-financial transactions.

Websites

A list of useful websites is included below for students interested in a career in accounting and who wish to find out more information.

i) Accountancy Institutes

Association of Chartered Certified Accountants (ACCA)
www.accaglobal.com

Chartered Institute of Management Accountants (CIMA)
www.cimaglobal.com

Chartered Institute of Public Finance and Accounting (CIPFA)
www.cipfa.org.uk

Institute of Chartered Accountants in England and Wales (ICAEW)
www.icaew.co.uk

Chartered Accountants in Ireland (CAI)
www.chartered accountants.ie

Institute of Chartered Accountants of Scotland (ICAS)
www.icas.org.uk

Association of Accounting Technicians (AAT)
www.aat.co.uk

ii) Accounting Firms

PriceWaterhouseCoopers
www.pwcglobal.com

Ernst & Young
www.ey.com

KPMG
www.kpmg.com

Deloitte
www.deloitte.com

Discussion Questions

Questions with numbers in blue have answers at the back of the book.

Q1 What is the importance, if any, of accounting?

Q2 Can you think of three business decisions for which managers would need accounting information?

Q3 What do you consider to be the main differences between financial and management accounting?

Q4 Discuss the idea that as society changes so does accounting.

Q5 'Managers should only supply financial information to the "current" shareholders of companies; no other user groups have any rights at all to information, particularly not the general public or government.' Discuss.

Go online to discover the extra features for this chapter at
www.wiley.com/college/jones

SECTION A

Financial Accounting: The Techniques

In this section, we look at the accounting techniques which underpin the preparation and interpretation of the financial statements. Chapter 2 sets the scene for this section, explaining the essential background. It deals with the nature and importance of financial accounting and introduces some of the basic concepts and terminology.

In these initial chapters, we focus primarily on the financial statements of the sole trader as these are the most straightforward. In Chapter 3, the key accounting techniques of the accounting equation, double-entry bookkeeping and the trial balance are introduced. The double-entry section of this chapter is *self-contained and can be passed over by those students not wishing to study bookkeeping in depth*. In Chapters 4 and 5, the essential nature, function and contents of the income statement and statement of financial position are discussed. This will enable students more fully to appreciate the importance of the income statement and statement of financial position before their preparation from the trial balance is explained in Chapter 6. In Chapter 7, we prepare the income statement and statement of financial position (balance sheet) of partnerships and limited companies. The final two chapters look at the statement of cash flows (Chapter 8) and the interpretation of accounts (Chapter 9) primarily from the perspective of limited companies. The statement of cash flows is the third most important financial statement for a company. Finally, in Chapter 9 we look at 16 ratios commonly used to assess an organisation's performance.

Chapter 2

The accounting background

'Living up to his reputation, he brooks no nonsense, adds no frills. A murmured thank you to the chair, then: "Let us never forget that we are all of us in business for one thing only. To make a profit." The hush breaks, the apprehension goes. Audibly, feet slide forward and chairs ease back. Orthodoxy has been established. The incantation has been spoken. No one is going to be forced to query the framework of his world, to face the terrible question, why?'

Graham Cleverly, *Managers and Magic* (1971), Longman, pp. 25–6.

Learning Outcomes

After completing this chapter you should be able to:

- Explain the nature of financial accounting.
- Appreciate the basic language of accounting.
- Identify the major accounting conventions and concepts.

Go online to discover the extra features for this chapter at
www.wiley.com/college/jones

Chapter Summary

- Financial accounting is about providing users with financial information so that they can make decisions.
- Key accounting terminology includes income, expenses, equity or capital, assets and liabilities.
- The three major financial statements are the income statement (also known as the profit and loss account), statement of financial position (also known as the balance sheet) and statement of cash flows (also known as the cash flow statement).
- The most widely agreed objective is to provide information for decision making.
- The most important external users for companies are the shareholders.
- Four major accounting conventions are entity, money measurement, historic cost and periodicity.
- Three major accounting concepts are going concern, accruals and consistency.
- Prudence is a fourth much-disputed accounting concept.

Introduction

Financial accounting is the process by which financial information is prepared and then communicated to the users. It is a key element in modern business. For limited companies, it enables the shareholders to receive from the managers an annual set of accounts which has been independently checked by auditors. For sole traders and partnerships, it allows the tax authorities to have a set of accounts which is often prepared by independent accountants. There are thus three parties to the production and dissemination of the financial accounts: the preparers, the users and the independent accountants. The broad objective of financial accounting is to provide information for decision making. Its preparation is governed by basic underpinning principles called accounting conventions and accounting concepts.

Financial Accounting

Once a year, company shareholders receive through the post an annual report containing the company's annual accounts. These comprise the key financial statements as well as other financial and non-financial information. Sole traders and partnerships annually prepare a set of financial statements for the tax authorities. Managers will also use these financial statements to evaluate the performance of the business over the past year. The whole process is underpinned by a set of overarching accounting principles (i.e., accounting conventions and accounting concepts) and by detailed accounting measurement and disclosure rules. Essentially, financial accounting is concerned with providing financial information to users so that they can make decisions. Definition 2.1 provides a more formal definition from the International Accounting Standards Board (a regulatory body which seeks to set accounting standards which will be used worldwide) applicable to all commercial, industrial and business reporting enterprises as well as a fuller definition from the Chartered Institute of Management Accountants.

DEFINITION 2.1

Financial Accounting

Working definition

The provision of financial information to users for decision making.

Formal definitions

'The objective of general purpose financial reporting is to provide financial information about the reporting entity that is useful to existing and potential investors, lenders and other creditors in making decisions about providing resources to the entity. Those decisions involve buying, selling or holding equity and debt instruments, and providing or settling loans and other forms of credit.'

Source: International Accounting Standards Board (2010), *The Conceptual Framework for Financial Reporting*.

'Classification and recording of the monetary transactions of an entity in accordance with established concepts, principles, accounting standards and legal requirements and their presentation, by means of income statements, balance sheets [statements of financial position] and cash flow statements [statements of cash flows], during and at the end of an accounting period.'

Source: Chartered Institute of Management Accountants (2005), *Official Terminology*. Reproduced by Permission of Elsevier.

SOUNDBITE 2.1

Money

'Money never meant anything to us. It was just sort of how we kept the score.'

Nelson Bunker Hunt, *Great Business Quotations*, R. Barron and J. Fisk

Source: The Book of Business Quotations (1991), p. 155.

Financial accounting meets the common needs of a wide range of users. It does not, however, provide all the information users may need. An important additional role of financial accounting is that it shows the stewardship of management (i.e., how successfully they run the company). Shareholders may use this information to decide whether or not to sell their shares.

At a still broader level, accounting allows managers to assess their organisation's performance. It is a way of seeing how well they have done or, as Soundbite 2.1 shows, of keeping the score. The main financial statements for sole traders, partnerships and companies are the income statement (profit and loss account) and the statement of financial position (balance sheet). These contain details of income, expenses, assets, liabilities and equity or capital. For companies (and often for other businesses), these two statements are accompanied by a statement of cash flows (cash flow statement), which summarises a company's cash flows. Generally, the principal user is assumed to be the shareholder. These three statements are sent to shareholders once a year in a document called an annual report. However, managers need more detailed and more frequent information to run a company effectively. Monthly accounts and accounts for different parts of the business are, therefore, often drawn up.

PAUSE FOR THOUGHT 2.1

Annual Financial Accounts

Why do sole traders, partnerships and limited companies produce financial accounts?

There are several reasons. First, those running the business wish to assess their own performance and regular, periodic accounts are a good way to do this. Second, businesses may need to provide third parties with financial information. In the case of sole traders and partnerships, the tax authorities need to assess the business's profits. Bankers may also want regular financial statements if they have loaned money. Similarly, companies are accountable not only to their shareholders, but to other users of accounts.

Language of Accounting

Accounting is a language. As with all languages, it is important to understand the basics. Five basic accounting terms (income, expenses, assets, liabilities and equity or capital) are introduced here as well as the three main financial statements: the income statement (the profit and loss account), the statement of financial position (balance sheet) and the statement of cash flows (cash flow statement). These concepts are explained more fully later in the book.

Income

Income is essentially the revenue earned by a business. Sales revenue is a good example. Income is income, even if goods and services have been delivered but customers have not yet paid. Income thus differs from cash received. Revenues are closely watched by analysts. Deloitte, a leading professional accountancy firm, for example, analyses football sales annually. An extract from its 2009/10 analysis is given in Real-World View 2.1.

REAL-WORLD VIEW 2.1

Europe's Premier Leagues

- Despite significant economic headwinds, the European football market grew by 4% to €16.3 billion in 2009/10.
- The 'big five' leagues' revenues grew by 5% to €8.4 billion, with all five leagues demonstrating revenue growth. Broadcasting revenue was the main driver of growth (up 8%) and now stands at over €4 billion.
- The Premier League increased its revenue to almost €2.5 billion in 2009/10. The gap to the second highest revenue generating league, the Bundesliga, now exceeds €800m.
- The Bundesliga's revenue grew 6% to €1,664m, driven by an impressive increase in commercial revenues, and the largest average attendance (42,700) in European football.

Source: Deloitte (13 June 2011) as reproduced in www.accountacyageinsight.com/abstract/football-finance-highlights.

Expenses

Expenses are the costs incurred in running a business. Examples are telephone, business rates and wages. The nature of expenses varies from business to business. Real-World View 2.2 shows that the biggest expense for football clubs is their wages. Expenses are expenses, even if goods and services have been consumed but the business has still not paid for them. Expenses are, therefore, different from cash paid.

REAL-WORLD VIEW 2.2

Football Club Expenses

It takes a lot to convince a former Conservative cabinet minister that wage caps are necessary. Yet that is the impact football had on our former chairman, Lord Mawhinney.

Instinctively, I don't believe in salary controls. It is all a little bit too 'Soviet' for my liking. But as far as league football is concerned, it looks like being a necessary evil.

It is necessary because people leave their business brains behind when they enter the emotionally charged world of football. Clubs are chasing a dream – they all want to gain promotion or win something for their fans. In doing so, the usual rules of business go out the window.

REAL-WORLD VIEW 2.2 (*continued*)

At the Football League, we spend a great deal of time devising ways of protecting clubs from themselves.

....

In the Championship during the 2007/08 season, the ratio of total wages against turnover was between 58% and 124%, averaging at 87%, up from 79% in the previous year. Last season's figures are expected to be even higher. It should be, at worst, between 60% and 70%.

Indeed, player wages in the 2008/09 tax year totalled £197m, some 24% higher than in 2007/08 and 45% higher than those in 2006/07.

It is clear to everyone in the game that clubs spend too much of their income on player wages.

Source: Tad Detko, Fever Pitch, *Accountancy Magazine*, May 2010, p. 18. Copyright Wolters Kluwer (UK) Ltd.

Assets

Assets are essentially items owned (or leased) by the business which will bring economic benefits. An example might be a building or inventory awaiting resale. Assets may be held for a long time for use in the business (such as motor vehicles) or alternatively be short-term assets (such as inventory) held for immediate resale. As Real-World View 2.3 shows, a solid asset base often underpins a successful company.

REAL-WORLD VIEW 2.3

Assets

With assets of £2.6 billion and 2,300 staff, Pennon is a 'bog standard' utility with a waste disposal business bolted on the side. For investors this need not be a turn-off. Pennon generates oodles of cash relative to its size, and – like all utilities – gives most of it to shareholders in the form of dividends.

Source: Philip Aldrick, Pennon's Safe Enough but Doesn't Hold Water for Growth Prospects, *Daily Telegraph,* 10 December 2004, p. 36.

Liabilities

Liabilities are amounts the business owes to a third party. An example might be money owed to the bank following a bank loan. Alternatively, the company may owe money to the suppliers of goods (known as trade payables or creditors).

Equity (Capital)

Equity equals the assets of a business less its liabilities to third parties. Equity represents the owner's interest in the business. In effect, equity is a liability as it is owed by the business to the owner. Owners may be sole traders, partners or shareholders. Under IFRS terminology 'equity' is preferred to 'capital'.

Income Statement

An income statement, at its simplest, records the income and expenses of a business over time. Income less expenses equals profit. By contrast, where expenses are greater than income, losses will occur. It is important (as Real-World View 2.4 shows) for even the world's largest companies to ensure that income (or revenue) exceeds expenses (or costs). The net profit (or net loss) in the income statement is added to (or subtracted from) equity in the statement of financial position. Over the years the accepted terminology has changed. The income statement was formally known as the profit and loss account. Under IFRS, there is a separation of profit generated from continuing operation such as sales and other comprehensive income (for example, gains on foreign exchange translations, property valuation and actuarial gains (i.e., from pensions)). IAS 1 permits two presentations. First, one statement called the 'statement of comprehensive income' (this combines both profits from continuing operations (i.e., the buying and selling of goods) and other comprehensive income). Alternatively, two statements can be provided. First, an income statement for continuing operations (income from other sources such as profit on the sale of investments) and then a statement of comprehensive income. Given the nature of this introductory book, I generally use the income statement as small businesses (sole traders, partnerships and non-listed limited companies) do not usually have other comprehensive income. For listed companies, however, I do sometimes use 'statement of comprehensive income', even though I do not deal in any depth with 'other comprehensive income' in this book. In this book, I follow current usage and reserve statement of comprehensive income for a separate statement showing items such as gains from foreign currency. This is explained more fully in Chapter 7.

REAL-WORLD VIEW 2.4

Revenues and Expenses

HSBC has outlined plans to cut costs by as much as $3.5 bn (£2.1 bn) over the next three years as part of an attempt to boost its returns to shareholders. … Analysts at Bank of America, Merill Lynch, said the envisaged cuts could shave close to 10pc off the bank's total cost base, with HSBC looking to reduce costs as a proportion of revenues from 55.2 pc today to 48pc – 52pc by 2013 … Among the businesses that will benefit from the plan is wealth management, with HSBC targeting annual revenues of $4 bn as it looks to grab a large slice of the profits from managing the money of the world's richest people. HSBC aims to shave costs by up to $3.5 bn in three years.

Source: Daily Telegraph, 12 May 2011, p. 1.

PAUSE FOR THOUGHT 2.2

Accounting Terms

Can you think of two examples of income, and three examples of expenses, assets and liabilities which a typical business might have?

These are many and varied. A few examples are given below:

Income	*Expenses*	*Assets*	*Liabilities*
Sales of goods	Telephone	Buildings	Bank loan
Sales of assets	Business rates	Motor cars	Trade payables
Bank interest earned	Electricity	Furniture	
	Repairs	Inventory	
	Petrol consumed	Trade receivables	

Company Snapshot 2.1 shows a reconstruction of the summary consolidated income statement for Marks & Spencer plc in 2010. The full statement can be seen in Appendix 2.1. From Company Snapshot 2.1 it can be seen that expenses are deducted from sales and other income to give profit before taxation. Once taxation has been deducted, we arrive at the profit for the year (£523 million for 2010 and £507 million for 2009). The 2010 accounts of Marks & Spencer plc follow the IFRS format set out by the International Accounting Standards Board for listed companies. In Appendix 2.4, the income statement for Volkswagen, also prepared using International Accounting Standards, is provided.

Statement of Financial Position (Balance Sheet)

A statement of financial position records the assets, liabilities and equity of a business at a certain point in time. Assets less liabilities will equal equity. Equity is thus the owners' interest in the business. The statement of financial position for Marks & Spencer as at 3rd April 2010 is presented in Company Snapshot 2.2. Here the assets are added together and then the liabilities are taken away. The net assets (i.e., assets less liabilities) equal the total equity employed by the business. A statement of financial position (balance sheet) in a listed company format following international accounting standards is presented for Volkswagen in Appendix 2.5. This is prepared using a format where the total assets are totalled; these then equal total equity and liabilities. This approach is commonly used by non-UK companies under International Financial Reporting Standards. UK companies more typically use a net assets approach as demonstrated already by Marks and Spencer in Appendix 2.2 and in Company Snapshot 7.4 by the British company AstraZeneca. This approach is used in this book.

COMPANY SNAPSHOT 2.1

Marks & Spencer Summarised Consolidated Income Statement

Marks & Spencer

Summary income statement for the 53 weeks ended 3rd April, 2010

	2010	2009
	£m	£m
Revenue	9,537	9,062
Add: Other income	(149)	(164)
	9,388	8,898
Less: Expenses	(8,685)	(8,192)
Profit before taxation	703	706
Taxation	(180)	(199)
Profit for the year	523	507

Note: The income statement has been simplified and reconstructed. The original summary income statement can be found as Appendix 2.1 at the back of this chapter. Appendix 2.1 also includes the consolidated statement of comprehensive income.

Source: Marks & Spencer plc, *Annual Review and Summary Financial Statements 2010*, p. 78.

COMPANY SNAPSHOT 2.2

Illustration of a Summarised Consolidated Statement of Financial Position

Marks & Spencer

Summary statement of financial position for the 53 weeks as at 3rd April, 2010

	As at 3 April 2010	As at 29 March 2009 as restated
	£m	£m
ASSETS		
Non-current assets		
Intangible assets	453	400
Property, plant and equipment	4,722	4,834
Other non-current assets	458	634
	5,633	5,868

COMPANY SNAPSHOT 2.2 (*continued*)

Current assets	£m	£m
Inventories	613	536
Trade receivables	281	285
Cash	406	423
Other	220	146
	1,520	1,390
Total Assets	7,153	7,258
LIABILITIES		
Current liabilities		
Trade payables	1,154	1,074
Other	736	1,233
	1,890	2,307
Non-current liabilities	3,077	2,850
Total liabilities	4,967	5,157
Net assets	2,186	2,101
EQUITY	£m	£m
Equity shareholders' funds	2,169	2,082
Non-equity shareholders' funds	17	19
Total Equity	2,186	2,101

Note: The statement of financial position has been simplified and reconstructed. The original summary statement of financial position can be found as Appendix 2.2 at the back of this chapter.

Source: Marks & Spencer plc, *Annual Report and Financial Statements 2010*, p. 79.

Statement of Cash Flows

A statement of cash flows shows the cash inflows and outflows of the business. These are normally calculated by comparing the statements of financial position for two consecutive years. As Chapter 8 shows, this can be very complicated. The statement of cash flows which deals with actual historic cash flows can be compared to future cash flows that are presented in a cash budget. Company Snapshot 2.3 shows a summary statement of cash flows for Marks & Spencer for 2010. Cash flows are split into three categories: operating (such as buying and selling goods or paying wages), investing (such as buying and selling machinery or receiving interest or dividends on investments) and financing (such as borrowing money and paying interest on loans). Overall, Marks & Spencer has a positive net cash flow from operating activities of £1,229 million in 2010. In Appendix 2.3 the statement of cash flows for Marks and Spencer is reproduced. Then in Appendix 2.6, the statement of cash flows (cash flow statement) for Volkswagen, a German listed company following international accounting standards, is presented.

COMPANY SNAPSHOT 2.3

Illustration of a Summarised Consolidated Statement of Cash Flows

Marks & Spencer

Summary statement of cash flows for the 53 weeks ended 3rd April, 2010

	53 weeks ended 3 April 2010 £m	52 weeks ended 29 March 2009 as restated £m
Cash generated from operations	1,350	1,372
Tax paid	(121)	(81)
Net cash inflow from operating activities	1,229	1,291
Cash flows from investing activities	(530)	(597)
Cash flows from financing activities	(792)	(521)
Exchange rate changes	(2)	7
Net cash (out) inflow from activities	(95)	180
	£m	£m
Opening net cash	298	118
Net cash flow from activities	(95)	180
Closing net cash	203	298

Note: The statement of cash flows has been simplified and reconstructed. The original statement of cash flows can be found as Appendix 2.3 at the back of this chapter.

Source: Marks & Spencer plc, *Annual Report and Financial Statements 2010*, p. 81.

We will now look at three summary financial statements for a business called Gavin Stevens which we will meet in more depth in Chapter 3. Gavin Stevens runs a hotel and summary details of his income, expenses, assets, liabilities and equity are given below. At this stage, the financial statements for Gavin Stevens (see Figure 2.1) and for Simon Tudent (see Figure 2.2) are drawn up using only broad general headings. More detailed presentation is covered in later chapters.

Figure 2.1 Preparation of Summary Income Statement, Statement of Financial Position and Statement of Cash Flows for Gavin Stevens

Financial Information

Income	£8,930	Liabilities	£1,350
Expenses	£5,600	Opening equity	£200,000
Assets	£204,680	Closing equity	£203,330
Cash inflows	£204,465	Cash outflows	£117,550

(i) Income Statement (Profit and Loss Account)

Here we are concerned with determining profit by subtracting expenses from income. We call the profit, net profit.

	£
Income	8,930
Less: *Expenses*	5,600
Net Profit	3,330

(ii) Statement of Financial Position (Balance Sheet)

Here we deduct the assets from the liabilities to give net assets. This represents the owner's equity employed in the business.

	£
Assets	204,680
Liabilities	(1,350)
Net Assets	203,330

	£
Opening equity	200,000
Add: Profit	3,330
Closing equity	203,330

(iii) Statement of Cash Flows	£
Cash Inflows	204,465
Cash Outflows	(117,550)
Net cash inflow	86,915

We have a positive cash flow. In other words, our cash has increased by £86,915 over the year. Note that in accounting when figures such as liabilities and cash outflows are subtracted it is common to use brackets if the word 'less' is not used.

Student Example

In order to give a further flavour of the nature of the main accounting terms, this section presents the income and expenditure of Simon Tudent. Simon is a student.

Figure 2.2 A Student's Financial Statements

Simon has collected the following details of his finances for his first year at university and possessions on 31 December. He has already divided them into income, expenses, assets and liabilities.

Income	**£**
Wages received from working in Student Union (38 weeks at £50 per week)	1,900
Gift from grandparents	12,000
Wages owing from Student Union (2 weeks at £50 per week – also an asset because he is owed it)	100

Assets	**£**
Second-hand car worth probably	700*
Cash at bank at start of year	2,500*
Computer worth about	150*
CD player worth about	200*

*All possessions at start of year.

Expenses	**£**
University tuition fees	9,000
Hall of residence fees	3,000
Money spent on books	600
Money spent on entertainment	1,000
Petrol used in car	500
Phone calls	100
Car repairs	1,000
Car expenses	1,200
General	150

Liabilities	**£**
Owes parents £150 for loan this year	150
Student loan from government	9,000
Maintenance loan	4,300

Note: Simon's opening equity is simply his opening assets less any opening liabilities. For simplicity, we assume that they are worth the same as at the start and as at the end of the year (except for cash at bank).

From the information shown above, we can present three financial statements, shown below and on the next page.

1. An income statement or profit and loss account (strictly, for a student we should call this an income and expenditure statement).
2. A statement of financial position or balance sheet (strictly, for a student we should call this an assets and liabilities statement).
3. A statement of cash flows or cash flow statement.

S. Tudent
Income Statement (profit and loss account) for the Year Ended 31 December

Income	**£**	**£**
Student union wages (note: includes £100 owing)		2,000
Gift from grandparents		12,000
		14,000

Figure 2.2 A Student's Financial Statements (*continued*)

Less Expenses	£	£
University tuition fees	9,000	
Hall of residence fees	3,000	
Books	600	
Entertainment	1,000	
Petrol	500	
Phone calls	100	
Car repairs	1,000	
Car expenses	1,200	
General	150	16,550
Net Deficit		(2,550)

Note that this statement deals with all income and expenses earned and incurred, not just with cash paid and received. We deduct all the expenses from the income and ascertain that S. Tudent has a net deficit. In business, this would be called a net loss.

S. Tudent
Statement of Financial Position (Balance Sheet) as at 31 December

Assets	£	£	
Cash at bank			
(balance from statement of cash flows)		13,300	
Second-hand car		700	
Computer		150	
CD player		200	
Owed by student union		100	
Total Assets		14,450	
Liabilities			
Parental Loan	(150)		
Government loans (9,000 + 4,300)	(13,300)		
Total Liabilities		(13,450)	
Net Assets		1,000*	
Capital Employed		£	
Opening equity		3,550*	Note: these two
Net deficit		(2,550)	figures balance
Closing equity		1,000*	

*Opening possessions (£700 + £2,500 + £150 + £200)

We are simply listing the assets and liabilities. The assets less liabilities give net assets. This also equals equity, also known as capital employed. The opening equity is simply opening assets less opening liabilities. Note that opening equity less the net deficit gives closing equity. A student loan is a liability because it is owed to the government. It is not income. In this case, as with many students, the position for the year is that the student has a net deficit. However, this can be seen as a current sacrifice for future benefits. In fact, this student is lucky for without the grandparents' contribution his net position would be of net liabilities.

Figure 2.2 A Student's Financial Statements (*continued*)

S. Tudent
Statement of Cash Flows (Cash Flow Statement) Year ended 31 December

	£	£
Bank balance at start of year		2,500
Add Receipts:		
Maintenance loan	4,300	
Student loan	9,000	
Student Union	1,900	
Loan from parents	150	
Gift from grandparents	12,000	27,350
		29,850
Less Payments:		
Books	600	
Entertainment	1,000	
Petrol used	500	
Phone calls	100	
Car repairs	1,000	
Car expenses	1,200	
General	150	
Hall fees	3,000	
University fees	9,000	16,550
Bank balance at end of year (balancing figure)		13,300

Note that we are simply recording all cash received and paid. We were not given the closing bank figure. However, it must be £13,300: opening cash of £2,500 plus receipts of £27,350 gives £29,850 less £16,550 payments.

PAUSE FOR THOUGHT 2.3

Student Loan

Students are often granted loans by the government. Why would a student loan from the government or a loan from one's parents be a liability, but a gift from parents be income?

This is because the loans must be repaid. They are, therefore, liabilities. When they are repaid, in part or in full, the liability is reduced. By contrast, a gift will be income as it does not have to be repaid.

From S. Tudent's financial statements, it can thus be seen that the net deficit (£2,550) occurs twice in the income statement and in the capital employed section of S. Tudent's financial position. This figure thus provides a link between these two statements. The closing figure of the bank balance in the statement of cash flows also appears under current assets in the statement of financial position. It should be noted that although most of the individual items of payments and expenses are the same, in this example, normally they will not be - it is just that for simplification we have assumed that there are no amounts owing.

Why Is Financial Accounting Important?

Financial accounting is a key control mechanism. All businesses prepare and use financial information in order to help them measure their performance. It is also useful in a business's relationship with third parties. It enables sole traders and partnerships to provide accounting information to the tax authorities or bank. For the limited company, it makes company directors accountable to company shareholders. For small businesses, the accounts are normally prepared by independent qualified accountants. In the case of large businesses, such as limited companies, the accounts are normally prepared by the managers and directors, but then audited by professional accountants. Auditing means checking the accounts are 'true and fair'. This term 'true and fair' is elusive and slippery. It is probably best considered to mean faithfully representing the underlying economic transactions of a business. The independent preparation and/or auditing of the financial accounts by accountants and auditors is an essential task in the protection of the users. The tax authorities need to ensure that the sole traders and partnership accounts have been properly prepared by an expert. Similarly, the shareholders need to have confidence that the managers have prepared a 'true and fair' account. For shareholders, this is particularly important as they are not usually directly involved in running the business. They provide the money, then stand back and allow the managers to run the company. So how can shareholders ensure that the managers are not abusing their trust? Bluntly, how can the shareholders make sure they are not being 'ripped off' by the managers? Auditing is one solution.

PAUSE FOR THOUGHT 2.4

Directors' Self-Interest

How might the directors of a company serve their own interests rather than the interests of the shareholders?

Both directors and shareholders want to share in a business's success. Directors are rewarded by salaries and other rewards, such as company cars, profit-related bonuses or lucrative pensions. Shareholders are rewarded by receiving cash payments in the form of dividends or an increase in share price. The problem is that the more the directors take for themselves, the less there will be left for the shareholders. So if directors pay themselves large bonuses, the shareholders will get smaller dividends.

Accounting Principles

There are several accounting principles which underpin the preparation of the accounts. For convenience, we classify them here into accounting conventions and accounting concepts (see Figure 2.3). Essentially, conventions concern the whole accounting process, while

Figure 2.3 Accounting Principles

Accounting Conventions	*Accounting Concepts*
• Entity • Monetary measurement • Historic cost • Periodicity	• Going concern • Matching (or accruals) • Consistency • Prudence (a disputed and controversial concept)

concepts are assumptions which underpin the actual accounts preparation. There are four generally recognised accounting conventions and four generally recognised 'potential' accounting concepts.

Accounting Conventions

Entity

The entity convention simply means that a business has a distinct and separate identity from its owners. This is fairly obvious in the case of a large limited company where shareholders own the company and managers manage the company. However, for a sole trader, such as a small baker's shop, it is important to realise that there is a theoretical distinction between personal and business assets. The business is treated as a separate entity from the owner. The business's assets less third-party liabilities represent the owner's equity or capital.

Monetary Measurement

Under this convention only items which can be measured in financial terms (for example, in pounds or dollars) are included in the accounts. If a company pollutes the atmosphere, this is not included in the accounts, since this pollution has no measurable financial value. However, a fine imposed for pollution is measurable and should be included in the accounts. A recent innovation in accounting is that a market in carbon emissions is emerging.

Historical Cost

Businesses may trade for many years. The historical cost convention basically states that the amount recorded in the accounts will be based on the *original* amount paid for a good or service. If, for example, we purchased a building for £1 million in 1970, that is the cost recorded in the accounts even though the building might now be worth £10 million. Nowadays, in the UK, and under International Financial Reporting Standards (IFRS), there are frequently departures from historical cost. For example, many companies remeasure land and buildings to reflect their increase in value. Company Snapshot 2.4 shows that Tesco plc prepared its accounts using the historical cost convention. It also shows that it used fair value (which is effectively a market value) for some financial assets and liabilities.

COMPANY SNAPSHOT 2.4

Historical Cost Convention: Basis of Preparation of Financial Statements

The financial statements are presented in Pounds Sterling, generally rounded to the nearest million. They are prepared on the historical cost basis, except for certain financial instruments, share-based payments, customer loyalty programmes and pensions that have been measured at fair value.

Source: Tesco Plc, *Annual Report and Financial Statements 2010,* p. 10.

Periodicity

This simply means that accounts are prepared for a set period of time. Audited financial statements are usually prepared for a year. Financial statements prepared for internal management are often drawn up more frequently. This means, in effect, that sometimes rather arbitrary distinctions are made about the period in which accounting items are recorded.

Accounting Assumptions or Concepts

There are four generally recognised potential accounting concepts. The International Accounting Standards Board recognises two overriding underlying assumptions (going concern and accruals). The UK Companies Act, however, recognises in addition two extra assumptions: consistency and prudence. However, the IASB has severe reservations about prudence, which is the most contentious of the concepts.

Going Concern

This concept assumes the business will continue into the foreseeable future. Assets, liabilities, income and expenses are thus calculated on this basis. If you are valuing a specialised machine, for example, you will value the machine at a higher value if the business is ongoing than if it is about to go bankrupt. If it were bankrupt, the machine would only have scrap value. In Company Snapshot 2.5, we can see that J.D. Wetherspoon's directors have assured themselves that the company is a going concern.

COMPANY SNAPSHOT 2.5

Going Concern

The Directors have made enquiries into the adequacy of the Company's financial resources, through a review of the Company's budget and medium-term financial plan, including capital expenditure plans, cash flow forecasts; they have satisfied themselves that the Company will continue in operational existence for the foreseeable future. For this reason, they continue to adopt the going-concern basis in preparing the Company's financial statements.

Source: J.D. Wetherspoon plc, *Annual Report 2010,* p. 55.

Accruals

The accruals concept (often known as the matching concept) recognises income and expenses when they are accrued (i.e., earned or incurred) rather than when the money is received or paid. Income is matched with any associated expenses to determine the appropriate profit or loss. A telephone bill owing at the accounting year end is thus treated as an expense for this year even if it is paid in the next year. If the telephone bill is not received by the year end, then the amount of telephone calls will be estimated. Alternatively, if rent is paid in advance, this will be treated as a payment in advance rather than as an expense of the year.

Consistency

This concept states that similar items will be treated similarly from year to year. Thus consistency attempts to stop companies choosing different accounting policies in different years. If they do this, then it becomes more difficult to compare the results of one year to the next.

Prudence

This is the most contentious of the four accounting concepts. Indeed, the IASB in the latest version of its Conceptual Framework in 2010 has replaced it completely. Prudence introduces an element of caution into accounting. Income and profits should only be recorded in the books when they are *certain* to result in an inflow of cash. By contrast, provisions or liabilities should be made *as soon as they are recognised*, even though their amount may not be known with certainty. Prudence is contentious because it introduces an asymmetry into the accounting process. Potential incomes are treated differently from potential liabilities. Some accountants believe that prudence is an out-of-date concept, while others feel that it is needed to stop management providing an over-optimistic view of the accounts. However, the IASB feels that prudence conflicts with a neutral view of accounts. It is, therefore, undesirable as it introduces bias into accounting.

PAUSE FOR THOUGHT 2.5

Personal Finances

Draw up a set of financial statements for yourself for the last twelve months.

I hope they are not too gruesome!

Conclusion

Financial accounting, along with management accounting, is one of the two main branches of accounting. Its main objective is to provide financial information to users for decision making. Shareholders, for example, are provided with information to assess the stewardship of managers so that they can then make decisions such as whether to buy or sell their shares. Understanding the accounting language is a key requisite to understanding accounting itself. Four accounting conventions (entity, money measurement, historical cost and periodicity) and three accounting concepts (going concern, accruals and consistency) underpin financial accounting. In addition, many people believe prudence is an important accounting concept.

Discussion Questions

Questions with numbers in blue have answers at the back of the book.

Q1 What is financial accounting and why is its study important?

Q2 **Formal definitions**

'The objective of general purpose **financial reporting** is to provide financial information about the **reporting entity** that is useful to existing and potential investors, lenders and other creditors in making decisions about **providing resources to the entity.** Those decisions involve buying, selling or holding equity and debt instruments, and providing or settling loans and other forms of credit.'

International Accounting Standards Board (IASB) (2010), *The Conceptual Framework for Financial Reporting.*

Discuss the key aspects *highlighted in bold* of this formal definition of the objective of general purpose financial reporting as formulated by the IASB in its conceptual framework.

Q3 Sole traders, partnerships and limited companies all have different users who need financial information for different purposes. Discuss.

Q4 Classify the following as an income, an expense, an asset or a liability:

(a) Friend owes business money
(b) Football club's gate receipts
(c) Petrol used by a car
(d) Photocopier
(e) Revenue or Sales
(f) Telephone bill outstanding
(g) Long-term loan
(h) Cash
(i) Wages
(j) Equity or capital

Q5 State whether the following are true or false. If false, explain why.

(a) Assets and liabilities show how much the business owns and owes.
(b) The income statement shows the income, expenses and thus the net assets of a business.
(c) Stewardship is now recognised as the primary objective of financial accounting.
(d) When running a small business, the owner must be careful to separate business from private expenditure.
(e) The matching and prudence accounting concepts sometimes conflict.

Numerical Questions

Questions with numbers in blue have answers at the back of the book.

Q1 Sharon Taylor has the following financial details:

Revenue	£8,000	Assets	£15,000
General expenses	£4,000	Liabilities	£3,000
Trading expenses	£3,000	Cash outflows	£12,000
Cash inflows	£10,000	Closing equity	£12,000
Opening equity	£11,000		

Required: Prepare Sharon Taylor's
(a) Income Statement (Profit and Loss Account)
(b) Statement of Financial Position (Balance Sheet)
(c) Statement of Cash Flows

Q2 Priya Patel is an overseas student studying at a British University. Priya has the following financial details:

	£		£
Tuition fees paid	16,840	Food paid	550
Hall of residence fees paid	8,000	General expenses paid	180
Money spent on books	160	Parental loan during year	5,000
Money spent on entertainment	500	Gift from grandparents	15,000
Money earned from part-time job	4,800	*State of affairs at the start of the year:*	
Phone calls paid	100	Cash at bank	8,600
		Music system*	200

*Still worth £200 at end of year.

Required: Priya's:
(a) Income Statement (Profit and Loss Account)
(b) Statement of Financial Position (Balance Sheet)
(c) Statement of Cash Flows

Appendix 2.1: Illustration of a Consolidated Income Statement for Marks & Spencer plc 2010

Consolidated income statement

	Notes	53 weeks ended 3 April 2010 £m	52 weeks ended 28 March 2009 £m
Revenue	2, 3	**9,536.6**	9,062.1
Operating profit	2, 3	**852.0**	870.7
Finance income	6	**12.9**	50.0
Finance costs	6	**(162.2)**	(214.5)
Profit on ordinary activities before taxation	4	**702.7**	706.2
Analysed between:			
Before property disposals and exceptional items		**694.6**	604.4
Profit on property disposals	2, 3	**8.1**	6.4
Exceptional costs	5	**—**	(135.9)
Exceptional pension credit	5, 11	**—**	231.3
Income tax expense	7	**(179.7)**	(199.4)
Profit for the year		**523.0**	506.8
Attributable to:			
Equity shareholders of the Company		**526.3**	508.0
Minority interests		**(3.3)**	(1.2)
		523.0	506.8
Basic earnings per share	8A	**33.5p**	32.3p
Diluted earnings per share	8B	**33.2p**	32.3p
Non-GAAP measure:			
Adjusted profit before taxation (£m)	1	**694.6**	604.4
Adjusted basic earnings per share	8A	**33.0p**	28.0p
Adjusted diluted earnings per share	8B	**32.7p**	28.0p

Appendix 2.1 Marks & Spencer Income Statement *(continued)*

Consolidated statement of comprehensive income

	53 weeks ended 3 April 2010 £m	52 weeks ended 28 March 2009 £m
Profit for the year	**523.0**	506.8
Other comprehensive income:		
Foreign currency translation differences	**(17.4)**	33.1
Actuarial losses on retirement benefit schemes	**(251.6)**	(927.1)
Deferred tax on retirement benefit scheme	**71.7**	254.9
Cash flow and net investment hedges		
– fair value movements in equity	**52.1**	304.8
– reclassified and reported in net profit	**(119.8)**	(206.8)
– amount recognised in inventories	**4.8**	(8.6)
Tax on cash flow hedges and fair hedges	**25.9**	(29.3)
Other comprehensive income for the year, net of tax	**(234.3)**	(579.0)
Total comprehensive income/(loss) for the year	**288.7**	(72.2)
Attributable to:		
Equity shareholders of the Company	**292.0**	(71.0)
Minority interests	**(3.3)**	(1.2)
	288.7	(72.2)

Source: Marks and Spencer plc, *Annual Report and Financial Statements 2010*, p. 78.

Appendix 2.2: Illustration of a Consolidated Statement of Financial Position for Marks and Spencer plc 2010

Consolidated statement of financial position

	Notes	As at 3 April 2010 £m	Restated as at 28 March 2009 £m
Assets			
Non-current assets			
Intangible assets	13	**452.8**	400.3
Property, plant and equipment	14	**4,722.0**	4,834.0
Investment property	15	**22.4**	24.8
Investment in joint ventures	16	**11.5**	13.8
Other financial assets	17	**3.0**	3.0
Trade and other receivables	18	**287.7**	336.8
Derivative financial instruments	22	**132.9**	254.0
Deferred tax assets	24	**0.7**	1.6
		5,633.0	5,868.3
Current assets			
Inventories		**613.2**	536.0
Other financial assets	17	**171.7**	53.1
Trade and other receivables	18	**281.4**	285.2
Derivative financial instruments	22	**48.1**	92.6
Cash and cash equivalents	19	**405.8**	422.9
		1,520.2	1,389.8
Total assets		**7,153.2**	7,258.1
Liabilities			
Current liabilities			
Trade and other payables	20	**1,153.8**	1,073.5
Borrowings and other financial liabilities	21	**482.9**	942.8
Partnership liability to the Marks & Spencer UK Pension Scheme	21	**71.9**	71.9
Derivative financial instruments	22	**27.1**	76.2
Provisions	23	**25.6**	63.6
Current tax liabilities		**129.2**	78.9
		1,890.5	2,306.9

Appendix 2.2 Marks and Spencer Statement of Financial Position (*continued*)

		£m	£m
Non-current liabilities			
Retirement benefit deficit	11	**366.5**	152.2
Trade and other payables	20	**280.3**	243.8
Borrowings and other financial liabilities	21	**2,278.0**	2,117.9
Partnership liability to the Marks & Spencer UK Pension Scheme	21	—	68.0
Derivative financial instruments	22	—	3.0
Provisions	23	**25.5**	40.2
Deferred tax liabilities	24	**126.5**	225.5
		3,076.8	2,850.6
Total liabilities		**4,967.3**	5,157.5
Net assets		**2,185.9**	2,100.6
Equity			
Called-up share capital – equity	25	**395.5**	394.4
Share premium account		**247.5**	236.2
Capital redemption reserve		**2,202.6**	2,202.6
Hedging reserve		**11.6**	62.6
Other reserve		**(5,970.5)**	(5,970.5)
Retained earnings		**5,281.9**	5,156.4
Total shareholders' equity		**2,168.6**	2,081.7
Minority interests in equity		**17.3**	18.9
Total equity		**2,185.9**	2,100.6

The financial statements were approved by the Board and authorised for issue on 24 May 2010. The financial statements also comprise the notes on pages 82 to 111.

Stuart Rose Chairman

Ian Dyson Group Finance and Operations Director

Source: Marks and Spencer plc, *Annual Report and Financial Statements 2010*, p. 79.

Appendix 2.3: Illustration of a Consolidated Statement of Cash Flows for Marks and Spencer plc 2010

Consolidated cash flow information

Illustration of Statement of cash flows
Marks and Spencer plc for 2010

	Notes	53 weeks ended 3 April 2010 £m	52 weeks ended 28 March 2009 £m
Consolidated statement of cash flows			
Cash flows from operating activities			
Cash generated from operations	28	1,349.7	1,371.9
Tax paid		(120.7)	(81.3)
Net cash inflow from operating activities		1,229.0	1,290.6
Cash flows from investing activities			
Acquisition of subsidiaries, net of cash acquired		(5.4)	—
Purchase of property, plant and equipment		(352.0)	(540.8)
Proceeds from sale of property, plant and equipment		20.9	58.3
Purchase of intangible assets		(77.5)	(121.6)
Purchase of non-current financial assets		—	(4.4)
Purchase of current financial assets		(118.3)	(1.1)
Interest received		2.7	12.7
Net cash outflow from investing activities		(529.6)	(596.9)
Cash flows from financing activities			
Interest paid		(163.4)	(197.1)
Cash inflow/(outflow) from borrowings		30.7	(25.8)
(Repayment)/drawdown of syndicated bank facility		(529.4)	108.1
Issue of medium-term notes		397.2	—
Redemption of medium-term notes		(200.4)	—
Payment of liability to the Marks & Spencer UK Pension Scheme		(68.0)	(15.1)
Decrease in obligations under finance leases		(17.0)	(1.0)
Equity dividends paid		(236.0)	(354.6)
Shares issued on exercise of employee share options		12.4	5.3
Shares purchased in buy back		—	(40.9)
Purchase of own shares by employee trust		(19.0)	—
Net cash outflow from financing activities		(792.9)	(521.1)

Appendix 2.3 Marks & Spencer Statement of Cash Flows (*continued*)

		£m	£m
Net cash (outflow)/inflow from activities		(93.5)	172.6
Effects of exchange rate changes		(2.1)	7.8
Opening net cash		298.3	117.9
Closing net cash	29	202.7	298.3

	Notes	53 weeks ended 3 April 2010 £m	52 weeks ended 28 March 2009 £m
Reconciliation of net cash flow to movement in net debt			
Opening net debt		(2,490.8)	(3,077.7)
Net cash (outflow)/inflow from activities		(93.5)	172.6
Increase in current financial assets		118.3	1.1
Decrease/(increase) in debt financing		386.9	(66.2)
Partnership liability to the Marks & Spencer UK Pension Scheme (non-cash)		—	539.6
Exchange and other non-cash movements		10.7	(60.2)
Movement in net debt		422.4	586.9
Closing net debt	29	(2,068.4)	(2,490.8)

Source: Marks and Spencer plc, *Annual Report and Financial Statements 2010*, p. 81.

Appendix 2.4: Illustration of a Consolidated Income Statement for Volkswagen 2009

Consolidated Financial Statements of the Volkswagen Group

Income Statement of the Volkswagen Group
for the Period January 1 to December 31, 2009

€ million	Note	2009	2008
Sales revenue	1	**105,187**	**113,808**
Cost of sales	2	–91,608	–96,612
Gross profit		**13,579**	**17,196**
Distribution expenses	3	–10,537	–10,552
Administrative expenses	4	–2,739	–2,742
Other operating income	5	7,904	8,770
Other operating expenses	6	–6,352	–6,339
Operating profit		**1,855**	**6,333**
Share of profits and losses of equity-accounted investments	7	701	910
Finance costs	8	–2,268	–1,815
Other financial result	9	972	1,180
Financial result		**–595**	**275**
Profit before tax		**1,261**	**6,608**
Income tax income/expense	10	–349	–1,920
current		–1,145	–2,338
deferred		796	418
Profit after tax		**911**	**4,688**
Minority interests		–49	–65
Profit attributable to shareholders of Volkswagen AG		960	4,753
Basic earnings per ordinary share in €	**11**	**2.38**	**11.92**
Basic earnings per preferred share in €	**11**	**2.44**	**11.98**
Diluted earnings per ordinary share in €	**11**	**2.38**	**11.88**
Diluted earnings per preferred share in €	**11**	**2.44**	**11.94**

Source: *Volkswagen Group Annual Report 2009*, p. 204. Copyright Volkswagen AG (Investor Relations).

Appendix 2.5: Illustration of a Consolidated Balance Sheet (Statement of Financial Position) for Volkswagen 2009

Balance Sheet of the Volkswagen Group as of December 31, 2009

€ million	Note	Dec. 31, 2009	Dec. 31, 2008
Assets			
Noncurrent assets			
Intangible assets	12	12,907	12,291
Property, plant and equipment	13	24,444	23,121
Leasing and rental assets	14	10,288	9,889
Investment property	14	216	150
Equity-accounted investments	15	10,385	6,373
Other equity investments	15	543	583
Financial services receivables	16	33,174	31,855
Other receivables and financial assets	17	3,747	3,387
Noncurrent tax receivables	18	685	763
Deferred tax assets	18	3,013	3,344
		99,402	**91,756**
Current assets			
Inventories	19	14,124	17,816
Trade receivables	20	5,692	5,969
Financial services receivables	16	27,403	27,035
Other receivables and financial assets	17	5,927	10,068
Current tax receivables	18	762	1,024
Marketable securities	21	3,330	3,770
Cash and cash equivalents	22	20,539	9,474
Assets held for sale	23	—	1,007
		77,776	**76,163**
Total assets		**177,178**	**167,919**
Equity and Liabilities			
Equity	**24**		
Subscribed capital		1,025	1,024
Capital reserves		5,356	5,351
Retained earnings		28,901	28,636
Equity attributable to shareholders of Volkswagen AG		35,281	35,011
Minority interests		2,149	2,377
		37,430	37,388

Appendix 2.5 Volkswagen Balance Sheet (*continued*)

Noncurrent liabilities			
Noncurrent financial liabilities	25	36,993	33,257
Other noncurrent liabilities	26	3,028	3,235
Deferred tax liabilities	27	2,224	3,654
Provisions for pensions	28	13,936	12,955
Provisions for taxes	27	3,946	3,555
Other noncurrent provisions	29	10,088	9,073
		70,215	**65,729**
Current liabilities			
Current financial liabilities	25	40,606	36,123
Trade payables	30	10,225	9,676
Current tax payables	27	73	59
Other current liabilities	26	8,237	8,545
Provisions for taxes	27	973	1,160
Other current provisions	29	9,420	8,473
Liabilities associated with assets held for sale	23	—	766
		69,534	**64,802**
Total equity and liabilities		**177,178**	**167,919**

Source: Volkswagen Group Annual Report 2009, p. 206. Copyright Volkswagen AG (Investor Relations).

Appendix 2.6: Illustration of a Consolidated Cash Flow Statement (Statement of Cash Flows) for Volkswagen 2009

Cash Flow Statement of the Volkswagen Group for the Period January 1 to December 31, 2009

€ million	2009	2008
Cash and cash equivalents at beginning of period (excluding time deposit investments)	**9,443**	**9,914**
Profit before tax	1,261	6,608
Income taxes paid	–529	–2,075
Depreciation and amortization of property, plant and equipment, intangible assets and investment property[1]	5,028	5,198
Amortization of capitalized development costs[1]	1,586	1,392
Impairment losses on equity investments[1]	16	32
Depreciation of leasing and rental assets[1]	2,247	1,816
Gain/loss on disposal of noncurrent assets	–547	37
Share of profit or loss of equity-accounted investments	–298	–219
Other noncash expense/income	727	765
Change in inventories	4,155	–3,056
Change in receivables (excluding financial services)	465	–1,333
Change in liabilities (excluding financial liabilities)	260	815
Change in provisions	1,660	509
Change in leasing and rental assets	–2,571	–2,734
Change in financial services receivables	–719	–5,053
Cash flows from operating activities	**12,741**	**2,702**
Investments in property, plant and equipment, intangible assets and investment property	–5,963	–6,896
Additions to capitalized development costs	–1,948	–2,216
Acquisition of equity investments	–3,989	–2,597
Disposal of equity investments	1,320	–1
Proceeds from disposal of property, plant and equipment, intangible assets and investment property	153	95
Change in investments in securities	989	2,041
Change in loans and time deposit investments	–236	–1,611

Appendix 2.6 Volkswagen Cash Flow Statement (*continued*)

Cash flows from investing activities	**–9,675**	**–11,183**
Capital contributions	4	218
Dividends paid	–874	–722
Capital transactions with minority interests	–392	–362
Other changes	23	–3
Proceeds from issue of bonds	15,593	7,671
Repayment of bonds	–10,202	–8,470
Change in other financial liabilities	1,405	9,806
Finance lease payments	–23	–15
Cash flows from financing activities	**5,536**	**8,123**
Effect of exchange rate changes on cash and cash equivalents	190	–113
Net change in cash and cash equivalents	**8,792**	**–471**
Cash and cash equivalents at end of period (excluding time deposit investments)	**18,235**	**9,443**

Cash and cash equivalents at end of period (excluding time deposit investments)	18,235	9,443
Securities and loans (including time deposit investments)	7,312	7,875
Gross liquidity	**25,547**	**17,318**
Total third-party borrowings	–77,599	–69,555
Net liquidity	**–52,052**	**–52,237**

[1]Net of impairment reversals.
[2]Prior-period amount adjusted.
Source: *Volkswagen Group Annual Report 2009*, p. 208. Copyright Volkswagen AG (Investor Relations).

Go online to discover the extra features for this chapter at **www.wiley.com/college/jones**

Chapter 3

Recording: Double-entry bookkeeping

'Old accountants never die, they just lose their balance.'

Anon.

Learning Outcomes

After completing this chapter you should be able to:

- Outline the accounting equation.
- Understand double-entry bookkeeping.
- Record transactions using double-entry bookkeeping.
- Balance off the accounts and draw up a trial balance.

Go online to discover the extra features for this chapter at **www.wiley.com/college/jones**

Chapter Summary

- Double-entry bookkeeping is an essential underpinning of financial accounting.
- The accounting equation provides the structure for double-entry.
- Assets and expenses are increases in debits recorded on the left-hand side of the 'T' (i.e., ledger) account.
- Income and equity are increases in credits recorded on the right-hand side of the 'T' (i.e., ledger) account.
- Debits and credits are equal and opposite entries.
- Initial recording in the books of account using double-entry, balancing off and preparing the trial balance are the three major steps in double-entry bookkeeping.
- The trial balance is a listing of all the balances from the accounts.
- The debits and credits in a trial balance should balance.
- In larger businesses, there will be books of prime entry such as the revenue (sales) day book and the purchases day book.

REAL-WORLD VIEW 3.1

Kissing Your Accountant

It has been a week for displays of affection in the market. The darlings of the entertainment industry have long been accustomed to hugging and kissing in public – anyone who has watched the Oscars ceremony knows this only too well. Now, this tendency towards overtly physical contact has spread into the financial world. The latest way to convey to the market that a deal is truly wonderful is for the leading figures to share a moment of intimacy.

The chief executives of Time Warner and AOL were photographed cuddling up after announcing their tie up. Chris Evans was even seen planting a smacker on his accountant after pocketing a cool £75m, when Scottish Media Group bought out Ginger Productions. Of course, if I had made £75m I might even be tempted to kiss my accountant – despite the fact that he still hasn't completed my income tax return and the January 31 deadline is getting ever closer.

Source: James Montier, Showbiz values come to the City, *The Guardian*, 15 January 2000, p. 31. Guardian Newspapers Limited 2000. Reproduced by permission of James Montier.

Introduction

Accounting is a blend of theory and practice. One of the key elements to understanding the practice of accounting is double-entry bookkeeping (see Definition 3.1). Although mysterious to the uninitiated, double-entry bookkeeping, in fact, is a mechanical exercise. It is a way of systematically recording accounting transactions into an organisation's accounting books.

DEFINITION 3.1

Double-Entry Bookkeeping

Working definition

A way of systematically recording the financial transactions of a company so that each transaction is recorded twice.

Formal definition

'Most commonly used system of bookkeeping based on the principle that every financial transaction involves the simultaneous receiving and giving of value, and is therefore recorded twice.'

Source: Chartered Institute of Management Accountants (2005), *Official Terminology*. Reproduced by Permission of Elsevier.

In a way it is like a business diary where all the financial transactions are recorded. Therefore, in essence, double-entry bookkeeping is the systematic recording of income, expenses, assets, liabilities and equity. Double-entry bookkeeping's importance lies in the fact that the income statement (also known as the profit and loss account) and statement of financial position (also known as the balance sheet) are prepared only after the accounting transactions have been recorded. The accounting equation and double-entry bookkeeping apply to all businesses. In this chapter, unless otherwise specified, the terminology used applies to sole traders, partnerships and non-listed companies. In this chapter the double-entry process is described up to the trial balance stage. Then, in Chapter 6, we show how the main financial statements (the income statement and the statement of financial position) are prepared from the trial balance.

The Accounting Equation

The reason why each transaction is recorded twice in the accounting books is not that accountants like extra work. In effect, it is a method of checking that the entries have been made correctly. As we will see later in this chapter, a trial balance can be prepared which helps to check that the bookkeeping transactions have been made properly.

At the heart of the double-entry system is the accounting equation. This starts from the basic premise that assets equal liabilities. Liabilities are, in effect, claims that somebody has over assets. It then logically builds up in complexity, as follows:

Step 1. | Assets = Liabilities |

If there is an asset of £1, then somebody must have a claim over that £1. This can either be a third party (such as the bank) or the owner of the business. There is thus a basic equality. For every asset, there is a liability.

Step 2. It should be appreciated that equity is a distinct type of liability because it is owed to the owner of a business. If we expand our accounting equation to formally distinguish between claims which owners have over a business (i.e., equity) and claims which others have over the business (i.e., third-party liabilities), we now have:

Assets = Liabilities + Equity

Accountants sometimes use the term 'Capital' to describe the amount invested by the owner. However, for consistency in this book the term equity is used. In a company, like Tesco (see Company Snapshot 3.1), the equity is share capital and will have been invested by shareholders.

Step 3. Assets = Liabilities + Equity + Profit

When an organisation earns a profit, its assets increase. Profit is on the same side as liabilities because profit is owed to the owner. Profit thus also increases the owner's share in the business. If a loss is made, assets will decrease, but the principle of equality still holds.

Step 4. Assets = Liabilities + Equity (+Income − Expenses)

All we have done is broken down profit into its constituent parts (i.e., income less expenses). We have still maintained the basic equality.

Step 5. Assets + Expenses = Liabilities + Equity + Income

We have now rearranged the accounting equation by adding expenses to assets. We have still preserved the accounting equation.

Step 6. In accounting terms, **assets** and **expenses** are recorded using **debit entries** and **income, liabilities** and **equity** are recorded using **credit entries**. Each page of each book of account has a debit side (left-hand side) and a credit side (right-hand side).

PAUSE FOR THOUGHT 3.1

The Accounting Equation

John decides to start a business and puts £10,000 into a business bank account. He also borrows £5,000 from the bank. How does this obey the accounting equation?

The asset here is easy. It is £15,000 cash. There is also clearly a £5,000 liability to the bank. However, the remaining £10,000, at first glance, is more elusive. A liability does, however, exist. This is because of the entity concept where the business and John are treated as different entities. Thus, the business owes John £10,000. We therefore have:

Asset		Liability		Equity
£15,000 in bank	=	£5,000 owed to bank	+	£10,000 owed to John

Where a business has a liability to its owner, this is known as equity.

This division of the page is called a 'T' account, with debits being on the left and credits on the right. Thus:

'T' Account (ledger account)	
Assets and expenses on the left-hand side DEBIT	Incomes, liabilities and capital on the right-hand side CREDIT

COMPANY SNAPSHOT 3.1

Share Capital

Note 29 Called up Share Capital

	2011		2010	
	Ordinary shares of 5p each		Ordinary shares of 5p each	
	Number	£m	Number	£m
Allotted, called up and fully paid:				
At beginning of year	7,985,044,057	399	7,895,344,018	395
Share options	36,535,102	2	62,329,535	3
Share bonus awards	24,888,933	1	27,370,504	1
At end of year	8,046,468,092	402	7,985,044,057	399

During the financial year, 37 million (2010 – 62 million) shares of 5p each were issued in relation to share options for aggregate consideration of £97m (2010 – £166m).

During the financial year, 25 million (2010 – 27 million) shares of 5p each were issued in relation to share bonus awards for consideration of £1m (2010 – £1m).

Between 27 February 2011 and 15 April 2011 options over 2,137,647 ordinary shares have been exercised under the terms of the Savings-related Share Option Scheme (1981) and the Irish Savings-related Share Option Scheme (2000). Between 27 February 2011 and 15 April 2011, options over 1,020,924 ordinary shares have been exercised under the terms of the Executive Share Option Schemes (1994 and 1996) and the Discretionary Share Option Plan (2004).

As at 26 February 2011, the Directors were authorised to purchase up to a maximum in aggregate of 802.1 million (2010 – 790.1 million) ordinary shares.

The owners of ordinary shares are entitled to receive dividends as declared from time to time and are entitled to one vote per share at the meetings of the Company.

Source: Tesco Plc, *Annual Report and Financial Statements 2011*, p. 140.

Tutorial Note: Share options and share bonus awards are methods of company remuneration. Share options give employees the right to purchase shares, usually at a discount. Share bonuses are usually awarded if employees meet their bonus targets.

PAUSE FOR THOUGHT 3.2

Illustration of Accounting Equation

A firm starts the year with £10,000 assets and £10,000 liabilities (£6,000 third-party liabilities and £4,000 owner's equity). During the year, the firm makes £5,000 profit (£9,000 income, £4,000 expenses). Show how the accounting equation works.

	Accounting equation	*Transaction*
(1)	Assets = Liabilities	£10,000 = £10,000
(2)	Assets = Liabilities + Equity	£10,000 = £6,000 + £4,000
(3)	Assets = Liabilities + Equity + Profit	£15,000 = £6,000 + £4,000 + £5,000
(4)	Assets = Liabilities + Equity + (Income − Expenses)	£15,000 = £6,000 + £4,000 + (£9,000 − £4,000)
(5)	Assets + Expenses = Liabilities + Capital + Income	£15,000 + £4,000 = £6,000 + £4,000 + £9,000

'T' Account		'T' Account	
Assets + Expenses	Liabilities + Equity + Income	£15,000 + £4,000	£6,000 + £4,000 + £9,000

The 'T' account is central to the concept of double-entry bookkeeping. In turn, double-entry bookkeeping is the backbone of financial accounting. As Helpnote 3.1 shows, it is underpinned by three major rules.

HELPNOTE 3.1

Basic Rules of Double-Entry Bookkeeping

1. For every transaction, there must be a *debit and a credit entry*.
2. These debit and credit entries are *equal* and *opposite*.
3. In the *cash book* all accounts *paid in* are recorded on the *debit* side, whereas all amounts *paid out* are recorded on the *credit* side.

In practice, there are many types of asset, liability, equity, income and expense. Figure 3.1 provides a brief summary of some of these.

Figure 3.1 does not provide an exhaustive list of all assets and liabilities. For instance, it only deals with tangible assets (literally assets you can touch). It thus ignores intangible assets (literally assets you cannot touch) such as royalties or goodwill. However, for now, this provides a useful framework. Intangible assets are most often found in the accounts of companies and are discussed later. More detail on the individual items in Figure 3.1 is provided in later chapters.

Figure 3.1 Summary of Some of the Major Types of Assets, Liabilities and Equity, Income and Expenses

Four Major Types of Items

1. Assets
2. Liabilities and equity
3. Income
4. Expenses

---

1. Assets

Essentially items owned or leased by a business which will bring economic benefits. Two main sorts of tangible assets (i.e., assets with a physical existence):

I. ***Non-current assets***

These can be divided into intangible assets such as patents or goodwill and tangible assets: property, plant and equipment. These are infrastructure assets *not* used in day-to-day trading. They are assets in use usually over a long period of time.

i. Motor vehicles
ii. Land and buildings
iii. Fixtures and fittings
iv. Plant and machinery

II. ***Current assets***

These are assets used in day-to-day trading

i. Inventory (Stock)
ii. Trade receivables (Debtors)
iii. Cash

2. Liabilities

Essentially these can be divided into:
I. Short-term and long-term third-party liabilities; and
II. Capital which is a liability owed by the business to the owner.

I. ***Third-party liabilities***

(a) ***Short-term (current liabilities)***

(i) Trade payables (creditors)
(ii) Bank overdraft
(iii) Proposed taxation (companies only)

(b) ***Long-term (non-current liabilities)***

(i) Bank loan repayable after several years
(ii) Mortgage loan

II. ***Equity***

Equity is a liability because the business owes it to the owner. Owner's equity (capital) is increased by profits, but reduced by losses.

3. Income

This is the day-to-day revenue earned by the business, e.g., sales.

4. Expenses

These are the day-to-day costs of running a business, e.g., rent and rates, electricity, wages.

PAUSE FOR THOUGHT 3.3

Debits and Credits

What do the terms 'debit' and 'credit' actually mean?

Debit and credit have their origins in Latin terms (*debeo*, I owe and *credo*, I make a loan). Debtor (one who owes, i.e., a customer) and creditor (one who is owed, i.e., a supplier) have the same origins. Over time, these terms have changed so that nowadays perhaps we have the following:

Debit = An entry on the left-hand side of a 'T' account. Records principally increases in either assets or expenses. However, may also record decreases in liabilities, equity or income.

Credit = An entry on the right-hand side of a 'T' account. Records principally increases in liabilities, equity or income. However, may also record decreases in assets or expenses.

HEALTH WARNING

Those students not wishing to gain an in-depth knowledge of double-entry bookkeeping can miss out pages 62–74. Appendix 3.1 provides a copy of the full example from initial entries, through to double-entry accounts and trial balance.

Worked Example

Let us now look at an example. Gavin Stevens has decided to open a hotel to cater for conferences and large functions.

1 January	G. Stevens invests £700,000 equity into a business bank account.	
2 January	Buys and pays for a hotel	£610,000
	Buys and pays for a second-hand delivery van	£3,000
	Makes purchases for cash	£2,000
	Makes purchases on credit from Hogen	£1,000
	Makes purchases on credit from Lewis	£2,000
3 January	Returns goods costing £500 to Hogen	
3 January	Credit sales to Ireton £4,000 for a large garden party	
	Credit sales to Hepworth £5,000 for a business conference	
4 January	Pays electricity bill	£300
	Pays wages	£1,000
5 January	Ireton returns a crate of wine costing £70 to G. Stevens	
7 January	G. Stevens pays half of the bills outstanding and half of the debtors pay him	

Figure 3.2 Recording the Transactions

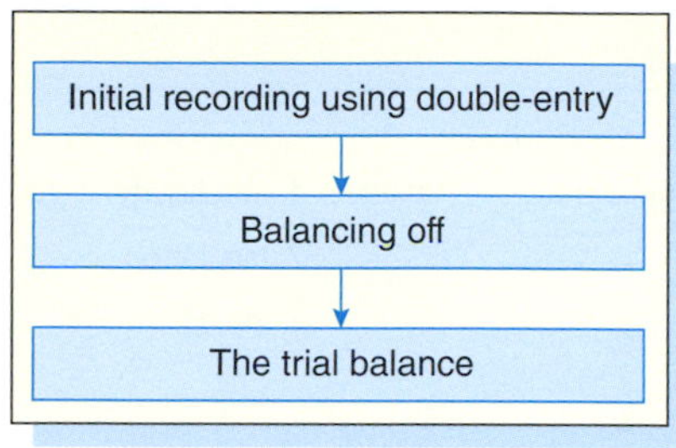

It is now time to enter the transactions for Gavin Stevens into the books of account. This will be done in the next section. As Figure 3.2 shows, there are three main parts to recording the transactions (recording, balancing off and the trial balance).

The bookkeeping role is an essential function of an accountant. However, as Real-World View 3.2 explains, the accountant who is only a bookkeeper is very rare. Most of an accountant's work is the more challenging job of analysing and interpreting the information.

REAL-WORLD VIEW 3.2

Keepers of the Books

As Keeper of the Books...the accountant has a rational and useful role. But the accountant who sticks to it is a rare fish. Certainly the officers of the established institutions would claim that it was a minor part of their usefulness. After all, it doesn't offer much in the way of power or esteem to an ambitious or intelligent man – and Valerie Barden's studies showed accountants on the whole as more intelligent than the average manager.

Source: Graham Cleverly (1971), *Managers and Magic (as amended)*, Longman, London, p. 39.

Step 1 The Initial Recording Using Double-Entry Bookkeeping

The individual amounts are directly entered into two different ledger accounts, **one on each side.** Thus, on 1st January we credit the equity (capital) account with £700,000, but debit the bank account with £700,000. This represents the initial £700,000 capital invested. We record three items: (1) date of transaction, (2) **account which is equal and opposite** to complete the double-entry and (3) amount. Each 'T' account (i.e., ledger page in the books of account) is treated separately. So that the transactions are easier to follow, each separate transaction is given a letter. Thus, the first transaction (investing £700,000 equity) is recorded as 'A' on the credit (i.e., right-hand side) in the equity account and also as 'A' on the debit (i.e., left-hand side) in the bank account (see Figure 3.3). For standardisation purposes, I use the term equity for sole traders (rather than capital, the term sometimes used).

It must be remembered that all organisations will structure their accounts books in slightly different ways. In particular, very small businesses may not keep any proper books of accounts, just filing the original invoices and passing them on to their accountants. Nonetheless all businesses will keep records of cash received and cash paid. However, bigger

Figure 3.3 Recording Gavin Stevens' Entries Using Double-Entry Bookkeeping

Equity

	£		£
		1 Jan. Bank	700,000 A

Bank

	£		£
1 Jan. Equity	700,000 A	2 Jan. Hotel	610,000 B
7 Jan. Ireton	1,965 M	2 Jan. Van	3,000 C
7 Jan. Hepworth	2,500 N	2 Jan. Purchases	2,000 D
		4 Jan. Electricity	300 J
		4 Jan. Wages	1,000 K
		7 Jan. Hogen	250 O
		7 Jan. Lewis	1,000 P

Revenue

	£		£
		3 Jan. Ireton	4,000 H
		3 Jan. Hepworth	5,000 I

Purchases

	£		£
2 Jan. Bank	2,000 D		
2 Jan. Hogen	1,000 E		
2 Jan. Lewis	2,000 F		

Sales Returns

	£		£
5 Jan. Ireton	70 L		

Purchases Returns

	£		£
		3 Jan. Hogen	500 G

Electricity

	£		£
4 Jan. Bank	300 J		

Wages

	£		£
4 Jan. Bank	1,000 K		

Hotel

	£		£
2 Jan. Bank	610,000 B		

Van

	£		£
2 Jan. Bank	3,000 C		

Ireton (trade receivable or debtor)

	£		£
3 Jan. Revenue	4,000 H	5 Jan. Sales returns	70 L
		7 Jan. Bank	1,965 M

Hepworth (trade receivable or debtor)

	£		£
3 Jan. Revenue	5,000 I	7 Jan. Bank	2,500 N

Hogen (trade payable or creditor)

	£		£
3 Jan. Purchases returns	500 G	2 Jan. Purchases	1,000 E
7 Jan. Bank	250 O		

Lewis (trade payable or creditor)

	£		£
7 Jan. Bank	1,000 P	2 Jan. Purchases	2,000 F

HELPNOTE 3.2

Note that each entry in Figure 3.3 appears on both sides (i.e., as a debit and a credit, equal and opposite) of different accounts. For example, equity of £200,000 is a credit in the equity account of £200,000 and a debit in the bank account of £200,000. Each account represents one page. So, for example, the sales account has nothing on the left-hand side of the page.

businesses will keep day books (such as the revenue or sales day book and purchases day book) in which they will list their credit sales and credit purchases.

In most businesses, the initial transactions are now recorded using a computer system. The individual ledger accounts are then stored in the computer. However, it is necessary to appreciate the underlying processes involved. These are now explained, both for Gavin Stevens and more generally. If we look at the double-entry in terms of debit and credit for Gavin Stevens, we have the following (see Figure 3.4).

Figure 3.4 Debit and Credit Table for Gavin Stevens

Account	Debit	Credit
Equity	–	Liability to owner increases by £700,000
Bank	Assets increase through capital introduced and money from trade receivables	Assets decrease through payments to suppliers and payments of expenses
Revenue	–	Income increases through credit sales £9,000
Purchases	Expenses increase through £2,000 cash purchases and £3,000 credit purchases	–
Revenue returns	Income reduced when customers return £70 goods	–
Purchases returns	–	Expenses reduced when £500 goods returned to supplier
Electricity	Expenses increase by £300	–
Wages	Expenses increase by £1,000	–
Hotel	Assets increase by £610,000	–
Van	Assets increase by £3,000	–
Ireton	Asset of trade receivable increases by £4,000	Asset reduced by returns of £70 and receipt of £1,965
Hepworth	Asset of trade receivable increases by £5,000	Asset reduced by receipt of £2,500
Hogen	Trade payable decreases by payment of £250 and returns of £500	Trade payable to third party increases by £1,000
Lewis	Liability decreases by payment of £1,000	Trade payable to third party increases by £2,000

Step 2 Balancing Off

Helpnotes 3.3 and 3.4 provide a number of rules to guide us through double-entry bookkeeping. When all the entries for a period have been completed then it is time to balance off

HELPNOTE 3.3

Double-Entry Checks

Because of the way double-entry is structured, a number of rules can guide us when we make the initial entries. We are using four accounts for revenue, purchases, revenue returns and purchases returns to make the entries clear.

1. Revenue and purchases
   There will normally never be a debit in a revenue account or a credit in a purchases account. Assets and liabilities never pass through these accounts

2. Returns
   Revenue returns and purchases returns have their own accounts. You will never find a credit in a revenue returns account or a debit in a purchases returns account

3. Assets and expenses
   When making the initial entries you never credit a non-current asset such as property, plant and equipment or expenses account

4. The bank account represents cash at bank. We always talk of cash received, and cash paid. Given the number of cash transactions the normal business conducts, there would normally be a separate cash book. The totals from the cash book would be summarised and then transferred to the bank account.

Bank account

In	*Out*
Equity invested	Cash paid for purchases
Cash from revenue	Cash paid for property, plant and equipment such as cars
	Cash paid for expenses such as:
	Wages paid
	Rent paid
	Electricity paid
	Light and heat paid

Finally, if all else fails and you are still struggling with double-entry then Helpnote 3.4 may be useful.

HELPNOTE 3.4

The Bank Account

If you are having trouble remembering your double-entry, work back from the bank account; remember:

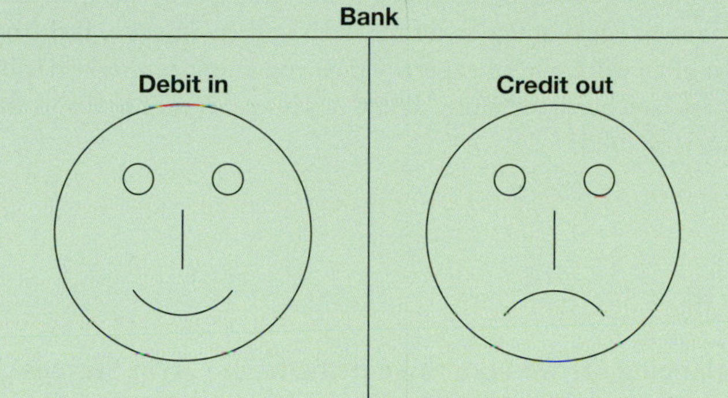

The smiling face represents money received so the business is better off. By contrast, the grumpy face represents money out, so the business is worse off.

the accounts and carry forward the new total to the next period. We are, in effect, signalling the end of an accounting period. It is convenient to carry all the figures forward. These carried forward figures will form the basis of the trial balance. However, the **revenue, purchases, revenue returns, purchases returns** and **expenses** accounts will then be **closed off** on the last day of the accounting period as they will *not* be carried forward to the next period. This is because in the next period all we are concerned with is that period's income and expenses. **The statement of financial position items will be brought forward** on the first day of the new accounting period. This is because assets, liabilities and equity continue from accounting period to accounting period. Accounting periods may be weekly, monthly or annually. The aim of balancing off is threefold.

1. To prepare a trial balance from which we will prepare the statement of financial position and income statement.
2. To close down income and expenses accounts which relate to the previous period.
3. To bring forward to the next period the assets, liabilities and equity balances.

First of all the accounts are balanced off. We then close off the revenue and expenses items to the income statement.

PAUSE FOR THOUGHT 3.4

The Trial Balance I

Why should the trial balance balance?

A trial balance is simply a list of all the balances on the individual accounts. If the double-entry process has been completed correctly, each debit will be matched by an equal and opposite credit entry. There will thus be equal amounts on the debit and credit sides. If the trial balance fails to balance – and it often will even for experts – then you know a mistake has been made in the double-entry process. You need, therefore, to find it. This process of trial and error is the reason why a trial balance is so called.

To illustrate balancing off we take three items from Gavin Stevens' accounts: revenue (an income statement item), electricity (an income statement item) and the bank account (a statement of financial position item). We balance off after the first week. We will then draw up a trial balance.

1. Income statement items

Revenue

	£		£
		3 Jan. Ireton	4,000
7 Jan. Bal. c/f	9,000	3 Jan. Hepworth	5,000
	9,000		9,000
7 Jan. Transfer to income statement	9,000	7 Jan. Bal. b/f	9,000

Note that the balance (bal.) would be carried forward (c/f) above the totals and brought forward (b/f) below them.

2. Income statement item

Electricity

	£		£
4 Jan. Bank	300	7 Jan. Bal. c/f	300
	300		300
7 Jan. Bal. b/f	300	7 Jan. Transfer to income statement	300

3. Statement of financial position item

Bank

	£		£
1 Jan. Capital	700,000	2 Jan. Hotel	610,000
7 Jan. Ireton	1,965	2 Jan. Van	3,000
7 Jan. Hepworth	2,500	2 Jan. Purchases	2,000
		4 Jan. Electricity	300
		4 Jan. Wages	1,000
		7 Jan. Hogen	250
		7 Jan. Lewis	1,000
		7 Jan. Bal. c/f	86,915
	£704,465		£704,465
8 Jan. Bal. b/f	£86,915		

Note that there is no need to close off the bank account because it will be used at the start of the next period. However, note **the date is the starting date for the next period.**

NOW GO BACK TO THE DOUBLE-ENTRY STAGE ON PAGE 64 AND COMPLETE THE 'T' ACCOUNTS SHOWN THERE. MAKE SURE YOU UNDERSTAND HOW TO BALANCE OFF PROPERLY. THEN CHECK YOUR ANSWER WITH THE ANSWER BELOW ON PAGES 70 AND 71.

HELPNOTE 3.5

Balancing Off

1 Always find which side has the greatest total (in the case below, £250) (a)
2 Record the greatest total twice, once on the debit side and once on the credit side (b)
3 Carry forward the balancing figure (bal. c/f) (c)
4 Bring forward the balancing figure (bal. b/f) (d)
5 For trading and profit and loss account items, only transfer the balance (e)

In this case, we use a telephone account for period to 31 January.

Balancing off a telephone account

	£		£
1 Jan. Telephone	250 (a)	31 Jan. Bal. c/f	250 (c)
	250 (b)		250 (b)
31 Jan. Bal. b/f	250 (d)	31 Jan. Transfer to income statement	250 (e)

The completed 'T' accounts are shown in Figure 3.5. The *balancing off* is shown in *italics* for ease of understanding. We have abbreviated balance brought forward (to Bal. b/f), balance carried forward (to Bal. c/f) and transfer to income statement (to IS). Note that statement of financial position items brought forward (Bal. b/f) are brought forward on the first day of the new accounting period, i.e. 8th January. Those students not wishing to gain an in-depth knowledge of double-entry bookkeeping can miss out pages 62–74. Appendix 3.1 provides a copy of the full example from initial entries, through to double-entry accounts and trial balance.

Figure 3.5 Completed Double-Entry Bookkeeping Entries for Gavin Stevens

Equity

	£		£
7 Jan. Bal. c/f	700,000	1 Jan. Bank	700,000
	700,000		*700,000*
		8 Jan. Bal. b/f	700,000

Bank

	£		£
1 Jan. Equity	700,000	2 Jan. Hotel	610,000
7 Jan. Ireton	1,965	2 Jan. Van	3,000
7 Jan. Hepworth	2,500	2 Jan. Purchases	2,000
		4 Jan. Electricity	300
		4 Jan. Wages	1,000
		7 Jan. Hogen	250
		7 Jan. Lewis	1,000
		7 Jan. Bal. c/f	86,915
	704,465		*704,465*
8 Jan. Bal. b/f	86,915		

Revenue

	£		£
		3 Jan. Ireton	4,000
7 Jan. Bal. c/f	9,000	3 Jan. Hepworth	5,000
	9,000		*9,000*
7 Jan. To income statement	9,000	*7 Jan. Bal. b/f*	9,000

Purchases

	£		£
2 Jan. Bank	2,000		
2 Jan. Hogen	1,000		
2 Jan. Lewis	2,000	*7 Jan. Bal. c/f*	5,000
	5,000		*5,000*
7 Jan. Bal. b/f	5,000	*7 Jan. To Income statement*	5,000

Revenue Returns

	£		£
5 Jan. Ireton	70	*7 Jan. Bal. c/f*	70
	70		*70*
7 Jan. Bal. b/f	70	*7 Jan. To income statement*	70

Purchases Returns

	£		£
7 Jan. Bal. c/f	500	3 Jan. Hogen	500
	500		*500*
7 Jan. To income statement	500	*7 Jan. Bal. b/f*	500

Electricity

	£		£
4 Jan. Bank	300	*7 Jan. Bal. c/f*	300
	300		*300*
7 Jan. Bal. b/f	300	*7 Jan. To income statement*	300

Wages

	£		£
4 Jan. Bank	1,000	*7 Jan. Bal. c/f*	1,000
	1,000		*1,000*
7 Jan. Bal. b/f	1,000	*7 Jan. To income statement*	1,000

Hotel

	£		£
2 Jan. Bank	610,000	*7 Jan. Bal. c/f*	610,000
	610,000		*610,000*
8 Jan. Bal. b/f	610,000		

Van

	£		£
2 Jan. Bank	3,000	*7 Jan. Bal. c/f*	3,000
	3,000		*3,000*
8 Jan. Bal. b/f	3,000		

Figure 3.5 Completed Double-Entry Bookkeeping Entries for Gavin Stevens (*continued*)

Ireton (trade receivable)

	£		£
3 Jan. Revenue	4,000	5 Jan. Sales Returns	70
		7 Jan. Bank	1,965
		7 Jan. Bal. c/f	1,965
	4,000		4,000
8 Jan. Bal. b/f	1,965		

Hepworth (trade receivable)

	£		£
3 Jan. Revenue	5,000	7 Jan. Bank	2,500
		7 Jan. Bal. c/f	2,500
	5,000		5,000
8 Jan. Bal. b/f	2,500		

Hogen (trade payable)

	£		£
3 Jan. Purchases Returns	500	2 Jan. Purchases	1,000
7 Jan. Bank	250		
7 Jan. Bal. c/f	250		
	1,000		1,000
		8 Jan. Bal. b/f	250

Lewis (trade payable)

	£		£
7 Jan. Bank	1,000	2 Jan. Purchases	2,000
7 Jan. Bal. c/f	1,000		
	2,000		2,000
		8 Jan. Bal. b/f	1,000

Note: We have closed off the income statement as at 7th January (revenue, purchases, revenue returns, purchases returns, electricity, wages) so that we can transfer these accounts to the income statement on that day. Statement of financial position items are, however, brought forward on 8th January ready for the new period. In practice, we would probably not bring forward accounts with only one entry in, such as equity.

Step 3 Trial Balance

DEFINITION 3.2

Trial Balance

Working definition
A listing of debit and credit balances to check the correctness of the double-entry system.

Formal definition
'A list of account balances in a double-entry accounting system. If the records have been correctly maintained, the sum of the debit balances will equal the sum of the credit balances, although certain errors such as the omission of a transaction or erroneous entries will not be disclosed by a trial balance.'

Source: Chartered Institute of Management Accountants (2000), *Official Terminology*. Reproduced by Permission of Elsevier.

The trial balance for Gavin Stevens may now be prepared. *Prepare your own answer before you look at the 'answer' shown in Figure 3.6.* The full Gavin Stevens' example from initial entries, through to double-entry accounts and the trial balance is shown in Appendix 3.1.

Figure 3.6 Gavin Stevens: Trial Balance as at 7th January

	Debit	Credit
	£	£
Hotel	610,000	
Van	3,000	
Revenue		9,000
Purchases	5,000	
Equity		700,000
Revenue returns	70	
Purchases returns		500
Bank	86,915	
Electricity	300	
Wages	1,000	
Ireton	1,965	
Hepworth	2,500	
Hogen		250
Lewis		1,000
	710,750	710,750

Note that the **debit items** in Figure 3.6 are either **assets** or **expenses** and the **credit items** are **income, liabilities** or **equity**. This conforms to the accounting equation:

$$\text{Assets} + \text{Expenses} = \text{Liabilities} + \text{Equity} + \text{Income}$$

These balances are analysed for Gavin Stevens in Figure 3.7.

Figure 3.7 Analysis of Gavin Stevens' Trial Balance

Assets	Hotel, van, bank, trade receivables (Ireton, Hepworth)
Expenses	Purchases, Revenue returns, electricity, wages
Income	Revenue, purchases returns
Liabilities	Trade payables (Hogen, Lewis)
Equity	Equity

Essentially, the trial balance is a check on the accuracy of the double-entry process. If the double-entry has been done properly, the trial balance will balance. If it does not, as Soundbite 3.1 shows, there is an error somewhere. Ideally, the books are then checked to find the error. Even when the trial balance balances, as Pause for Thought 3.5 shows, the accounts may not be totally correct.

SOUNDBITE 3.1

Trial Balance

Nowadays, you hear a lot about fancy accounting methods, like LIFO and FIFO, but back then we were using the ESP method, which really sped things along when it came time to close those books. It's a pretty basic method: if you can't make your books balance you take however much they're off by and enter it under the heading ESP, which stands for Error Some Place.

Sam Walton in *Sam Walton* p. 53

Source: The Executive's Book of Quotations (1994), pp. 3–4.

PAUSE FOR THOUGHT 3.5

The Trial Balance II

If the trial balance balances, that is the end of all my problems; I now know the accounts are correct. Is this true?

....

Unfortunately, this is not true! Although you can be happy that the trial balance does indeed balance, you must still be wary. There are several types of error (listed below) which may have crept in, perhaps at the original double-entry bookkeeping stage.

1. **Error of omission**
   You have omitted an entry completely. The trial balance will still balance, but your accounts will not be correct.
2. **Reverse entry**
   If you have completely reversed your entry and entered a debit as a credit, and vice versa, then your trial balance will balance, but incorrectly.
3. **Wrong amount**
   If the wrong figure (say £300 for the van instead of £3,000) was entered in the accounts, the books would still balance, but at the wrong amount.
4. **Wrong account**
   One of the entries might have been entered in the wrong account; for example, the van might be recorded in the electricity account.
5. **Compensating errors**
   If you make errors which cancel each other out, your trial balance will once more wrongly balance.

Day Books and Ledgers

Modern businesses are often very complex. There is a need to record the bookkeeping entries into books of account. The main book of account is the general ledger. This records all the accounts which will feed into the trial balance that will form the basis for the preparation of the income statement and statement of financial position. However, given the volume of transactions, often subsidiary records are kept such as the revenue and purchases day books, the revenue returns and purchases returns books and the revenue and purchases ledgers which are used to record individual transactions for trade receivables and trade payables. Note we use the terms revenue ledgers and revenue day book for consistency with the rest of the book, but they are also commonly known as the sales ledger and sales day book. The revenue returns and purchases returns books are also known as the returns inwards and returns outwards books. These balances are then transferred to the main ledger.

In large businesses, a set of subsidiary records may be kept such as revenue and purchases day books and the revenue and purchases ledger. These can be called books of prime entry. These are illustrated in Figure 3.8 below.

Control accounts will be used by companies to reconcile the balances in individual trade receivable and trade payable accounts with the totals taken from the revenue day book and

Figure 3.8 Demonstration of the Use of Day Books and Ledgers

Bamber Limited purchases and sells goods for his outdoor and climbing business. At the start of April 2014, he has the following purchases and revenues all on credit. Then at the end of April 2014, he pays his bills and his customers pay him.

(i) Set up the appropriate day books and ledgers.

(ii) Balance these accounts off at the end of April.

(iii) Transfer the amounts to the general ledger.

April 1 Buys goods for £3,000, £5,000 and £7,000 from Peters, Chen and Norton.

April 2 Returns good to Chen and Norton worth £500 and £600.

April 3 Sells goods to Jones, Khan and Smith for £4,000, £6,500 and £7,500.

April 10 Khan and Smith return goods worth £2,000 and £500.

April 20 Pays Peters £2,500, Chen £4,000 and Norton £6,000.

April 24 Receives £3,000 from Jones, £3,000 from Khan and £5,000 from Smith.

Day books and ledgers

(a) Day Books

Purchases Day Book

		£
April 1	Peters	3,000
April 1	Chen	5,000
April 1	Norton	7,000
April 30	To Purchases Account, General Ledger	15,000

Revenue Day Book

		£
April 3	Jones	4,000
April 3	Khan	6,500
April 3	Smith	7,000
April 30	To Revenue Account, General Ledger	17,500

Figure 3.8 Demonstration of the Use of Day Books and Ledgers (*continued*)

Purchases Returns Day Book

		£
April 2	Chen	500
April 2	Norton	600
April 30	To Purchases Returns Account, General Ledger	1,100

Revenue Returns Day Book

		£
April 10	Khan	2,000
April 10	Smith	500
April 30	To Revenue Returns Account, General Ledger	2,500

(b) Ledgers

Purchases Ledger

Peters

		£		£
April 20	Cash Book	2,500	April 1 Purchases	3,000
April 30	Bal c/f	500	Day Book	
		3,000		3,000
			May 1 Bal b/f	500

Chen

		£		£
April 2 Purchases Returns Day Book		500		
April 20	Cash Book	4,000	April 1 Purchases	5,000
April 30	Bal c/f	500	Day Book	
		5,000		5,000
			May 1 Bal b/f	500

Norton

		£		£
April 2 Revenue Returns Day Book		600		
April 20	Cash Book	6,000	April 1 Purchases	7,000
April 30	Bal c/f	400	Day Book	
		7,000		7,000
			May 1 Bal b/f	400

Revenue Ledger

Jones

	£		£
April 3 Revenue Day Book	4,000	April 24 Cash Book	3,000
		April 30 Bal c/f	1,000
	4,000		4,000
May 1 Bal b/f	1,000		

Khan

	£		£
April 3 Revenue Day Book	6,500	April 10 Revenue Returns Day Book	2,000
		April 24 Cash Book	3,000
		April 30 Bal c/f	1,500
	6,500		6,500
May 1 Bal b/f	1,500		

Figure 3.8 Demonstration of the Use of Day Books and Ledgers (*continued*)

Smith

	£		£
		April 10 Revenue Returns Day Book	500
April 3 Revenue Day Book	7,000	April 24 Cash Book	5,000
		April 30 Bal c/f	1,500
	7,000		7,000
May 1 Bal b/f	1,500		

Balances from Purchases and Revenue Ledgers

Purchases Ledger	£	Revenue Ledger	£
Peters	500	Jones	1,000
Chen	500	Khan	1,500
Norton	400	Smith	1,500
	1,400 cr		4,000 dr

Therefore, in the General Ledger account we have the following balances.

Purchases Account

	£		£
April 30 Purchases Day Book	15,000	April 30 Bal c/f	15,000
	15,000		15,000
May 1 Bal b/f	15,000		

Revenue Account

	£		£
April 30 Bal c/f	17,500	April 30 Revenue Day Book	17,500
	17,500		17,500
		May 1 Bal b/f	17,500

Revenue Returns Account

	£		£
April 30 Revenue Returns Book	2,500	April 30 Bal c/f	2,500
	2,500		2,500
May 1 Bal b/f	2,500		

Purchases Returns Account

	£		£
April 30 Bal c/f	1,100	April 30 Purchases Returns Book	1,100
	1,100		1,100
		May 1 Bal b/f	1,100

Cash Book

	£		£
April 24 Jones	3,000	April 20 Peters	2,500
April 24 Khan	3,000	April 20 Chen	4,000
April 30 Smith	5,000	April 20 Norton	6,000
April 30 Bal c/f	1,500		
	12,500		12,500
		May 1 Bal b/f	1,500

Note: For simplification and completeness we show the cash book which has a credit balance showing the company is overdrawn by £1,500. We summarise the double-entry process below in a trial balance just to show that despite the day books, the books still balance.

Figure 3.8 Demonstration of the Use of Day Books and Ledgers (*continued*)

Bamber Limited Trial Balance as at 30 April 2013

	£	£
Purchases Ledger (Trade payables)		1,400
Revenue Ledger (Trade receivables)	4,000	
Purchases account	15,000	
Revenue account		17,500
Revenue Returns	2,500	
Purchases Returns		1,100
Cash book		1,500
	21,500	21,500

revenue returns book and the purchases day book and purchases returns book. This is, in effect, a reconciliation account. Control accounts work on the principle that if we know the opening and closing balances and the movements in and out of the accounts then everything should balance.

If we look at both the revenue and purchases ledger control accounts, we would have the following with **made up amounts.**

Revenue ledger control (trade receivables)

	£		£
Opening trade receivables (revenue ledger)	20,000	Cash received (cash book)	10,000
Add revenue (general ledger)	5,000	Revenue returns (general ledger)	3,000
		Closing trade receivables (revenue ledger)	12,000
	25,000		25,000

Purchases ledger control (trade payables)

	£		£
Cash paid (cash book)	15,000	Opening trade payables (purchases ledger)	12,000
Purchases returns (general ledger)	2,000		
Closing trade payables (purchases ledger)	9,000	Add purchases (general ledger)	14,000
	26,000		26,000

We have thus taken the opening and closing balances from the revenue and purchases ledgers while the revenue and purchases come from the totals taken from the day books and transferred to the revenue and purchases accounts in the general ledger. We will also record the totals from the revenue returns (for trade receivables) and purchases returns (for trade payables). The cash received and paid are taken from the cash book. Overall, therefore, if there is an error in the trade receivables or trade payables, the control accounts will not balance.

We illustrate this below for a revenue ledger control account in the general ledger account and a purchases ledger control account in Figure 3.9.

Figure 3.9 Control Accounts

Hebson Ltd has the following balances relating to the revenue and purchases for January 2014.

Trade receivables	1.1.2014	£85,000
Trade payables	1.1.2014	£68,000
Cash received for trade receivables January 2014		£28,000
Cash paid for trade payables January 2014		£32,000
Revenue		£65,000
Purchases		£62,000
Revenue returns		£3,000
Purchases returns		£2,000
Closing trade receivables		£119,000
Closing trade payables		£100,000

Draw up the trade receivables and trade payables control accounts and advise Hebson if there is a problem.

Revenue Ledger Control Account

	£		£
Opening trade receivables	85,000	Revenue returns	3,000
Revenue	65,000	Cash received	28,000
		Closing trade receivables	119,000
	150,000		150,000

Purchases Ledger Control Account

	£		£
Purchases returns	2,000	Opening trade payables	68,000
Cash paid	32,000	Purchases	62,000
Closing trade payables	100,000		
	134,000		130,000

We can advise Hebson that the revenue ledger control account balances, and, therefore, the revenue ledger has been correctly drawn up. However, we have made an error in the purchases ledger of £4,000 (£134,000 – £130,000) which needs to be found.

HEALTH WARNING

Those students who did not wish to gain an in-depth knowledge of double-entry bookkeeping can restart here.

Computers

Double-entry bookkeeping is obviously very labour-intensive; therefore, computerised packages, such as *Sage*, are very popular. Normally, an entry is keyed into the bank account (e.g., hotel £610,000) or into a trade receivable or trade payable account (e.g., sales to Ireton £4,000). The computer automatically completes the entries. Revenue, purchases and bank transactions are standard and, therefore, only require one entry by the user. For non-standard items both a debit and a credit entry is recorded. The computer, after all the transactions have been input, can produce a trial balance, an income statement and the statement of financial position. Nowadays, there are numerous software packages which help with bookkeeping and accounts production. Organisations purchase off-the-shelf accounting packages and specialised accountancy packages customised for their particular businesses.

At first sight, therefore, computerised accounting packages which perform the double-entry transactions and then prepare the income statement and statement of financial position would seem to be a gift from heaven. They are quick, efficient and save labour. However, there are problems. The principal one is that, as many organisations have found to their cost, if you put rubbish into the computer, you get rubbish out. In other words, computer operators who are unskilled in accounting can create havoc with the accounts. To enter items correctly, it is necessary to have an understanding of the accounting process. Otherwise, disasters may occur with meaningless accounts. Therefore, unfortunately, understanding double-entry bookkeeping is just as important in this computer age.

Conclusion

The double-entry process is a key part of financial accounting. Without understanding double-entry, it is difficult to get to grips with accounting itself. However, there is no need to be scared of double-entry. Essentially, it means that for every transaction which is entered on one side of a ledger account, an equal and opposite entry is made in another ledger account. These entries are called debit and credit. All the debits will equal all the credits. This is proved when the accounts are balanced off. The balance from each account is then listed in a trial balance. The trial balance shows that the double-entry process has been completed. However, a balanced trial balance does not necessarily guarantee that the double-entry has been correctly carried out (for example, there may be some errors of omission). Once the trial balance has been prepared, it is possible to complete the income statement and the statement of financial position.

Discussion Questions

Questions with numbers in blue have answers at the back of the book.

Q1 Why is double-entry bookkeeping so important?

Q2 How do you think that the books of account kept by different businesses might vary?

Q3 Computerisation means that there is no need to understand double-entry bookkeeping. Discuss.

Q4 How much trust can be placed in a trial balance which balances?

Q5 Why are there usually more debit balances in a trial balance than credit balances?

Q6 State whether the following are true or false. If false, explain why.
- (a) We debit cash received, but credit cash paid.
- (b) Revenue is debited to a revenue account, but purchases are credited to a purchases account.
- (c) If a business purchases a car for cash, we debit the car account and credit the bank account.
- (d) Purchases, hotel, electricity and wages are all debits in a trial balance.
- (e) Revenue, rent paid and equity are all credits in a trial balance.

Numerical Questions

Questions with numbers in blue have answers at the back of the book.

Q1 From the following accounting figures show the six steps in the accounting equation:
opening assets £25,000, opening liabilities £25,000 (£15,000 third party and £10,000 equity), profit £15,000 (income £60,000, expenses £45,000).

Q2 Show the debit and credit accounts of the following transactions in the ledger and what effect (i.e., increase/decrease) they have on assets, liabilities, equity, income and expenses.
The first one is done as an illustration.

(a) Pay wages of £7,000

Debit effect	*Credit effect*
Wages: increases an expense	Bank: decreases an asset

(b) Introduces £10,000 equity by way of a cheque.
(c) Buys a car for £9,000 by cheque.
(d) Pays electricity bill of £300.
(e) Sales for £9,000 cash.
(f) Purchases £3,000 on credit from A. Taylor.

Q3 You have the following details for A. Bird of transactions with customers and suppliers.

(a) 1 June credit purchases of £8,000, £6,000 and £5,000 from Robin, Falcon and Sparrow, respectively.
(b) 4 June A. Bird returns goods unpaid of £1,000 and £2,000 to Robin and Falcon, respectively.
(c) 6 June A. Bird makes credit sales of £4,000, £7,000 and £6,000 to Thrush, Raven and Starling, respectively.
(d) 7 June Starling returns £1,000 goods unpaid which are faulty.

Required:

(i) Write up the relevant ledger accounts.
(ii) Balance off the accounts on 7 June for the income statement. Bring them forward on 7 June; however, there is no need actually to transfer them to the income statement.
(iii) Bring forward balances for assets and liabilities on 8 June.

Q4 Balance off the following four accounts from four different businesses at the month end. Transfer the balances for revenue and purchases to the trading account.

(i) Revenue

	£		£
		8 June Bank	1,000
		9 June Brown	2,000

(ii) Purchases

	£		£
1 June Bank	500		
30 June Patel	9,500		

(iii) Bank

	£		£
3 June Cash Sales	500	1 June Wages	800
		7 June Rent	300
		8 June Purchases	200

(iv) R. Smith (trade receivable)

	£		£
1 June Sales	800	3 June Rev. Rets.	1,000
		4 June Bank	3,000

Rev. Rets. represents revenue returns.

Q5 John Frier has the following transactions during a six-month period to 30 June.

(a) Invests £10,000 in the business on 1 January.
(b) Buys a motor van for £4,000 on 8 February by cheque.
(c) Purchases £8,000 goods on credit from A. Miner on 10 March.
(d) Pays A. Miner £3,000 on 12 April.
(e) Sells £9,000 credit sales to R. Army on 7 May.
(f) Receives £4,500 in cash on 10 June from R. Army.

Required: On 30 June prepare John Frier's:

(i) Ledger accounts
(ii) Trial balance after balancing off the accounts. Bring forward revenue and purchases on 30 June, but there is no need to transfer the income statement items.

Q6 Katherine Jones sets up a small agency that markets and distributes goods. She has the following regular credit customers (Edwards, Smith and Patel) and regular suppliers of credit goods (Johnston and Singh). She has the following transactions in the first week of July.

1 July Invests £195,000 equity into the business.
2 July Buys some premises for £75,000 by cheque.
Buys office equipment for £9,000 by cheque.
Buys goods from Johnston for £3,000 and from Singh for £1,000, both are on credit.
Cash purchases of £7,000.
3 July Sales of £10,000, £9,000 and £7,000 are made on credit to Edwards, Smith and Patel, respectively.
4 July Returns £500 goods unpaid to Johnston as they were damaged.
5 July Pays wages £4,000 and bills for electricity £2,000 and telephone £1,000.
7 July Settles half of the outstanding trade payables and receives half of the money outstanding from trade receivables.

Q6 Katherine Jones *(continued)*

Required: Prepare Katherine Jones':

(i) Ledger accounts. Balance off the income statement items on 7 July. However, there is no need to transfer the income statement items.

(ii) Trial balance after balancing off the accounts.

Q7 R. Poon was having a whale of a time trying to get a trial balance for his company Redwar. He had the following transactions during the month of May. He asks you to prepare the book entries and a trial balance.

1 May	Invests £8,000 in his business bank account.
2 May	Purchases £2,000 goods for cash from N. Yuwit.
	£4,000 of goods on credit from S. Eal.
	£1,000 of goods on credit from P. Olar.
4 May	Sells £1,500 goods for cash to A.R.C. Tic.
	£5,000 goods on credit to H. Unter.
	£3,000 goods on credit to M. Dick.
7 May	M. Dick returns £2,000 goods unpaid saying that they were rotting.
8 May	R. Poon sends M. Dick's £2,000 goods (that he had originally purchased from S. Eal for £1,800) back unpaid because he can't stand the smell.
10 May	Purchases another £1,200 of goods on credit from S. Eal.
11 May	H. Unter buys on credit £1,600 of goods from R. Poon.
15 May	R. Poon receives bank interest of £250.
20 May	R. Poon pays S. Eal the amount owing.
20 May	R. Poon pays P. Olar £750.
21 May	R. Poon receives £2,000 from H. Unter.
21 May	R. Poon receives £800 from M. Dick.
31 May	R. Poon pays by cheque wages £800, rent £500, electricity £75 and stationery £25.

Required: Prepare R. Poon's:

(i) Ledger accounts.

(ii) Trial balance after balancing off the accounts. Bring forward the income statement items on 31 May, but there is no need actually to transfer the income statement items.

Q8 Jay Shah has the following balances as at 31 December in his accounts.

	£		£
Equity	45,300	Purchases returns	500
Motor car	3,000	Bank	3,600
Building	70,000	Electricity	1,400
Office furniture	400	Business rates	1,800
A. Smith (trade receivable)	250	Rent	1,600
J. Andrews (trade payable)	350	Wages	3,500
T. Williams (trade payable)	550	Long-term loan	9,000
G. Woolley (trade receivable)	150	Revenue	100,000
		Purchases	70,000

Q8 Jay Shah *(continued)*

Required:
(i) Jay Shah's trial balance as at 31 December.
(ii) An indication of which balances are assets, liabilities, equity, income or expenses.

Q9 Mary Symonds, a management consultant has the following balances from the accounts on 30 September.

	£		£
Office	80,000	Equity	28,150
Long-term loan	3,000	Electricity	1,600
Van	3,500	Telephone	3,400
H. Mellet (trade receivable)	650	Repairs	300
R. Edwards (trade receivable)	1,300	Business rates	900
P. Morgan (trade payable)	1,400	Computer	3,000
Y. Karbhari (trade payable)	600	Travel	4,000
Consultancy fees	70,000	Stationery	800
Cash at bank	3,700		

Required: Mary Symonds' trial balance as at 30 September.

Q10 The following trial balance for Rajiv Sharma as at 31 December has been incorrectly prepared.

	£	£
Shop		55,000
Machinery	45,000	
Car		10,000
Revenue	135,000	
Purchases	80,000	
Opening inventory		15,000
Trade receivables		12,000
Trade payables	8,000	
Long-term loan	16,000	
General expenses		300
Telephone	400	
Light and heat	300	
Repairs		400
	284,700	92,700

Required: A corrected trial balance as at 31 December.
Helpnote: If you rearrange the balances and the trial balance irritatingly still doesn't balance, remember equity.

Q11 Rachel Thomas's trial balance balances as follows:

	£	£
Revenue		100,000
Shop	60,000	
Van	50,000	
Purchases	60,000	
Equity		172,800
Bank	100,000	
General expenses	1,000	
Return inwards	300	
Repairs	800	
A. Bright (trade receivable)	2,000	
B. Dull (trade payable)		1,600
Telephone	300	
	274,400	274,400

Unfortunately, Rachel Thomas's bookkeeper was not very experienced. The following transactions were incorrectly entered:

(a) Purchase of a computer for £3,000 cash completely omitted.
(b) Credit sales of £800 to A. Bright forgotten.
(c) A photocopier worth £800 wrongly debited to the shop account.
(d) £300 credited to B. Dull's account should have been charged to A. Bright as it was a sales return.
(e) The van really cost £5,000, but had wrongly been recorded as costing £50,000 in both the van and bank accounts.

Required: A corrected trial balance as at 31 December.

Q12 Which of the following balances extracted from the books on 31 December would be used as a basis for next year's accounts?

	£		£
Equity employed	9,200	Trade receivables	700
Rent and rates	1,000	Trade payables	1,400
Buildings	7,000	Bank	600
Telephone	1,500	Inventory	1,300
Revenue	100,000	Purchases	80,000
Computer	1,000		

Q13 Norton Limited purchases and sells goods for his mobility business. At the start of May 2014, he has the following purchases and revenue all on credit. Then at the end of May 2014, he pays his bills and his customers pay him.

(a) Set up the purchases day book, revenue day book, revenue returns book and purchases returns book.
(b) Set up the purchases and revenue ledgers.
(c) Balance these accounts off at the end of May.
(d) Transfer the amounts to the general ledger.

May 1 Buys goods for £4,000, £6,000 and £10,000 from Robin, Sparrow and Hare.
May 6 Returns goods to Robin and Sparrow of £2,000 and £1,000.
May 10 Sells goods to Fox, Rabbit and Hare for £5,000, £6,000 and £7,000.
May 12 Fox and Rabbit return £1,500 and £800 goods.
May 18 Pays Robin, £1,500, Sparrow £2,500 and Hare £8,000.
May 25 Receives £3,000 from Fox, £2,500 from Rabbit and £6,000 from Hare.

Q14 Delaware Ltd has the following balances relating to revenue and purchases for January 2014.

Trade receivables	1.1.2014	£96,300
Trade payables	1.1.2014	£71,600
Cash received for trade receivables January 2014		£50,000
Cash paid for trade payables January 2014		£40,500
Revenue		£70,700
Purchases		£30,300
Revenue returns		£2,000
Purchases returns		£1,500
Closing trade receivables	31.1.2014	£118,000
Closing trade payables	31.1.2014	£60,000

Required: Draw up the trade receivables and trade payables control accounts and advise Delaware Ltd.

APPENDIX 3.1: Complete Worked Example for Gavin Stevens

Let us now look at an example. Gavin Stevens has decided to open a hotel to cater for conferences and large functions.

1 January	G. Stevens invests £700,000 equity into a business bank account.	
2 January	Buys and pays for a hotel	£610,000
	Buys and pays for a second-hand delivery van	£3,000
	Makes purchases for cash	£2,000
	Makes purchases on credit from Hogen	£1,000
	Makes purchases on credit from Lewis	£2,000
3 January	Returns goods costing £500 to Hogen	
3 January	Credit sales to Ireton £4,000 for a large garden party	
	Credit sales to Hepworth £5,000 for a business conference	
4 January	Pays electricity bill	£300
	Pays wages	£1,000
5 January	Ireton returns a crate of wine costing £70 to G. Stevens	
7 January	G. Stevens pays half of the bills outstanding and half of the debtors pay him	

Completed Double-Entry Bookkeeping Entries for Gavin Stevens

Equity

	£		£
7 Jan. Bal. c/f	700,000	1 Jan. Bank	700,000
	700,000		700,000
		8 Jan. Bal. b/f	700,000

Bank

	£		£
1 Jan. Equity	700,000	2 Jan. Hotel	610,000
7 Jan. Ireton	1,965	2 Jan. Van	3,000
7 Jan. Hepworth	2,500	2 Jan. Purchases	2,000
		4 Jan. Electricity	300
		4 Jan. Wages	1,000
		7 Jan. Hogen	250
		7 Jan. Lewis	1,000
		7 Jan. Bal. c/f	86,915
	704,465		704,465
8 Jan. Bal. b/f	86,915		

Revenue

	£		£
		3 Jan. Ireton	4,000
7 Jan. Bal. c/f	9,000	3 Jan. Hepworth	5,000
	9,000		9,000
7 Jan. To income statement	9,000	*7 Jan. Bal. b/f*	9,000

Purchases

	£		£
2 Jan. Bank	2,000		
2 Jan. Hogen	1,000		
2 Jan. Lewis	2,000	*7 Jan. Bal. c/f*	5,000
	5,000		5,000
7 Jan. Bal. b/f	5,000	*7 Jan. To Income statement*	5,000

Completed Double-Entry Bookkeeping Entries for Gavin Stevens (*continued*)

Revenue Returns

	£		£
5 Jan. Ireton	70	*7 Jan. Bal. c/f*	70
	70		70
7 Jan. Bal. b/f	70	*7 Jan. To income statement*	70

Purchases Returns

	£		£
7 Jan. Bal. c/f	500	3 Jan. Hogen	500
	500		500
7 Jan. To income statement	500	*7 Jan. Bal. b/f*	500

Electricity

	£		£
4 Jan. Bank	300	*7 Jan. Bal. c/f*	300
	300		300
7 Jan. Bal. b/f	300	*7 Jan. To income statement*	300

Wages

	£		£
4 Jan. Bank	1,000	*7 Jan. Bal. c/f*	1,000
	1,000		1,000
7 Jan. Bal. b/f	1,000	*7 Jan. To income statement*	1,000

Hotel

	£		£
2 Jan. Bank	610,000	*7 Jan. Bal. c/f*	610,000
	610,000		610,000
8 Jan. Bal. b/f	610,000		

Van

	£		£
2 Jan. Bank	3,000	*7 Jan. Bal. c/f*	3,000
	3,000		3,000
8 Jan. Bal. b/f	3,000		

Ireton (trade receivable)

	£		£
3 Jan. Revenue	4,000	5 Jan. Sales Returns	70
		7 Jan. Bank	1,965
		7 Jan. Bal. c/f	1,965
	4,000		4,000
8 Jan. Bal. b/f	1,965		

Hepworth (trade receivable)

	£		£
3 Jan. Revenue	5,000	7 Jan. Bank	2,500
		7 Jan. Bal. c/f	2,500
	5,000		5,000
8 Jan. Bal. b/f	2,500		

Hogen (trade payable)

	£		£
3 Jan. Purchases Returns	500	2 Jan. Purchases	1,000
7 Jan. Bank	250		
7 Jan. Bal. c/f	250		
	1,000		1,000
		8 Jan. Bal. b/f	250

Lewis (trade payable)

	£		£
7 Jan. Bank	1,000	2 Jan. Purchases	2,000
7 Jan. Bal. c/f	1,000		
	2,000		2,000
		8 Jan. Bal. b/f	1,000

Gavin Stevens: Trial Balance as at 7th January

	Debit	Credit
	£	£
Hotel	610,000	
Van	3,000	
Revenue		9,000
Purchases	5,000	
Equity		700,000
Revenue returns	70	
Purchases returns		500
Bank	86,915	
Electricity	300	
Wages	1,000	
Ireton	1,965	
Hepworth	2,500	
Hogen		250
Lewis		1,000
	710,750	710,750

Go online to discover the extra features for this chapter at **www.wiley.com/college/jones**

Chapter 4

Main financial statements: The Income Statement (Profit and Loss Account)

'Around here you're either expense or you're revenue.'

Donna Vaillancourt, Inc. (March 1994) *The Wiley Book of Business Quotations* (1998), p. 90.

Learning Outcomes

After completing this chapter you should be able to:

- Explain the nature of the income statement.
- Understand the individual components of the income statement.
- Outline the layout of the income statement.
- Evaluate the nature and importance of profit.

Go online to discover the extra features for this chapter at
www.wiley.com/college/jones

Chapter Summary

- One of three main financial statements.
- Consists of revenue, cost of sales and other expenses.
- Cost of sales is essentially opening inventory plus purchases less closing inventory.
- Gross profit is revenue less cost of sales.
- Net profit is income less cost of sales less other expenses.
- Profit is determined by income earned less expenses incurred, not cash received less cash paid.
- Profit is an elusive concept.
- Capital expenditure (i.e., on non-current assets such as motor vehicles) is treated differently to revenue expenditure (i.e., an expense such as telephone line rental).
- Profit is useful when evaluating an organisation's performance.

Introduction

The income statement (often known as profit and loss account) is one of the three most important financial statements. Effectively, it records an organisation's income and expenses and is prepared from the trial balance. For UK companies, it is required by the Companies Act 1985. An income statement seeks to determine an organisation's profit (i.e., income less expenses) over a period of time. It is thus concerned with measuring an organisation's performance. Different organisations will have different income statements. Indeed, they also have slightly different names. In this chapter, we focus on understanding the purpose, nature, contents and layout of the income statement of the sole trader. The preparation of the income statement of the sole trader from the trial balance is covered in Chapter 6. In Chapter 7 we investigate the preparation of the income statements of partnerships and limited companies. In this chapter, I have used the term 'income statement', which is recommended by the International Accounting Standards Board. I prefer this to the term statement of comprehensive income, which is also international accounting terminology, as the latter includes items such as gains on foreign exchange, which is outside the scope of this book. Sometimes the term profit and loss account is used for sole traders, partnerships or non-listed companies. However, to avoid confusion I use the term 'income statement' for all those business enterprises.

Context

The income statement, along with the statement of financial position and statement of cash flows, is one of the three major financial statements. It is prepared from the trial balance and presents an organisation's income and expenses over a period of time. This period may vary. Many businesses prepare a monthly income statement for internal management purposes.

Annual accounts are prepared for external users like shareholders or the tax authorities. From now on we generally discuss a yearly income statement. By contrast, the statement of financial position presents an organisation's assets, liabilities and equity and is presented at a particular point in time. The statement of cash flows shows the cash inflows and outflows of a business.

SOUNDBITE 4.1

Profits

'You must deodorise profits and make people understand that profit is not something offensive, but as important to a company as breathing.'

Sir Peter Parker, quoted in the *Sunday Telegraph* (5 September 1976)

Source: The Book of Business Quotations (1991), p. 183.

The major parts of the income statement are:

$$\text{Income} - \text{Expenses} = \text{Profit}$$

As Soundbite 4.1 above shows, profits are central to evaluating an organisation's performance. The profit figure is extremely important as it is used for a variety of purposes. It is used as an overall measure of performance and for more specific purposes, such as the basis by which companies distribute dividends to shareholders or as a starting point for working out taxation payable to the government. An organisation's profit performance is closely followed by analysts and by the press. In Real-World View 4.1, for example, HSBC have produced record results.

REAL-WORLD VIEW 4.1

Profit Performance

HSBC Enters History Books with £10 Billion Profit

Banking group HSBC stepped into another row about profits yesterday when it announced the largest earnings in British corporate history, alongside bumper payouts for its top executives. The company said it made pre-tax profits of £10 billion last year – 35pc more than in 2003 and higher than the £9.3 billion profits declared by oil giant Shell last month.

Source: Andrew Cave, *Daily Telegraph*, 1 March 2005, p. 38.

Definitions

As Definition 4.1 indicates, an income statement represents the income less the expenses of an organisation. Essentially, income represents money earned by the organisation (for example, revenue or sales), while expenses represent the costs of generating these sales (for example, purchases) and of running the business (for example, telephone expenses). Definition 4.1 gives a working and a formal definition of an income statement and an official definition from the Chartered Institute of Management Accountants.

DEFINITION 4.1

Definition of an Income Statement (Profit and Loss Account)

Working definition
The statement detailing the income less the expenses of an organisation over a period of time, giving profit.

Formal definition
'A key financial statement which represents an organisation's income less its expenses over a period of time and thus determines its profit so as to give a 'true and fair' view of an organisation's financial affairs.'

Formal definition (CIMA (2005) *Official Terminology*)
'Financial statement including all the profits and losses recognised in a period, unless an accounting standard requires inclusion elsewhere.'

Source: Chartered Institute of Management Accountants (2000), *Official Terminology*. Reproduced by Permission of Elsevier.

Broadly, a working definition of income is the revenue and other gains earned by a business, while expenses are the costs incurred running a business. The International Accounting Standards Board formally defines income and expenses using the concept of an increase or a decrease in economic benefit (i.e., does it increase the wealth of the business). Incomes are thus increases in economic benefit (i.e., inflows or increases in assets or decreases in third-party liabilities) which increase owners' equity. Expenses are decreases in economic benefit (i.e., outflows or decreases in assets or increases in third-party liabilities) that decrease owners' equity. Both working and formal definitions are provided in Definition 4.2.

DEFINITION 4.2

Income

Working definition
Revenue and other gains earned by a business.

Formal definition
'Increases in economic benefits during the accounting period in the form of inflows or enhancements of assets or decreases of liabilities that result in increases in equity.'

Source: International Accounting Standards Board (2010), *Conceptual Framework for Financial Reporting.*

Expenses

Working definition
Costs incurred running a business.

Formal definition
'Decreases in economic benefits during the accounting period in the form of outflows or depletions of assets or incurrences of liabilities that result in decreases in equity.'

Source: International Accounting Standards Board (2010), *Conceptual Framework for Financial Reporting.*

Layout

The income statement is nowadays conventionally presented in a vertical format (such as in Figure 4.1). Here we begin with revenue (sales) and then deduct the expenses. In the UK, the 1985 Companies Act sets out several possible formats, which are still broadly followed. For sole traders or partnerships, a full income statement is sometimes prepared using all the figures from the trial balance. Often, however, the income statement is presented in summary form, with many individual revenues and expenses grouped together. For companies presenting their results to the shareholders in the annual report, the exact relationship to the original trial balance is often unclear. Examples of Marks & Spencer plc and AstraZeneca plc income statements (profit and loss accounts) are given in Company Snapshots 2.1 (in Chapter 2) and 7.1 in Chapter 7 respectively.

By contrast the income statement (sometimes called the trading and profit and loss account) of the sole trader is more clearly derived from the trial balance. In this section we explain the theory behind this in more detail. In the following section the main terminology is explained. In order to be more realistic, we use the adapted income statement of a real person, a sole trader who runs a public house (pub). This is presented in Figure 4.1.

Figure 4.1 Sole Trader's Income Statement

R. Beer *Income Statement for the Year Ended 31 March 2014*		
	£	£
Revenue		100,425
Less *Cost of Sales*		
Opening inventory	3,590	
Add Purchases	58,210	
	61,800	
Less Closing inventory	2,200	59,600
Gross Profit		40,825
Add *Other Income*		
Gaming machine		2,000
Less *Expenses*		42,825
Wages	8,433	
Rates and water	3,072	
Insurance	397	
Electricity	2,714	
Telephone	292	
Advertising	172	
Motor expenses	530	
Darts team expenses	1,865	
Repairs and renewals	808	
Laundry	1,174	
Music and entertainment	3,095	
Licences	604	
Guard dog expenses	385	
Garden expenses	1,716	
Sundry expenses	1,648	
Accounting	800	
Depreciation	6,770	34,475
Net Profit		8,350

The corresponding statement of financial position (balance sheet) for R. Beer is presented in the next chapter in Figure 5.2. In Chapter 6, we show how to prepare an income statement from the trial balance.

Main Components

Figure 4.2 shows the six main components of the income statement (revenue or sales, cost of sales, gross profit, other income, expenses and net profit) of a sole trader.

These six components are shown in Figure 4.3. In the first column, an overview definition is provided. This is followed by some general examples and then, whenever possible, a specific example. These components are then discussed in more detail in the text. The same order is used as for R. Beer's income statement.

Figure 4.2 Overview of Income Statement

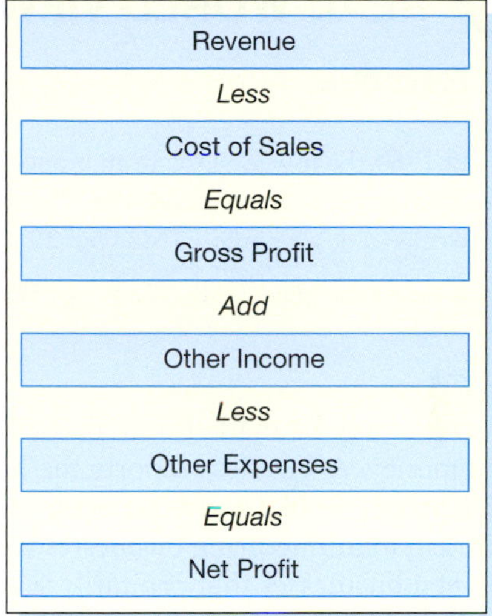

Revenue or Sales

Generating sales is a key ingredient of business success. However, the nature of sales varies considerably from organisation to organisation. For companies, the word 'revenue' or sometimes 'turnover' is used for sales. In this book, for consistency, we use the term revenue in the financial statements and sales more generally. However, practice in this area is variable. Essentially, revenue is the income that an organisation generates from its operations. For example, Brook Brothers in Real-World View 4.2 sold clothes.

Figure 4.3 Main Components of the Income Statement (Trading and Profit and Loss Account)

	Overview	*General Examples*	*Specific Examples*
Revenue (sales)	Income earned from selling goods (may be reduced by sales returns, i.e., goods returned by customers)	Sales	e.g., Sales of beer, food
Cost of Sales	The costs directly incurred in selling goods	1. Opening inventory 2. Purchases (may be reduced by purchases returns, i.e., goods returned to supplier) 3. Closing inventory	e.g., Barrels of beer a pub has at start of year e.g., Purchases of beer e.g., Barrels of beer a pub has left at end of year
Gross Profit	Revenue less cost of sales	Measures gain of organisation from buying and selling	e.g., The direct profit a pub makes by reselling the beer
Other Income	Non-trading income which a firm has earned	1. Income from investments 2. Income from sale of property, plant and equipment	e.g., Interest received from deposit account at bank e.g., Profit on selling a car for more than it was recorded in the accounts
Expenses	Items indirectly incurred in selling the goods	1. Light and heat 2. Employees' pay	e.g., Electricity e.g., Wages and salaries
Net Profit	Sales less cost of sales less expenses	Measures gain of organisation from all business activities	e.g., The profit a pub makes after taking into account all the pub's expenses

REAL-WORLD VIEW 4.2

Revenue

In 1964 the lower Manhattan branch of Brook Brothers was robbed, and the thieves got away with clothes worth $200,000. One clerk remarked: 'If they had come during our sale two weeks ago, we could have saved 20 percent.'

Source: Peter Hay (1988), *The Book of Business Anecdotes*, Harrap Ltd, London, p. 100.

Sales may be made for credit or for cash. Credit sales create debtors, who owe the business money. A business reports the balance that these debtors owe as an asset called 'trade receivables'. Some businesses, such as supermarkets, have predominantly cash customers. By contrast, manufacturing businesses will have largely credit customers. A further distinction is between businesses that primarily sell goods (for example, supermarkets which supply food) and those which supply services (for example, a bank). Revenue is very diverse. In Company Snapshot 4.1, for example, Stagecoach Plc's revenue for 2011 is shown divided up into UK Bus and Rail, and North America.

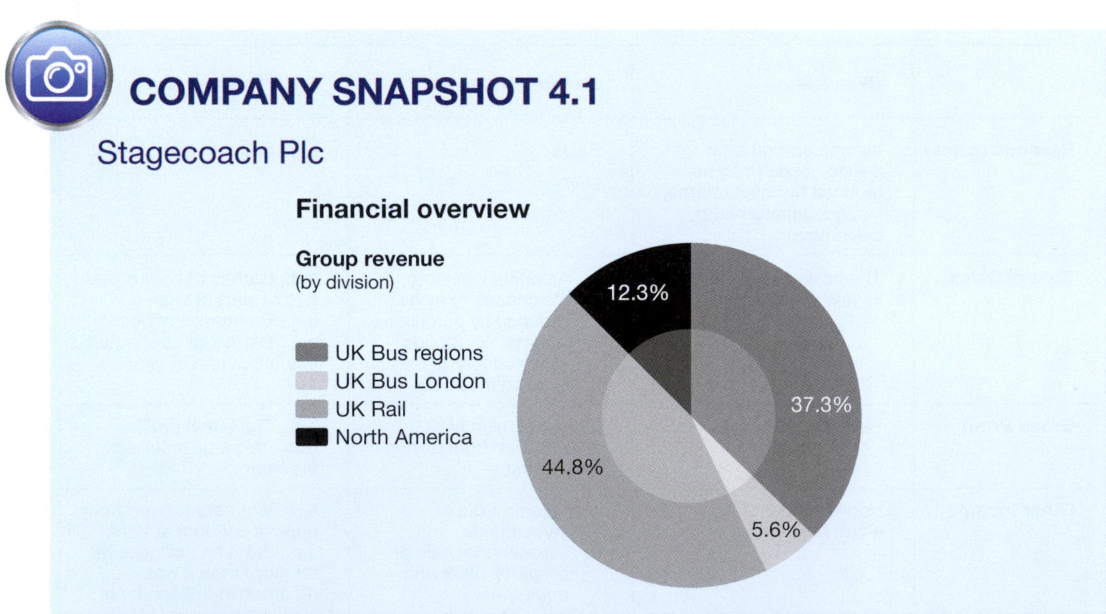

Source: Stagecoach Group plc, *Annual Report and Financial Statements, 2011.*

In the modern world, both developed and developing countries have varied businesses with varied revenue. For example, banks can have interest earned, football clubs gate receipts, merchandising and television broadcasts. Companies like the UK's Independent Television (ITV) are dependent on advertising revenues. If revenues increase or decrease then this can affect their share price quite dramatically as is the case in Real-World View 4.3.

REAL-WORLD VIEW 4.3

Revenue and Share Price

ITV was yesterday's worst performer in the FTSE100 after it said advertising revenues could fall by as much as 20pc in June. Adam Crozier, ITV's chief executive, said advertising revenues plunged by 9pc in May and predicted a fall of between 15pc and 20pc in June, blaming 'continued economic uncertainty' and tough comparatives with last year's World Cup.

Source: Amanda Andrews, ITV June ad sales may fall by 20pc, *Daily Telegraph*, 12 May 2011, p. 33.

Revenue recognition is a topic that has concerned accountants for generations. In many cases, it is not straightforward to determine the exact timing or nature of a sale. An illustration of this is when should a sale be recognised on a leasing contract? There are many similar examples which accountants continue to wrestle with.

The great variety of revenue is indicated in Figure 4.4 which provides an overview of the different types of revenue. This figure is for guidance only. The division between credit and cash is, in particular, very rough and ready.

Figure 4.4 Selected Industrial Sectors for 2010

Sector	*Example of Revenue*	*Credit/cash*	*Goods/services*
Agriculture, forestry and fishing	Farm produce	Credit	Goods
Manufacturing	Manufactured goods	Credit	Goods
Construction	Buildings	Credit	Goods
Motor trades	New cars or car repairs	Cash and credit	Goods
Wholesale*	Food wholesaler*	Credit	Goods
Retail	Supermarket	Cash and credit card	Goods
Hotels and catering	Hotels	Cash and credit card	Services
Transport and storage	Taxi fares	Cash	Services
Finance and income	Interest earned	Not applicable	Services
Property and business services	Rents	Cash and credit	Services

*Wholesale businesses act as middlemen between manufacturers and customers. They buy from manufacturers and sell on to retailers

Source: Office for National Statistics licensed under the Open Government Licence v.1.0.

Revenue is reduced by sales returns. These are simply goods which are returned by customers, usually because they are faulty or damaged. Company Snapshot 4.2 demonstrates the revenue for Christian Dior, a French company, famous for fashion, fragrance and jewellery. Interestingly, Christian Dior analyses its revenue in three ways: by business group, globally and by currency.

COMPANY SNAPSHOT 4.2

Revenue for Christian Dior

Financial highlights

CONSOLIDATED REVENUE BY BUSINESS GROUP
(EUR millions)

2008	2009	Business group	2009
4%	4%	Christian Dior Couture	717
17%	15%	Wines and Spirits	2,740
34%	36%	Fashion and Leather Goods	6,302
16%	15%	Perfumes and Cosmetics	2,741
5%	4%	Watches and Jewelry	764
24%	26%	Selective Retailing	4,533
		Other activities and eliminations	(52)
			17,745

CONSOLIDATED REVENUE BY GEOGRAPHIC REGION OF DELIVERY
(EUR millions)

2008	2009	Region	2009
15%	15%	France	2,597
24%	22%	Europe (excluding France)	3,918
22%	22%	United States	3,913
10%	10%	Japan	1,752
20%	23%	Asia (excluding Japan)	4,012
9%	8%	Other markets	1,553
			17,745

CONSOLIDATED REVENUE BY CURRENCY
(EUR millions)

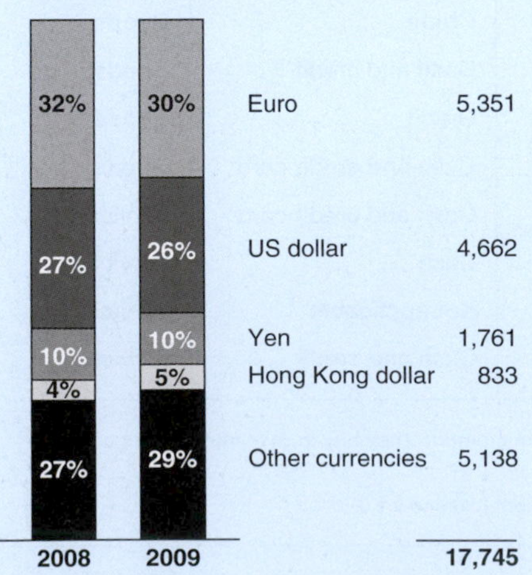

Source: Christian Dior, *Annual Report 2009*, p. 6.

PAUSE FOR THOUGHT 4.1

Revenue Recognition

When is a sale not a sale?

At first glance, the question when is a sale actually made might seem straightforward. For example, a street trader selling fruit and vegetables for cash makes a sale when he exchanges the fruit for cash. However, if we delve more deeply then defining a sale can be more complex. For tangible goods which are bought and sold, the date of sale is usually the despatch date. However, complications can arise; what if the customer has the right to return the goods anytime within the next year? On long-term contracts which might last for years, when do you attribute the profit? In practice, therefore, the exact point at which you recognise revenue can be problematic.

Cost of Sales

Cost of sales is essentially the expense of directly providing the goods for sale. Cost of sales is normally primarily found in businesses which buy and sell goods rather than those which provide services. The main component of cost of sales is purchases. However, purchases are adjusted for other items such as purchases returns (goods returned to suppliers), carriage inwards (i.e., the cost of delivering the goods from the supplier), and, of particular importance, inventory. Company Snapshot 4.3 shows the cost of sales for J. Sainsbury plc.

COMPANY SNAPSHOT 4.3

Cost of Sales

Cost of sales consists of all costs to the point of sale including warehouse and transportation costs and all the costs of operating retail outlets.

Supplier incentives, rebates and discounts are recognised within cost of sales based on the expected entitlement at the balance sheet date. The accrued value at the reporting date is included in prepayments and accrued income.

Source: J. Sainsbury plc, *Annual Report and Financial Statements 2010*, p. 53. Reproduced by kind permission of Sainsbury's Supermarkets Ltd.

In businesses that manufacture products, rather than buy and sell goods, the cost of revenue is more complicated. It will contain, for example, those costs which can be directly related to manufacturing. Figure 4.5 presents a detailed example of cost of sales.

Figure 4.5 Cost of Sales

John Green, a retailer, runs a small business. He has the following details of a week's trading: Opening inventory £2,000, carriage inwards £100, purchases £9,000, purchases returns £300, closing inventory £3,800.
(i) What is his cost of sales? (ii) Why do we adjust for inventory?

	£	£
Cost of Sales:		
Opening inventory		2,000
Add Purchases	9,000	
Less Purchases returns	300	
	8,700	
Add Carriage inwards	100	8,800
		10,800
Less Closing inventory		3,800
Cost of Sales		7,000

i. Cost of sales is thus £7,000. Note that we have adjusted (i) for goods returned to the supplier £300, (ii) for carriage inwards which is the cost of delivering the goods from the supplier (i.e., like 'postage' on goods), and (iii) for closing inventory.
ii. We need to match the revenue with the actual costs directly incurred in generating them. Essentially, opening inventory represents purchases made last period, but not used. They were not, therefore, directly involved in generating last period's revenue. Similarly, closing inventory represents this year's purchases which have not been used. They will, therefore, be used to generate the next period's, rather than this period's, revenue.

Helpnote: When presenting cost of sales we subtract purchases returns and closing inventory. We indicate this using the word 'less'. As a result, we do not put these figures in brackets.

Gross Profit

Gross profit is simply revenue (sales) less cost of sales. It is a good measure of how much an organisation makes for every £1 of goods sold. In other words, the mark-up an organisation is making. Mark-ups and margins are discussed in Pause for Thought 4.2.

Businesses watch their cost of sales and their gross profit margins very closely. Gross profit is determined by taking cost of sales from revenue (this section of the income statement is sometimes called the trading account).

Other Income

This is basically income from activities other than trading. So it might be interest from money in a bank or building society (interest received). Or it might be dividends received from an investment or profit on sale of a particular item of plant, property and equipment. In the case of the R. Beer example it was income from the gaming machine. Sometimes organisations report operating profits. Operating profit is concerned with trading activities (e.g., revenue, purchases and expenses). Other income would be excluded.

Expenses

Expenses are many and varied. They are simply the costs incurred in meeting revenue. Some companies itemise their expenses in their accounts. For example, British Airways in 2009 list

PAUSE FOR THOUGHT 4.2

Gross Profit, Mark-ups and Gross Margins

We give three examples below.

Business A operates on a mark-up of 50% on cost of sales. If its cost of sales was £60,000, how much would you expect gross profit to be?

	Mark-up		Gross margin
	%	£	%
Revenue	150	90,000	100
Cost of sales	100	60,000	67
Gross profit	50	30,000	33

It is thus £30,000.

Business B has £400,000 revenue and a mark-up of 33% of cost of sales. What would you expect its gross profit to be?

	Mark-up		Gross Margin
	%	£	%
Revenue	133⅓	400,000	100
Cost of Sales	100	300,000	75
Gross Profit	33⅓	100,000	25

It is thus £100,000.

Business C has revenue of £500,000 and a gross profit margin of 20%. What would you expect gross profit to be?

	Mark-up		Gross Margin
	%	£	%
Revenue	125	500,000	100
Cost of Sales	100	400,000	80
Gross Profit	25	100,000	20

It is thus £100,000.

We can thus see that businesses can talk in terms of mark-ups or gross margin. Mark-up starts from cost of sales whereas gross margin starts from revenues. Thus, a gross margin is a percentage of sales whereas mark-up is a percentage of cost of sales. Both mark-up and gross margin are, therefore, different ways of expressing the same thing.

PAUSE FOR THOUGHT 4.3

Trading Account

In the accounts of sole traders, the income statement is often presented using a fully unabridged format. The income statement is sometimes called the trading, profit and loss account. This begs the question:

What actually is the trading account and why is it so called?

The trading account is the initial part of the sole trader's income statement (or trading and profit and loss account). In other words, revenue less cost of sales. As we can see below, it deals with the revenue and purchases of goods and gives gross profit.

	£	£	£
Revenue			100,000
Less Revenue returns			10,000
			90,000
Less *Cost of Sales*			
Opening inventory		8,000	
Add Purchases	50,000		
Less Purchases returns	4,000	46,000	
		54,000	
Less Closing inventory		2,000	52,000
Gross Profit			38,000

It is termed a trading account because it gives details of an organisation's direct trading income (i.e., buying and selling goods) rather than non-trading income (e.g., bank interest) or expenses. Nowadays, because of the growth of businesses which have little inventory (e.g., service companies), the trading account is becoming less important.

their main expenses in their income statement (see Company Snapshot 4.4). Some common expenses are listed below.

- Accountants' fees
- Advertising
- Insurance
- Light and heat
- Petrol consumed
- Sales commission
- Business rates
- Rent paid
- Repairs and renewals
- Telephone bill

COMPANY SNAPSHOT 4.4

Expenses

Employee costs (£ million)	2,166	2,277
Depreciation, amortisation and impairment	692	714
Aircraft operating lease costs	68	81
Fuel and oil costs	2,055	1,931
Engineering and other aircraft costs	451	414
Landing fees and en route charges	528	517
Handling charges, catering and other operating costs	977	930
Selling costs	359	436
Currency differences	6	18
Accommodation, ground equipment and IT costs	576	618
Total expenditure on operations before non-recurring items	7,878	7,936

Source: British Airways Annual Report 2007/8, p. 78. Reproduced by Permission.

Most expenses *are* a result of a cash payment (e.g., rent paid) or *will* result in a cash payment (e.g., rent owing). However, depreciation is a non-cash payment. It represents the expense of using property, plant and equipment, such as motor vehicles, which wear out over time. The topic of depreciation is dealt with in more detail in Chapter 5.

Net Profit

Net profit is simply the amount left over after cost of sales and expenses have been deducted from revenue. It is a key method of measuring a business's performance. It is often expressed as a percentage of revenue, giving a net profit to revenue ratio.

Profit

The concept of profit seems a simple one, at first. Take a barrow boy, Jim, selling fruit and vegetables from his barrow in Manchester. If he buys £50 of fruit and vegetables in the morning and by the evening has sold all his goods for £70, Jim has made a profit of £20. However, in practice profit measurement is much more complicated and often elusive. Although there is a set of rules which guide the determination of income and expenses, there are also many assumptions which underpin the calculation of profit. The main factors which complicate matters are:

- the accruals or matching concept
- estimation
- changing prices
- the wearing out of assets

Soundbite 4.2 shows that profit, and profit generation, is central to any successful business.

SOUNDBITE 4.2

Successful Profit Generation

'Mining companies with strong balance sheets invariably turn to acquisitions and BHP, after the rebound in commodity prices in 2009, has an embarrassment of riches. The company has little debt and was generating profits at a rate of £20m a day in its last reporting period.'

Source: Nils Pratley, Viewpoint, *The Guardian,* 18 August 2012, p. 25.

Accruals or Matching Concept

It is essential to appreciate that the whole purpose of the income statement is to match income earned and expenses incurred. This is the accruals or matching concept which we saw in Chapter 2. Income earned and expenses incurred are not the same as cash paid and cash received. We have already seen that depreciation is a non-cash item. However, it is also important to realise that for many other income and expense items the cash received and paid during the year are not the same as income earned and expenses incurred. When we are attempting to arrive at income earned and expenses incurred we have to estimate certain items such as amounts owing (known as accruals). We also need to adjust for items paid this year which will, in fact, be incurred next year (for example, rent paid in advance).

Estimating

Accounting is often about estimation. This is because we often have uncertain information. For example, we may estimate the outstanding telephone bill or the value of closing inventory.

Changing Prices

If the price of a non-current asset (such as property, plant and equipment) rises then we have a gain from holding that asset. Indeed, property is often revalued. Is this gain profit? Well yes, in the sense that the organisation has gained. But no, in that it is not a profit from trading. This whole area is clouded with uncertainty. There are different views. Normally such property, plant and equipment gains are only included in the accounts when the plant, property and equipment are sold.

Wearing Out of Assets

Assets wear out and this is accounted for by the concept of depreciation. However, calculating depreciation involves a lot of assumptions; for example, length of asset life. Profit is thus contingent upon many adjustments, assumptions and estimates. All in all, therefore, the determination of profit is more an art than a science.

It is true to say that different accountants will calculate different profits. And they might all be correct! It is, however, also true that despite the assumptions needed to arrive at profits, profits are a key determinant by which businesses of all sorts are judged. Real-World View 4.4, for example, shows the profits of leading UK football clubs in 2008.

REAL-WORLD VIEW 4.4

Football Clubs' Profits

Top 20 Premier League Clubs' Financial Information 2008

Club	Revenue £'000	Operating profit/(loss) before player trading £'000	Net funds/ (debt) £'000
Arsenal	209,294	48,473	(318,073)
Aston Villa	75,639	4,821	(72,261)
Birmingham City	49,836	12,829	2,414
Blackburn Rovers	56,395	6,567	(16,918)
Bolton Wanderers	59,072	(5,002)	(53,542)
Chelsea	213,648	(30,878)	(710,562)
Derby County	48,558	12,328	(21,811)
Everton	75,650	6,809	(36,752)
Fulham	53,670	(1,979)	(192,823)
Liverpool	164,222	28,350	(299,838)
Manchester City	82,295	(1,598)	(137,532)
Manchester United	257,116	71,758	(649,429)
Middlesbrough	47,952	(1,826)	(93,842)
Newcastle United	100,866	(11,692)	(245,053)
Portsmouth	71,556	(6,323)	(50,106)
Reading	58,023	12,529	(42,313)
Sunderland	63,597	11,142	(71,231)
Tottenham Hotspur	114,788	27,461	(29,702)
West Ham United	n/a	n/a	n/a
Wigan Athletic	43,455	(2,805)	(66,412)
Totals	**1,845,632**	**180,964**	**(3,105,786)**

Source: Deloitte *Annual Review of Football Finance (2009).*

Sometimes, an asset will have lost more value than is accounted for via depreciation. In this case, the value of the asset may be written down. This is called impairment.

Listed Companies

Listed companies in Europe follow International Financial Reporting Standards (IFRS) for their group accounts. Under IFRS, companies should present an income statement (sometimes called the profit and loss account). Under IFRS, sales are conventionally termed revenue. The listed company is covered in depth in Chapter 7.

Capital and Revenue Expenditure

One example of the many decisions which an accountant must make is the distinction between capital and revenue expenditure. Capital expenditure is usually associated with items in the statement of financial position, such as property, plant and equipment; in other words, assets which may last for more than one year (e.g., land and buildings, plant and machinery, motor vehicles, and fixtures and fittings). By contrast, revenue expenditure is usually associated with income statement items such as telephone, light and heat or purchases. This appears simple, but sometimes it is not. For example, to a student, is this book a capital or a revenue expenditure? Well, it has elements of both. A capital expenditure in that you may keep it for reference. A revenue expenditure in that its main use will probably be over a relatively short period of time. So we can choose! Often when there is uncertainty, small-value items are charged to the profit and loss account. Interestingly, the WorldCom accounting scandal involved WorldCom incorrectly treating £2.5 billion of revenue expenditure as capital expenditure. This had the effect of increasing profit by £2.5 billion.

DEFINITION 4.3

Capital and Revenue Expenditure

Capital expenditure
A payment to purchase an asset with a continuing use in the business such as an item of property, plant and equipment.

Revenue expenditure
A payment for a current year's good or services such as purchases for resale or telephone expenses.

Limitations

So does the income statement provide a realistic view of the performance of the company over the year, especially of profit? The answer is, maybe! The income statement does list income and expenses and thus arrives at profit. However, there are many estimates, which means that the profit figure is inherently subjective. At the end of a year, for example, there is a need to estimate the amount of phone calls made. This brings subjectivity into the estimation of profit. Another example is that the loss in value of property, plant and equipment is not accurately measured. Similarly, the valuation of inventory is very subjective. It should be noted that given the wealth of detail in companies' accounts, the figures presented are generally summarised.

Interpretation

The income statement, despite its limitations, is often used for performance comparisons between companies and for the same company over time. These performance comparisons can then be used as the basis for investment decisions. Profitability ratios are often used to assess a company's performance over time or relative to other companies (for example, profit is often measured against revenue or capital employed). Ratios are more fully explained in Chapter 9.

Conclusion

The income statement presents an organisation's income and expenses over a period. It allows the determination of both gross and net profit. In many ways, making a profit is the key to business success (as Soundbite 4.3 shows). Gross profit is essentially an organisation's profit from trading. Net profit represents profit after all expenses have been taken into account. It is important to realise that the income statement is concerned with matching revenues earned with expenses incurred. It is not, therefore, a record of cash paid less cash received. Profit is not a precise absolute figure: it depends on many estimates and assumptions. However, despite its subjectivity, profit forms a key element in the performance evaluation of an organisation.

SOUNDBITE 4.3

Profits

'Nobody ever got poor taking a profit.'

Cary Reich, *Financier: André Meyer*, p. 119

Source: The Executive's Book of Quotations (1994), p. 233.

Discussion Questions

Questions with numbers in blue have answers at the back of the book.

Q1 Why is the income statement such an important and useful financial statement to such a variety of users?

Q2 'There is not just one profit; there are hundreds of profits.' Do you agree with this statement, taking into account the subjectivity inherent in calculating profit?

Q3 The matching principle is essential to the calculation of accounting profit. Discuss.

Q4 Over time, with the decline of the manufacturing company and rise of the service company, inventory, cost of sales and gross profit are becoming less important. Discuss.

Q5 State which of the following statements is true and which false? If false, explain why.

(a) Profit is income earned less expenses paid.
(b) Revenue less cost of sales less expenses will give net profit.
(c) Revenue returns are returns by suppliers.
(d) If closing inventory increases so will gross profit.
(e) The purchase of an item of property, plant or equipment is known as a capital expenditure.

Numerical Questions

Questions with numbers in blue have answers at the back of the book.

Q1 Joan Smith has the following details from her accounts year ended 31 December 2013.

Revenue	£100,000	Purchases	£60,000	General expenses	£10,000
Opening Inventory	£10,000	Closing Inventory	£5,000	Other expenses	£8,000

Required: Draw up Joan Smith's income statement (trading and profit and loss account) for the year ended 31 December 2013.

Q2 Dale Reynolds has the following details from his accounts for the year ended 31 December 2013.

	£		£
Opening inventory	5,000	Closing inventory	8,000
Purchases	25,000	Purchases returns	2,000
Revenue	50,000	Sales returns	1,000
Carriage inwards	1,000		

Required: Draw up Dale Reynolds' trading account for the year ended 31 December 2013.

Q3 Mary Scott has the following details for the year to 31 December 2013.

	£		£
Revenue	200,000	Income from investments	3,000
Opening inventory	5,000	Wages	4,000
Purchases	100,000	Insurance	2,500
Closing inventory	3,000	Electricity	3,500
Advertising	3,500	Telephone	4,000
Motor expenses	1,500	Purchases returns	1,000
Repairs	800	Revenue returns	2,000
Sundry expenses	2,400		

Required: Draw up Mary Scott's income statement (trading and profit and loss account) for the year ended 31 December 2013.

Q4 Given the following different scenarios, calculate revenue, gross profit and cost of sales from the information available.

(a) Revenue £100,000, gross margin 25%.
(b) Revenue £200,000, mark-up 30%.
(c) Cost of sales £50,000, gross margin 25%.
(d) Cost of sales £40,000, mark-up 20%.

Q5 Good, Bad and Ugly are three businesses. Calculate their Gross Profit.

(a) Good has £375,000 revenue and a mark-up of 25% of cost of sales.
(b) Bad has revenue of £600,000 and a gross profit margin of 30%.
(c) Ugly has £200,000 cost of sales and a mark-up of 40% on cost of sales.

Go online to discover the extra features for this chapter at
www.wiley.com/college/jones

Chapter 5

Main financial statements: The statement of financial position (balance sheet)

'Creative accounting practices gave rise to the quip: "A balance sheet is very much like a bikini bathing suit. What it reveals is interesting, what it conceals is vital."'

Abraham Briloff, *Unaccountable Accounting*, Harper & Row (1972). *The Wiley Book of Business Quotations* (1998), p. 351.

Learning Outcomes

After completing this chapter you should be able to:

- Explain the nature of a statement of financial position.
- Understand the individual components of a statement of financial position.
- Outline the layout of a statement of financial position.
- Evaluate the usefulness of a statement of financial position.

Go online to discover the extra features for this chapter at **www.wiley.com/college/jones**

Chapter Summary

- One of three main financial statements.
- Consists of assets, liabilities and equity.
- Assets are most often non-current (e.g., property, plant and equipment such as land and buildings, plant and machinery, motor vehicles, and fixtures and fittings) or current (e.g., inventory, trade receivables, cash).
- Liabilities can be current (e.g., trade payables, short-term loans) or non-current (e.g., long-term loans).
- Listed companies have a special terminology and presentational format for the statement of financial position.
- A sole trader's equity is opening equity plus profit for the period less drawings.
- In modern statements of financial position, a vertical format is most popular.
- A statement of financial position's usefulness is limited by missing assets and inconsistent valuation.
- Different business organisations will have differently structured statements of financial position (e.g., sole traders and limited companies).
- Statements of financial position are used as a basis for determining liquidity.

Introduction

The statement of financial position, along with the income statement and statement of cash flows, is one of the most important financial statements. However, it is only in the last century that the income statement or profit and loss account gained in importance. Before then, the statement of financial position ruled supreme. There is great debate on whether you should give pre-eminence to the statement of financial position so that the income statement becomes the secondary statement or vice versa. The statement of financial position is prepared from an organisation's trial balance. It consists of assets, liabilities and equity. For UK companies, it is required by the Companies Act 2006. The statement of financial position seeks to measure an organisation's net assets at a particular point in time. It developed out of concepts of stewardship and accountability. Although useful for assessing liquidity, statements of financial position do not actually represent an organisation's market value. In this chapter, the primary focus will be on understanding the purpose, nature and contents of the statement of financial position. The preparation of the statement of financial position of sole traders, partnerships and limited companies from the trial balance is covered in depth in Chapters 6 and 7, respectively. For listed companies, a different terminology and presentation is adopted. This is mentioned in this chapter, but dealt with in more depth in Chapter 7.

Context

The statement of financial position is one of the key financial statements. It is prepared from the trial balance at a particular point in time, which can be any time during the year. The statement of financial position is usually prepared for shareholders at either 31 December or 31 March. The statement of financial position has three main elements: assets, liabilities and equity. Essentially, the assets less the third-party liabilities (i.e., net assets) equal the owner's equity. Thus,

$$\boxed{\text{Assets} - \text{Liabilities} = \text{Equity}}$$

Alternatively:

$$\boxed{\text{Assets} = \text{Liabilities} + \text{Equity}}$$

The statement of financial position and income statement are complementary (see Figure 5.1). The income statement shows an organisation's performance over the accounting period, normally a year. It is thus concerned with income, expenses and profit. A statement of financial position, by contrast, is a snapshot of a business at a particular point in time. It thus focuses on assets, liabilities and equity.

Figure 5.1 Comparison of Income Statement and Statement of Financial Position

	Income Statement (Profit and Loss Account)	***Statement of Financial Position (Balance Sheet)***
Preparation source	Trial balance	Trial balance
Main elements	Income, expenses, profit	Assets, liabilities, equity
Period covered	Usually a year	A point in time
Main focus	Profitability	Net assets

As Soundbite 5.1 shows, the statement of financial position provides basic information which helps users to judge the value of a company.

SOUNDBITE 5.1

Statement of Financial Position

'The market is mostly a matter of psychology and emotion, and all that you find in the statement of financial position [balance sheets] is what you read into them; we've all guessed to one extent or another, and when we guess wrong they say we're crooks.'

Major L.L.B. Angas, *Stealing the Market*, p. 15

Source: The Executive's Book of Quotations (1994), p. 179.

Definitions

As Definition 5.1 shows, a statement of financial position is essentially a collection of the assets, liabilities and equity of an organisation at a point in time. It is prepared so as to provide a true and fair view of the organisation.

DEFINITION 5.1

Statement of Financial Position (Balance Sheet)

Working definition

A collection of the assets, liabilities and equity of an organisation at a particular point in time.

Formal definition

'Statement of the financial position of an entity at a given date disclosing the assets, liabilities and accumulated funds (such as shareholders' contributions and reserves) prepared to give a true and fair view of the financial state of the entity at that date.'

Source: Chartered Institute of Management Accountants (2005), *Official Terminology.* Reproduced by Permission of Elsevier.

PAUSE FOR THOUGHT 5.1

Net Assets

If the assets were £20,000 and the liabilities to third parties were £10,000, what would (a) net assets and (b) equity be?

....

The answer would be £10,000 for both. This is because net assets equals assets less liabilities and equity equals net assets.

Broadly, assets are the things an organisation owns or leases; liabilities are things it owes. Assets can bring economic benefits by either being sold (for example, inventory) or being used (for example, a car). Equity (sometimes known as ownership interest) is accumulated wealth. Equity is effectively a liability of the business because it is 'owed' to the owner: standard setters more formally define assets in terms of rights to future economic benefits and liabilities as obligations. Equity (ownership interest) is what is left over. In other words, assets less third-party liabilities equal owner's equity. By formally defining assets and liabilities, the statement of financial position tends to drive the income statement. In the income statement, as we will see in Figure 5.2, an individual's closing equity is represented by opening equity plus net profit less drawings (i.e., money taken out of a business by the owner). In Definition 5.2 we present both formal and working definitions of assets, third-party liabilities and equity (ownership interest).

DEFINITION 5.2

Assets

Working definition
Items owned or leased by a business.

Formal definition
'An asset is a resource controlled by the enterprise as a result of past events and from which future economic benefits are expected to flow to the entity.'

Source: International Accounting Standards Board (2010), *Conceptual Framework for Financial Reporting*.

Liabilities

Working definition
Items owed by a business.

Formal definition
'A liability is a present obligation of the enterprise arising from past events, the settlement of which is expected to result in an outflow from the entity of resources embodying economic benefits.'

Source: International Accounting Standards Board (2010), *Conceptual Framework for Financial Reporting*.

Equity (Capital or Ownership Interest)

Working definition
The funds (assets less liabilities) belonging to the owner(s).

Formal definition
'Equity is the residual interest in the assets of the entity after deducting all its liabilities.'

Source: International Accounting Standards Board (2010), *Conceptual Framework for Financial Reporting*.

Layout

Traditionally, the statement of financial position was always arranged with the assets on the right-hand side of the page and the liabilities on the left-hand side of the page. However, now the vertical format is most often used. For UK companies, the use of the vertical format was set out in the 2006 Companies Acts. Examples of Marks & Spencer plc's and AstraZeneca plc's statements of financial position are given in Company Snapshots 2.2 (in Chapter 2) and 7.4 (in Chapter 7), respectively. However, most other organisations now commonly use the vertical format. This sets out the assets and liabilities at the top. The equity employed is then put at the bottom. This modern format is the one which this book will use from now on. However, Appendix 5.1 (at the end of this chapter) gives an example of the traditional 'horizontal' format which readers may occasionally encounter.

In order to be more realistic, we continue to use the example of R. Beer (see p. 94 in Chapter 4), a sole trader who runs a public house. R. Beer's statement of financial position is given in Figure 5.2. In Chapter 6, we show the mechanics of the preparation of the statement of financial position from the trial balance. The purpose of this section is to explain the theory behind the presentation.

Figure 5.2 Sole Trader's Statement of Financial Position

R. Beer Statement of Financial Position as at 31 March 2014	
ASSETS	
Non-Current Assets	
Property, Plant and Equipment	£
Land and buildings	71,572
Plant and machinery	3,500
Furniture and fittings	5,834
Motor car	3,398
Total non-current assets	84,304
Current Assets	
Inventory	2,200
Trade receivables	100
Prepayments	50
Bank	3,738
Cash	340
Total current assets	6,428
Total Assets	90,732
LIABILITIES	
Current Liabilities	
Trade payables	(3,900)
Accruals	(91)
Short-term loans	(1,000)
Total current liabilities	(4,991)
Non-current Liabilities	(6,500)
Total Liabilities	(11,491)
Net Assets	79,241
EQUITY	£
Opening equity	80,257
Add Net profit	8,350
	88,607
Less Drawings	9,366
Closing equity	79,241

Main Components

Figure 5.3 lists the main components commonly found in the statement of financial position of a sole trader. It provides some general examples and, wherever possible, a specific example.

Figure 5.3 Main Components of the Statement of Financial Position

	Overview	General Examples	Specific Examples
Non-current Assets (Property, plant and equipment)	Assets used to run the business long-term	1. Land and buildings 2. Plant and machinery 3. Fixtures and fittings 4. Motor vehicles	Public house, factory Lathe Computer, photocopier Car, van
Current Assets (i.e., short-term assets) (i) Inventories	Goods purchased and awaiting use or produced awaiting sale	1. Finished goods 2. Work in progress 3. Raw materials	Tables manufactured and awaiting sale Half-made tables Raw wood awaiting manufacture
(ii) Trade Receivables	Amounts owed to company	Trade receivables	Customers who have received goods, but not yet paid
(iii) Prepayments	Amounts paid in advance	Prepayments for services	Insurance prepaid
(iv) Cash and bank	Physical cash Money deposited on short-term basis with a bank	Cash in till Cash and bank deposits	Petty cash Current account in credit
Current Liabilities (i.e., amounts falling due within one year) (i) Trade Payables	Money owed to suppliers	Trade payables	Amounts owing for raw materials
(ii) Accruals	Amounts owed to the suppliers of services	Accruals for services	Amounts owing for electricity or telephone
(iii) Loans	Amounts borrowed from third parties and repayable within a year	Short-term loans from financial institutions	Bank loan
Non-current liabilities	Amounts borrowed from third parties and repayable after a year	Long-term loans from financial institutions	Loan secured, for example, on business property
Equity (Owner's Capital Employed)	Originally, the money the sole trader introduced into the business. Normally represents the net assets (i.e., assets less liabilities)	The equity at the start of the year and equity at the end of the year are generally known as opening and closing equity	The opening and closing equity represent the opening and closing net assets
(i) Profit	The profit earned during the year	Taken from the income statement, represents income less expenses	Net profit for year
(ii) Drawings	Money taken out of the business by the owner. A reduction of owner's equity	Living expenses	Owner's salary or wages

The main components of the statement of financial position are then discussed in the text. The same order is used as for R. Beer's statement of financial position. Finally, in Figure 5.6 on page 122, we summarise the major valuation methods used for the main assets. An overview of the structure of the statement of financial position is shown in Figure 5.4.

Figure 5.4 Overview of a Statement of Financial Position

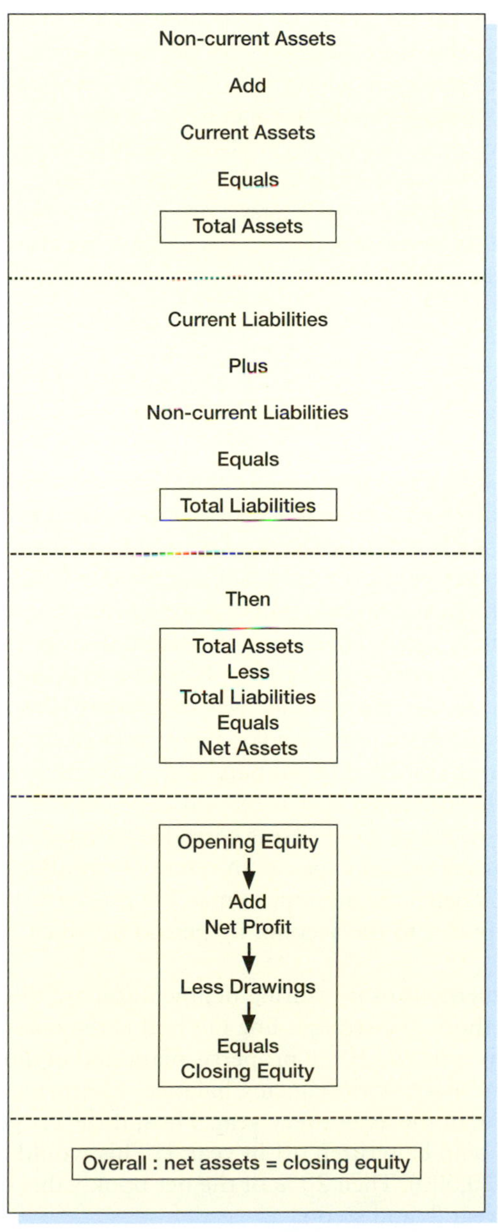

PAUSE FOR THOUGHT 5.2

Statement of Financial Position

Why does a balance sheet (i.e., statement of financial position) balance?

This is a tricky question! For the answer we need to think back to the trial balance. The trial balance balances with assets and expenses on one side and income, liabilities and equity on the other. Essentially, the statement of financial position is a rewritten trial balance. It includes all the individual items from the trial balance in terms of the assets, liabilities and equity. It also includes all the income and expense items. However, all of these are included only as one figure: 'profit' (i.e., all the income items less all the expense items). This is illustrated in the student example from pages 34–38 in Chapter 2. Incidentally, a balance sheet was probably originally called a balance sheet not because it balances, but because it is a list of all the individual balances from the trial balance.

Non-current Assets

These are the assets that a business uses for its continuing operations. Non-current assets can be divided into tangible assets and intangible assets. It is normal to recognise four main types of tangible assets more usually called property, plant and equipment or fixed assets (intangible assets, i.e. those which do not physically exist, are discussed in Chapter 7): land and buildings, plant and machinery, fixtures and fittings, and motor vehicles. For sole traders, these different types of asset are separately listed. However, for presentation purposes they are aggregated into one heading for listed companies. Property, plant and equipment are traditionally valued at historical cost. In other words, if a machine was purchased 10 years ago for £100,000, this £100,000 was originally recorded in the books. Every year of the property, plant and equipment's useful life, an amount of the original purchase cost will be allocated as an expense in the income statement. This allocated cost is termed depreciation. Thus, depreciation simply means that a proportion of the original cost is spread over the life of the property, plant and equipment and treated as an annual expense. In essence, this allocation of costs relates back to the matching concept. There is an attempt to match a proportion of the original cost of the property, plant and equipment to the accounting period in which property, plant and equipment were used up.

The most common methods of measuring depreciation are the straight line method and the reducing balance method. The straight line method is the one used in Figure 5.5. Essentially, the same amount is written off the property, plant and equipment every year over the estimated useful life of the asset. With reducing balance, a set percentage is expensed or written off the net book value of the asset every year. Thus, if the set percentage was 20%, then in Figure 5.5 £20,000 would be written off in year 1. This would leave a net book value of £80,000 (£100,000 − £20,000). Then 20% of the net book value of £80,000 (i.e., £16,000) would be written off in year 2, and so on.

Figure 5.5 Illustrative Example on Depreciation

A machine was purchased 10 years ago for £100,000. Estimated useful life 20 years. We will assume the depreciation is equally allocated over 20 years. What would be the total depreciation (known as accumulated depreciation) after 12 years and at how much would the machine be recorded in the statement of financial position? The machine is estimated to have no scrap value after 20 years.

Statement of Financial Position			
Non-current Assets	*Cost*	*Accumulated depreciation*	*Net book value*
	£	£	£
Property, Plant and Equipment	100,000	(60,000)	40,000

In the statement of financial position, the original cost (£100,000) is recorded, followed by accumulated depreciation (i.e., depreciation over the 12 years: 12 × £5,000 = £60,000). The term 'net book value' simply means the amount left in the books after writing off depreciation. It is important to note that the net book value does not equal the market value. Indeed, it may be very different. In the income statement only one year's depreciation (£100,00 ÷ 20 years) of £5,000 is recorded each year.

Note: This topic is discussed more fully in Chapter 6.

Companies have great flexibility when choosing appropriate rates of depreciation. These rates should correspond to the useful lives of the assets. So, for example, if the directors believe an item of property, plant and equipment has a useful life of five years, they would choose a straight line rate of depreciation of 20%. Company Snapshot 5.1 gives the rates of depreciation used by Manchester United plc.

COMPANY SNAPSHOT 5.1

Depreciation

Depreciation is provided on tangible assets at annual rates appropriate to the estimated useful lives of the assets, as follows:

	Reducing Balance	Straight Line
Freehold buildings	1.33%	75 years
Computer equipment and software (included within plant and machinery)	33%	3 years
Plant and machinery	20–25%	4–5 years
General fixtures and fittings	15%	7 years

Tangible fixed assets acquired prior to 31 July 1999 are depreciated on a reducing balance basis at the rates stated above.

Tangible fixed assets acquired after 1 August 1999 are depreciated on a straight line basis at the rates stated above.

Source: Manchester United Ltd, *Annual Report 2010*, p. 60.

Interestingly, up until 1999 the club used the reducing balance method, which is relatively uncommon in the UK. However, it has now changed to the more conventional straight line depreciation.

Finally, it is important to realise that nowadays, many businesses regularly revalue some non-current assets such as property, plant and equipment every five years. Businesses can also revalue their non-current assets whenever they feel it is necessary (or, alternatively, devalue them if they have lost value). Where revaluations occur, the depreciation is based on the revalued amount. A devaluation of non-current assets is generally called an impairment. Indeed, the term impairment is used more generally for the loss of value of assets.

Current Assets

Current assets are those assets which a company owns which are essentially short-term. They are normally needed to perform the company's day-to-day operations. The five most common forms of current assets are inventories, trade receivables, prepayments, cash and bank.

1. Inventories (Stocks)

Inventories are an important business asset. This is especially so in manufacturing businesses. Inventories can be divided into three categories: raw materials, work-in-progress and finished goods (see, for example, Company Snapshot 5.2).

COMPANY SNAPSHOT 5.2

Inventories (Stocks)

	2010 EURm	2009 EURm
Raw materials, supplies and other	326	346
Work in progress	477	435
Finished goods	502	388
Total	1,305	1,169

Source: Nokia, *Annual Report 2010*, p. 45.

HELPNOTE 5.1

Inventory or Inventories or Stock

The terminology in this area can be difficult and often confusing. Generally, inventories or inventory is the terminology used under IFRS. In this book, I try to be consistent. I use inventory in general discussion and for sole traders and partnerships as they are likely to have only 'one' sort of inventory. For limited companies, I generally use inventories as they may carry multiple stocks.

Each category represents a different stage in the production process.

- *Raw materials.* These are the inventories a company has purchased and are ready for use. A carpenter, for example, might have wood awaiting manufacture into tables.
- *Work-in-progress.* These are partially completed inventories, sometimes called inventories in process. They are neither raw materials nor finished goods. They may represent partly manufactured goods such as tables with missing legs. Some of the costs of making the tables should be included.
- *Finished goods.* These represents inventories at the other end of the manufacturing process; for example, finished tables. Cost includes materials and other manufacturing costs (e.g., labour and manufacturing overheads).

Inventories at the year-end are often determined after a stocktake. As Real-World View 5.1 shows, inventories can often represent a substantial percentage of a company's net assets. This is especially true for Rolls-Royce, a manufacturing company. By contrast, Vodafone and Nokia carry relatively little inventories.

REAL-WORLD VIEW 5.1

The Importance of Inventories (Stock) Valuation

Company	Inventories Value	Net Assets	Inventories ÷ Net Assets
	£m[1]	£m[1]	%
Nokia	€2,523	39,123	6.4
Astra Zeneca	$1,750	$20,821	8.0
Tesco	2,729	14,681	18.5
Sainsbury	702	4,966	14.1
Marks & Spencer	613	2,186	28.0
Rolls-Royce	2,432	3,782	64.3
Vodafone	433	90,810	0.004
J.D. Wetherspoon	20	162	12.3
Volkswagen	€14,124	€37,430	37.8

Source: 2009/10 Annual Reports.

1. Unless indicated Astra Zeneca, Volkswagen and Nokia report in $ or €.

Generally, inventories are valued at the lower of cost or net realisable value (i.e., the value they could be sold for). In the case of work-in-progress and finished goods, cost could include some overheads (i.e., costs associated with making the tables). The valuation methods used for non-current assets are presented in Figure 5.6.

Figure 5.6 Summary of the Valuation Methods Used for Property, Plant and Equipment and Inventories

Property, Plant and Equipment	Normally valued at historical cost, or revaluation less depreciation. Historical cost is the original purchase price of the assets. Revaluation is the value of the property, plant and equipment as determined, usually by a surveyor, at a particular point in time.
Inventories	Inventories are generally valued at the lower of cost (i.e., what a business paid for it) and the amount one would realise if one sold it (called net realisable value). For a business with work-in-progress or finished goods inventories, an appropriate amount of overheads is included.

Different Inventory Valuation Measures: FIFO, LIFO, AVCO

The inclusion of production overheads in finished goods inventory is one key problem in inventory valuation. Another difficulty, which primarily concerns raw material inventory, is the choice of inventory valuation methods. There are three main methods: FIFO (first-in-first-out), LIFO (last-in-first-out) and AVCO (average cost). All three are permitted in management accounting and for inventory valuation in the financial accounts in the US. However, in the UK, and under IFRS, only FIFO and AVCO are permitted for inventory valuation in financial accounting.

Inventory valuation is not quite as easy as it may at first seem. It depends on which assumptions you make about the inventory sold. Is the inventory you buy in first, the first to be sold (first-in-first-out (FIFO))? Or is the inventory you buy in last, sold first (last-in-first-out (LIFO))? If the purchase price of inventory changes then this assumption matters.

In Figure 5.7, we investigate an example of the impact that using FIFO or LIFO has upon the valuation of raw materials inventory. We also include a third method, AVCO (average cost), which takes the average purchase price of the goods as their cost of sale.

It should be appreciated that inventory valuation is distinct from physical inventory management. In most businesses, good business practice dictates that you usually physically issue the oldest inventory first (i.e., adopt FIFO). However, in inventory valuation you are allowed to choose what is acceptable under the regulations.

Figure 5.7 Costing for Inventory Valuation and for Cost-Plus Pricing

Inventory co purchases its inventory on the first day of the month. It starts with no inventory. Its purchases and revenue over the first three months are as follows:

		Kilos	*Cost per kilo*	*Total cost*
January 1	*Purchases*	*10,000*	*£1.00*	*£10,000*
February 1	*Purchases*	*15,000*	*£1.50*	*£22,500*
March 1	*Purchases*	*20,000*	*£2.00*	*£40,000*
		45,000		*£72,500*
March 31	*Revenue*	*(35,000)*		
March 31	*Closing inventory*	*10,000*		

Figure 5.7 Costing for Inventory Valuation and for Cost-Plus Pricing (*continued*)

What is the closing inventory valuation using FIFO, LIFO and AVCO?

(i) **FIFO:** Here, the first inventory purchased is the first sold. The 35,000 kilos sold, therefore, used up all the January inventory (10,000 kilos), and the February inventory (15,000 kilos), and 10,000 kilos of the March inventory. We, therefore, have left in inventory 10,000 kilos of material valued at the March purchase price of £2.00 per kilo. Closing inventory is, therefore, 10,000 × £2 = £20,000.

(ii) **LIFO:** Here the last inventory purchased is assumed to be the first to be sold. The 35,000 kilos sold, therefore, used up:

20,000	kilos from March
15,000	kilos from February
35,000	

We, therefore, have remaining 10,000 kilos from January at £1 per kilo = £10,000.

(iii) **AVCO:** Here the inventory value is pooled and the average cost of purchase is taken as the cost of the goods sold. We purchased 45,000 kilos for £72,500 (i.e., £1.611 per kilo). The cost of our inventory is, therefore, 10,000 kilos × average cost £1.611 = £16,110.

We can, therefore, see that our inventory *valuations* vary considerably.

	£
FIFO	20,000
LIFO	10,000
AVCO	16,110

2. Trade Receivables (Debtors)

Trade receivables are sales which have been made, but for which the customers have not yet paid. If all transactions were in cash, there would be no trade receivables. Trade receivables at the year end are usually adjusted for those customers who it is believed will not pay. These are called a variety of terms such as bad and doubtful debts, impaired receivables, irrecoverable debts. In this book, for consistency, we use provision for the impairment of receivables. Bad debts are those debts which will definitely not be paid. Doubtful debts have an element of uncertainty to them. Usually, businesses estimate a certain proportion of their debts as doubtful debts. These bad and doubtful debts are also included in the income statement.

PAUSE FOR THOUGHT 5.3

Bad and Doubtful Debts

Can you think of any reasons why bad and doubtful debts might occur?

There may be several reasons; for example, bankruptcies, disputes over the goods supplied or cash flow problems. Most businesses constantly monitor their trade receivables to ensure that bad debts are kept to a minimum.

PAUSE FOR THOUGHT 5.4

FIFO, LIFO and AVCO and Cost of Sales

Do you think that using a different inventory valuation method in Figure 5.7 on pages 122 and 123 would affect cost of sales or profit?

Yes!! Whichever valuation method is used, both cost of sales and profit are affected. Essentially, the cost of purchases will be split between inventory and cost of sales.

	Total cost	*Cost of sales*	*Inventory*
	£	£	£
FIFO	72,500	52,500 (N1)	20,000
LIFO	72,500	62,400 (N2)	10,000
AVCO	72,500	56,390 (N3)	16,110

			£
(N1) FIFO represents:	January	10,000 kilos at £1.00	10,000
	February	15,000 kilos at £1.50	22,500
	March	10,000 kilos at £2.00	20,000
			52,500

			£
(N2) LIFO represents:	February	15,000 kilos at £1.50	22,500
	March	20,000 kilos at £2.00	40,000
			62,500

			£
(N3) AVCO represents:		35,000 kilos at £1.611	56,390

Profit is affected because if cost of sales is less, inventory, and thus profit, is higher and vice versa. In this case, using FIFO will show the greatest profit as its cost of sales is lowest. LIFO will show the lowest profit. AVCO is in the middle!

3. Prepayments

Prepayments are those items where a good or service has been paid for in advance. A common example of this is insurance. A business might, for example, pay £1,000 for a year's property insurance on 1 October. If the accounts are drawn up to 31 December, then at 31 December there is an asset of nine months' insurance (January–September) paid in advance, which is £750. The £750 represents an asset as it represents a future benefit to the firm.

4. Cash and bank

This is the actual money held by the business. Cash comprises petty cash and unbanked cash. Bank comprises money deposited at the bank or on short-term loan. For limited companies the term cash and cash equivalents is often used. This recognises that sometimes businesses own assets that can be turned into cash at relatively short notice, such as short-term deposits. As Soundbite 5.2 shows, money has long been the topic of humour.

SOUNDBITE 5.2

Money

They say money can't buy happiness, but it can facilitate it. I thoroughly recommend having lots of it to anybody.

Malcolm Forbes (*Daily Mail*, 20 June 1988)

Source: The Book of Business Quotations (1991), p. 158.

Current Liabilities

These are the amounts which the organisation owes to third parties. For a sole trader, there are three main types.

1. Trade Payables (Creditors)

These are the amounts which are owed to suppliers for goods and services received, but not yet paid (for example, raw materials).

2. Accruals

'Accruals' is accounting terminology for expenses owed at the financial reporting date. Accruals comply with the basic accounting concept of matching. In other words, because an expense has been incurred, but not yet paid, there is no reason to exclude it from the income statement. Accruals are amounts owed, but not yet paid, to suppliers for services received. Accruals relate to expenses such as telephone or light and heat. For example, we might have paid the telephone bill up to 30 November. However, if our year end was 31 December then we might owe, say, another £250 for telephone. Importantly, accruals do *not* relate to purchases of trade goods owing: these are trade payables.

3. Loans

Loans are the amounts which a third party, such as a bank, has loaned to the company on a short-term basis and which are due for repayment within one year.

The current assets less the current liabilities is, in effect, the operating capital of the business. It is commonly known as a business's working capital. Businesses try to manage their working capital as efficiently as possible. A working capital cycle exists (see Figure 5.8), where cash is used to purchase goods which are then turned into inventory. This inventory is then sold and cash is generated. Successful businesses will sell their goods for more than

Figure 5.8 The Working Capital Cycle

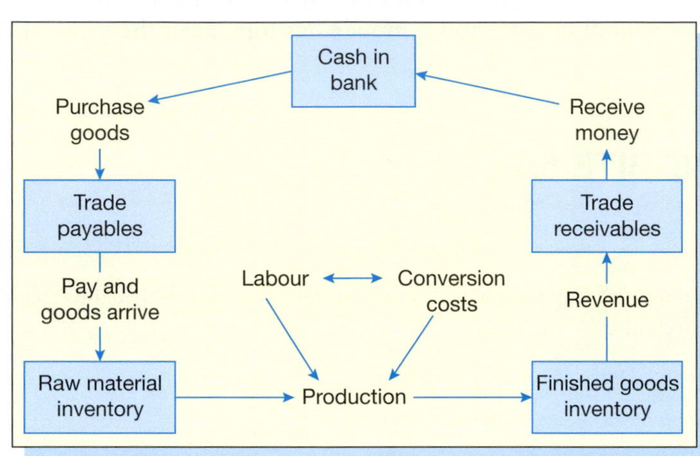

their total cost, thus generating a positive cash flow. In most businesses, current assets will be greater than current liabilities: current assets less current liabilities is sometimes calculated. This is known as net current assets. In some cases, a business may have more current liabilities than current assets. Instead of being net current assets, this section becomes net current liabilities. This is the situation with Tesco in 2005; see Company Snapshot 5.3.

COMPANY SNAPSHOT 5.3

Current Assets and Current Liabilities

Current assets	£m	£m	£m	£m
Inventories	1,309	—	1,309	1,199
Trade and other receivables	1,002	(233)	769	811
Cash and cash equivalents	1,146	—	1,146	1,100
	3,457	(233)	3,224	3,110
Current liabilities				
Trade and other payables	(5,374)	417	(4,957)	(3,986)
Short-term borrowings	(477)	(5)	(482)	(847)
Current tax payable	(221)	—	(221)	(308)
	(6,072)	412	(5,660)	(5,141)
Net current liabilities	(2,615)	179	(2,436)	(2,031)

Source: Tesco, *2004/5 Restatement of Financial Information under International Financial Reporting Standards* (IFRS), p. 7.

Loans give rise to debt. Many leading companies have large debts. As Soundbite 5.3 shows, debt is a particular problem for football clubs globally, especially in the English Premier League.

SOUNDBITE 5.3

Debts

Liverpool and Manchester United, English football's two most successful clubs, have a combined net debt of nearly £1bn. In March, Sepp Blather, President of FIFA (Fédération Internationale de Football Association) summed it up succinctly when he said: 'I think something is wrong with the Premier League'.

Source: Accountancy Magazine, Alex Blyth, Game Over, May 2010, p. 20.

Non-current Liabilities

Non-current liabilities are liabilities that the organisation owes and must repay after more than one year. Put simply, they are a company's borrowings. The most common are long-term loans. The total assets of a business less current liabilities and non-current liabilities give the total net assets of the business. Total net assets represent the total equity employed by a business.

PAUSE FOR THOUGHT 5.5

BORROWING

Companies often borrow money. However, it is worth reflecting on the reasons why they borrow and the differential impacts that borrowing might have on profitable and less profitable/unprofitable companies.

Why Borrow?

Companies as they grow may need funds. They often need money now for investments such as buildings or infrastructure projects which will be hopefully profitable in future years. However, they may not have enough money in the bank to expand so they have a simple choice to either not expand or borrow money to expand.

Contingent Liabilities

These are liabilities that sometimes occur in organisations. They are contingent because they are dependent on the occurrence of an event (for example, the outcome of a law suit). These contingent liabilities may or may not happen. They are thus not included in double-entry process or main financial statements. Instead, they are included in the notes to accounts if they are probable or possible.

Equity (Capital Employed)

For a sole trader the owner's equity or capital employed is opening equity plus profit less drawings. Thus for R. Beer it is:

Equity	£
Opening equity	80,257
Add Profit	8,350
	88,607
Less Drawings	9,366
Closing equity	79,241

Opening equity is that equity at the start of the year (e.g., 1 April 2014). In essence, it represents the total net assets at the start of the year (i.e., all the assets less all the liabilities). If the business had made a loss, opening equity would have been reduced. It is important to realise that the profit (or loss) recorded under owner's equity represents the net profit (or loss) as determined from the income statement. It is, thus, a linking figure.

PAUSE FOR THOUGHT 5.6

Equity (Capital)

A chip shop owner, B. Atter, has opening equity of £19,500. His income is £100,000 and expenses are £90,000. He has taken out £15,000 to live on. His financial position has improved over the year. True or false?

Unfortunately, for B. Atter, the answer is false. If we quickly draw up his capital employed:

Equity (Owner's capital employed)	£
Opening equity	19,500
Add Profit (i.e., income less expenses)	10,000
	29,500
Less Drawings	15,000
Closing equity	14,500

His capital has declined by £5,000 over the year.

Profit is the profit as determined from the income statement (i.e., revenue less cost of sales and other expenses). Drawings is the money that R. Beer has taken out of the business

SOUNDBITE 5.4

Capital

'Capital isn't scarce; vision is.'

Michael Milken (junk-bond creator)

Source: The Executive's Book of Quotations (1994), p. 47.

for his own personal spending. Finally, closing equity is equity at the statement of financial position date. It must be remembered at all times that:

Assets − Liabilities = Equity

Businesses need capital to operate. However, the capital needs to be used wisely (see Soundbite 5.4).

PAUSE FOR THOUGHT 5.7

Financial Position

Angela Roll, a baker, has the following assets and liabilities. Non-current assets £59,000, current assets £12,000, current liabilities £8,000 and non-current liabilities £7,000. What are her net assets? Is it true that her total assets are £50,000?

Net assets are £56,000:

	£
Non-current Assets	59,000
Current Assets	12,000
Total Assets	71,000
Current Liabilities	(8,000)
Non-current Liabilities	(7,000)
Total Liabilities	(15,000)
Net Assets	56,000

Total assets are £71,000

Limitations

To the casual observer, it looks as if the statement of financial position places a market value on the net assets of the organisation. Unfortunately, this is wrong. Very wrong! To understand why, one must look at the major components of the statement of financial position. The statement of financial position is a collection of individual assets and liabilities. These individual assets and liabilities are usually not valued at a real-world market value, so neither is the statement of financial position as a whole. Taking the property, plant and equipment, for example, only selected property, plant and equipment are revalued. These valuations are neither consistent nor necessarily up to date. There is, therefore, a considerable amount of subjectivity involved in their valuation. Also depreciation does not accurately measure the loss in value of property, plant and equipment (nor is it supposed to). The statement of financial position is thus a tangle of assets all measured in different ways.

Another problem, especially for companies, is that significant assets are not shown in the statement of financial position. All the hard work of an owner to generate revenue and goodwill will only be recognised when the business is sold. Many key items that drive corporate value, such as know-how and market share, are also not recorded (see Real-World View 5.2). Neither is the value of human assets recorded! For example, what is the greatest asset of football clubs? You might think it was the footballers like David Beckham, Wayne Rooney or Andy Carroll. However, conventionally these players would not be valued as assets on the statement of financial position unless they have been transferred from another club. Nor, in the case of zoos, would the animals bred in captivity be valued.

REAL-WORLD VIEW 5.2

Missing Assets

In many respects, the current reporting model is more suited to a manufacturing economy than one based on services and knowledge. For example, it does a good job measuring historical costs of physical assets, like plant and equipment. But it ignores many of the key drivers of corporate value, such as know-how and market share. The result is incomplete, or distorted, information about a company's worth, and diminished relevance to investors.

Source: Dennis M. Nally, *The Future of Financial Reporting* (1999), International Financial Reporting Conference From Web http://www.amazon.co.uk/exec/abidos/ASIN.

In addition to these assets which are not required to be shown on the statement of financial position, there is concern that many companies are deliberately omitting assets, and more importantly liabilities from their financial statements. This is shown in Soundbite 5.5.

SOUNDBITE 5.5

Off-Balance Sheet Financing

'It is child's play, particularly for bankers who devised complex structures to keep assets and, more importantly, the related liabilities off the balance sheet [statement of financial position].'

Source: David Cairns, Accounting Standards and the Financial Crisis, *Accountancy Magazine*, March 2010, p. 67.

Interpretation

Given the above limitations, any meaningful interpretation of amounts recorded in the statement of financial position is difficult. However, ratios are often used in an attempt to understand a company's financial performance better. For example, ratios derived from the statement of financial position are used to assess the financial position of a business. These ratios are dealt with in more depth in Chapter 9. Here we just briefly comment on liquidity (i.e., cash position) and long-term capital structure.

The statement of financial position records both current assets and current liabilities. These can be used to assess the short-term liquidity (i.e., short-term cash position) of a business. There are a variety of ratios such as the current ratio (current assets divided by current liabilities) and quick ratio (current assets minus inventories then divided by current liabilities) which do this. In addition, the statement of financial position records the long-term capital structure of a business. It is particularly useful in determining how dependent a business is on external borrowings. In Soundbite 5.6, for example, excessive borrowing created a statement of financial position where there was negative net worth.

SOUNDBITE 5.6

Statement of Financial Position (Balance Sheet)

MCI's balance sheet [statement of financial position] looked like Rome after the Visigoths had finished with it. We had a $90-million negative net worth, and we owed the bank $100 million, which was so much that they couldn't call the loan without destroying the company.

W.G. McGowgan, *Henderson Winners*, p. 187

Source: The Executive's Book of Quotations (1994), p. 81.

Listed Companies

Listed Companies in Europe follow International Financial Reporting Standards. Their statements of financial position are presented differently from those of sole traders or partnerships. Several examples of listed companies' statements of financial position are given in this book (see, for example, Marks and Spencer in Appendix 2.2, Volkswagen in Appendix 2.5 and AstraZeneca in Company Snapshot 7.4). They are all slightly different as there is no standardised format.

In this book, we use a standardised terminology for simplification and ease of understanding. Therefore, we use the listed companies' terminology throughout. However, sometimes an alternative terminology is used. We present this in Figure 5.9. For sole traders and partnerships traditionally more detail is given in the main financial statements. Listed companies are covered in more depth in Chapter 7.

Figure 5.9 Terminology

Terminology for Listed Companies	Sole Traders, Partnerships, Non-Listed Companies (alternative terminology permissible)
Property, plant and equipment	Fixed assets
Inventories	Stocks
Trade receivables	Debtors
Trade payables	Creditors
Equity	Capital and reserves/Ownership interest
Non-current liabilities	Long-term liabilities

Conclusion

The statement of financial position is a key financial statement. It shows the net assets of a business at a particular point of time. The three main constituents of the statement of financial position are assets (non-current and current), liabilities (current and non-current) and equity. Normally a vertical statement of financial position is used to portray these elements. The statement of financial position itself is difficult to interpret because of missing assets and inconsistently valued assets. However, it is commonly used to assess the liquidity position of a firm.

Discussion Questions

Questions with numbers in blue have answers at the back of the book.

Q1 The statement of financial position and income statement provide complementary, but contrasting information. Discuss.

Q2 What are the main limitations of the statement of financial position and how can they be overcome?

Q3 Is the statement of financial position of any use?

Q4 Are the different elements of the statement of financial position changing over time; for example, as manufacturing industry gives way to service industry?

Q5 State whether the following are true or false. If false, explain why.
- (a) A statement of financial position is a collection of assets, liabilities and equity.
- (b) Inventory, bank and trade payables are all current assets.
- (c) Total net assets are property, plant and equipment plus current assets less current liabilities.
- (d) Total net assets equal closing equity.
- (e) An accrual is an amount prepaid; for example, rent paid in advance.

Numerical Questions

Questions with numbers in blue have answers at the back of the book.

Q1 The following financial details are for Jane Bricker as at 31 December 2013.

	£		£
Equity 1 January 2013	5,000	Profit	12,000
Drawings	7,000		

Required: Jane Bricker's capital employed as at 31 December 2013.

Q2 Alpa Shah has the following financial details as at 30 June 2014.

	£		£
Non-current assets	100,000	Current liabilities	30,000
Current assets	50,000	Non-current liabilities	20,000

Required: Alpa Shah's total net assets as at 30 June 2014.

Q3 Jill Jenkins has the following financial details as at 31 December 2013.

	£		£
Inventory	18,000	Cash	4,000
Trade receivables	8,000	Trade payables	12,000

Required: Jill Jenkins' net current assets as at 31 December 2013.

Q4 Janet Richards has the following financial details as at 31 December 2013.

	£		£
Land and buildings	100,000	Trade payables	15,000
Plant and machinery	60,000	Long-term loan	15,000
Inventory	40,000	Opening equity	200,000
Trade receivables	30,000	Net profit	28,000
Cash	20,000	Drawings	8,000
		Closing equity	220,000

Required: Janet Richards' Statement of financial position as at 31 December 2013.

Appendix 5.1: Horizontal Format of Statement of Financial Position

R. Beer's Statement of Financial Position as at 31 March 2014 (presented in horizontal format)

	£	£		£	£
Equity			**Non-Current Assets**		
Opening equity		80,257	Property, Plant and Equipment		
Add Profit		8,350	Land and buildings		71,572
		88,607	Plant and machinery		3,500
Less Drawings		9,366	Furniture and fittings		5,834
Closing equity		79,241	Motor vehicles		3,398
Long-term loan		6,500	*Total Non-current assets*		84,304
		85,741			
Current Liabilities			**Current Assets**		
Creditors	3,991		Inventory	2,200	
Loan	1,000	4,991	Trade receivables	100	
			Prepayments	50	
			Bank	3,738	
			Cash	340	6,428
		90,732			90,732

Go online to discover the extra features for this chapter at **www.wiley.com/college/jones**

Chapter 6

Preparing the financial statements

'Mr Evans was the chief accountant of a large manufacturing concern. Every day, on arriving at work, he would unlock the bottom drawer of his desk, peer at something inside, then close and lock the drawer. He had done this for 25 years. The entire staff was intrigued but no one was game to ask him what was in the drawer. Finally, the time came for Mr Evans to retire. There was a farewell party with speeches and a presentation. As soon as Mr Evans had left the buildings, some of the staff rushed into his office, unlocked the bottom drawer and peered in. Taped to the bottom of the drawer was a sheet of paper. It read, "The debit side is the one nearest the window".'

R. Andrews, *Funny Business, C.A. Magazine,* April 2000, p. 26. Copyright The Institute of Chartered Accountants of Scotland.

Learning Outcomes

After completing this chapter you should be able to:

- Show how the trial balance is used as a basis for preparing the financial statements.
- Prepare the income statement (profit and loss account) and the statement of financial position (balance sheet).
- Understand the post-trial balance adjustments commonly made to the accounts.
- Prepare the income statement (profit and loss account) and the statement of financial position (balance sheet) using post-trial balance adjustments.

Go online to discover the extra features for this chapter at **www.wiley.com/college/jones**

Chapter Summary

- The trial balance when rearranged creates an income statement and a statement of financial position.
- The income statement presents revenue, cost of sales, other income and other expenses.
- The statement of financial position consists of assets, liabilities and equity.
- Revenue less cost of sales less other expenses gives net profit.
- There are five main post trial-balance adjustments to the accounts: closing inventory, accruals, prepayments, depreciation, and bad and doubtful debts.
- In addition, there may be a profit or loss on the sale of property, plant and equipment.
- All five adjustments are made twice to maintain the double-entry: first, in the income statement and second, in the statement of financial position.

Introduction

A trial balance is prepared after the bookkeeping process of recording the financial transactions in a double-entry form. The bookkeeping stage is really one of aggregating and summarising the financial information. The next step is to prepare the income statement (profit and loss account) and the statement of financial position (balance sheet) from the trial balance. In essence, the income statement sets out income less expenses and thus determines profit. Meanwhile, the statement of financial position presents the assets and liabilities, including equity. The two statements are seen as complementary. Chapters 4 and 5 discussed the nature and purpose of the income statement and the statement of financial position. This present chapter looks at the mechanics of how we prepare the final accounts from the trial balance. It is thus a continuation of Chapter 3. These mechanics are the same for sole traders, partnerships and companies. However, in companies the final unabridged accounts are then used to provide summarised accounts for publication.

Main Financial Statements

Essentially, the two main financial statements rearrange the items in the trial balance. The profit for the year effectively links the income statement and the statement of financial position. In the **income statement profit is income less expenses paid**, while in the **statement of financial position, closing equity add drawings less opening equity gives profit.** Looked at another way, profit represents the increase in equity over the year. Profit is a key figure in the accounts and plays a vital part in linking the income statement to the statement of financial position. Profit is often reported graphically by companies in their annual reports. Stage Coach plc's profit figure is given in Company Snapshot 6.1.

COMPANY SNAPSHOT 6.1

Operating Profit

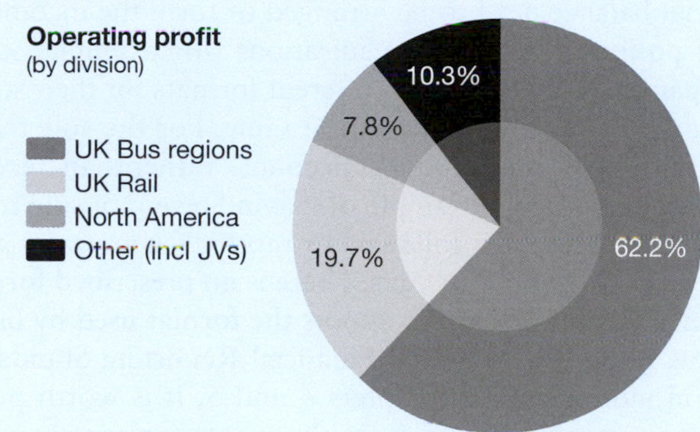

Source: Stagecoach Group plc, *Annual Report and Financial Statements 2011*.

PAUSE FOR THOUGHT 6.1

Accounting Equation and Financial Statements

What is the relationship between the accounting equation, income statement and statement of financial position?

In essence, the accounting equation develops into the financial statements. Remember from Chapter 3 that the expanded accounting equation was:

$$\text{Assets} + \text{Expenses} = \text{Liabilities} + \text{Equity} + \text{Income}$$

Rearrange thus:

$$\underbrace{\text{Assets} - (\text{Liabilities} + \text{Equity})}_{\text{Statement of financial position}} = \underbrace{\text{Income} - \text{Expenses}}_{\text{Income statement}}$$

Trial Balance to the Income Statement (Profit and Loss Account) and the Statement of Financial Position (Balance Sheet)

The elements of the trial balance need to be arranged to form the income statement and the statement of financial position. Different organisations (for example, sole traders, partnerships and limited companies) all have slightly different formats for their statement of financial position. However, the basic structure remains the same. For the sole trader, sometimes the terminology used is 'trading and profit and loss account', rather than 'income statement'. For illustrative purposes, we continue the example of Gavin Stevens, a sole trader, who is setting up a hotel. The format used here is that followed by most UK companies and broadly adheres to the requirements of the UK Companies Acts. There is **no prescribed format** for sole traders, therefore, **for consistency this book broadly adopts the format used by listed companies that follow the requirements of the International Financial Reporting Standards.** The individual items were explained in more detail in Chapters 4 and 5. It is worth pointing out that the statement of cash flows is usually derived from the income statement and the statement of financial position once they have been prepared and *not* from the trial balance (see Chapter 8).

Gavin Stevens, Continued

In Chapter 3, we prepared the trial balance. We now can use this to prepare the income statement and the statement of financial position. However, when we prepare the financial accounts we also need to collect information on the amount of inventory and on any expenses which are yet to be paid or have been paid in advance. In this example, we set out more details about inventory, amounts owing for telephone and amounts prepaid for electricity in the notes to the trial balance. It is important to realise that none of these items has so far been entered into the books. We deal with these adjustments in more depth later in this chapter.

Gavin Stevens
Trial Balance as at 7 January

		Debit	Credit
		£	£
Hotel		610,000	
Van		3,000	
Revenue			9,000
Purchases		5,000	
Equity			700,000
Revenue returns		70	
Purchases returns			500
Bank		86,915	
Electricity		300	
Wages		1,000	
Trade receivables	Ireton	1,965	
	Hepworth	2,500	
Trade payables	Hogen		250
	Lewis		1,000
		710,750	710,750

Notes:

1. Gavin Stevens does not use all the catering supplies. He estimates that the amount of catering supplies left as closing inventory is £50.
2. There is a special arrangement with the electricity company in which Gavin Stevens pays £300 in advance for a quarter. By 7 January he has used £50 which means he has prepaid £250. This is known as a prepayment.
3. There is a telephone bill yet to be received. However, Gavin Stevens estimates that he owes £100. This is known as an accrual.

We now prepare the income statement following the steps in Helpnote 6.1.

HELPNOTE 6.1

Presentational Guide to the Four Steps (Given as A–D in Gavin Stevens' Income Statement (Trading and Profit and Loss Account))

In terms of presentation, we should note:

- We must first determine cost of sales (Step A). This is, at its simplest, opening stock add purchases less closing inventory. Purchases must be adjusted for purchases returns.
- Sales less cost of sales gives gross profit (Step B). Sales must be adjusted for revenue returns.
- We list and total all expenses (Step C).
- We determine net profit (Step D) by taking expenses away from gross profit.

Gavin Stevens
Income Statement (Trading and Profit and Loss Account) for the Week Ended 7 January

	£	£	£		
Revenue			9,000		
Less Revenue returns			70		
			8,930		
Less *Cost of Sales*				A	
Opening inventory		–			**Trading account**
Add Purchases	5,000				
Less Purchases returns	500	4,500			
Less Closing inventory		50	4,450		
Gross Profit			4,480	B	
Less *Expenses*				C	
Electricity		50			
Wages		1,000			**Profit and loss account**
Telephone		100	1,150		
Net Profit			3,330	D	

Points to notice:

1. All the figures are from the trial balance except for closing inventory £50, electricity £50 and telephone £100 (calculated from notes) and profit £3,330 (calculated).
2. The first part of the statement down to gross profit (B) (revenue less cost of sales (A)) is sometimes called the trading account. It deals with revenue and purchases. Essentially sales returns and purchases returns are deducted from revenue and purchases, respectively. Inventory is simply unsold purchases.
3. Gross profit (B) is revenue minus cost of sales.
4. Net profit (D) is revenue minus cost of sales minus other expenses (C).
5. Net profit of £3,330 increases equity in the statement of financial position. It is the balancing item, simply income minus expenses.

We now prepare the statement of financial position following the steps in Helpnote 6.2.

HELPNOTE 6.2

Presentational Guide to the Five Steps (Given as A–E in Gavin Stevens' Statement of Financial Position (Balance Sheet))

In terms of presentation, we should note:

- All the property, plant and equipment (i.e., tangible non-current assets) are added together (Step A).
- Total assets (non-current assets and current assets) are determined next. This will give total assets (Step B).
- The total liabilities are determined. This is current liabilities and non-current liabilities added together (Step C).
- Total assets less total liabilities gives net assets (Step D).
- Equity is determined. Effectively, net profit is added to opening equity to give closing equity (Step E).

Gavin Stevens
Statement of Financial Position (Balance Sheet) as at 7 January

TOTAL ASSETS		
Non-current Assets		
Property, plant and equipment	£	
Hotel	610,000	
Van	3,000	
Total non-current assets	613,000	A
Current Assets		
Inventory	50	
Trade receivables (£1,965 + £2,500)	4,465	

Electricity prepayment	250	
Bank	86,915	
Total current assets	91,680	
Total Assets	704,680	B
TOTAL LIABILITIES		
Current Liabilities		
Trade payables (£250 + £1,000)	(1,250)	
Telephone bill accrued	(100)	
Total Liabilities	(1,350)	C
Net Assets	703,330	D
EQUITY	£	
Opening equity	700,000	
Add Net profit	3,330	
Closing equity	703,330	E

Points to notice:

1. Thus, in this example we have:
   A = The sum total of the non-current assets (property, plant and equipment) £613,000.
   B = The total assets £704,680 (£613,000 non-current assets plus £91,680 current assets).
   C = Total liabilities (in this case the current liabilities of £1,350 as there are no non-current liabilities).
   D = Net assets £703,330 (total assets £704,680 (B) less total liabilities £1,350 (C)).
   E = Equity £703,330 (opening equity plus net profit).
2. All figures are from the trial balance except for closing inventory £50, electricity prepayment £250, telephone bill (from notes) and profit £3,330 (balancing figure). Except for electricity, all *these* figures are the same in the income statement. Electricity is different because, in effect, we are splitting up £300. Thus:
   Total paid £300 = £50 used up as an expense in the income statement, and £250 not used up recorded as an asset in the statement of financial position.
3. Our statement is divided into non-current assets, current assets, current liabilities and equity.
4. The trade receivables are the trial balance figures for Ireton and Hepworth; the trade payables are those for Hogen and Lewis.
5. Our opening equity plus our net profit gives us our closing equity. In other words, the business 'owes' Gavin Stevens £700,000 at 1 January, but £703,330 at 7 January.
6. Net profit of £3,330 is found in the income statement. It is the balancing item. As we saw from Pause for Thought 6.1, the profit can be seen as the increase in net assets over the year. Or, alternatively, it can be viewed as assets less liabilities less opening equity.
7. The statement of financial position balances. In other words, total net assets equals closing equity.

PAUSE FOR THOUGHT 6.2

Accounting Equation and Gavin Stevens

How does the Gavin Stevens example we have just completed fit the accounting equation?

If we take our expanded accounting equation:

Assets + Expenses = Liabilities + Equity + Income

and rearrange it,

Assets − (Liabilities + Equity) = Income − Expenses

Now, if we substitute the figures from Gavin Stevens, we have:

Non-current assets (£613,000) + Current assets (£91,680) − ((Current liabilities (£1,350) + Opening equity (£700,000)) = Income (£8,930) − (Cost of sales (£4,450) + Expenses (£1,150))

∴ £613,000 + £91,680 − (£1,350 + £700,000) = £8,930 − (£4,450 + £1,150)
∴ £704,680 − £701,350 = £8,930 − £5,600
∴ £3,330 = £3,330

The £3,330 represents net profit. This net profit, therefore, provides a bridge between the statement of financial position and the income statement.

Adjustments to Trial Balance

The trial balance is prepared from the books of account and is then adjusted for certain items. These items represent estimates or adjustments which typically do not form part of the initial double-entry process. Five of the main adjustments are **closing inventory, accruals, prepayments, depreciation,** and **bad and doubtful debts**. The mechanics of their accounting treatment is discussed here. However, the items themselves are discussed in more depth in Chapters 4 and 5 on the income statement and the statement of financial position.

Inventories (Stock)

Inventories are an important asset to any business, especially manufacturing businesses. Stock control systems in large businesses can be very complex and sophisticated. In most sole traders and in many other businesses it is normal not to record the detailed physical movements (i.e., purchases and sales of inventory). Inventory is not, therefore, formally recorded in these organisations in the double-entry process. However, at the financial reporting date inventory is counted and valued and the accounting records updated. To maintain the double-entry, the asset of inventory is entered twice: *first* in the trading part of the income statement; and *second*, in the current assets section of the statement of financial position. These two figures for accounting purposes cancel out and thus the double-entry is maintained. Last year's closing inventory figure becomes the current year's opening inventory figure. The term inventories is often used in listed company accounts to denote the fact that a company may have many individual inventories. An alternative commonly used term is stock.

Accruals

Accruals are the amounts we owe to the suppliers of services such as the telephone or light and heat. In small businesses, accruals are normally excluded from the initial double-entry process. We adjust for accruals so that we will arrive at the expenses incurred for the year not just the amount paid. Accruals appear in the final accounts in two places. *First*, the amount owing is included in the income statement under expenses. *Second*, a matching amount is included under current liabilities in the statement of financial position. The double-entry is thus maintained. Figure 6.1 gives an example of accruals and prepayments (payments in advance for services).

Prepayments

Prepayments represent the amount paid in advance to the suppliers of services; for example, rent paid in advance. In many ways prepayments are the opposite of accruals. Whereas accruals must be added to the final accounts to achieve the matching concept, a prepayment must be deducted. The amount paid in advance is treated as an asset which will be used up at a future date. We adjust for prepayments so that we will arrive at the expenses incurred for the year and not include payments for future years.

Figure 6.1 Accruals and Prepayments

From the following information calculate the income statement and the statement of financial position entries for:

1. Electricity

Mary Christmas has received and paid three electricity bills for the year (£300, £400, £550) from the supplier Webelect. The bills are received on 31 March, 30 June and 30 September. They are paid at the end of the next month. Another bill of £600 received on 30 December is yet to be paid.

2. Rent

The quarterly rent for Mary Christmas's offices is £300 payable in advance to Rentco plc. The first payment is made on 1st January when the business starts, the last on 31st December.

1. Electricity

Effectively, the total bill incurred for the year is the amount paid (£300 + £400 + £550) £1,250 and the amount due £600. Therefore, the total bill is £1,850; this is included in the income statement. In the statement of financial position, £600 is included as an accrual.

2. Rent

The amount paid is 5 × £300 = £1,500.

However, only £1,200 relates to this year and should go in the income statement. The £300 balance is a prepayment in the statement of financial position.

Income Statement		Statement of Financial Position	
EXPENSES	£	**ASSETS**	£
Electricity	1,850	**Current Assets**	
Rent	1,200	Rent prepaid	300
		LIABILITIES	
		Current Liabilities	
		Electricity owing	600

For Mary Christmas, we can also prepare T accounts to show the effect of these transactions (see Figure 6.2).

Figure 6.2 Example of Bookkeeping Entries For Accruals for Mary Christmas

Webelect Supplier Account

		£			£
30.4.2013	Cash Book	300	31.3.2013	Electricity	300
31.7.2013	Cash Book	400	30.6.2013	Electricity	400
31.10.2013	Cash Book	550	30.9.2013	Electricity	550
31.12.2013	Bal c/f	600	30.12.2013	Electricity	600
		1,850			1,850
			1.1.2014 Bal b/f		600

Electricity

		£			£
31.3.2013	Webelect	300	31.12.2013	Income Statement	1,850
30.6.2013	Webelect	400			
30.9.2013	Webelect	550			
31.12.2013	Webelect	600			
		1,850			1,850

Cash Book (extracts)

		£			£
31.12.2013 Bal c/f		1,250	30.4.2013	Webelect	300
			31.7.2013	Webelect	400
			31.10.2013	Webelect	550
		1,250			1,250
			1.1.2014	Bal b/f	1,250

We can thus see that at the end of the year the Electricity bill for the year is taken from the Electricity account and is £1,850 and that the amount brought forward is £600 from the Webelect supplier account, which is the accrual. The Cash book is given for information and shows a £1,250 credit balance.

For the prepayment for Mary Christmas, we can also complete double-entry bookkeeping entry. This is illustrated in Figure 6.3.

Depreciation

As we saw in Chapter 5, property, plant and equipment wear out over time and depreciation seeks to recognise this. Depreciation in the accounts is simply recording this – twice. *First*, a proportion of the original cost is allocated as an expense in the income statement. *Second*, an equivalent amount is deducted from the property, plant and equipment in the statement of financial position (see Figure 6.4). The double entry for this process can be seen in Figure 6.7 on page 151. Essentially, depreciation for each year is entered into a depreciation account as a debit. The credit is entered into the provision for depreciation account. The depreciation account balance is transferred to each year's income statement. The provision for depreciation account is cumulative and goes into the statement of financial position.

Figure 6.3 Example of Bookkeeping Entries for Prepayments for Mary Christmas

Rentco Plc

	£			£
1.1.2013 Cash Book	300	1.1.2013	Rent	300
1.4.2013 Cash Book	300	1.4.2013	Rent	300
1.7.2013 Cash Book	300	1.7.2013	Rent	300
1.10.2013 Cash Book	300	1.10.2013	Rent	300
31.12.2013 Cash Book	300	31.12.2013 Bal c/f		300
	1,500			1,500
1.1.2014 Bal b/f	300			

Cash Book (extracts)

	£			£
31.12.2013 Bal c/f	1,500	1.1.2013	Rentco	300
		1.4.2013	Rentco	300
		1.7.2013	Rentco	300
		1.10.2013	Rentco	300
		31.12.2013	Rentco	300
	1,500			1,500
		1.1.2014 Bal b/f		1,500

Rent Account

	£			£
1.1.2013 Rent	300	31.12.2013	Income Statement	1,200
1.4.2013 Rent	300			
1.7.2013 Rent	300			
1.10.2013 Rent	300			
	1,200			1,200

We can thus see that the debit entries in the rent account reflect the fact that the charge for the year is £1,200, which is transferred to the income statement. The £300 in Rentco plc's account represents the prepayment and is carried forward on 31st December 2013 as a debit balance to signify that it is an asset.

PAUSE FOR THOUGHT 6.3

Accruals and Prepayments

Can you think of four examples of accruals and prepayments?

We might have, for example:

Accruals	*Prepayments*
Electricity owing	Rent paid in advance
Business rates owing	Prepaid electricity on meter
Rent owing	Prepaid standing charge for telephone
Telephone owing	Insurance paid in advance

Figure 6.4 Example of Depreciation

A business has five assets shown at cost. Ten per cent of the original cost of each asset has been allocated as depreciation. Record the transactions in the accounts.

	£
Premises	80,000
Machine	75,000
Office furniture	12,000
Computer	1,500
Motor van	6,000

There are two parts to this. **First,** we record 10% of the original cost as an expense in the expenses section of the income statement (for example, premises: 10% £80,000 = £8,000).

Income Statement (Year 1)

Expenses	£
Depreciation on premises	8,000
Depreciation on machine	7,500
Depreciation on office furniture	1,200
Depreciation on computer	150
Depreciation on motor van	600

Second, we record the original cost, total depreciation (called accumulated depreciation) and net book value (original cost less depreciation) in the statement of financial position. Note that accumulated depreciation is recorded in brackets – this shows it is being taken away.

Statement of Financial Position (Year 1)

Property, Plant and Equipment	£ *Cost*	£ *Accumulated depreciation*	£ *Net book value*
Premises	80,000	(8,000)	72,000
Machine	75,000	(7,500)	67,500
Office furniture	12,000	(1,200)	10,800
Computer	1,500	(150)	1,350
Motor van	6,000	(600)	5,400
	174,500	(17,450)	157,050

In next year's trial balance, the cost and accumulated depreciation figures would be recorded. The *accumulated depreciation* is often called *provision for depreciation*. This example records only one year's depreciation. However, in future years, there will be more depreciation, which is why it is called accumulated depreciation.
In the following year, we also have 10% depreciation. The income statement is thus the same.

Income Statement (Year 2)

Expenses	£
Depreciation on premises	8,000
Depreciation on machine	7,500
Depreciation on office furniture	1,200
Depreciation on computer	150
Depreciation on motor van	600

In the statement of financial position, however, we *add* this year's depreciation to the accumulated depreciation figure. Thus, for premises we add £8,000 and £8,000 to arrive at £16,000. We, therefore, have:

Statement of Financial Position (Year 2)

Property, Plant and Equipment	£ *Cost*	£ *Accumulated depreciation*	£ *Net book value*
Premises	80,000	(16,000)	64,000
Machine	75,000	(15,000)	60,000
Office furniture	12,000	(2,400)	9,600
Computer	1,500	(300)	1,200
Motor van	6,000	(1,200)	4,800
	174,500	(34,900)	139,600

In essence, we have merely added the two years' depreciation figures. Thus, for premises, our opening figure for accumulated depreciation was £8,000. We then added this year's depreciation to arrive at £16,000. The net book value is simply the residual figure.

For ease of understanding these same figures are used in our comprehensive example, Live Wire, later in this chapter.

Rentokil Initial plc's property, plant and equipment (as recorded in its 2009 statement of financial position) are given as an illustration in Company Snapshot 6.2. As you can see, they can be quite complex. In essence, however, two years' accounts are shown: 2008 and 2009. The amounts recorded at cost are shown and then adjusted for additions and disposals at cost. Adjustments for depreciation and impairment (where there is a write-down in the value of an asset over and above depreciation) are shown. The cost less the depreciation and impairment equals the net book value.

COMPANY SNAPSHOT 6.2

Property, Plant and Equipment

	Land and Buildings £m	Equipment for rental £m	Other plant and equipment £m	Vehicles and office equipment £m	Total £m
Cost					
At 1 January 2008	182.5	463.0	266.2	212.2	1,123.9
Exchange differences	40.2	137.9	61.0	47.2	286.3
Additions	13.3	136.8	29.9	49.6	229.6
Disposals	(9.6)	(64.6)	(30.8)	(52.3)	(157.3)
Acquisition of companies and businesses[1]	(1.0)	0.1	0.5	1.2	0.8
Reclassifications	(4.1)	—	2.3	1.8	—
At 31 December 2008	221.3	673.2	329.1	259.7	1,483.3
At 1 January 2009	221.3	673.2	329.1	259.7	1,483.3
Exchange differences	(12.2)	(37.2)	(19.1)	(10.1)	(78.6)
Additions	4.1	122.1	16.4	33.0	175.6
Disposals	(6.5)	(93.4)	(17.5)	(43.4)	(160.8)
Acquisition of companies and businesses[1]	—	—	—	0.2	0.2
Disposal of companies and businesses	—	(3.4)	(0.4)	(1.1)	(4.9)
Reclassifications	(0.2)	—	—	0.2	—
At 31 December 2009	206.5	661.3	308.5	238.5	1,414.8
Accumulated depreciation and impairment					
At 1 January 2008	(35.5)	(251.4)	(166.8)	(109.0)	(562.7)
Exchange differences	(10.6)	(78.0)	(38.3)	(26.6)	(153.5)
Disposals	4.8	63.2	28.7	44.0	140.7
Reclassifications	0.1	—	—	(0.1)	—
Depreciation charge	(6.2)	(115.7)	(23.4)	(41.3)	(186.6)
At 31 December 2008	(47.4)	(381.9)	(199.8)	(133.0)	(762.1)

COMPANY SNAPSHOT 6.2 (*continued*)

At 1 January 2009	(47.4)	(381.9)	(199.8)	(133.0)	(762.1)
Exchange differences	3.1	21.1	12.0	6.3	42.5
Disposals	2.8	91.6	14.9	38.0	147.3
Disposal of companies and businesses	—	3.2	0.4	0.8	4.4
Depreciation charge	(8.1)	(133.5)	(26.0)	(43.0)	(210.6)
At 31 December 2009	(49.6)	(399.5)	(198.5)	(130.9)	(778.5)
Net Book Value	£m	£m	£m	£m	£m
At 1 January 2008	147.0	211.6	99.4	103.2	561.2
At 31 December 2008	173.9	291.3	129.3	126.7	721.2
At 31 December 2009	156.9	261.8	110.0	107.6	636.3
The net carrying amounts of assets held under finance leases are as follows:					
At 31 December 2008	10.2	—	0.3	15.2	25.7
At 31 December 2009	3.9	0.4	0.4	14.1	18.8

[1]*Included within acquisition of companies and businesses are fair value adjustments to prior periods of (£0.1 million)(2008: £0.6 million). Refer to note 30 for further details on fair value adjustments.*

The category of equipment for rental consists of equipment leased by the group to third parties under operating leases.

Source: Rentokil Initial plc, *Annual Report 2009*, p. 62.

Tutorial Note: Exchange differences arise when, for example, transactions are carried out in different currencies or company results of overseas subsidiaries are translated from one currency to another.

Bad and Doubtful Debts

This is the last of the five adjustments. Bad and doubtful debts are also considered in Chapter 5 on the statement of financial position. Essentially, some debts *may* not be collected. These are termed doubtful debts.

Other debts *will almost certainly not* be collected; they are called bad or irrecoverable debts. The accounting entries to record this are in the income statement as an expense and in the statement of financial position as a reduction in trade receivables. Some businesses, such as building societies and banks, typically carry a high level of bad and doubtful debts. Company Snapshot 6.3 shows the bad and doubtful debts for Vodafone, the UK mobile phone company.

When considering the accounting treatment of bad and doubtful debts, it is crucial to distinguish between bad and doubtful debts.

1. Bad Debts

Bad debts are recorded as an expense in the income statement and written off trade receivables in the statement of financial position (see Figure 6.5).

COMPANY SNAPSHOT 6.3

Doubtful Debts

The Group's trade receivables are stated after allowances for bad and doubtful debts based on management's assessment of creditworthiness, an analysis of which is as follows:

	2010 £m	2009 £m
1 April	874	664
Exchange movements	(27)	101
Amounts charged to administrative expenses	465	423
Trade receivables written off	(383)	(314)
31 March	**929**	**874**

The carrying amounts of trade and other receivables approximate their fair value. Trade and other receivables are predominantly non-interest bearing.

Source: Vodafone Group plc, *Annual Report 2010,* p. 99. VODAFONE and the Vodafone logo are trade marks of the Vodafone Group.

Figure 6.5 Illustrative Example of Bad Debts

A business has trade receivables of £4,800, but estimates that bad debts will be £320.

Income Statement	£
Expenses	
Bad debts	320
Statement of Financial Position	
ASSETS	
Current Assets	
Trade receivables less bad debts	
(£4,800 - £320)	4,480

For ease of understanding, these same figures are used in our comprehensive example, Live Wire, later in this chapter.

2. Provision for the impairment of receivables

A 'provision for the impairment of receivables' is set up by a business for those debts it is dubious about collecting. The word 'impairment' indicates that it is doubtful whether the full money will be recovered for the trade receivables. This provision is *always* deducted from trade receivables in the statement of financial position. However, only **increases or decreases** in the provision are entered in the income statement. An *increase* is recorded as an *expense* and a *decrease* as an *income* (see Figure 6.6). Where there are both bad and doubtful debts

Figure 6.6 Illustrative Example of Doubtful Debts

A business has trade receivables of £4,800. There is a provision for the impairment of receivables of 10% of trade receivables. Last year trade receivables were £2,400 and the provision for the impairment of receivables was £240 (£480 - £240).

Income Statement	£
Expenses	
Increase in provision for the impairment of receivables	240
Statement of Financial Position	
ASSETS	
Current Assets	
Trade receivables	4,800
Provision for the impairment of receivables	(480)
Net trade receivables	4,320

For ease of understanding, these same figures are used in our comprehensive example, Live Wire, later in this chapter.

then either the provision for the impairment of trade receivables is calculated first and then bad debts are deducted or vice versa. There are arguments both ways. In this example the provision for the impairment of receivables is calculated first. In effect, using this method, bad debts are those debts which are definitely irrecoverable.

Debts

'A small debt makes a man your debtor, a large one makes him your enemy.'

Seneca (Ad Lucilium xix)

Source: The Executive's Book of Quotations (1994), p. 80.

Sale of an item of plant, property or machinery

When we sell items of plant, property or machinery, the amount that we receive for the asset will be unlikely to be the same as its net book value. We, therefore, will need to adjust the books for the profit or loss on the sale. Let us take the example of Horner Ltd. Horner buys three trucks (A, B and C) for £100,000 each on 1st January 2011. They are depreciated at the rate of 10% per annum. Horner sells Truck A on 31st December 2011 for £85,000. Truck B is sold on 31st December 2012 for £75,000 and truck C for £80,000 on 31st December 2013.

If we have to prepare the accounts for three years, we can use 'T' accounts (see Figure 6.7). We show the accounts for property, plant and equipment, depreciation, provision for depreciation and disposals account: property, plant and equipment.

Figure 6.7 Sale of Plant, Property or Machinery Illustrated with Bookkeeping Entries

Property, Plant and Equipment (at cost)

	£		£
1.1.2011 Cash Truck A	100,000	31.12.2011 Disposals	100,000
1.1.2011 Cash Truck B	100,000	31.12.2011 Bal c/f	200,000
1.1.2011 Cash Truck C	100,000		
			300,000
	300,000	31.12.2012 Disposals	100,000
1.1.2012 Bal b/f	200,000	31.12.2012 Bal c/f	100,000
	200,000		200,000
1.1.2013 Bal b/f	100,000	31.12.2013 Disposals	100,000
	100,000		100,000

Depreciation Account

	£		£
31.12.2011 Prov for Dep Truck A	10,000	31.12.2011 Income Statement	30,000
31.12.2011 Prof for Dep Truck B	10,000		
31.12.2011 Prov for Dep Truck C	10,000		
	30,000		30,000
31.12.2012 Prov for Dep Truck B	10,000	31.12.2012 Income Statement	20,000
31.12.2012 Prov for Dep Truck C	10,000		
	20,000		20,000
31.12.2012 Prov for Dep Truck C	10,000	31.12.2013 Income Statement	10,000
	10,000		10,000

Provision for Depreciation Account

	£		£
31.12.2011 Disposals	10,000	31.12.2011 Depreciation	30,000
31.12.2011 Bal c/f	20,000		
	30,000		30,000
31.12.2012 Disposals	20,000	1.1.2012 Bal b/f	20,000
31.12.2012 Bal c/f	20,000	31.12.2012 Depreciation	20,000
	40,000		40,000
31.12.2013 Disposals	30,000	1.1.2013 Bal b/f	20,000
		31.12.2013 Depreciation	10,000
	30,000		30,000

Disposals Account: Property, Plant and Equipment

	£		£
31.12.2011 Property, Plant and Equipment	100,000	31.12.2011 Prov for Dep A/C	10,000
		31.12.2011 Cash	85,000
		31.12.2011 Loss to Income Statement	5,000
	100,000		100,000
31.12.2012 Property, Plant and Equipment	100,000	31.12.2012 Prov for Dep A/C	20,000
		31.12.2012 Cash	75,000
		31.12.2012 Loss to Income Statement	5,000
	100,000		100,000
31.12.2013 Property, Plant and Equipment	100,000	31.12.2013 Prov for Dep A/C	30,000
31.12.2013 Profit to Income Statement	10,000	31.12.2013 Cash	80,000
	110,000		110,000

We can now prepare extracts from the income statement and statement of financial position.

(i) **Year 1**

Income Statement Extracts
Year ending 31 December 2011

	£
Depreciation	(30,000)
Loss on Disposal of PPE	(5,000)
	(35,000)

Statement of Financial Position Extracts as at 31.12.2011 for Property, Plant and Equipment (PPE)

	Cost	Accumulated Depreciation	Net Book Value
	£	£	£
PPE	200,000	(20,000)	180,000

We can thus see that in the first year, when we sell lorry A, there was a loss on disposal of £5,000. The cost was £100,000 less allocated depreciation of £10,000. We thus might have expected to receive £90,000, but instead we received only £85,000. It should be stressed that this is a book loss.

(ii) **Year 2**

Income Statement Extracts
Year ending 31 December 2012

	£
Depreciation	(20,000)
Loss on Disposal of PPE	(5,000)
	(25,000)

Statement of Financial Position Extracts as at 31.12.2012 for Property, Plant and Equipment (PPE)

	Cost	Accumulated Depreciation	Net Book Value
	£	£	£
PPE	100,000	(20,000)	80,000

In the second year, when we sell lorry B, there is also a book loss on disposal of £5,000. This is because the cost £100,000 less allocated depreciation of £20,000 is worth £80,000. However, instead of receiving this, we only received £75,000.

(iii) **Year 3**

Income Statement Extracts
Year ending 31 December 2013

	£
Depreciation	(10,000)
Profit on Disposal of PPE	10,000
	-

Statement of Financial Position Extracts as at 31.12.2013 for Property, Plant and Equipment (PPE)

	Cost	Accumulated Depreciation	Net Book Value
	£	£	£
PPE	-	-	-

In the third year, we sell lorry C. In this case, however, we have a profit. This is because the cost was £100,000 with accumulated depreciation equalling £30,000. However, we received £80,000 for it which is £10,000 more than the book value.

Common Items Found in the Final Account

It is now time to introduce some items commonly found in accounts. These are briefly explained in Figure 6.8. Mainly we focus on the accounts of a sole trader. Goodwill and other intangible assets (i.e., assets that we cannot touch) such as brands are discussed in more detail in Chapter 12.

Figure 6.8 Introducing Common Items Found in the Final Accounts

Item	Explanation	Location
Bank overdraft	This is where the business owes the bank money. Too many students are in this position!	Statement of financial position Current liabilities
Carriage inwards	This is usually found in manufacturing businesses. It is a cost of purchasing raw materials. It refers to the days when goods were brought in by horse and carriage.	Income statement Trading account Added to purchases
Carriage outwards	Similar to carriage inwards, except that it is an expense incurred by the business when selling goods.	Income statement Profit and loss account Expenses
Discount allowed	This is discount allowed by the business to customers for prompt payment. In other words, instead of paying, say £100, the customer pays £95. The sale £100 is recorded as normal, but discount allowed is recorded separately.	Income statement Profit and loss account Expenses
Discount received	Similar to discount allowed. However, it is received by the business from the supplier for paying promptly. The business, therefore, pays less. The purchase is recorded as normal, the discount received is recorded separately.	Income statement Profit and loss account Other income
Drawings	This is money which the sole trader or owner takes out for his or her living expenses. It is, in effect, the owner's salary. It is really a withdrawal of equity.	Statement of financial position Capital employed **Note:** Do *not* put in expenses
Income receivable*	This is income which is received by the business from a third party. Examples include dividends receivable from companies or interest receivable from the bank. Income received is a narrower term found in the statement of cash flows.	Income statement Profit and loss account Other income
Interest payable*	This is the reverse of income receivable. It is interest payable by the business to outsiders, especially on bank loans. Interest paid is a narrower term found in the statement of cash flows.	Income statement Profit and loss account Expenses
Long-term loan	This is a loan not repayable within a year. The loan may be with a bank or other organisation. Sometimes long-term loans are called debentures.	Statement of financial position Non-current liabilities

* Income receivable and interest payable are broader phrases than interest received and interest paid. They include interest earned yet to be received and interest incurred yet to be paid, respectively.

Note: We have divided the income statement into two parts, a trading account and a profit and loss account. These terms are sometimes used in the accounts of sole traders and partnerships and in the unabridged income statements of companies.

Comprehensive Example

We now close this chapter with a comprehensive example. This example includes most items normally found in the accounts of a sole trader. We use the example of a small engineering business run by Live Wire, which buys and sells electrical products. The trial balance is provided in Figure 6.9(a), and then in Figure 6.9(b) are the income statement, the statement of financial position and the explanatory notes.

Figure 6.9 Worked Example of a Sole Trader's Accounts

(a)

Live Wire
Trial Balance as at 31 December 2013

	Debit £	Credit £
Revenue		250,000
Revenue returns	800	
Purchases	100,000	
Purchases returns		600
Carriage inwards	200	
Carriage outwards	300	
Discounts allowed	150	
Discounts receivable		175
Dividends receivable		225
Interest receivable		100
Drawings	26,690	
Advertising	1,250	
Telephone	2,150	
Wages	27,000	
Electricity	3,700	
Business rates	1,500	
Travelling expenses	1,200	
Van repairs	650	
Petrol	3,800	
General expenses	1,200	
Insurance	1,500	
Premises at cost	80,000	
Accumulated depreciation as at 1 January 2013		8,000
Machine at cost	75,000	
Accumulated depreciation as at 1 January 2013		7,500
Office furniture at cost	12,000	
Accumulated depreciation as at 1 January 2013		1,200
Computer at cost	1,500	
Accumulated depreciation as at 1 January 2013		150

Figure 6.9 Worked Example of a Sole Trader's Accounts (*continued*)

	£	£
Motor van at cost	6,000	
Accumulated depreciation as at 1 January 2013		600
Opening inventory	9,000	
Cash at bank	7,050	
Bank overdraft		3,600
Trade receivables	4,800	
Provision for the impairment of receivables as at 1 January 2013		240
Trade payables		9,800
Long-term loan		15,600
Interest payable	1,150	
Equity		70,800
	368,590	368,590

You have the following extra information:

(i) Closing inventory at 31 December 2013 was £8,600.

(ii) Of the insurance £500 was paid in advance.

(iii) Live Wire still owes £450 for the telephone.

(iv) Depreciation is charged at 10% on the cost of the property, plant and equipment (i.e., £8,000 for premises, £7,500 for machine, £1,200 for office furniture, £150 for computer and £600 for motor van). The accumulated depreciation is the depreciation charged to date.

(v) Bad debts are £320. They have not yet been written off. The provision for the impairment of receivables has increased from £240 to £480 and is 10% of trade receivables.

Required: Live Wire's Income Statement for year ended 31 December 2013 and Statement of Financial Position as at 31 December 2013.

(b)

Live Wire
Income Statement Year Ended 31 December 2013

	£	£	£
Revenue			250,000
Less Revenue returns			800
			249,200
Less *Cost of Sales*			
Opening inventory		9,000	
Add Purchases	100,000		
Carriage inwards	200		
	100,200		
Less Purchases returns	600	99,600	
		108,600	
Less Closing inventory (Note 2)		8,600	100,000
Gross Profit			149,200
Add *Other Income*			
Discounts receivable		175	
Dividends receivable		225	
Interest receivable		100	500
			149,700

Figure 6.9 Worked Example of a Sole Trader's Accounts (*continued*)

	£	£	£
Less *Expenses*			
Carriage outwards		300	
Discounts allowed		150	
Advertising		1,250	
Telephone (Note 3)		2,600	
Wages		27,000	
Electricity		3,700	
Business rates		1,500	
Travelling expenses		1,200	
Van repairs		650	
Petrol		3,800	
General expenses		1,200	
Insurance (Note 4)		1,000	
Interest payable		1,150	
Depreciation (Note 5)			
Premises		8,000	
Machine		7,500	
Office furniture		1,200	
Computer		150	
Motor van		600	
Bad debts (Note 6)		320	
Provision for the impairment of receivables (Note 7)		240	63,510
Net Profit			86,190

Live Wire

Statement of Financial Position as at 31 December 2013

	£	£	£
ASSETS	Cost	Accumulated depreciation (Note 5)	Net book value
Non-current assets			
Property, plant and equipment			
Premises	80,000	(16,000)	64,000
Machine	75,000	(15,000)	60,000
Office furniture	12,000	(2,400)	9,600
Computer	1,500	(300)	1,200
Motor van	6,000	(1,200)	4,800
	174,500	(34,900)	139,600

Figure 6.9 Worked Example of a Sole Trader's Accounts (*continued*)

	£	£	£
Current Assets			
Inventory (Note 2)		8,600	
Trade receivables less provision for the impairment of receivables (Notes 6, 7)		4,000	
Prepayments (Note 4)		500	
Cash at bank		7,050	20,150
Total Assets			159,750
LIABILITIES			
Current Liabilities			
Trade payables		(9,800)	
Bank overdraft		(3,600)	
Accruals (Note 3)		(450)	(13,850)
Non-current Liabilities			(15,600)
Total Liabilities			(29,450)
Net Assets			130,300
EQUITY			£
Opening equity			70,800
Add Net profit			86,190
			156,990
Less Drawings			(26,690)
Closing equity			130,300

Notes:

1. All the figures in Live Wire's accounts, except for closing inventory, telephone, insurance, depreciation, and bad and doubtful debts are as listed in the trial balance. The figures for profit and closing equity are calculated as balancing figures.
2. Closing inventory of £8,600 is recorded in the trading account (top part of the income statement) and in the statement of financial position.
3. The telephone expense is adjusted for the £450 owing. In the income statement, the expense increases to £2,600 (£2,150 + £450). In the statement of financial position, the £450 owing becomes an accrual.
4. The insurance is adjusted for the £500 paid in advance. The expense in the income statement thus becomes £1,000 (£1,500 − £500). The £500 is recorded as a prepayment in current assets in the statement of financial position.
5. The depreciation for the year, which was the same as in Figure 6.4, has been recorded twice: *first,* under expenses in the income statement, and *second*, in the statement of financial position under property, plant and equipment. The double-entry is thus maintained.
6. The £320 for bad debts has been recorded twice: *first*, under expenses in the income statement, and *second*, under current assets (trade receivables) in the statement of financial position. The double-entry is thus completed (see also Figure 6.5).
7. Doubtful debts represents the increase in the provision for the impairment of receivables from £240 to £480. The increase of £240 is recorded twice. *First*, under expenses in the income statement, and *second*, as part of the £480 deduction from trade receivables under current assets in the statement of financial position. The double-entry is thus completed (see also Figure 6.6).

Conclusion

The two main financial statements – the income statement and the statement of financial position – are both prepared from the trial balance. The income statement focuses on income, such as sales or dividends receivable, and expenses, such as telephone or electricity. The statement of financial position, by contrast, focuses on assets, liabilities and owner's capital or equity. In both financial statements, profit becomes the balancing figure. After the trial balance has been prepared, the accounts are often adjusted for items such as closing inventory, accruals (amounts owing), prepayments (amounts prepaid), depreciation (the wearing out of property, plant and equipment), and bad and doubtful debts. In each case, we adjust the accounts twice: *first* in the income statement and *second* in the statement of financial position. The double-entry and the symmetry of the accounts are thus maintained.

Discussion Questions

Questions with numbers in blue have answers at the back of the book.

Q1 What is a sole trader and why is it important for the sole trader to prepare a set of financial statements?

Q2 'Profit is the figure which links the income statement and the statement of financial position.' Discuss.

Q3 Why do we need to carry out post trial-balance adjustments when we are preparing the final accounts?

Numerical Questions

The numerical questions which follow are graded in difficulty. Those at the start are about as complex as the illustrative example, Gavin Stevens. They gradually become more complex, until the final questions equate to the illustrative example, Live Wire.

Questions with numbers in blue have answers at the back of the book.

Q1 Michael Anet has the following trial balance.

M. Anet
Trial Balance as at 31 December 2013

	Debit	Credit
	£	£
Hotel	40,000	
Van	10,000	
Revenue		25,000
Purchases	15,000	
Equity		51,900
Bank	8,000	
Electricity	1,500	
Wages	2,500	
A. Brush (Trade receivable)	400	
A. Painter (Trade payable)		500
	77,400	77,400

Required: Prepare Michael Anet's income statement for the year ended 31 December 2013 and statement of financial position as at 31 December 2013.

Q2 Paul Icasso has the following trial balance.

P. Icasso
Trial Balance as at 31 March 2014

	Debit	Credit
	£	£
Hotel	50,000	
Van	8,000	
Revenue		35,000
Purchases	25,000	
Revenue returns	3,000	
Purchases returns		4,000
Equity		60,050
Bank	9,000	
Electricity	1,000	
Advertising	800	
Trade receivable Shah	1,250	
Trade receivable Chan	2,250	
Trade payable Jones		1,250
	100,300	100,300

Required: Prepare Paul Icasso's trading and income statement for the year ended 31 March 2014 and a statement of financial position as at 31 March 2014.

Q3 Rose Ubens buys and sells goods. Her trial balance is presented below.

R. Ubens
Trial Balance as at 31 December 2013

	Debit	Credit
	£	£
Opening inventory	3,600	
Building	20,400	
Motor van	3,500	
Trade receivables	2,600	
Trade payables		3,800
Cash at bank	4,400	
Electricity	1,500	
Advertising	300	
Printing and stationery	50	
Telephone	650	
Rent and rates	1,200	
Postage	150	
Drawings	7,800	
Equity		19,950
Revenue		88,000
Purchases	66,000	
Revenue returns	800	
Purchases returns		1,200
	112,950	112,950

Note:
1. Closing inventory is £4,000

Required: Prepare Rose Ubens' income statement for the year ended 31 December 2013 and a statement of financial position as at 31 December 2013.

Q4 Clara Onstable has prepared her trial balance as at 31 December. She has the following additional information.

(a) She pays £240 rent per month. She has paid £3,600, the whole year's rent plus three months in advance.

(b) She has paid insurance costs of £480. However, she has paid £120 in advance.

Required: Prepare the extracts for the final accounts.

Q5 Vincent Gogh, a shopkeeper, has the following trial balance.

V. Gogh
Trial Balance as at 31 December 2013

	Debit	Credit
	£	£
Revenue		40,000
Revenue returns	500	
Purchases	25,000	
Purchases returns		450
Opening inventory	5,500	
Trade receivables	3,500	
Trade payables		1,500
Cash at bank	1,300	
Long-term loan		3,700
Motor car	8,500	
Shop	9,000	
Business rates	1,000	
Rent	600	
Electricity	350	
Telephone	450	
Insurance	750	
General expenses	150	
Wages	10,500	
Drawings	12,900	
Equity		34,350
	80,000	80,000

You also have the following additional information.
1. Closing inventory as at 31 December 2012 is £9,000.
2. V. Gogh owes £350 for electricity.
3. £200 of the rent is paid in advance.

Required: Prepare V. Gogh's income statement for the year ended 31 December 2013 and a statement of financial position as at 31 December 2013.

Q6 Leonardo Da Vinci, who sells computers, has extracted the following balances from the accounts.

L. Da Vinci
Trial Balance as at 30 September 2013

	Debit £	Credit £
Revenue		105,000
Revenue returns	8,000	
Purchases	70,000	
Purchases returns		1,800
Opening inventory of computers	6,500	
Drawings	8,500	
Trade receivables	12,000	
Trade payables		13,000
Cash at bank	1,800	
Long-term loan		6,600
Discounts allowed	300	
Carriage inwards	250	
Business premises	18,000	
Motor van	7,500	
Computer	1,500	
Wages	32,500	
Electricity	825	
Telephone	325	
Insurance	225	
Rent	1,250	
Business rates	1,000	
Equity		44,075
	170,475	170,475

You have the following additional information.
1. Closing inventory of computers as at 30 September 2013 is £7,000.
2. Da Vinci owes £175 for the telephone and £1,200 for electricity.
3. The prepayments are £25 for insurance and £250 for rent.

Required: Prepare Da Vinci's income statement for the year ended 30 September 2013 and a statement of financial position as at 30 September 2013.

Q7 Helen Ogarth is preparing her accounts for the year to 31 December 2013. On 1 January 2013 she purchased the following property, plant and equipment.

	£
Buildings	100,000
Machine	50,000
Motor van	20,000

She wishes to write off the following amounts for depreciation.

	£
Buildings	10,000
Machine	3,000
Motor van	2,000

Required: Prepare the appropriate extracts for the statement of financial position and income statement.

Q8 Michael Atisse, a carpenter, has the following trial balance as at 31 December 2013.

	Debit £	Credit £
Work done		50,000
Purchases of materials	25,000	
Opening inventory of tools	650	
Motor expenses	3,550	
Trade receivables	1,000	
Trade payables		4,000
Cash at bank	3,600	
Long-term loan		16,800
Building at cost	52,300	
Motor car at cost	8,000	
Computer at cost	6,300	
Office equipment at cost	10,200	
Business rates	1,300	
Electricity	900	

Q8 Michael Atisse (*continued*)

	Debit	Credit
	£	£
Interest on loan	1,600	
Drawings	5,200	
Telephone	1,200	
Equity		50,000
	120,800	120,800

You have the following additional information.
1. Closing inventory of tools £4,500
2. Depreciation is to be written off the property, plant and equipment as follows:

Buildings	£3,000
Motor car	£2,000
Computer	£1,400
Office equipment	£1,800

Required: Prepare M. Atisse's income statement for the year ended 31 December 2013 and the statement of financial position as at 31 December 2013.

Q9 Clare Analetto, an antiques dealer, has the following trial balance as at 31 December 2013.

	Debit	Credit
	£	£
Revenue		100,000
Revenue returns	5,000	
Purchases	70,000	
Purchases returns		6,000
Opening inventory of antiques	9,000	
Trade receivables	16,800	
Business rates	800	
Trade payables		14,000
Cash at bank	17,100	
Long-term loan		12,000
Bank interest receivable		850
Rent	2,050	
Electricity	1,950	

Q9 Claire Analetto (*continued*)

	Debit £	Credit £
Insurance	1,250	
Loan interest	1,200	
General expenses	1,025	
Motor van expenses	1,800	
Premises at cost	60,000	
Machinery at cost	16,500	
Office equipment at cost	1,750	
Motor car at cost	2,050	
Drawings	8,200	
Repairs to antiques	1,300	
Telephone	500	
Equity		85,425
	218,275	218,275

You also have the following notes to the accounts.

1. Closing inventory of antiques is £7,000.
2. Depreciation for the year is to be charged at 2% on premises, 10% on machinery, 15% on office equipment and 25% on the motor car.

Required: Prepare C. Analetto's income statement for the year ended 31 December 2013 and the statement of financial position as at 31 December 2013.

Q10 Michelle Angelo has trade receivables of £40,000 at the year end. However, she feels that £4,000 is irrecoverable.

Required: Prepare the appropriate statement of financial position and income statement extracts.

Q11 Simon Eurat, who runs a taxi business, has the following trial balance.

S. Eurat
Trial Balance as at 30 June 2014

	Debit £	Credit £
Cash overdrawn at bank		1,500
Long-term loan		3,550
Receipts		28,300
Diesel and oil	8,250	
Taxi repairs and service	3,950	
Radio hire	3,400	
Road fund licences	2,300	
Buildings at cost	68,000	
Taxis at cost	34,500	
Business rates	450	
Electricity	1,300	
Telephone	1,250	
Trade receivables	100	
Trade payables for motor repairs		1,800
Insurance on buildings	1,300	
General expenses	850	
Drawings	9,600	
Bank interest	150	
Equity		103,250
Wages	3,000	
	138,400	138,400

You have the following additional information.

1. 10% of the trade receivables are considered irrecoverable.
2. £800 of the insurance is prepaid.
3. There is £250 owing for electricity and £300 owing for telephone.
4. Depreciation on taxis is to be 25% on cost and on buildings 2% on cost.

Required: Prepare S. Eurat's income statement for the year ended 30 June 2014 and statement of financial position as at 30 June 2014.

Q12 Rebecca Odin has the following details of her property, plant and equipment.

	Cost	*Accumulated depreciation as at 31 December 2012*
	£	£
Buildings	102,000	8,000
Machinery	65,000	6,500
Motor car	8,000	4,000
Computer	9,000	2,700

She charges depreciation at 2% per annum on cost for buildings, 10% per annum on cost for machinery, 25% per annum on cost for the motor car and 15% per annum on cost for the computer.

Required: Prepare the appropriate extracts for:

(a) the statement of financial position as at 31 December 2012.

(b) the income statement for year ended 31 December 2013 and for the statement of financial position as at 31 December 2013.

Q13 Deborah Urer owns a small bar. Her trial balance as at 30 June 2014 is set out below.

	Debit	Credit
	£	£
Takings from sales of beer, wine and spirits		145,150
Purchases of beer, wine and spirits	83,250	
Discounts receivable		450
Dividends receivable		150
Drawings	26,400	
Advertising	3,600	
Motor expenses	1,750	
Telephone	2,800	
Electricity	1,250	
Insurance	1,900	
General expenses	2,250	
Repairs	350	
Premises at cost	20,340	
Accumulated depreciation as at 1 July 2013		6,300
Bar equipment at cost	8,200	
Accumulated depreciation as at 1 July 2013		2,500

Q13 D. Urer (*continued*)

	Debit £	Credit £
Bar furniture at cost	5,600	
Accumulated depreciation as at 1 July 2013		1,800
Motor car at cost	3,600	
Accumulated depreciation as at 1 July 2013		2,000
Trade receivables	220	
Provision for the impairment of receivables		20
Loan interest	650	
Trade payables		3,650
Cash at bank	4,350	
Long-term loan		6,500
Wages	2,560	
Business rates	2,450	
Opening inventory	5,500	
Equity		8,500
	177,020	177,020

You also have the following additional information.

1. Closing inventory is £6,250.
2. There is £200 owing for electricity and £300 of the insurance is prepaid.
3. Bad debts are £25 to be written off this year.
4. The provision for the impairment of receivables is to be increased to £25 on 30 June 2014.
5. There are the following depreciation charges:
   2% on premises
   10% on bar equipment and bar furniture
   25% on motor car

Required: Prepare D. Urer's income statement for the year ended 30 June 2014 and the statement of financial position as at 30 June 2014.

Q14 Bernard Ruegel has drawn up a trial balance which is presented below.

B. Ruegel
Trial Balance as at 30 September 2013

	Debit £	Credit £
Carriage inwards	350	
Carriage outwards	180	
Discounts allowed	80	
Discounts receivable		75
Revenue		208,275
Revenue returns	185	
Purchases	110,398	
Drawings	38,111	
Purchases returns		98
Interest receivable		790
Advertising	1,987	
Telephone	476	
Wages and salaries	10,298	
Electricity	1,466	
Rent	2,873	
Cash at bank	21,611	
Travelling expenses	1,288	
Van repairs	1,471	
Petrol	2,187	
Business rates	2,250	
General expenses	1,921	
Insurance	1,100	
Premises at cost	50,981	
Accumulated depreciation as at 1 October 2012		28,300
Machine at cost	21,634	
Accumulated depreciation as at 1 October 2012		8,200
Office furniture at cost	8,011	
Accumulated depreciation as at 1 October 2012		2,386
Computer at cost	2,980	
Accumulated depreciation as at 1 October 2012		1,200
Motor van at cost	2,725	
Accumulated depreciation as at 1 October 2012		1,725
Accumulated depreciation as at 1 October 2012		1,980

Q14 B. Rueghel (*continued*)

	Debit	Credit
	£	£
Opening inventory	11,211	
Loan interest	1,500	
Bank overdraft		8,933
Trade receivables	11,000	
Provision for the impairment of receivables		850
Trade payables		4,279
Long-term loan		14,811
Equity		31,758
	313,660	313,660

You have the following extra information:

1. Closing inventory is £13,206.
2. There are the following amounts owing: advertising £325, telephone £125, carriage outwards £20, general expenses £37, wages and salaries £560.
3. The following amounts are prepaid: travelling expenses £288, electricity £76, insurance £250.
4. It is business policy to treat 10% of total trade receivables as doubtful.
5. There is a bad debt of £600 to be provided in addition to the provision.
6. It has been decided to write down the property, plant and equipment to the following net book value amounts as at 30 September 2013.

	£
Premises	21,081
Machine	12,434
Office furniture	4,151
Computer	125
Motor van	275
Motor car	1,599

Required: Prepare, taking the necessary adjustments into account, the income statement for the year ended 30 September 2013 and the statement of financial position as at 30 September 2013.

Q15 Peter Piper has four gas bills in the year for £400 on 31 March 2013, £500 on 30 June 2013, £600 on 30 September 2013 and £700 on 31 December 2013. Bills are paid to GasCo a month later.

Required: Draw up and balance off the accounts for GasCo, Gas and the cash book (extracts).

Q16 Papa rents his office block from Property Plc for £2,000 per month. His policy then changes so he pays for January and February 2013 at the end of each month. Then he pays six months in advance on 1 March 2013 and 1 September 2013.

Required: Prepare his accounts for Property Plc, the rent account and the cash book extracts.

Q17 Delivery Co buys two vans (A and B) on 1 January 2011 for £50,000 each and van C for £60,000 on 1 July 2011. They are depreciated at the rate of 20% per annum. Delivery Co sells van A on 31 December 2011 for £35,000 and van B is sold on 30 June 2012 for £20,000. Van C is not sold.

Required:

(a) Prepare the Property, Plant and Equipment Account, Depreciation Account and Disposals Account for 2011, 2012 and 2013.

(b) Prepare the income statement and statement of financial position extracts for 2011, 2012 and 2013.

Go online to discover the extra features for this chapter at
www.wiley.com/college/jones

Chapter 7

Partnerships and limited companies

'Corporation, [i.e. Company] An ingenious device for obtaining individual profit without individual responsibility.'

Ambrose Bierce, *The Devil's Dictionary*, p. 29.

Learning Outcomes

After completing this chapter you should be able to:

- Explain the nature of partnerships and limited companies.
- Outline the distinctive accounting features of partnerships and limited companies.
- Demonstrate how to prepare the accounts of partnerships and limited companies.
- Understand the differences between listed and non-listed companies preparing accounts under IFRS for SMEs.

Go online to discover the extra features for this chapter at **www.wiley.com/college/jones**

Chapter Summary

- Sole proprietors, partnerships and limited companies are the main forms of business enterprise.
- A partnership is more than one person working together.
- Partnership accounts must share out the profit and equity between the partners.
- Sharing out profit, capital and current accounts are special partnership features.
- A limited company is based on the limited liability of the shareholders (i.e., they lose only their initial investment if things go wrong).
- A limited company's special features are taxation, dividends and equity employed split between share capital and reserves.
- In company accounts it is common to find intangible assets (i.e., assets you cannot touch) such as goodwill or patents.
- Limited companies may be private or public.
- A listed company's accounts will follow International Financial Reporting Standards.
- Annual reports are sent to shareholders. They are also increasingly put on a company's website.

Introduction

The three most common types of business enterprise are sole traders, partnerships and public corporations. For example, in 2009, in the UK, there were about 449,800 sole proprietors (or sole traders), 277,200 partnerships and 1,236,900 companies and public corporations (Office for National Statistics, 2009). Of these 1,256 were listed companies. So far in this book, we have focused on sole traders. Sole traders are, typically, relatively small enterprises owned by one person. Their businesses and accounts tend to be less complicated than those of either partnerships or companies. They are thus ideal for introducing the basic principles behind bookkeeping and final accounts. In this chapter, we now look at the income statement and the statement of financial position of partnerships and limited companies. The statement of cash flows prepared by companies is covered in Chapter 8. Partnerships are normally larger than sole traders. However, basically their accounts are similar to those of the sole trader. This reflects the fact that partners, like sole traders, generally own and run their own businesses. For companies, however, the owners provide the equity, but the directors run the company. This divorce of ownership and management is reflected in the accounts of limited companies. In certain respects, particularly the equity or capital employed, the accounts of limited companies thus appear quite different to those of partnerships and sole traders. From 1 January 2005, listed companies (i.e., companies quoted on a national stock exchange) in the UK and other European Union countries had to follow accounting standards set by the International Accounting Standards Board. Increasingly, IFRS are being used for other reporting entities. In the UK, from 2015, medium-sized companies can choose between adopting IFRS or adopting FRS 102 (UK generally accepted accounting principles) with its reduced disclosures. The smallest UK companies will continue to use simplified versions of UK standards.

Context

In this section, we briefly set out the main features of sole traders, partnerships and limited companies. The main points are summarised in Figure 7.1 using the UK as an example. In essence, the differences between these three types of business enterprise can be traced back to size and capital structure. In terms of size, sole traders are normally smaller than partnerships, which are usually smaller than companies. This greater size causes accounting to be more complicated for companies than for sole traders.

Figure 7.1 Sole Traders, Partnerships and Limited Companies Compared

Feature	*Sole Traders*	*Partnerships*	*Limited Companies*
Business			
(i) Owners	Sole traders	Partners	Shareholders
(ii) Run company	Sole traders	Partners	Directors
(iii) Statutory accounting legislation	No specific act	Partnership Act, 1890	Companies Acts
(iv) Number of owners	1	Since 2002 no restriction on numbers	Private 1–50; Public 2 upwards
(v) Liability	Unlimited	Unlimited, except for limited partners	Limited
(vi) Approximate number in UK* in 2009	449,800	277,200	1,236,900
(vii) Size of turnover in UK*	(a) 64% under £100,000 (b) 1% over £1m	(a) 33% under £100,000 (b) 7% over £1m	(a) 33% under £100,000 (b) 22% over £1m
Accounting			
(i) Main external users of accounts	Tax authorities, bank	Tax authorities, bank	Tax authorities for small, private companies, shareholders for public companies
(ii) Main financial statements	Income statement (also called trading and profit and loss account) and statement of financial position (also called balance sheet)	Income statement (also called trading and profit and loss and appropriation account) and statement of financial position (also called balance sheet)	Income statement, statement of financial position and statement of cash flows
(iii) Main differences in income statement from sole trader	–	Appropriation account shares out profit	Income statement has dividends and taxation (IFRS for SMEs) or taxation but not dividends (full IFRS)
(iv) Main differences in net assets from sole trader	–	None	Companies, when in groups, may have goodwill. They are also likely to have other intangible assets such as patents or brands. In current liabilities, and taxation payable
(v) Main differences in equity or owners' capital from sole trader		Capital and current accounts record partners' share of equity invested and profit	Equity essentially divided into share capital and reserves

*From Office for National Statistics, UK Business: activity, size and location, 2009

An important distinction between the three businesses is the capital structure. Sole traders and most partners own and run their businesses. They provide the capital, although they may borrow money. The main problem for partnerships is simply the fair allocation of both the equity and profit to the partners. For companies, the owners provide the equity whereas the directors run the company. The concept of limited liability for companies means that shareholders can only lose the money they initially invested. This is the great advantage that companies have over sole traders and partnerships. Many small businesses, therefore, prefer to convert from sole traders or partnerships to unlisted companies. They then gain potential protection from their creditors should the businesses fail. These unlisted companies are generally not listed and their shares are not publicly traded on the stock market.

Partnerships

Introduction

Partnerships may be seen as sole traders with multiple owners. Many sole traders take on partners to help them finance and run their businesses. As in all human relationships, when partners are well matched, partnerships can prove very successful businesses. However, when they are ill-suited, problems can occur (see Soundbite 7.1). Except for certain occupations (such as firms of accountants or solicitors) the maximum number of partners in the UK is 20. An important aspect of both sole traders and partnerships is that liability is generally unlimited. (There is an exception, if you are a limited partner. Limited partners can lose only the equity invested. However, they do not participate in running the company and there must be at least one unlimited liability partner.) In other words, if a business goes bankrupt the personal assets of the owners are *not* ring-fenced. Bankrupt partners may have to sell their houses to pay their creditors. Recently, however, for professional partnerships, particularly accounting partnerships, a new organisational form, the limited liability partnership (LLP), has been created. For these organisations, liability is capped.

Sole traders and partners prepare accounts for use in their own personal internal management, but also for external users, such as the tax authorities and banks. The key issue which underpins partnerships is how the partners should split any profits. The ratio in which the profits are split is called the profit sharing ratio or PSR. Partnerships traditionally have used the terms 'trading and profit and loss and appropriation account'

SOUNDBITE 7.1

Partners

'The history of human achievement is rich with stories of successful partnerships – while the history of human failure is rife with tales of fruitless competition and wilful antagonisms.'

Margaret E. Mahoney, *The Commonwealth Fund* (Annual Report 1987)

Source: The Executive's Book of Quotations (1994), p. 212.

and 'balance sheet' for their financial statements. However, for consistency with the rest of the book I use the terms 'income statement' and 'statement of financial position'. I also use equity rather than capital. However, I still refer to the appropriation account as a section at the bottom of the partnership income statement.

It is in the appropriation account that the allocation of profits between the partners is presented. The appropriation, or 'sharing out', account appears after the calculation of net profit. In other words, we add a section at the bottom of the income statement.

REAL-WORLD VIEW 7.1

Partnerships

Occasionally partners have more in common than business interests: their names seem to complement each other. The following curious and apt names of partnerships were collected from old English signs and business directories: Carpenter & Wood; Spinage & Lamb; Sage & Gosling; Rumfit & Cutwell, and Greengoose & Measure, both tailors; Single & Double; Foot and Stocking, Hosiers. One is not quite sure whether to believe that Adam & Eve were two surgeons who practised in Paradise Row, London, though Buyers & Sellers did have a shop in Holborn.

'Sometimes the occupation of persons harmonizes admirably with their surnames,' a nineteenth-century antiquarian continues: Gin & Ginman are innkeepers; so is Alehouse; Seaman is the landlord of the Ship Hotel, and A. King holds the 'Crown and Sceptre' resort in City Road. Portwine and Negus are licensed victuallers, one in Westminster and the other in Bishopsgate Street. Mixwell's country inn is a well-known resort. Pegwell is a shoemaker, so are Fitall and Treadaway, likewise Pinch; Tugwell is a noted dentist; Bird an egg merchant; Hemp a sherriff's officer; Captain Isaac Paddle commands a steamboat; Mr. Punt is a favourite member of the Surrey wherry [rowing] club; Laidman was formerly a pugilist; and Smooker or Smoker a lime burner; Skin & Bone were the names of two millers in Manchester; Fogg and Mist china dealers in Warwick street: the firm afterward became Fogg & Son, on which it was naturally enough remarked that the 'son had driven away the mist.' Mr. I. Came, a wealthy shoemaker in Liverpool, who left his immense property to public charities, opened his first shop on the opposite side of the street to where he had started as a servant, and inscribed a sign: 'I CAME from over the way.'

Finally, Going & Gonne was the name of a well-known banking house in Ireland, and on their failure in business someone wrote:

'Going & Gonne are now both one
For Gonne is going and Going's gone.'

Source: Peter Hay (1988), *The Book of Business Anecdotes*, Harrap Ltd, London, pp. 119–20.

The main elements of the basic appropriation account are salaries and the sharing of the profit. Salaries are allocated to the partners before the profit is shared out. Note that for partners, salaries are an appropriation *not* an expense. Figure 7.2 demonstrates the process.

Figure 7.2 Main Elements in the Partnership Appropriation Account

Main Elements	***Explanation***	***Layout***			
				£	£
Net Profit	Profit as calculated from income statement	Net profit before appropriation			18,000
		Less:			
Salaries	The amount which each partner earns must be deducted from net profit before profit sharing	Salaries	A	5,500	
			B	3,500	9,000
					9,000
Residual Profit	The profit share for each individual	Profit	A	6,000	
			B	3,000	9,000

Two partners, A and B, share £18,000 net profit. The profit sharing ratio is 2:1. Their salaries are £5,500 and £3,500, respectively. The example is continued in Figure 7.3.

Partners' equity can be divided into two parts: capital accounts and current accounts. Each partner needs to keep track of his or her own equity.

PAUSE FOR THOUGHT 7.1

Partners' Profit Sharing

Why are profits not just split equally between partners?

Superficially, it might seem that the partners might just split the profit equally between them. So if a partnership of two people earns £30,000, each partner's share is £15,000. Unfortunately, life is not so simple! In practice, profit sharing is determined by a number of factors, such as how hard each partner works, their experience and the equity each partner has contributed. It might, therefore, be decided that the profit sharing ratio or PSR was 2:1. In this case, one partner would take £20,000; the second would take £10,000.

Capital Accounts

These accounts represent the long-term capital invested into the partnership by the individual partners. When new partners join a partnership, it is conventional for them to 'buy their way' into the partnership. This initial equity introduced can be seen as purchasing their share of the net assets of the business they have joined. This initial equity remains unchanged in the accounts unless the partners specifically introduce or withdraw long-term equity. It represents the amount which the business 'owes' the partners.

Current Accounts

In contrast to the capital accounts, current accounts are not fixed. Essentially, they represent the partners' share of the profits of the business since they joined, less their withdrawals. In basic current accounts, the main elements are the opening balances, salaries, profit for year, drawings and closing balances. These elements are set out in Figure 7.3. This continues Figure 7.2, with drawings of £12,000 for A and £10,000 for B. It is important to realise that the salaries are credited (or added) to the partners' current account rather than physically paid. The partners physically withdraw cash, which is known as drawings. Drawings are essentially sums taken out of the business by the partners as living expenses.

Figure 7.3 Main Elements in Partners' Current Accounts

Main Elements	*Explanation*	*Layout*		
			A £	B £
Opening Balances	Amount of profits brought forward from last year. Normally a credit balance, and is the amount the business owes the partner	Opening balances	7,000	6,000
Salaries	The amount which the partners earn by way of salary	Add: Salaries	5,500	3,500
Profit Share	Amount of the profit attributable to partner. Determined by profit sharing ratio	Profit	6,000	3,000
			18,500	12,500
Drawings	Amount the partners take out of the business to live on	Less: Drawings	12,000	10,000
Closing Balances	The amount of profits carried forward to next year. This is usually the balance owed to the partner	Closing balances	6,500	2,500

PAUSE FOR THOUGHT 7.2

Debit Balances on Current Accounts

What do you think a negative or debit balance on a partner's current account means?

This means that the partner owes the partnership money! A current account represents the partner's account with the business. It is increased by or credited with (i.e., the business owes the partner money) the partner's salary and share of profit. The account is then debited (or reduced) when the partner takes money out (i.e., drawings). If the partner takes out more funds than are covered by the salary and profit share, a debit balance is created. It is, in effect, like going overdrawn at the bank. A partner with a debit balance owes rather than is owed capital.

Partnership Example: Stevens and Turner

Let us imagine that Gavin Stevens has traded for several years. The year is now far into the future 20XX. He has now teamed up with Diana Turner. Both partners have invested £135,000 equity into their capital accounts. Their salaries are £12,000 for Stevens and £6,000 for Turner. Their current accounts stand at £8,000 (credit) Stevens, £9,000 (credit) Turner. They share residual profits in Stevens' favour 2:1. Their opening trial balance is below.

Stevens and Turner: Partnership Trial Balance as at 31 December 20XX

		£	£
Capital accounts	Stevens		135,000
	Turner		135,000
Current accounts	Stevens		8,000
	Turner		9,000
Drawings	Stevens	18,000	
	Turner	13,500	
Hotel		610,000	
Vans		30,200	
Opening inventory		5,000	
Trade receivables		15,000	
Trade payables			20,000
Bank		20,300	
Electricity		1,850	
Wages		12,250	
Telephone		350	
Long-term loan			350,000
Revenue			270,000
Purchases		195,000	
Other expenses		5,550	
		927,000	927,000

Notes:

1. Closing inventory is £10,000.
2. For simplicity, we are ignoring all other post-trial balance adjustments such as depreciation, bad and doubtful debts, accruals and prepayments.
3. Salaries are £12,000 for Stevens and £6,000 for Turner. These are 'notional' salaries in that the money is not actually paid to the partners. Instead it is credited to their accounts.

Using this trial balance we now prepare, in Figure 7.4, the income statement (with an appropriation account) and the statement of financial position.

Figure 7.4 Stevens and Turner Partnership Accounts Year Ended 31 December 20XX

Stevens and Turner
Income Statement for the Year Ended
31 December 20XX

	£	£
Revenue		270,000
Less Cost of Sales		
Opening inventory	5,000	
Add Purchases	195,000	
	200,000	
Less Closing inventory	10,000	190,000
Gross Profit		80,000
Less Expenses		
Electricity	1,850	
Wages	12,250	
Telephone	350	
Other expenses	5,550	20,000
********		
Net profit before appropriation		60,000
Less Salaries		
Stevens	12,000	
Turner	6,000	18,000
		42,000
Profits:		
Stevens	28,000	
Turner	14,000	
Net Profit		42,000
********		

Note: The net profit is calculated as for a sole trader. The profit is then shared out between the partners. This appropriation is shown between the asterisks.

Stevens and Turner
Statement of Financial Position as at 31 December 20XX

ASSETS	£
Non-current Assets	
Property, Plant and Equipment	
Hotel	610,000
Vans	30,200
Total non-current assets	640,200

Figure 7.4 Stevens and Turner Partnership Accounts Year Ended 31 December 20XX (*continued*)

Current Assets			£
Inventory			10,000
Trade receivables			15,000
Bank			20,300
Total current assets			45,300
Total Assets			685,500
LIABILITIES			
Current Liabilities			
Trade payables			(20,000)
Non-current Liabilities			(350,000)
Total Liabilities			(370,000)
Net Assets			315,500

* *

	Stevens	Turner	
EQUITY	£	£	£
Capital Accounts	135,000	135,000	270,000
Current Accounts			
Opening balances	8,000	9,000	
Add			
Salaries	12,000	6,000	
Profit share	28,000	14,000	
	48,000	29,000	
Less Drawings	18,000	13,500	
Closing balances	30,000	15,500	45,500
Total Partners' Funds			315,500

* *

Note: The total net assets part of the statement of financial position is drawn up as for a sole trader. The capital and current accounts show the amounts due to the partners. They are distinctive to partnership accounts and are shown between the asterisks.

Limited Companies

The Basics

Limited companies are a popular form of legal business entity. As Real-World View 7.2 indicates, in actual fact a 'company' does not physically exist. It is a collection of people and assets. However, companies do have a legal existence. The essence of limited companies lies in the fact that the shareholders' (i.e., owners') liability is limited. This means that owners are only liable to lose the amount of money they have initially invested. For example, if a shareholder invests £500 in a company and the company goes bankrupt, then £500 is all the shareholder will lose. All the shareholder's personal possessions (for example, house or car) are safe! This is a great advantage over partnerships and sole traders where the liability is unlimited.

REAL-WORLD VIEW 7.2

The Company

A second major feature of the orthodox creed is the ascription of supernatural existence to the 'company'. Objectively and rationally speaking, the 'company' does not exist at all, except in so far as it is a heterogeneous collection of people. In order to facilitate the mutual ownership and use of assets, and for other technical reasons, the corporation is treated in law as a person. It is a legal fiction, but a fiction nonetheless.

Source: Graham Cleverly (1971), *Managers and Magic*, Longman Group Limited, London, p. 31.

PAUSE FOR THOUGHT 7.3

Limited Liability

For suppliers, and particularly lenders, limited liability can be bad news as their money may be less secure. Can you think of any ways they may seek to counter this?

....

A fact that is often overlooked is that in small companies, limited liability is often not seen as a bonus to those who have close connections with the company. Suppliers may be less certain that they will be paid and bankers more worried about making loans. In many cases, unlimited liability is replaced by other control mechanisms. For example, suppliers may want to be paid in cash or have written guarantees of payment. Bankers will often secure their loans against the property of the business and, in many cases, against the personal assets of the owners. So the owners may not avoid losing their personal possessions in a bankruptcy after all.

The mechanism underpinning a limited liability company is the share. The total equity of the business is divided into these shares (literally a 'share' in the equity of the business). For instance, a business with share capital of £500,000 might divide this share capital into 500,000 shares of £1 each. These shares may then be bought and sold. Subsequently, they will probably be bought or sold for more or less than £1. For instance, Sheilah might sell 50,000 £1 shares to Mary for £75,000. There is thus a crucial difference between the face value of the shares (£1 each in this case) and their trading value (£1.50 each in this case).

The face value of the shares is termed **nominal value**. The trading value is termed **market price**. If market price increases, it is the individual shareholder *not* the company that benefits.

The risk for the shareholders is that they will lose the equity they have invested. The reward is twofold. First, shareholders will receive dividends (i.e., annual payments based on profits) for investing their capital. The dividends are the reward for investing their money in the company rather than, for example, investing in a bank or building society where it would earn interest. The second reward is any potential growth in share price. For example, if Sheilah originally purchased the shares for £50,000, she would gain £25,000 when she sold them to Mary.

It is important to realise that the shareholders own the company; they do not run the company. Running the company is the job of the directors. This division is known as the 'divorce of ownership and control'. In many small companies, however, the directors own most of the shares. In this case, although in theory there is a separation of ownership and control, in practice there is not.

There are two types of company in the UK. The private limited company and the public limited company. The main features are outlined in Figure 7.5.

Figure 7.5 Features of Private Limited Companies (Ltds) and Public Limited Companies (plcs) in the UK

Feature	*Private Limited Company*	*Public Limited Company*
Names	Ltd after company name	PLC after company name
Number of shareholders	1 upwards	2 to unlimited
Share trading	Restricted	Unrestricted
Stock market listing	No	Usually
Authorised share capital	No minimum	At least £50,000
Size	Usually small to medium enterprises	Usually medium to large enterprises
Accounts	Follow National Standards	Follow International Accounting Standards

The essential difference is that private limited companies are usually privately controlled and owned whereas public limited companies are large corporations usually trading on the stock market. Their shares can thus be bought and sold by individuals external to the companies themselves. The major companies world wide such as British Petroleum, Toyota and Coca-Cola are all, in essence, public limited companies. (Even though laws vary from country to country, they are broadly equivalent.) In these large companies, the managers are, in theory, accountable to the shareholders. In practice, many commentators doubt this accountability.

There are several reasons why companies prepare accounts. First, the detailed accounts (normally comprising an income statement, a statement of financial position and a statement of cash flows) will be used by management for internal management purposes. They will often be prepared monthly. The published accounts which are sent to the shareholders will usually be prepared annually.

The second reason is to comply with the Companies Act 2006. This lays down certain minimum statutory requirements which are supplemented by accounting standards and stock exchange regulations. Companies following these accounting requirements will normally prepare and send their shareholders published accounts containing an income statement, statement of financial position and (except for small companies which are exempt) a statement of cash flows.

These accounts are prepared using a standardised format. For large companies, these accounts are sent out to shareholders as part of the annual reporting package. This is dealt with in detail in Chapter 12; however, it is briefly introduced later in this chapter. Companies, as part of their statutory reporting requirements, will also submit a set of accounts to the Registrar of Companies.

Third, as well as preparing accounts for shareholders, companies may also provide accounts to other users who have an interest in the company's affairs. Of particular importance is the role of corporation tax. The statutory accounts are usually used as the starting point for assessing this tax, which was introduced in 1965 and is payable by companies on their profits. It is calculated according to a complicated, and often-changing, set of tax rules. 'Accounting' profit is usually adjusted to arrive at 'taxable' profit. Unlike partnerships and sole traders, who are assessed for income tax as individuals, companies are assessed for corporation tax as taxable entities themselves.

Finally, especially for large companies, there may be a wide range of potential users of the accounts such as employees, customers, banks and suppliers. Their information needs were discussed in Chapter 1. The accounts of medium and large companies are usually prepared by the directors and then audited by independent accountants. This is so that the shareholders and other users can be assured that the accounts are 'true and fair'. The auditors' report is a badge of quality.

PAUSE FOR THOUGHT 7.4

Abridged Company Accounts

Companies often prepare a full, detailed set of accounts for their internal management purposes. Why would they not wish to supply these to their shareholders?

For internal management purposes, detailed information is necessary to make decisions. However, in the published accounts, directors are careful what they disclose. In a public limited company, anybody can buy shares and thus receive the published accounts. Directors do not wish to give away any secrets to potential competitors just because they own a few shares. In actual fact, the Companies Acts requirements allow the main details to be disclosed in a way that is sometimes not terribly informative. There are many levels at which accounts can be summarised. Figure 7.8 shows a very high level of summary, while Figure 7.17 is more like the level of detail which companies typically supply in their annual reports.

A distinctive feature of many companies is that they are organised into groups. This book does not cover the preparation of group accounts (which are often complex and complicated and best left to more specialist textbooks). Interested readers might try Alexander, Britton and Jorissen (2011) *International Financial Reporting and Analysis*. For now we merely note that many medium and large companies are not, in fact, single entities, but are really many individual companies working together collectively. There is, usually, one overall company which is the controlling company. This is further discussed in Chapter 12.

Distinctive Accounting Features of Limited Companies

The essence of the income statements of sole traders, partnerships and limited companies is the same. However, there are some important differences. The most important difference between a sole trader and a partnership is that for partnerships the profit is divided (this is formally known as appropriated) between the partners. Many UK companies still follow UK GAAP. Manchester United is a good example and its income statement and statement of financial position (balance sheet) are presented in Appendices 7.1 and 7.2 at the end of this chapter. As you will see, these statements use UK GAAP terminology such as stock for inventories. Many people in the UK still prefer these terms.

For limited companies, there is an abridged, standardised format set out by the 2006 Companies Act for non-listed companies. For listed companies, the format is similar, but is prepared under International Financial Reporting Standards. An illustration of the formats for the four business entities is given in Figure 7.6.

Figure 7.6 Differences between Income Statements of Sole Traders, Partnerships and Limited Companies

Sole Traders: Income Statement (also known as Trading and Profit and Loss Account)		*Partnerships: Income Statement (also known as Trading and Profit and Loss and Appropriation Account)*		*Non-Listed Limited Companies: Income Statement reporting under IFRS for SMEs*		*Listed Companies: Income Statement*	
	£		£		£		£
Revenue	200,000	Revenue	200,000	Revenue	200,000	Revenue	200,000
Cost of Sales	(100,000)	Cost of Sales	(100,000)	Cost of Sales	(100,000)	Cost of Sales	(100,000)
Gross Profit	100,000	*Gross Profit*	100,000	*Gross Profit*	100,000	*Gross Profit*	100,000
Other Income	10,000	Other Income	10,000	Other Income	10,000	Other Income	10,000
	110,000		110,000		110,000		110,000
Expenses	(60,000)	Expenses	(60,000)	Expenses	(60,000)	Expenses	(60,000)
Net Profit	50,000	*Net Profit*	50,000	*Profit before Tax*	50,000	*Profit before Tax*	50,000
				Taxation	(20,000)	Taxation	(20,000)
		Partner A	25,000	*Profit after Tax*	30,000	*Profit for the period*	30,000
		Partner B	25,000	Dividends	(15,000)		
			50,000	Retained Profit	15,000		

Be careful of the limited companies' format. There are several possible variations and the examples in Figure 7.6 have been grossly simplified for comparison purposes. The income statements of listed companies may be called by a variety of names. For small and medium-sized entities (SMEs), they may be called the Statement of Comprehensive Income

PAUSE FOR THOUGHT 7.5

Limited Companies' Income Statement (Profit and Loss Account)

Why do you think limited companies produce only abbreviated figures for their shareholders?

The answer to this is twofold. First of all, many limited companies are large and complicated businesses. They need to simplify the financial information provided. Otherwise, the users of the accounts might suffer from information overload. Second, for public limited companies, there is the problem of confidentiality. Remember that a company is owned by shareholders. Anybody can buy shares. A competitor, for example, could buy shares in a company. Companies would not wish to give away all the details of their revenue and expenses to a potential competitor. Therefore, they summarise and limit the amount of information they provide. Limited companies, therefore, publicly provide abridged (or summarised) accounts rather than full ones using all the figures from the trial balance.

and Retained Earnings. This may include dividends. For listed companies, there may be an income statement and then a separate Statement of Other Comprehensive Income dealing with non-operating income such as property revaluations or foreign exchange differences. Alternatively, the limited company may produce a Statement of Comprehensive Income which combines both statements. Dividends will be recorded separately. Generally in this book we will use the term 'the income statement' for ease of understanding.

The special nature of limited companies leads to several distinctive differences between the accounts of limited companies and those of sole traders and partnerships, both in the income statement and in the statement of financial position. We now deal with four special features of a company: taxation, dividends, the formats and long-term capital. We also discuss intangible assets which can occur in the accounts of sole traders and partnerships, but are much more common in company accounts.

SOUNDBITE 7.2

Taxation

'The art of taxation consists in so plucking the goose as to obtain the largest possible amount of feathers with the smallest possible amount of hissing.'

Jean-Baptiste Colbert

Source: The Book of Business Quotations (1998), p. 257.

1. Taxation

As previously noted, companies pay corporation tax. As Soundbite 7.2 shows, taxation has never proved very popular. For companies, taxation is assessed on annual taxable profits. Essentially, these are the accounting profits adjusted to comply with taxation rules. The accounting consequences of taxation on the income statement and statement of financial position are twofold.

- In the income statement, *the amount for taxation for the year is recorded.*
- In the statement of financial position, under current liabilities, *the liability for the year is recorded as proposed taxation.*

It is important to note that for companies there is no direct record of taxation paid in the income statement or statement of financial position. Taxation paid appears in the statement of cash flows. This is illustrated in Pause for Thought 7.6 (page 188).

2. Dividends

A reward for shareholders for the capital they have invested is the dividends they receive. Recent changes in accounting treatment have led to the virtual elimination of proposed dividends from the accounts. Therefore, in this book for consistency all dividends will be treated as paid. In the case of non-listed companies which are reporting under IFRS for SMEs, the following treatment is used. *All dividends for the year* are recorded in the income statement. This feeds into the retained earnings at the end of the year. There is thus no separate disclosure in the statement of financial position. However, in some cases a statement of changes in equity may be prepared.

Note that for listed companies or companies reporting under full IFRS, *no* dividends are recorded in the income statement. There are two possible ways of treating these in the statement of financial position. First, they may be deducted from shareholders' equity in the statement of financial position. Alternatively, and more usually, they may be recorded in a statement of changes in equity. These alternatives are shown in Figure 7.7 below.

Figure 7.7 Treatment of Dividends Paid in the Statement of Financial Position for a Listed Company under IFRS

Tutin Plc has opening retained earnings of £250,000, a profit for the year of £100,000 with preference dividends and ordinary dividends paid of £8,000 and £6,000, respectively, for the year ended 31 December 2012. Other reserves are £300,000.

i) Deduction from reserves.

Statement of Financial Position for Tutin Plc as at 31 December 2013

Reserves	£	£	£
Capital reserves			300,000
Other reserves			
Opening retained earnings		250,000	
Retained earnings for year	100,000		
Less: Dividends paid	(14,000)	86,000	
Closing retained earnings			336,000
Total Equity			636,000

ii) Separate Statement of Changes in Equity

Statement of Changes in Equity for Tutin Plc for the year ended 31 December 2013

	£	£
Opening retained earnings		250,000
Retained earnings for year	100,000	
Less: Dividends Paid	(14,000)	86,000
Closing retained earnings		336,000

This is then taken to the statement of financial position as shown below

Statement of Financial Position for Tutin Plc as at 31 December 2013

	£
Reserves	
Capital Reserves	
Other reserves	300,000
Retained earnings	336,000
Total Equity	636,000

PAUSE FOR THOUGHT 7.6

Taxation Paid

If you have details of the income statement charge for taxation and the opening and closing liabilities, how do you calculate the amount actually paid?

One becomes a detective. Take this example: opening taxation payable £800, closing taxation payable £1,000, income statement taxation expense £3,000. Our opening liability of £800 plus this year's charge of £3,000 equals £3,800. At the end of the year, however, we only owe £1,000. We must, therefore, have paid £2,800. This logic underpins the calculation of tax paid in the statement of cash flows, covered in Chapter 8.

Many companies, like J. Sainsbury plc (the UK supermarket group) pay interim dividends as payments on account during the accounting year and then final dividends once the accounts have been prepared and the actual profit is known. Only the paid dividends are recognised in the financial statements as is illustrated in Company Snapshot 7.1.

COMPANY SNAPSHOT 7.1

Dividends

	2010 pence per share	2009 pence per share	2010 £m	2009 £m
Amounts recognised as distributions to equity holders in the year:				
Final dividend of prior financial year	**9.60**	9.00	**167**	155
Interim dividend of current financial year	4.00	3.60	74	63
	13.60	12.60	241	218

After the balance sheet date, a final dividend of 10.20 pence per share (2009:9.60 pence per share) was proposed by the Directors in respect of the 52 weeks to 20 March 2010, resulting in a total final proposed dividend of £189 million (2009: £167 million). The proposed final dividend has not been included as a liability at 20 March 2010.

Source: J. Sainsbury plc, *Annual Report and Financial Statements 2010*, p. 63. Reproduced by kind permission of Sainsbury's Supermarkets Ltd.

3. Formats and Terminology

There are, rather confusingly, a variety of formats used by companies. Non-listed companies may follow either IFRS format, or national UK standards, or, if appropriate, IFRS for SMEs. These were covered in Figure 7.6.

The presentational formats for IFRS can be broadly categorised as falling into (1) a total assets and a total equity and liabilities format followed by most European companies and (2) a net assets format followed by most UK companies. These different formats are outlined in Figure 7.8.

Figure 7.8 Different Statement of Financial Position Structures for Sole Traders, Partnerships and Limited Companies

Sole Traders and Partnerships		Companies (1) Net Assets Format		Companies (2) Assets and Liabilities Format	
	£		£		£
ASSETS		**ASSETS**		**ASSETS**	
Non-current Assets	80,000	**Non-current Assets**	80,000	**Non-current Assets**	80,000
Current Assets	80,000	**Current Assets**	80,000	**Current Assets**	80,000
Total Assets	160,000	*Total Assets*	160,000	*Total Assets*	160,000
LIABILITIES		**LIABILITIES**		**EQUITY AND LIABILITIES**	
Current Liabilities	(20,000)	**Current Liabilities**	(20,000)	**Equity***	120,000
Non-Current Liabilities	(20,000)	**Non-Current Liabilities**	(20,000)	**Non-current Liabilities**	20,000
Total Liabilities	(40,000)	*Total Liabilities*	(40,000)	*Total Liabilities*	20,000
Net Assets	120,000	*Net Assets*	120,000		
Equity*	120,000	**Equity***	120,000	**Total Equity and Liabilities**	160,000
		Approach used in this book for sole traders, partnerships and companies			

Note: * A breakdown of the Equity figure for the three business types is presented in Figure 7.11.

UK listed companies prefer to subtract total liabilities from total assets to arrive at net assets which equals equity (Assets − Liabilities = Equity). By contrast, European listed companies prefer to record total assets and then to add equity to liabilities (Assets = Equity and Liabilities). Although the totals are different, the individual figures are the same. Examples of the two different approaches are given in Company Snapshot 7.4 on page 203 (net assets equals equity approach) and Appendix 2.5 in Chapter 2 (total assets equals total equity and liabilities approach). The situation is further complicated by the fact that instead of totalling all the assets and liabilities and then striking a balance, some UK companies present a net figure for net current assets. This is illustrated below.

	£	£
Non-current assets		80,000
Current assets	80,000	
Current liabilities	(20,000)	
Net current assets		60,000
Non-current liabilities		(20,000)
Net assets		120,000

In this book, the net assets approach has been used for sole traders, partnerships and companies as followed by UK listed companies as presented in Figure 7.8. This is considered the simplest and easiest to understand.

In terms of terminology, there is a variety of usages. For limited companies, for consistency, and to reflect better the real economic situation, I use inventories not inventory. Also under equity, I use the sub-heading capital and reserves.

4. Long-Term Capital

The long-term capital of a company can be categorised into share capital (comprising ordinary and preference shares) and loan capital (often called debentures). We can see the differences between these in Figure 7.9. This is portrayed diagrammatically in Figure 7.10.

Figure 7.9 Different Types of Long-Term Capital of a Company

Features	Ordinary Shareholders	Preference Shareholders	Debenture holders
Type of capital	Share	Share	Loan
Ownership	Own company	Do not own company	Do not own company
Risk	Lose money invested first	Lose money invested after ordinary shareholder	Often loans secured on assets
Reward	Dividends and growth in the market value of the share	Usually fixed dividends	Interest payable
Accounting treatment for non-listed companies	Under Equity	Under Equity	Under Liabilities as a non-current liability
Accounting treatment for listed companies	Under Equity	Under Equity	Deducted from net assets

Figure 7.10 Long-Term Capital Structure of a Company

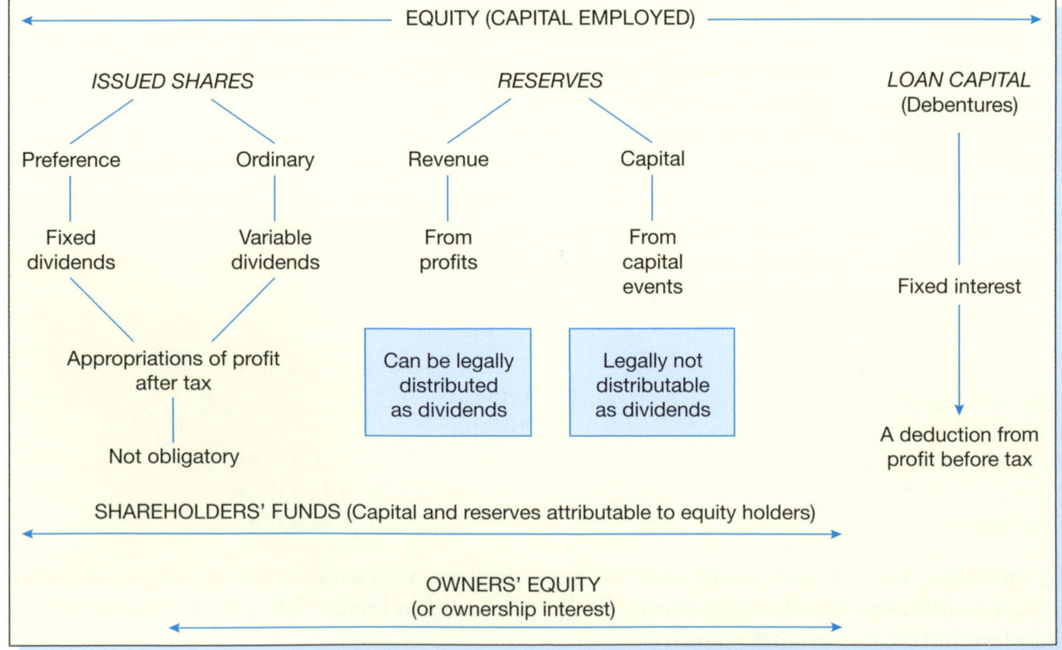

In terms of capital structure, the basic financing structure of a company can be split into that owned by the shareholders in terms of capital and reserves and that provided by debentures in terms of loan capital. The ordinary shareholders' equity is represented by ordinary shares and reserves.

Essentially, ordinary shareholders own the company by way of owning shares and, therefore, take the most risk and, potentially, gain the most reward. The risk is that the company may fail and they may therefore lose their money while the reward is in terms of dividends and an increase in the value of their shares if they wished sell. Preference shareholders normally receive a fixed dividend, whereas debenture holders receive interest. Debentures are long-term loans. Neither preference shareholders nor debenture holders are owners of the company.

As Figure 7.11 below shows, the limited company's equity (capital employed) is presented differently from that of the sole trader or partnership. For a limited company, the equity is not adjusted for drawings. Excluding long-term capital, a company's equity is essentially represented by share capital and reserves.

Unfortunately, there are many different types of share capital and reserves. Figure 7.12 below provides a quick overview of these.

Figure 7.11 Owner's Equity (Capital Employed) for Sole Trader, Partnerships and Limited Companies

Sole Trader		*Partnership*		*Limited Company*	
	£		£		£
Opening equity	100,000	Capital Accounts	100,000	Share Capital	100,000
Add Net Profit	50,000	Current Accounts	20,000	Reserves	20,000
	150,000	*Total Partners' Funds*	120,000	*Total Equity (total shareholders' funds)*	120,000
Less Drawings	30,000				
Closing Equity	120,000				

Figure 7.12 Overview of the Main Terminology of a Limited Company's Share Capital and Reserves, and Loan Capital

Term	*Explanation*
Share Capital	The capital of the company divided into shares.
Authorised share capital	The amount of share capital that a company is allowed to issue to its shareholders.
Called-up share capital	The amount of issued capital that has been fully paid to the company by shareholders. For example, a share may be issued for £1.50 and paid in three equal installments. After two installments are paid, the called-up share capital will be £1.
Issued share capital	The amount of share capital actually issued.
Ordinary (equity) share capital	The amount of share capital relating to the shareholders who own the company and are entitled to ordinary dividends.
Preference share capital	The amount of share capital relating to shareholders who are not owners of the company and are entitled to fixed dividends.

Figure 7.12 Overview of the Main Terminology of a Limited Company's Share Capital and Reserves, and Loan Capital (*continued*)

Market value	The value the shares will fetch on the open market. This may differ significantly from their nominal value.
Nominal value	The face value of the shares, usually their original issue price.
Reserves	The accumulated profits (revenue reserves) or capital gains (capital reserves) to shareholders.
Capital reserves	Reserves which are not distributable to shareholders as dividends; for example, the share premium account or revaluation reserve.
General reserve	A reserve created to deal with general, unspecified contingencies such as inflation.
Retained earnings	The accumulated profits of a listed company.
Revaluation reserve	A capital reserve created when Property, Plant and Equipment are revalued at more than the original purchase cost. The revaluation is a gain to the shareholders.
Revenue reserves	Reserves that are distributable to shareholders as dividends; for example, the income statement, general reserve.
Share premium account	A capital reserve created when new shares are issued for more than their nominal value. For example, if shares were issued for £150,000 and the nominal value was £100,000, the share premium account would be £50,000.
Total equity	The share capital and reserves which are owned by ordinary and preference shareholders.
Loan capital	Money loaned to the company by third parties. They are not owners of the company and are entitled to interest not dividends.
Debentures	Just another name for a long-term loan. Debentures may be secured or unsecured.
Secured and unsecured loans	Secured loans are loans which are secured on (or guaranteed by) the assets of the company. Unsecured loans are loans which are not secured on the assets.

Share capital represents the amount that the shareholders have directly invested. The amount a company is allowed to issue (authorised share capital) is determined in a company document called the Memorandum of Association. The amount actually issued is the issued share capital. It is important to emphasise that the face value for the shares is not its market value. If you like, it is like buying and selling stamps. The Penny Black, a rare stamp, was issued at one penny (nominal value), but you would have to pay a fortune for one today (market value). Shareholders' funds is an important figure in the statement of financial position and is equivalent to net assets (Company Snapshot 7.2 shows the shareholders' funds for Tesco PLC).

Reserves are essentially gains to the shareholder. Capital reserves are gains from activities such as issuing shares at more than the nominal value (share premium account) or revaluing property, plant and equipment (revaluation reserve). They cannot be paid out as dividends. By contrast, revenue reserves, essentially accumulated profits, are distributable.

COMPANY SNAPSHOT 7.2

Fame - company report of Tesco PLC

Tesco PLC

Waltham Cross, EN8 9SL (England)

Publicly quoted

This company is the GUO of the Corporate Group

Registered no 00445790

Status Active

Evolution of: Shareholders' Funds (2001–2010)

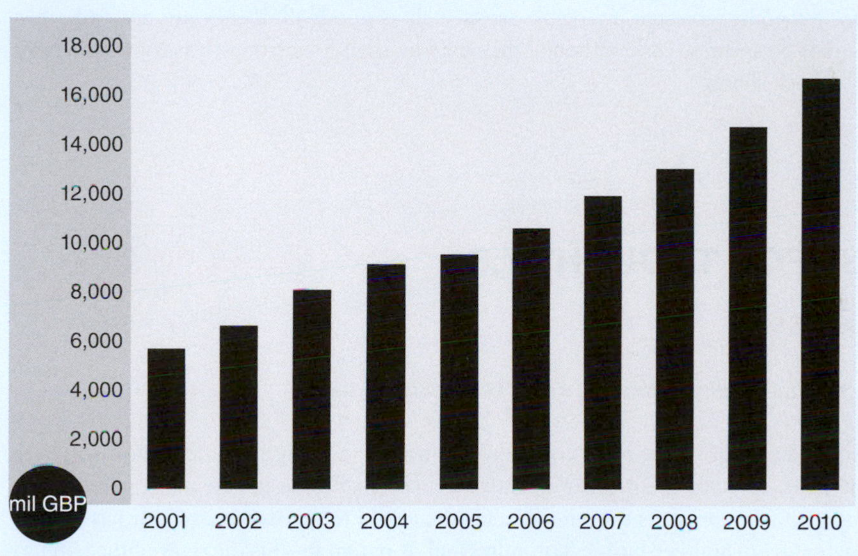

Source: Fame Database. Company report of Tesco PLC. Evolution of: Shareholders' Funds (2001–2010) published by Bureau van Dijk.

5. Intangible Assets

Intangible assets are literally non-current assets one cannot touch. They are thus in direct contrast to tangible non-current assets (plant, property and equipment) such as land and buildings, plant and machinery, fixtures and fittings and motor vehicles which are highly visible. They can occur in all businesses, but are most common in companies. Intangible assets are increasing in value and frequency as organisations become more knowledge-based. As the old manufacturing firms which are heavily dependent on property, plant and equipment decline and the new information technology businesses arise, the balance of assets in companies changes. There are now many types of intangible assets, such as goodwill. Goodwill is covered in more depth in Chapter 12.

PAUSE FOR THOUGHT 7.7

The Nature of Reserves

Can you spend reserves?

No! Reserves are not cash. Reserves are in fact amounts which the business owes to the shareholders. They represent either accumulated profits (retained earnings) or gains to the shareholders such as an issue of shares above the nominal value (share premium account) or the revaluation of property, plant and equipment (revaluation account). Reserves are represented by net assets. However, these assets may be non-current assets or current assets. They do not have to be cash. They may, for example, represent intangible assets such as goodwill. If they are not cash, they obviously cannot be spent as cash, although they may be used for certain treasury transactions such as buying back shares.

PAUSE FOR THOUGHT 7.8

Intangible Assets

Apart from goodwill, can you think of any other intangible assets?

There are many, but four of the most common are brands, copyrights, patents and software development costs. Perhaps the most frequently occurring of these is patents. A patent is an intangible asset which represents the amount a firm has paid to register a patent or has paid to purchase a patent from another business or individual. A patent itself is the right of the patent's owner to exploit the invention for a period of time. Patents are recorded in the statement of financial position under intangible assets.

Accounting Treatment For Limited Companies

Income Statement

Essentially, the income statement is calculated as normal. We then have to appropriate (or distribute) some of the profit to the government by way of tax. In addition, non-listed companies preparing a statement of comprehensive income and retained earnings under IFRS for SMEs distribute dividends to their shareholders. For listed companies and companies following IFRS, dividends are not recorded in the income statement. This is demonstrated in Figure 7.13.

Figure 7.13 Limited Companies' Appropriation Account Format

The income statement was prepared as normal. The profit was £100,000. The tax for the year was £40,000 and dividends are £25,000.

Unlisted Limited Co. Ltd (following IFRS for SMEs) Income Statement (extract)		**Unlisted and Listed Limited Co. Ltd (following IFRS) Income Statement (extract)**	
	£		£
Profit before Taxation (calculated as normal)	100,000	*Profit before Taxation (calculated as normal)*	100,000
Taxation	(40,000)	Taxation	(40,000)
Profit after Taxation	60,000	*Profit for the year*	60,000
Dividends for year	(25,000)		
Retained Profit	35,000		

Statement of Financial Position

In the statement of financial position, the main differences between a sole trader or partnership and a company are (i) that taxation payable is recorded under current liabilities; (ii) in the presentation of equity (capital employed); and (iii) that limited companies are more likely than sole traders or partnerships to have intangible assets such as goodwill or patents. The current liabilities presentation is relatively straightforward, so only the presentation of equity format is given here (see Figure 7.14).

Figure 7.14 Limited Companies Equity (Capital Employed) Format

Limited Co. Ltd has the following details of equity.

Ordinary share capital	£100,000	*Retained earnings*	£15,000
Preference share capital	£50,000	*Share premium account*	£5,000
		Revaluation reserve	£6,000

EQUITY	£	£
Capital and Reserves		
Share Capital		
Ordinary share capital		100,000
Preference share capital		50,000
		150,000
Reserves		
Capital reserves		
Share premium account	5,000	
Other reserves		
Revaluation reserve	6,000	
Retained earnings	15,000	26,000
Total Equity		176,000

Intangible assets are recorded in the statement of financial position under non-current assets. The more conventional non-current assets, such as land and buildings, are then recorded as property, plant and equipment.

Limited Company Example: Stevens, Turner Ltd

In order to demonstrate a more comprehensive example of the preparation of a limited company's accounts, we now turn again to the accounts of Gavin Stevens. When we last met Gavin Stevens he had formed a partnership with Diana Turner and they were trading as a partnership, Stevens and Turner (see Figure 7.4). We now assume that many years into the future in the year 20X1, the partnership has turned into a non-listed company. The trial balance is listed below.

Stevens, Turner Ltd: Trial Balance as at 31 December 20X1

	£000	£000
Ordinary share capital (£1 each)		300
Preference share capital (£1 each)		150
Share premium account		25
Revaluation reserve		30
General reserve		20
Retained earnings as at 1 January 20X1		50
Long-term loan		80
Land and buildings	550	
Patents	50	
Motor vehicles	50	
Opening inventories	10	
Trade receivables	80	
Trade payables		54
Bank	75	
Electricity	8	
Ordinary dividends	6	
Preference dividends	3	
Wages	50	
Telephone	7	
Revenue		350
Purchases	150	
Loan interest	8	
Other expenses	12	
	1,059	1,059

Notes:

1. Closing inventories are £25,000.
2. For simplicity, we are ignoring all other post-trial balance adjustments such as depreciation, bad and doubtful debts, accruals and prepayments.
3. Also for ease of understanding, we do not include non-operating items here such as revaluation of property, plant and equipment and gains or losses from foreign currency.
4. The following is not recorded in the trial balance: taxation payable £26,000.

We will now prepare the company accounts (see Figure 7.15). **The distinctive elements of a limited company's accounts are bordered by asterisks.** It is important to realise that in this section we are preparing the **full accounts for internal management purposes.** We are preparing the accounts here assuming Gavin Stevens is now an unlisted company following IFRS for SMEs in Figure 7.15. However, in Figure 7.16 we present the accounts of the company as if it were a listed company following full IFRS. You will note that only the treatment of dividends is different. These are listed separately in bold at the bottom of Figure 7.15 in the statement of comprehensive income and retained earnings. Also in the case of a listed company in Figure 7.16 we adjust for dividends in a statement of changes in equity. We could have prepared a separate statement of changes in equity in Figure 7.15. However, given its simplicity we recorded the opening and closing retained earnings in the statement of financial position. These are, in effect, alternative treatments. In Figure 7.17, we show the published accounts of Stevens, Turner assuming they are a public limited company.

I. Presentation as the accounts of a non-listed company following IFRS for SMEs (unabridged)

Figure 7.15 Stevens, Turner Ltd: Accounts for Year Ended 31 December 20X1

Stevens, Turner Ltd

Statement of Comprehensive Income and Retained Earnings for the Year Ended 20X1

	£000	£000
Revenue		350
Less Cost of Sales		
Opening Inventories	10	
Add Purchases	150	
	160	
Less Closing Inventories	25	135
Gross Profit		215
Less Expenses		
Electricity	8	
Wages	50	
Telephone	7	
Loan Interest	8	
Other expenses	12	85
******		
Profit before Taxation		130
Taxation[1]		(26)
Profit after Taxation		104
Ordinary dividends		**(6)**
Preference dividends		**(3)**
Retained Profit		95
******		

Figure 7.15 Stevens, Turner Ltd: Accounts for Year Ended 31 December 20X1 (*continued*)

Stevens, Turner Ltd

Statement of Financial Position as at 31 December 20X1

		£000	£000
ASSETS			
Non-current Assets			
Intangible Assets			
Patents			50
Property, Plant and Equipment			
Land and buildings			550
Motor vehicles			50
			600
Total non-current assets			650
Current Assets			
Inventory			25
Trade receivables			80
Bank			75
Total current assets			180
Total Assets			830
LIABILITIES			
Current Liabilities			
Trade payables			54
Taxation payable[1]			26
Total Current Liabilities			80
Non-current Liabilities			80
Total Liabilities			160
Net Assets			670
EQUITY			
Capital and Reserves	£000	£000	£000
Share Capital		*Authorised*	*Issued*
Ordinary share capital		350	300
Preference share capital		200	150
		550	450

Figure 7.15 Stevens, Turner Ltd: Accounts for Year Ended 31 December 20X1 (*continued*)

Reserves	£000	£000	£000
Capital reserves			
Share premium account		25	
Other reserves			
Revaluation reserve		30	
General reserve		20	
Opening retained earnings	50		
Retained earnings for year	95		
Closing retained earnings		145	220
Total Equity			670

Note 1: In this case, the amount payable equals the charge for the year. This will not always be so.

II. Presentation as the accounts of a listed company following IFRS (unabridged)

Figure 7.16 Stevens, Turner Plc: Accounts for the Year Ended 31 December 20X1

Stevens, Turner plc

Income Statement for the Year Ended 20X1

	£000	£000
Revenue		350
Less Cost of Sales		
Opening Inventories	10	
Add Purchases	150	
	160	
Less Closing Inventories	(25)	(135)
Gross Profit		215
Less Expenses		
Electricity	8	
Wages	50	
Telephone	7	
Loan Interest	8	
Other expenses	12	(85)
Profit before Taxation		130
Taxation[1]		(26)
Profit for the year		104

Figure 7.16 Stevens, Turner Plc: Accounts for the year ended 31 December 20X1 (*continued*)

Stevens, Turner plc

Statement of Financial Position as at 31 December 20X1

		£000
ASSETS		
Non-current Assets		
Intangible Assets		
Patents		50
Property, plant and equipment		
Land and buildings		550
Motor vehicles		50
		600
Total non-current assets		650
Current Assets		
Inventory		25
Trade receivables		80
Bank		75
Total current assets		180
Total Assets		830
LIABILITIES		
Current Liabilities		
Trade payables		54
Taxation payable[1]		26
Total current liabilities		80
Non-current Liabilities		80
Total Liabilities		160
Net Assets		670
EQUITY		
Capital and Reserves	£000	£000
Share Capital	*Authorised*	*Issued*
Ordinary share capital	350	300
Preference share capital	200	150
	550	450

Figure 7.16 Stevens, Turner Plc: Accounts for the Year Ended 31 December 20X1 (*continued*)

Reserves	£000	£000
Capital reserves		
Share premium account	25	
Other reserves		
Revaluation reserve	30	
General reserve	20	
Retained earnings	145	220
Total Equity		670

Note 1:
In this case, the amount payable equals the charge for the year. This will not always be so.

Stevens, Turner plc
Statement of Changes in Equity for the year ended 31 December 20X1

	£000	£000
Opening Retained Earnings		50
Profit for year	104	
Less Dividends	(9)	95
Closing Retained Earnings		145

Limited Companies: Published Accounts

The internal company accounts are not suitable for external publication. The published accounts which are sent to shareholders are incorporated in a special document called an annual report and have several special features: they are standardised and abridged and have supplementary notes.

- *Standardised*. Published accounts use special Companies Acts' formats. In actual fact, these formats are broadly used throughout this book for consistency and to aid understanding.
- *Abridged*. The Companies Acts' formats mean that the details are summarised.
- *Supplementary notes*. Supplementary notes are used to flesh out the details of the main accounts.
- *Annual report*. In the case of public limited companies, an annual report is sent to shareholders. Increasingly, the annual report is also put onto a company's website. The website will include the financial statements, but also much more information. A separate chapter is devoted to the annual report (Chapter 12), given its importance, with Figure 12.4 providing some corporate website addresses.

Company Snapshots 7.3 and 7.4 that follow on pages 202 and 203 show the income statement and statement of financial position for a UK company, AstraZeneca, in 2009. They have been prepared using International Financial Reporting Standards and using dollars rather than pounds.

COMPANY SNAPSHOT 7.3

Income Statement for a Limited Company

Consolidated Statement of Comprehensive Income for the year ended 31 December

	Notes	2009 $m	2008 $m	2007 $m
Revenue	1	**32,804**	31,601	29,559
Cost of sales		**(5,775)**	(6,598)	(6,419)
Gross profit		**27,029**	25,003	23,140
Distribution costs		**(298)**	(291)	(248)
Research and development		**(4,409)**	(5,179)	(5,162)
Selling, general and administrative costs	2	**(11,332)**	(10,913)	(10,364)
Other operating income and expense	2	**553**	524	728
Operating profit	2	**11,543**	9,144	8,094
Finance income	3	**462**	854	959
Finance expense	3	**(1,198)**	(1,317)	(1,070)
Profit before tax		**10,807**	8,681	7,983
Taxation	4	**(3,263)**	(2,551)	(2,356)
Profit for the period		**7,544**	6,130	5,627
Other Comprehensive Income:				
Foreign exchange arising on consolidation		**388**	(1,336)	492
Foreign exchange differences on borrowings forming net investment hedges		**(68)**	291	(40)
Gain/(loss) on cash flow hedge in connection with debt issue		**1**	1	(21)
Net available for sale gains/(losses) taken to equity		**2**	2	(9)
Actuarial loss for the period		**(569)**	(1,232)	(113)
Income tax relating to components of Other Comprehensive Income	4	**192**	368	33
Other Comprehensive Income for the period, net of tax		**(54)**	(1,906)	342
Total Comprehensive income for the period		**7,490**	4,224	5,969
Profit attributable to:				
Owners of the Parent		**7,521**	6,101	5,595
Non-controlling interests		**23**	29	32
Total Comprehensive income attributable to:				
Owners of the Parent		**7,467**	4,176	5,934
Non-controlling interests		**23**	48	35
Basic earnings per $0.25 Ordinary Share	5	**$5.19**	$4.20	$3.74
Diluted earnings per $0.25 Ordinary Share	5	**$5.19**	$4.20	$3.73

COMPANY SNAPSHOT 7.3 (*continued*)

	Notes	2009 $m	2008 $m	2007 $m
Weighted average number of Ordinary Shares in issue (millions)	5	**1,448**	1,453	1,495
Diluted weighted average number of Ordinary Shares in issue (millions)	5	**1,450**	1,453	1,498
Dividends declared and paid in the period	21	3,026	2,767	2,658

All activities were in respect of continuing operations.
$m means millions of US dollars.

Source: AstraZeneca PLC, *Annual Report and Form 20-F information 2009*, p. 124.

The specific requirements for published company accounts are complex and beyond the scope of this book. All European listed companies must prepare their accounts in accordance with International Financial Reporting Standards. The presentation of the accounts differs from that conventionally used for sole traders and partnerships. However, Figure 7.17 on page 205 is a summary of what Stevens, Turner plc might look like. It is prepared using the same information from the trial balance for Stevens Turner Ltd presented earlier in this chapter.

COMPANY SNAPSHOT 7.4

Statement of Financial Position for a Limited Company

Consolidated Statement of Financial Position at 31 December

	Notes	2009 $m	2008 $m	2007 $m
Assets				
Non-current assets				
Property, plant and equipment	7	**7,307**	7,043	8,298
Goodwill	8	**9,889**	9,874	9,884
Intangible assets	9	**12,226**	12,323	11,467
Derivative financial instruments	16	**262**	449	117
Other investments	10	**184**	156	182
Deferred tax assets	4	**1,292**	1,236	1,044
		31,160	31,081	30,992
Current assets				
Inventories	11	**1,750**	1,636	2,119
Trade and other receivables	12	**7,709**	7,261	6,668

COMPANY SNAPSHOT 7.4 (*continued*)

Other investments	10	**1,484**	105	91
Derivative financial instruments	16	**24**	—	—
Income tax receivable		**2,875**	2,581	2,251
Cash and cash equivalents	13	**9,918**	4,286	5,867
		23,760	15,869	16,996
Total assets		**54,920**	46,950	47,988
Liabilities				
Current liabilities				
Interest-bearing loans and borrowings	14	**(1,926)**	(993)	(4,280)
Trade and other payables	17	**(8,687)**	(7,178)	(6,968)
Derivative financial instruments	16	**(90)**	(95)	(31)
Provisions	18	**(1,209)**	(600)	(387)
Income tax payable		**(5,728)**	(4,549)	(3,552)
		(17,640)	(13,415)	(15,218)
Non-current liabilities				
Interest-bearing loans and borrowings	14	**(9,137)**	(10,855)	(10,876)
Derivative financial instruments	16	**—**	(71)	—
Deferred tax liabilities	4	**(3,247)**	(3,126)	(4,119)
Retirement benefit obligations	23	**(3,354)**	(2,732)	(1,998)
Provisions	18	**(477)**	(542)	(633)
Other payables	17	**(244)**	(149)	(229)
		(16,459)	(17,475)	(17,855)
Total liabilities		**(34,099)**	(30,890)	(33,073)
Net assets		**20,821**	16,060	14,915
Equity				
Capital and reserves & attributable to equity holders of the Company				
Share capital	20	**363**	362	364
Share premium account	19	**2,180**	2,046	1,888
Capital redemption reserve	19	**94**	94	91
Merger reserve	19	**433**	433	433
Other reserves	19	**1,392**	1,405	1,378
Retained earnings	19	**16,198**	11,572	10,624
		20,660	15,912	14,778
Non-controlling interests	19	**161**	148	137
Total equity	19	**20,821**	16,060	14,915

The Financial Statements on pages 124 to 186 were approved by the Board of Directors on 28 January 2010 and were signed on its behalf by:

David R Brennan Director

Simon Lowth Director

Source: AstraZeneca PLC, *Annual Report and Form 20-F Information 2009*, p. 125.

Figure 7.17 Stevens, Turner Ltd: Accounts Presented as Published Accounts of a Public Limited Company

Stevens, Turner plc

Income Statement for the year ended 31 December 20X1

	£000
Revenue[1]	350
Cost of Sales	(135)
Gross Profit	215
Administrative expenses	(85)
Profit before Taxation	130
Taxation	(26)
Profit for year[2,3]	104

Stevens, Turner plc

Statement of Financial Position as at 31 December 20X1

	Notes	
ASSETS		£000
Non-current assets		
Property, plant and equipment	1	600
Goodwill and intangible assets		50
Total non-current assets		650
Current Assets		
Inventory		25
Trade receivables		80
Bank		75
Total current assets		180
Total Assets		830
LIABILITIES		
Current Liabilities	2	80
Non-current Liabilities		80
Total Liabilities		160
Net Assets		670
EQUITY		£000
Capital and Reserves		
Called-up share capital[4]	3	450
Share premium account		25
Other reserves	4	50
Retained earnings		145
Total Equity		670

Figure 7.17 Stevens, Turner Ltd: Accounts Presented as Published Accounts of a Public Limited Company (*continued*)

Stevens, Turner plc

Statement of Changes in Equity for the year ended 31 December 20X1

	£000	£000
Opening Retained Earnings		50
Profit for year	104	
Less Dividends	(9)	95
Closing Retained Earnings		145

Notes to the accounts

1. Property, Plant and Equipment	£000	**3. Called-up Share Capital**[3]	£000
Land and buildings	550	Ordinary share capital	300
Motor vehicles	50	Preference share capital	150
	600		450
2. Current Liabilities		**4. Other Reserves**	
Trade receivables	54	Revaluation reserve	30
Taxation payable	26	General reserve	20
	80		50

We have thus summarised the accounts of Stevens, Turner plc and supplemented them with notes to the accounts. The main figures can thus easily be identified. There are some points of interest, indicated by the superscript notes in Figure 7.17.

1. Revenue may also be called 'sales' or 'turnover'.
2. No dividends are shown in the income statement. Dividends paid are deducted in the statement of changes in equity. Dividends proposed are not recorded.
3. There is no non-operating income recorded here. If there was, it would be either recorded as other comprehensive income under profit for the year or alternatively in a second statement called Statement of Other Comprehensive Income.
4. Called-up share capital has a technical meaning (see Figure 7.12). However, for convenience, it can be taken here as issued share capital.

Conclusion

Partnerships and limited companies are important types of business organisation. Partnerships are broadly similar to sole traders, except that there is the problem of how to divide the equity and profit between the partners. Limited companies, unlike partnerships or sole traders, are based on the concept of limited liability. The principal differentiating features in the accounts of companies are corporation tax, dividends and the division of equity (capital employed) into share capital and reserves. Limited companies may be either private limited companies or public limited companies. It is the latter which are quoted on the stock exchange. The presentation and format of published public limited companies differ from those of the other types of business organisation.

Discussion Questions

Questions with numbers in blue have answers at the back of the book.

Q1 Why do you think that three different types of business enterprise (sole traders, partnerships and limited companies) exist?

Q2 Discuss the view that the accounts of partnerships are much like those of sole traders except for the need to share out the equity and profit between more than one partner.

Q3 Distinguish between a private limited company and a public limited company. Is there any difference between the users of the accounts of each type of company?

Q4 Why is the distinction between capital and revenue reserves so important for a company?

Q5 State whether the following are true or false. If false, explain why.
- (a) Drawings are an expense recorded in the partners' trading, profit and loss and appropriation account (i.e., a separate section of the income statement called the appropriation account).
- (b) Partners' current accounts report the yearly short-term movements in partners' equity or capital.
- (c) The nominal value of a company's shares is the amount the shares will fetch on the stock market.
- (d) An unsecured loan is secured on specific assets such as the company's machinery.
- (e) Reserves can be spent on the purchase of property, plant and equipment.

Numerical Questions

These questions are separated into those on (A) partnerships and (B) limited companies. Within each section, they are graded in difficulty.

Questions with numbers in blue have answers at the back of the book.

A Partnerships

Q1 Two partners, Peter Tom and Sheila Thumb, have the following details of their accounts for the year ended 31 December 2013.

			£	
Net profit before appropriation: £100,000	Capital accounts:	Tom	8,000	
Profit sharing ratio: 3 Tom, 1 Thumb		Thumb	6,000	
Salaries: Tom £10,000, Thumb £30,000	Current accounts:	Tom	3,000	cr
Drawings: Tom £25,000, Thumb £30,000		Thumb	1,000	dr

Required: Prepare the relevant income statement and statement of financial position extracts.

Q2 J. Waite and P. Watcher's trial balance as at 30 November 2013 is set out below.

		£	£
Capital accounts:	Waite		88,000
	Watcher		64,000
Current accounts:	Waite	2,500	
	Watcher		12,000
Drawings:	Waite	13,300	
	Watcher	6,300	
Land and buildings at cost		166,313	
Motor vehicles at cost		65,000	
Opening inventory		9,000	
Trade receivables		12,000	
Trade payables			18,500
Bank		6,501	
Electricity		3,406	
Wages		14,870	
Telephone		1,350	
Rent and business rates		6,660	
Long-term loan			28,000
Revenue			350,000
Purchases		245,000	
Interest on loan		2,800	
Other expenses		5,500	
		560,500	560,500

Q2 Waite and Watcher (*continued*)

Notes:

1. Closing inventory is £15,000.
2. Salaries are £18,000 for Waite and £16,000 for Watcher.
3. There is £300 owing for rent.
4. Depreciation for the year is £2,000 on land and buildings and £3,000 on motor vehicles. The business was started on 1 December 2012.
5. The split of profits is 3 Watcher:2 Waite.

Required: Prepare the income statement for year ended 30 November 2013 and the statement of financial position as at 30 November 2013.

Q3 Cherie and Tony's trial balance as at 31 December 2013 is set out below.

		£	£
Capital accounts:	Cherie		30,000
	Tony		35,000
Current accounts:	Cherie		26,000
	Tony		18,500
Drawings	Cherie	21,294	
	Tony	18,321	
Land and buildings at cost		203,500	
Plant and machinery at cost		26,240	
Land and buildings accumulated depreciation as at 1 January 2013			12,315
Plant and machinery accumulated depreciation as at 1 January 2013			9,218
Trade receivables		18,613	
Trade payables			2,451
Bank		25,016	
Electricity		1,324	
Wages		12,187	
Telephone		1,923	
Insurance		1,318	
Long-term loan			83,000
Revenue			251,800
Revenue returns		340	
Purchases		128,317	
Purchases returns			206
Other expenses		1,497	
Opening inventory		8,600	
		468,490	468,490

Q3 Cherie and Tony (*continued*)

Notes:

1. Closing inventory is £12,000.
2. £197 of the other expenses was prepaid and £200 is owed for the telephone.
3. Salaries will be £12,000 for Cherie and £10,000 for Tony.
4. Depreciation is fixed at 2% on the cost of land and buildings and 10% on the cost of plant and machinery.
5. Profits are shared in the ratio 2 for Cherie and 1 for Tony.

Required: Prepare the income statement for the year ended 31 December 2013 and the statement of financial position as at 31 December 2013.

Q4 Sister and Sledge are trading in partnership, sharing profits and losses in the ratio of 2:1, respectively. The partners are entitled to salaries of Sister £6,000 per annum and Sledge £5,000 per annum. There is the following additional information:

(1) Inventory as at 31 December 2013 was valued at £8,800.
(2) Staff salaries owing £290.
(3) Advertising paid in advance £200.
(4) Provision for the impairment of receivables to be increased to £720.
(5) Provision should be made for depreciation of 2% on land and buildings on cost, and for fixtures and fittings at 10% on cost.

Trial Balance as at 31 December 2013

	£	£
Capital accounts:		
Sister		12,500
Sledge		5,000
Current accounts:		
Sister		1,500
Sledge	600	
Drawings:		
Sister	9,800	
Sledge	6,700	
Long-term loan		40,250
Land and buildings at cost	164,850	
Inventory as at 1 January 2013	9,500	
Fixtures and fittings at cost	12,500	
Purchases	126,000	
Cash at bank	3,480	
Revenue		305,400
Trade receivables	9,600	
Carriage inwards	200	
Carriage outwards	300	
Staff salaries	24,300	

Q4 Sister and Sledge (*continued*)

	£	£
Trade payables		26,300
General expenses	18,200	
Provision for the impairment of receivables		480
Advertising	5,350	
Discounts receivable		120
Discounts allowed	350	
Rent and business rates	2,850	
Land and buildings accumulated depreciation as at 1 January 2013		9,750
Fixtures and fittings accumulated depreciation as at 1 January 2013		3,500
Electricity	4,500	
Telephone	5,720	
	404,800	404,800

Required: Prepare the income statement for the year ended 31 December 2013 and the statement of financial position as at 31 December 2013.

B Limited Companies

i Non-Listed Companies Reporting under IFRS for SMEs

Q5 Red Devils Ltd has the following extracts from its accounts.

Red Devils Ltd
Trial Balance as at 30 November 2013

	£	£
Gross profit for year		150,000
7% Debentures		200,000
6% Preference share capital (£150,000 authorised)		150,000
£1 Ordinary share capital (£400,000 authorised)		250,000
Share premium account		55,000
Property, plant and equipment	680,900	
Ordinary dividends	25,000	
Preference dividends	9,000	
General expenses	22,100	
Directors' fees	19,200	
Trade receivables	4,700	
Trade payables		46,200
Bank	5,300	
Retained earnings as at 1 December 2012		9,000
General reserve as at 1 December 2012		11,000
Inventories as at 30 November 2013	105,000	
	871,200	871,200

Q5 Red Devils (*continued*)

Notes:
1. An audit fee is to be provided of £7,500.
2. The debenture interest for the year has not been paid.
3. The directors propose to transfer £3,500 to the general reserve. (Note: transfers are recorded in the statement of comprehensive income.)
4. Corporation tax of £17,440 is to be provided on the profit for the year.

Required: Prepare for internal management purposes:
(a) The statement of comprehensive income and retained earnings (income statement) for the year ended 30 November 2013.
(b) The statement of financial position as at 30 November 2013.

Q6 **Superprofit Ltd.**

Trial Balance as at 31 December 2013

	£000	£000
Ordinary share capital		210
Preference share capital		25
Share premium account		40
Revaluation reserve		35
General reserve		15
Retained earnings as at 1 January 2013		28
Long-term loan		32
Land and buildings	378	
Patents	12	
Motor vehicles	47	
Opening inventories	23	
Trade receivables	18	
Trade payables		45
Bank	31	
Electricity	12	
Insurance	3	
Wages	24	
Ordinary dividends	9	
Preference dividends	3	
Telephone	5	
Light and heat	8	
Revenue		351
Purchases	182	
Other expenses	26	
	781	781

Q6 Superprofit Ltd. (*continued*)

Notes (all figures in £000s):
1. Closing inventories are £26.
2. The following had not yet been recorded in the trial balance:
(a) Taxation payable £13
(b) Interest on long-term loan £4
(c) Auditors' fees £2
(d) The authorised share capital is ordinary share capital £250, preference share capital £50.
3. The business started trading on 1 January 2013. Depreciation for the year is £18 for land and buildings and £7 for motor vehicles.

Required: Prepare for *internal management purposes* the income statement for year ended 31 December 2013 and the statement of financial position as at 31 December 2013.

ii Companies Reporting under Full IFRS

Q7 Lindesay Trading plc

Trial Balance as at 31 March 2014

	£000	£000
Ordinary share capital		425
Preference share capital		312
Share premium account		18
Revaluation reserve		27
General reserve as at 1 April 2013		13
Retained earnings as at 1 April 2013		17
Long-term loan		87
Land and buildings at cost	834	
Patents	25	
Motor vehicles at cost	312	
Opening inventories as at 1 April 2013	10	
Trade receivables	157	
Trade payables		121
Ordinary dividends	19	
Preference dividends	9	
Bank	186	
Electricity	12	
Wages and salaries	183	
Telephone	5	
Revenue		1,500
Insurance	6	
Purchases	750	

Q7 **Lindesay Trading plc** (*continued*)

	£000	£000
Other expenses	125	
Land and buildings accumulated depreciation as at 1 April 2014		25
Motor vehicles accumulated depreciation as at 1 April 2014		88
	2,633	2,633

Notes (all figures in £000s):

1. Closing inventories are £13.
2. The following are not recorded in the trial balance: Taxation payable £58.
3. Authorised share capital was £500 for ordinary share capital and £400 for preference share capital.
4. There was £45 owing for wages and salaries.
5. Debenture interest was £8.
6. Of the insurance £1 was prepaid.
7. The proposed auditors' fees are £3.
8. A transfer to the general reserve was made of £16.
9. Depreciation is to be £17 on land and buildings and £60 on motor vehicles.

Required: Prepare for *internal management purposes* the income statement for the year ended 31 March 2014 and the statement of financial position as at 31 March 2014.

Q8 The following trial balance was extracted from the books of Leisureplay plc, a listed company, for the year ended 31 December 2013.

	£000	£000
Ordinary share capital (£1 each)		700,000
Preference share capital (£1 each)		80,000
Debentures		412,000
Retained earnings as at 1 January 2013		98,000
Share premium account		62,000
Revaluation reserve		70,000
General reserve		18,000
Freehold premises at cost	1,550,000	
Motor vehicles at cost	18,000	
Furniture and fittings at cost	8,000	
Freehold premises accumulated depreciation as at 1 January 2013		102,000
Motor vehicles accumulated depreciation as at 1 January 2013		9,350
Furniture and fittings accumulated depreciation as at 1 January 2013		1,100
Inventories as at 1 January 2013	5,000	
Cash at bank	183,550	
Provision for the impairment of receivables		1,000
Purchases/revenue	500,000	800,000
Trade receivables/payables	28,900	7,000
Revenue returns/purchases returns	3,500	3,800
Carriage inwards	60	
Carriage outwards	70	
Bank charges	20	
Rates	4,280	
Salaries	5,970	
Wages	3,130	
Travelling expenses	1,980	

Q8 **Leisureplay** (*continued*)

	£000	£000
Preference dividends	5,000	
Ordinary dividends	25,000	
Discount allowed	20	
Discount received		15
General expenses	8,100	
Gas, electricity	9,385	
Printing, stationery	1,850	
Advertising	2,450	
	2,364,265	2,364,265

Notes (all figures are in 000s):

(a) Inventories as at 31 December 2013 are £12,000

(b) Depreciation is to be charged as follows:
   (i) Freehold premises 2% on cost
   (ii) Motor vehicles 10% on cost
   (iii) Furniture and fittings 5% on cost

(c) There is the following payment in advance:
   General expenses £500

(d) There are the following accrued expenses:
   Business rates £300
   Advertising £550
   Auditors' fees £250

(e) Authorised ordinary share capital is £1,000,000 £1 shares, and authorised preference share capital is 100,000 £1 shares.

(f) Taxation has been calculated as £58,500.

(g) Debenture interest should be charged at 10%.

(h) Provision for the impairment of receivables is increased to £1,600 and a bad debt of £400 is to be written off. You should calculate out the provision first.

(i) The ordinary and preference dividends should be deducted from retained earnings.

Required: Prepare for *internal management purposes* the income statement for Leisureplay plc for the year ended 31 December 2013 and statement of financial position as at 31 December 2013 using International Financial Reporting Standards.

Q9 You have the following summarised trial balance for Stock High plc as at 31 March 2014. Further details are provided in the notes.

	£000	£000
Revenue		1,250
Cost of sales	400	
Administrative expenses	200	
Distribution expenses	150	
Patents	50	
Land and buildings at cost	800	
Motor vehicles at cost	400	
Land and buildings accumulated depreciation as at 1 April 2013		140
Motor vehicles accumulated depreciation as at 1 April 2013		150
Long-term loan		60
Retained earnings as at 1 April 2013		36
Share premium account		25
Revaluation reserve		30
General reserve		25
Ordinary share capital		450
Preference share capital		100
Taxation paid	86	
Ordinary dividends paid	50	
Trade payables		12
Inventories as at 31 March 2014	20	
Trade receivables	100	
Cash	22	
	2,278	2,278

Notes (in £000s except for note 3):

1. At the statement of financial position date £8 is owing for taxation.
2. Depreciation is to be charged at 2% on cost for land and buildings (used for administration) and 20% on cost for motor vehicles (used for selling and distribution).
3. Authorised share capital is 600,000 £1 ordinary shares and £150,000 £1 preference shares.

Required: Prepare the income statement and statement of changes in equity for the year ended 31 March 2014 and the statement of financial position for the year ended 31 March 2014 as they would appear in the published accounts prepared under International Financial Reporting Standards.

Appendix 7.1: Example of an Income Statement (Profit and Loss Account) using UK GAAP (Manchester United Ltd)

Manchester United Limited

Consolidated profit and loss account

	Note	**Year ended 30 June 2009 £'000**	Year ended 30 June 2008 £'000
Turnover: Group and share of joint venture		**278,476**	257,116
Less: Share of joint venture		—	(877)
Group turnover	2	**278,476**	256,239
Operating expenses–other	3	**(230,481)**	(212,928)
Operating expenses–exceptional items	4	**(837)**	(490)
Total operating expenses		**(231,318)**	(213,418)
Group operating profit		**47,158**	42,821
Analysed as:			
Group operating profit before depreciation and amortisation of players' registrations and goodwill		**92,789**	86,005
Depreciation		**(7,427)**	(7,271)
Amortisation of players' registrations		**(37,641)**	(35,481)
Amortisation of goodwill		**(563)**	(432)
		47,158	42,821
Share of operating profit in:			
- Joint venture		—	2
- Associate		—	91
Total operating profit: Group and share of joint venture and associate		**47,158**	42,914
Profit on disposal of associate		—	1,209
Profit on disposal of players		**80,724**	21,831
Profit before interest and taxation		**127,882**	65,954
Net interest (payable)/receivable	5	**(236)**	462
Profit on ordinary activities before taxation		**127,646**	66,416
Tax on profit on ordinary activities	7	**(34,768)**	(19,916)
Profit on ordinary activities after taxation		**92,878**	46,500
Equity minority interest		**83**	254
Profit for the financial year	21	**92,961**	46,754

Source: Manchester United Limited, *Annual Report and Financial Statements for the year end 30 June 2009*, p. 9.

Appendix 7.2: Example of a Statement of Financial Position (Balance Sheet) using UK GAAP (Manchester United Ltd)

Manchester United Limited

Consolidated balance sheet

	Note	**At 30 June 2009** £'000	At 30 June 2008 £'000
Fixed assets			
Intangible assets – goodwill	9a	**7,337**	7,900
Intangible assets – players' registrations	9b	**113,406**	92,739
Tangible assets	10	**160,683**	166,813
		281,426	267,452
Current assets			
Stock	12	**279**	283
Debtors – amounts falling due within one year	13	**174,094**	118,748
Debtors – amounts falling due after more than one year	13	**12,650**	10,460
Cash at bank and in hand		**150,530**	49,745
		337,553	179,236
Creditors – amounts falling due within one year	14	**(88,409)**	(65,487)
Net current assets		**249,144**	113,749
Total assets less current liabilities		**530,570**	381,201
Creditors – amounts falling due after more than one year	15	**(17,877)**	(15,934)
Provision for liabilities and charges			
Deferred taxation	17a	**(17,568)**	(351)
Other provisions	17b	**(1,091)**	(1,335)
Accruals and deferred income			
Deferred grant income	18	**(380)**	(448)
Other deferred income	19	**(111,757)**	(71,976)
Net assets		**381,897**	291,157
Capital and reserves			
Called up share capital	20	**26,519**	26,519
Share premium reserve	21	**7,756**	7,756
Other reserves	21	**1,674**	3,696
Profit and loss reserve	21	**348,892**	256,047
Total shareholders' funds	22	**384,841**	294,018
Minority interests		**(2,944)**	(2,861)
Capital employed		**381,897**	291,157

The financial statements on pages 9 to 40 were approved by the board of directors on 30 September 2009 and signed on its behalf by:

M Bolingbroke
Director

Source: Manchester United Limited, *Annual Report and Financial Statements for the year end 30 June 2009*, p. 11.

Go online to discover the extra features for this chapter at **www.wiley.com/college/jones**

Chapter 8

Main financial statement: The statement of cash flows

'Cash is King. It is relatively easy to "manufacture" profits but creating cash is virtually impossible.'

UBS Phillips and Drew (January 1991), *Accounting for Growth*, p. 32.

Learning Outcomes

After completing this chapter you should be able to:

- Explain the nature of cash and the statement of cash flows.
- Demonstrate the importance of cash flow.
- Investigate the relationship between profit and cash flow.
- Outline the direct and indirect methods of the statement of cash flows preparation.

Go online to discover the extra features for this chapter at **www.wiley.com/college/jones**

Chapter Summary

- Cash is key to business success.
- Cash flow is concerned with cash received and cash paid, unlike profit which deals with income earned and expenses incurred.
- Reconciling profit to cash flow means adjusting for movements in working capital and for non-cash items, such as depreciation.
- Large companies provide a statement of cash flows as the third major financial statement.
- Sole traders, partnerships and small companies may, but are not required to, prepare a statement of cash flows.
- The two ways of preparing a statement of cash flows are the direct and the indirect methods.
- Most companies use the indirect method of preparing a statement of cash flows.
- Listed companies use a different format than other business organisations.
- When controlling cash it is important to use a bank reconciliation statement.

Introduction

Cash is king. It is the essential lubricant of business. Without cash, a business cannot pay its employees' wages or pay for goods or services. As Real-World View 8.1 shows, at its most extreme, this can lead to the failure of a business. A business records cash in the bank account in the books of account. Small businesses may sometimes prepare a statement of cash flows directly from the bank account. More usually, however, the statement of cash flows is prepared indirectly by deducing the figures from the income statement and the statement of financial position. The statement of cash flows, at its simplest, records the cash inflows and cash outflows classified under certain headings such as cash flows from operating (i.e., trading) activities. All companies (except small ones) must prepare a statement of cash

REAL-WORLD VIEW 8.1

Cash Bloodbath

With last week's collapse of Boo.com – the first big liquidation of a dot.com company in Europe – the internet gold rush has taken on the appearance of a bloodbath. The company's principal failing – and there were many, it was burning cash at a rate of $1m a week – was to forget that in the new economy the old rules still apply.

Source: Accountancy Age, 25 May 2000, p. 26.

flows in line with financial reporting regulations. However, some sole traders, partnerships and smaller companies also provide them, often at the request of their bank. As Real-World View 8.2 shows, banks are well aware of the importance of cash. As well as preparing the statement of cash flows on the basis of past cash flows, businesses will continually monitor their day-to-day cash inflows and outflows. Statements of cash flows essentially record what has happened over the reporting period. Companies also prepare cash budgets which look to the future. Cash management, therefore, concerns the past, present and future activities of a business.

REAL-WORLD VIEW 8.2

Cash Flow

Bankers *do* know about cash flow. They have to live with it on Friday, every Friday, in any number of companies up and down the country. Where there is insufficient cash to pay the wages, really agonising decisions result. Should the company be closed, with all the personal anguish it will cause, or should it be allowed to limp on, perhaps to face exactly the same agonising dilemma in as little as a week's time?

Source: B. Warnes (1984), *The Genghis Khan Guide to Business*, Osmosis Publications, London, p. 6.

Importance of Cash

Cash is the lifeblood of a business. Cash is needed to pay the wages, to pay the day-to-day running costs, to buy inventory and to buy new property, plant and equipment. The generation of cash is, therefore, essential to the survival and expansion of businesses. Money makes the world go round! In many ways, the concept of cash flow is easier to understand than that of profit. Most people are more familiar with cash than profit. Cash is, after all, what we use in our everyday lives. At its most stark, if a business runs out of cash it will not be able to pay its trade payables and it will cease trading. As Jack Welch, a successful US businessman, has said, 'There's one thing you can't cheat on and that's cash and Enron didn't have any cash for the last three years. Accounting is odd, but cash is real stuff. Follow the cash' (*The Guardian*, 27 February 2002, p. 23). Ken Lever, a member of the UK's Accounting Standards Board agrees (*Accountancy Age*, 24 February 2011, p. 5). Cash flow is the key. 'A lot of businesses see cash as an afterthought. There is a tendency to get side-tracked by accounting metrics.'

It is far easier to manipulate profit than it is to manipulate cash flow. This is highlighted by Real-World Views 8.3 and 8.4. In Real-World View 8.3, Phillips and Drew, a firm of city fund managers (now called UBS Global Management), basically state that cash is essential to business success.

REAL-WORLD VIEW 8.3

Importance of Cash I

In the end, investment and accounting all come back to cash. Whereas "manufacturing" profits is relatively easy, cash flow is the most difficult parameter to adjust in a company's accounts. Indeed, tracing cash movements in a company can often lead to the identification of unusual accounting practices. The long term return of an equity investment is determined by the market's perception of the stream of dividends that the company will be able to pay. We believe that there should be less emphasis placed on the reported progression of earnings per share and more attention paid to balance sheet movements, dividend potential and, most important of all, cash.

Source: UBS Phillips and Drew (January 1991), *Accounting for Growth*, p. 1.

This was as true in 1991 as it was in 2011, as Real-World View 8.4 shows.

REAL-WORLD VIEW 8.4

Importance of Cash II

Even more important than earnings coverage, though, is free cash flow coverage. Whereas earnings are in some part an accounting fiction, free cash flow is cold, hard fact. Free cash flow can be used for real purposes, including paying debts, investing in new capacity and paying dividends. Therefore, we tried to pick out companies whose free cash flow had improved or was stable over recent years – as well as those in the opposite situation.

Source: D.M. Hand, Die hard dividends, *Investors Chronicle*, 21–27 October 2011, p. 24. Financial Times Ltd.

HELPNOTE

Free cash flow is defined as:

'Cash flow from operations after deducting interest, tax, preference dividends and ongoing capital expenditure, but excluding capital expenditure associated with strategic acquisitions and/or disposals and ordinary share dividends' (CIMA, 2009, *Official Terminology*).

Context

The statement of cash flows is the third of the key financial statements which medium and large companies provide. It summarises the company's cash transactions over time. At its simplest, the cash flow is related to the opening and closing cash balances:

$$\text{Opening cash} + \text{Inflows} - \text{Outflows} = \text{Closing cash}$$

Cash inflows are varied, but may, for example, be receipts from revenue or interest from a bank deposit account. Cash outflows may be payments for goods or services, or for capital expenditure items such as motor vehicles.

All *large* companies are required to provide a statement of cash flows. There are two methods of preparation. The first is the **direct method**, which categorises cash flow by function; for example, receipts from revenue. A statement of cash flows, using the direct method, can be prepared from the bank account and is the most readily understandable. The second method is the **indirect method**. This uses a 'detective' approach. It deduces cash flow from the existing statements of financial position and income statement and reconciles operating profit to operating cash flow. The statement of cash flows, using the indirect method, is not so readily comprehensible. Unfortunately, this is the method most often used.

PAUSE FOR THOUGHT 8.1

Yes, But What Exactly is Cash?

Cash is cash! However, there are different types of cash, such as petty cash, cash at bank, bank deposit accounts, or deposits repayable on demand or with notice. How do they all differ?

The basic distinction is between cash and bank. However, the terms are often used loosely and interchangeably. Cash is the cash available. In other words, it physically exists; for example, a fifty-pound note. Petty cash is money kept specifically for day-to-day small expenses, such as purchasing coffee. Cash at bank is normally kept either in a current account (which operates via a cheque book for normal day-to-day transactions) or in a deposit account (basically a store for surplus cash). The term cash and cash equivalents is often used to refer to cash at bank and that held in short-term (say up to 30 days) deposit accounts. Deposits repayable on demand are very short-term investments which can be repaid within one working day. Deposits requiring notice are accounts where the customer must give a period of notice for withdrawal (for example, 30 days).

Cash and the Bank Account

As we saw in Chapter 4, cash is initially recorded in the bank account. In large businesses, a separate book is kept called the cash book. Debits are essentially good news for a company in that they increase cash in the bank account, whereas credits are bad news in that they decrease cash in the bank account. For an individual looking at their bank statements, however, it is the other way round. From the bank account it is possible to prepare a simple statement of cash flows.

PAUSE FOR THOUGHT 8.2

Cash Inflows and Outflows

What might be some examples of the main sources of cash inflow and outflow for a small business?

Cash Inflow	Cash Outflow
Cash from customers for goods	Payments to suppliers for goods
Interest received from bank deposit account	Payments for services, e.g., telephone, light and heat
Cash from sale of property, plant and equipment	Repay bank loans
Cash introduced by owner	Payments for property, plant and equipment, e.g., motor vehicles
Loan received	Interest paid on bank loan

Let us take the example once more of Gavin Stevens' bank account (see Figure 8.1). As Figure 8.1 shows, we have essentially summarised the figures from the bank account and reclassified them under certain headings.

For sole traders and partnerships, there is no regulatory requirement for a statement of cash flows in the UK. Small companies are also exempt. Many organisations do, nevertheless, prepare one. From 1 January 2015, UK non-listed companies are regulated by accounting standards: section 7 Statement of Cash Flows from FRS102. However, UK listed companies, like all European listed companies, follow International Accounting Standard IAS 7. The objective of this standard is to require the provision of information about the historical changes in cash and cash equivalents of an entity by means of a statement of cash flows which classifies cash flows during the period as operating, investing and financing activities. The statement of cash flows is a primary financial statement and ranks along with the statement of financial position and income statement. These standards lay down certain main headings for categorising cash flows (see Figure 8.2).

In Appendix 8.1, the main headings for the cash flow statement (note it is called the cash flow statement rather than the statement of cash flows) as required by the UK's accounting standards are given. This can be used by sole traders, partnerships and some non-listed companies.

We use three headings for listed companies (see Figure 8.2 on page 228): (1) Cash flows from operating activities (which covers flows from operating activities and taxation);

Figure 8.1 Simple Statement of Cash Flows for Gavin Stevens

Taking Gavin Stevens' bank account:

Bank

	£		£
1 Jan. Equity	700,000	2 Jan. Hotel	610,000
7 Jan. Ireton	1,965	2 Jan. Van	3,000
7 Jan. Hepworth	2,500	2 Jan. Purchases	2,000
		4 Jan. Electricity	300
		4 Jan. Wages	1,000
		7 Jan. Hogen	250
		7 Jan. Lewis	1,000
		7 Jan. Bal. c/f	86,915
	704,465		704,465
8 Jan. Bal. b/f	86,915		

From the bank account, we can summarise the main cash flows and record them in a statement of cash flows, as follows:

Gavin Stevens
Statement of Cash Flows up to 7 January

	£	£
Opening Cash Balance		–
Add *Inflows*		
Capital invested (1)	700,000	
Trading (2)	4,465	704,465
Less *Outflows*		
Capital expenditure (3)	613,000	
Trading (4)	4,550	617,550
Closing Cash Balance		86,915

Notes:

(1) Represents the initial capital investment. Often termed a 'financing' cash flow.

(2) Represents money received from trade receivables (Ireton £1,965 and Hepworth £2,500). Often termed cash inflow from a 'trading' or 'operating' activity.

(3) Represents the purchase of property, plant and equipment (hotel £610,000 and van £3,000). Often termed cash flow from 'investing' activities.

(4) Represents the money paid for goods and services (purchases £2,000, electricity £300, wages £1,000, Hogen £250, Lewis £1,000). Often termed cash outflow from a 'trading' or 'operating' activity.

(2) Cash flows from investing activities (which covers capital expenditure and financial investment, acquisitions and disposals, interest received and dividends received); and (3) Cash flows from financing activities. Unfortunately, these headings are very cumbersome and often lack transparency.

Figure 8.2 Main Headings for the Statement of Cash Flows using IFRS

	Simplified Meaning	*Examples of Inflows*	*Examples of Outflows*
Cash flows from operating activities	i. Cash flows from the normal trading activities of a business ii. Cash paid to government for taxation	i. Cash for sale of goods. ii. Taxation refunds	i. Payment for purchases of goods ii. Expenses paid iii. Taxation paid
Cash flows from investing activities	i. Cash flows relating to the purchase and sale of a. property, plant and equipment. b. investments ii. Payments for the purchase or sale of other companies	i. Interest received ii. Dividends received iii. Receipts for sale of property, plant and equipment e.g. motor vehicles iv. Sale of investments v. Cash received for sale of another company	i. Payments for property, plant and equipment e.g. motor vehicles. ii. Purchase of investments iii. Cash paid to buy another company
Cash flows from financing activities	i. Cash received from shareholders ii. Cash flows relating to the issuing or buying back of shares or loan capital iii. Dividends companies pay to shareholders	i. Cash received from the issue of: a. shares b. loans	i. Cash paid to buy back shares or to repay loans ii. Dividends paid iii. Interest paid

The details of IAS 7 are well summarised in Real-World View 8.5 by Paul Klumpes and Peter Welch.

REAL-WORLD VIEW 8.5

Cash Flow Statements

According to the International Accounting Standards Committee Foundation's Technical Summary of IAS 7: 'The objective of this standard is to require the provision of information about the historical changes in cash and cash equivalents of an entity by means of a statement of cash flows which classifies cash flows during the period as operating, investing and financing activities.'

Summarising the three cashflow categories:

- Operating: principal revenue-producing activities of the entity.
- Investing: acquisition and disposal of long-term assets and other investments (including subsidiaries).
- Financing: activities that result in changes in the size and composition of equity and borrowings.

REAL-WORLD VIEW 8.5 (*continued*)

Crucially, IAS 7 allows two options for the reporting of operating activities:

- Direct method: major classes of gross cash receipts and payments are disclosed.
- Indirect method: profit and loss adjusted for the effects of non-cash transactions, any deferrals/accruals of operating cashflows and any income and expense items associated with investing or financing cashflows.

The operating section of a bank's cashflow statement is more complex than that of a non-financial firm. A bank's core services – taking in deposits and other funds and using those funds to make loans and investments – are themselves cashflows. These are also captured in the operating segment as operating asset and liability flows. In broad terms, a bank's operating cashflow is therefore made up of two main components:

- The adjustment of profit (normally profit before tax) for non-cash items, tax paid, etc.
- The operating asset and liability flows – the asset-related movements in loans and investments, and liability-related movements in deposits and wholesale funding such as debt securities.

Despite their importance to understanding a bank's financial health, all the UK and Eurozone banks we surveyed were using the indirect method to report their operating asset and liability flows on a net basis. Yet in most cases, the net change can already be calculated or estimated, by comparing the value of the item (for example, loans and advances to customers) in the end period balance sheet with its value in the preceding period balance sheet. This leaves the cashflow statement communicating little new information.

Source: Paul Klumpes and Peter Welch, Call for Clarity, *Accountancy Magazine*, October 2009, pp. 34–5.

Tutorial Note: Cash equivalents are short-term, highly liquid assets such as one-day bonds.

Relationship between Cash and Profit

Cash and profit are fundamentally different. In essence, cash flow and profit are based on different principles. Cash flow is based on cash received and cash paid (see Figure 8.3). By contrast, profit is concerned with income earned and expenses incurred.

Figure 8.3 Cash Flow and Profit

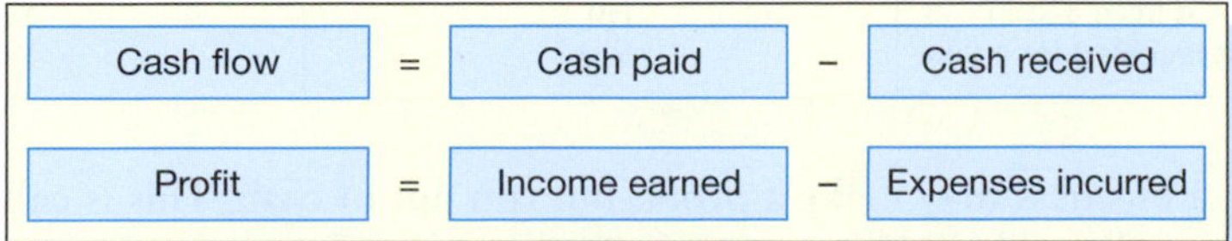

In a sense, the difference between the two merely results from the timing of the cash flows. For example, a telephone bill owing at the year end is included as an accrued expense in the income statement, but is not counted as a cash payment. However, next year the situation will reverse and there will be a cash outflow, but no expense.

An important difference between profit and cash flow is depreciation. Depreciation is a non-cash flow item. The related cash flows occur only when property, plant or equipment is bought or sold. Real-World View 8.6 demonstrates this.

REAL-WORLD VIEW 8.6

Cash Loss vs. Stated Loss

As always, there is the need to distinguish between a stated loss, per the profit and loss account [income statement] and a cash loss. One company the author handled was running at an apparently frightening loss of £25,000 per month, but on closer examination there was not too much to worry about. It had a £30,000 monthly depreciation provision. It was in reality producing a cash-positive profit of £5,000 per month. It had *years* of life before it. This gave all the time needed to get the operation right.

Source: B. Warnes (1984) *The Genghis Khan Guide to Business*, Osmosis Publications, London, p. 63.

Figure 8.4 shows how some common items are treated in the income statement and statement of cash flows. Some items, such as sale of goods for cash, appear in both. However, amounts owing, such as a telephone bill, appear only in the income statement. By contrast, money received from a loan only affects the statement of cash flows.

Figure 8.4 Demonstration of How Some Items Affect the Income Statement and Some Affect the Statement of Cash Flows

Transaction	*In Income Statement*	*In Statement of Cash Flows*
i. Sale of goods for cash	Yes	Yes
ii. Sale of goods on credit	Yes	No
iii. Telephone bill for year owing	Yes	No
iv. Telephone bill for year paid	Yes	Yes
v. Cash purchase of property, plant and equipment	No	Yes
vi. Profit on sale of property, plant and equipment	Yes	No
vii. Cash from sale of property, plant and equipment	No	Yes
viii. Money received from a loan	No	Yes
ix. Bank interest received for a year	Yes	Yes

Sometimes, a business may make a profit, but run out of cash. This is called overtrading and happens especially when a business starts trading.

PAUSE FOR THOUGHT 8.3

Overtrading, Cash Flow vs. Profit

A company, Bigger is Better, doubles its revenue every month.

Month	1	2	3	4
	£000	£000	£000	£000
Revenue	10	20	40	80
Purchases	(8)	(16)	(32)	(64)
Profit	2	4	8	16

It pays its purchases at once, but has to wait two months for its customers to pay for the revenue. The bank, which has loaned £10,000, will close down the business if it is owed £50,000. What happens?

Month	1	2	3	4
	£000	£000	£000	£000
Cash at bank	10	2	(14)	(36)
Cash in	–	–	10	20
Cash out	(8)	(16)	(32)	(64)
Cash at bank	2	(14)	(36)	(80)

The result: Bye-bye, Bigger is Better. Even though the business is trading profitably, it has run out of cash. This is because the first cash is received in month 3, but the cash outflows start at once.

Preparation of Statement of Cash Flows

In this section, we present the two methods of preparing a statement of cash flows (the direct and indirect methods). In Figure 8.5 and Appendix 2, a statement of cash flows is prepared for a sole trader using the **direct method**, which classifies *operating* cash flows by function or type of activity (e.g., receipts from customers). In Figure 8.5 the statement of cash flows is prepared using IFRS while Appendix 8.2 illustrates UK GAAP. In essence, this resembles the statement of cash flows for Gavin Stevens in Figure 8.1. We assume a bank has requested a statement of cash flows and that it is possible to extract the figures directly from the company's accounting records. Figure 8.6 then compares the direct and indirect methods of preparing the statement of cash flows. In Figure 8.7 we then look at some of the adjustments made to profit to arrive at cash flow. This is followed with an illustrative example in Figure 8.8, Collette Ash. We then present the statement of cash flows for a company using the more conventional **indirect method used by most companies** in Figure 8.9, following IFRS format. In Appendix 8.3, we prepare the statement of cash flows using UK GAAP. In this case, we derive the operating cash flow from the income statement and the statement of financial position.

In this book we focus on presentation using IFRS, but it worth briefly comparing the UK and IFRS cash flow statements. The primary difference between the two is in the main headings. In the most commonly used indirect method there are five main headings under which the cash flows are classified using UK GAAP, but only three using IFRS.

UK GAAP

1. Net cash flows from operating activities.
2. Returns on investment and servicing of finance.
3. Taxation.
4. Capital expenditure and financial investment.
5. Equity dividends paid.
6. Financing.

IFRS

1. Cash flows from operating activities.
2. Cash flows from investing activities.
3. Cash flows from financing activities.

In particular, under UK GAAP dividends and taxation are separately disclosed.

Figure 8.5 Preparation of a Sole Trader's Statement of Cash Flows Using the Direct Method Using IFRS Format

You have extracted the following aggregated cash figures from the accounting records of Richard Hussey, who runs a book shop. The bank has requested a statement of cash flows. Prepare Hussey's statement of cash flows for the year ended 31 December 2013.

	£		£
Cash receipts from customers	150,000	Interest received	850
Cash payments to suppliers	60,000	Interest paid	400
Cash payments to employees	30,000	Cash from sale of motor car	3,000
Cash expenses	850	Payment for new motor car	4,350
Loan received and paid into the bank	8,150		

Richard Hussey

Statement of Cash Flows for the Year Ended 31 December 2013

Cash Flows from Operating Activities	£	£
Receipts from customers	150,000	
Payments to suppliers	(60,000)	
Payments to employees	(30,000)	
Expenses	(850)	59,150
Cash Flows from Investing Activities		
Interest received	850	
Sale of motor car	3,000	
Purchase of motor car	(4,350)	(500)
Cash Flows from Financing Activities		
Interest paid	(400)	
Loan	8,150	7,750
Increase in Cash		66,400

Direct Method

This method of preparing statements of cash flows is relatively easy to understand. However, in practice it is used far less than the indirect method. It is made of functional flows such as payments to suppliers or employees. These are usually extracted from the cash book or bank account. Figure 8.5 demonstrates the direct method using IFRS format.

We used the headings in Figure 8.2 which relate to the presentation of the statement of cash flows using IFRS. We use this as the main presentational format for ease of understanding. However, Appendix 8.2 gives the traditional format using UK Accounting Standards. The **net cash inflow from operating activities** represents all the cash flows relating to trading activities (e.g., buying or selling goods). By contrast, **returns on investments and servicing of finance** deals with interest received or paid, resulting from money invested or money borrowed. **Capital expenditure and financial investment** are concerned with the cash spent on, or received from, buying or selling property, plant or equipment. Finally, **financing** represents a loan paid into the bank.

PAUSE FOR THOUGHT 8.4

Profit and Positive Cash Flow

If a company makes a profit, does this mean that it will have a positive cash flow?

No! Not necessarily. A fundamental point to grasp is that if a company makes a profit this means that its assets *will increase*, but this increase in assets *will not necessarily be in the form of cash*. Assets other than cash may increase (e.g., property, plant and equipment, inventory or trade receivables) or liabilities may decrease. This can be shown by a quick example. Noreen O. Cash has two assets: inventories £25,000 and cash £50,000. Noreen makes a profit of £25,000, but invests it all in inventories. We can, therefore, compare the two statements of financial position.

	Before	*After*		*Before*	*After*
	£	£		£	£
Inventories	25,000	50,000	Equity	75,000	75,000
Cash	50,000	50,000	Profit	–	25,000
	75,000	100,000		75,000	100,000

There is a profit, but it does not affect cash. The increase in profit is reflected in the increase in inventories.

From Richard Hussey's statement of cash flows it is clear that cash has increased by £66,400. However, the statement also clearly shows the separate components such as a positive operating cash flow of £59,150. By looking at the statement of cash flows, Richard Hussey can quickly gain an overview of where his cash has come from and where it has been spent. The principles underlying the direct method of preparation are similar to those used in the construction of a cash budget.

Indirect Method

The most common method of preparing the statement of cash flows is the indirect method. This method, which can be more difficult to understand than the direct method, has three steps.

- First, *we must adjust profit before taxation to arrive at operating profit.*
- Second, *we must reconcile operating profit to operating cash flow by adjusting for changes in working capital and for other non-cash flow items such as depreciation.* By adjusting the operating profit to arrive at operating cash flow, we effectively bypass the bank account. Instead of directly totalling all the operating cash flows from the bank account, we work indirectly from the figures in the income statement and the opening and closing statements of financial position. *This reconciliation is done either as a separate calculation or in the statement of cash flows.*
- Third, *we can prepare the statement of cash flows.*

These steps are outlined in Figure 8.6 and the direct and indirect methods are compared. We will now look in more detail at the first two steps. Figure 8.7 summarises these adjustments and then Figure 8.8, Collette Ash, illustrates them. We then work through a full example, Any Company plc, in Figure 8.9. Figure 8.9 uses the IFRS format while in Appendix 8.3 we present the statement of cash flows using the more traditional UK format. Essentially, the method of preparation in the two figures is identical, but the presentation differs.

Figure 8.6 Comparison of Direct and Indirect Methods of Preparing Statement of Cash Flows

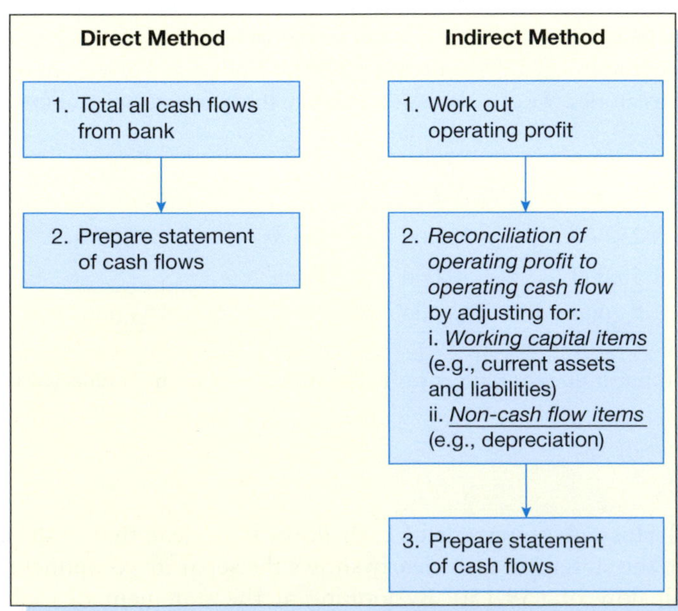

1. Calculation of Operating Profit by Adjusting Profit before Taxation

In the indirect method, we need to calculate operating cash flow (i.e., net cash flow from operating activities). To do this we need to first calculate operating profit so that we can reconcile operating profit to operating cash flow. Operating profit is calculated by *adjusting profit before taxation to operating profit*. The profit before tax figure must be adjusted by adding interest paid and deducting interest received. (Strictly, these items are called interest payable and interest receivable; for simplicity we call them in this section interest paid and interest received: see Figure 6.5 on page 149 for an explanation of this.) These items can, under IAS 7, be treated as either (i) operating activities or (ii) interest paid as a financing activity and interest received as an investing activity. In either case they must be separately disclosed. In this book I treat them as financing and investing flows respectively, as that seems most logical. Thus, they will appear in our statement of cash flows as follows: interest received under cash flows from investing activities and interest paid under cash flows from financing activities. For listed companies, this adjustment is recorded under the heading *Cash Flows from Operating Activities*.

2. Reconciliation of Operating Profit to Operating Cash Flow

It is possible to identify two main types of adjustment needed to adjust operating profit to operating cash flow: (i) *working capital adjustments* and (ii) *non-cash flow items*, such as depreciation. It is important to emphasise that we need to consider operating cash flow and operating profit. The term 'operating' is used in accounting broadly to mean trading activities such as buying or selling goods or services. For listed companies, we start from profit before taxation not operating profit. Taxation paid is also deducted under *Cash Flow from Operating Activities*.

(i) Working Capital Adjustments Effectively, working capital adjustments represent short-term timing adjustments between the income statement and statement of cash flows. They principally concern inventory, trade receivables and trade payables. Essentially, an increase in inventory, trade receivables or prepayments (or a decrease in trade payables or accruals) means less cash flowing into a business for the current year. For example, when trade receivables increase there is a delay in receiving the money. There is thus less money in the bank. By contrast, a decrease in inventory, trade receivables or prepayments (or an increase in trade payables or accruals) will mean more cash flowing into the business.

(ii) Non-Cash Flow Items Two major items are depreciation and profit or loss on the sale of property, plant and equipment. These two items are recorded in the income statement, but not in the statement of cash flows. **Depreciation** (which has reduced profit) must be **added back to profit** to arrive at cash flow. By contrast, **profit on sale of property, plant and equipment** (which has increased profit) must be **deducted from profit** to arrive at *Operating Cash Flow*. Cash actually spent on purchasing property, plant and equipment or received from selling property, plant and equipment is included for listed companies under *Cash Flows from Investing Activities* in the statement of cash flows.

Figure 8.7 provides examples of both working capital and non-cash flow adjustments.

Figure 8.7 Summary of Adjustments Made to Profit to Arrive at Cash Flow

Item	*Effect on Cash Flow*	*Adjustment*
i. Working Capital (Source: **Comparison of opening and closing statements of financial position)** Increase in inventories Increase in trade receivables Increase in prepayments Decrease in trade payables Decrease in accruals	All of these **reduce** cash flow as more 'cash' is tied up in working capital (i.e., current assets less current liabilities)	**Deduct from profit** to arrive at cash flow
Decrease in inventories Decrease in trade receivables Decrease in prepayments Increase in trade payables Increase in accruals	All of these **increase** cash flow as less cash is tied up in working capital (i.e., current assets less current liabilities)	**Add to profit** to arrive at cash flow
ii. Non-Cash Flow Items (Source: **Income statement)** Depreciation Loss on sale of property, plant and equipment	Have **no effect** on cash flow, but were deducted from profit as expenses	**Add back to profit** to arrive at cash flow
Profit on sale of property, plant and equipment	Has **no effect** on cash flow, but increased profit as other income	**Deduct from profit** to arrive at cash flow

Figure 8.8, Collette Ash, on the next page now demonstrates the first two steps (calculation of operating profit and reconciliation of operating profit to operating cash flow). *The increases or decreases in working capital items are established by comparing the individual current assets and current liabilities in the opening and closing statement of financial position*. By contrast, the *non-cash flow items (depreciation and profit on sale of property, plant and equipment) are taken from the income statement.*

In straightforward cases this can be done in the statement of cash flows itself. Otherwise, as here, it can be done separately and the net figure, in this case £100,950, is taken to the statement of cash flows.

Figure 8.8 Illustration of Profit Adjustments

Collette Ash has the following extracts from her business income statement for the year ending 31 December 2013 and the statements of financial position as at 31 December 2012 and 31 December 2013. Reconcile her operating profit to her operating statement of cash flows.

Income Statement	£	**Statements of Financial Position**	31.12.2012	31.12.2013
Profit before Taxation	95,000	**Current Assets**	£	£
After deducting:		Inventory	4,000	5,300
Depreciation	3,000	Trade receivables	3,250	3,000
Interest paid	10,000	Prepayments	350	300
After adding:		Cash	6,300	10,500
Profit from sale of property, plant and equipment	1,000	**Current Liabilities**	(1,850)	(1,750)
	5,000	Trade payables	(650)	(700)
Interest received		Accruals		

i. Calculation of Operating Profit

Before reconciling operating profit to operating cash flow, we must adjust our profit before taxation for interest paid and interest received, which are financing and investment rather than operating items. As explained above they can both be treated as either operating activities **or** interest paid as a financing activity and interest received as an investing activity. In this book I treat them as financing and investing flows respectively. Interest paid has already been deducted in calculating profit before taxation and interest received has already been credited to profit. We must reverse these entries. We, therefore, have:

	£
Profit before Taxation	95,000
Add Interest paid	10,000
Less Interest received	(5,000)
Operating Profit	100,000

ii. Reconciliation of Operating Profit to Operating Cash Flow

We are now in a position to adjust the operating cash flow for all changes in working capital and for all non-cash flow items (i.e., depreciation and profit on sale of property, plant and equipment).

C. Ash
Reconciliation of Operating Profit to Operating Cash Flow

	£	£
Operating Profit		100,000
Add:		
Decrease in trade receivables	250	
Decrease in prepayments	50	
Increase in accruals	50	
Depreciation	3,000	3,350
Deduct:		
Increase in inventory	(1,300)	
Decrease in trade payables	(100)	
Profit on sale of property, plant and equipment	(1,000)	(2,400)
Cash Flows from Operating Activities		100,950

The three-stage process is now illustrated in Figure 8.9, which shows the calculation of a statement of cash flows for Any Company plc. The income statement and statement of financial position are provided. This is done by following IFRS. A statement of cash flows prepared under UK GAAP is recorded as Appendix 8.2. Then steps 1–3 which follow show how a statement of cash flows would be prepared using the indirect method.

Figure 8.9 Preparation of the Statement of Cash Flows of Any Company plc using the Indirect Method Using IFRS

Any Company plc
Income Statement for the Year Ended 31 December 2013

	£000
Profit before Taxation (see note below)	150
Taxation	(30)
Profit for year	120

Note: This is after having added interest received of £15,000 to profit and having deducted interest paid of £8,000 from profit.

Statements of Financial Position

	31 December 2012		31 December 2013	
	£000	£000	£000	£000
ASSETS				
Non-current Assets				
Patents		30		50
Property, plant and equipment				
Cost	300		500	
Accumulated depreciation	(50)	250	(60)	440
Total non-current assets		280		490
Current Assets				
Inventories	50		40	
Trade receivables	20		45	
Prepayments	25		30	
Cash	45	140	40	155
Total Assets		420		645
LIABILITIES				
Current Liabilities				
Trade payables	(35)		(15)	
Accruals	(5)	(40)	(10)	(25)
Non-current Liabilities		(80)		(110)
Total Liabilities		(120)		(135)
Net Assets		300		510
EQUITY				
Capital and Reserves		£000		£000
Ordinary share capital		250		360
Retained earnings		50		150
Total Equity		300		510

Notes:

1. There are no disposals of property, plant and equipment. Therefore, the increases in property, plant and equipment between 2012 and 2013 are purchases of property, plant and equipment.
2. Taxation in the income statement equals the amounts actually paid. This will not always be so.
3. Dividends paid for the year were £20,000.

Figure 8.9 Preparation of the Statement of Cash Flows of Any Company plc using the Indirect Method Using IFRS (*continued*)

Any Company plc
Income Statement for the Year Ended 31 December 2013

Cash Flows from Operating Activities	£000	£000
Net Profit before Taxation		150
Add:		
Interest paid (1)	8	
Decrease in inventories (2)	10	
Increase in accruals (2)	5	
Depreciation (3)	10	33
Deduct:		
Interest received (1)	(15)	
Increase in trade receivables (2)	(25)	
Increase in prepayments (2)	(5)	
Decrease in trade payables (2)	(20)	
Taxation paid (4)	(30)	(95)
Net Cash from Operating Activities		88
Cash Flows from Investing Activities		
Patents purchased	(20)	
Plant and machinery purchased	(200)	
Interest received	15	
Net Cash used in Investing Activities		(205)
Cash flows from Financing Activities		
Increase in non-current liabilities	30	
Interest paid	(8)	
Increase in share capital	110	
Equity dividends paid	(20)	
Net Cash from Financing Activities		112
Net Decrease in Cash		(5)
		£000
Opening Cash and Cash Equivalent(5)		45
Decrease in cash		(5)
Closing Cash and Cash Equivalent(5)		40

Some explanatory help:

1. Interest paid and interest received are added back and deducted, respectively, under operating activities. Interest received is then treated as a cash flow from investing activities and interest paid as a cash flow from financing activities. Note that interest paid can also be treated as an operating flow. Also note the different treatment from a non-listed company prepared under UK GAAP where they are both recorded under Returns on Investments and Servicing of Finance.
2. These items are all movements in working capital taken as increase or decrease from the statement of financial position.
3. Depreciation is a non-cash flow item taken from increase in accumulated depreciation in the statement of financial position.
4. Taxation paid is recorded under operating activities not under *Taxation* as per a non-listed company using UK GAAP.
5. Cash and cash equivalents represents cash in hand, balances with banks as well as short-term investments.

An example of a statement of cash flows for AstraZeneca, a UK listed company, is given in Company Snapshot 8.1. There is also a statement of cash flows for Manchester United prepared under UK GAAP in Appendix 8.4. This has a very different format from the format of AstraZeneca that is prepared under IFRS.

COMPANY SNAPSHOT 8.1

Statement of Cash Flows for AstraZeneca, a Limited Company

Consolidated Statement of Cash Flows for the year ended 31 December

	Notes	2009 $m	2008 $m	2007 $m
Cash flows from operating activities				
Profit before tax		**10,807**	8,681	7,983
Finance income and expense	3	**736**	463	111
Depreciation, amortisation and impairment		**2,087**	2,620	1,856
Increase in trade and other receivables		**(256)**	(1,032)	(717)
Decrease in inventories		**6**	185	442
Increasel(decrease) in trade and other payables and provisions		**1,579**	637	(168)
Other non-cash movements		**(200)**	87	901
Cash generated from operations		**14,759**	11,641	10,408
Interest paid		**(639)**	(690)	(335)
Tax paid		**(2,381)**	(2,209)	(2,563)
Nat cash inflow from operating activities		**11,739**	8,742	7,510
Cash flows from investing activities				
Acquisitions of business operations	22	**–**	–	(14,891)
Movement in short term investments and fixed deposits		**(1,371)**	1	894
Purchase of property, plant and equipment		**(962)**	(1,095)	(1,130)
Disposal of property, plant and equipment		**138**	38	54
Purchase of intangible assets		**(624)**	(2,944)	(549)
Disposal of intangible assets		**269**	–	–
Purchase of non-current asset investments		**(31)**	(40)	(35)
Disposal of non current asset investments		**3**	32	421
Interest received		**113**	149	358

COMPANY SNAPSHOT 8.1 (*continued*)

		$m	$m	$m
Payments made by subsidiaries to non-controlling interests		(11)	(37)	(9)
Net cash outflow from investing activities		(2,476)	(3,896)	(14,887)
Nat cash inflow/outflow before financing activities		9,263	4,846	(7,377)
Cash flows from financing activities				
Proceeds from issue of share capital		135	159	218
Re-purchase of shares		–	(610)	(4,170)
Issue of loans		–	787	9,692
Repayment of loans		(650)	–	(1,165)
Dividends paid		(2,977)	(2,739)	(2,641)
Movement in short term borrowings		(137)	(3,959)	4,117
Nat cash (outflow)/inflow from financing activities		(3,629)	(6,362)	6,051
Net increase/(decrease) in cash and cash equivalents in the period		5,634	(1,516)	(1,326)
Cash and cash equivalents at beginning of the period		4,123	5,727	6,989
Exchange rate effects		71	(88)	64
Cash and cash equivalents at the end of the period	13	9,828	4,123	5,727

Source: AstraZeneca plc, *Annual Report and Form 20-F Information 2009*, p. 127.

All the adjusted figures, therefore, involved comparing the two statements of financial position or taking figures directly from the income statement. In Figures 8.8 and 8.9, the *taxation* in the income statement was *assumed to be the amounts paid*. This will not always be so. Where this is not the case, it is necessary to do some detective work to arrive at cash paid! This is illustrated for tax paid in Figure 8.10.

Sometimes there may be cases where a dividend has been declared, but not paid during the year. In this case, one would do a similar exercise. However, given the rarity of this, it is not considered here in detail.

Essentially, we find the total liability by adding the amount owing at the start of the year to the amount incurred during the year recorded in the income statement. If we then deduct the amount owing at the end of the year, we arrive at the amount paid.

Figure 8.10 Deducing Cash Paid for Tax – the Sherlock Holmes Approach

If we have only details of tax payable and the amount for the year, *we need to deduce* tax paid by a bit of detective work. For example, S. Holmes Ltd has the following information:

Income Statement (extracts)		**Statements of Financial Position** (extracts)		
			Opening	Closing
	£		£	£
Tax	9,000	Tax payable	6,500	7,500

How much did S. Holmes pay for taxation?

Effectively, we know the opening and closing amounts owing and the income statement expense. The amount paid is the balance figure, which is £8,000.

Opening liability	+	Income statement	−	Amount paid	=	Closing liability
£6,500	+	£9,000	−	£8,000	=	£7,500

Or for those who like 'T' accounts.

Tax account

	£		£
Amount paid	8,000	Opening liability	6,500
Closing liability	7,500	Income statement	9,000
	15,500		15,500

In Company Snapshot 8.2, J.D. Wetherspoon's 2010 statement of cash flows is presented. We can see that in 2010 there was a cash inflow from operating activities of £110.4 million. There was also a net investment in new pubs of £53.8 million (under cash flows from investing activities). Finally, Wetherspoon financed its operations mainly by bank loans of £87.6 million. Overall, Wetherspoon's cash increased by £2.5 million. Wetherspoon also reports its free cash flow (£71.3 million). Essentially, this is a company's cash flow from ongoing activities excluding financing. Cash flow statements can thus provide important insights into a business's inflows and outflows of cash. In Chapter 9, we cover the interpretation of the cash flow statement.

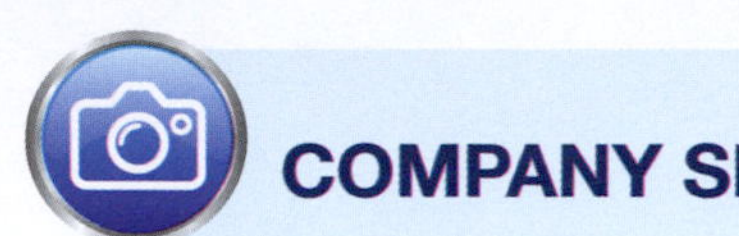

COMPANY SNAPSHOT 8.2

Statement of Cash Flows for J.D. Wetherspoon plc

J D Wetherspoon plc, company number: 1709784

	Notes	52 weeks ended 25 July 2010 £000	52 weeks ended 25 July 2010 £000	52 weeks ended 26 July 2009 £000	52 weeks ended 26 July 2009 £000
Cash flows from operating activities					
Cash generated from operations	8	**153,405**	153,405	171,850	171,850
Interest received		**9**	9	460	460
Interest paid		**(30,252)**	(30,252)	(35,317)	(35,317)
Corporation tax paid		**(21,617)**	(21,617)	(20,497)	(20,497)
Gaming machine VAT receipt		**14,941**		–	
Purchase of own shares for share-based payments		**(6,129)**	(6,129)	(6,003)	(6,003)
Net cash inflow from operating activities		**110,357**	95,416	110,493	110,493
Cash flows from investing activities					
Purchase of property, plant and equipment		**(21,778)**	(21,778)	(9,546)	(9,546)
Purchase of intangible assets		**(2,294)**	(2,294)	(1,453)	(1,453)
Proceeds on sale of property, plant and equipment		**170**		495	
Investment in new pubs and pub extensions		**(53,804)**		(36,899)	
Purchase of lease premiums		**(3,935)**		(931)	
Net cash outflow from investing activities		**(81,641)**	(24,072)	(48,334)	(10,999)
Cash flows from financing activities					
Equity dividends paid	10	**(26,174)**		(10,439)	
Proceeds from issue of ordinary shares		**523**		580	
Advances/(repayments) under bank loans	9	**87,586**		(44,051)	
Repayment of US private placement	9	**(86,742)**		–	
Advances under finance leases	9	**9,092**		–	
Finance costs on new loan	9	**(7,626)**		(208)	
Finance lease principal payments	9	**(2,898)**		(889)	
Net cash outflow from financing activities		**(26,239)**		(55,007)	
Net increase in cash and cash equivalents	9	**2,477**		7,152	
Opening cash and cash equivalents	17	**23,604**		16,452	
Closing cash and cash equivalents	17	**26,081**		23,604	
Free cash flow	7		**71,344**		99,494
Free cash flow per ordinary share	7		**51.3p**		71.7p

Source: J.D. Wetherspoon plc, *Annual Report and Accounts 2010*, p. 11.

Most companies comment on their cash flow in their annual reports. Sainsbury's, for example, summarises and comments on its cash flow activities in Company Snapshot 8.3.

COMPANY SNAPSHOT 8.3

Cash Flows from Operating Activities

Net debt and cash flow

Sainsbury's net debt as at 20 March 2010 was £1,549 million (March 2009: £1,671 million), a reduction of £122 million from the 2009 year-end position. The reduction was driven by the cash generated from the capital raised in June 2009 and strong operational cash flows, including another good working capital performance, offset by capital expenditure on the acceleration of the store development programme and outflows for taxation, interest and dividends. The resolution of a number of outstanding items contributed to a lower tax payment than in 2008/09, and interest payments benefited from lower interest rates on inflation linked debt as a result of a lower RPI than last year.

Sainsbury's expects year-end net debt to increase to around £1.9 billion in 2010/11, in line with its increased capital expenditure from the plan to deliver 15 per cent space growth in the two years to March 2011.

Summary cash flow statement for the 52 weeks to 20 March 2010	2009/10 £m	2008/09 £m
Operating cash flows before changes in workinq capital	**1,114**	1,039
Changes in working capital	**92**	167
Cash generated from operations	**1,206**	1,206
Net interest paid	**(96)**	(118)
Corporation tax paid	**(89)**	(160)
Cash flow before appropriations	**1,021**	928
Purchase of non-current assets	**(1,057)**	(994)
Investment in joint ventures	**(2)**	(291)
Disposal of non-current assets	**139**	390
Proceeds from issue of shares	**250**	15
Receipt of new debt	**123**	165
Net dividends paid	**(239)**	(215)
Increase/(decrease) in cash and cash equivalents	**235**	(2)
Increase in debt	**(115)**	(157)
IAS 32 and IAS 39 adjustments and other movements	**2**	(9)
Movement in net debt	**122**	(168)
Opening net debt	**(1,671)**	(1,503)
Closing net debt	**(1,549)**	(1,671)

COMPANY SNAPSHOT 8.3 (*continued*)

Working capital

Sainsbury's has continued to manage working capital closely and cash generated from operations includes a further year-on-year improvement in working capital of £92 million. This has been achieved through tight management of inventories, which are up less than two per cent on last year, and continued improvement of trade cash flows.

Source: J. Sainsbury plc, *Annual Report 2010*, p. 19. Reproduced by kind permission of Sainsbury's Supermarkets Ltd.

Bank Reconciliation Statements

A standard control measure carried out by most businesses at weekly or monthly intervals is the bank reconciliation statement. Put simply, this statement attempts to check that the company's bank account is correct by comparing it with the bank statement. There are several legitimate reasons why the bank account and the bank statement may differ. These are set out below:

1. Items entered in the bank account, but not yet entered into the bank statement, for example:
   (i) Cheques written by the company, but not yet received by the bank (i.e., not yet cashed).
   (ii) Cheques received by the company, but not yet received at the bank (i.e., not yet credited). Although cheques are becoming less important, they are still important for smaller businesses.
2. Items entered into the bank statement, but which by their nature do not appear in the bank account, for example:
   (i) Standing orders
   (ii) Direct debits
   (iii) Bank charges

A simple example for Woolley plc is given below.

Figure 8.11 Bank Reconciliation Statement

i. Bank Account for Woolley plc

Bank A/C

	£		£
1st January Bal b/f	3,500	1st January cheque paid 43001 Pike	450
2nd January cheque received Prior	200	2nd January cheque paid 43002 Helliar	250
3rd January cheque received Carnegie	600	3rd January cheque paid 43003 Richards	300
4th January cheque received Peters	300	4th January cheque paid 43004 Slack	400
5th January cheque received Jones	500	5th January cheque paid 43005 Okzan	300
6th January cheque received Khan	400	6th January cheque paid 43006 Shah	400
7th January cheque received Burritt	800	7th January cheque paid 43007 Mohamed	600
	6,300	7th January Bal c/f	3,600
			6,300

Figure 8.11 Bank Reconciliation Statement (*continued*)

ii. Bank Statement for Woolley plc

	Dr	Cr	Balance
			£
1st January Balance			3,500
Direct Debit	300		3,200
3rd January 43001	450		2,750
3rd January 43002	250		2,500
3rd January, Prior		200	2,700
4th January 43004	400		2,300
4th January, Peters		300	2,600
4th January 43005	300		2,300
6th January, Jones		500	2,800
7th January, Khan		400	3,200
Standing Order	500		2,700

We, therefore, need to reconcile our bank statement that shows £2,700 with the bank account balance of £3,600 as recorded in our books.

iii. Bank Reconciliation Statement for January

	£	£
Bank statement closing balance		2,700
Add back:		
Items on bank statement, but not in bank account		
Direct debit	300	
Standing order	500	800
		3,500
Deduct:		
Items on bank account but not on bank statement		
Cheques not yet debited:	£	
Richards 43003	300	
Shah 43006	400	
Mohamed 43007	600	(1,300)
		2,200
Cheques not yet credited:		
Carnegie	600	
Burritt	800	1,400
Bank account closing balance		3,600

Conclusion

Cash and cash flow are at the heart of all businesses. Cash flow is principally concerned with cash received and cash paid. It can thus be contrasted with profit which is income earned less expenses incurred. Cash is initially entered into the bank account or cash book. Companies usually derive the statement of cash flows from the income statement and statements of financial position, not the cash book. This is known as the indirect method of cash flow preparation. The statement of cash flows, after the income statement and the statement of financial position, is the third major financial statement. As well as preparing a statement of cash flows based on past cash flows, managers will constantly monitor current cash flows and forecast future cash flows. Cash is much harder to manipulate than profits. 'Accounting sleight of hand might shape profits whichever way a management team desires, but it is hard to deny that a cash balance is what it is. No more, no less' (E. Warner, *The Guardian*, 16 February 2002, p. 26).

Discussion Questions

Questions with numbers in blue have answers at the back of the book.

Q1 At the start of this chapter, it was stated that 'cash is king' and that it is relatively easy 'to manufacture profits, but virtually impossible to create cash'. Discuss this statement.

Q2 What is the relationship between profit and cash flow?

Q3 The direct method of preparing the statement of cash flows is the easiest to understand, but most companies use the indirect method. Why do you think this might be so?

Q4 Preparing a statement of cash flows using the indirect method is like being an accounting detective. Discuss this view.

Q5 State whether the following are true or false. If false, explain why.

(a) Depreciation and profit from sale of property, plant and equipment are both non-cash flow items and must be added back to operating profit to arrive at operating cash flow.

(b) Inventory, trade receivables and property, plant and equipment are all items of working capital.

(c) Decreases in current assets such as inventory, trade receivables and prepayments must be added back to profit to arrive at cash flow.

(d) We need to adjust profit before taxation for non-operating items (such as interest paid or received) to arrive at operating profit for non-listed companies.

(e) The indirect method of preparing the statement of cash flows is seldom used by large companies.

Numerical Questions

These questions are designed to gradually increase in difficulty. Questions with numbers in blue have answers at the back of the book. For consistency and ease of understanding, students should use the format required under International Reporting Standards for all questions whether they relate to sole traders, partnerships or companies.

Q1 Bingo has the following items in its accounts:

(a) Dividends payable
(b) Cash from loan
(c) Sale of goods on credit
(d) Purchase of goods for cash
(e) Cash purchase of property, plant and equipment
(f) Cash on sale of motor car
(g) Loan repaid
(h) Taxation payable
(i) Receipts from share capital issue
(j) Bank interest paid

Required: Are the above items recorded in the income statement, the statement of cash flows, or both? If these items appear in the statement of cash flows, state which heading would be most appropriate when using the direct method (e.g., net cash inflow from operating activities) under IFRS.

Q2 The cash flows below were extracted from the accounts of Peter Piper, a music shop owner.

	£		£
Loan repaid	25,000	Purchase of office equipment	15,000
Sale of property	25,000	Interest paid	350
Interest received	1,150	Payments to suppliers	175,000
Payments to employees	55,000	Expenses paid	10,000
Receipts from customers	250,000		

Required: Prepare a statement of cash flows using the **direct** method for the year ended 31 December 2013. Prepare a separate reconciliation statement from operating profit to operating cash flow.

Q3 The *cash flows* below were extracted from the accounts of Picasso and Partners, a painting and decorating business.

	£		£
Bank interest paid	1,000	Purchase of a building	88,000
Loan received	9,000	Sale of office furniture	2,300
Cash for sale of a motor car	4,000	Payment for a motor car	12,000
Interest received	300		

Required: Prepare a statement of cash flows under the **indirect** method for the year ended 31 December 2013. Prepare a separate reconciliation statement from operating profit to operating cash flow. You know that the operating profit was £111,000 with £75,000 of working capital adjustments to be deducted and £15,000 of non-cash adjustments to be added back to arrive at operating cash flow. The operating profit has already been adjusted for the interest paid and received (so do not adjust again!).

Q4 Diana Rink Ltd, a chain of off-licences, has the following extracts from the accounts.

Income Statement for 2013

	£
Operating profit	95,000
Depreciation for year	8,000
Profit on sale of property, plant and equipment	3,500

Statements of Financial Position as at 31 December

	2012	2013
	£	£
Current Assets		
Inventories	19,000	16,000
Trade receivables	10,000	11,150
Prepayments	5,000	3,500
Cash	10,000	3,250
Current Liabilities		
Trade payables	1,700	2,000
Accruals	750	1,000

Required: Prepare a statement which reconciles operating profit to operating cash flow.

Q5 Brian Ridge Ltd, a construction company, has extracted the following *cash flows* from its books as at 30 November 2013.

	£		£
Operating profit	25,000	Interest paid	500
Increase in inventories over year	3,500	Increase in non-current liabilities	4,600
Increase in trade receivables over year	1,300	Purchase of plant and machinery	18,350
Increase in trade payables over year	800	Share capital issued	3,200
		Dividends paid	550
Depreciation for year	6,000	Purchase of patents	1,650
Tax paid	23,500		
Interest received	3,000		

Required: Prepare a statement of cash flows using the indirect method. The operating profit has already been adjusted for the interest paid and received (so do not adjust again!). You should first prepare a reconciliation of operating profit to operating cash flow.

Q6 You have the following extracts from the income statement account and statement of financial position for Grow Hire Ltd, a transport company.

Grow Hire Ltd
Income Statement Year Ended 31 December 2013 (extracts)

	£000
Profit before Taxation (Note)	112,000
Taxation paid	(33,600)
Profit for year	78,400

Grow Hire Ltd
Statements of Financial Position as at 31 December 2012 and 31 December 2013

	2012		2013	
ASSETS	£000	£000	£000	£000
Non-Current Assets				
Patents		8,000		42,200
Property, plant and equipment				
Cost	144,000		164,000	
Accumulated depreciation	(28,000)	116,000	(44,000)	120,000
Total non-current assets		124,000		162,200

Q6 **Grow Hire** (*continued*)

Current Assets				
Inventory	112,000		110,000	
Trade receivables	18,000		11,000	
Cash	7,000	137,000	10,000	131,000
Total Assets		261,000		293,200
LIABILITIES				
Current Liabilities				
Trade payables	(45,000)		(20,000)	
Accruals	(4,000)	(49,000)	(5,000)	(25,000)
Non-Current Liabilities		(16,000)		(28,000)
Total Liabilities		(65,000)		(53,000)
Net Assets		196,000		240,200

Capital and Reserves	£000	£000
Share capital	177,000	178,600
Retained earnings	19,000	61,600
Total shareholders' funds	196,000	240,200

There were no sales of property, plant and equipment during the year.

Notes (in £000s):

1. Profit is after adding interest received £13,000 and deducting interest paid £6,500.
2. Dividends paid were £35,800.
3. There were no sales of property, plant and equipment during the year.

Required: Prepare a statement of cash flows using the indirect method for the year ended 31 December 2013.

Q7 You have the following information regarding taxation for Brain and Co., a software house:

Income Statement (Extract) From Year to 31 December 2013		**Statement of Financial Position (Extracts) as at 31 December**		
			2012	2013
	£		£	£
Profit before Taxation	106,508	**Current Liabilities**		
Taxation	(51,638)	Tax payable	50,320	65,873
Profit for year	54,870			

Required: Calculate tax paid.

Q8 A construction company, Expenso plc, has the following summaries from the income statement and statement of financial position for the year ended 30 September 2013:

	£000
Revenue	460,750
Cost of Sales	(328,123)
Gross Profit	132,627
Other Income	
Interest received	868
	133,495
Expenses includes interest paid £85,000	(123,478)
Profit before Taxation	10,017
Taxation	(3,005)
Profit for Year	7,012

Expenso plc
Statement of Financial Position as at 30 September

	2012		2013	
	£000	£000	£000	£000
ASSETS				
Non-current Assets				
Property, Plant and Equipment				
Land and buildings:				
Cost	20,000		26,000	
Accumulated depreciation	(7,000)		(8,000)	
Net book value	13,000		18,000	
Plant and machinery:				
Cost	25,000		30,000	
Accumulated depreciation	(8,500)		(10,000)	
Net book value	16,500	29,500	20,000	38,000
Intangible Assets				
Patents		4,000		4,500
Total non-current assets		33,500		42,500
Current Assets				
Inventories	2,800		6,400	
Trade receivables	3,200		4,500	
Cash	8,800	14,800	1,500	12,400
Total Assets		48,300		54,900

Q8 Expenso *(continued)*

	2012		2013	
	£000	£000	£000	£000
LIABILITIES				
Current Liabilities				
Trade payables	(4,600)		(5,000)	
Accruals	(400)		(350)	
Taxation	(4,200)		(3,200)	
	(9,200)		(8,550)	
Non-current Liabilities	(12,100)		(12,505)	
Total Liabilities		(21,300)		(21,055)
Net Assets		27,000		33,845
EQUITY				
Capital and Reserves		£000		£000
Share capital		18,630		22,568
Retained earnings		8,370		11,277
Total Equity		27,000		33,845

Notes (in £000s):

1. There were no sales of property, plant and equipment during the year.
2. The dividends paid during the year were £4,105. They have been deducted from retained earnings.

Required: Prepare a statement of cash flows using the indirect method for the year ended 30 September 2013; this should include the adjustment to net profit before taxation.

Q9 **Required:** From the bank account and bank statement for Petrel, who runs a small plumbing business, for March, draw up a bank reconciliation statement.

(a) **Bank Account for Petrel**

Bank A/C

	£		£
1 March Bal b/f	2,100	3 January cheque 28376 paid Lumsdon	350
3 March cheque received Bird	300	6 January cheque 28368 paid Aylett	250
14 March cheque received Burke	200	9 January cheque 28353 paid Jones	300
23 March cheque received Edwards	850	9 January cheque 28366 paid Roberts	500
24 March cheque received Lowe	350	12 January cheque 28360 paid Baggott	600
28 March cheque received Davies	450	15 January cheque 28361 paid Corden	750
30 March cheque received Howegate	650	18 January cheque 28350 paid Milligan	650
		31 January Bal c/f	1,500
	4,900		4,900

(b) **Bank Statement for Petrel**

	Dr	**Cr**	**Balance**
			£
1 January Balance			2,100
Direct Debit	360		1,740
5 March 28376	350		1,390
10 March 28368	250		1,140
11 March Bird		300	1,440
12 March 28353	300		1,140
23 March Edwards		850	1,990
26 March 28366	500		1,490
30 March Lowe		350	1,840
30 March Davies		450	2,290
Standing Order	600		1,690

Appendix 8.1: Main Headings for the Cash Flow Statement (Statement of Cash Flows) for Sole Traders, Partnerships and some Non-Listed Companies under UK GAAP

A Sole Trader's, Partnership's and Non-Listed Company's	Simplified Meaning	Examples of Inflows	Examples of Outflows
Net Cash Flows from Operating Activities[1]	Cash flows from the normal trading activities of a business	i. Cash for sale of goods	i. Payments for purchases of goods ii. Expenses paid
Returns on Investments and Servicing of Finance	Cash received from investments or paid on loans	i. Interest received ii. Dividends received	i. Interest paid
Taxation	Cash paid to Government for taxation	i. Taxation refunds	i. Taxation paid
Capital Expenditure and Financial Investment	Cash flows relating to the purchase and sale of: i. property, plant and equipment ii. investments	i. Receipts for sale of property, plant and equipment e.g., motor vehicles ii. Sale of investments	i. Payments for property, plant and equipment e.g., motor vehicles ii. Purchase of investments
Acquisitions and Disposals[2]	Cash flows arising from the purchase or sale of other companies	i. Cash paid to buy another company	i. Cash received for sale of another company
Equity Dividends Paid	Dividends companies pay to shareholders	None	Dividends paid
Management of Liquid Resources[3]	Current asset investments readily turned into cash	Cash withdrawn from 7-day deposit account	Cash paid into a 7-day deposit account
Financing	Cash flows relating to the issuing or buying back of shares or loan capital	Cash received from the issue of: i. shares ii. loans	Cash paid to buy back: i. shares ii. loans

Notes:

1. Where cash flow is positive we use the term net cash inflow. Where it is negative we use net cash outflow.
2. This item mainly applies to groups of companies. They are outside the scope of this chapter.
3. For simplification, this item is not incorporated into any of the examples.

Appendix 8.2: Preparation of a Sole Trader's Cash Flow Statement Using the Direct Method Using UK Format

You have extracted the following aggregated cash figures from the accounting records of Richard Hussey, who runs a book shop. The bank has requested a cash flow statement. Prepare Hussey's cash flow statement for year ended 31 December 2013.

	£		£
Cash receipts from customers	150,000	Interest received	850
Cash payments to suppliers	60,000	Interest paid	400
Cash payments to employees	30,000	Cash from sale of motor car	3,000
Cash expenses	850	Payment for new motor car	4,350
Loan received and paid into the bank	8,150		

Richard Hussey
Cash Flow Statement Year Ended 31 December 2013

	£	£
Net Cash Inflow from Operating Activities		
Receipts from customers	150,000	
Payments to suppliers	(60,000)	
Payments to employees	(30,000)	
Expenses	(850)	59,150
Returns on Investments and Servicing of Finance		
Interest received	850	
Interest paid	(400)	450
Capital Expenditure and Financial Investment		
Sale of motor car	3,000	
Purchase of motor car	(4,350)	(1,350)
Financing		
Loan	8,150	8,150
Increase in Cash		66,400

Appendix 8.3: Preparation of the Cash Flow Statement of Any Company Ltd using the Indirect Method Using UK GAAP

To ease understanding, we use IFRS terminology rather than that permitted under UK GAAP.

	2013
	£000
Profit before Taxation (see note below)	150
Taxation	(30)
Profit for year	120

Note:
This is after having added interest received of £15,000 to profit and having deducted interest paid of £8,000 from profit.

Statements of Financial Position

	31 December 2012		31 December 2013	
	£000	£000	£000	£000
ASSETS				
Non-current Assets				
Patents		30		50
Property, Plant and Equipment				
Cost	300		500	
Accumulated depreciation	(50)	250	(60)	440
Total non-current assets		280		490
Current Assets				
Inventories	50		40	
Trade receivables	20		45	
Prepayments	25		30	
Cash	45	140	40	155
Total Assets		420		645
LIABILITIES				
Current Liabilities				
Trade payables	(35)		(15)	
Accruals	(5)	(40)	(10)	(25)
Non-current Liabilities		(80)		(110)
Total Liabilities		(120)		(135)
Net assets		300		510

Appendix 8.3 Preparation of the Cash Flow Statement of Any Company Ltd using the Indirect Method Using UK GAAP (*continued*)

EQUITY		
Capital and Reserves	£000	£000
Ordinary share capital	250	360
Retained earnings	50	150
Total Equity	300	510

Notes:

1. There are no disposals of property, plant and equipment. Therefore, the increase in property, plant and equipment between 2012 and 2013 are purchases of property, plant and equipment.
2. Taxation in the income statement equals the amounts actually paid. This will not always be so.
3. Dividends paid for the year were £20,000.

Step 1: Calculation of Operating Profit

We need first to adjust net profit before taxation (£150,000) taken from profit and loss account, by adding back interest paid (£8,000) and deducting interest received (£15,000). These items are investment not operating flows. This is because we wish to determine operating or trading profit. Thus:

	£000
Net Profit before Taxation	150
Add Interest paid	8
Deduct Interest received	(15)
Operating profit	143

Step 2: Reconciliation of Operating Profit to Operating Cash Flow

This involves taking the company's operating profit and then adjusting for:

(i) Movement in working capital (e.g., increase or decrease in inventory, trade receivables, prepayments, trade payables and accruals).

(ii) Non-cash flow items such as depreciation, and profit or loss on sale of property, plant and equipment.

	£000	£000
Operating Profit		143
Add		
Decrease in inventories (1)	10	
Increase in accruals (1)	5	
Depreciation (2)	10	25
Deduct:		
Increase in trade receivables (1)	(25)	
Increase in prepayments (1)	(5)	
Decrease in trade payables (1)	(20)	(50)
Net Cash Inflow from Operating Activities		118

(1) Represents increases, or decreases, in the current assets and current liabilities sections between the two statements of financial position (i.e., movements in working capital).

(2) Difference in accumulated depreciation in the two statements of financial position represents depreciation for year (i.e., represents a non-cash flow item).

Appendix 8.3 Preparation of the Cash Flow Statement of Any Company Ltd using the Indirect Method Using UK GAAP (*continued*)

Step 3: Cash Flow Statement year ended 31 December

This involves deducing the relevant figures in the cash flow statement by using the existing figures from the income statement and the opening and closing statements of financial position. We start from net cash inflow calculated in Step 2.

	£000	£000
Net Cash Inflow from Operating Activities		
(see above)		118
Returns on Investments and Servicing of Finance		
Interest received (1)	15	
Interest paid (1)	(8)	7
Taxation		
Taxation paid (1)	(30)	(30)
Capital Expenditure and Financial Investment		
Patents purchased (2)	(20)	
Property, plant and equipment purchased (2)	(200)	(220)
Equity Dividends Paid (1)	(20)	(20)
Financing		
Increase in non-current liabilities (2)	30	
Increase in share capital (2)	110	140
Decrease in Cash (2)		(5)
		£000

	£000
Opening Cash	45
Decrease in cash	(5)
Closing Cash	40

Notes:

1. Figure from income statement.
2. Represents increase or decrease from statement of financial position.

Some explanatory help:

1. Operating profit is adjusted for interest paid and interest received, then both are included under returns on investments and servicing of finance. In a listed company under IFRS we have included interest paid under financing flows and interest received under investing flows.
2. There are six headings recorded here rather than three using IFRS.
3. Depreciation is a non-cash flow item.
4. Taxation paid is recorded under taxation not under operating activities as under IFRS.

Appendix 8.4: Example of Statement of Cash Flows (Cash Flow Statement) Using UK GAAP (Manchester United Ltd)

Manchester United Limited
Consolidated cash flow statement

	Note	Year ended 30 June 2009		Year ended 30 June 2008	
		£000	£000	£000	£000
Net cash inflow from operating activities			**112,133**		94,629
Returns on investments and servicing of finance					
Interest received		**1,259**		1,011	
Interest paid		**(1,186)**		(471)	
Net cash inflow from returns on investments and servicing of finance			**73**		540
Taxation received/(paid)			**236**		(205)
Capital expenditure and financial investment					
Proceeds from sale of players' registrations		**99,180**		19,301	
Purchase of players' registrations		**(55,220)**		(45,751)	
Proceeds from sale of tangible fixed assets		**28**		183	
Purchase of tangible fixed assets		**(3,810)**		(16,754)	
Net cash inflow/(outflow) from capital expenditure and financial investment			**40,178**		(43,021)
Acquisitions and disposals					
Purchase of shares in subsidiary undertaking		—		(2,615)	
Net cash acquired with subsidiary undertaking		—		113	
Proceeds from sale of investment in associated company		—		1,581	
Net cash outflow from acquisitions and disposals			—		(921)

Appendix 8.4 Example of Statement of Cash Flows (Cash Flow Statement) Using UK GAAP for Manchester United (*continued*)

		£000	£000	£000	£000
Cash inflow before use of liquid resources and financing			**152,620**		51,022
Financing					
Increase in borrowings		**25,000**		8,000	
Repayment of borrowings		**(25,215)**		—	
Purchase of loan stock		**—**		(750)	
Loans to parent company		**(51,620)**		(70,656)	
Net cash outflow from financing			**(51,835)**		(63,406)
Increase/(decrease) in cash in the year	23		**100,785**		(12,384)

Source: Manchester United Ltd, *Annual Report and Financial Statements for the year end 30 June 2009*, p. 13.

Go online to discover the extra features for this chapter at **www.wiley.com/college/jones**

Chapter 9

Interpretation of accounts

'More money has been lost reaching for yield than at the point of a gun.'

Raymond Revoe Jr, *Fortune,* 18 April 1994, *Wiley Book of Business Quotations* (1998), p. 192.

Learning Outcomes

After completing this chapter you should be able to:

- Explain the nature of accounting ratios.
- Appreciate the importance of the main accounting ratios.
- Calculate the main accounting ratios and explain their significance.
- Understand the limitations of ratio analysis.

Go online to discover the extra features for this chapter at **www.wiley.com/college/jones**

Chapter Summary

- Ratio analysis is a method of evaluating the financial information presented in accounts.
- Ratio analysis is performed after the bookkeeping and preparation of final accounts.
- There are six main types of ratio: profitability, efficiency, liquidity, gearing, cash flow and investment.
- Three important profitability ratios are return on capital employed (ROCE), gross profit ratio and net profit ratio.
- Four important efficiency ratios are trade receivables collection period, trade payables collection period, inventory turnover ratio and asset turnover ratio.
- Two important liquidity ratios are the current ratio and the quick ratio.
- Five important investment ratios are dividend yield, dividend cover, earnings per share (EPS), price earnings ratio and interest cover.
- Ratios can be viewed collectively using Z scores or pictics.
- For some predominately non-profit oriented businesses, it is appropriate to use non-standard ratios, such as performance indicators.
- Four limitations of ratios are that they must be used in context, the absolute size of the business must be considered, ratios must be calculated on a consistent and comparable basis and international comparisons must be made with care.

Introduction

The interpretation of accounts is the key to any in-depth understanding of an organisation's performance. Interpretation is basically when users evaluate the financial information, principally from the income statement and statement of financial position, so as to make judgements about issues such as profitability, efficiency, liquidity, gearing (i.e., amount of indebtedness), cash flow, and success of financial investment. The analysis is usually performed by using certain 'ratios' which take the raw accounting figures and turn them into simple indices. The aim is to try to measure and capture an organisation's performance using these ratios. This is often easier said than done!

Context

The interpretation of accounts (or ratio analysis) is carried out after the initial bookkeeping and preparation of the accounts. In other words, the transactions have been recorded in the books of account using double-entry bookkeeping and then the financial statements have been drawn up (see Figure 9.1). For this reason, the interpretation of accounts is often known as financial statement analysis. The financial statements which form the

Figure 9.1 Main Stages in Accounting Process

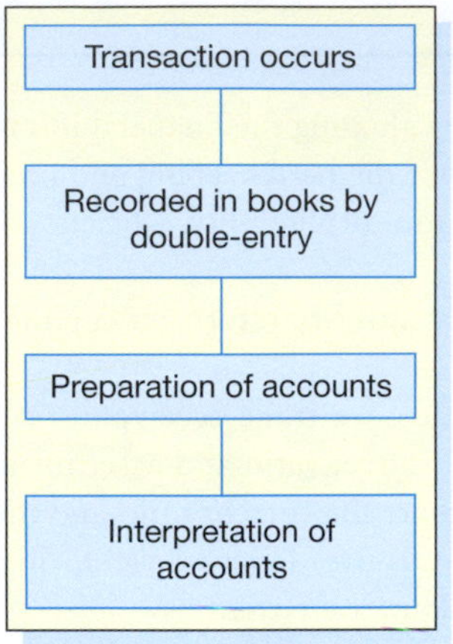

basis for ratio analysis are principally the income statement and the statement of financial position.

Overview

Two useful techniques, when interpreting a set of accounts, are (i) vertical and horizontal analysis and (ii) ratio analysis. Vertical and horizontal analysis involves comparing key figures in the financial statements. In vertical analysis, key figures (such as revenue in the income statement and total net assets in the statement of financial position) are set to 100%. Other items are then expressed as a percentage of 100. In horizontal analysis, the company's income statement and statement of financial position figures are compared across years. We return to vertical and horizontal analysis later in the chapter. For now, we focus on ratio analysis.

Broadly, ratio analysis can be divided into six major areas: profitability, efficiency, liquidity, gearing, cash flow and investment. The principal features are represented diagrammatically in Figure 9.3, but set out in more detail in Figure 9.2 on the following page. These ratios are then discussed later on in this chapter.

It is important to appreciate that there are potentially many different ratios. The actual ratios used will depend on the nature of the business and the individual preferences of users. The interpretation of accounts and the choice of ratios are thus inherently subjective. The ratios in Figure 9.2 have been chosen because generally they are appropriate for most businesses and are commonly used.

The 16 ratios, therefore, cover six main areas. Each of the above ratios can yield many more; for example, the gross profit ratio in Figure 9.2 is currently divided by revenue. However, gross profit per employee (divide by number of employees) or gross profit per share (divide by number of shares) are also possible. The fun and frustration of ratio analysis is that there are no fixed rules. In the UK, none of the ratios, except for earnings per share, is a regulatory requirement.

Figure 9.2 Principal Features of the Main Areas of the Interpretation of Accounts

Main Area	*Main Source of Ratios*	*Main Ratios*	*Overview Definition*
1. Profitability	Mainly derived from income statement	1. Return on capital employed (ROCE)	Profit before tax and loan interest / Average capital employed
		2. Gross profit ratio	Gross profit / Revenue
		3. Net profit ratio	Net profit before tax / Revenue
2. Efficiency	Mixture of income statement and statement of financial position	1. Trade receivables collection period	Average trade receivables / Credit sales
		2. Trade payables collection period	Average trade payables / Credit purchases
		3. Inventory turnover ratio	Cost of sales / Average inventories
		4. Asset turnover ratio	Revenue / Average total assets
3. Liquidity	Mainly from statement of financial position	1. Current ratio	Current assets / Current liabilities
		2. Quick ratio	Current assets–inventories / Current liabilities
4. Gearing	Mainly from statement of financial position	1. Gearing ratio	Long-term borrowing / Total long-term capital
5. Cash flow	Statement of cash flows	1. Cash flow ratio	Total cash inflows / Total cash outflows
6. Investment	Mainly share price and income statement information	1. Dividend yield	Dividend per ordinary share / Share price
		2. Dividend cover	Profit after tax and preference shares / Ordinary dividends
		3. Earnings per share	Profit after tax and preference dividends / Number of ordinary shares
		4. Price/earnings ratio	Share price / Earnings per share
		5. Interest cover	Profit before tax and loan interest / Loan interest

Figure 9.3 Main Ratios

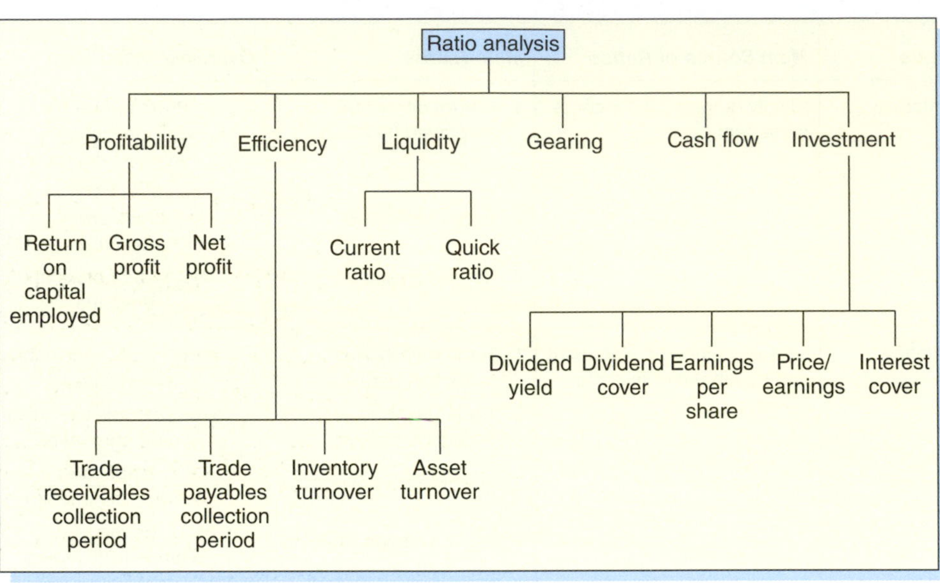

Importance of Ratios

Once the managers have prepared the accounts, then many other groups, such as investment analysts, will wish to comment on them. This is expressed in Soundbite 9.1. Different users will be interested in different ratios. For example, shareholders are primarily interested in investment ratios that measure the performance of their shares. By contrast, lenders may be interested primarily in liquidity (i.e., can the company repay its loan?). Ratios are important for three main reasons. First, they provide a quick and easily digestible snapshot of an organisation's achievements. It is much easier to glance at a set of ratios and draw conclusions from them than plough through the often quite complex financial statements. Second, ratios provide a good yardstick by which it is possible to compare one company with another (i.e., inter-firm comparisons) or to compare the same company over time (intra-firm comparisons). Third, ratio analysis takes account of size. One company may make more absolute profit than another. At first glance, it may, therefore, seem to be doing better than its competitor. However, if absolute size is taken into account, it may in fact be performing less well.

SOUNDBITE 9.1

'Captains of industry change things. We merely comment on them. Somebody has to bring the news of the relief of Mafeking.'

Angus Phaure, August, *County Natwest Business*, October 1990

Source: The Book of Business Quotations (1991), p. 13.

PAUSE FOR THOUGHT 9.1

Ratios and Size

Two companies, David and Goliath, have net profits of £1 million and £100 million. Is it obvious that Goliath is doing better than David?

No! We need to take into account the size of the two businesses. David may be doing worse, but then again . . . Imagine that David's revenue was £5 million, while Goliath's revenue was £5,000 million. Then, in £ millions,

	David	Goliath
$\frac{\text{Net profit}}{\text{Revenue}}$	$\frac{1}{5} = 20\%$	$\frac{100}{5,000} = 2\%$

Suddenly, Goliath's performance does not look so impressive. Size means everything when analysing ratios.

Closer Look at Main Ratios

It is now time to look in more depth at the main categories of ratio and at individual ratios. The ratios are mainly derived from the accounts of John Brown Plc. Although John Brown is a limited company, many of the ratios are also potentially usable for partnerships or sole traders. John Brown's financial statements are given at the back of this chapter as Appendix 9.1. They have been prepared for internal use and thus have more detail than in published accounts.

Some ratios (return on capital employed, trade receivables and trade payables collection period, inventory turnover and asset turnover) use average figures from two years' accounts. In practice, two years' figures are not always available. In this case, as for John Brown, the closing figures are used on their own. When this is done, then any conclusions must be drawn cautiously. In order to place the interpretation of key ratios in context, I have, wherever the information was available, referred to figures calculated from the UK's top publicly quoted companies. As there was no one authoritative up-to-date source I have used three main sources. First, information collected from Fame and Extel, two corporate databases, in July 2005. Second, where these sources were not available I used information from Fame and Extel November 2011. Third, I have used data from Jones and Finley (2011), which was based on a widespread sample of EU and Australian companies using IFRS. This article ('Have IFRS Made a Difference to Intra-country Financial Reporting Diversity?') was published in *The British Accounting Review*. The reader should be aware, however, that the way in which these sources calculate ratios may differ from the exact ratios in the book; they should thus be seen as guidelines rather than definitive figures.

Profitability Ratios

The profitability ratios seek to establish how profitably a business is operating. Profit is a key measure of business success and, therefore, these ratios are keenly watched by both internal users, such as management, and external users, such as shareholders. There are three main profitability ratios (return on capital employed, gross profit ratio and net profit ratio). The figures used are from John Brown Plc (see Appendix 9.1).

(i) Return on Capital Employed

This ratio considers how effectively a company uses its capital employed. It compares net profit to capital employed. A problem with this ratio is that different companies often use different versions of capital employed. At its narrowest, a company's capital employed is ordinary share capital and reserves. At its widest, it might equal ordinary share capital and reserves, preference shares, long-term loans (i.e., debentures) and current liabilities. Different definitions of capital employed necessitate different definitions of profits.

The most common definition measures *profit before interest and tax* against *long-term financing* (i.e., ordinary share capital and reserves, preference share capital and non-current liabilities). Therefore, for John Brown we have:

$$\frac{\text{Profit before tax and loan interest}}{\text{Long-term capital (ordinary share capital and reserves, preference share capital and long-term loans)}} = \frac{50 + 10}{150 + 65 + 50 + 70} = \frac{60}{335} = 17.9\%$$

Essentially, the 17.9% indicates the return which the business earns on its capital. The key question is: could the capital be used anywhere else to gain a better return? In this example, with only one year's statement of financial position, we can only take one year's capital employed. If we have an opening and a closing statement of financial position, we can take the average capital employed over the two statements of financial position. As Real-World View 9.1 shows, this is a good return on capital, which has varied in recent years from 8.9% to 14.9%.

REAL-WORLD VIEW 9.1

Return on Capital Ratios

The return on capital varies with the economic cycle, for example, the *Investors Chronicle* in October 2011 states that:

'The latest official figures show that non-financial companies' net return on capital in the second quarter was 12.1%. Although this is below the pre-recession peak of 14.9%, it's well above the recessionary trough of 10.6%.'

In addition, it was pointed out that this is still higher than the 1990s where, for example, in 1992 it was 8.4%.

Source: The Paradox of Corporate Profits, Chris Dillow, *Investors Chronicle,* 14–20 October, 2011, p.12. Financial Times.

(ii) Gross Profit Ratio

The gross profit ratio (or gross profit divided by revenue) is a very useful ratio. It calculates the profit earned through trading. It is particularly useful in a business where inventory is purchased, marked up and then resold. For example, a retail business selling car batteries (see Figure 9.4) may well buy the batteries from the manufacturer and then add a fixed percentage as mark-up. In the case of pubs, it is traditional to mark up the purchase price of beer by 100% before reselling to customers.

In the case of John Brown, the gross profit is

$$\frac{\text{Gross profit}}{\text{Revenue}} = \frac{100}{200} = 50\%$$

This is the *direct* return that John Brown makes from buying and selling goods.

Figure 9.4 Gross Profit Illustration

Snowfield batteries buys car batteries from a wholesaler for £40 each and resells them for £60 each. What will Snowfield's gross profit be?

It will simply be revenue (£60) – purchases (£40) = gross profit (£20). Expressed as a percentage this is $\frac{20}{60} = 33.33\%$.

This is useful because Snowfield will know that its gross profit ratio should be 33.33%. If it is not, then there may be a problem, such as theft of inventory.

(iii) Net Profit Ratio

The net profit ratio (or net profit divided by revenue) is another key financial indicator. Whereas gross profit is calculated *before* taking administrative and distribution expenses into account, the net profit ratio is calculated *after* such expenses. Be careful with net profit as it is a tricky concept without a fixed meaning. Some people use it to mean profit before interest and tax, others to mean profit after interest but before tax, and still others profit after tax. For John Brown, some alternatives are:

$$\frac{\text{Net profit before taxation}}{\text{Revenue}} = \frac{50}{200} = 25\%$$

$$\frac{\text{Net profit after taxation}}{\text{Revenue}} = \frac{35}{200} = 17.5\%$$

The most popularly used alternative is net profit before taxation. This assumes that taxation is a factor that cannot be influenced by a business. This is the ratio which will be used from now on. As Real-World View 9.2 shows, most companies have traditionally, and still today, operate on net profit margins of less than 10%. Across the top UK 250 public limited companies this ratio was 11.4% in July 2005.

REAL-WORLD VIEW 9.2

Net Profit Margins

However as we have already said profits are only likely to be a comparatively minor factor in cash flow anyway. After-tax profits in even the most spectacularly successful company will rarely run at more than about 10% of annual turnover and most companies will operate at well below this figure, say, 7% or 8% before tax.

Source: B. Warnes (1984) *The Genghis Khan Guide to Business,* Osmosis Publications London, p. 66.

Efficiency Ratios

The efficiency ratios look at how effectively a business is operating. They are primarily concerned with the efficient use of assets. Four of the main efficiency ratios are explained below (trade receivables collection period, trade payables collection period, inventory turnover and asset turnover). The first two are related in that they seek to establish how long customers take to pay and how long it takes the business to pay its suppliers. The figures used are from John Brown (see Appendix 9.1 at the end of this chapter).

(i) Trade Receivables Collection Period (Debtors Collection Period)

This ratio seeks to measure how long customers take to pay their debts. Obviously, the quicker a business collects and banks the money, the better it is for the company. This ratio can be worked out on a monthly, weekly or daily basis. This book prefers the daily basis as it is the most accurate method. The calculation for John Brown follows:

$$\text{Daily basis} = \frac{\text{Average trade receivables}}{\text{Credit sales per day}} = \frac{40}{200/365} = 73 \text{ days}$$

It, therefore, takes 73 days for John Brown to collect its debts. It is important to note that 'credit' sales (i.e., not cash sales) are needed for this ratio to be fully effective. This information, although available internally in most organisations, may not be readily ascertainable from the published accounts. Normally, the average of opening and closing trade receivables is used to approximate average trade receivables. When this figure is not available (as in this case), we just use closing trade receivables. Across the top 250 UK plcs it took 52 days to collect money from trade receivables in July 2005.

(ii) Trade Payables Collection Period (Creditors Collection Period)

In many ways, this is the mirror image of the trade receivables collection period. It calculates how long it takes a business to pay its trade payables. The slower a business is to pay, the longer the business has the money in the bank! As with the trade receivables collection period, we can calculate this ratio either monthly, weekly or daily. Once more, we prefer the daily basis. This is calculated below for John Brown.

$$\text{Daily basis} = \frac{\text{Average trade payables}}{\text{Credit purchases per day}} = \frac{50}{100/365} = 183 \text{ days}$$

It is usually not possible to establish accurately the figure for credit purchases from the published accounts. In John Brown, cost of sales is used as the nearest equivalent to credit purchases (remember that cost of sales is opening inventory add purchases less closing inventory). However, it should be noted that if two years' accounts are available, we can deduce purchases as the following example shows for Bamber. Bamber has opening inventory £800, closing inventory £600 and cost of sales £1,400.

	£
Opening inventory	800
Plus purchases	1,200
	2,000
Less Closing inventory (from year 2)	(600)
Cost of sales	1,400

As with the trade receivables collection ratio, strictly we should use average trade payables for the year (i.e., normally, the average of opening and closing trade payables). If this is not available, as in this case, we use closing trade payables.

It is often important to compare the trade receivables and trade payables ratios. For John Brown, this is:

$$\frac{\text{Trade receivables collection period (in days)}}{\text{Trade payables collection period (in days)}} = \frac{73 \text{ days}}{183 \text{ days}} = 0.40$$

In other words John Brown collects its cash from trade receivables in 40% of the time that it takes to pay its trade payables. The management of working capital is effective. However, this is not necessarily a good thing as supplier goodwill may be lost.

PAUSE FOR THOUGHT 9.2

Trade Receivables and Trade Payables Collection Period

Businesses whose trade receivables collection periods are much less than their trade payables collection periods are managing their working capital well. Can you think of any businesses which might be well placed to do this?

Businesses which sell direct to customers, generally for cash, would be prime examples. Pubs and supermarkets operate on a cash basis, or with short-term credit (cheques or credit cards). Their trade receivables collection period is very low. However, they may well take their time to pay their suppliers. If they have a high turnover of goods, they may collect the money for their goods from customers before they have even paid their suppliers.

(iii) Inventory Turnover Ratio (Stock Turnover Ratio)

This ratio effectively measures the speed with which inventory moves through the business. This varies from business to business and product to product. For example, crisps and chocolate have a high inventory turnover, while diamond rings have a low inventory turnover. Strictly this ratio compares cost of sales to average inventories. Where this figure is not available, we use the next best thing, closing inventory. Thus for John Brown, we have:

$$\frac{\text{Cost of sales}}{\text{Average inventories}} = \frac{100}{60} = 1.66 \text{ times}$$

John Brown, therefore, holds inventory for 219 days (365 ÷ 1.66) until it is sold. This is a very slow turnover.

(iv) Asset Turnover Ratio

This ratio compares revenue to total assets employed (i.e., property, plant and equipment and current assets). Businesses with a large asset infrastructure, perhaps a steel works, have lower ratios than businesses with minimal assets, such as management consultancy or dot.com businesses. Once more, where the information is available, it is best to use average total assets. For John Brown, average total assets are not available; we therefore use this year's total assets:

$$\frac{\text{Revenue}}{\text{Average total assets}} = \frac{200}{395} = 0.51 \text{ times}$$

In other words, every year John Brown generates about half of its total assets in revenue. This is very low. There are many other potential asset turnover ratios where revenue is compared to, for example, non-current assets or net assets.

If we take these three ratios together, we can gain an insight into how efficient our cash cycle is. Thus, if we hold inventory for 219 days (inventory turnover ratio) and then debtors take 73 days to pay (trade receivables collection period), all in all it takes us 292 days to receive our money, while we pay suppliers in 183 days. Some businesses can manage to receive their cash from customers before they pay them.

Liquidity Ratios

Liquidity ratios are derived from the statement of financial position and seek to test how easily a firm can pay its debts. Loan creditors, such as bankers who have loaned money to a business, are particularly interested in these ratios. There are two main ratios (the current ratio and quick ratio). Once more we use John Brown (see Appendix 9.1).

(i) Current Ratio

This ratio tests whether the short-term assets cover the short-term liabilities. If they do not, then there will be insufficient liquid funds to pay current liabilities as they fall due. For John Brown this ratio is:

$$\frac{\text{Current assets}}{\text{Current liabilities}} = \frac{120}{60} = 2$$

In other words, the short-term assets are double the short-term liabilities. John Brown is well covered. Across the top 250 UK plcs, this ratio was 2.16 in July 2005. In other words, current assets were double current liabilities.

(ii) Quick Ratio

This is sometimes called the 'acid test' ratio. It is a measure of extreme short-term liquidity. Basically, inventories are sold, turning into trade receivables. When the debtors pay, the business gains cash. The quick ratio excludes inventory, the least liquid (i.e., the least cash-like) of the current assets, to arrive at an immediate test of a company's liquidity. If the creditors come knocking on the door for their money, can the business survive? For John Brown we have:

$$\frac{\text{Current assets} - \text{inventories}}{\text{Current liabilities}} = \frac{120 - 60}{60} = 1.0$$

For John Brown, the answer is yes. John Brown has just enough trade receivables and cash to cover its immediate liabilities. Across the top 250 UK plcs in July 2005 this ratio was 1.80.

Gearing

Like liquidity ratios, gearing ratios are derived from the statement of financial position. Gearing is also often known as leverage. Gearing effectively represents the relationship between the equity and the debt capital of a company. Essentially, equity represents the funding provided by owners (i.e., ordinary shareholders). By contrast, debt capital is that supplied by external parties (normally preference shareholders and loan holders).

So far, so good. However, the role of preference share capital and short-term liabilities is worth discussing. First, preference share capital is technically part of shareholders' funds, but preference shareholders *do not own* the company and usually receive a fixed dividend. We therefore treat them as debt. Second, current liabilities and short-term loans, to some extent, do finance the company. However, generally gearing is concerned with *long-term* borrowing. Figure 9.5 now summarises shareholders' funds and long-term borrowings:

Figure 9.5 Main Elements of the Gearing Ratio

Ordinary Shareholders' Funds	***Long-term Borrowings***
Ordinary share capital	Preference share capital
Share premium account	Long-term loans (also known as debentures)
Revaluation reserve	Other non-current liabilities
General reserve	
Retained earnings	
Other reserves	

We can now calculate the gearing ratio for John Brown. The preferred method used in this book is to compare long-term borrowings to total long-term capital employed (i.e., equity funding plus long-term borrowings). Thus we have for John Brown:

$$\frac{\text{Long-term borrowings}}{\text{Total long-term capital}} = \frac{\text{Preference share capital and debentures}}{\text{ordinary share capital, retained earnings and preference share capital and long-term loans}}$$

$$= \frac{50 + 70}{150 + 65 + 50 + 70} = \frac{120}{335} = 36\%$$

In other words, 36% (or 36 pence in every £1) of John Brown is financed by long-term non-ownership capital. Essentially, the more highly geared a company, the more risky the situation for the owners when profitability is poor. This is because interest on long-term borrowings will be paid first. Thus, if profits are poor, there may be little, if anything, left to pay the dividends of ordinary shareholders. Conversely, if profits are booming, there will be relatively more profits left for the ordinary shareholders since the return to the 'lenders' is fixed. When judging the gearing ratio, it is thus important to bear in mind the overall profitability of the business. According to Jones and Finley (2011) this ratio was 72.67% in 2006 for their sample of EU and Australian companies.

Cash Flow

The cash flow ratio, unlike the other ratios we have considered so far, is prepared from the statement of cash flows, not the income statement or statement of financial position. There are many possible ratios, but the one shown here simply measures total cash inflows to total cash outflows. Figure 9.6 shows the situation using IFRS whereas Appendix 9.2 illustrates the situation using the UK GAAP cash flow statement.

Figure 9.6 The Cash Flow Ratio Using IFRS Format

Any Company Ltd has the following cash inflows and outflows in £000s.

	Inflows		Outflows
Cash Flows from Operating Activities	80		
Cash Flows from Investing Activities			205
Cash Flows from Financing Activities	120		—
Total Cash Flows	200		205

$$\frac{\text{Total cash inflows}}{\text{Total cash outflows}} \quad \frac{200}{205} = 0.98$$

Other commonly used cash flow ratios are cash flow cover (net operating cash flow divided by annual interest payments), total debt to cash flow and cash flow per share.

Investment Ratios

The investment ratios differ from the other ratios, as they focus specifically on returns to the shareholder (dividend yield, earnings per share and price/earnings ratio) or the ability of a company to sustain its dividend or interest payments (dividend cover and interest cover). The ratios once more are calculated from John Brown (see Appendix 9.1). The first four ratios covered below are mainly of concern to the shareholders. The fifth, interest cover, is of more interest to the holders of long-term loans. Many companies give details of investment ratios in their annual reports. Company Snapshot 9.1 shows the earnings per share, dividends per share and dividend cover for Manchester United from 2000 to 2004.

COMPANY SNAPSHOT 9.1

Investment Ratios

Earnings per share (pence)	7.4	11.5	9.6	5.5	4.6
Dividends per share (pence)	2.65	4.00	3.10	2.00	1.90
Dividend cover (times)	2.8	2.9	3.1	2.8	2.4

Source: Manchester United Ltd, *Annual Report 2004*, p. 81.

(i) Dividend Yield

This ratio shows how much dividend the ordinary shares earn as a proportion of their market price. The market price for the shares of leading public companies is shown daily in many newspapers, such as (in the UK) the *Financial Times*, the *Guardian*, the *Telegraph* or *The Times*. Dividend yield can be shown as net or gross of tax (dividends are paid net after deduction of tax; gross is inclusive of tax). The calculation of gross dividend varies according to the tax rate and tax rules. For simplicity, we just show the *net* dividend yield.

For John Brown, the dividend yield is:

$$\frac{\text{Dividend per ordinary share}}{\text{Share price}} = \frac{\pounds10\text{m} \div 150\text{m shares}}{\pounds0.67} = \frac{0.067}{\pounds0.67} = 10\%$$

The dividend yield is perhaps comparable to the interest at the bank or building society. However, the increase or decrease in the share price over the year should also be borne in mind. The return from the dividend combined with the movement in share price is often known as the total shareholders' return. Across the top 200 UK plcs in November 2001, the dividend yield was 4.1%.

(ii) Dividend Cover

This represents the 'safety net' for ordinary shareholders. It shows how many times profit available to pay ordinary shareholders' dividends covers the actual dividends. In other words, can the current dividend level be maintained easily? For John Brown we have:

$$\frac{\text{Profit after tax and preference dividends}}{\text{Ordinary dividends}} = \frac{30}{10} = 3.0$$

Thus, dividends are covered three times by current profits. As Company Snapshot 9.2 shows, Manchester United's dividend is well covered by profit available. Across the top 200 UK plcs in November 2001, dividend cover was 2.5.

COMPANY SNAPSHOT 9.2

Dividends

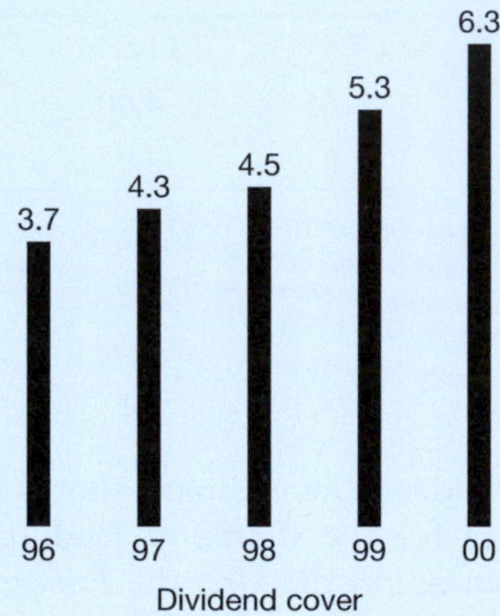

Source: Manchester United Ltd, *Annual Report 2004,* p. 64.

(iii) Earnings per Share (EPS)

Earnings per share (EPS) is a key measure by which investors measure the performance of a company. Its importance is shown by the fact that it is required to be shown in the published accounts of listed companies (unlike the other ratios). It measures the earnings attributable to a particular ordinary share. For John Brown it is:

$$\frac{\text{Profit after tax and preference dividends}}{\text{Number of ordinary shares}} = \frac{30}{150} = 20\text{p}$$

Each share thus earns 20 pence. Company Snapshot 9.3 shows that GSK's EPS was 32.1p in 2010. In this case, the number of ordinary shares is adjusted for the fact that some share options may be taken up to create new shares. This is called diluted EPS. Across the top 250 UK plcs in July 2005, EPS was 32.0 pence.

(iv) Price/Earnings (P/E) Ratio

This is another key stock market measure. It uses EPS and relates it to the share price. A high ratio means a high price in relation to earnings and indicates a fast-growing, popular company in which the market has confidence. A low ratio usually indicates a slower-growing, more established company. If we look at John Brown, we have:

$$\frac{\text{Share price}}{\text{Earnings per share}} = \frac{67}{20} = 3.35$$

COMPANY SNAPSHOT 9.3

15 Earnings per Share

	2010 pence	2009 pence	2008 pence
Basic earnings per share	**32.1**	109.1	88.6
Adjustment for major restructuring	**21.8**	12.1	16.1
Basic earnings per share before major restructuring	**53.9**	121.2	104.7
Diluted earnings per share	**31.9**	108.2	88.1
Adjustment for major restructuring	**21.6**	12.1	16.0
Diluted earnings per share before major restructuring	**53.5**	120.3	104.1

Basic and adjusted earnings per share have been calculated by dividing the profit attributable to shareholders by the weighted average number of shares in issue during the period after deducting shares held by the ESOP Trusts and Treasury shares. The trustees have waived their rights to dividends on the shares held by the ESOP Trusts.

Adjusted earnings per share is calculated using results before major restructuring earnings. The calculation of results before major restructuring is described in Note 1 'Presentation of the financial statements'.

Diluted earnings per share have been calculated after adjusting the weighted average number of shares used in the basic calculation to assume the conversion of all potentially dilutive shares. A potentially dilutive share forms part of the employee share schemes where its exercise price is below the average market price of GSK shares during the period and any performance conditions attaching to the scheme have been met at the balance sheet date.

The numbers of shares used in calculating basic and diluted earnings per share are reconciled below.

Weighted average number of shares in issue	**2010 millions**	2009 millions	2008 millions
Basic	**5,085**	5,069	5,195
Dilution for share options	**43**	39	31
Diluted	**5,128**	5,108	5,226

Source: GlaxoSmithKline, *Annual Report 2010.*

This indicates that the earnings per share is covered three times by the market price. In other words, it will take more than three years for current earnings to cover the market price. Across the top 200 UK plcs in November 2000, the P/E ratio was 36.

The P/E ratio is shown in the financial pages of newspapers along with dividend yield and the share price. In Real-World View 9.3, we show details from the *Daily Telegraph* for the aerospace and defence, automobiles and parts, and banks' industrial sectors. This shows that the P/E ratio for aerospace and defence ranged from 10.7 to 145.2, while for banks it was much lower, from 6.8 to 15.00. This probably reflects the more cautious attitude of the stock market to banks following the financial crisis of recent years.

REAL-WORLD VIEW 9.3

Company Share Details

52 week High (pence)	52 week Low (pence)	Stock	Price (pence)	+ or –	Yld	P/E
AEROSPACE & DEFENCE						⬇ 0.01%
364	248	BAE Systems	$278\frac{1}{2}$*	$+\frac{3}{4}$	6.3	10.7
$736\frac{1}{2}$	485	Chemring ♦	518	$-11\frac{1}{2}$	2.3	11.8
$245\frac{1}{2}$	$168\frac{1}{2}$	Cobham Gp ♦	178	$+5\frac{5}{8}$	3.6	12.6
$39\frac{1}{4}$	9	Hampson Inds	9	$-\frac{1}{4}$	9.8	–
$136\frac{1}{4}$	$96\frac{3}{4}$	Qinetiq Gp ♦	$117\frac{1}{2}$	$+1\frac{1}{4}$	1.4	145.2
$709\frac{1}{2}$	$557\frac{1}{2}$	Rolls-Royce	$709\frac{1}{2}$	$+9\frac{1}{2}$	2.3	–
1895	1305	Ultra ♦	1605	+15	2.2	15.1
$512\frac{1}{2}$	$289\frac{1}{2}$	UMECO	$289\frac{1}{2}$	$-\frac{1}{2}$	6.3	64.4
AUTOMOBILES & PARTS						⬇ 4.92%
245	157	GKN	186	$-9\frac{1}{4}$	2.8	9.8
BANKS						⬆ 1.34%
$54\frac{1}{4}$	6	Bank of Ireland	$8\frac{3}{4}$	$+\frac{3}{8}$	36.7	–
$333\frac{1}{2}$	$138\frac{3}{4}$	Barclays	$179\frac{1}{2}$	$+4\frac{3}{8}$	3.1	7.9
731	$473\frac{1}{2}$	HSBC	$522\frac{1}{2}$	$+2\frac{1}{4}$	4.6	15.0
$71\frac{3}{4}$	$27\frac{1}{2}$	Lloyds Banking Gp	$33\frac{1}{4}$	$+1\frac{1}{8}$	–	–
49	$19\frac{3}{4}$	Ryl Bk Scot	$24\frac{1}{2}$	$+\frac{3}{4}$	–	–
859	$452\frac{3}{4}$	Santander	$535\frac{1}{2}$	$+11\frac{1}{2}$	10.2	6.8
1959	$1169\frac{1}{2}$	Standard Chart	1409	+19	3.1	10.9

Source: Daily Telegraph, 20 October, 2011.

Note: The figures from left to right show the 52 week highs and lows of the share, the price on 20 October, the change since 19 July, the dividend and the P/E (price/earnings) ratio.

(v) Interest Cover

This ratio is of particular interest to those who have loaned money to the company. It shows the amount of profit available to cover the interest payable on long-term borrowings. Long-term borrowings can be defined as either preference shares and long-term loans or simply long-term loans. We will use only *long-term loans* here. This ratio is similar to dividend cover. It represents a safety net for borrowers. How much could profits fall before they failed to cover interest?

However, it is worth pointing out that interest is paid out of cash, not profit. For John Brown, we have:

$$\frac{\text{Profit before tax and loan interest}}{\text{Loan interest}} = \frac{50 + 10}{10} = 6$$

Loan interest is thus covered six times (i.e., well covered). Profits would have to fall dramatically before interest was not covered. Over the top 250 UK public limited companies in July 2005, this ratio was 23.56. Tesco's interest cover is shown in Company Snapshot 9.4. An alternative to this ratio is cash flow cover, which is net operating cash flow divided by annual interest payments.

COMPANY SNAPSHOT 9.4

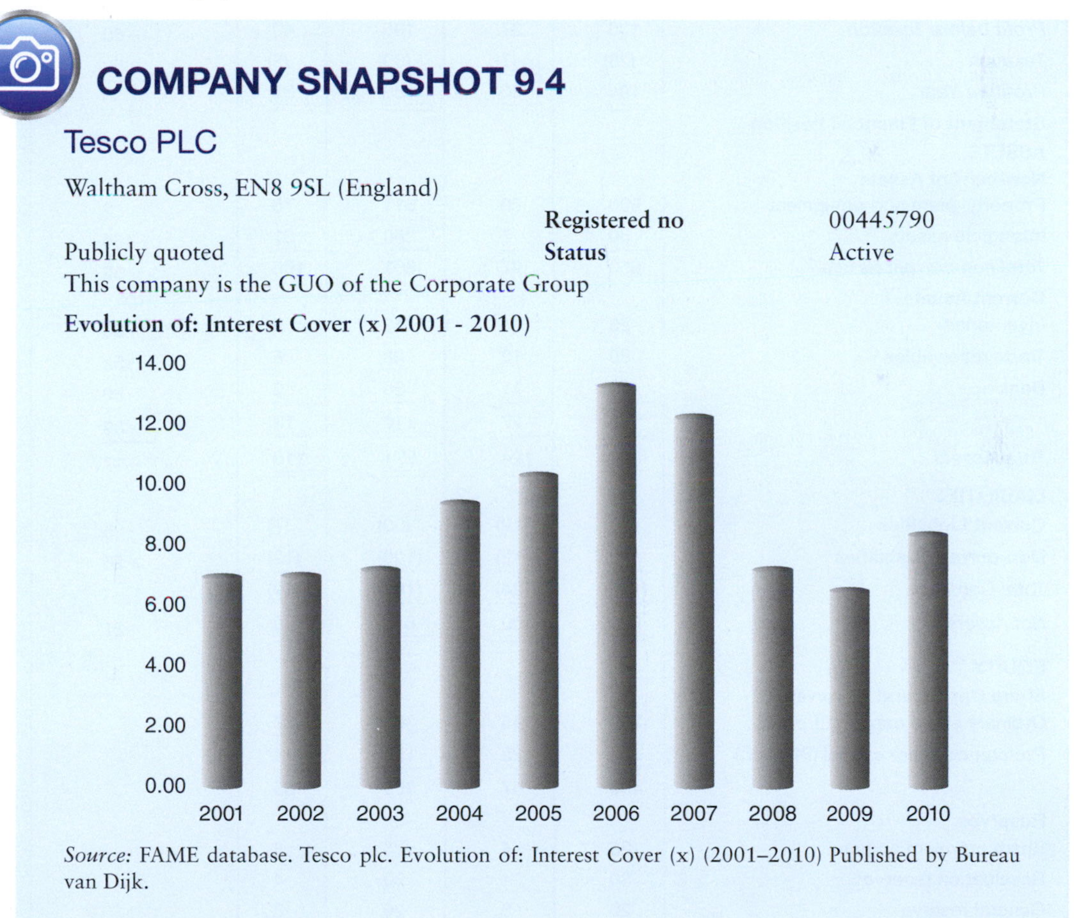

Source: FAME database. Tesco plc. Evolution of: Interest Cover (x) (2001–2010) Published by Bureau van Dijk.

Worked Example

Having explained 16 ratios, it is now time to work through a full example. In order to do this, we use the summarised accounts of Stevens, Turner plc in Figure 9.7 (last seen in Chapter 7). Although adapted slightly, these are essentially the accounts in Figure 7.15 for 20X1; however, we now have an extra year 20X2. The main change is that there are now two years' figures and percentages.

Figure 9.7 Illustrative Example on Interpretation of Accounts

Summarised figures for Stevens, Turner plc 20X1 and 20X2					
	20X1	20X1	20X2	20X2	(Increase/decrease)
	£000	%	£000	%	%
Income Statements					
Revenue (all credit)	350	100	450	100	+29
Cost of Sales (all credit)	(135)	(39)	(150)	(33)	+11
Gross Profit	215	61	300	67	+40
Loan interest	(8)	(2)	(10)	(2)	+25
Administrative expenses	(77)	(22)	(95)	(22)	+23
Profit before Taxation	130	37	195	43	+50
Taxation	(26)	(7)	(39)	(8)	+50
Profit for Year	104	30	156	35	+50
Statement of Financial Position					
ASSETS					
Non-current Assets					
Property, plant and equipment	600	90	611	75	+2
Intangible assets	50	7	250	31	+400
Total non-current assets	650	97	861	106	+32
Current Assets					
Inventories	25	4	42	5	+68
Trade receivables	80	12	38	5	−52
Bank	75	11	30	3	−60
	180	27	110	13	−39
Total Assets	830	124	971	119	+17
LIABILITIES					
Current Liabilities	(80)	(12)	(60)	(7)	−25
Non-current Liabilities	(80)	(12)	(100)	(12)	+25
Total Liabilities	(160)	(24)	(160)	(19)	–
Net Assets	670	100	811	100	+21
EQUITY					
Share Capital and Reserves					
Ordinary share capital (£1 each)	300	45	300	37	–
Preference share capital (£1 each)	150	22	150	18	–
	450	67	450	55	–
Reserves					
Share premium account	25	4	25	3	–
Revaluation reserve	30	4	30	4	–
General reserve	20	3	20	3	–
	75	11	75	10	
Retained earnings	154		301		
Less: Ordinary dividends	(6)		(12)		
Preference dividends	(3)		(3)		
Net retained earnings	145	22	286	35	+97
	220	33	361	45	+64
Total Equity	670	100	811	100	+21
Market Price	£1		£1.50		

Vertical and Horizontal Analysis

Before calculating the ratios it is useful to perform vertical and horizontal analysis.

Vertical Analysis

Vertical analysis is where key figures in the accounts (such as revenue, statement of financial position totals) are set to 100%. The other figures are then expressed as a percentage of 100%. For example, cost of sales for 20X1 is 135; it is thus 39% of revenue (i.e., 135 of 350). Vertical analysis is a useful way to see if any figures have changed markedly during the year. Real-World View 9.4 presents a graph using vertical analysis for Tesco's 2010 results. In this case, total assets are shown as 100%. In addition, Tesco's liquidity ratio (probably current ratio) and gearing are compared to that of other retailers.

REAL-WORLD VIEW 9.4

Vertical Analysis at Tesco

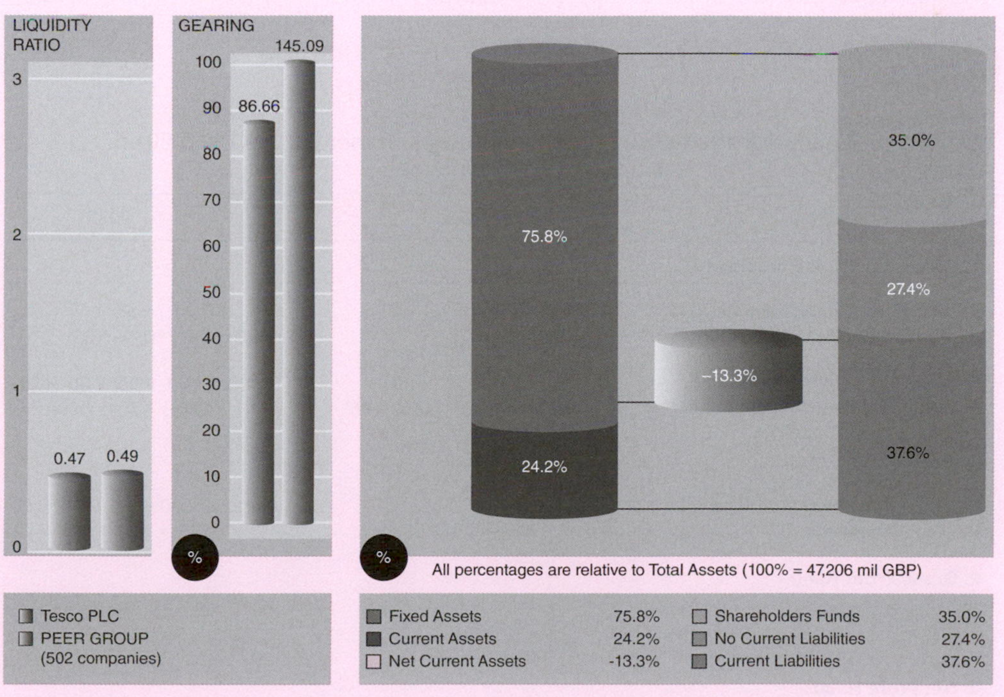

Source: FAME Database. Tesco plc. Structure of the balance sheet 2010. Published by Bureau van Dijk.

In Stevens, Turner plc, in 20X2, we can see from the income statement that loan interest and administrative expenses represent 2% and 22% of revenue, whereas in the statement of financial position, in 20X2, property, plant and equipment represent 75% of total net assets. We need to assess whether or not these figures appear reasonable.

Horizontal Analysis

Whereas vertical analysis compares the figures within the same year, horizontal analysis compares the figures across time. Thus, for example, we see that revenue has increased from £350,000 in 20X1 to £450,000 in 20X2, a 29% increase. We need to investigate any major changes which look out of line. For example, why have there been so many changes in current assets: inventories, trade receivables, and cash have all changed markedly (i.e., inventories up 68%, trade receivables down 52% and bank down 60%)? These may represent normal trading changes, or then again...

Interpretation

We will now work through the various categories of ratio (shown in Figures 9.8 to 9.13). We present them in tables and then make some observations. When reading these it needs to be borne in mind that normally these observations would be set in the context of the industry in which the company operates and in the economic context. They should, therefore, be taken as illustrative not definitive. We will use the available data. This is most comprehensive for 20X2 (as we can use the 20X1 comparative data).

(i) Profitability Ratios

Figure 9.8 Profitability Ratios for Stevens, Turner plc 20X1 and 20X2

Ratios	20X1	20X2
1. Return on Capital Employed		
$\frac{\text{Profit before tax and loan interest}}{\text{Average capital employed}^{a}}$	$\frac{130+8}{750^{**}} = 18.4\%$	$\frac{195+10}{(911^{*}+750^{**}) \div 2} = 24.7\%$
[a](i.e., ordinary share capital and reserves, preference share capital and long-term capital, i.e., long-term creditors)	**(i.e., 300 + 25 + 30 + 20 + 145 + 150 + 80)	*(i.e., 300 + 25 + 30 + 20 + 286 + 150 + 100)
In 20X1, only one year-end figure is available		**(i.e., 300 + 25 + 30 + 20 + 145 + 150 + 80)
2. Gross Profit Ratio		
$\frac{\text{Gross Profit}}{\text{Revenue}}$	$\frac{215}{350} = 61.4\%$	$\frac{300}{450} = 66.7\%$
3. Net Profit Ratio		
$\frac{\text{Net profit before tax}}{\text{Revenue}}$	$\frac{130}{350} = 37.1\%$	$\frac{195}{450} = 43.3\%$

Brief Discussion

Essentially, these profitability ratios tell us that Stevens, Turner plc's return on capital employed is running at between 18% and 25%, having increased over the year. This represents the return from the net assets of the company. Meanwhile, the business is operating on a high gross profit margin. This has also increased over the year. Finally, the net profit ratio has also increased, perhaps because the relative cost of sales has reduced.

(ii) Efficiency Ratios

Figure 9.9 Efficiency Ratios for Stevens, Turner plc 20X1 and 20X2

Ratios	20X1	20X2
1. Trade Receivables Collection Period		
$\frac{\text{Average trade receivables}}{\text{Credit sales per day}}$	$\frac{80^*}{350 \div 365} = 83$ days	$\frac{(80 + 38)^* \div 2}{450 \div 365} = 48$ days
	*only year-end figure available	*average of two year-end figures
2. Trade Payables Collection Period		
$\frac{\text{Average trade payables}}{\text{Credit purchases per day}^*}$	$\frac{80^*}{135 \div 365} = 216$ days	$\frac{(80 + 60)^* \div 2}{150 \div 365} = 170$ days
*in this case cost of sales	*only year-end figure available	*average of two year-end figures
3. Inventory Turnover Ratio		
$\frac{\text{Cost of sales}}{\text{Average inventories}}$	$\frac{135}{25^*} = 5.4$ times	$\frac{150}{(25 + 42)^* \div 2} = 4.48$ times
	*only year-end figure available	*average of two year-end figures
4. Asset Turnover Ratio		
$\frac{\text{Revenue}}{\text{Average total assets}}$	$\frac{350}{50 + 600 + 180^*} = 0.42$ times	$\frac{450}{(50 + 250) + (600 + 611) + (180 + 110)/2^*} = 0.50$ times
(i.e., intangible, property, plant and equipment and current)	*the intangible assets, property, plant and equipment and current assets figures for 20X1	*the intangible assets, property, plant and equipment and current assets figures for 20X1 and 20X2 averaged (i.e., ÷ 2)

Brief Discussion

There have been substantial reductions in the trade receivables and trade payables collection periods. Trade receivables are now paid in 48 rather than 83 days. By contrast, Stevens,

Turner pays its trade payables in 170 days not 216 days. By receiving money more quickly than paying it, Stevens, Turner is benefiting as its overall bank balance is healthier. However, it must be careful not to antagonise its suppliers as 170 days is a long time to withhold payment. Inventory is moving more slowly this year than last. However, each inventory item is still replaced 4½ times each year. Finally, the asset turnover ratio is disappointing. Revenue is considerably lower than total assets, even though there is some improvement over the year.

(iii) Liquidity Ratios

Figure 9.10 Liquidity Ratios for Stevens, Turner plc 20X1 and 20X2

Ratios	20X1	20X2
1. Current Ratio		
$\frac{\text{Current assets}}{\text{Current liabilities}}$	$\frac{180}{80} = 2.2$	$\frac{110}{60} = 1.8$
2. Quick Ratio		
$\frac{\text{Current assets - inventories}}{\text{Current liabilities}}$	$\frac{180 - 25}{80} = 1.9$	$\frac{110 - 42}{60} = 1.1$

Brief Discussion

There is a noted deterioration in both liquidity ratios. The current ratio has fallen from 2.2 to 1.8. Meanwhile, the quick ratio has declined from 1.9 to 1.1. While not immediately worrying, Stevens, Turner needs to pay attention to this.

(iv) Gearing Ratio

Figure 9.11 Gearing Ratio for Stevens, Turner plc 20X1 and 20X2

Ratio	20X1	20X2
$\frac{\text{Long term borrowings*}}{\text{Total long-term capital**}}$	$\frac{230^*}{750^{**}} = 30.7\%$	$\frac{250^*}{911^{**}} = 27.4\%$
*Preference shares and long-term loans (i.e., long-term creditors)	*150 + 80 = 230	*150 + 100 = 250
**Preference shares, long-term loans (i.e., long-term creditors), ordinary shares, share premium account, revaluation reserve, general reserve, retained earnings.	**150 + 80 + 300 + 25 + 30 + 20 + 145 = 750	**150 + 100 + 300 + 25 + 30 + 20 + 286 = 911

Brief Discussion

Gearing has declined over the year from 30.7% to 27.4%. In 20X2, 27.4 pence in the £ of the long-term capital employed is from borrowed money, rather than 30.7 pence last year. This change is due to the increase in retained earnings during the year.

(v) Cash Flow Ratio

Figure 9.12 Cash Flow Ratio for Stevens, Turner plc 20X1 and 20X2

From the statement of financial position and income statements in Figure 9.7, we can determine the statement of cash flows. From this statement of cash flows we can work out the cash inflows and cash outflows.

Stevens, Turner plc
Statement of Cash Flows Year Ended 31.12.20X2

	£000	£000
Cash Flows from Operating Activities		
*Net Profit before Taxation and Loan Interest**		205
Add:		
Decrease in trade receivables	42	42
Deduct:		
Increase in inventories	(17)	
Decrease in trade payables	(20)	
Taxation paid	(39)	(76)
Net Cash Inflow from Operating Activities		171
Cash Flows from Investing Activities		
Purchase of intangible assets	(200)	
Purchase of property, plant and equipment	(11)	(211)
Cash Flows from Financing Activities		
Increase in loan capital	20	
Dividends paid	(15)	
Interest paid	(10)	(5)
Decrease in Cash		(45)

	£000
Opening Cash and Cash Equivalents	75
Decrease in cash	(45)
Closing Cash and Cash Equivalents	30

Therefore our cash flow ratio is:

	Cash Inflows £000	Cash Outflows £000
Net Cash Inflow from Operating Activities	171	
Cash Flows from Investing Activities		211
Cash Flows from Financing Activities	5	
	176	211

$$\frac{\text{Total cash inflows}}{\text{Total cash outflows}} = \frac{176}{211} = 0.83$$

*For simplicity, we assume no depreciation.

(vi) Investment Ratios

Figure 9.13 Investment Flow Ratios for Stevens, Turner plc 20X1 and 20X2

Ratios	20X1	20X2
1. Dividend Yield		
$\frac{\text{Dividend per ordinary share*}}{\text{Share price}}$	$\frac{2*}{100p} = 2\%$	$\frac{4*}{150p} = 2.67\%$
*Net ordinary dividend divided by number shares	*6 ÷ 300 = 2p	*12 ÷ 300 = 4p
2. Dividend Cover		
$\frac{\text{Profit after tax and preference dividends}}{\text{Ordinary dividends}}$	$\frac{101}{6} = 16.8$ times	$\frac{153}{12} = 12.8$ times
3. Earnings per Share		
$\frac{\text{Profit after tax and preference dividends}}{\text{Number of ordinary shares}}$	$\frac{101}{300} = 33.7p$	$\frac{153}{300} = 51p$
4. Price/Earnings Ratio		
$\frac{\text{Share price}}{\text{Earnings per share}}$	$\frac{100}{33.7} = 3.0$	$\frac{150}{51} = 2.9$
5. Interest Cover		
$\frac{\text{Profit before tax and loan interest}}{\text{Loan interest}}$	$\frac{130 + 8}{8} = 17.2$ times	$\frac{195 + 10}{10} = 20.5$ times

Brief Discussion

More cash is flowing out than is flowing in. The main reason for this is the purchase of property, plant and equipment. The dividend yield is quite low at around 2% to 3%. However, it must be remembered that the share price has increased rapidly by 50p, and it is unusual to have strong capital growth and high dividends at the same time. Both dividend cover and interest cover are high. If necessary the company has the potential to increase dividends and interest. Earnings per share (EPS) has increased over the year and is now running at an improved 51 pence. It is this rise in EPS which may have fuelled the share price increase. The P/E ratio, however, is still very modest at 2.9.

Company Specific Ratios

The ratios provided in this chapter are widespread, but there is no standard set of ratios that are used for all companies. This makes sense as, for example, an airline will operate very differently from a mobile phone operator and ratios need to reflect this. In Company Snapshot 9.5 the key ratios and economic indicators used by Nokia, the mobile phone operator, are recorded. As can be seen, some ratios are relatively standard (e.g., return on capital employed), but some are more specialised (e.g., R&D expenditure as a % of net sales).

COMPANY SNAPSHOT 9.5

Key Ratios in Practice

NOKIA

Key ratios and economic indicators	2010	2009	2008	2007	2006
Net sales, EURm	42,446	40,984	50,710	51,058	41,121
Change, %	3.6	−19.2	−0.7	24.2	20.3
Exports and foreign subsidiaries, EURm	42,075	40,594	50,348	50,736	40,734
Salaries and social expenses, EURm	6,947	6,734	6,847	5,702	4,206
Operating profit, EURm	2,070	1,197	4,966	7,985	5,488
% or net sales	4.9	2.9	9.8	15.6	13.3
Financial income and expenses, EURm	−285	−265	−2	239	207
% of net Sales	0.7	0.6	—	0.5	0.5
Profit before tax EURm	1,786	962	4,970	8,268	5,723
% of net sales	4.2	2.3	9.8	16.2	13.9
Profit from continuing operations. EURm	1,850	891	3,988	7,205	4,306
% of net sales	4.4	2.2	7.9	14.1	10.5
Taxes, EURm	443	702	1,081	1,522	1,357
Dividends, EURm	1,498	1,498	1,520	2,111	1,761
Capital expenditure, EURm	679	531	889	715	650
% of net sales	1.6	1.3	1.8	1.4	1.6
Gross investments, EURm	836	683	1,166	1,017	897
% of net sales	2.0	1.7	2.3	2.0	2.2
R&D expenditure, EURm	5,863	5,909	5,968	5,647	3,897
%of net sales	13.8	14.4	11.8	11.1	9.5
Average personnel	129,355	123,171	121,723	100,534	65,324
Non-interest bearing liabilities, EURm	16,591	14,483	16,833	18,208	10,103
Interest-bearing liabilities, EURm	5,279	5,203	4,452	1,090	249
Return on capital employed, %	11.0	6.7	27.2	54.8	46.1
Return on equity, %	13.5	6.5	27.5	53.9	35.5
Equity ratio, %	42.8	41.9	42.3	46.7	54.0
Net debt to equity, %	−43	−25	−14	−62	−69

Source: Nokia, *Annual Report 2010*, p. 79.

Report Format

Students are often required to write a report on the performance of a company using ratio analysis. A report is not an essay! It has a pre-set style, usually including the following features:

- Terms of reference
- Title
- Introduction
- Major sections
- Recommendations
- Appendices

Figure 9.14 illustrates a *concise* overall report on Stevens, Turner plc for 20X1 and 20X2.

Figure 9.14 Illustrative Report on Financial Performance of Stevens, Turner plc for 20X2

Report on the Financial Performance of Stevens, Turner plc Year Ended 20X2

1.0 Terms of Reference

The Managing Director requested a report on the financial performance of Stevens, Turner plc for the year ended 20X2 using appropriate ratio analysis.

2.0 Introduction

The income statement, statement of financial position and cash flow data were used to prepare 16 ratios to assess the company's performance for 20X2. The 20X2 financial results were compared to those in 20X1. The underpinning ratios with their calculations are presented in the appendix. This report briefly covers the profitability, efficiency, liquidity, gearing, cash flow and investment ratios.

3.0 Profitability

The company has traded quite profitably over the year. This has been helped by the substantial increase in revenue (+29%) which has increased faster than cost of sales (+11%). The return on capital employed and gross profit ratios have increased over the year from 18.4% to 24.7%, and from 61.4% to 66.7%, respectively. The net profit ratio improved from 37.1% to 43.3%. This ratio is extremely good.

4.0 Efficiency

The collection of money from trade receivables is still quicker than the payment of trade payables (48 days vs 170 days), which is good for cash flow. Both collection periods have declined over the year. This means that debtors are paying quicker, but that we are also paying our trade payables quicker. The inventories are turned over 4.48 times per year, which is usual for this type of business. Finally, the asset turnover ratio appears quite low. However, once more this reflects the nature of the business.

5.0 Liquidity

Liquidity is an area to watch for the future. Both the current ratio and quick ratio have declined markedly over the year (from 2.2 to 1.8, and 1.9 to 1.1, respectively). This has been caused by a fall in trade receivables and particularly by cash at the bank. While this is not immediately worrying, this ratio should not be allowed to slip any further.

6.0 Cash flow

The cash flow ratio is 0.79. More cash is flowing out than is coming in. The main reason appears to be the purchase of property, plant and equipment. This investment has also meant that there is less cash at the bank. As a result liquidity has fallen.

7.0 Gearing

The dependence on outside borrowing has declined during the year from 30.7% to 27.4%. This is good news. It means that if liquidity falls further the company can borrow money if necessary.

8.0 Investment

Both dividends and loan interest remain well covered (respectively 12.8 times and 20.5 times). Overall, shareholders are receiving a good return for their investment. Share price has increased by 50 pence, which compensates for the low dividend yield of 2.67%. The earnings per share remains a healthy 51p (up from 33.7p). Finally, the P/E ratio has remained steady at 2.9.

9.0 Conclusions

Overall, Stevens, Turner plc has had a good year in terms of profitability, investment performance, gearing, and efficiency ratios. The one area we really need to pay attention to is cash flow and liquidity. While not immediately worrying, this area should be carefully monitored.

Appendix 1 (Extract)

1. Return on capital employed	20X1	20X2
$\frac{\text{Net profit before tax and loan interest}}{\text{Average capital employed}}$	$\frac{138}{750} = 18.4\%$	$\frac{205}{830} = 24.7\%$

Note: All the ratios are calculated in Figures 9.8 to 9.13.

A real report would be longer than this, but this report gives a good insight into the use of report format.

Holistic View of Ratios

So far we have looked at individual ratios. However, although useful, one ratio on its own may potentially be misleading or may even be manipulated through creative accounting. Therefore, there have been attempts to look at ratios collectively. Two main approaches are briefly discussed here.

1. The Z Score Model

The idea behind this model, which was first developed in the US, is to select ratios which when combined have a high predictive power. In the UK, an academic, Richard Taffler, developed the model using two groups of failed and non-failed companies. After a comprehensive study of accounts, he produced a model for listed industrial companies. This model proved successful in distinguishing between those companies which would go bankrupt and those companies which would not.

2. Pictics

Pictics are an ingenious way of presenting ratios. Essentially, each pictic is a face. The different elements of the face are represented by different ratios. Real-World View 9.5 demonstrates two pictics.

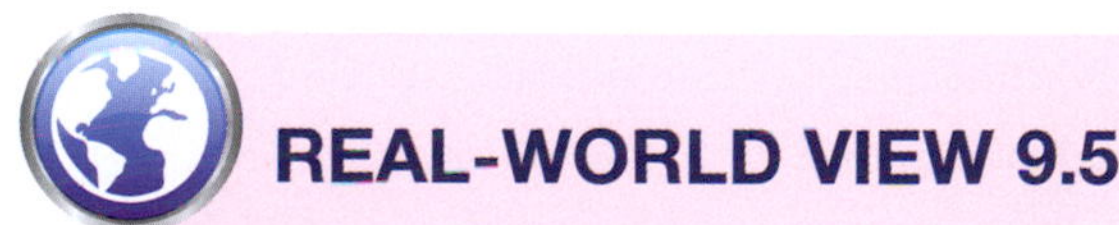

REAL-WORLD VIEW 9.5

Pictics

Source: Richard Taffler, Changing Face of Accountancy, *Accountancy Age*, 2 May 1996, p. 17.

The face on the left represents a successful business while that on the right is an unsuccessful business. The size of the smile represents profitability while the length of the nose represents working capital. Pictics are an easy way of presenting multi-dimensional information. Although it is easy to dismiss pictics as a joke, they have proved remarkably successful in controlled research studies.

Performance Indicators

The conventional mix of ratios may be unsuitable for some businesses, in particular those where non-financial performance is very important. Examples of such organisations include the National Health Service and the railways. Such businesses use customised performance measures, often called performance indicators. For the National Health Service, indicators such as number of operations, or bed occupancy rate, may be more important than net profit.

PAUSE FOR THOUGHT 9.3

Performance Indicators

Which performance indicators do you think would be useful when assessing the performance of individual railway operating companies?

Potentially, there are many performance indicators. For example:

- Percentage of trains late
- Miles per passenger
- Volume of freight moved
- Passengers per train
- Number of complaints
- Number of accidents

Organisations like the rail companies need to balance financial considerations (such as making profits for shareholders) with non-financial factors (such as punctuality). As Company Snapshot 9.6 shows, rail operating companies consider factors such as punctuality and UK rail customer satisfaction. They may also consider factors such as passenger and train numbers and income from fares and subsidies.

COMPANY SNAPSHOT 9.6

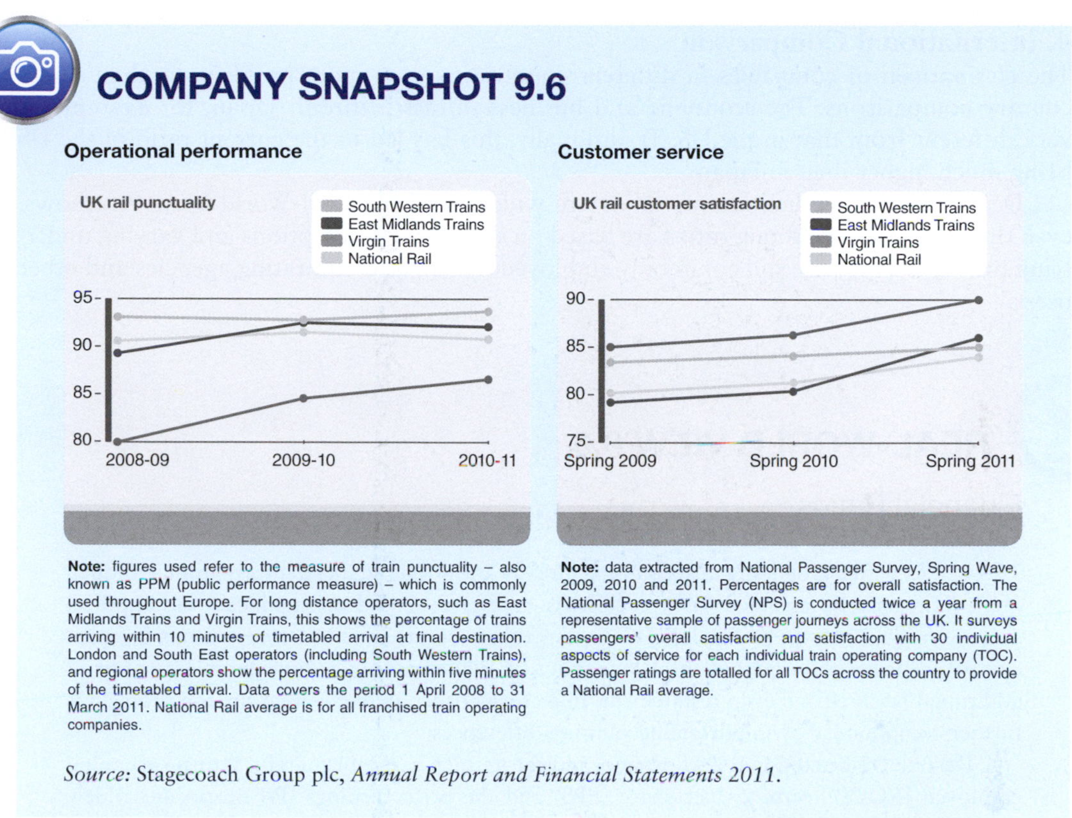

Note: figures used refer to the measure of train punctuality – also known as PPM (public performance measure) – which is commonly used throughout Europe. For long distance operators, such as East Midlands Trains and Virgin Trains, this shows the percentage of trains arriving within 10 minutes of timetabled arrival at final destination. London and South East operators (including South Western Trains), and regional operators show the percentage arriving within five minutes of the timetabled arrival. Data covers the period 1 April 2008 to 31 March 2011. National Rail average is for all franchised train operating companies.

Note: data extracted from National Passenger Survey, Spring Wave, 2009, 2010 and 2011. Percentages are for overall satisfaction. The National Passenger Survey (NPS) is conducted twice a year from a representative sample of passenger journeys across the UK. It surveys passengers' overall satisfaction and satisfaction with 30 individual aspects of service for each individual train operating company (TOC). Passenger ratings are totalled for all TOCs across the country to provide a National Rail average.

Source: Stagecoach Group plc, *Annual Report and Financial Statements 2011.*

Limitations

Ratio analysis can be a useful financial tool. However, certain problems associated with ratio analysis must be appreciated.

1. Context

Ratios must be used in context. They cannot be used in isolation, but must be compared with past results or industry norms. Unless such a comparative approach is adopted, ratio analysis is fraught with danger.

2. Absolute Size

Ratios give no indication of the relative size of the result. If net profit is 10%, we do not know if this is 10% of £100 or 10% of £1 million. Both the ratio *and* the size of the organisation need to be taken into account.

3. Like with Like

We must ensure that we are comparing like with like. The accounting policies of different companies differ and this needs to be appreciated. If companies A and B, for example, use a different rate of depreciation then a net profit of 10% for company A may equal 8% for company B.

4. International Comparison

The comparison of companies in different countries is even more problematic than same-country comparisons. The economic and business infrastructure in Japan, for example, is very different from that in the US. Traditionally, this has led to the current ratio in the US being much higher than in Japan.

Despite the above limitations, ratios are widely used. As Real-World View 9.6 shows, even though these accounting ratios are based on significant assumptions and varying underlying principles, they are still commonly employed by banks, credit rating agencies and other users.

REAL-WORLD VIEW 9.6

Financial Ratios

Those of us with a grounding in accounting already know that financial information, although often (and naively) assumed to be precise, is necessarily based on significant assumptions and varying underlying principles. This means that accurate financial comparisons between companies (even those within the UK) cannot be made without a considerable amount of additional research and even restatement. In a cross-border analysis situation, the problem is further compounded by important accounting differences.

Despite this, traditional performance indicators such as profit margin, return on capital employed (ROCE), earnings per share (EPS) and the price earnings (P/E) ratio are widely published and used in decision making, often one suspects without any great attention being paid to what lies behind them. For example, banks, credit rating agencies, auditors, investment analysts, merger and acquisition teams and the financial press all use such financial ratios in their daily work.

Source: This article was published in *Management Accounting* by authors: M. Gardiner and K. Bagshaw, Financial Ratios: Can You Trust Them?, September 1997, page 30. ISSN - 0025-1682. Copyright Chartered Institute of Management Accountants (CIMA), 1997. Reproduced by Permission.

5. Validity of the Data

The reliability of the ratio analysis also depends on the reliability of the underlying data. This needs to be complete, comparable and accurate. This is particularly difficult for international comparisons.

Conclusion

Ratio analysis is a good way to gain an overview of an organisation's activities. There is a whole range of ratios on profitability, efficiency, liquidity, gearing, cash flow and investment. Taken together these ratios provide a comprehensive view of a company's financial activities.

They are used to compare a company's performance over time as well as to compare different companies' financial performance. For certain businesses, particularly those not so profit orientated, performance indicators provide a useful alternative to ratios. Performance indicators are often also used to supplement ratio analysis. When calculating ratios, care is necessary to ensure that the underlying figures have been drawn up in a consistent and comparable way. However, when used carefully, ratios are undoubtedly very useful.

Discussion Questions

Questions with numbers in blue have answers at the back of the book.

Q1 What do you understand by ratio analysis? Distinguish between the main types of ratio analysis.

Q2 Do the advantages of ratio analysis outweigh the disadvantages? Discuss.

Q3 'Each of the main financial statements provides a distinct set of financial ratios.' Discuss this statement.

Q4 Devise a set of non-financial performance indicators which might be appropriate for monitoring:
(a) The Police
(b) The Post Office (now known as Royal Mail in the UK)

Q5 State whether the following are true or false. If false, explain why.

(a) Gross profit ratio $= \frac{\text{Gross profit}}{\text{Revenue}}$

(b) Net profit ratio $= \frac{\text{Net profit after taxation}}{\text{Average capital employed}}$

(c) Current ratio $= \frac{\text{Current assets} - \text{inventories}}{\text{Current liabilities}}$

(d) Debtors collection period $= \frac{\text{Trade receivables}}{\text{Credit sales per day}}$

(e) Asset turnover ratio $= \frac{\text{Revenue}}{\text{Property, plant and equipment}}$

(f) Dividend yield $= \frac{\text{Dividend per ordinary share}}{\text{Revenue}}$

(g) Earnings per share $= \frac{\text{Profit after tax and preference dividends}}{\text{Number of ordinary shares}}$

Numerical Questions

Questions with numbers in blue have answers at the back of the book.

Q1 The information below is from the accounts of John Parry, a sole trader.

Income Statement for the Year Ended 31 December 2013

	£	£
Revenue		150,000
Less *Cost of Sales*		
Opening inventory	25,000	
Add Purchases	75,000	
	100,000	
Less Closing inventory	30,000	70,000
Gross Profit		80,000
Less Expenses		30,000
Net Profit		50,000

Other information	31.12.2012	31.12.2013
	£	£
Total assets	50,000	60,000
Closing equity	300,000	500,000
Trade receivables	18,000	19,000
Trade payables	9,000	10,000

Note: All of John Parry's sales and purchases are on credit.

Required: Calculate the following profitability and efficiency ratios:

(a) Return on capital employed
(b) Gross profit ratio
(c) Net profit ratio
(d) Trade receivables collection period
(e) Trade payables collection period
(f) Inventory turnover ratio
(g) Asset turnover ratio

Q2 Henry Mellett has the following extracts from his statement of financial position as at 31 March 2013:

	£
Current Assets	
Inventory	18,213
Trade receivables	12,407
Cash	1,283
Current Liabilities	
Trade payables	14,836
Non-current liabilities	30,000
Net assets	150,000

Required: Calculate the following ratios:
(a) **Current ratio** (b) Quick ratio (c) Gearing ratio

Q3 Jane Edwards Ltd has prepared its statement of cash flows under the direct method. It has the following main cash flows:

	£		£
Cash from customers	125,000	Dividends paid	8,000
Cash paid to employees	18,300	Taxation paid	16,000
Cash paid to suppliers	9,250	Purchase of property, plant and equipment	80,000
Issue of shares	29,000		
Buy back loan	8,000	Sales of property, plant and equipment	35,000

Required: Calculate the cash flow ratio.

Q4 From the following information for Clatworthy plc calculate the investment ratios as indicated:

	£000
Revenue	1,000
Profit before Taxation	750
(after charging loan interest of £40,000)	
Taxation	(150)
Profit for Year	600

Note: *Preference dividends for the year were £20,000* and ordinary dividends were £40,000.

Market price ordinary shares £1.25. Number of ordinary shares in issue are 500,000.

Required:
(a) Dividend yield
(b) Dividend cover
(c) Earnings per share
(d) Price/earnings ratio
(e) Interest cover

Q5 The abridged accounts for N.O. Hope plc are given below.

Income Statements	**2012**	**2013**
	£000	£000
Revenue	400	440
Cost of Sales	(300)	(330)
Gross Profit	100	110
Administrative expenses	(15)	(25)
Distribution expenses	(5)	(10)
Profit before Taxation	80	75
Taxation	(16)	(15)
Profit for the year	64	60

Statements of Financial Position		
ASSETS		
Non-current Assets	£000	£000
Property, plant and equipment	120	235
Intangible assets	20	20
Total non-current assets	140	255
Current Assets		
Inventories	80	40
Trade receivables	40	20
Bank	20	10
Total current assets	140	70
Total Assets	280	325
LIABILITIES		
Current Liabilities	(70)	(75)
Non-current Liabilities	(20)	(40)
Total Liabilities	(90)	(115)
Net Assets	190	210
EQUITY		
Capital and Reserves	£000	£000
Share Capital		
Ordinary share capital (£1 each)	120	125
Preference share capital (£1 each)	17	17
	137	142

Q5 N.O. Hope plc (*continued*)

	£000	£000
Reserves		
Capital reserves		
Share premium account	10	10
Revaluation reserve	10	10
Other reserves		
General reserve	8	8
Retained earnings	25	40
	53	68
Total Equity	190	210

1. Retained earnings were after taking into account dividends of £46,000 for 2012 and £45,000 for 2013.

Required: Prepare a horizontal and vertical analysis. Highlight three figures that may need further enquiry.

Q6 The following two non-listed companies, Alpha Industries and Beta Industries, operate in the same industrial sector. You have extracted the following ratios from their accounts:

	Alpha	Beta
Return on capital employed	9%	20%
Gross profit ratio	25%	25%
Net profit ratio	7%	14%
Current ratio	2.1	1.7
Quick ratio	1.7	1.3
Price/Earnings ratio	4	8
Dividend cover	2	4

Required: Compare the financial performance of the two companies. All other things being equal, which company would you expect to have the higher market price?

Q7 Anteater plc has produced the following summary accounts:

Income Statement for the Year Ended 31 December 2013

	£000
Revenue	1,000
Cost of sales	(750)
Gross Profit	250
Administrative expenses	(117)
Distribution expenses	(30)
Operating profit	103
Debenture interest	(3)
Profit before Taxation	100
Taxation	(20)
Profit for Year	80

Statement of Financial Position as at 31 December 2013

	£000	£000
ASSETS		
Non-current Assets		
Property, plant and equipment		420
Current Assets		
Inventories	40	
Trade receivables	50	
Cash	30	120
Total Assets		540
LIABILITIES		
Current Liabilities		(40)
Non-current Liabilities		(100)
Total Liabilities		(140)
Net Assets		400
EQUITY		
Capital and Reserves		
Share Capital		£000
Ordinary share capital (£1 each)		300
Preference share capital (£1 each)		20
		320

Q7 Anteater plc (*continued*)

	£000
Reserves	
Capital reserves	
Share premium account	10
Other reserves	
Retained earnings[1]	70
Total Equity	400

Share price £2.00.

[1]Note that preference dividends of £10,000 and ordinary dividends of £40,000 have been charged to retained earnings.

Required: From the above accounts prepare the following ratios:
(a) Profitability ratios
(b) Efficiency ratios
(c) Liquidity ratios
(d) Gearing ratio
(e) Investment ratios

Q8 You are an employee of a medium-sized, light engineering company. Your managing director, Sara Potter, asks you to analyse the accounts of your company, Turn-a-Screw Ltd, with a competitor, Fix-it-Quick.

Income Statement for the Year Ended 31 December 2013

	Turn-a-Screw	Fix-it-Quick
	£000	£000
Revenue	2,500	2,800
Cost of Sales	(1,000)	(1,200)
Gross Profit	1,500	1,600
Administrative expenses (includes loan interest)	(900)	(1,170)
Distribution expenses	(250)	(200)
Profit before Taxation	350	230
Taxation	(76)	(46)
Profit for the year	274	184
Note: You have the following additional information for dividends		
Preference dividends	(30)	(20)
Ordinary dividends	(124)	(94)

Q8 Turn-a-Screw (*continued*)

Statement of Financial Position as at 31 December 2013

	Turn-a-Screw		Fix-it-Quick	
	£000	£000	£000	£000
ASSETS				
Non-current assets				
Property, plant and equipment		1,820		1,765
Current Assets				
Inventories	120		115	
Trade receivables	100		115	
Cash	10	230	25	255
Total Assets		2,050		2,020
LIABILITIES				
Current Liabilities		(190)		(225)
Non-current Liabilities				
Long-term loans (10% interest)		(250)		(400)
Total Liabilities		(440)		(625)
Net Assets		1,610		1,395
EQUITY				
Capital and Reserves		£000		£000
Share Capital				
Ordinary share capital (£1 each)		850		860
Preference share capital (£0.50 each)		300		200
		1,150		1,060
Reserves				
Capital reserves				
Share premium account		125		—
Other reserves				
Retained earnings		335		335
Total equity		1,610		1,395
Share price		£1.44		£1.00

Required: Using the accounts of the two companies calculate the appropriate:

(a) Profitability ratios
(b) Efficiency ratios
(c) Liquidity ratios
(d) Gearing ratio
(e) Investment ratios

Briefly comment on your main findings for each category.

Q9 You have been employed temporarily by a rich local businessman, Mr Long Pocket, as his assistant. He has been told at the golf club that Sunbright Enterprises plc, a locally based company, would be a good return for his money. The last five years' results are set out below.

Income Statements for the Year Ended 31 December

	2009	2010	2011	2012	2013
	£000	£000	£000	£000	£000
Revenue	1,986	2,001	2,008	2,010	2,012
Cost of Sales	(1,192)	(1,221)	(1,406)	(1,306)	(1,509)
Gross Profit	794	780	602	704	503
Expenses (including loan interest)	(633)	(648)	(487)	(606)	(437)
Profit before Taxation	161	132	115	98	66
Taxation	(32)	(26)	(23)	(19)	(13)
Profit for Year	129	106	92	79	53

Statement of Financial Position as at 31 December

	2009	2010	2011	2012	2013
	£000	£000	£000	£000	£000
ASSETS					
Non-current Assets					
Property, plant, and equipment	500	580	660	780	878
Current Assets					
Inventories	24	26	27	45	68
Trade receivables	112	120	121	130	134
Cash	25	24	30	21	9
Total current assets	161	170	178	196	211
Total Assets	661	750	838	976	1,089
LIABILITIES					
Current Liabilities	(83)	(90)	(111)	(126)	(210)
Non-current Liabilities (10% interest)	(100)	(110)	(120)	(130)	(150)
Total Liabilities	(183)	(200)	(231)	(256)	(360)
Net Assets	478	550	607	720	729

Q9 Sunbright Enterprises plc (*continued*)

EQUITY					
Capital and Reserves	£000	£000	£000	£000	£000
Share Capital					
Ordinary share capital (£1 each)	250	250	250	300	300
Preference share capital (£1 each)	88	88	88	100	100
	338	338	338	400	400
Reserves					
Capital reserves					
Share premium account	12	12	12	25	25
Other reserves					
Retained earnings	128	200	257	295	304
Total Equity	478	550	607	720	729
Share price	£1.10	£1.08	£1.07	£1.05	£0.95

Note: You have the following details of dividends over the last five years which have been deducted from the retained earnings.

	2009	2010	2011	2012	2013
	£000	£000	£000	£000	£000
Preference dividends	(8)	(8)	(8)	(9)	(9)
Ordinary dividends	(25)	(26)	(27)	(32)	(35)

Required: Analyse the last five years' financial results for the company and calculate the appropriate ratios. Present your advice as a short report.

Note: Horizontal analysis, vertical analysis and a calculation of the cash flow ratio are not required.

Appendix 9.1: John Brown Plc

John Brown Plc has the following abridged results prepared for internal management use for the year ending 31 December 2013. The income statement and the statement of financial position are presented below.

John Brown Plc
Income Statement for the Year Ended 31 December 2013

	£m	£m
Revenue		200
Cost of sales		(100)
Gross Profit		100
Less *Expenses*		
General	40	
Loan interest	10	50
Profit before Taxation		50
Taxation		(15)
Profit for the year		35

Note: You have the following information for dividends. Preference dividends (10%) are £5m and ordinary dividends are £10m.

APPENDIX 9.1: John Brown Plc (*continued*)

Statement of Financial Position as at 31 December 2013

	£m	£m
ASSETS		
Non-current Assets		
Property, plant and equipment		275
Current Assets		
Inventories	60	
Trade receivables	40	
Cash	20	120
Total Assets		395
LIABILITIES		
Current Liabilities		
Trade payables		(50)
Proposed tax		(10)
		(60)
Non-current Liabilities		(70)
Total Liabilities		(130)
Net Assets		265
EQUITY		
Capital and Reserves		
Share Capital		£m
Ordinary share capital (1.50m £1 shares)		150
Preference share capital (50m £1 shares)		50
		200
Reserves		
Opening retained earnings		45
Retained earnings for the year		20
Closing retained earnings		65
Total Equity		265

At 31 December 2012 the market price of the ordinary shares was 67p.

APPENDIX 9.2: The Cash Flow Ratio using UK GAAP

Any Company Ltd has the following cash inflows and outflows in £000s:

	Inflows	Outflows
Net Cash Inflow from Operating Activities	118	
Returns on Investments and Servicing of Finance	15	8
Taxation		30
Capital Expenditure and Financial Investment		220
Equity Dividends Paid		20
Financing	140	
Totals	273	278

Therefore, our cash flow ratio is:

$$\frac{\text{Total cash inflows}}{\text{Total cash outflows}} = \frac{273}{278} = 0.98$$

To all intents and purposes, our total cash inflows thus match our total cash outflows.

Go online to discover the extra features for this chapter at **www.wiley.com/college/jones**

SECTION B

Financial Accounting: The Context

In Section A, we looked at the accounting techniques which underpin the preparation and interpretation of the financial statements of sole traders, partnerships and limited companies. These techniques do not exist in a vacuum. In this section, we examine five crucial aspects of the context in which these accounting techniques are applied.

Chapter 10 investigates the regulatory and conceptual frameworks within which accounting operates. The regulatory framework provides a set of rules and regulations which govern accounting. The conceptual theory is broader and seeks to set out a theoretical framework to underpin accounting. Then, in Chapter 11, the main potential alternative measurement systems which can underpin the preparation of accounts are laid out. This chapter shows how using different measurement systems can yield different profits and different valuations of the statement of financial position.

The annual report, the main way in which public limited companies communicate financial information to their shareholders, is discussed in Chapter 12. This chapter outlines the nature, context and function of the annual report. Both the content and the presentation of the annual report are examined.

Chapters 13 and 14 then investigate two interesting aspects of financial accounting: creative accounting and international accounting. Creative accounting explores the flexibility within accounting and shows how managers may manipulate financial information out of self-interest. Finally, Chapter 14 provides a broad international view of accounting. It shows that different countries have different accounting environments. Moreover, this chapter also shows the progress which has been made towards the harmonisation of accounting practices both in the UK and worldwide. Particularly, the role of the International Accounting Standards Board is investigated.

Chapter 10

Regulatory and conceptual frameworks

'Regulation is like salt in cooking. It's an essential ingredient – you don't want a great deal of it, but my goodness you'd better get the right amount. If you get too much or too little you'll soon know.'

Sir Kenneth Berrill, *Financial Times* (6 March 1985), *The Book of Business Quotations* (1991), p. 47.

Learning Outcomes

After completing this chapter you should be able to:

- Outline the traditional corporate model.
- Understand the regulatory framework.
- Explain corporate governance.
- Understand the conceptual framework.

Go online to discover the extra features for this chapter at **www.wiley.com/college/jones**

Chapter Summary

- Directors, auditors and shareholders are the main parties in the traditional corporate model.
- The regulatory framework provides a set of rules and regulations for accounting.
- At the international level, the International Accounting Standards Board provides a broad regulatory framework of International Accounting Standards. This applies to all European listed companies, including UK companies.
- In the UK, the two main sources of regulation are the Companies Acts and accounting standards.
- Financial statements must give a true and fair view of the financial position and performance of the reporting entity.
- The UK accounting standards-setting regime operates under the Financial Reporting Council. It consists of the Codes and Standards Committee, the Accounting Council, the Audit and Assurance Council and the Financial Reporting Review Panel.
- Corporate governance is the system by which companies are directed and controlled.
- A conceptual framework is a coherent and consistent set of accounting principles which will help in standard setting.
- Some major elements in a conceptual theory are the objectives of accounting, users, user needs, information characteristics and measurement models.
- The most widely agreed objective is to provide information for decision making.
- Users include shareholders and analysts, lenders, creditors, customers and employees.
- Key information characteristics are relevance and faithful representation, which are enhanced by comparability, verifiability, timeliness and understandability.

Introduction

So far, we have looked at accounting practice – focusing on the preparation and interpretation of the financial statements of sole traders, partnerships and limited companies. In particular, we considered practical aspects of accounting such as double-entry bookkeeping, the trial balance, the income statement (profit and loss account), the statement of financial position (balance sheet), the statement of cash flows (cash flow statement) and ratio analysis. Accounting practice does not, however, take place in a vacuum. It is bounded both by a regulatory framework and a conceptual framework. These frameworks have grown up over time to bring order and fairness into accounting practice. They have been devised principally in relation to limited companies, but are also relevant to some extent to sole traders and partnerships.

The regulatory framework is essentially the set of rules and regulations which govern corporate accounting practice. At the international level, the regulatory framework is provided by the International Accounting Standards Board. This applies to all European listed companies, including UK companies. In the UK, regulations are set down mainly by government in Companies Acts and by independent private sector regulation in accounting standards. These cover small and medium-sized companies. The conceptual framework seeks to set out a theoretical and consistent set of accounting principles by which financial statements can be prepared.

Traditional Corporate Model: Directors, Auditors and Shareholders

In what I term the traditional corporate model, there are three main groups (directors, auditors and shareholders). As Figure 10.1 shows, these three groups interact. This interaction is explained in more detail below.

Figure 10.1 The Traditional Corporate Model

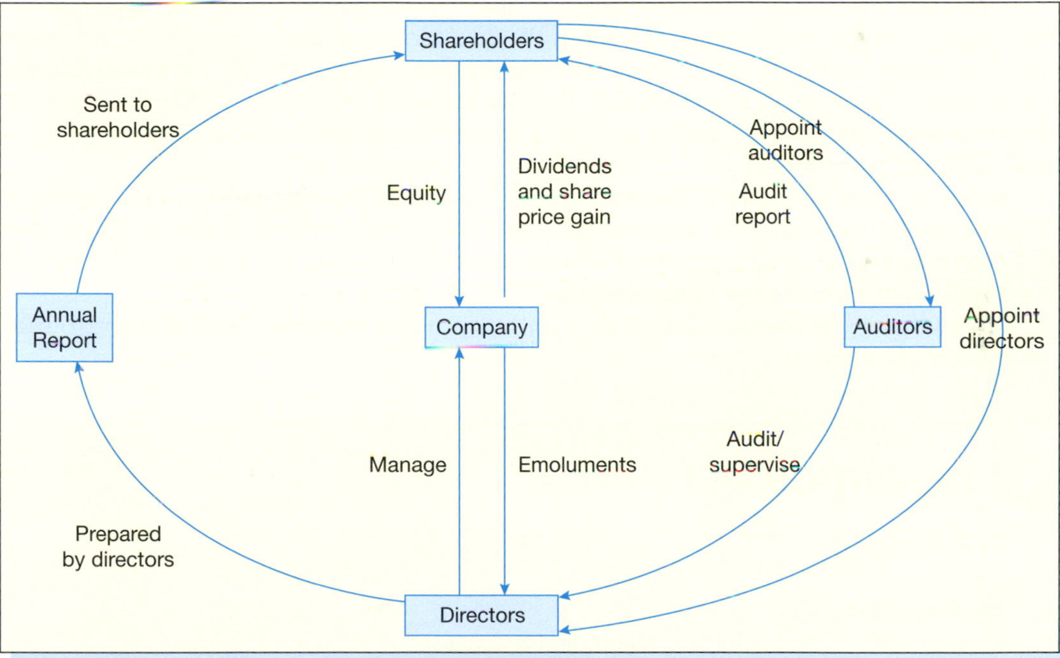

The directors are responsible for preparing the accounts – in practice this is usually delegated to the accounting managers. These accounts are then checked by professionally qualified accountants, the auditors. Finally, the accounts are sent to the shareholders.

1. Directors

The directors are those responsible for running the business. They are accountable to the shareholders, who in theory appoint and dismiss them. The relationship between the directors and shareholders is sometimes uneasy. The shareholders own the company, but it is the directors who run it. This relationship is often termed a 'principal–agent' relationship. The shareholders are the principals and the directors are the agents. The principals delegate the management of the company to directors. However, the directors are still responsible to the shareholders.

The directors are responsible for preparing the accounts which are sent to the shareholders. These accounts, prepared annually, allow the shareholders to assess the performance of the company and of the directors. They also provide information to shareholders to enable them to make share trading decisions (i.e., to hold their shares, to buy more shares or to sell their shares). As a reward for running the company, the directors receive emoluments. These may take the form of a salary, profit-related bonuses or other benefits in kind such as share options or company cars.

2. Auditors

Unfortunately, human nature being human nature, there is a problem with such arm's-length transactions. In a nutshell, how can the shareholders trust accounts prepared by the directors? For example, how can they be sure that the directors are not adopting creative accounting in order to inflate profits and thus pay themselves inflated profit-related bonuses? One way is by external auditing.

The auditors are a team of professionally qualified accountants. They are appointed by the shareholders on the recommendation of the directors. It is their job to check and report on the accounts. This checking and reporting involves extensive work verifying that the transactions have actually occurred, that they are recorded properly and that the monetary amounts in the accounts do indeed provide a true and fair view of the company's financial position and performance.

A key aspect of the external auditors is that they should be independent of management. This means, for example, that they should not be friends or relatives of management. Also, they must be careful in their provision of non-audit services and consulting as these could potentially compromise their independence.

An audit (see Definition 10.1) is thus an independent examination and report on the accounts of a company.

DEFINITION 10.1

The Audit

Working definition

An independent examination and report on the accounts.

Formal definition

'The systematic independent examination of a business's, normally a company's, accounting systems, accounting records and financial statements in order to provide a report on whether or not they provide a true and fair view of the business's activities.'

CIMA definition

'Systematic examination of the activities and status of an entity, based primarily on investigation and analysis of its systems, contracts and rewards.'

Source: Chartered Institute of Management Accountants (2005), *Official Terminology.* Reproduced by Permission of Elsevier.

For their time and effort the auditors are paid often quite considerable sums. The auditors prepare a formal report for shareholders. This is part of the annual report. In Company Snapshot 10.1 we attach an auditors' report prepared by PricewaterhouseCoopers, the auditors of Sainsbury plc, on Sainsbury's 2010 accounts.

COMPANY SNAPSHOT 10.1

Independent Auditors' report to the members of J Sainsbury plc

We have audited the financial statements of J Sainsbury plc for the 52 weeks ended 20 March 2010 which comprise the Group income statement, the Group and Company Statements of comprehensive income, the Group and Company Balance sheets, the Group and Company Cash flow statements, the Group and Company Statement of changes in equity and the related notes. The financial reporting framework that has been applied in their preparation is applicable law and International Financial Reporting Standards ('IFRSs') as adopted by the European Union and, as regards the Company financial statements, as applied in accordance with the provisions of the Companies Act 2006.

Respective responsibilities of Directors and Auditors

As explained more fully in the Statement of Directors' responsibilities set out on page 43, the Directors are responsible for the preparation of the Annual Report, the Remuneration report and financial statements. The Directors are responsible for being satisfied that the financial statements give a true and fair view. Our responsibility is to audit the financial statements in accordance with applicable law and International Standards on Auditing (UK and Ireland). Those standards require us to comply with the Auditing Practices Board's Ethical Standards for Auditors.

This report, including the opinion, has been prepared for and only for the Company's members as a body in accordance with Chapter 3 of Part 16 of the Companies Act 2006 and for no other purpose. We do not, in giving this opinion, accept or assume responsibility for any other purpose or to any other person to whom this report is shown or into whose hands it may come save where expressly agreed by our prior consent in writing.

Scope of the audit of the financial statements

An audit involves obtaining evidence about the amounts and disclosures in the financial statements sufficient to give reasonable assurance that the financial statements are free from material misstatement, whether caused by fraud or error. This includes an assessment of: whether the accounting policies are appropriate to the Group's and the Company's circumstances and have been consistently applied and adequately disclosed; the reasonableness of significant accounting estimates made by the Directors; and the overall presentation of the financial statements.

Opinion on financial statements

In our opinion:

- the financial statements give a true and fair view of the state of the Group's and of the Company's affairs as at 20 March 2010 and of the Group's profit and the Group's and Company's cash flows for the 52 weeks then ended;

COMPANY SNAPSHOT 10.1 (*continued*)

- the Group financial statements have been properly prepared in accordance with IFRSs as adopted by the European Union;
- the Company financial statements have been properly prepared in accordance with IFRSs as adopted by the European Union and as applied in accordance with the provisions of the Companies Act 2006; and
- the financial statements have been prepared in accordance with the requirements of the Companies Act 2006 and, as regards the Group financial statements, Article 4 of the IAS Regulation.

Opinion on other matters prescribed by the Companies Act 2006
In our opinion:

- the part of the Remuneration report to be audited has been properly prepared in accordance with the Companies Act 2006; and
- the information given in the Directors' report for the financial year for which the financial statements are prepared is consistent with the financial statements.

Matters on which we are required to report by exception
We have nothing to report in respect of the following:

Under the Companies Act 2006 we are required to report to you if, in our opinion:

- adequate accounting records have not been kept by the Company, or returns adequate for our audit have not been received from branches not visited by us; or
- the Company financial statements and the part of the Remuneration report to be audited are not in agreement with the accounting records and returns; or
- certain disclosures of Directors' remuneration specified by law are not made: or
- we have not received all the information and explanations we require for our audit.

Under the Listing Rules we are required to review:

- the Directors' statement, set out on page 28, in relation to going concern; and
- the parts of the Statement of corporate governance relating to the Company's compliance with the nine provisions of the June 2008 Combined Code specified for our review.

Robert Milburn (Senior Statutory Auditor)
for and on behalf of PricewaterhouseCoopers LLP
Chartered Accountants and Statutory Auditors
London
12 May 2010

Source: J. Sainsbury Plc, *Annual Report and Financial Statements 2010,* p. 44. Reproduced by kind permission of Sainsbury's Supermarkets Ltd.

This auditors' report thus confirms that the directors of J. Sainsbury plc have prepared a set of financial statements which have given a true and fair view of the company's accounts as at 20 March 2010. This is known as a clean audit report. In this case, therefore, the auditors have not drawn the shareholders' attention to any discrepancies. A qualified auditors' report, by contrast, would be an adverse opinion on some aspect of the accounts; for example, compliance with a particular accounting standard. Shareholders of Sainsbury can thus draw comfort from the fact that the auditors believe the accounts do give a true and fair view and faithfully reflect the economic performance of the company over the year.

3. Shareholders

The shareholders (in the US known as the stockholders) own the company. They have provided funding to the business in exchange for shares. Their reward is twofold. First, they may receive an annual dividend, which is simply a cash payment from the company based on profits. Second, they may benefit from any increase in the share price over the year. However, companies may make losses and share prices can go down as well as up, so this reward is not guaranteed. In the developed world, more and more companies are owned by large institutions (such as investment trusts or pension funds) rather than private shareholders.

The shareholders of the company receive an annual audited statement of the company's performance. This is called the annual report. It comprises the financial statements and also a narrative explanation of corporate performance. Included in this annual report is an auditors' report.

It is important to realise that shareholders are only liable for the equity which they contribute to a company. This equity is known as *share capital* (i.e., the capital of a company is divided into many shares). These shares limit the liability of shareholders and so we have limited liability companies. Shares, once issued, are bought or sold by shareholders on the stock market. This enables people who are not involved in the day-to-day running of the business to own shares. This division between owners and managers is often known as the divorce of ownership and control. It is a fundamental underpinning of a capitalist society.

PAUSE FOR THOUGHT 10.1

Risk and Reward

In the corporate model, each of the three groups is rewarded for its contributions. This is called the 'risk and reward model'. Can you work out each group's risk and reward?

	Contribution (risk)	*Reward*
Shareholders	Share capital	Dividends and increase in share price
Directors	Time and effort	Salaries, bonuses, benefits-in-kind such as cars or share options
Auditors	Time and effort	Auditors' fees

Regulatory Framework

The corporate model of directors, shareholders and auditors is one of checks and balances. The directors manage the company, receive directors' emoluments and recommend the appointment of the auditors to the shareholders. The shareholders own the company, but do not run it, and rely upon the auditors to check the accounts. Finally, the auditors are appointed by shareholders on the recommendation of the directors. They receive an auditors' fee for the work they undertake when they check the financial statements prepared by managers.

PAUSE FOR THOUGHT 10.2

Checks and Balances

Is auditing enough to stop company directors pursuing their own interests at the expense of the shareholders?

Auditing is a powerful check on directors' self-interest. The directors prepare the accounts and the auditors check that the directors have correctly prepared them and that they give a 'true and fair' view. However, there are problems. The auditors, although technically appointed by the shareholders at the company's *annual general meeting* (i.e., a meeting called once a year to discuss a company's accounts), are recommended by directors. Auditors are also paid, often huge fees, by the company. The auditors do not wish to upset the directors and lose those fees. Given the flexibility within accounts, there is a whole range of possible accounting policies which the directors can choose. The regulatory framework helps to narrow this range of potential accounting policies and gives guidance to both directors and auditors. The auditors can, therefore, point to the rules and regulations if they feel that the directors' accounting policies are inappropriate. The regulatory framework is, therefore, a powerful ally of the auditor.

This system of checks and balances is fine, in principle. However, it is rather like having two football teams and a referee with no rules. The regulatory framework, in effect, provides a set of rules and regulations to ensure fair play. As Definition 10.2 shows, at the national level, these rules and regulations may originate from the government, the accounting standard setters or, more rarely, for listed companies, the stock exchange. The principal aim of the regulatory framework is to ensure that the financial statements present a true and fair view of the financial performance and position of the organisation.

DEFINITION 10.2

The National Regulatory Framework

Working definition
The set of rules and regulations which govern accounting practice, mainly prescribed by government and the accounting standard-setting bodies.

Formal definition
'The set of legal and professional requirements with which the financial statements of a company must comply. Company reporting is influenced by the requirements of law, of the accounting profession and of the Stock Exchange (for listed companies).'

Source: Chartered Institute of Management Accountants (2000), *Official Terminology.* Reproduced by Permission of Elsevier.

SOUNDBITE 10.1

Regulations

'If you destroy a free market you create a black market. If you have ten thousand regulations, you destroy all respect for the law.'

Winston S. Churchill

Source: The Book of Unusual Quotations (1959), pp. 240–41.

In most countries, including the UK, the main sources of authority for the regulatory framework are either via the government through companies legislation or via accounting standard-setting bodies through accounting standards. In the UK, since 2012, this is through the Accounting Council. As Soundbite 10.1 suggests, there is a need not to overregulate. At the international level, there is a set of International Financial Reporting Standards (IFRS) issued by the International Accounting Standards Board (IASB). This is a non-governmental organisation that sets global accounting standards worldwide. It is dealt with in more depth in Chapter 14. The IASB is steadily growing in importance. Its standards are aimed primarily at large international companies (see Chapter 14 for a fuller discussion of IFRS). However, nowadays many other entities use IFRS. European listed companies must comply with IFRS.

International Accounting Standards

Over the last decade, both in the UK and in other European (and indeed non-European) countries, the role of the International Accounting Standards Board has grown in importance. The IASB has published International Accounting Standards (IAS) or International Financial Reporting Standards which are dealt with in more depth in Chapter 14. However, it is important to set the scene here.

From 2005, IAS (issued by the International Accounting Standards Committee up to 2001) and IFRS (issued by the International Accounting Standards Board from 2001) have been used by UK listed companies in their group accounts. These standards are based on a conceptual framework set out by the International Accounting Standards Board (see section later in this chapter).

However, these international standards are being used by more and more organisations such as the UK's National Health System and publicly accountable organisations. Also globally IFRS are now being used widely, for example, by countries in the European Union.

Regulatory Framework in the UK

Most countries have a national regulatory framework that exists alongside IFRS. For example, in the UK, there are two main sources of authority for regulation: the Companies Acts and accounting standards. There are some additional requirements from the Stock Exchange for listed companies, but given their relative unimportance, they are not discussed further here.

In the UK, as in most countries, the regulatory framework has evolved over time. As accounting has grown more complex, so has the regulatory framework which governs it. At first, the only requirements that companies followed were those of the Companies Acts. However, in 1970 the first accounting standards set by the Accounting Standards Steering Committee were issued. Today, UK companies must adhere both to the requirements of Companies Acts and to accounting standards. For non-listed companies these are set by the Accounting Council (formerly the Accounting Standards Board (ASB)), for listed companies by the International Accounting Standards Board. The UK accounting standards are increasingly becoming less influential. However, from January 2015 the smallest UK companies will continue to use a simplified version of UK standards, FRSSE (Financial Reporting Standard for Smaller Entities), while other non-listed companies will use a standard based on IFRS, FRS 102, for small and medium-sized enterprises (IFRS for SMEs). Alternatively, these companies can adopt IFRS. The overall aim of this regulatory framework is to protect the interests of all those involved in the corporate model. Specifically, there is a need to provide a 'true and fair view' of a company's affairs.

True and Fair View

Section 404 of the 2006 Companies Act requires that for companies following the Companies Acts Group Accounts (rather than IFRS Group Accounts): 'the accounts must give a true and fair view of the state of affairs as at the end of the financial year, and the profit or loss for the financial year, of the undertakings included in the consolidation as a whole, so far as concerns members of the company'. The 'true and fair' concept is thus of overriding importance. Unfortunately, it is a particularly nebulous concept which has no easy definition. A working definition is, however, suggested in Definition 10.3. In essence, there is a presumption that the accounts will reflect the underpinning economic reality. Generations of accountants have struggled unsuccessfully to pin down the exact meaning of the phrase. In general, to achieve a true and fair view, accounts should comply with the Companies Acts and accounting standards.

Occasionally, however, where compliance with the law would not give a true and fair view, a company may override the legal requirements. However, the company would have to demonstrate clearly why this was necessary.

DEFINITION 10.3

Working Definition of a 'True and Fair View'

A set of financial statements which faithfully, accurately and truly reflect the underlying economic transactions of an organisation.

Companies Acts

Companies Acts are Acts of Parliament which lay down the legal requirements for companies including regulations for accounting. There has been a succession of Companies Acts which have gradually increased the reporting requirements placed on UK companies. Initially, the Companies Acts provided only a broad legislative framework. However, later Companies Acts (CAs), especially the CA 1981, have imposed a significant regulatory burden on UK companies. The CA 1981 introduced the European Fourth Directive into UK law. Effectively, this Directive was the result of a deal between the United Kingdom and other European Union members. The United Kingdom exported the true and fair view concept, but imported substantial detailed legislation and standardised formats for the income statement (profit and loss account) and statements of financial position (balance sheets). The CA 1981, therefore, introduced a much more prescriptive 'European' accounting regulatory framework into the UK. The latest Companies Act is the CA 2006 which has introduced IFRS into British law. Group Accounts may be prepared in accordance with Section 404 (Companies Act Group Accounts) or in accordance with international accounting standards (IFRS Group Accounts).

Accounting Standards

Whereas Companies Acts are governmental in origin, accounting standards are set by non-governmental bodies. Accounting standards were introduced, as Real-World View 10.1 indicates, to improve the quality of UK financial reporting.

REAL-WORLD VIEW 10.1

Introduction of Accounting Standards

Inflation accounting was, in fact, only one part of a bigger move towards accounting standards – a move that was itself controversial. Standards had been proposed a few years earlier to limit the scope for judgement in the preparation of accounts. They were the profession's response to a huge City row when GEC chief executive Arnold Weinstock restated the profits of AEI, a company he had just taken over, from mega millions down to zero.

The City was outraged and demanded more certainty in accounts so it could have more faith in public profit figures.

Standards were the result and, though taken for granted now, many saw them as the death knell for the profession, precisely because they limited the scope for professional judgement. Many believed the profession had been permanently diminished when its ability to make judgements was curtailed.

Source: Anthony Hilton, Demands for Change, *Accountancy Age*, 11 November 2004, p. 25.

At the international level, International Financial Reporting Standards (IFRS) are set by the International Accounting Standards Board. These are now mandatory for all European listed companies in their group accounts. The US market does not accept IFRS at present without reconciliation to US GAAP. However, there have been discussions between the IASB and the US Financial Accounting Standards Board (FASB) about convergence. UK non-listed companies may still follow UK accounting standards. The role of the IASB is discussed in more detail in Chapter 14.

The UK's accounting setting regime has evolved over time. The current regulatory framework was set up in 1990, reorganised in 2004 and then again in July 2012. In 2004, the structure consisted of a Financial Reporting Council which supervised five boards regulating accounting, accountants and auditing: the Auditing Practices Board, Accounting Standards Board, Financial Reporting and Review Panel, Investigation and Discipline board and Professional Oversight Board. The new FRC structure set up in July 2012 is shown in Figure 10.2. The main elements that concern accounting are the Codes and Standards Committee, the Accounting Council, the Financial Reporting Review Panel and the Audit and Assurance Council.

There was much concern in the accounting community about the abolition of the Accounting Standards Board. Effectively, it has been replaced by the Accounting Council.

Figure 10.2 UK's Regulatory Framework

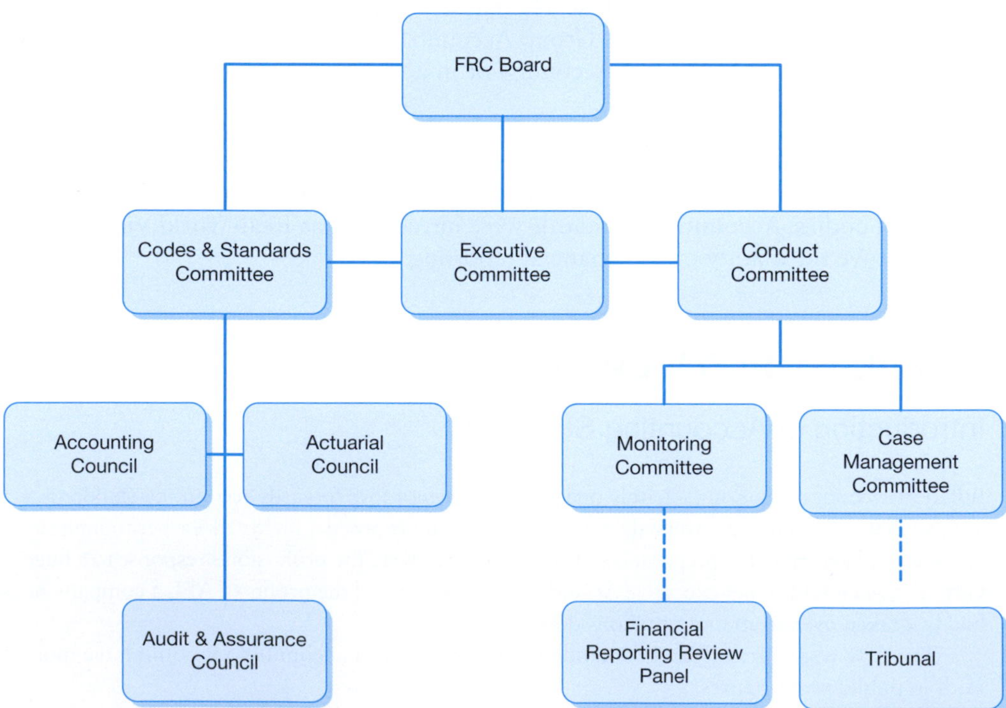

Source: © Financial Reporting Council Ltd (FRC). Adapted and reproduced with the kind permission of the Financial Reporting Council. All Rights reserved. www.frc.org.uk

1. Financial Reporting Council (FRC)

The Financial Reporting Council is a supervisory body which ensures that the overall system is working. As can be seen in Figure 10.2, the FRC supervises a Codes and Standards Committee, an Executive Committee and a Conduct Committee. The main accounting functions come under the Codes and Standards Committee in terms of the Accounting Council and Audit and Assurance Council. In addition, the Financial Reporting Review Panel comes under the Monitoring Committee. These are discussed more fully below.

2. Codes and Standards Committee

This was established in 2012. It is responsible for advising the FRC board on monitoring an effective framework of UK codes and standards for corporate governance, stewardship, accounting, auditing and assurance and actuarial technical standards. This board is advised by the Accounting Council (including accounting and accounting narratives), the Audit and Assurance Council, and the Actuarial Council.

3. Accounting Council

The Accounting Council took over from the ASB in 2012. It is the engine of the accounting standards process. In the UK, accounting standards are called Financial Reporting Standards (FRS). The Accounting Council issues FRS which are applicable to the accounts of all UK companies not following IFRS and are intended to give a true and fair view. These Financial Reporting Standards have replaced most of the Standard Statements of Accounting Practice which were issued from 1970 to 1990 by the Accounting Council's and the ASB's predecessor, the Accounting Standards Committee. Listed companies follow IFRS issued by the International Accounting Standards Board. Other publicly accountable UK entities are increasingly following IFRS. The Accounting Council collaborates with accounting standard setters from other countries and particularly with the International Accounting Standards Board. As Definition 10.4 shows, in essence, accounting standards are pronouncements which must normally be followed in order to give a true and fair view. The Accounting Council has taken over the role of the Urgent Issues Task Force (UITF). As accounting standards take time to develop, the Accounting Council needs to react quickly to new situations. Recommendations are made to curb undesirable interpretations of accounting standards or to prevent accounting practices which the Accounting Council considers undesirable.

DEFINITION 10.4

Accounting Standards

Working definition

Accounting pronouncements which must be followed in order to give a true and fair view within the regulations.

Formal definition

'Accounting standards are authoritative statements of how particular types of transaction and other events should be reflected in financial statements and accordingly compliance with accounting standards will normally be necessary for financial statements to give a true and fair view.'

Source: Foreword to *Accounting Standards*, Accounting Standards Board (1993), para. 16.

4. Audit and Assurance Council

This body, created in 2012, advises the FRC board and the Codes and Standards Committee on audit and assurance matters.

Accounting standards are mandatory in that accountants are expected to observe them. They cover specific technical accounting issues such as inventory, depreciation, and research and development. These standards essentially aim to improve the quality of accounting in the UK. They narrow the areas of difference and variety in accounting practice, set out minimum disclosure standards and disclose the accounting principles upon which the accounts are based. Overall, accounting standards provide a comprehensive set of guidelines which preparers and auditors can use when drawing up and verifying the financial statements.

5. The Financial Reporting Review Panel (FRRP)

The FRRP investigates contentious departures from accounting standards. It reports to the Monitoring Committee. It is the 'detective' arm of the regulatory framework. The FRRP questions the directors of the companies investigated. The last resort of the FRRP is to take miscreant companies to court to force them to revise their accounts. However, so far the threat of court action has been enough. The FRRP began as a reactive body only responding to complaints. However, recently the FRRP has become more proactive as Real-World View 10.2 explains.

REAL-WORLD VIEW 10.2

FRRP

When it was set up in 1990 to deal with the scandals of the eighties, the government had decided that self-regulation was the best option. It is a strategy that Sir Bryan describes as highly successful 'because the people in the system knew they had to make it work because of the alternative'.

But since Enron, Parmalat et al, the pressure's on to up the ante. Enhancements include a new proactive approach to uncovering accounting cock-ups in the books of listed UK companies, with 300 sets of accounts slated for investigation by the Financial Reporting Review Panel (FRRP) this year.

Source: Insider, *Accountancy Age*, 1 April 2004, p. 15.

In 2005, for example, the FRRP investigated the accounts of MG Rover. This company was run by four businessmen and then subsequently collapsed. There were suspicions of accounting impropriety and, therefore, the FRRP looked into its finances. As Real-World View 10.3 shows, this triggered a government enquiry.

REAL-WORLD VIEW 10.3

FRRP and MG Rover

The Phoenix Four, the Midlands businessmen behind the collapsed MG Rover Group, are to be investigated by the Department of Trade and Industry, which has set up an independent inquiry into the affairs of the former car maker.

The inquiry was announced yesterday by Alan Johnson, the Trade and Industry Secretary. He ordered the inquiry after receiving an initial report into the company's finances by the Financial Reporting and Review Panel (FRRP), part of the accountancy watchdog, the Financial Reporting Council.

A clean bill of health for MG Rover, and its associated companies, would have left the Government little choice but to close the case. But Mr Johnson said the FRRP report 'raises a number of questions that need to be answered'. He said the public interest demanded a more detailed account of what went on at MG Rover Group, which collapsed into administration in April with the loss of more than 5000 jobs.

Source: Damian Reece, DTI Opens MG Rover Investigation, *Financial Times*, 1 June 2005, p. 57.

Corporate Governance

From the 1990s, corporate governance has grown in importance. Effectively, corporate governance is the system by which companies are directed and controlled (see Real-World View 10.4).

REAL-WORLD VIEW 10.4

Corporate Governance

Corporate governance is the system by which companies are directed and controlled. Boards of directors are responsible for the governance of their companies. The shareholders' role in governance is to appoint the directors and the auditors and to satisfy themselves that an appropriate governance structure is in place. The responsibilities of the board include setting the company's strategic aims, providing the leadership to put them into effect, supervising the management of the business and reporting to shareholders on their stewardship. The board's actions are subject to laws, regulations and the shareholders in general meeting.

Within that overall framework, the specifically financial aspects of corporate governance (the committee's remit) are the way in which boards set financial policy and oversee its implementation, including the use of financial controls, and the process whereby they report on the activities and progress of the company to the shareholders.

Source: Report of the Committee on the Financial Assets of Corporate Governance (1992), Gee and Co., p. 15.

The financial aspects of corporate governance relate principally to internal controls, the way in which the board of directors functions and the process by which the directors report to the shareholders on the activities and progress of the company. Corporate governance came to prominence in the UK after the failure of Polly Peck, which went insolvent after a major fraudulent misstatement of the accounts. Polly Peck is discussed in detail in Chapter 13. The Cadbury Committee was set up and in 1992 made several recommendations such as the separation of CEO and Chairman, that there should be non-executive directors and that there should be an audit committee. Several other corporate committees followed in the UK including the Greenbury Committee (1995) on executive compensation, the Hampel Committee (1998) which recommended a combined code and the Turnbull Committee (1999) which suggested directors should be responsible for finance and auditing controls. In addition, since 2003 there have been several other reports. The Higgs review focused on the role of non-executive directors. Paul Myners looked at the role of institutional investors and the Walker review focused on the banking industry. Then in 2010 a stewardship code was issued by the Financial Reporting Council.

The continuing interest in corporate governance arises in part for two reasons. First, there have been some unexpected failures of major companies such as Polly Peck, Maxwell Communications, WorldCom, Enron and Parmalat. In the US, in particular, this has led to the Sarbanes-Oxley Act (see Soundbite 10.2). The Sarbanes-Oxley Act was the US government's response to Enron and WorldCom. Since 2004, all US companies have submitted details of their internal control systems to the US Security Exchange Council (SEC). These control systems are also audited. Second, there have been extensive criticisms in the press of 'fat-cat' directors. These directors, often of privatised companies (i.e., companies which were previously state-owned and run), are generally perceived to be paying themselves huge and unwarranted salaries.

SOUNDBITE 10.2

Corporate Governance

'Sarbanes-Oxley was brought in to ward off any future Enrons by, effectively, creating a vast network of internal controls and regulations that would, the legislators intended, make Enron-scale corporate deceptions impossible.'

Source: Robert Bruce, Winds of Change, *Accountancy Magazine*, February 2010, p. 27.

As a result of the Cadbury Committee and other subsequent committees, there were attempts to tighten up corporate governance in the UK. In particular, there was a concern with the amount of information companies disclosed, with the role of non-executive directors (i.e., directors appointed from outside the company), with directors' remuneration, with audit committees (committees ideally controlled by non-executive directors which oversee the appointment of external auditors and deal with their reports), with relations with institutional investors and with systems of internal financial control set up by management.

Companies are very concerned to demonstrate their good corporate governance structure. In the UK, the Financial Reporting Council in 2012 revised the UK's Corporate Governance Code. This sets out principles of good corporate governance. Public companies need to disclose how they have complied with the code. Marks and Spencer plc, for example, has aligned its governance with the themes in this Code: leadership's effectiveness, accountability, communication and remuneration. Marks and Spencer has outlined its governance structure in its 2010 annual report (see Company Snapshot 10.2).

In the annual report, companies now set out extensive details of directors' remuneration and disclose information about corporate governance. The auditors review these corporate governance elements to check that they comply with the principles of good governance and code of best practice as set out in the London Stock Exchange's rules. Company Snapshot 10.3 presents part of J.D. Wetherspoon's corporate governance statement which relates to internal control. The directors acknowledge their responsibility to establish controls such as those to protect against the unauthorised use of assets.

Internationally, there are two main approaches to corporate governance: rules-based and principles-based. The US adopts a rules-based approach as set out in the Sarbanes-Oxley Act. By contrast, the UK takes a more principles-based approach. Companies in the UK comply with the regulations or explain why they are not complying (usually termed a comply or explain approach).

COMPANY SNAPSHOT 10.2

Governance Structures: Marks and Spencer

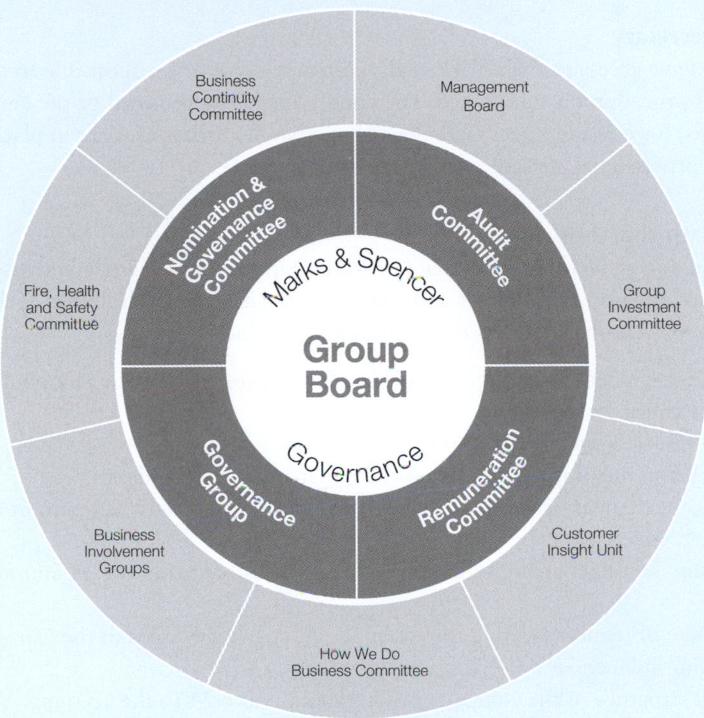

Source: Marks and Spencer plc, *Annual Report and Financial Statements 2010*.

COMPANY SNAPSHOT 10.3

Corporate Governance

Nomination committee

A formal nomination committee has been established, comprising John Herring (chairman), Debra van Gene, Elizabeth McMeikan and Sir Richard Beckett. The nomination committee meets as appropriate and considers all possible board appointments and also the re-election of directors, both executive and non-executive. No director is involved in any decision about his or her own re-appointment. Under the terms of the Code, one of the members of the committee was not independent.

COMPANY SNAPSHOT 10.3 (*continued*)

The terms of reference of the nomination committee are available on request.

Company secretary

All directors have access to the advice of the company secretary, responsible to the board for ensuring that procedures are followed. The appointment and removal of the company secretary is reserved for consideration by the board as a whole. Procedures are in place for seeking independent professional advice, at the Company's expense.

Relations with shareholders

The board takes considerable measures to ensure that all board members are kept aware of both the views of major shareholders and changes in the major shareholdings of the Company. Efforts made to accomplish effective communication include:

- Annual general meeting, considered to be an important forum for shareholders to raise questions with the board
- Regular feedback from the Company's stockbrokers
- Interim, full and ongoing announcements circulated to shareholders
- Any significant changes in shareholder movement being notified to the board by the company secretary, when necessary
- The company secretary maintaining procedures and agreements for all announcements to the City
- A programme of regular meetings between investors and directors of the Company, including the senior independent director, as appropriate
- The capital structure of the company is described in note 24 to the accounts.

Risk management

The board is responsible for the Company's risk-management process.

The internal audit department, in conjunction with the management of the business functions, produces a risk register annually. This register has been compiled by the business using a series of facilitated control and risk self-assessment workshops, run in conjunction with internal audit. These workshops were run with senior management from the key business functions.

The identified risks are assessed based on the likelihood of a risk occurring and the potential impact to the business, should the risk occur. The head of internal audit determines and reviews the risk assessment process and will communicate the timetable annually.

The risk register is presented to the audit committee every six months, with a schedule of audit work agreed on, on a rolling basis. The purpose of this work is to review, on behalf of the Company and board, those key risks and the systems of control necessary to manage such risks.

The results of this work are reported back to relevant senior management and the audit committee. Where recommendations are made for changes in systems or processes to reduce risk, internal audit will follow up regularly to ensure that the recommendations are implemented.

COMPANY SNAPSHOT 10.3 (*continued*)

Internal control

During the year, the Company and the board continued to support and invest in resource to provide an internal audit and risk-management function. The system of internal control and risk mitigation is deeply embedded in the operations and the Company culture. The board is responsible for maintaining a sound system of internal control and reviewing its effectiveness. The function can only manage, rather than entirely eliminate, the risk of failure to achieve business objectives. It can provide only reasonable and not absolute assurance against material misstatement or loss. Ongoing reviews, assessments and management of significant risks took place throughout the year under review and up to the date of the approval of the annual report and accords with the Turnbull Guidance (Guidance on Internal Control).

The Company has an internal audit function which is discharged as follows:

- Regular audits of the Company stock
- Unannounced visits to retail units
- Monitoring systems which control the Company cash
- Health & safety visits, ensuring compliance with Company procedures
- Reviewing and assessing the impact of legislative and regulatory change
- Annually reviewing the Company's strategy, including a review of risks facing the business
- Risk-management process, identifying key risks facing the business (Company Risk Register).

The Company has key controls, as follows:

- Clearly defined authority limits and controls over cash-handling, purchasing commitments and capital expenditure
- Comprehensive budgeting process, with a detailed 12-month operating plan and a mid-term financial plan, both approved by the board
- Business results are reported weekly (for key times), with a monthly comprehensive report in full and compared with budget
- Forecasts are prepared regularly throughout the year, for review by the board
- Complex treasury instruments are not used; decisions on treasury matters are reserved by the board
- Regular reviews of the amount of external insurance which it obtains, bearing in mind the availability of such cover, its costs and the likelihood of the risks involved
- Regular evaluation of processes and controls in relation to the Company's financial reporting requirements.

The directors confirm that they have reviewed the effectiveness of the system of internal control. Directors' insurance cover is maintained.

Keith Down
Company Secretary
10 September 2010

Source: J.D. Wetherspoon plc, *Annual Report and Accounts 2010*, p. 68.

Conceptual Framework

DEFINITION 10.5

Conceptual Framework

The development of a coherent and consistent set of accounting principles which underpin the preparation and presentation of financial statements.

Since the 1960s, standard-setting bodies (such as the Financial Accounting Standards Board (FASB), in the USA, the International Accounting Standards Board (IASB) and the Accounting Standards Board (1990–2012) in the UK) have sought to develop a conceptual framework or statement of principles which will underpin accounting practice. As Definition 10.5 shows, the basic idea of a conceptual framework is to create a set of fundamental accounting principles which will help in standard setting.

A major achievement of the search for a conceptual theory has been the emergence of the decision-making model. As Real-World View 10.5 sets out, there is a need to provide decision-useful information to investors. In accounting, a conceptual framework has developed over time. In 1989, the IASC published a *Framework for the Preparation and Presentation of Financial Statements*. The aim of the conceptual framework is to assist the IASB in developing standards, help other standard setters and assist preparers, auditors and users in interpreting and understanding financial statements. The six essential components of a conceptual framework are broadly agreed by all three major standard-setting bodies: objectives, users, user needs, elements of financial statements, information characteristics and measurement principles with concepts of capital maintenance. These components are briefly discussed below. The various elements of the financial statements such as financial position (assets, liabilities, and equity) and performance (income and expenses), have been discussed already in Section A. The IASB updated its conceptual framework and its latest version was published in 2010.

REAL-WORLD VIEW 10.5

Conceptual Framework

First – and of fundamental importance – all involved in global financial reporting must have a common mission or objective. At the heart of that mission is a conceptual framework which must focus on the investor, provide decision-useful information, and assure that capital is allocated in a manner that achieves the lowest cost in our world markets. I believe we all have an understanding and acceptance of providing decision-useful information for investors, but not all standard setters and not all standards yet reflect that mission.

Source: International Accounting Standards Board, *IASC Insight*, p. 12.

1. Objectives

The IASB has determined that '[t]he objective of general purpose financial reporting is to provide financial information about the reporting entity that is useful to existing and potential investors, lenders and other creditors in making decisions about providing resources to the entity. Those decisions involve buying, selling or holding equity and debt instruments, and providing or settling loans and other forms of credit' (Conceptual Framework, IASB, 2010, OB2). This replaces the previous objective that had been agreed by the US Financial Accounting Standards Board (FASB) and the International Accounting Standards Board (IASB): 'The objective of financial statements is to provide information about the financial position, performance and changes in financial position of an entity that is useful to a wide range of users in making economic decisions' (*Framework for the Preparation and Presentation of Financial Statements*, IASB, 1999, para. 12). It will be seen that the 2010 definition is more investor-focused than that in 1999. This approach to accounting is widely known as the decision-making model (see Figure 10.3). In other words, the basic idea of accounting is to provide accounting information to users which fulfils their needs, thus enabling them to make decisions. Encompassed within this broad definition is the idea that financial statements show how the managers have accounted for the resources entrusted to them by the shareholders. This accountability is often called stewardship. To enable stewardship and decision making, the information must have certain information characteristics and use a consistent measurement model.

Figure 10.3 Decision-Making Model

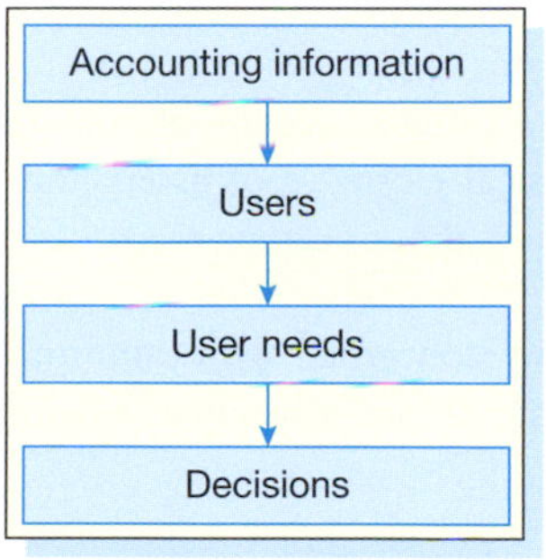

In the UK, the ASB (1990–2012) had developed a Statement of Principles. The Statement takes a broader definition of the objectives of financial reporting than either the FASB or the IASB. 'The objective of financial statements is to provide information about the reporting entity's financial position, performance and changes in financial position that is useful to a wide range of users for assessing the stewardship of the entity's management and for making economic decisions' (Accounting Standards Board, *Statement of Principles*, 1999). Thus, the ASB (now the Accounting Council) sees the *objective of financial reporting* as (i) the *stewardship of management* and (ii) *making economic decisions*.

Stewardship and decision making are discussed in more depth in Chapter 12. However, at this stage it is important to introduce them. Stewardship is all about accountability. It seeks to make the directors accountable to the shareholders for their stewardship or management of the company. Corporate governance is one modern aspect of stewardship.

Decision making, by contrast, focuses on the need for shareholders to make economic decisions, such as to buy or sell their shares. As performance measurement and decision making have grown in importance, so has the income statement. In a sense, decision making and stewardship are linked, as information is provided to shareholders so that they can make decisions about the directors' stewardship of the company. There has been much debate as to whether stewardship or decision making should be given primacy when drawing up financial statements.

Essentially, stewardship and decision making are user-driven and take the view that accounting should give a 'true and fair' view of a company's accounts. By contrast, the public relations view suggests that there are behavioural reasons why managers might seek to prepare accounts that favour their own self-interest. Self-interest and 'true and fair' may well conflict. In this section, we focus only on the officially recognised roles of accounting (stewardship and decision making). Discussion of the public relations role and the conflicting multiple accounting objectives is covered in Chapter 12.

PAUSE FOR THOUGHT 10.3

Stewardship and Decision Making

Why are assets and liabilities most important for stewardship, but profits most important for decision making?

Stewardship is about making individuals accountable for assets and liabilities. In particular, stewardship focuses on the physical existence of assets and seeks to prevent their loss and/or fraud. Stewardship is, therefore, about keeping track of assets rather than evaluating how efficiently they are used.

Decision making is primarily concerned with monitoring performance. Therefore, it is primarily concerned with whether or not a business has made a profit. It is less concerned with tracking assets.

2. Users

The main users are usually considered to be the present and future shareholders. Indeed, shareholders are the only group required by law to be sent an annual report. Shareholders comprise individual and institutional shareholders. Besides shareholders, there are a number of other users. In its most recent version of the Conceptual Framework (2010), the IASB focuses on existing and potential investors, lenders and other creditors. However, before this the IASB identified a wider set of users including:

- lenders, such as banks or loan creditors
- suppliers and other trade creditors (i.e., trade payables)
- employees and employee organisations

- customers
- governments and their agencies
- general public
- analysts and advisers.

In addition to this list we can add:

- academics
- management
- pressure groups such as Friends of the Earth.

Broadly, we can see that this list is broadly the same as that discussed in Chapter 1 (see Figure 1.3). In Chapter 1, however, we distinguished between internal users (management and employees) and external users (the rest). All of these users will need the information to appraise the performance of management and also to make decisions.

Generally the accounts are pitched at the shareholders. Their primary requirement is to acquire economic information so that they can make economic decisions. Satisfying the interests of shareholders is generally thought to cover the main concerns of the other groups. The annual report adopts a general purpose reporting model. This provides a comprehensive set of information targeted at all users. It does not, therefore, specifically target the needs of one user group.

3. User Needs

User needs vary. However, commonly users will want answers to questions such as:

- How well is management running the company?
- How profitable is the organisation?
- How much cash does it have in the bank?
- Is it likely to keep trading?

The IASB looks at the needs of external users and believes that user needs will be focused on economic decisions such as to:

- Decide to buy, hold or sell shares
- Assess the stewardship or accountability of management
- Assess the ability of the entity to pay the wages
- Assess the security for monies lent
- Determine tax policy
- Determine distributable profits and dividends
- Prepare and use national income statistics
- Regulate an entity's activities.

In order to answer these questions, users will need information on the profitability, liquidity, efficiency and gearing of the company. This is normally provided in the three key financial statements: the income statement, the statement of financial position and the statement of cash flows. Users will also be interested in the softer, qualitative information provided, for example, in accounting narratives such as the chairman's statement.

4. Qualitative Information Characteristics

In order to be useful to users, the financial information needs to possess certain characteristics. The UK's Accounting Standards Board, now replaced by the Accounting Council, focuses on four principal characteristics: relevance, reliability, comparability and understandability. The ASB then classified these characteristics into those relating to content (relevance and reliability) and those relating to presentation (comparability and understandability) (see Figure 10.4).

Figure 10.4 Overview of Information Characteristics (Accounting Council)

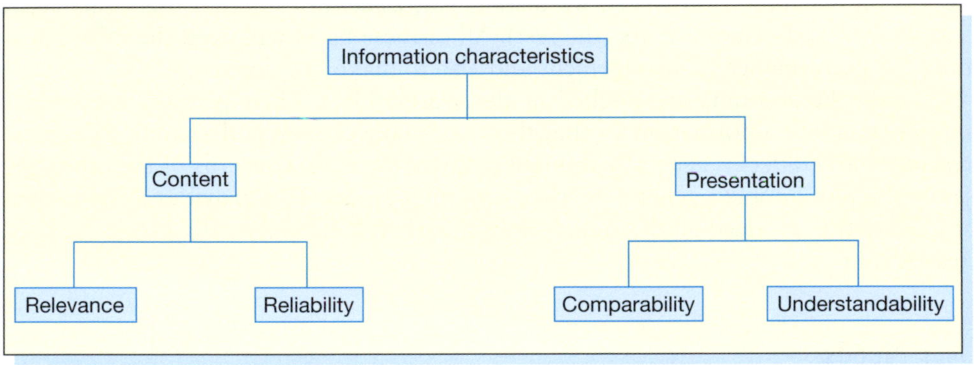

Information characteristics
Content
Presentation
Relevance
Reliability
Comparability
Understandability

This approach was also adopted by the IASB, but it has now refined its position. The IASB now sees two fundamental qualitative characteristics: relevance and faithful representation. There are then a further four characteristics that enhance relevance and faithful representation: comparability, verifiability, timeliness and understandability (see Figure 10.5).

Figure 10.5 Overview of Information Characteristics (ASB)

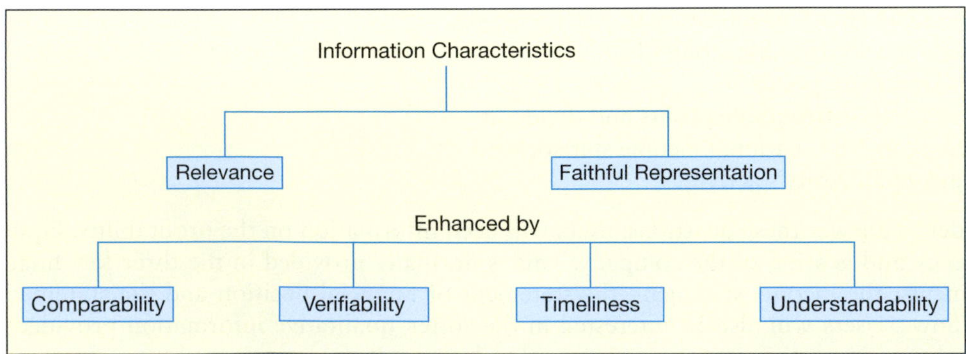

The major change in the latest conceptual framework is the replacement of reliability by representational faithfulness. The IASB abandoned 'reliability' because it believed there was a lack of common understanding of the term.

A. Fundamental Qualitative Characteristics

Relevance. Relevant information is that which affects users' economic decisions. Relevance is a prerequisite of usefulness. Examples of relevance are information that helps to predict future events or to confirm or correct past events. The relevance of financial information in the financial statements crucially depends on its materiality. If information is immaterial (i.e., will not affect users' decisions), then, in practice, it does not need to be reported. Materiality is thus best considered as a threshold or cut-off point rather than being a primary qualitative information characteristic in its own right.

Faithful Representation. Financial reports represent economic phenomena in numbers and words. Like relevance, faithful representation is a prerequisite of usefulness. Three characteristics underpin information that is representationally faithful (i.e., information that validly describes the underlying events). First, information must be complete in that all necessary information should be included. Second, reliable information must be neutral, i.e., not biased. Third, faithful representation dictates that there are no errors or omissions in the information. The IASB did not see substance over form as a separate component of faithful representation. This was because a legal form which did not represent economic substance automatically violated representational faithfulness.

B. Supplementary Enhancing Qualitative Characteristics

Comparability. Accounts should be prepared on a consistent basis and should disclose accounting policies. This will then allow users to make inter-company comparisons and intra-company comparisons over time.

Verifiability. This means that different knowledgeable and independent observers could reach consensus, although not necessarily complete agreement. However, the key is that they could arrive at similar decisions.

Timeliness. This means that information should be available to decision makers in time to influence their decisions. However, some information will have a long time span, for instance, when used to assess trends over time.

Understandability. Information that is not understandable is useless. Therefore, information must be presented in a readily understandable way. In practice, this means conveying complex information as simply as possible rather than 'dumbing down' information. Whether financial information is understandable will depend on the way in which it is characterised, aggregated, classified and presented.

The IASB and ASB (Accounting Council) recognise that trade-offs are inevitable where conflicts arise between information characteristics. For example, out-of-date information may be useless. Therefore, some detail (e.g., faithful representation) may be sacrificed to speed of reporting (e.g., timeliness). In addition, the benefits derived from information should exceed the costs of providing it. Cost is described by the IASB as a pervasive constraint.

Prudence
Another concept which was, at one time, thought to underpin reliability is prudence. Prudent information is where assets or income are not deliberately overstated or expenses and liabilities deliberately understated. There is currently much discussion about prudence. On the one hand some believe that prudence is a sensible counter-balance against the potential over-optimism of managers. Others, by contrast, argue that a prudent view mitigates against an objective view of a business. However, the IASB has omitted prudence from its latest version of the conceptual framework. It considers that prudence would be inconsistent as it would introduce bias. However, it did state that it has sometimes been considered desirable to counteract excessively optimistic management estimates.

PAUSE FOR THOUGHT 10.4

The Debate about Prudence

Prudence is a much debated concept. There are two main views. Many commentators believe that prudence is very useful as it balances the managerial tendency to provide over-optimistic accounts. It is, therefore, a valuable safeguard for credit and shareholders. This is certainly the view of the UK's House of Lords Committee which investigated banks and bank auditing in 2011. By contrast, others, including the IASB, think that accounts should be neutral and without bias. Therefore, as prudence introduces a negative bias into the accounts, it should not underpin accounts. The House of Lords Report criticised IFRS as an 'inferior system' which inhibited the auditors' ability to exercise judgement.

Both sides feel strongly!! Which view do you support?

5. Measurement Model

The objectives, users, user needs and information characteristics have proved relatively easy to agree upon. However, the choice of an appropriate measurement model for profit measurement and asset determination has caused much controversy. The measurement basis that underpins financial statements remains a modified form of historical cost. In other words, income, expenses, assets and liabilities are recorded at the date of their original monetary transaction. Unfortunately, although historical cost is relatively well understood and easy to understand, it understates assets and overstates profits, especially in times of inflation. Most commentators agree that historical cost, therefore, is flawed. However, there is no consensus on a suitable replacement. The alternative measurement models are more fully discussed in Chapter 11.

PAUSE FOR THOUGHT 10.5

Critics of the Conceptual Framework

The conceptual framework has been criticised for not achieving very much and being a social document rather than a theory document. What do you think these criticisms mean and are they fair?

The conceptual framework has brought into being the decision-making model. However, there is little agreement on the appropriate measurement model for accounting. In other words, should we continue to use historical cost or should we move towards some alternative measurement model that perhaps accounts for the effects of inflation? Critics have seen this failure to agree on a measurement model as a severe blow to the authority of the conceptual framework. In addition, there is concern that the conceptual framework has not really developed a theoretically coherent and consistent set of accounting principles at all. These critics argue that the conceptual framework is primarily descriptive – just describing what already exists. A descriptive framework is not a theoretical framework. Finally, some critics argue that the real reason for the search for a conceptual framework is to legitimise and support the notion of a standard-setting regime independent of government. The conceptual framework should thus be seen as a social document which supports the existence of an independent accounting profession.

Conclusion

In order to appreciate accounting practice properly, we need to understand the regulatory and conceptual frameworks within which it operates. These frameworks were primarily devised for published financial statements, such as those in the corporate annual report. The regulatory framework is the set of rules and regulations which governs corporate accounting practice. The International Accounting Standards Board sets International Financial Reporting Standards. These are followed by all European listed companies, including UK companies. The two major strands of the UK's regulatory framework are the Companies Acts and accounting standards. The UK's accounting standards regulatory framework consists of five elements: the Financial Reporting Council, the Codes and Standards Committee, the Accounting Council, the Audit and Assurance Council and the Financial Reporting Review Panel. Corporate governance is the system by which companies are governed.

A conceptual framework is an attempt to create a set of fundamental accounting principles which will help standard setting. A major achievement of the search for a conceptual framework has been the emergence of the decision-making model. The essence of this is that the objective of financial statements is to provide financial information useful to a wide range of users for making economic decisions. A second objective is to provide financial information for assessing the stewardship of managers. In order to be useful, the IASB believes this information must have relevance and faithful representation enhanced by comparability, verifiability, timeliness and understandability. Although there is general agreement on the essentials of a decision-making model, there is little consensus on which measurement model should underpin the decision-making process.

Selected Reading

The references below will give you further background. They are roughly divided into those on the regulatory framework and those on the conceptual framework.

Regulatory Framework

Bartlett, S.A. and M.J. Jones (1997) Annual Reporting Disclosures 1970–90: An Exemplification, *Accounting, Business and Financial History*, Vol. 7, No. 1, pp. 61–80.

This article looks at how the accounts of one firm, H.P. Bulmers (Holdings) plc, the cider makers, were affected by changes in the regulations from 1970 to 1990.

International GAAP 2012: Generally Accepted Accounting Practice under International Financial Reporting Standards, Ernst and Young 2012. A very thorough and complete look at IFRS.

Solomon, J.F. (2007) *Corporate Governance and Accountability*, John Wiley and Sons Ltd, Chichester.

Provides an overview of corporate governance.

The Combined Code (1998) London Stock Exchange, June.

This provides a comprehensive set of recommendations arising from the various corporate governance reports (i.e., Cadbury, Greenbury, Hampel). UK-listed companies now follow these.

The Financial Aspects of Corporate Governance (The Cadbury Committee Report) (1992), Gee and Co.

The first, and arguably the most influential, report into corporate governance. Authoritative.

UK and International GAAP (2004), Ernst and Young, Butterworth.

Provides a very comprehensive guide to UK and IFRS standards as well as to the ASB's *Statement of Principles*. This guide is updated annually.

Conceptual Framework

Outlines of Potential Conceptual Frameworks by Professional Bodies

Accounting Standards Board (1999) Statement of Principles, *Accountancy.*

This synopsis offers a good, quick insight into current thinking in the UK about a conceptual theory. The Accounting Council has taken over responsibility for this.

Accounting Standards Setting Committee (ASSC) (1975) *The Corporate Report* (London).

A benchmark report which outlined the Committee's – at the time groundbreaking – thoughts about the theory of accounting. Easy to read.

Financial Accounting Standards Board (FASB) (1978), *Statement of Financial Accounting Concepts No. 1, Objectives of Financial Reporting by Business Enterprises* (Stanford, FASB).

Offers an insight into the US view of a conceptual theory.

International Accounting Standards Board (IASB) (2000), *Framework for the Preparation and Presentation of Financial Statements* in International Accounting Standards, 2000.
The IASB's early thoughts on a conceptual theory.

International Accounting Standards Board (IASB) (2010), *Conceptual Framework for Financial Reporting*.
A very influential document outlining the IASB's latest views.

Discussion Questions

Questions with numbers in blue have answers at the back of the book.

Q1 What is the role of directors, shareholders and auditors in the corporate model?

Q2 What is the decision-making model? Assess its reasonableness.

Q3 Discuss the view that if a regulatory framework did not exist it would have to be invented.

Q4 Companies often disclose 'voluntary' information over and above that which they are required to do. Why do you think they do this?

Q5 What is a conceptual framework and why do you think so much effort has been expended to try to find one?

Go online to discover the extra features for this chapter at **www.wiley.com/college/jones**

Chapter 11

Measurement systems

'What is a Cynic? A man who knows the price of everything and the value of nothing.'

Oscar Wilde, *Lady Windermere's Fan* (1892), *Wiley Book of Business Quotations* (1998), p. 349.

Learning Outcomes

After completing this chapter you should be able to:

- Explore the importance of accounting measurement systems.
- Critically evaluate historical costing.
- Investigate the alternatives to historical costing.

Go online to discover the extra features for this chapter at **www.wiley.com/college/jones**

Chapter Summary

- Measurement systems determine asset valuation and profit measurement.
- The capital maintenance concept is concerned with maintaining the capital of a company.
- Historical cost, which records items at their original cost, is the most widely used measurement system.
- Current purchasing power adjusts historical cost for changes in the purchasing power of money (i.e., inflation).
- Replacement cost is based on the cost of replacing assets.
- Realisable value is based on the orderly sale value of the assets.
- Present value is based on the present value of the discounted net cash inflows of an asset.
- Modifications to historical cost are the valuing of inventory at the lower of cost or net realisable value or, in the UK, the revaluation of property, plant and equipment.
- Fair value is based on the amount that a market participant would pay for the assets.

Introduction

Measurement systems underpin not only profit, but also asset valuation. Essentially, a measurement system is the way in which the elements in the accounts are valued. Traditionally, historical cost has been the accepted measurement system. Income, expenses, assets and liabilities have been recorded in the accounting system at cost at the time that they were first recognised. Unfortunately, historical cost, although easy to use, has several severe limitations; for example, it does not take inflation into account. However, although the limitations of historical cost accounting are well known, accountants have been unable to agree on any of the main alternatives such as current purchasing power, replacement cost, realisable value, present value or fair value. A variety of measurement systems are, therefore, used.

SOUNDBITE 11.1

Measurement

'What you measure is what you get.'

Robert S. Kaplan and David P. Norton, *Harvard Business Review*, January–February, 1992

Source: The Wiley Book of Business Quotations (1998), p. 295.

Overview

Measurement systems are the processes by which the monetary amounts of items in the financial statement are determined. These systems are fundamental to the determination of profit and to the measurement of net assets. In essence, the measurement system determines the values obtained. Potentially, there are six major measurement systems: historical cost, current purchasing power, replacement cost, realisable value, present value and fair value (see Figure 11.1).

Figure 11.1 The Alternative Measurement Systems

Measurement System	*Explanation*	*Capital Maintenance System*
Historical Cost Systems		
i. *Historical cost*	Monetary amounts recorded at the date of original transaction.	Financial capital maintenance.
ii. *Current purchasing power*	Historical cost adjusted by general changes in purchasing power of money (e.g., inflation), often measured using the retail price index (RPI).	Financial capital maintenance.
Current Value Systems		
i. *Replacement cost*	Assets valued at the amounts needed to replace them with an equivalent asset.	Physical capital maintenance.
ii. *Realisable value*	Assets valued at the amount they would fetch in an orderly sale.	Physical capital maintenance.
iii. *Present value*	Assets valued at the discounted present values of future cash inflows.	Physical capital maintenance.
iv. *Fair value*	Assets valued at the amount that a market participant would pay for them.	Physical capital maintenance.

Measurement systems are underpinned by the idea of capital maintenance (see Figure 11.2). Capital maintenance determines that a profit is made only after capital is maintained. This capital can be monetary (monetary capital maintenance) or physical (physical capital maintenance).

Figure 11.2 Capital Maintenance Concepts

What exactly is a capital maintenance concept and why is it important?

A capital maintenance concept is essentially a way of determining whether the 'capital' of a business has improved, deteriorated or stayed the same over a period of time. There are two main capital maintenance concepts (*financial capital maintenance* and *physical capital maintenance*).

Under financial capital maintenance we are primarily concerned with monetary measurement; in particular, the measurement of the net assets. This is true using both historical cost and current purchasing power. For example, under *historical cost* the capital maintenance unit is based on actual monetary units (i.e., actual pounds in the UK). Under *current purchasing power*, it is actual pounds adjusted by the rate of inflation. In both cases, if our closing net assets (as measured in £s) are higher than our opening net assets we make a profit.

Under physical capital maintenance, the physical productive capacity (i.e., operating capacity of the business) must be maintained. For example, can we still produce the same amount of goods or services at the end of a period as we could at the start? We maintain the operating capacity in terms of *replacement costs, realisable values, fair values* or *present values* (i.e., discounted future cash flows). For example, under replacement costs, we are concerned with valuing the operating capacity of the business at the replacement cost of individual assets and liabilities.

Historical cost and current purchasing power both stem from the normal bookkeeping practice of recording transactions at the date they occur in monetary amounts. For current purchasing power, these amounts are then adjusted by the general changes in the purchasing power of money. Under both measurement systems the concern is to maintain the monetary amount of the enterprise's net assets. In both cases, we are therefore concerned with financial capital maintenance. *Replacement cost, realisable value, present value and fair value are sometimes known as current value systems*. They seek to maintain the physical (or operating) capital of the enterprise. The first three systems differ in how they seek to do this. Replacement cost measures assets at the amount it would cost to *replace* them with an equivalent asset. Realisable value (also known as net realisable value or settlement value) measures assets at their sale value. Present value measures the business at the present values of the future net cash flows. These three current value systems can be combined into a 'value to the business' model.

A fourth measurement system, fair value, has recently grown in influence. This is sometimes known as a mark-to-market model as it seeks to capture an asset's market value. These market values may be based on quoted prices in active markets. Fair value is most usually associated with valuing complex financial instruments such as those used by financial institutions. It is similar to realisable value, but ignores transaction costs and takes a market-based rather than an entity perspective. It takes into account a market participant's ability to generate economic benefits by using the asset in the best way possible. It can be defined as the price that will be received when selling the asset or that is paid to transfer a liability between players in the market. See Definition 11.1 for a formal definition of fair value. Fair value has been a particularly contentious topic as many commentators have suggested that fair value accounting facilitated the asset bubble which led to the global financial crisis. This is because the asset's valuation was based on rising property prices. As property prices rose, so did the value of the company assets. Both became overinflated and when the property prices fell, so did the company assets, which many think exacerbated the financial collapse. Given its dependence on market prices, fair value is crucially dependent on the reliability of active markets. A detailed description of fair value and the value to the business model (sometimes called current value accounting) are beyond the scope of this book.

DEFINITION 11.1

Fair Value

'The price that would be received to sell an asset or paid to transfer a liability in an orderly transaction between market participants at the measurement date (i.e. an exit price).'

International Financial Reporting Standards IFRS13, May 2011, para. 9.

It is, however, important to realise two fundamental points. First, historical cost still remains the most common measurement basis adopted by enterprises. Second, although historical cost is much criticised, there is no consensus about which measurement system, if any, should replace it. Disagreement on measurement systems is where attempts to arrive at a consensual conceptual theory have all foundered.

Measurement Systems

In this section, we have discussed two of the most important measurement systems: historical cost and replacement cost. Readers interested in the other three measurement systems are referred to more advanced texts such as Geoffrey Whittington's *Inflation Accounting: An Introduction to the Debate*.

Historical Cost

Historical cost has always been the most widely used measurement system. Essentially, transactions are recorded in the books of account at the date the transaction occurred. This original cost is maintained in the books of account and not updated for any future changes in value that might occur. To illustrate, if we paid £5,000 for a building in 1980, this will be the cost that is shown in the statement of financial position when we prepare our accounts in 2014. This is even when the building has increased in value to say £20,000 through inflation. The depreciation will be based on the original value of the asset (i.e., £5,000 not £20,000).

The main strength of historical cost is that it is objective. In other words, you can objectively verify the original cost of the asset. You only need to refer to the original invoice. In addition, historical cost is very easy to use and to understand. Finally, historical cost enables businesses to keep track of their assets.

There is, however, one crucial problem with historical cost. It uses a fixed monetary capital maintenance system, which does not take inflation into account. This failure to take into account changing prices can cause severe problems. In particular, as Soundbite 11.2 shows, it may not accurately value a company's worth.

SOUNDBITE 11.2

Historical Cost Accounting's Limitations

'Historical cost-based financial reporting is not the most efficient way of reflecting a company's true value.'

Mike Starr, Chairman of American Institute of Certified Public Accountants Committee on Enhanced Business Reporting

Source: Nicholas Neveling, Consortium Urges Reporting Reforms, *Accountancy Age*, 17 February 2005, p. 11.

Replacement Cost

Replacement cost attempts to place a realistic value on the assets of a company. It is concerned with maintaining the operating capacity of a business. Essentially, replacement cost asks the question: what would it cost to replace the existing business assets with identical, equivalent assets at today's prices?

Replacement cost is an alternative method of measuring the assets and profits of a business rather than principally a method of tackling inflation. In the Netherlands, replacement costing was successfully used by many businesses, such as Heineken. As Company Snapshot 11.1 shows, Heineken in 2004 valued its property, plant and equipment at replacement cost based on expert valuation. Dutch companies are still permitted to use replacement costing under Dutch law. However, Heineken now uses IFRS and has, therefore, discontinued replacement costing in its more recent accounts. Indeed, the problem for the Dutch is not so much the difficulties of using replacement cost, but of convincing the rest of the world that it is a worthwhile system.

PAUSE FOR THOUGHT 11.1

Historical Cost and Asset-Rich Companies

The statements of financial position of asset-rich companies, such as banks, may not reflect their true asset values, if prepared under historical cost accounting. Why do you think this might be?

If we take banks and building societies as examples of asset-rich companies, these businesses have substantial amounts of prime location property. Almost in every town, banks occupy key properties in central locations. These properties were also often acquired many years ago, indeed possibly centuries ago. Using strict historical cost, these buildings would be recorded in the statement of financial position at very low amounts. This is because over time, money values have changed. If a prime site was purchased for £1,000 in 1700, that might have been worth a lot then. Today, it might be worth say £400 million. Thus, property, plant and equipment will be radically understated, unless revalued.

COMPANY SNAPSHOT 11.1

Replacement Cost and Heineken

Property, Plant and Equipment (Tangible Fixed Assets)
Except for land, which is not depreciated, tangible fixed assets are stated at replacement cost less accumulated depreciation. The following average useful lives are used for depreciation purposes:

Buildings	30–40 years
Plant and equipment	10–30 years
Other fixed assets	5–10 years

The replacement cost is based on appraisals by internal and external experts, taking into account technical and economic developments. Other factors taken into account include the experience gained in the construction of breweries throughout the world. Grants received in respect of investments in tangible fixed assets are deducted from the amount of the investment. Projects under construction are included at cost.

Source: Heineken, *Annual Report 2004*, pp. 84–5. Copyright Heineken H.V.

The main problem with replacement cost is that although the concept is very simple, in practice it is often difficult to arrive at an objective value for the replacement assets. However, in many cases specific indices are available for certain classes of assets, allowing more accurate valuations.

Deficiencies of Historical Cost Accounting

Figure 11.3 on the next page shows how historical cost accounting can give a misleading impression of the profit for the year and of the value of assets in the statement of financial position. In particular, strictly following historical cost will have the effect of:

(i) encouraging companies to pay out more dividends to shareholders than is wise,
(ii) making companies appear more profitable than they really are, and
(iii) impairing the ability of companies to replace their assets.

In practice, many UK companies now use a modified form of historical cost accounting. This involves revaluing property, often every five years. Depreciation is then based on the revised valuation. However, in some other countries, such as the US, Germany and France, there is still a closer adherence to historical cost.

Illustrative Example of Different Measurement Systems

In Figure 11.4 on page 346, we pull together some of the threads and show how the valuation of an individual asset can vary considerably depending upon the chosen measurement system.

We can, therefore, see that different measurement systems give different asset valuations There are thus six different valuations ranging from £2,500 to £9,947. Realisable value, which is an exit value, gives the lowest valuation at £2,500 while present value, which looks to the future earnings of the company, is £9,947.

The most objective of the measurement systems are probably historical cost and current purchasing power.

	£
• Historical cost	6,000
• Current purchasing power	7,200
• Realisable value	2,500
• Replacement cost	4,000
• Present value	9,947
• Fair value	3,000

It is important to note that, in practice, each measurement system itself could potentially yield many different asset valuations, depending on the underlying assumptions and estimations. For example, present value is crucially dependent on the estimated discount rate (10%), the estimated future cash flows (£4,000), and the timing of those cash flows.

Figure 11.3 The Deficiencies of Historical Cost Accounting

A company's only asset is a building, purchased 10 years ago for £20,000. The replacement cost for an equivalent building is now £200,000. The company, which deals only in cash, has profits of £10,000 per annum before depreciation; it distributes 50% of its profits as dividends. The asset is depreciated over 20 years.

(i) Historical Cost Accounts in year 10

Income Statement		Statement of Financial Position	
	£		£
Profit before depreciation	10,000	Property, plant and equipment	20,000
Depreciation	(1,000)	Accumulated depreciation	(10,000)
Profit for year	9,000	Total property, plant and equipment	10,000
		Cash	55,000
		Net assets	65,000

(a) Over the first ten years, the company's net cash inflow is £100,000 (£10,000 × 10), minus £45,000 in dividends leaving £55,000 cash in the company. This looks healthy.

(b) The shareholders are happy receiving an annual dividend.

(c) Return on capital employed (taking closing net assets) is:

$$\frac{£9{,}000}{£65{,}000} = 13.8\%$$

Everything, therefore, seems pretty good. Unfortunately, the company has only £65,000 in net assets, which is not enough to replace the property, plant and equipment which will cost £200,000!

(ii) Replacement Cost Accounts in year 10

Income Statement		Statement of Financial Position	
	£		£
Profit before depreciation	10,000	Property, plant and equipment	200,000
Depreciation	(10,000)	Accumulated depreciation	(100,000)
	–	Total property, plant and equipment	100,000
		Cash	100,000
		Net assets	200,000

(a) In this case, the company makes no profit because the increased depreciation has wiped out all the profits. There is no profit out of which to pay dividends. If the company had paid out dividends during the 10 years, it would have no money left to replace the property, plant and equipment.

(b) The net worth has risen considerably. This is a plus for the company. However, not paying out dividends is a considerable minus.

(c) There is no return on capital employed!

Suddenly, everything appears less rosy. However, the firm can continue in business because it can just about replace its property, plant and equipment (in actual fact, its net assets equal the amount needed to replace the property, plant and equipment). This assumes that the building could be sold for £100,000!

Figure 11.4 Example of Different Measurement Systems

JoJo bought a van two years ago for £10,000. She expects to keep the van for five years. The used van guide states the van is now worth £2,500. If sold, the general price in an active market for such vans is £3,000. Replacement cost for a van in a similar condition is £4,000. The future net cash flows will be £4,000 for the next three years (assume the cash flows occur at the end of the year) and she can borrow money at 10%. The retail price index was 100 when the van was bought and it is 120 now.

	Appropriate value £
Historical Cost	
We base our calculations on the original historical cost of £10,000. Using straight line depreciation (£10,000 ÷ 5) = £2,000 p.a. *Thus*, £10,000 − £4,000 (*two years' depreciation*)	6,000
Current Purchasing Power	
We base our calculation on the original historical cost less depreciation. In the calculation above, this was £10,000 – £4,000 = £6,000. We then adjust this for inflation. This is measured using the retail price index, which has increased from 100 to 120.	
$£6{,}000 \times \frac{\textit{Closing RPI}}{\textit{Opening RPI}}\left(\frac{120}{100}\right)$	7,200
Realisable Value	
In this case, our calculations are based upon the amount of money we would receive for the van if we sold it. *Used van guide*	2,500
Replacement Cost	
In this case, we base our calculations on the amount it would cost to replace the van with a similar asset in a similar condition. *Similar value asset*	4,000
Present Value	
Here, we are interested in looking at the future cash flows generated by the asset. We then discount them back to today's value.	

£	Discount Factor*	£
4,000	0.9091	3,636
4,000	0.8264	3,306
4,000	0.7513	3,005
		9,947

Present value: 9,947

Fair Value

Fair value: with Fair Value we are interested in the current price which this asset would reach in an active market. We ignore transaction cases. This is similar to net realisable value. — 3,000

*10% interest discounted back, assumes cash flow is on the last day of each year.

Real Life

The merits of historical cost accounting and the advantages and disadvantages of the competing alternative measurement systems have been debated vigorously for at least 40 years. However, with some rare exceptions, most companies worldwide still mainly use historical cost.

This is not to say that experimentation has not occurred. In the Netherlands, for example, Philips, one of the world's leading companies, used replacement cost accounting for over a generation. Finally, Philips abandoned replacement cost, not because of replacement cost's inadequacies, but because of the failure of international financial analysts to understand Philips' accounts. There are, however, still non-listed companies in the Netherlands which use replacement cost. In the UK too, there were a few companies, usually ex-privatised utilities with extensive infrastructure assets, such as British Gas, which until recently used replacement costs.

In both the UK and the US in the 1970s, there were serious attempts to replace historical cost accounting initially with current purchasing power, but later with current value accounting (a mixture of the three current value systems). These methods were thought to be superior to historical cost accounting when dealing with inflation, which was at that time quite high. They were also believed to provide a more realistic valuation of company assets. In the end these attempts failed. The reasons for their failure were quite complex. However, in general, accountants preferred the objectivity of a tried-and-tested, if somewhat flawed, historical cost system to the subjectivity of the new systems. In addition, rates of inflation fell.

The role of accounting measurement in the recent global credit crunch has aroused a lot of attention. This is particularly true of the role of fair value. When the value of financial assets declined then their fair value reduced and so did the valuation of the companies. Whereas some onlookers felt that accounting measurement was only measuring what had happened, others felt that accounting measurement had contributed to the economic problems by eroding company value.

Although the backbone of the accounts is historical cost, there is some limited use of alternative measurement systems (see Figure 11.5). As we pointed out earlier, many UK

Figure 11.5 Use of Alternative Measurement Systems

'The measurement basis most commonly adopted by enterprises in preparing their financial statements is historical cost. This is usually combined with other measurement bases. For example, inventories are usually carried at the lower of cost and net realisable value, marketable securities may be carried at market value and pension liabilities are carried at their present value. Furthermore, some enterprises use the current cost basis as a response to the inability of the historical cost accounting model to deal with the effects of changing prices of non-monetary assets.'

Source: International Accounting Standards Board (2011), *Conceptual Framework*, para. 4.56.

companies revalue their property every five years. This is particularly common in companies that have a great deal of property, such as hotel chains. However, this periodic revaluation of property means that UK accounts are prepared on a different basis to those in countries, such as France (using French domestic principles) or the US, where periodic revaluations are not permitted. Revaluations are, however, permitted under IFRS.

Conclusion

Different measurement systems will give different figures in the accounts for profit and net assets. The mostly widely used measurement system, historical cost, records and carries transactions in the accounts at their original amounts. Historical cost, however, does not deal well with changes in asset values resulting from, for example, inflation. There are four other traditional main measurement systems (current purchasing power, replacement cost, realisable value, present value). Current purchasing power adjusts historical cost for general changes in the purchasing power of money. Replacement cost records assets at the amounts needed to replace them with equivalent assets. Realisable value records assets at the amounts they would fetch in an orderly sale. Finally, present value discounts future cash inflows to today's monetary values. Although historical cost is the backbone of the accounting measurement systems, there are departures from it, such as the valuation of inventory at the lower of cost or realisable value. In particular, in the UK, many companies revalue their property. A relatively recent new measurement system is fair value, the price the asset would rate in an active market. This is similar to net realisable value. The role of fair value in the credit crunch has been hotly debated.

Selected Reading

The topic of accounting measurement systems can be extremely complex. The first two readings below have been deliberately selected because they are quite accessible to students. Students wishing for a fuller insight into the debate are referred to the book by Geoffrey Whittington below.

1. Accounting Standards Steering Committee (1975), *The Corporate Report*, Section 7, pp. 61–73.
   Although now 40 years old, this report provides a very good, easy-to-read, introduction to the topic.
2. International Accounting Standards Board (IASB) (2011), 'Conceptual Framework', in *International Financial Reporting* (2011), paras 4.54–4.65.
   It presents more modern thinking on the topics and is reasonably easy to follow.

For the Enthusiast

Whittington, G. (1983) *Inflation Accounting: An Introduction to the Debate* (Cambridge University Press).

For students who enjoy a challenge. Gives a thorough grounding in the inflation debate, which is at the heart of choosing different measurement systems.

Discussion Questions

Questions with numbers in blue have answers at the back of the book.

Q1 'Accounting measurement systems are the skeleton of the accounting body.' Critically evaluate this statement.

Q2 Why is historical cost still so widely used, if it is so deeply flawed?

Q3 What is the difference between a financial capital maintenance concept and a physical capital maintenance concept?

Q4 Why do many UK companies revalue their property? How might this affect profit?
Why is this practice unusual internationally?

Go online to discover the extra features for this chapter at **www.wiley.com/college/jones**

Chapter 12

The annual report

'It is a yearly struggle: the conflict between public relations experts determined to put a sunny face on somewhat drearier figures, and those determined to tell it like it is, no matter how many "warts" there are on the year's story. The annual report is a vital instrument designed – ideally – to tell the story of a company, its objectives, where the company succeeded or failed, and what the company intends to do next year.'

Kirsty Simpson, 'Glossy, expensive and useless', *Australian Accountant*, September 1997, pp. 16–18.

Learning Outcomes

After completing this chapter you should be able to:

- Explain the nature of the annual report.
- Outline the multiple, conflicting objectives of the annual report.
- Discuss the main contents of the annual report.
- Evaluate how the annual report is used for impression management.

Go online to discover the extra features for this chapter at **www.wiley.com/college/jones**

Chapter Summary

- The annual report is a key corporate financial communication document.
- It is an essential part of corporate governance.
- It serves multiple, and sometimes conflicting, roles of stewardship/accountability, decision making and public relations.
- It comprises key audited financial statements: income statement (i.e., profit and loss account), statement of financial position (i.e., balance sheet), and statement of cash flows (i.e., cash flow statement).
- It normally includes at least 22 identifiable sections.
- It includes important non-audited sections such as the chairman's statement.
- Most important companies provide group accounts.
- Goodwill is an important intangible asset in many group accounts.
- Managers use the annual report for impression management.

Introduction

The annual report is well entrenched as a core feature of corporate life. This yearly-produced document is the main channel by which directors report corporate annual performance to their shareholders. All leading companies worldwide produce an annual report. In the UK, both listed and unlisted companies produce one. Many other organisations, such as the British Broadcasting Corporation, now also produce their own versions of the annual report. Indeed, the Labour Government produced the first governmental annual report in 1998. Traditionally, the annual report was a purely statutory document. The modern annual report, however, now has multiple functions, including a public relations role. Modern reports comprise a mixture of voluntary and statutory, audited and unaudited, narrative and non-narrative, financial and non-financial information. They are also governed by a regulatory framework which includes Companies Acts and accounting standards. The modern annual report has become a complex and sophisticated business document. In particular, European listed companies now follow International Financial Reporting Standards. As most publicly available annual reports are those of listed companies, the terminology laid down by the IASB will be used in this chapter.

Definition

In essence, an annual report is a document produced to fulfil the duty of the directors to report to shareholders. It is produced annually and is a mixture of financial and non-financial information. As Definition 12.1 shows, it is a report containing both audited financial information and unaudited, non-financial information.

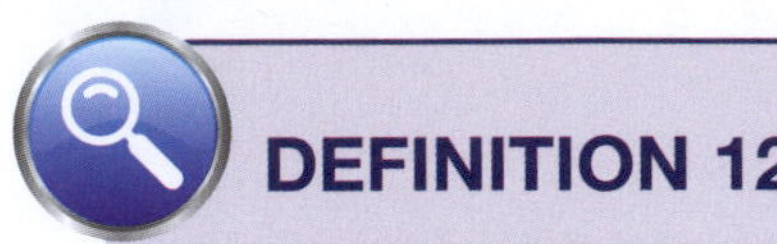

DEFINITION 12.1

Annual Report

Working definition
A report produced annually by companies comprising both financial and non-financial information.

Formal definition
'A document produced annually by companies designed to portray a 'true and fair' view of the company's annual performance, with audited financial statements prepared in accordance with companies legislation and other regulatory requirements, and also containing other non-financial information.'

CIMA definition
'Package of information including a management report, an auditor's report and a set of financial statements with supportive notes. In the case of companies these are drawn up for a period which is called the accounting reference period, the last day of which is known as the reporting date.'

Source: Chartered Institute of Management Accountants (2005), *Official Terminology*. Reproduced by Permission of Elsevier.

Context

The annual report has evolved over time into an important communications document, especially for large publicly listed companies. Surveys have consistently shown that it is one of the most important sources of financial information. It plays a critical confirmatory role. The earliest annual reports arose out of the need to make directors accountable to their shareholders. The main financial statement was the statement of financial position. In order to ensure that the financial statements fairly represented corporate performance, the annual report was audited. The annual report, therefore, has always played a key role in the control of the directors by the shareholders. The central role of the annual report in external reporting can be seen in Figure 12.1.

In essence, the directors are responsible for the preparation of the financial statements from the accounting records. The actual preparation is normally carried out by accounting staff. An annual report is then compiled, often with the help of a company's public relations department and graphic designers. These graphic designers are responsible for the layout and design of the annual report (providing, for example, colourful graphs and photographs). The annual report's financial content is then audited and disseminated

Figure 12.1 The Annual Report

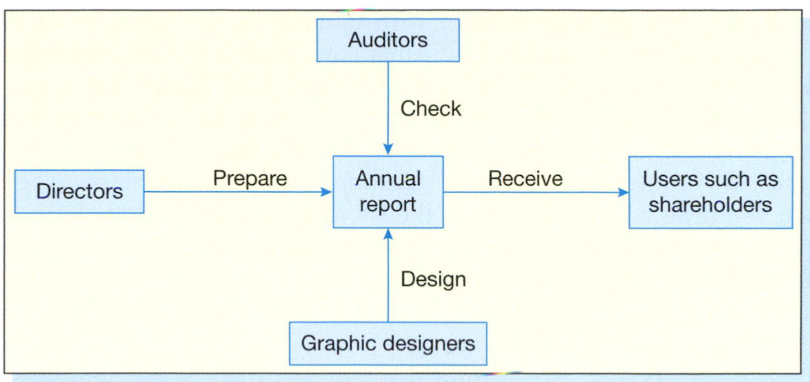

to the main users, principally the shareholders. As discussed in Chapter 10, much of the annual report is mandated by a regulatory framework consisting principally of the requirements of the Companies Acts and accounting standards.

Multiple Roles

The annual report is a social as well as a financial document. Therefore, as society evolves, so does the annual report. The earliest annual reports were stewardship documents. Today's annual report is much more complex, being an amalgam of stewardship and accountability, decision making and public relations. These concepts are discussed below. The first two roles are those traditionally recognised by standard setters. Although it is important to realise that nowadays the IASB prefers decision making rather than stewardship. However, the public relations role is more driven by preparer self-interest.

(i) Stewardship and Accountability

Effectively, stewardship involves the directors reporting their actions to the shareholders. This reflects the origins of financial reporting. In the middle ages, the stewards who managed the estates used to render an annual account of the master's assets (for example, livestock and cereals) to the lord of the manor. The main aim of the accounts, or annual statement, was thus for the lord of the manor to keep a check on the steward's activities. In particular, there was a concern that the steward should not defraud the lord of the manor. An important aspect of stewardship is this accountability. Accountability is traditionally seen as referring to the control and safeguarding of the assets of a company.

Gradually, as the economy became more sophisticated so did the accountability mechanisms. At first, there was a rudimentary statement of assets and liabilities, showing how much the organisation owned and owed. This gradually evolved into the modern statement of financial position. However, the fundamental aim was still to account for the assets and liabilities of the organisation. Accountability tended to diminish in importance with the rise of decision making.

An important modern aspect of stewardship is corporate governance. Essentially, in both Europe and the US, several well-publicised corporate financial scandals (e.g., Polly Peck, Maxwell) led to a growing concern with monitoring the activities of directors. In addition, the privatisation of the utilities created considerable concern over the salaries of so-called 'fat-cat directors'. Real-World Views 12.1 and 12.2 discuss this issue. As can be seen, this issue is apparently perennial and refuses to go away. The committees which looked at corporate governance in the 1990s all stressed the role that corporate financial communication could play in increasing directors' accountability to shareholders. The accounting scandals such as Enron and WorldCom in the US and Parmalat in Italy have reawakened interest in corporate governance. There has been increasing concern with auditor independence and the need for effective audit committees.

REAL-WORLD VIEW 12.1

Directors' Pay: The Continuing Debate

Directors' pay has long been a problem for politicians in the UK. For example, Alex Brummer stated that Stephen Byers, a UK politician, had called for world-class salaries for world-class performance. However, as Brummer pointed out at the time:

'The trouble is that it fits only a handful of the executives and companies in the Guardian's pay survey. Of the 35 or so directors in the million-pounds-plus pay club only a handful – such as those at the drugs companies SmithKline Beecham and Glaxo Wellcome – deliver a world class product.'

Brummer further pointed out that others, for example, Bob Mendelsohn of Royal and Sun Alliance took home £2.4million without being world class.

Since then directors' pay fuelled by generous remuneration schemes sanctioned by generous remuneration committees have continued to soar. A particular bone of contention has been bank bonuses where bankers, widely seen as failing society and causing the global financial crisis, are still walking away with huge salaries. This caused a rare shareholders revolt at Barclays in 2012.

Source: Alex Brummer, Time is Up for World Class Waffle, *The Guardian*, 20 July 1999.

REAL-WORLD VIEW 12.2

Director's Pay:

Bob Diamond, the new boss of Barclays, has refused to bow to MPs' demands that he waives his 2010 bonus, which could be as much as £8m.

Speaking yesterday, Mr Diamond said he had forgone his bonus in 2008 and 2009 and would decide 'with my family' whether to do so again. He added: 'There was a period of remorse and apology for banks and I think that period needs to be over.'

In a lengthy and sometimes irascible session before the Treasury Select Committee, Mr Diamond attacked the MPs for being 'wrong and unfair' about British banks.

'I really resent the fact that you refer to this as blackjack or casino banking or rogue trading,' he said. 'It's wrong, it's unfair, it's a poor choice of words. We have some fantastically strong financial institutions in this country and frankly they deserve better.'

The banker had been called to appear before the committee to discuss bank competition, but was mostly grilled on pay, leading him to make an impassioned defence of the industry.

He warned that the government could not expect bonuses to be 'isolated' and targeted for regulation and 'assume it won't have consequences'.

He told the MPs that shareholders had not asked for information about this year's bonus pool but were 'very involved' in the process.

Source: Louise Armistead and Harry Wilson, MPs try to shame Barclays boss on pay, *Daily Telegraph*, 12 January 2011, p. 23.

PAUSE FOR THOUGHT 12.1

'Fat Cat' Directors

There has been a great furore about the salaries of 'fat-cat' directors. What justification do you think they tend to give for their salaries? What do their critics argue?

The directors' view

Conventionally, directors argue that they are doing a complex and difficult job. They are running world-class businesses and they, therefore, need to be paid world-class salaries. They also create and add shareholder value because of increased share prices and, therefore, they deserve to be well paid.

The critics' view

Yes, but if the directors are paid on the basis of performance, then we would expect them not to get big bonuses when their organisations are doing less well. However, generally this does not happen. Also, much of the increase in share prices that directors ascribe to themselves is often caused by a general rise in the stock market. This debate has intensified because of the financial crisis and credit crunch. Many believe it is unfair, for example, for bankers to pay themselves big salaries when they are widely perceived to be responsible for the current economic downturn.

(ii) Decision Making

In the twentieth century, decision making has increasingly replaced stewardship as the main role of accounting. This reflects wider developments in society, business and accounting. In particular, decision making is associated with the rise of the modern industrial company.

Industrialisation led to increasingly sophisticated businesses and to the creation of the limited liability company with its divorce of ownership and control. Shareholders were no longer involved in the day-to-day running of the business. They were primarily interested in increases in the value of their share price and in any dividends they received. These dividends were based on profits. Consequently, the income statement became more important relative to the statement of financial position. The primary interest of shareholders shifted from cash and assets to profit. Thus, performance measurement and decision making replaced asset management and stewardship as the prime objective of financial information.

PAUSE FOR THOUGHT 12.2

Engines of Capitalism

Limited liability companies have been called the engines of capitalism. Why do you think this is so?

Effectively, limited liability companies are very good at allowing capital to be allocated throughout an economy. There are several advantages to investors. First, they can invest in many companies not just one. Second, they can sell their shares very easily, assuming a buyer can be found. Third, they stand to lose only the amount of capital they have originally invested. Their personal assets are thus safe.

These new shareholder concerns were officially recognised by two reports in the 1960s and 1970s in the US and the UK. Both reports, *A Statement of Basic Accounting Theory* (American Accounting Association, 1966) in the US and *The Corporate Report* (Accounting Standards Steering Committee, 1975) in the UK, proved turning points in the development of accounting. Before then stewardship had been the generally acknowledged role of accounting. After them, decision-usefulness was generally recognised as the prime criterion. In a sense, decision making and stewardship are linked, for shareholders need to make decisions about how well the directors have managed the company.

In a nutshell, the purpose of the annual report was recognised to be:

> 'to communicate economic measurements of and information about the resources and performance of the reporting entity useful to those having reasonable rights to such information.' (*The Corporate Report*, 1975, para. 3.2)

The decision-making model had been born!

As Definition 12.2 shows, the modern objective of accounting is still recognised as providing users with information so that they can make decisions.

For the shareholder, these economic decisions might involve the purchase or sale of shares. Other users will have different concerns. For example, banks might be principally interested in whether or not to lend a company more money.

DEFINITION 12.2

Decision Making Objective of Annual Report

Working definition

Providing users, especially shareholders, with financial information so that they can make decisions such as buying or selling their shares.

Formal definition

'The objective of general purpose financial reporting is to provide financial information about the reporting entity that is useful to existing and potential investors, lenders and other creditors in making decisions about providing resources to the entity.'

Source: International Accounting Standards Board (2010), *The Conceptual Framework for Financial Reporting*.

(iii) Public Relations Role

The public relations role reflects the annual report's development over the last 20 years as a major marketing tool. Company management has come to realise that the annual report represents an unrivalled opportunity to 'sell' the corporate image. In part, this only reflects human nature. We all wish to look good. It is a rare person who never attempts to massage the truth; for example, at a job interview. The public relations role of annual reports does, however, provoke strong reactions by some commentators (see Real-World View 12.3).

REAL-WORLD VIEW 12.3

Public Relations and the Annual Report

Queen Isabella was said to have washed only three times in her life, and only once voluntarily. That was when she was married. The other two times were at her birth and death. No wonder Columbus left to discover a new world. Why this olfactory analysis of history? Because this is the time of year when we are inundated with corporate annual reports, and in most of them the letter to the shareholders smells as wretched as Queen Isabella must have.

One of the sad truths about malodorous things is that people tend to get used to them in time. But I'll never become accustomed to the public-relations pap I read in most annual reports. Every year tens of thousands of stale, vapid, and uninspired letters to shareholders appear in elaborate annual reports. They are printed on expensive paper whose gloss and sheen are exceeded only by the glitzy words of the professional PR writer who ghosted the message. They will be read by shareholders who don't understand them – or believe them. Quite often they are hype. Sometimes they are dull. Some are boastful, others apologetic. And they are generally ambiguous.

Source: Sal Marino, *Industry Week*, 5 May 1997, p. 12. Reproduced with permission.

Conflicting Objectives

The standard-setting organisations generally only recognise the first two objectives of financial statements (also by implication of annual reports): stewardship and decision making. Indeed, there is currently heated debate within the accounting community about the relative importance of stewardship vis-à-vis decision making. In effect, these two objectives clash with the public relations role. This is because the stewardship and decision-making roles rely upon the notion of providing a neutral and objective view of the company. However, the public relations view is where managers seek to present a favourable, not a neutral, view of a company's activities. This causes stress, particularly if a company did not perform as well as market analysts had predicted. In these cases, as we see in Chapter 13, there is great pressure for the company management to indulge in impression management.

PAUSE FOR THOUGHT 12.3

Stewardship or Decision Making

There are broadly two schools of thought about the basic objectives of accounting. First, there are those who think that accounting is all about decision making. This is generally the line followed by the IASB. Others, however, are less convinced. For example, Professor David Myddelton ('Yesterday', *Accountancy Magazine*, March 2010, p. 22) disagrees with the modern-day assumption that the primary purpose of company accounts is decision-usefulness for investors, and presents three main reasons for doing so:

> 'First, companies publish their accounts much later than nearly all of the many other sources of information for investors. Second, Modern Portfolio Theory of investment implies that a fully-diversified investor need not care much about the results of any specific company. Asset allocation and portfolio re-balancing are far more important.'

And his third reason concludes:

> '. . . the vast majority of entities producing accounts do not have investors who are even remotely considering buying or selling shares in them.'

Some commentators often think that more credence should be given to accountability. In particular, that directors should be accountable to their shareholders. The Accounting Community is thus divided.

So what do you think? Should accounting be primarily about decision making?

Main Contents of the Annual Report

Every annual report is unique. The average annual report ranges from about 40–80 pages with many having substantially more pages. Indeed, some annual reports, such as HSBC, run into hundreds of pages. Perhaps unsurprisingly, therefore, the modern annual report is often criticised for being too complex. A company's report presents a wide variety of corporate financial and non-financial information. The traditional financial statements (e.g., statement of financial position, statement of comprehensive income (or income statement and statement of comprehensive income), statement of cash flows) and accompanying financial information (such as notes to accounts) are normally audited. Other parts, such as the chairman's statement, are not. Nowadays, they also are normally positioned at the back of the annual report with the more contextual qualitative information such as the chairman's statement appearing at the front. However, auditors generally review this qualitative information to ensure it is consistent with the audited accounts. In addition, the report is a mixture of voluntary and mandatory (i.e., prescribed by regulation) information, and narrative and non-narrative information. In Figure 12.2, the main sections of a typical annual report are outlined. Although based on UK financial reporting practice, in the main these sections are also found in most European listed companies.

Figure 12.2 Main Sections of a Typical Annual Report

Section	*Audited*	*Narrative (N)*	*Mandatory (M)*
	Formally	*Non-Narrative (NN)*	*Voluntary (V)*
1. Statement of comprehensive income (or income statement and statement of comprehensive income)	Yes	NN	M
2. Statement of financial position	Yes	NN	M
3. Statement of cash flows	Yes	NN	M
4. Statement of changes in equity	Yes	NN	M
5. Note on reconciliation of net cash flow to movement in net debt	Yes	NN	M
6. Note on historical cost profits and losses	Yes	NN	M
7. Accounting policies	Yes	N	M
8. Notes to the accounts	Yes	N	M
9. Principal subsidiaries	No	N	M
10. Business Review	No	N	M
11. Chairman's statement	No	N	V
12. Directors' report	No	N	M
13. Review of operations	No	N	V
14. Social and environmental accounting statement	No	N	V
15. Statement of corporate governance	No	N	M
16. Directors' Remuneration Report	No	N	M
17. Auditors' report	Not applicable	N	M
18. Statement of directors' responsibilities for the financial statements	No	N	M
19. Shareholder information	No	N	V
20. Highlights	No	NN	V
21. Historical summary	No	NN	V
22. Shareholder analysis	No	NN	V

Figure 12.3 Overview of the Annual Report

Contents				
Audited			*Non-audited*	
Main statements	Subsidiary Statements	Explanatory material	Narrative	Non-narrative
1. Statement of comprehensive income (SOCI) (or income statement and statement of comprehensive income) 2. Statement of financial position 3. Statement of cash flows	4. Statement of changes in equity 5. Note on reconciliation of net cash flow to movement in net debt 6. Note on historical cost profits and losses	7. Accounting policies 8. Notes to the accounts 9. Principal subsidiaries	10. Business Review 11. Chairman's statement 12. Directors' report 13. Review of operations 14. Social and environmental accounting statement 15. Statement of corporate governance 16. Directors' remuneration report 17. Auditors' report 18. Statement of directors' responsibilities for the financial statements 19. Shareholder information	20. Highlights 21. Historical summary 22. Shareholder analysis

A growing trend is for companies to produce multiple reports. Some companies produce an annual report which contains only financial statements aimed at sophisticated investors and another report entitled 'Annual Review' which contains simplified financial information and discussion. Companies also may produce separate environmental, corporate responsibility or sustainability reports. These deal with non-financial markets. For example, the environmental report might deal with issues such as pollution, recycling and biodiversity. This is particularly true of large listed companies both in the UK, Europe and the US. Indeed a recent development is the International Integrated Reporting Committee (IIRC), an influential group of business leaders, academics, accountants and regulators who aim to develop a global reporting framework that embraces environmental and financial issues. Integrated reporting is particularly advanced in South Africa where companies produce a separate integrated report that has financial information side by side with environmental data. In addition, many companies produce web-based financial information. For simplicity, however, we assume for the rest of this chapter that a company produces only the traditional annual report.

The main sections of the annual report can be divided into audited and non-audited statements. These are shown in Figure 12.3 and discussed below. In the text, various illustrative figures are included from the annual report of Tesco, a UK listed company, and from the annual report of the Finnish listed company, Nokia.

The Audited Statements

Nine audited financial sections are normally included by most UK companies in their annual reports. The first three (the statement of comprehensive income (see Chapter 4), the statement of financial position (see Chapter 5) and the statement of cash flows (see Chapter 8)) have already been covered in depth earlier. As Soundbite 12.1 shows, they are still very important despite the growth in non-audited material. They are, therefore, only lightly touched on here. The remaining audited statements are all comparatively recent. They can be divided into subsidiary statements and explanatory material. All the sections are presented in a relatively standard way, following guidance laid down in the Companies Acts and accounting standards.

SOUNDBITE 12.1

The Accounting Numbers

'For all their flaws – and I accept that some can be rather colourful – the numbers in reports and accounts do give you a good solid picture of how the company has actually performed – the cashflow, the strength of the balance sheet, the level of debt.'

Source: Ian Fraser, More than Words, *Accountancy Magazine,* November 2009, p. 39.

Main Statements

1. Statement of Comprehensive Income (SOCI) or Income Statement and Statement of Comprehensive Income (also known as Profit and Loss Account). The statement of comprehensive income is widely recognised as one of the two primary financial statements. It focuses on the revenue earned and expenses incurred by the business during the accounting period as well as non-trading items. Importantly, this is not the same as cash received and cash paid. European listed companies follow guidelines for the SOCI as laid down by IAS 1 *Presentation of Financial Statements*. UK non-listed companies will follow FRS 102, Section 3, Financial Statement Presentation, although they may choose to follow IFRS. An illustration of the income statement for AstraZeneca is given in Company Snapshot 7.3 in Chapter 7.

The SOCI may be presented as one statement; alternatively it can be presented as two statements: first, the income statement dealing with trading items and arriving at profit for the year and second, the statement of comprehensive income dealing with other items. Practice varies between companies with some companies producing just one statement of comprehensive income whereas others present an income statement and then a statement of comprehensive income. *In this book, we generally present the income statement as one statement*. Other non-trading items are typically outside the scope of this book. As one statement, the statement of comprehensive income deals with profit from trading as well as dealing with *non-trading gains and losses* in a unified statement. The SOCI attempts to highlight all shareholder gains and losses (i.e., not just those from trading). These gains and losses might, for example, be surpluses on property revaluation. Alternatively, as in the case of Tesco in 2010 (see Company Snapshot 12.1), there may be a gain on foreign currency translations, losses on pensions or losses on hedging (insuring against) cash flows. Tesco's statement of comprehensive income just shows the non-trading gains and losses. Tesco also produced a separate income statement.

COMPANY SNAPSHOT 12.1

Statement of Comprehensive Income

Group statement of comprehensive income

Year ended 27 February 2010	notes	52 weeks 2010 £m	53 weeks 2009 Restated* £m
Change in fair value of available-for-sale financial assets and investments		1	3
Currency translation differences		343	(275)
Total loss on defined benefit pension schemes	28	(322)	(629)
(Losses)/gains on cash flow hedges:			
Net fair value (losses)/gains		(168)	505
Reclassified and reported in the Group Income Statement		5	(334)
Tax relating to components of other comprehensive income	6	54	375
Total other comprehensive income		(87)	(355)
Profit for the year		2,336	2,138
Total comprehensive income for the year		2,249	1,783
Attributable to:			
Owners of the parent		2,222	1,784
Minority interests		27	(1)
		2,249	1,783

*See note 1 Accounting policies.

Source: Tesco PLC, *Annual Report and Financial Statements 2010*, p. 71.

2. *The Statement of Financial Position.* It is much debated whether the statement of financial position or the income statement are the most important for decision making. The statement of financial position focuses on assets, liabilities and shareholders' funds (i.e., equity or capital employed) at a particular point in time (the reporting date). The statement of financial position, along with the income statement, is prepared from the trial balance. The statement of financial position is commonly used to assess the liquidity of a company, whereas the income statement focuses on profit. An illustration of the statement of financial position for AstraZeneca is given in Company Snapshot 7.4 in Chapter 7.

3. *Statement of Cash Flows.* Unlike the previous two statements, which use the matching basis and are prepared from the trial balance, the statement of cash flows is usually prepared by deduction from the income statement and statements of financial position. It is a relatively new statement; for example, introduced in the UK in 1991. The objective of the statement of cash flows is to report and categorise cash inflows and outflows during a particular period. In Company Snapshot 12.2, Tesco PLC's Statement of Cash Flows for 2010 is given (note that Tesco still prefer to use the old UK GAAP terminology, cash flow statement).

COMPANY SNAPSHOT 12.2

Tesco PLC's Cash Flow Statement (Statement of Cash Flows)

Year ended 27 February 2010	notes	52 weeks 2010 £m	53 weeks 2009 £m
Cash flows from operating activities			
Cash generated from operations	31	5,947	4,978
Interest paid		(690)	(562)
Corporation tax paid		(512)	(456)
Net cash from operating activities		4,745	3,960
Cash flows from investing activities			
Acquisition of subsidiaries, net of cash acquired		(65)	(1,275)
Proceeds from sale of property, plant and equipment		1,820	994
Purchase of property, plant and equipment and investment property		(2,855)	(4,487)
Proceeds from sale of intangible assets		4	–
Purchase of intangible assets		(163)	(220)
Increase in loans to joint ventures		(45)	(242)
Investments in joint ventures and associates		(4)	(30)
Investments in short-term and other investments		(1,918)	(1,233)
Proceeds from sale of short-term investments		1,233	360
Dividends received		35	69
Interest received		81	90
Net cash used in investing activities		(1,877)	(5,974)
Cash flows from financing activities			
Proceeds from issue of ordinary share capital		167	130
Increase in borrowings		862	7,387
Repayment of borrowings		(3,601)	(2,733)
Repayment of obligations under finance leases		(41)	(18)
Dividends paid		(968)	(883)
Dividends paid to minority interests		(2)	(3)
Own shares purchased		(24)	(265)
Net cash from financing activities		(3,607)	(3,615)
Net (decrease) increase in cash and cash equivalents		(739)	1,601
Cash and cash equivalents at beginning of year		3,509	1,788
Effect of foreign exchange rate changes		49	120
Cash and cash equivalents at end of year	19	2,819	3,509

Source: Tesco PLC, *Annual Report and Financial Statements 2010*, p. 74.

Subsidiary Statements

4. Statement of Changes in Equity. This statement highlights major changes to the ownership claims of shareholders. These include profit (or loss) for the year, annual dividends and new share capital. In Tesco's statement of changes in equity (Company Snapshot 12.3), Tesco has chosen to show all the changes in other comprehensive income (thus replicating the information shown in the statement of comprehensive income in Company Snapshot 12.1) and then show the share and dividend movements. It could have just begun with the total comprehensive income of £2249 m.

COMPANY SNAPSHOT 12.3

Tesco PLC's Statement of Changes in Equity

	ATTRIBUTABLE TO OWNERS OF THE PARENT										
	Issued share capital £m	Share premium £m	Other reserves £m	Capital redemption reserve £m	Hedging reserve £m	Translation reserve £m	Treasury shares £m	Retained earnings £m	Total £m	Minority interest £m	Total equity £m
At 28 February 2009 (restated*)	395	4,638	40	13	175	173	(229)	7,644	12,849	57	12,906
Profit for the year	–	–	–	–	–	–	–	2,327	2,327	9	2,336
Other comprehensive income											
Change in fair value of available-for-sale financial assets	–	–	–	–	–	–	–	1	1	–	1
Currency translation differences	–	–	–	–	–	325	–	–	325	18	343
Loss on defined benefit schemes	–	–	–	–	–	(2)	–	(320)	(322)	–	(322)
Loss on cash flow hedges	–	–	–	–	(163)	–	–	–	(163)	–	(163)
Tax on components of other comprehensive income	–	–	–	–	–	(33)	–	87	54	–	54
Total other comprehensive income	–	–	–	–	(163)	290	–	(232)	(105)	18	(87)
Total comprehensive income	–	–	–	–	(163)	290	–	2,095	2,222	27	2,249
Transactions with owners											
Purchase of treasury shares	–	–	–	–	–	–	(24)	–	(24)	–	(24)
Share-based paymens	–	–	–	–	–	–	73	168	241	–	241
Issue of shares	4	163	–	–	–	–	–	–	167	–	167
Purchase of minority interest	–	–	–	–	–	–	–	91	91	3	94
Dividends paid to minority interests	–	–	–	–	–	–	–	–	–	(2)	(2)
Dividends authorised in the year	–	–	–	–	–	–	–	(968)	(968)	–	(968)
Tax on items charged to equity	–	–	–	–	–	–	–	18	18	–	18
Transactions with owners	4	163	–	–	–	–	49	(691)	(475)	1	(474)
At 27 February 2010	399	4,801	40	13	12	463	(180)	9,048	14,596	85	14,681

COMPANY SNAPSHOT 12.3 (*Continued*)

ATTRIBUTABLE TO OWNERS OF THE PARENT

	Issued share capital £m	Share premium £m	Other reserves £m	Capital redemption reserve £m	Hedging reserve £m	Translation reserve £m	Treasury shares £m	Retained earnings £m	Total £m	Minority interest £m	Total equity £m
At 23 February 2008	393	4,511	40	12	4	245	(204)	6,814	11,815	87	11,902
IFRIC 13 restatement	–	–	–	–	–	–	–	(29)	(29)	–	(29)
At 23 February 2008 (restated*)	393	4,511	40	12	4	245	(204)	6,785	11,786	87	11,873
Profit for the year	–	–	–	–	–	–	–	2,133	2,133	5	2,138
Other comprehensive income											
Change in fair value of available-for-sale investments	–	–	–	–	–	–	–	3	3	–	3
Currency translation differences	–	–	–	–	–	(269)	–	–	(269)	(6)	(275)
Loss on defined benefit schemes	–	–	–	–	–	(2)	–	(627)	(629)	–	(629)
Gains on cash flow hedges	–	–	–	–	171	–	–	–	171	–	171
Tax on components of other comprehesive income	–	–	–	–	–	199	–	176	375	–	375
Total other comprehensive income	–	–	–	–	171	(72)	–	(448)	(349)	(6)	(355)
Total comprehensive income	–	–	–	–	171	(72)	–	1,685	1,784	(1)	1,783
Transaction with owners											
Purchase of treasury shares	–	–	–	–	–	–	(165)	–	(165)	–	(165)
Share-based payments	–	–	–	–	–	–	140	68	208	–	208
Issue of shares	3	127	–	–	–	–	–	–	130	–	130
Share buy-backs	(1)	–	–	1	–	–	–	–	–	–	–
Purchase of minority interest	–	–	–	–	–	–	–	–	–	(26)	(26)
Dividends paid to minority interests	–	–	–	–	–	–	–	–	–	(3)	(3)
Fair value reserve arising on acquisition of Tesco Bank	–	–	–	–	–	–	–	(71)	(71)	–	(71)
Dividends authorised in the year	–	–	–	–	–	–	–	(883)	(883)	–	(883)
Tax on items charged to equity	–	–	–	–	–	–	–	60	60	–	60
Transaction with owners	2	127	–	1	–	–	(25)	(826)	(721)	(29)	(750)
At 28 February 2009 (restated*)	395	4,638	40	13	175	173	(229)	7,644	12,849	57	12,906

* See note 1 Accounting policies.

Source: Tesco PLC, *Annual Report and Financial Statements 2010*, p. 73.

5. *Note on Reconciliation of Net Cash Flow to Movement in Net Debt*. This statement seeks to reconcile the increase in cash flow calculated from the statement of cash flows to the net debt. As Tesco's 2010 statement (Company Snapshot 12.4) shows, it specifies increases and decreases in debt and cash flow.

COMPANY SNAPSHOT 12.4

Tesco PLC's Reconciliation of Net Cash Flow to Movement in Net Debt Note

Year ended 27 February 2010	note	52 weeks 2010 £M	53 weeks 2009 £M
Net (decrease)/increase in cash and cash equivalents		(739)	1,601
Investment in Tesco Bank		(230)	–
Elimination of net increase in Tesco bank cash and cash equivalents		(167)	(37)
Debt acquired on acquistion of Homever		–	(611)
Transfer of joint venture loan receivable on acquisition of Tesco Bank		–	(91)
Net cash inflow (outflow) from debt and lease financing		2,780	(4,636)
Dividend received from Tesco Bank		150	–
Increase in short-term investments		81	873
Increase in joint venture loan receivables		45	242
Other non-cash movements		(249)	(759)
Decrease/(increase) in net debt in the year		1,671	(3,418)
Opening net debt	32	(9,600)	(6,182)
Closing net debt	32	(7,929)	(9,600)

NB. The reconciliation of net cash flow to movement in net debt note is not a primary statement and does not form part of the cash flow statement and forms part of the notes to the financial statements.

Source: Tesco PLC, *Annual Report and Financial Statements 2010*, p. 74.

6. *Note on Historical Cost Profits and Losses*. If the accounts are prepared under the historical cost convention then the original cost of assets is recorded in the accounts. However, sometimes assets, particularly property, will be revalued. These assets are not then included in the accounts at their original purchase price. Depreciation on the revalued property will then be more than on the original cost. This note records any such differences caused by departures from the historical cost convention. Tesco records its property, plant and equipment at cost so there is no note on historical cost profits and losses.

Explanatory Material

7. *Accounting Policies*. Companies must describe the accounting policies they use to prepare the financial statements. The flexibility inherent within accounting means that companies

have a choice of accounting policies in areas such as foreign currencies, goodwill, pensions, sales and inventories. Different accounting policies will result in different accounting figures. Nokia's policy on inventories is given as an illustration (see Company Snapshot 12.5).

COMPANY SNAPSHOT 12.5

Policy on Inventories

Inventories are stated at the lower of cost or net realisable value. Cost is determined using standard cost, which approximates actual cost, on a FIFO (first in first out) basis. Net realisable value is the amount that can be realised from the sale of the inventory in the normal course of business after allowing for the costs of realisation.

In addition to the cost of materials and direct labour, an appropriate proportion of production overhead is included in the inventory values.

An allowance is recorded for excess inventory and obsolescence based on the lower of cost or net realisable value.

Source: Nokia, *Annual Report 2010*, p. 24. Reproduced by permission.

8. *Notes to the Accounts.* These notes provide additional information about items in the accounts. They are often quite extensive. For example, in Tesco's 2004 annual report the main three financial statements take up three pages, but the 34 notes take up a further 24 pages. These notes flesh out the detail of the three main financial statements. They cover a variety of topics. For example, the first six Tesco notes cover prior year adjustment, segmental analysis, operating profit, employee profit-sharing, profit on ordinary activities before taxation, and employment costs. The notes to accounts can be crucial. 'The numbers are just part of the story. The balance sheet is just a snapshot. It captures some of the picture but not all of it so that's why the notes to the accounts are important' (Jill Treanor, *The Guardian*, 6 March 2000, p. 28).
9. *Principal Subsidiaries.* Most large companies consist of many individual companies arranged as the parent (or holding company) and its subsidiaries. Collectively, they are known as groups (see later in this chapter for a fuller explanation of groups). In the case of a group, there will be a listing of the parent (i.e., main) company's subsidiary companies (i.e., normally those companies where over 50% of the shares are owned by the parent company) and associate companies (normally where between 20% and 50% of shares are owned by the parent company).

The Non-Audited Sections

The amount of non-audited information in annual reports has mushroomed over the last 30 years. It has caught even experienced observers by surprise. Narrative information has grown in importance over the last generation until as Deloitte (2010) point out, almost half of the annual report is narrative (see Real-World View 12.4).

The non-audited information is extremely varied, but can be broadly divided into narrative and non-narrative information. The *narrative* information consists mainly of the chairman's statement, the directors' report, the business review and the auditors' report.

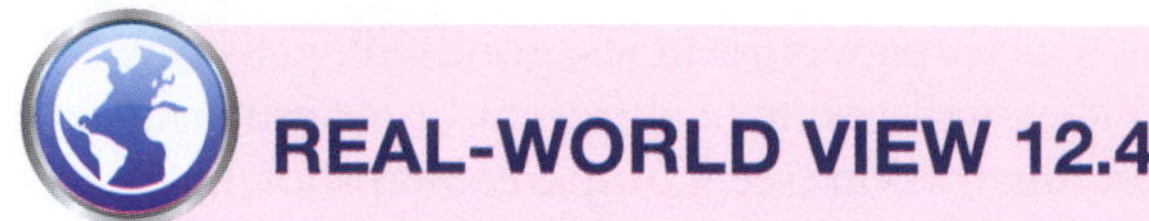

REAL-WORLD VIEW 12.4

Accounting Narratives

The balance of narrative versus financial statements as a proportion of the total annual report has shifted slightly from the prior year. As shown in figure 2, below, financial statements now represent on average 2% more of the total report than last year at 48% (2008: 46%). The overall shift is to an increase in length of the financial statements. The larger companies continue to devote more of the report to narrative information than the middle and smaller companies, with total narrative of 56%, 50% and 45% respectively (2008: 59%, 51 % and 47% respectively). The relative decline between 2008 and 2009 may be due to the factors referred to above regarding information being moved to company websites or separate reports.

Figure 2 What is the balance of narrative and financial reporting in the annual report?

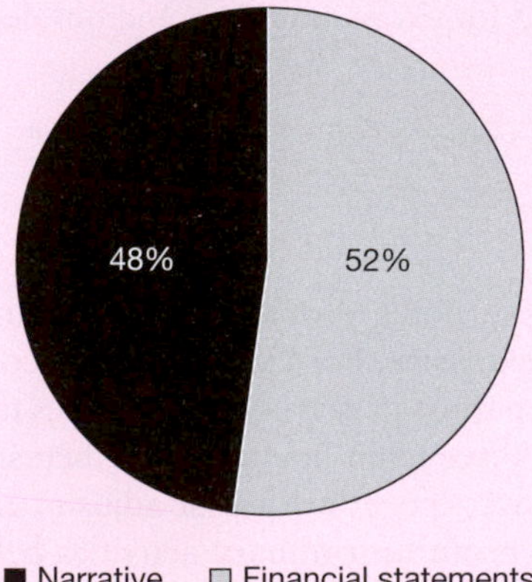

■ Narrative □ Financial statements

Source: Deloitte (2010) *A Telling Performance, Surveying Narrative Reporting in Annual Reports.*

SOUNDBITE 12.2

Narrative Reporting

'Indeed, the financial statements are becoming a technical appendix, play a supporting role to a evolving narrative.'

Source: Michael Power, *Accountancy Magazine*, February 2011, Pantomime Accounting, p. 22.

As Soundbite 12.2 shows, some argue that narrative reporting is now the key driver in an annual report. By contrast, the *non-narrative* information mainly comprises the highlights and the historical summary. Although these sections are not audited, the auditor is required to review the non-narrative information to see if there are material misstatements or material inconsistencies with the financial statements. If there are, the auditors consider whether any information needs to be amended. Unfortunately, all this is very subjective and, in reality, little guidance is given to auditors.

Narrative Sections

10. Business Review. The operating and financial review (OFR) represented a major innovation in UK financial reporting. For the first time, regulators formally recognised the importance of qualitative, non-financial information. It enabled companies to provide a formalised, structured and narrative explanation of financial performance. The ASB introduced the OFR as a voluntary statement in 1993. It had two parts: first, the operating review which discusses items such as a company's operating results, profit and dividends; second, the financial review which covers items such as capital structure and treasury policy. The OFR aimed to provide investors with more relevant information. In an interesting example of government interference in UK accounting, the Government in November 2005 decided to abolish the proposed mandatory status of the OFR. It has been replaced with a European piece of legislation, the Business Review. This is discussed in Pause for Thought 12.4. If a company has an OFR, this meets the European requirement for a Business Review. The aim of the Business Review, like that of the OFR, is to provide users with a balanced and comprehensive view of the company's activities, including any risks and uncertainties.

PAUSE FOR THOUGHT 12.4

The Operating and Financial Review (OFR)

The Operating and Financial Review is a document that was originally suggested by the UK's Accounting Standards Board. It was a document whereby companies could present an extended narrative on areas such as risks or social and environmental information. It was going to be made mandatory but then the Labour Government scrapped it. The Coalition Government in 2010, however, planned to reinstate it.

So what would you have done? Scrap it or reinstate it?

11. Chairman's Statement. This is the longest-established accounting narrative. It is provided voluntarily by nearly all companies. The chairman's statement provides a personalised overview of the company's performance over the past year. Most chairman's statements cover strategy, the financial performance and future prospects. It is also traditional for the chairman to thank the employees and retiring directors.

12. Directors' Report. The directors' report is prescribed by law. Its principal objective is to supplement the financial information with information that is considered vital for a full appreciation of the company's activities. Items presented here (or elsewhere in the accounts – an increasingly common practice) might include any changes in the company's activities, proposed dividends, and charitable and political gifts.

PAUSE FOR THOUGHT 12.5

Auditing the Accounting Narratives

Auditors check that the accounts give a true and fair view of the company's performance.

What difficulties do you think an auditor might have if called upon to audit the narrative sections of the annual report, such as the chairman's statement?

The main difficulty is deciding how to audit the written word. Usually, auditors audit figures. They can thus objectively trace these back to originating documentation. The problem with accounting narratives is that they are very subjective. How do you audit phrases such as 'We have had a good year' or 'Profit has increased substantially'?

13. *Review of Operations*. This section forms a natural complement to the chairman's statement. Whereas the chairman provides the overview, the chief executive reviews the individual business operations, often quite extensively. Normally, the chief executive discusses, in turn, each individual business or geographical segment.

14. *Social and Environmental Accounting Statement*. A growing number of companies are reporting social and environmental, social responsibility or sustainability information. For example, over 70% of the UK's top 350 listed companies report such information. This information is largely voluntary. Increasingly, companies are producing separate stand-alone environmental reports or sustainability reports. However, they may also include sections in their annual report. For example, J.D. Wetherspoon's in 2010 included a corporate social responsibility section in its 2010 annual report. This covered, inter alia, responsible drink retailing, the environment, and community and charitable activities.

SOUNDBITE 12.3

Sustainability Information

'Accounting mechanisms have not, for the moment at least, kept pace with our requirements for sustainability information.'

Prince Charles

Source: Accountancy Age, 2 June 2005, p. 12.

15. *Statement of Corporate Governance*. This statement arises out of the drive to make directors more accountable to their shareholders. The corporate governance statement is governed by stock market requirements. The issues usually covered are risk management, treasury management, internal controls, going concern and auditors. A major objective is to present a full and frank discussion of the directors' remuneration. Contained within this section is often a Directors' Remuneration Report. However, growing numbers of companies record this separately.

16. Directors' Remuneration Report. This includes details of directors' pay. It may include details of the remuneration committee, the remuneration policy and the main components of the directors' pay (for example: basic salary, incentives, bonuses, share options and performance-related pay). There is also a graph showing the company's total shareholder return with an appropriate stock market index (see Company Snapshot 12.6 for Tesco PLC's 2010 performance graph). This is headed total shareholder return. It compares Tesco's share price against the FTSE 100 and Eurofirst Food and Drug Index over a ten-year period. Tesco is shown to outperform these other indices. This graph helps shareholders to compare directors' remuneration to company performance.

COMPANY SNAPSHOT 12.6

Tesco PLC Performance Graph

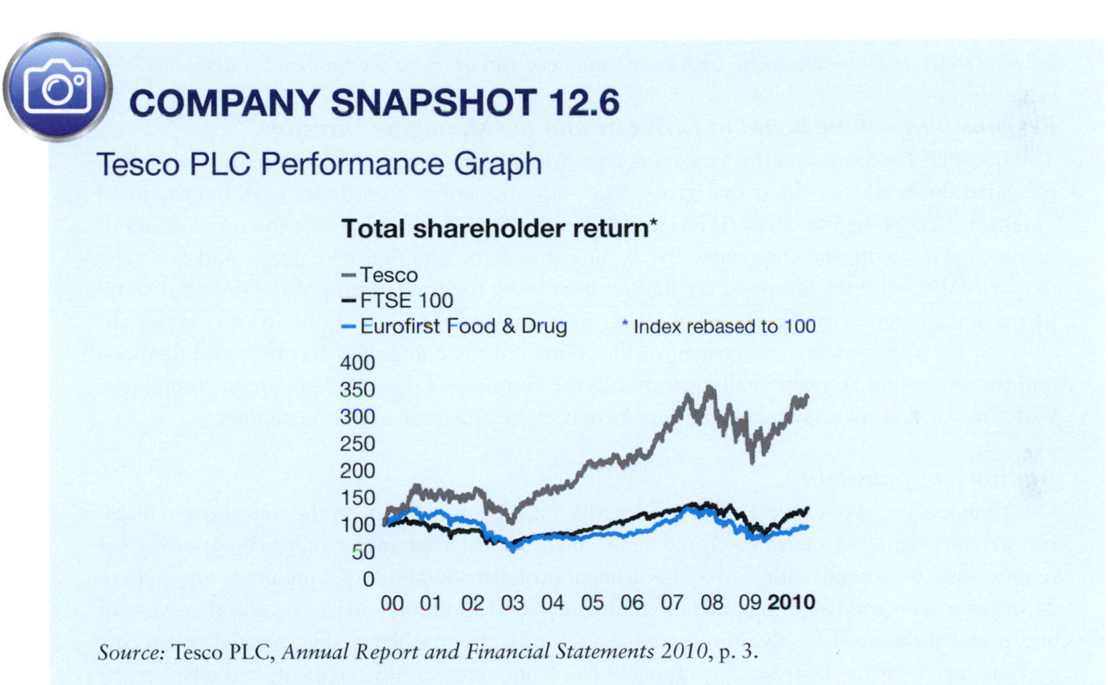

Source: Tesco PLC, *Annual Report and Financial Statements 2010*, p. 3.

17. Auditors' Report. The audit is an independent examination of the financial statements. An example of an auditors' report for Nokia, a Finnish company, is given in Company Snapshot 12.7. An example of a UK company's audit report is given for J. Sainsbury plc in Company Snapshot 10.1.

Companies are legally required to publish the auditors' report. In essence, the report states whether the financial statements present a 'true and fair view' of the company's activities over the previous financial year. It sets out the respective responsibilities of directors and auditors as well as spelling out the work carried out to arrive at the auditors' opinion.

The auditors' report thus outlines the respective responsibilities of directors and auditors, the basis of the audit opinion and how the auditors arrived at their opinion. PricewaterhouseCoopers, the auditors of Nokia, are one of the world's leading auditing partnerships.

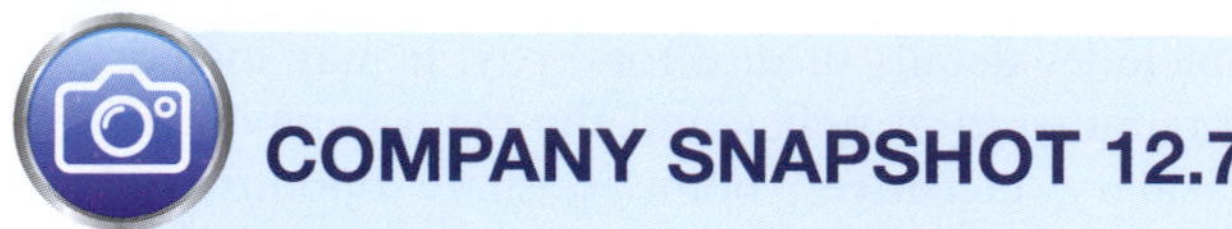

COMPANY SNAPSHOT 12.7

Independent Auditors' Report

To the Annual General Meeting of Nokia Corporation

We have audited the accounting records, the financial statements, the review by the Board of Directors and the administration of Nokia Corporation for the year ended 31 December 2010. The financial statements comprise the consolidated statement of financial position, income statement, statement of comprehensive income, cash flow statement, statement of changes in shareholder's equity and notes to the consolidated financial statements, as well as the parent company's balance sheet, income statement, cash flow statement and notes to the financial statements.

Responsibility of the Board of Directors and the Managing Director

The Board of Directors and the Managing Director are responsible for the preparation of consolidated financial statements that give a true and fair view in accordance with International Financial Reporting Standards (IFRS) as adopted by the EU, as well as for the preparation of financial statements and the review by the Board of Directors that give a true and fair view in accordance with the laws and regulations governing the preparation of the financial statements and the review by the Board of Directors in Finland. The Board of Directors is responsible for the appropriate arrangement of the control of the company's accounts and finances, and the Managing Director shall see to it that the accounts of the company are in compliance with the law and that its financial affairs have been arranged in a reliable manner.

Auditor's responsibility

Our responsibility is to express an opinion on the financial statements, on the consolidated financial statements and on the review by the Board of Directors based on our audit. The Auditing Act requires that we comply with the requirements of professional ethics. We conducted our audit in accordance with good auditing practice in Finland. Good auditing practice requires that we plan and perform the audit to obtain reasonable assurance about whether the financial statements and the review by the Board of Directors are free from material misstatement, and whether the members of the Board of Directors of the parent company and the Managing Director are guilty of an act or negligence which may result in liability in damages towards the company or have violated the Limited Liability Companies Act or the articles of association of the company.

An audit involves performing procedures to obtain audit evidence about the amounts and disclosures in the financial statements and the review by the Board of Directors. The procedures selected depend on the auditor's judgement, including the assessment of the risks of material misstatement, whether due to fraud or error. In making those risk assessments, the auditor considers internal control relevant to the entity's preparation of the financial statements and the review by the Board of Directors that give a true and fair view in order to design audit procedures that are appropriate in the circumstances, but not for the purpose of expressing an opinion on the effectiveness of the company's internal control. An audit also includes evaluating the appropriateness of accounting policies used and the reasonableness of

COMPANY SNAPSHOT 12.7 (*continued*)

accounting estimates made by management, as well as evaluating the overall presentation of the financial statements and the review by the Board of Directors.

We believe that the audit evidence we have obtained is sufficient and appropriate to provide a basis for our audit opinion.

Opinion on the consolidated financial statements

In our opinion, the consolidated financial statements give a true and fair view of the financial position, financial performance, and cash flows of the group in accordance with International Financial Reporting Standards (IFRS) as adopted by the EU.

Opinion on the company's financial statements and the review by the Board of Directors

In our opinion, the financial statements and the review by the Board of Directors give a true and fair view of both the consolidated and the parent company's financial performance and financial position in accordance with the laws and regulations governing the preparation of the financial statements and the review by the Board of Directors in Finland. The information in the review by the Board of Directors is consistent with the information in the financial statements.

Other opinions

We support that the financial statements should be adopted. The proposal by the Board of Directors regarding the distribution of the profit shown in the balance sheet is in compliance with the Limited Liability Companies Act. We support that the Members of the Board of Directors and the Managing Director should be discharged from liability for the financial period audited by us.

Helsinki, March 11, 2011

PricewaterhouseCoopers Oy
Authorised Public Accountants

Merja Lindh
Authorised Public Account

Source: Nokia, *Annual Report 2010*, p. 82. Reproduced by permission.

18. Statement of Directors' Responsibilities for the Financial Statements. This statement (see Company Snapshot 12.8) was introduced because of a general misconception by the general public of the purpose of an audit compared with the actual nature of an audit as understood by auditors. The directors must spell out their responsibilities which include (i) keeping proper accounting records; (ii) preparing financial statements in accordance with the Companies Act 2006; (iii) selecting suitable accounting policies consistently; (iv) stating whether Group and Company financial statements are following appropriate standards; (v) preparing the financial statements under the going concern basis and (vi) making reasonable and prudent judgements and estimates.

In the case of Tesco, in 2010, it is noteworthy that the Group financial statements are prepared following IFRS, as endorsed by the EU, while the parent company accounts are still prepared following UK GAAP.

COMPANY SNAPSHOT 12.8

Statement of Directors' Responsibilities

The Directors are required by the Companies Act 2006 to prepare financial statements for each financial year which give a true and fair view of the state of affairs of the company and the Group as at the end of the financial year and of the profit or loss for the financial year. Under that law the Directors are required to prepare the Group financial statements in accordance with International Financial Reporting Standards (IFRSs) as endorsed by the European Union (EU) and have elected to prepare the Company financial statements in accordance with UK Accounting Standards.

In preparing the Group and Company financial statements, the Directors are required to:

- select suitable accounting policies and then apply them consistently;
- make reasonable and prudent judgements and estimates;
- for the Group financial statements, state whether they have been prepared in accordance with IFRS, as endorsed by the EU.
- for the Company financial statements state whether applicable UK Accounting Standards have been followed; and
- prepare the financial statements on the going concern basis, unless it is inappropriate to presume that the Group and the Company will continue in business.

The Directors confirm that they have complied with the above requirements in preparing the financial statements.

The Directors are responsible for keeping proper accounting records which disclose with reasonable accuracy at any time, the financial position of the Company and the Group, and which enable them to ensure that the financial statements and the Directors' Remuneration Report comply with the Companies Act 2006, and as regards the Group financial statements, Article 4 of the IAS Regulation.

The Business Review includes a fair review of the business and important events impacting it, as well as a description of the principal risks and uncertainties of the business.

The Directors are responsible for the maintenance and integrity of the Annual Review and Summary Financial Statement and Annual Report and Financial Statements published on the Group's corporate website. Legislation in the UK concerning the preparation and dissemination of financial statements may differ from legislation in other jurisdictions.

The Directors have general responsibility for taking such steps as are reasonably open to them to safeguard the assets of the Group and of the Company and to prevent and detect fraud and other irregularities.

Source: Tesco PLC, *Annual Report and Financial Statement 2010*, p. 68.

19. Shareholder Information. Companies increasingly include a variety of shareholder information. This might, for example, include a financial calendar, share price details, shareholder analysis (see item 22) or notice of the AGM. The information may be narrative or non-narrative in nature.

Non-Narrative Sections

20. Highlights. This very popular feature normally occurs at the start of the annual report, often accompanied by graphs of selected figures. This section provides an at-a-glance summary of selected figures and ratios.

In Tesco's report (Company Snapshot 12.9), for example, group sales, group profit, profit before tax, earnings per share, dividends per share, group enterprise value (market capitalisation plus net debt) and return on capital employed are the financial ratios highlighted. The financial highlights may be seen as an abridged version of the historical summary.

21. Historical Summary. The historical summary is a voluntary recommendation of the stock exchange. Indeed, in the UK, it is one of the very few regulations set out by the stock exchange. Usually, companies choose to present five years of selected data from both the statement of financial position and the income statement.

22. Shareholder Analysis. In many ways this item supplements item 20, shareholder information. It provides detailed analysis of the shareholders; for example, by size of shareholding.

These 22 items are by no means exhaustive; for example, J.D. Wetherspoon's plc, the pub chain, provides a list of its Directors, officers and advisers.

Presentation

The style of the annual report is becoming much more important. Companies are increasingly presenting key financial information as graphs rather than as tables. This information is voluntary and generally often supplements the mandatory information. Many companies use graphs to provide oases of colour and interest in otherwise dry statutory documents. In many cases, the graphs are presented at the front along with the highlights. Tesco, for example, in 1999 provided five-year graphs of group sales, group operating profit, earnings per share, and operating cash flow and capital expenditure (see Company Snapshot 12.10 on page 377).

Photographs are also common in annual reports. These may be of employees or products. However, often they act as 'mood music' with no obvious relationship to the actual content of the report.

The increased use of the Internet provides many opportunities for companies to present their annual reports on their websites. Many companies are now experimenting with this new presentational format, often using varied presentational methods. Figure 12.4 on page 378 gives some well-known company websites and students are encouraged to visit them.

COMPANY SNAPSHOT 12.9

Financial Highlights

Group sales (including VAT)*	+6.8%
Underlying profit before tax	+10.1%
Group profit before tax	+10.4%
Underlying diluted earnings per share**	+9.1%
Diluted earnings per share	+9.8%
Dividend per share	+9.1%

All growth figures reported on a 52-week basis.

		2008/9‡	
52 weeks ended 27 February 2010	2009/10	52 weeks	53 weeks
Group sales (£m) (including VAT)*	**62,537**	58,570	59,426
Group revenue (£m) (excluding VAT)	**56,910**	53,115	53,898
Group trading profit (£m)	**3,412**	3,039	3,086
Underlying profit before tax (£m)	**3,395**	3,083	3,124
Group profit before tax (£m)	**3,176**	2,876	2,917
Underlying diluted earnings per share (p)	**31.66**	28.50	28.87
Dividend per share (p)	**13.05**	—	11.96
Group enterprise value (£bn) (market capitalisation plus net debt)	**41.4**	—	35.9
Return on capital employed	**12.1%**	—	12.8%

* Group sales (inc. VAT) excludes the accounting impact of IFRIC 13 (Customer Loyalty Programmes).
** Growth in underlying diluted EPS calculated on a constant tax rate basis.
‡ Restated for the impact of IFRIC 13 and IFRS 2.

Source: Tesco PLC, *Annual Report and Financial Statements 2010*, Inside Cover.

COMPANY SNAPSHOT 12.10

Financial Graphs

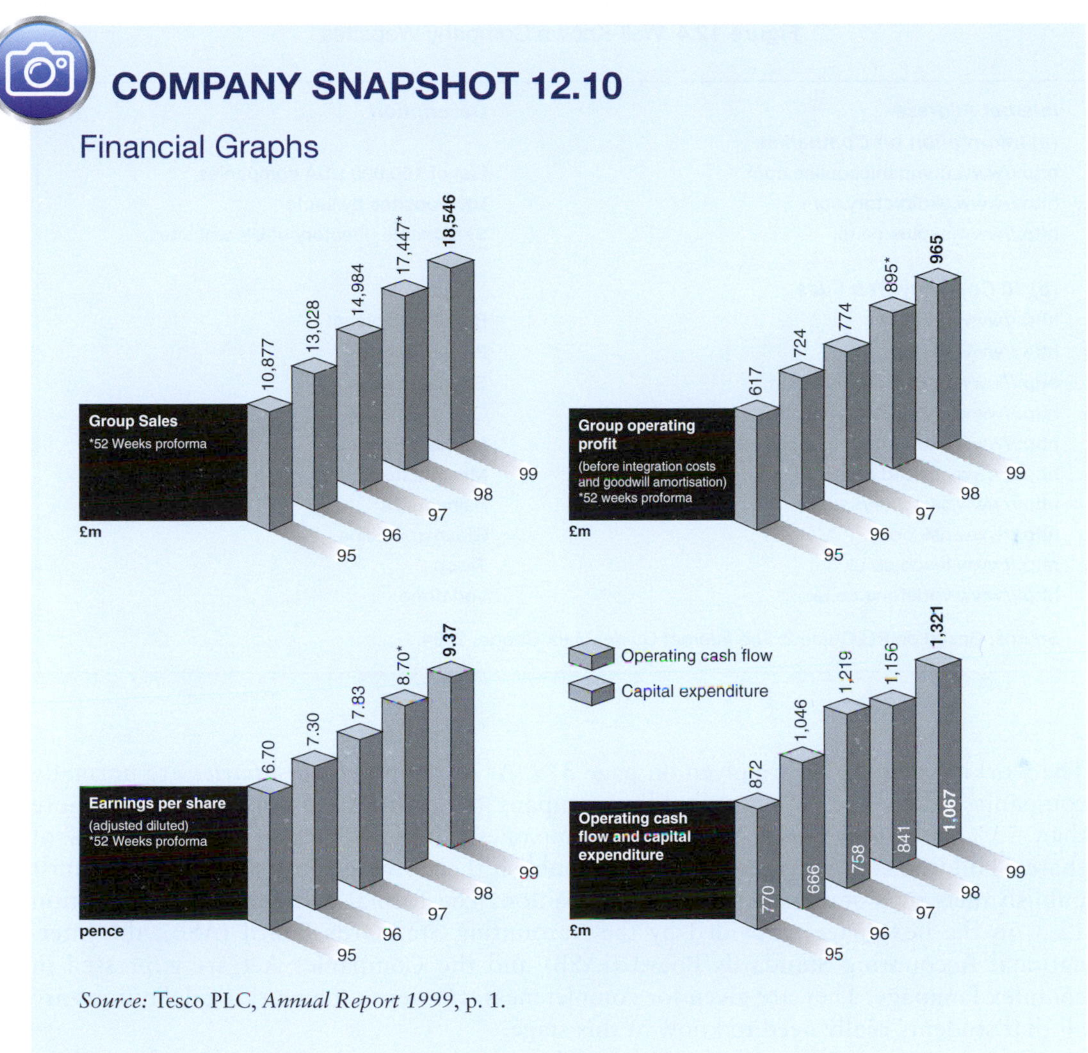

Source: Tesco PLC, *Annual Report 1999*, p. 1.

Group Accounts

Subsidiary and Associated Companies

An interesting feature of most of the world's largest companies is that they are structured as groups. This is because companies often buy other companies. All the companies must publish consolidated or group accounts which treat all companies in the group as one entity. It is the annual reports of these groups of companies such as Vodafone, Toyota or Wal-Mart that are most often publicly available. A group of companies is one where one or more companies is controlled by another. In many cases, these groups are extremely complex and complicated involving many hundreds of subsidiary and associated companies.

Figure 12.4 Well-Known Company Websites

Internet Address	***Description***
(a) Information on Companies	
http://www.companiesonline.com	List of 100,000 USA companies
http://www.ukdirectory.com	UK websites by sector
http://www.ukplus.co.uk	Searchable directory of UK websites
(b) 10 Company Web Sites	
http://www.bp.com	British Petroleum
http://www.bt.com	British Telecom
http://www.british-airways.com	British Airways
http://www.glaxowellcome.com	Glaxo Wellcome
http://www.marks-and-spencer.co.uk	Marks & Spencer
http://www.manutd.com	Manchester United
http://www.sainsburys.co.uk	Sainsbury's
http://www.gsk.com	Glaxosmithkline
http://www.tesco.co.uk	Tesco
http://www.vodafone.co.uk	Vodafone

Source: Based on PC Guide 2: *The Internet Guide*, Mark Goode, 2004.

The working definitions are given on page 379. At its simplest, *subsidiaries* are normally companies where the parent or holding company (i.e., top group company) owns more than 50% of shares and *associates* are companies where the parent owns 20–50% of shares. Holding companies do not need to publish their own income statement, but must publish their own statement of financial position. The formal definitions (see Definition 12.3 on the next page) provided by the Accounting Standards Board (ASB), the International Accounting Standards Board (IASB) and the Companies Act are expressed in complex language. They are given for completeness. However, the working definitions are all that students really need to know at this stage.

Group accounts are prepared using special accounting procedures, which are beyond the scope of this particular book (interested readers could try Elliot and Elliot, *Advanced Financial Accounting and Reporting*, or Alexander, Britton and Jorrisen, *International Financial Reporting and Analysis*). In essence, the group income statement and group statement of financial position attempt to portray the whole group's performance and financial position rather than that of individual companies.

Thus, in Figure 12.5 (see page 380), the group comprises seven companies. Company A is the parent company and owns over 50% of companies B and C, making them subsidiaries. Company B also owns more than 50% of the shares of companies B1 and B2. Companies B1 and B2 thus become sub-subsidiaries of Company A. These four companies (B, C, B1 and B2) are therefore consolidated as subsidiaries using normal accounting procedures. In addition, an appropriate proportion of companies D and E are taken into the group accounts since these two companies are associates as between 20% and 50% of the shares are held. Overall, therefore, we have the aggregate financial performance of the whole group. One group set of financial statements is prepared. It is these group accounts that are normally published in the annual report.

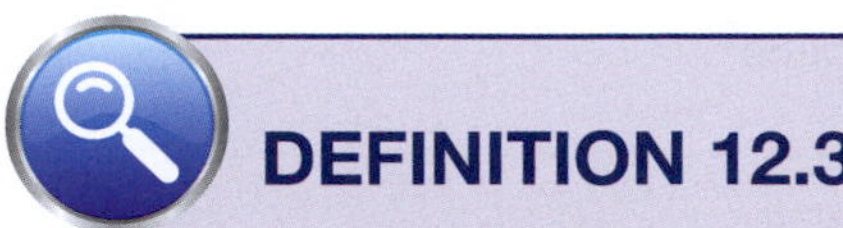

DEFINITION 12.3

1. Subsidiary Company

Working definition

A company where more than half the shares are owned by another company or which is effectively controlled by another company, or is a subsidiary of a subsidiary.

Formal definition

'A subsidiary is an entity, including an incorporated entity such as a partnership, that is controlled by another entity (known as the parent). Control is presumed to exist when the parent owns, directly or indirectly through subsidiaries, more than one half of the voting power of an enterprise unless, in exceptional circumstances, it can be clearly demonstrated that such ownership does not constitute control. Control also exists even when the parent owns one half or less of the voting power of an enterprise when there is:

(a) power over more than one half of the voting rights by virtue of an agreement with other investors;
(b) power to govern the financial and operating policies of the enterprise under a statute or an agreement;
(c) power to appoint or remove the majority of the members of the board of directors or equivalent governing body; or
(d) power to cast the majority of votes at meetings of the board of directors or equivalent governing body.'

Source: International Accounting Standards Board, 2010, IAS 27, *Consolidated and Separate Financial Statements*, paras 2 and 12.

2. Associated Company

Working definition

A company in which 20–50% of the shares are owned by another company or one in which another company has a significant influence.

Formal definition

'An associate is an entity, including an unincorporated entity such as a partnership, over which the investor has significant influence and that is neither a subsidiary nor an interest in a joint venture of the investor. If an investor holds, directly or indirectly (e.g., through subsidiaries), 20 per cent or more of the voting power of the investee, it is presumed that the investor does have significant influence, unless it can be clearly demonstrated that this is not the case. Conversely, if the investor holds, directly or indirectly (e.g., through subsidiaries), less than 20 per cent of the voting power of the investee, it is presumed that the investor does not have significant influence, unless such influence can be clearly demonstrated. A substantial or majority ownership by another investor does not necessarily preclude an investor from having significant influence.'

Source: International Accounting Standards Board, 2010, IAS 28, *Accounting for Investments in Associates*, paras 2 and 6.

Figure 12.5 Example of Group Structure

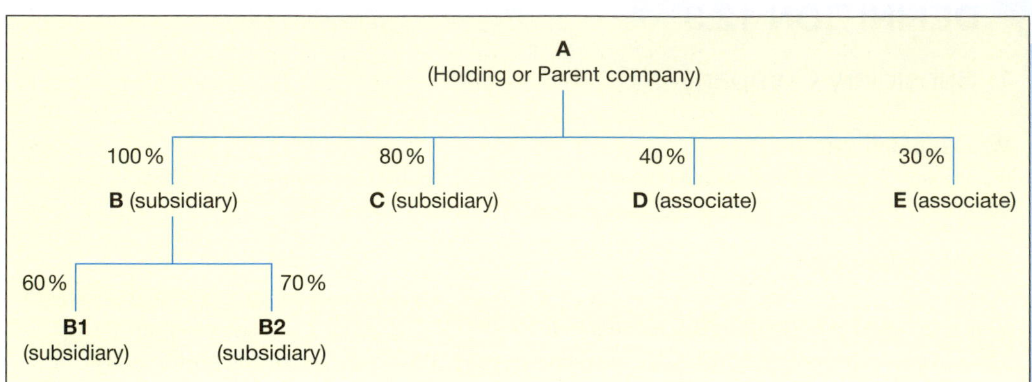

Goodwill

Goodwill is a particular feature of group companies. Goodwill is known as an intangible asset (i.e., one that you cannot touch). Goodwill, in accounting terms, is only recognised when one company takes over another. It represents the value of the whole business over and above the value of its individual assets and liabilities. This can often be quite considerable. European listed companies follow International Financial Reporting Standard 3 which states that goodwill is shown as an asset on the statement of financial position. It is then reviewed every year to see if the goodwill has lost value. If it has lost value, this value will be written off to the income statement. That annual review is called an impairment test. For UK non-listed companies, the UK standard requires a different treatment. The preferred treatment is that companies should write off goodwill to the income statement annually over a period of up to 20 years. This process of writing off goodwill is called amortisation. It is similar to depreciation. Non-listed companies are also permitted, if they can make a case, to write off goodwill over a period of greater than 20 years or even not at all.

PAUSE FOR THOUGHT 12.6

Group Accounts

Nowadays, most leading companies must prepare group accounts. Can you think of any problems they might encounter?

There are many! Many companies will have hundreds of subsidiaries. All the information must be supplied to head office. At head office, it must all be collected and collated. Different subsidiaries may have different year-end accounting dates, operate in different countries using different accounting policies and different currencies. Some of the subsidiaries will have been acquired or sold, or the shareholdings of the parent company will have changed, during the year. All these are potential problems.

Impression Management

Managers have significant incentives to try to influence the financial reporting process in their own favour. These incentives may be financial and non-financial. Financially, managers may be keen, for example, to maximise their own remuneration. If remuneration is based on profits, they may seek to adopt accounting policies that will increase rather than decrease profits. In non-financial terms, managers, like all human beings, will try to portray themselves in a good light. This may result, for example, in managers selectively disclosing only positive features of the annual performance.

In this section, three illustrative examples of impression management are discussed: creative accounting, narrative enhancement and use of graphs.

PAUSE FOR THOUGHT 12.7

Impression Management

Can you think of any non-accounting situations where human beings indulge in impression management?

There are many, just to take two: interviews and dating. At an interview, normal, sane candidates try to give a good impression of themselves in order to get the job. This may involve trying to stress their good points and downplay their bad points. When dating, you try to look good to impress your partner. Once more, most normal people will try to present themselves in a favourable light. You want to impress your dates not repel them.

Creative Accounting

Creative accounting will be dealt with more fully in Chapter 13. Put simply, creative accounting is the name given to the process whereby managers use the flexibility inherent within the accounting process to manipulate the accounting numbers. Flexibility within the accounting system is abundant. By itself, flexibility allows managers to choose those accounting policies that will give a true and fair view of the company's activities. However, there are also opportunities for managers to choose policies which portray themselves in a good light. The worst excesses are covered by the regulatory framework. To see how the flexibility within accounting can alter profit, we take inventory and depreciation as examples.

Inventory

In accounting terms:

$$\text{Assets} - \text{Liabilities} = \text{Equity}$$

In other words, if assets increase so will equity. As equity includes retained earnings, if we increase inventory we will increase retained earnings. Inventory is an easy asset to manipulate, if we wish to increase our profits. We could, for example, do an extremely thorough stocktake at the end of one year, recording and valuing items which normally would have been overlooked.

PAUSE FOR THOUGHT 12.8

Inventory and Creative Accounting

A company has one asset, inventory. Its abridged statement of financial position is set out below.

	£		£
Inventory	50,000	Equity	30,000
		Retained earnings	20,000
	50,000		50,000

If the company revalues its inventory to £60,000, what will happen to profit?

The answer is that profit increases by £10,000, as the new statement of financial position shows.

	£		£
Inventory	60,000	Equity	30,000
		Profit	30,000
	60,000		60,000

Depreciation

Depreciation is the expense incurred when property, plant and equipment is written down in value over its useful life. Unfortunately, estimates of useful lives vary. For example, if an asset has an estimated useful life of five years then depreciation, using a straight line basis, would be 20% per year. If the asset's estimated useful life was ten years, depreciation would be 10% per year. In other words, by extending the useful life, we halve the depreciation rate and halve the amount that is treated as an expense in the income statement. Managers can thus alter profit by choosing a particular rate of depreciation. They would argue that they are more fairly reflecting the useful life of the asset.

Narrative Enhancement

Narrative enhancement occurs when managements use the narrative parts of the annual report to convey a more favourable impression of performance than is actually warranted. They may do this by omitting key data or stressing certain elements. Many companies stress, for example, their 'good' environmental performance. Indeed, social and environmental disclosures are nowadays exceedingly common. Since such disclosures are voluntary and reviewed rather than audited, there is great potential for companies to indulge in narrative enhancement. This can be seen from Real-World View 12.5. In this, the news reported by Australian corporations is overwhelmingly positive, which is unlikely to be true in reality.

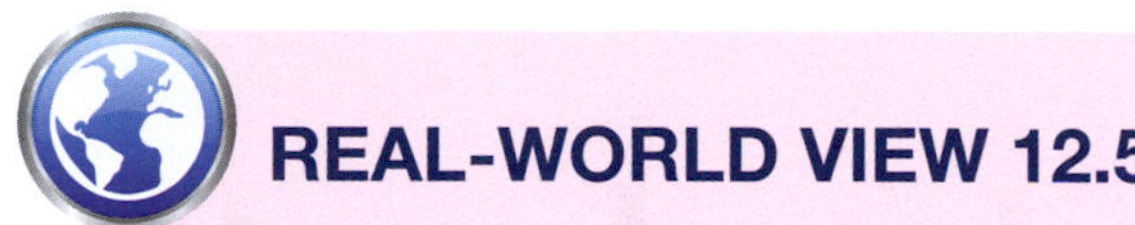

REAL-WORLD VIEW 12.5

Environmental Accounting

An interesting example of narrative measurement is given by Craig Deegan and Ben Gordon. They studied the environmental disclosure practices of Australian corporations.

The number of positive and negative words of environmental disclosure in annual reports from 1980 to 1991 are recorded for 25 companies. They find:

	1980	1985	1988	1991
Mean positive disclosure	12	14	20	105
Mean negative disclosure	0	0	0	7

They conclude:

'The environmental disclosures are typically self-laudatory, with little or no negative disclosures being made by all firms in the study.'

Source: Craig Deegan and Ben Gordon (1996), A Study of the Environmental Disclosure Practices of Australian Corporations, *Accounting and Business Research*, Vol 26, Issue 3, p. 198. Taylor & Francis. Reprinted by permission of the publisher (Taylor & Francis Ltd).

Graphs

Graphs are a voluntary presentational medium. Used well they are exceedingly effective. However, they also present managers with significant opportunities to manage the presentation of the annual report. For example, a variety of research studies show that managers are exceedingly selective in their use of graphs. They tend to display time-series trend graphs when performance is good, with these graphs presenting a rising trend of corporate performance. By contrast, when the results are poor, graphs are omitted.

Even when included, there is a potential for graphical misuse. The increase in the height of the graph should be proportionate to the increase in the data. However, graphs are often drawn more favourably than is warranted. For example, graphs may be (and often are) drawn with non-zero axes that enhance the perception of growth. Or graphs may simply be drawn inaccurately.

Currently, graphs are not regulated; therefore companies are free to use them creatively. An interesting example is shown in Company Snapshot 12.11. These five graphs represent the financial performance of Polly Peck. This company had spectacular results just before the company collapsed into a totally unexpected bankruptcy. Although not inaccurately drawn, they do present a very effective, and misleading, display. Who could guess that this company was about to fail? Certainly not the investors or even the auditors. Polly Peck is one of Britain's most important business scandals.

COMPANY SNAPSHOT 12.11

Creative Graphs

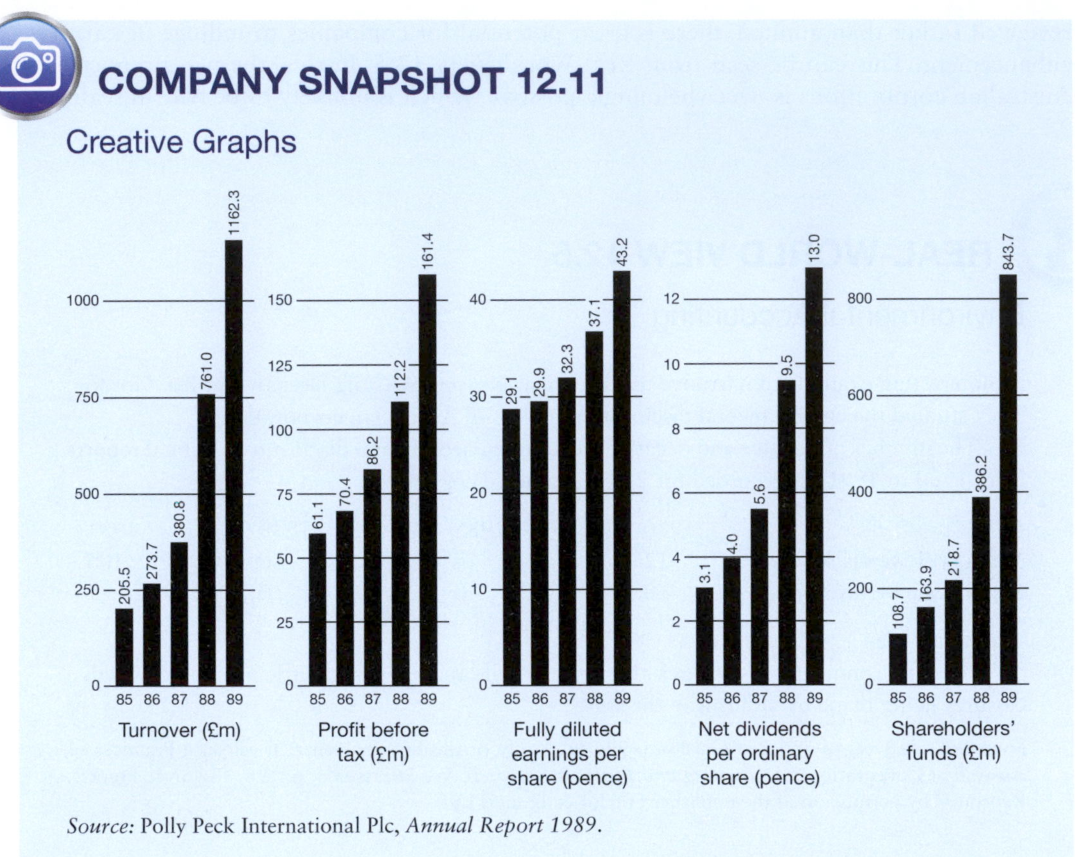

Source: Polly Peck International Plc, *Annual Report 1989*.

Conclusion

The annual report is a key part of the process by which managers report to their shareholders. It is central to the corporate governance process. There are three overlapping objectives: stewardship and accountability, decision making and public relations. The annual report is built around three core audited financial statements: the income statement, the statement of financial position and the statement of cash flows. However, in the UK another seven important audited financial statements are normally present: statement of total recognised gains and losses; reconciliation of movements in shareholders' funds; note on reconciliation of net cash flow to movement on net debt; note on historical cost profits and losses; accounting policies; notes to the accounts; and the principal subsidiaries. Most large enterprises are groups consisting of subsidiary and associated companies. The main accounts are therefore group accounts.

The modern annual report also consists of non-audited sections. These can be divided into narratives and non-narratives. In the UK, the ten narratives comprise the chairman's statement, the business review, the directors' report, the review of operations, the social and environment statement, the statement of corporate governance, the directors' remuneration report, the auditors' report, the statement of directors' responsibilities for the financial statements and shareholder information. The three non-narratives are the highlights, the historical summary and the shareholder analysis. As well as these sections, the modern annual report commonly uses graphs and photographs to enhance its presentation. Managements face many incentives to influence the financial reporting process in their favour. This can be done, for example, through creative accounting, narrative enhancement or the use of graphs.

Selected Reading

Unfortunately, there is no one book or article which really covers the modern annual report. Readers are referred to the following four sources which cover some valuable material.

1. Deloitte Touche Tohmatsu (2009) *A Telling Performance: Surveying Narrative Reporting in Annual Reports*.
   This publication takes a good look at the rapid growth of the narrative parts of the annual report.
2. Deegan, C. and Gordon, B. (1996) 'A Study of Environmental Disclosure Practices of Australian Companies', *Accounting and Business Research*, Vol. 26, No. 5, pp. 187–99.
   This article provides an interesting insight into how individual companies accentuate the good news and downplay bad news of their environmental activities.
3. The full Companies Act 2006 can be seen at http://www.legislation.gov.uk/ukpga/2006/46/contents. At this site there are also all the previous Companies Acts. Deloitte have produced a guide which specifically covers the Companies Acts. It is available at http://www.pwc.co.uk/eng/publications/practical_guide_to_companies_act_2006.html.
4. McKinstry, S. (1996) 'Designing the Annual Reports of Burton plc from 1930 to 1994', *Accounting, Organizations and Society*, Vol. 21, No. 1, pp. 89–111.
   This rather heavyweight article looks at how one company's annual reports have changed over time, concentrating particularly on the public relations aspects.

Discussion Questions

Questions with numbers in blue have answers at the back of the book.

Q1 Explain the role that the annual report plays in the corporate governance process.

Q2 Evaluate the stewardship/accountability, decision making and public relations roles of the annual report and identify any possible conflicts.

Q3 In your opinion, what are the six most important sections of the annual report. Why have you chosen these sections?

Q4 Why do companies prepare group accounts?

Q5 What do you understand by the term 'impression management'? Why do you think that managers might use the annual report for impression management?

Go online to discover the extra features for this chapter at
www.wiley.com/college/jones

Chapter 13

Creative accounting

'Every company in the country is fiddling its profits. Every set of published accounts is based on books which have been gently cooked or completely roasted. The figures which are fed twice a year to the investing public have all been changed to protect the guilty. It is the biggest con trick since the Trojan Horse.'

Ian Griffiths (1986), *Creative Accounting*, Sidgwick and Jackson, p. 1.

Learning Outcomes

After completing this chapter you should be able to:

- Explain the nature of creative accounting.
- Outline the managerial incentives for creative accounting.
- Demonstrate some common methods of creative accounting.
- Understand the real-life relevance of creative accounting.

Go online to discover the extra features for this chapter at **www.wiley.com/college/jones**

Chapter Summary

- Creative accounting involves managers using the flexibility within accounting to serve their own interests.
- The regulatory framework tries to ensure that accounts correspond to economic reality.
- Management will indulge in creative accounting, inter alia, to flatter profits, smooth profits or manage gearing.
- Revenue, inventories, depreciation, interest payable, and brands can all be managed creatively.
- In extreme cases, such as Parmalat, Polly Peck, WorldCom or Enron, creative accounting can contribute to bankruptcy.
- Several well-known publications, in particular, *Accounting for Growth, Creative Accounting, Fraud and International Accounting Standards*, have documented actual cases of creative accounting and fraud.
- Companies can also creatively manage the published version of their accounts through, for example, creative graphics.
- Regulators, such as the International Accounting Standards Board, try to curb creative accounting. This creates a creative accounting 'arms race'.

Introduction

Creative accounting became a hot topic in the late 1980s. Attention was drawn, by commentators such as Ian Griffiths (author of *Creative Accounting*), to how businesses use the flexibility inherent in accounting to manage their results. In itself, flexibility is good because it allows companies to choose accounting policies that present a 'true and fair view'. However, by the judicious choice of accounting policies and by exercising judgement, accounts can serve the interests of the preparers rather than the users. Creative accounting is not illegal but effectively, through creative compliance with the regulations, seeks to undermine a 'true and fair view' of accounting. Creative accounting can involve manipulating income, expenses, assets or liabilities through simple or exceedingly complex schemes.

SOUNDBITE 13.1

The Perennial Nature of Accounting Scandals

'Accounting scandals, creative accounting and fraud are perennial. They range from ancient Mesopotamia to the South Sea bubble in 1720 to Enron and Parmalat today. They occur in all eras and in all countries.'

Source: Michael Jones (2010), *Creative Accounting, Fraud and International Accounting Scandals*, p. 3.

The current regulatory framework can partially be seen as a response to creative accounting. It attempts to ensure that accounting represents economic reality and presents a true and fair view of the company's activities. However, new regulations bring new opportunities for creative compliance and thus creative accounting. As Real-World View 13.1 shows, even well-known companies are accused of questionable accounting.

REAL-WORLD VIEW 13.1

Microsoft and Cookie Jar Accounting

The Securities Exchange Commission (SEC), which has been cracking down on so-called 'cookie-jar' accounting, has mounted a probe of Microsoft's accounting for financial reserves . . .

The SEC customarily does not comment on its investigations. Microsoft, however, in an apparent attempt to prevent bad publicity and any negative effect on its stock price, recently revealed the existence of the probe in a conference call with analysts and reporters . . .

. . . Cookie-jar accounting is the practice of hiding assets in reserves when times are good so that they can be used as a fallback when times are bad. It is not illegal as such but the SEC is, nevertheless, adamant that there are limits beyond which a company cannot go. Specifically, the SEC has been targeting questionable accounting for restructuring charges and restructuring reserves. 'Some companies like the idea so much that they establish restructuring reserves every year', said Walter Schuetze, Chief of the SEC's enforcement division, in a recent speech.

Source: J.R. Peterson, Microsoft faced with SEC accounting probe, *The Accountant*, July 1999, p. 1. Reproduced by permission of Arvind Hickman, Group Editor, VRL Financial News. www.theaccountant-online.com.

The Microsoft example involves an interesting point. Should companies be prudent in good times so that they have reserves to fall back on in bad times? If they do so, they will be adopting different accounting policies depending on their results. In effect, they would be prudent. Many believe this is good; for example, if banks, in the recent financial crisis, had been more prudent, they would have been in a stronger position to cope with the credit crunch. However, prevailing practice in accounting does not permit such a prudent approach.

Enron, once the seventh biggest US company, which went into liquidation in 2001, is believed to have indulged in creative accounting. Other US companies such as WorldCom have been involved in accounting scandals in which creative accounting has played a contributory role. Indeed, Mulford and Comiskey in Michael Jones (2010) cite many more US companies (see Real-World View 13.2). Creative accounting also seems to have played an important role in banking failures in the recent credit crunch.

REAL-WORLD VIEW 13.2

US Accounting Scandals

The list of US firms involved in accounting scandals in recent years is frighteningly long. The names of many roll off one's tongue as readily as a list of professional athletes, musical artists or even movie stars. In contrast to athletes, musical artists and movie stars, however, these firms are famous for the wrong reasons. Consider names like Cendant Corp., Tyco International, Ltd or W.R. Grace & co. These are names of firms that readers may not have heard of had they not been involved in some form of accounting scandal.

Source: Michael Jones (2010), *Creative Accounting, Fraud and International Accounting Scandals*, p.3. Reproduced by permission of John Wiley & Sons Ltd.

Definition

Creative accounting is a slippery concept which evades easy definition. As Definition 13.1 shows, there are perhaps three key elements in creative accounting: flexibility, management of the accounts and serving the interests of managers. Sometimes, however, creative accounting is in the interests of users too; for example, where creative accounting keeps profits high and thus enables a company to maintain its share price and maintain or increase its dividend payments.

DEFINITION 13.1

Creative Accounting

Working definition
Using the flexibility within accounting to manage the measurement and presentation of the accounts so that they serve the interests of the preparers.

Formal definition
'Form of accounting which, while complying with all regulations and practices, nevertheless gives a biased impression (generally favourable) of an entity's performance and position.'

Source: Chartered Institute of Management Accountants (2005), *Official Terminology*. Reproduced by Permission of Elsevier.

(i) Flexibility

Accounting is very flexible. There are numerous choices, for example, for measuring depreciation, valuing inventory or recording revenue. This flexibility underpins the idea that the financial statements should give a 'true and fair view' of the state of affairs of the company and of the profit. Accounting policies should thus, in theory, be chosen to support a true and fair view. In many cases they are, but the flexibility within accounting does sometimes enable managers to present a more favourable impression of the company's performance than is perhaps warranted. Indeed, within accounting there is a continuum (see Figure 13.1).

Figure 13.1 Flexibility within Accounting

No flexibility →	Flexibility to give a 'true and fair' view →	Flexibility to give a creative view →	Flexibility to give a fraudulent view
↓	↓	↓	↓
Regulatory framework eliminates accounting choice	Working within regulatory framework to serve users' interests	Working within regulatory framework to serve preparers' interests	Working outside regulatory framework
← Within regulatory framework		→	← Outside regulatory framework →

This continuum starts with a completely standardised accounting system. This gives way to flexibility so as to present a true and fair view. Next we have flexibility to account creatively. Finally, there is fraud, which involves non-compliance with the regulations rather than 'bending' them. In the US, for example, WorldCom has been accused of fraudulently overstating profits by \$3.8bn (*Financial Times*, 26 June 2002, p. 1). Parmalat, Italy's eighth largest company in 2003, has been the centre of a corporate scandal. Executives were alleged by prosecutors to have used a forged Bank of America document to vouch for \$5 billion in assets and claimed the company had sold enough milk to Cuba to provide every Cuban with 55 gallons of milk for the year (Christopher Erdmann, *The Parmalat Scandal: Italy's Enron* (2004)).

SOUNDBITE 13.2

Methods of Creative Accounting and Fraud

'There are innumerable different methods of creative accounting. These arise because of the inherent flexibility within accounting. Each set of accounts consists of a myriad of different items of income, expenses, assets, liabilities and equity. For each different item there will be an accounting policy. As there are many accounting policies the opportunity arises to adapt and alter accounting policies so as to change the reported accounting figures.'

Source: Michael Jones (2010), *Creative Accounting, Fraud and International Accounting Scandals*, p. 43. Reproduced by permission of John Wiley & Sons Ltd.

(ii) Management of the Accounts

Unfortunately, in practice, the directors may choose accounting policies more to fulfil managerial objectives than to satisfy the requirements of users for a 'true and fair view'. Accounting thus becomes a variable to be managed rather than an instrument for providing true and fair information.

(iii) Interests of Managers

Accounting theory suggests that the aim of the accounts is to provide financial information to users so that they can make decisions. However, creative accounting privileges the interests of managers. Users *may*, indeed, benefit from creative accounting, but managers *will* definitely benefit.

PAUSE FOR THOUGHT 13.1

Users' and Preparers' Interests

How do you think the interests of regulators, users and preparers might conflict?

The aim of the regulators is that the financial statements should provide a 'true and fair view' of the accounts. This involves concepts of neutrality, lack of bias and faithfully representing external reality. In theory, users, such as shareholders, are likely to support this aim. Preparers, by contrast, are likely to wish to manage the accounts in their own interests. Preparers may thus indulge in reporting strategies such as profit smoothing or flattering profits, which keep share prices high. Interestingly, existing shareholders may support these strategies since they benefit from them through these higher share prices. However, other users and potential shareholders will be less happy.

Managerial Motivation

Managers have incentives to adopt creative accounting. Essentially, managers are judged, and rewarded, on the performance of their companies. It is, therefore, in managers' interests that their companies meet expectations. For example, if managers have profit-related bonuses, it makes sense for them to maximise their profits so they get bigger bonuses. Other managerial incentives might be the ownership of shares and share options, the need to smooth profits or to manage gearing. Mulford and Comiskey (2002, p. 6) cite the case of Green Tree Financial Corp whose annual share bonus was $28.5 million in 1994, $65.1 million in 1995 and $102.0 million in 1996. Such bonuses are exceedingly generous.

Shares and Share Options

Managers may own shares. They also may have share options which allow them to buy shares today at a set price and then sell them for a higher price at a future date. If the stock market expects a certain amount of profit from a company, then managers may wish to adopt creative accounting to deliver that profit. Otherwise, the share price will fall and the managers will lose out.

Profit Smoothing

The stock market prefers a steady progression in earnings to an erratic earnings pattern. Companies with erratic earnings typically have lower share prices than those with steadier performances. Their lower share price makes these companies more vulnerable to takeover than companies with smoother profit trends. Managers of companies that are taken over may lose their jobs. Therefore, managers have incentives to smooth profits. Current shareholders are also likely to benefit from profit smoothing as the share price remains high.

PAUSE FOR THOUGHT 13.2

Profit Smoothing

Two firms (A and B) in the same industry have the following profit trends. Which do you think might be favoured by the stock market?

Years	1	2	3	4
	£m	£m	£m	£m
A	1	2	4	8
B	4	(1)	15	(3)

At first glance, A looks the better bet. Its profits steadily rise, doubling each year.

However, company B, whose profits are irregular, actually makes the same cumulative profits as A (i.e., £15m). Overall, the stock market will probably favour A with its steady growth. Indeed, in year 4, company A might even be able to make a successful bid for B! Company A's share price at that date will probably be much higher than company B's.

Manage Gearing

As well as managing profits, companies have incentives to manage gearing or conceal debt. Companies may wish to borrow money. However, existing borrowers may put restrictions on the amount of any new debt that can be raised. Managers may attempt to circumvent these restrictions using creative accounting. Enron, for instance, attempted to conceal the amount of its liabilities.

The managerial incentives vary from firm to firm. For example, in some regulated industries (such as gas or water), managers may actually wish to reduce revenue and profits so as to stop the government putting price restrictions on them. In many cases, managers will wish to increase profits or assets. This can be done by increasing income or decreasing expenses in the case of profits and increasing assets or decreasing liabilities in the case of net assets. In other cases, managers will wish to smooth profits so as to provide a steady upward trend of profits so as to satisfy the needs of the stock market. The key point about managerial incentives is that they encourage managers to serve their own or the company's interests rather than present a true and fair view of the company's performance.

Methods of Creative Accounting

There are innumerable methods of creative accounting. These arise mainly from the flexibility of accounting and the existence of so many acceptable accounting policies. If you change your accounting policies, you will change your results. Indeed, as Robert Townsend suggests in Soundbite 13.3, one easy way of creative accounting is continually to change your accounting policies. In the US, WorldCom, which collapsed in 2002, was accused of repeatedly restating its accounts. However, the consistency concept does to some extent limit companies' abilities to do this.

SOUNDBITE 13.3

Restating your Figures

'The easiest way to do a snow job on investors (or on yourself) is to change one factor in the accounting each month. Then you can say, "It's not comparable with last month or last year. And we can't really draw any conclusion from the figures".'

Robert Townsend (1970) *Up the Organization*, Knopf

Source: The Wiley Book of Business Quotations (1998), p. 89.

Many creative accounting procedures are complex and often undetectable to the analyst. In this section, we will look at five of the more straightforward techniques. The aim is to give some illustrative examples rather than to present a comprehensive list. The worst excesses of creative accounting have been curbed by accounting standards and regulations that have been developed to try to ensure that the accounts correspond to economic reality. In many cases, some of the techniques listed will be used by management taking advantage of accounting's flexibility to give a true and fair view of the company's activities. In other cases, these techniques will be used creatively. To the onlooker it is generally difficult to distinguish these two contrasting uses. Motivation is the key distinguishing feature. Where managers attempt to serve their own interests rather than present a true and fair view, creative accounting is occurring.

Those readers who wish a more in-depth look at the subject are referred to Ian Griffiths' *New Creative Accounting*, Terry Smith's *Accounting for Growth*, and more recently my book, *Creative Accounting, Fraud and International Accounting Standards* (Michael Jones).

(i) Inflating Income

The problem is that revenue recognition is not as precise as cash flow (see Real-World View 13.3). When should we recognise a sale as a sale? This may, at first, seem a silly question. However, the date of sale is not always obvious. For example, is it when (i) we dispatch goods to a customer, (ii) we invoice the customer, or (iii) we receive the money? Normally, it is when we invoice the customer. However, in complex businesses there is often a fair degree of latitude about revenue recognition. If you take a big construction project (like Multiplex's building of Wembley Stadium), for example, when should you recognise revenue and take profits? There are rules to help in profit determination, but these rules still permit a good deal of flexibility. Another troublesome area associated with revenue recognition is warranty provision (i.e., setting aside money to deal with customer returns). You can deal with this, in advance, and estimate a provision or deal with it on an actual return-by-return basis. Moreover, warranties can be treated as a reduction in revenue or as an expense. The differing treatments can result in differing profits.

REAL-WORLD VIEW 13.3

Income Recognition

Accounting standards generally call for revenue to be recognized when it is earned and realizable. Earned revenue entails completion of the earnings process, including a valid order and delivery of the goods or services in question. Realizability requires that the selling company have a valid claim from a creditworthy customer.

The difference between premature revenue and fictitious revenue is one of degree. Premature revenue typically results from revenue recognition pursuant to a valid order but prior to delivery. Ficitious revenue results from the recognition of non-existent revenue. A valid customer order does not exist. Whether revenue is recognized as premature or fictitious, it is done outside the boundary of GAAP.

Source: C.W. Mulford and E.E. Comiskey (2010), p. 410, Creative Accounting and Scandals in the US in Michael Jones, *Creative Accounting, Fraud and International Accounting Scandals*. Reproduced by permission of John Wiley & Sons Ltd.

(ii) Inventories

Inventories provide a rich area for the creative accountant. The key feature about inventories is that if you increase your inventories you increase your profit (see Figure 13.2). The beauty of inventories is also that, in many businesses, inventories are valued once a year at an annual stock-take. When carrying out these stock-takes, it is relatively easy to take an optimistic or a pessimistic view of the value of inventories.

PAUSE FOR THOUGHT 13.3

Revenue Recognition

I was once involved in auditing a company selling agricultural machinery like combine harvesters. The company's year end was 30 June. Farmers wanted the machinery invoiced in March, but would pay in August when the machinery was delivered. Why do you think the farmers wished to do this and what revenue recognition policy was best for the company?

....

Essentially, this arrangement benefited both the company and the farmers. The company would take its revenue in March, arguing this was the invoice date. The revenue thus appeared before the June year end. The farmer would treat the purchase in March so that they could set off the machinery against taxation. As the tax year runs from April 6 to April 5, the farmers would hope to receive the capital allowances in one tax year, and pay for the machinery in the next tax year. Everybody was happy, but the company needed to wait for its money.

Figure 13.2 Inventories (Stock) as an Example of Creative Accounting

If there is only one asset, inventories, worth say £10 million, then if equity is £5 million and this year's profit is £5 million, then we have statement of financial position A:

Statement of Financial Position A

	£m		£m
Equity	5	Inventories	10
Profit	5		
	10		10

The company could:

(1) adopt a more generous inventories valuation policy, perhaps by lowering the provisions for obsolete inventories (increases inventories by £0.5 million), (2) do a particularly rigorous stock-take (increases inventories by £1.0 million previously unrecorded inventories). The statement of financial position now looks like statement of financial position B.

Statement of Financial Position B

	£m		£m
Equity	5.0	Inventories	11.5
Profit	6.5		
	11.5		11.5

Hey presto! We have increased our profits by £1.5 million.

(iii) Depreciation

Depreciation is the allocation of the cost of property, plant and equipment over time. It is an expense recorded in the income statement. If the amount of depreciation changes then so will profit. The depreciation process is subject to many estimations, such as the life of the asset, which may alter the depreciation charge. A simple example is given in Figure 13.3 below. In essence, lengthening expected lives boosts profits while reducing them reduces profits. If management lengthens the assets' lives because it judges that the assets will last longer, this is fair enough. If the motivation, however, is to boost profits then this is creative accounting.

Figure 13.3 Depreciation

A business makes a profit of £10,000. It has £100,000 worth of property, plant and equipment. Currently it depreciates them straight line over 10 years. However, the company is thinking of changing its depreciation policy to 20 years straight line. Will this affect profit?

	Original policy	New policy
	£	£
Profit before depreciation	10,000	10,000
Depreciation	(10,000)	(5,000)
Profit after depreciation	–	5,000

The answer is yes. By changing the depreciation policy, profit has increased by £5,000. In fact, the company looks much healthier.

The pace of technological change creates shorter asset lives. It would be assumed, therefore, that most companies would reduce their expected asset lives. However, as UBS Phillips and Drew point out below, in Real-World View 13.4, this is not necessarily so.

REAL-WORLD VIEW 13.4

Change of Depreciation Lives

Perhaps the simplest way of changing the depreciation level is by changing the life of the assets. In essence, lengthening an asset's life will reduce the level of depreciation. If management believes that the asset will last longer, then lengthening the asset life is perfectly legitimate. However, if it is done because management wants to reduce profit, then that is creative accounting.

Source: Michael Jones (2010), *Creative Accounting, Fraud and International Accounting Scandals*, p. 54. Reproduced by permission of John Wiley & Sons Ltd.

Finally, Smith (1992) draws attention to British Airports Authority's (BAA) decision to lengthen its terminal and runway lives. Runway lives lengthened from 23.5 years in 1990 to 100 years in 1998. Annual depreciation was thus reduced.

(iv) Brands

Brand valuation is a contentious issue within accounting. Some companies argue that it is appropriate to value brands so as better to reflect economic reality. By contrast, other observers believe that valuing brands is too subjective and judgemental and that the real motive behind brand valuation is for companies to boost asset values on the statement of financial position. Brand accounting is a relatively new phenomenon in the UK. The idea is that, in many cases, brands are worth incredible amounts of money (think, for example, of Guinness or Kit Kat). Indeed, it is estimated that Coca-Cola's brand name adds £2bn additional value to the company per year (Fiona Gilmore, *Accountancy Age*, May 2001).

Traditionally, brands have not formally been recognised as assets. They are, however, as Soundbite 13.4 shows, very valuable. From the mid-1980s, UK companies such as Grand Metropolitan and Cadbury started to include brands in their statements of financial position. These brands are assets and help to boost the assets in the statement of financial position. They are *not* amortised (i.e., written off).

SOUNDBITE 13.4

Brands

'A strong brand is part of what Warren Buffett has described as an "economic moat" around the company castle, helping to protect profits and margins.'

Source: A. Hall, Global Brand Winners, *Investors Chronicle*, 21–27 October, 2011, p. 54.

Traditional accountants are still suspicious of brands. This is because they are difficult to measure and, in essence, they are subjective. The situation in the UK is, therefore, something of an uneasy compromise. Acquired brands can be capitalised (i.e., included in the statements of financial position). However, companies are not permitted to capitalise internally generated brands. Overall, some companies capitalise their brands and some do not. There is also a great variety of ways in which brands are valued. In other words, there is great potential for creativity.

SOUNDBITE 13.5

Grasping Reality

'Some have suggested that Rolls-Royce accounts are fine because they meet with UK GAAP accounting rules, but let's remember that Enron complied with US rules. The question is whether you get a grasp of reality from the accounts, and I don't know that you do.'

Source: The Guardian, 12 February 2002, p. 23, Terry Macalister quoting Terry Smith of Collins Stewart brokers.

(v) Capitalisation of Costs such as Interest Payable

The capitalisation of costs involves the simple idea that a debit balance in the accounts can either be an expense or an asset. Expenses are deducted from revenue and reduce profit. Assets are capitalised. Property, plant and equipment are particularly important in this context. Only the depreciation charged on property, plant and equipment is treated as an expense and reduces profit. Therefore, it will often benefit companies to treat certain expenses as property, plant and equipment.

An example of this was until very recently interest costs. Where companies borrow money to construct property, plant and equipment, they can argue, and often do, that interest on borrowing should be capitalised. However, some commentators, such as Phillips and Drew ((1991) *Accounting for Growth*, p. 10), found this a dubious practice. Virtually every UK listed property company, with the notable exception of Land Securities, made use of capitalised interest in the 1990s (and often other costs as well) to defer the impact of developments on profits. While commercial property prices were rising rapidly, investors and banks did not worry about the amount of interest being capitalised. Indeed, Phillips and Drew pointed out that some UK companies would actually make a loss, not a profit, if they did not capitalise their interest. In the US, in 2001 WorldCom improperly capitalised huge amounts of expenses (this is shown in Real-World View 13.5).

REAL-WORLD VIEW 13.5

Capitalisation of Costs

The most high-profile case of companies improperly capitalising their expenses was in the USA. WorldCom is a US telecommunications firm. In 2001, it capitalised enormous amounts of costs. Analysts suspect these included wages and salaries of workers who maintained the telecom systems. As Matt Krantz (2002) [USA Today, 27th June], saw it, 'Worldcom used the gimmick to a level never before seen. The company showed a $1.4 billion profit in 2001, rather than a loss, by using what's essentially the oldest trick in the book. Put simply what WordCom did was treat revenue expenses such as painting a door as capital expenses such as replacing the door.'

Source: Michael Jones (2010), *Creative Accounting, Fraud and International Accounting Scandals*, p. 51. Reproduced by permission of John Wiley & Sons Ltd.

The capitalisation of interest is, however, now much more restricted as under IFRS, there is now provision that where the asset is not yet in the location and condition suitable for its intended use, borrowing costs can be capitalised as long as they are directly attributable. However, there is still obvious room for manoeuvre in defining terms such as directly attributable, asset and location and condition. In addition, there is still scope to capitalise some development costs such as in computer software.

Figure 13.4 Example of Creative Accounting

Creato plc
Income Statement for Year Ended 31 December 2013

	Notes	£000	£000
Revenue	1		100
Less *Cost of Sales*			
Opening inventories		10	
Add Purchases		40	
		50	
Less Closing inventories	2	15	35
Gross Profit			65
Less *Expenses*			
Depreciation	3	12	
Interest payable	4	15	
Other expenses		43	70
Loss for year			(5)

Notes
1. Creato has a prudent income recognition policy; a less conservative one would create an additional £10,000 sales.
2. Closing inventories could be valued, less prudently, at £18,000.
3. Depreciation is charged over five years; a few competitors charge depreciation over ten years even though this is longer than the realistic expected life.
4. Interest payable is interest on borrowings used to finance the company's activities. Part of this is a new factory. The company has estimated that between one third and two thirds could be directly attributed to the factory.

If we indulge in a spot of creative accounting, we can transform Creato plc's income statement.

Creato plc
Income Statement for Year Ended 31 December 2013

		£000	£000
Revenue	1		110
Less *Cost of Sales*			
Opening inventories		10	
Add Purchases		40	
		50	
Less Closing inventories	2	18	32
			78
Gross Profit			
Less *Expenses*			
Depreciation	3	6	
Interest payable	4	5	
Depreciation on capitalised interest payable	4	1	
Other expenses		43	55
Profit for year			23

Notes
1. We can simply boost revenue by £10,000 and be less conservative.
2. If we value closing inventories at £18,000, this will reduce cost of sales, thus boosting gross profit.
3. By doubling the life of our property, plant and equipment, we can halve the depreciation charge.
4. If we have borrowed the money to finance property, plant and equipment, then we can capitalise some of the interest payable. Interest payable thus reduces from £15,000 to £5,000 as we have taken a generous estimate of the amount directly attributable to the factory. We assume here that we will then depreciate this capitalised interest over ten years (this company's new policy for property, plant and equipment). Thus, we are charging £1,000 depreciation on the capitalised interest payable. We thus boost profit by £9,000 (i.e., £10,000 saved less £1,000 extra depreciation).

Hey presto! We have transformed a loss of £5,000 into a profit of £23,000.

Example

In order to demonstrate that creative accounting can make a difference, an example, Creato plc, is presented in Figure 13.4 (see page 400). Adjustments are made for revenue, inventories, depreciation and the capitalisation of interest.

Real Life

It should be stressed that creative accounting is very much a real-life phenomenon. Extensive research has demonstrated its existence. Of particular interest are two empirical studies: *Accounting for Growth* and *Company Pathology*. Although dating from the 1990s, these studies, which have not been repeated more recently, demonstrate quite clearly the existence of creative accounting. *Accounting for Growth* was published twice: first, by fund managers UBS Phillips and Drew in 1991 as a report and second by Terry Smith in 1992 as a book. It caused considerable controversy – in fact, it resulted in Terry Smith, one of the analysts responsible for the research, leaving UBS Phillips and Drew. Essentially, as Real-World View 13.5 shows, UBS Phillips and Drew wished to draw attention to the recent growth in creative accounting.

PAUSE FOR THOUGHT 13.4

Accounting for Growth

In their report, UBS Phillips and Drew identified the innovative accounting practices used by 165 UK companies. Why do you think this caused such a storm?

Before *Accounting for Growth* was published, there was much speculation about creative accounting. However, there was little systematic evidence. The Phillips and Drew report identified 165 leading companies (out of 185 they investigated) which had used at least one innovative accounting practice. It named names! The speculation turned into reality. The companies named were unhappy. As some of them were clients of UBS Phillips and Drew, some of the companies felt let down. The result of the storm was that Terry Smith left UBS Phillips and Drew and published his book, *Accounting for Growth*, on his own.

UBS Phillips and Drew analysed 185 UK listed companies. They identified 11 innovative (i.e., creative) accounting practices and drew up an accounting health check. They found that 165 companies used at least one innovative accounting practice, 17 used five or more and three used seven (see Real-World View 13.6). Interestingly, two of the high-scoring companies subsequently went bankrupt: Maxwell Communications and Tiphook.

REAL-WORLD VIEW 13.6

High Scores in Health Check

Companies using the most accounting techniques in Phillips and Drew's 'Health Check'

Company	**Sector**	**Frequency**
British-Aerospace	Engineering	7
Maxwell	Media	7
Burton Group	Stores	7
Dixons	Stores	6
Cable and Wireless	Telephone networks	6
Blue Circle	Building materials	5
TI Group	Engineering	5
Bookers	Food manufacturing	5
Asda	Food retailer	5
Granada	Leisure	5
Next	Stores	5
Sears	Stores	5
LEP	Business services	5
Laporte	Chemicals	5
British Airways	Transport	5
Tiphook	Transport	5
Ultramar	Oils	5

This article was published in *Management Accounting* by author: M.J. Jones, Accounting for Growth: Surviving the Accounting Jungle, February 1992, page 22, ISSN- 0025-1682. Copyright Chartered Institute of Management Accountants (CIMA), 1992. Reproduced by Permission.

In *Company Pathology* (1991), County NatWest WoodMac studied 45 'deceased' companies from 1989–90. They drew attention to questionable accounting practices, such as the capitalisation of interest. In only three out of the 45 cases did the audit report warn of the impending disaster. In only two out of the 45 cases did the pre-collapse turnover fall. Finally, in only six out of 45 cases did the last reported accounts show a loss. County NatWest WoodMac were quite scathing in their overall assessment. 'A downturn in earnings per share is a lagging rather than a leading indicator of trouble. Accounting Standards give companies far too much scope for creative accounting. One set of accounts were described by an experienced and well-qualified fund manager as "a complete joke". Auditors' reports seldom give warning of impending disaster' (p. 4).

In Germany, a real study of the findings of the German Financial Reporting Enforcement Panel (FREP) from 2005–6 had similar findings as Real-World View 13.7 shows. However,

REAL-WORLD VIEW 13.7

Auditors and Misstatements

It should be mentioned that in only three out of 25 cases had the auditors qualified their reports with respect to the misstatement mentioned by the FREP. In all other cases, the auditor either did not detect or did not report the misstatement in the audit opinion.

Source: Hansrudi Lenz (2010), p. 203, Accounting Scandals in Germany, in Michael Jones, *Creative Accounting, Fraud and International Accounting Scandals*. Reproduced by permission of John Wiley & Sons Ltd.

in the UK, given the active attention paid by the Accounting Standards setters to curbing creative accounting since the 1990s, many of the worst abuses have now been curtailed.

A recent book has looked at this area in great depth (Michael Jones: *Creative Accounting, Fraud and International Accounting Scandals*). This book looks at accounting scandals that occurred across 13 countries ranging from developed countries such as UK and US to developing countries such as China and India. Fifty-four individual cases were covered ranging from well-known, high-profile accounting scandals such as Enron, WorldCom and Polly Peck to other scandals that are less known globally, but scandals that were important in individual countries such as Bank of Crete in Greece, Comroad in Germany or Fermenta in Sweden. Individual countries were written by individual country experts. The book also showed how accounting scandals were perennial in nature with the earliest known scandal dating back to the second millennium BC in Mesopotamia.

The book isolated some motives for the scandals such as covering up bad performance and also for personal benefit. In addition, in many scandals there were charismatic persuaders such as Robert Maxwell in the UK or Bernard Ebbers at WorldCom. In the book, several popular methods of creative accounting and/or fraud were noted which were frequently used by companies such as recognising revenue early (premature revenue recognition), capitalising expenses, inflating inventory and off-balance sheet financing. In most cases, there were severe failings in either, or often both, internal control or external audit.

The book concluded by setting out a theoretical model to reduce creative accounting and fraud (see Figure 13.5). This showed that the potential for creative accounting and fraud was enhanced by strong motives (such as personal incentives or market-based incentives) and environmental opportunities (such as lax rules and regulations, poor supervision and inappropriate reward structures). It could potentially be reduced by environmental constraints and by better enforcement and higher ethical standards. Many companies already have a code of ethics and some examination bodies, such as the ACCA, have incorporated ethics modules into their examination syllabuses.

Figure 13.5 Theoretical model to reduce creative accounting and fraud

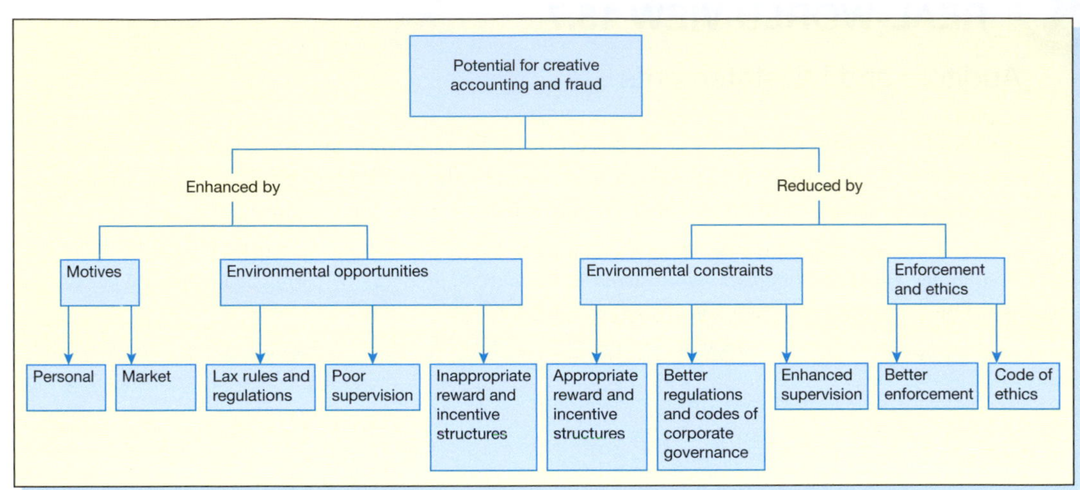

Source: Michael Jones (2010), *Creative Accounting, Fraud and International Accounting Scandals*, p. 500. Reproduced by permission of John Wiley & Sons Ltd.

Case Studies

(i) Polly Peck

An interesting example of a spectacular company collapse where creative accounting was present is Polly Peck. Polly Peck's demise is well-documented not only in Terry Smith's *Accounting for Growth*, but also in Trevor Pijper's *Creative Accounting: The Effect of Financial Reporting in the UK*.

Essentially, Polly Peck was one of the fastest expanding UK firms in the 1980s. It was headed by a charismatic chairman, Asil Nadir. It started off in food and electronics, and expanded rapidly. County NatWest Wood Mackenzie calculated that in the year to November 1989, Polly Peck's shares had grown faster than any other UK company. The 1989 results were full of optimism. For example, profit before tax had increased from £112 million to £161 million.

Indeed, the optimism continued in the 1990 interim results. Eleven days after their publication, and six days before the collapse, Kitcat and Aitken (city analysts) reported that profits would increase substantially.

The collapse of Polly Peck cannot be attributed solely to creative accounting. There was fraud and deception and, in addition, there was the blind faith of bankers and shareholders. The signs were there for those who wished to look. For example, debt rose from £65.9 million in 1985 to £1,106 million in 1989. However, creative accounting did play its part in two key areas. First, Polly Peck capitalised the acquired brands, such as Del Monte, and thus strengthened its statement of financial position. Second, and more seriously, the company indulged in currency mismatching. This is explained in Figure 13.6. This flattered Polly Peck's income statement at the expense of seriously damaging its statement of financial position. Asil Nadir, Chairman of Polly Peck, escaped to North Cyprus but in 2010 returned to the UK to face trial. He was convicted of theft in August 2012.

Figure 13.6 Polly Peck's Currency Mismatching

Polly Peck borrowed in Swiss francs, a strong currency, and paid back a low rate of interest. These borrowings were invested in Turkey, which had a weaker currency. Polly Peck was paid a high rate of interest. Unfortunately, however, the Turkish dinar depreciated against the Swiss franc. This meant that Polly Peck made capital losses of £44.7 million in 1989 on its borrowings. Meanwhile, its income statement had been flattered by £12.5 million (£68.1 million received less £55.6 million paid) because of the high rate of interest on the dinar deposits as compared with the low interest on the matched Swiss franc borrowings.

(ii) Enron

The spectacular collapse of Enron in December 2001 has brought creative accounting once more centre stage. Enron, at one time, was the seventh biggest US company. However, from August 2000 its share price began to fall as a result of doubts about the strength of its statement of financial position and significant sales of shares by managers. Enron's main business was to supply and make markets in oil and gas throughout the world. Enron first made profits on investments in technology and energy businesses followed by losses. Following these losses, Enron built up huge debts which have been estimated at $80 billion. From the accounts it was not obvious that these liabilities existed. They were buried in rather complex legal jargon (see Company Snapshot 13.1).

COMPANY SNAPSHOT 13.1

Extract from Enron's Notes to the Accounts

Enron is a guarantor on certain liabilities of unconsolidated equity affiliates and other companies totalling approximately $1,863 million at December 31, 2001, including $538 million related to EOTT trade obligations [EOTT Energy Partners]. The EOTT letters of credit and guarantees of trade obligation are secured by the assets of EOTT. Enron has also guaranteed $386 million in lease obligations for which it has been indemnified by an 'Investment Grade' company. Management does not consider it likely that Enron would be required to perform or otherwise incur any losses associated with the above guarantees. In addition, certain commitments have been made related to capital expenditures and equity investments planned in 2001.

Source: Enron, *Annual Report 2000*, Notes to the Accounts, p. 48.

In order to manipulate income, to avoid reporting losses and keep its debts off the group's statement of financial position, Enron set up special purpose entities (SPEs). Under US regulations, if the SPEs were not controlled by Enron and if outside equity capital controlled at least 3% of total assets then Enron would not have to bring the SPEs into its group accounts. It would thus not disclose its debts. Investors would not therefore realise the net indebtedness of the company. Many SPEs appear not to have been incorporated into the group accounts quite legally. However, in other cases it is alleged that control was held by Enron, not by third parties, and that Enron had provided third parties with funds so that the 3% was not truly held independently. If this is the case, there was prima facie false accounting and questions began to be raised about the role of Arthur Andersen, the company's auditors. The role of the auditors as independent safeguards of the investors appeared to have broken down. Arthur Andersen subsequently collapsed. Finally, it was reported in the press that Enron was receiving up-front payments for the future sales of natural gas or crude oil and effectively treating loans as revenue.

Overall, therefore, Enron demonstrates that even well-known companies still indulge in creative accounting. In Enron's case, however, like that of Polly Peck, the borderline between creative accounting and fraud became blurred.

Enron is the most famous case of creative accounting and has even given rise to a theatre production. In this, as Soundbite 13.6 shows, Andy Fastow, the chief financial officer, is shown as a key player.

SOUNDBITE 13.6

Enron

'This is the man who, when the accounts inexplicably showed the company going down the drain, began a long-term policy of losing debt through the most innovative and creative accounting techniques known to man. On stage, the companies are literally seen as Jurassic Park monsters hungrily eating up all of that nasty debt.'

Source: Philip Fisher, Trading Thin Air, *Accountancy Magazine,* 2009, p. 24.

(iii) Bank of Crete

The Bank of Crete was covered by George Kontos, Maria Krambia-Kapardis and Nikolas Milonas (as a chapter in Jones, *Creative Accounting, Fraud and International Accounting Standards*). It is an excellent example of how one man was able to take advantage of a weak internal control system. Koskotas, a Greek, was a fraudster. From the age of 15 to 25 he worked in the US and committed 64 mainly forgery offences as well as forging academic qualifications. Koskotas then returned to Greece. In 1979, he began work for the Bank of Crete. He impressed his bosses and became head of the bank's internal audit department in 1980. He then began to embezzle money from the bank. He stole US$1,155,000 and deposited them with the Westminster bank. His theft was not discovered and he then began systematically to misappropriate a total amount of what appears to have been about US$32 million. He managed to do this by exploiting weak internal controls; for example, reconciliations of inter-branch accounts. When he was suspected, he gathered together a group of employees and systematically forged letters and documents to cover his tracks. Eventually Koskotas was detected and found guilty. He served a 12-year jail sentence.

(iv) Banks

The role of creative accounting in the recent bank failures worldwide has caught the attention of many commentators. This is demonstrated by Simon Norton in Real-World View 13.8.

REAL-WORLD VIEW 13.8

Two Parts

Recent events have shown how complex financial instruments and funding arrangements can be used to manipulate the apparent strength of balance sheets when ratings agencies, investors and even management itself fail adequately to evaluate risk or 'stress test' trading or portfolio investment strategies. Leverage or borrowing against a healthy balance sheet is a sustainable and often wise business practice, but when this becomes over-leveraging or raising capital against overvalued or potentially highly volatile assets, the foundation stones of a funding crisis are put in place. Regulators who permit banks to weigh the risks accruing to their balance sheets through the use of their own internal risk measurement or value at risk models should not be surprised when it eventually transpires that the true levels of exposure to particular markets are either underplayed or underreported.

****

Nonetheless, the role of market psychology should not be overlooked in the context of creative accounting; the reality is that in booming markets investors and ratings agencies have a tendency to dilute their level of scrutiny of new business strategies. And when a firm is maintaining healthy returns even during a market downturn, those taking the shilling of its success are often too willing to overlook the thicket of 'red flags' which would suggest to the objective bystander that groundless exuberance or even worse, criminality, may be lurking in the undergrowth.

Source: Simon Norton (2010), pp. 450–1, Bank Failures and Accounting during the Financial Crisis of 2008–2009 in Michael Jones, *Creative Accounting, Fraud and International Accounting Scandals.* Reproduced by permission of John Wiley & Sons Ltd.

Banks, in particular, used many complex financial instruments such as derivatives and Collaterised Mortgage Obligations (CMOs) where groups of mortgages are bundled together and sold on to third parties. There were also collateralised debt obligations (CDOs) which allowed banks to shift debt off the statement of financial position and credit default swaps (CDSs). It is not necessary to go into the details here; indeed, some of the creative instruments were so complex that the Board of Directors often did not understand them. However, the end result was that the accounts often became very difficult to understand. In many cases, substantial liabilities were kept off the statement of financial position. It is not clear how much the use of these complex financial instruments or creative accounting contributed to the difficulties in which the banks found themselves or to specific instances of banking and financial institution scandals such as Lehman Brothers, Madoff Securities International or Bear Stearns. However, it does seem to have played a part. For instance, Lehman Brothers appears to have used the flexibility permitted by US Generally Accepted Accounting Principles to avoid writing down the value of its assets. As Real-World View 13.9 shows, Lehman's creativity exploited the weaknesses in US accounting standards. Meanwhile, Bear Stearns appears to have entirely lawfully used creative accounting to convert high-risk assets into lower-risk repackaged products.

REAL-WORLD VIEW 13.9

Lehman Brothers

At the height of the credit crisis Lehman Brothers was able temporarily to take $50bn (£32.7bn) from its balance sheet at key quarterly reporting dates to improve its financial leverage ratio with the aim of misleading investors.

It did this through Repo 105 and Repo 108 transactions, which were short-term repurchase agreements under which Lehman sold securities to a counterparty for cash, with a simultaneous agreement to repurchase the same or equivalent securities at a specific price at a later date. The cash received was used to temporarily pay down its liabilities and boost its leverage ratio.

Lehman exploited weaknesses in US Statement of Financial Accounting Standards No 140 (SFAS 140), Accounting for Transfers and Servicing of Financial Assets and Extinguishments of Liabilities. This allowed it to book Repo 105 and Repo 108 transactions as sales rather than as financing transactions, which would have kept assets on the balance sheet.

Source: Ian Sanderson, What Repo 105 Really Means, *Accountancy Magazine,* April 2010, p. 28. Copyright Wolters Kluwer (UK) Ltd.

Creative Presentation

As well as creative accounting, companies can present their accounts in a flattering way. One of the ways they can do this is by using graphs. There are three main ways graphs can be used: selectivity, measurement distortion and presentational enhancement. For example, they may use graphs only in years when the company has made a profit (the graph will show a rising trend). In selectivity, it has been shown by countless research studies (see Beattie and Jones, 2008) that companies select those graphs that will give a favourable rather than an unfavourable view of their financial performance. Measurement distortion is where graphs may be deliberately drawn so as to exaggerate a rising trend. In essence, the increase in the columns in a graph is drawn so that they are greater than the increase in the data. This may, for example, be done by using a non-zero axis. An example of creative graphical presentation is shown in Real-World View 13.10. In particular, it should be noted that the earnings per share graph is inconsistent with the other three. It is for three years, not four, and has a non-zero axis. The overall result is that it perhaps presents a more favourable view of the company's results than would otherwise be warranted. Finally, graphs may be subject to presentational enhancement; for example, attention may be drawn so as to place undue emphasis on certain features of the graph such as the last two columns in Real-World View 13.10 which have darker shading, (particularly 1989).

REAL-WORLD VIEW 13.10

Creative Graphs: T.I.P. Europe plc, 1989 Annual Report

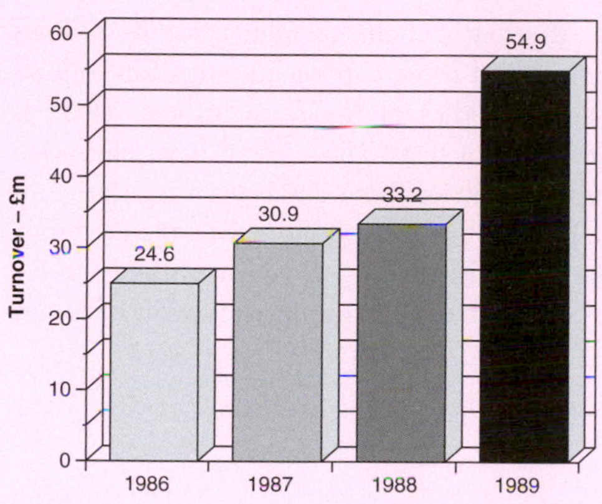

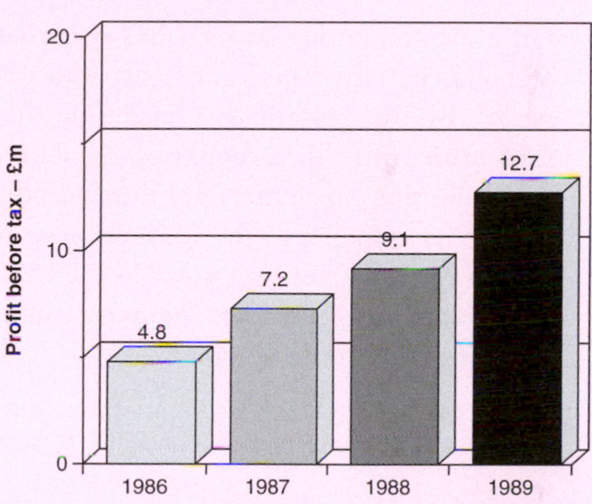

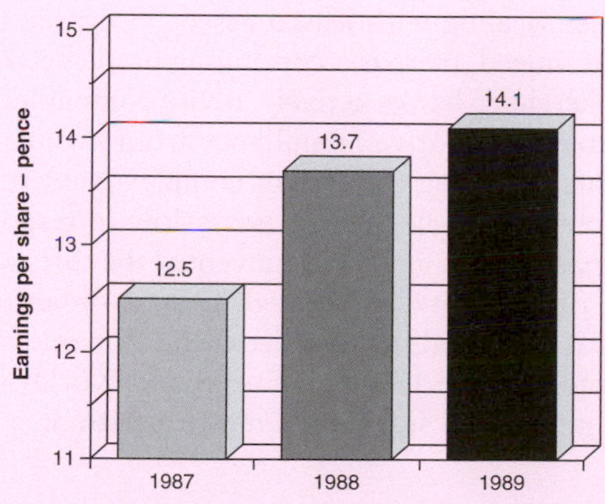

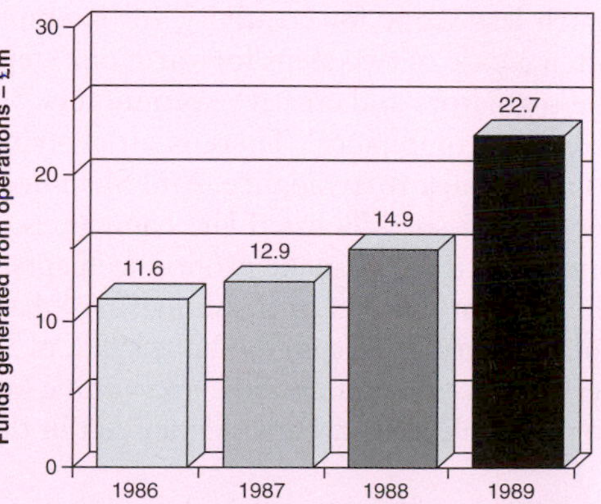

Extract(s) from ACCA Research Report No. 31, *'The Communication of Information Using Graphs in Corporate Annual Reports'* by Vivien Beattie and Michael Jones. This research was funded and published by the Certified Accountants Educational Trust (CAET). Extracts were reproduced with ACCA's kind permission.

Controlling Creative Accounting

One of the key objectives of the UK's Accounting Standards Board, which was set up in the 1990's, was to control creative accounting. The International Accounting Standards Board also shares this concern. As Real-World View 13.11 shows, creative accounting leads to regulation.

REAL-WORLD VIEW 13.11

Regulatory Response to Creative Accounting

Once an accounting scandal has occurred, the aftermath of the scandal typically follows a similar pattern. There is extensive media interest, and some sort of investigation follows (either by the government, accounting professional bodies or the fraud office). There is then criticism of the accounting regulations and often a trial. Then, often new legislation or accounting regulations are introduced. In most countries there has been a legislative or regulatory response to the accounting scandals. Perhaps the most famous was the introduction of the Sarbanes-Oxley Act in the USA. This has subsequently also formed the basis for changes in Japan. Perhaps the most common response has been the introduction of a new code of corporate governance.

Source: Michael Jones (2010), *Creative Accounting, Fraud and International Accounting Scandals*, p. 484. Reproduced by permission of John Wiley & Sons Ltd.

Since 1990, there has been a concerted attempt by regulators to curb creative accounting. Undoubtedly, they have made substantial progress in many areas. Companies now have much less scope for creativity, for example, when dealing with leased assets. However, it is often a case of two steps forward, one step back. Indeed, there is a continuing battle between the regulators and creative accountants. Some merchant banks actively advise companies on 'creative compliance'. There is an evolving pattern of creative compliance from avoidance, to rules, back to avoidance. Atul Shah documents this using the case of complex convertible securities issued by listed UK companies. He concludes: '[r]egulators were slow to respond, and when they did make pronouncements, companies once again circumvented the rules with the help of various professionals. A "dialectic of creativity" is created, from avoidance to rules to avoidance again' (Shah, 1998, p. 36). This continual struggle between companies and regulators causes a creative accounting 'arms race'. In the US, after Enron and WorldCom, for example, the Sarbanes-Oxley Act in the US introduced substantial new legislation.

Conclusion

Creative accounting emerged into the limelight in the 1980s. However, it is still alive and kicking today. As the collapse of Enron in 2001 clearly demonstrated, managers have incentives to manage their accounting profits so that they serve managerial, rather than shareholder, interests. This is possible because of the flexibility within accounting. There are numerous methods of creative accounting: some are extremely complex and others very simple. When used excessively, creative accounting can be positively dangerous; for example, it has contributed to corporate collapses. The regulators attempt, through accounting standards, to curb creative accounting. However, there is an ongoing battle as companies seek ways around the regulations.

Selected Reading

1. *Accounting for Growth*
   This report was a real accounting bombshell. It documents the use by 165 UK companies of 11 innovative accounting practices. The original report (see (a) below) was issued by UBS Phillips and Drew. Then Terry Smith published (b) below after he left UBS Phillips and Drew. Those who can't get hold of the original report/book, or who want a quick summary, could try Jones (c).
   (a) UBS Phillips and Drew (1991) *Accounting for Growth*.
   (b) Smith, T. (1992) *Accounting for Growth* (Century Business).
   (c) Jones, M.J. (1992) 'Accounting for Growth: Surviving the accounting jungle', *Management Accounting*, February, pp. 20–22.
2. County NatWest WoodMac (1991) *Company Pathology*.
   This report provides an interesting study into creative accounting by 45 companies.
3. Griffiths, I. (1986) *Creative Accounting* (Sidgwick and Jackson) and (1995) *New Creative Accounting* (Macmillan).
   Both very good reads which provide a journalist's view of the debate.
4. Pijper, T. (1993) *Creative Accounting: The Effect of Financial Reporting in the UK* (Macmillan). Another good overview of creative accounting.
5. Shah, A.K. (1998) 'Exploring the Influences and Constraints on Creative Accounting in the United Kingdom', *The European Accounting Review*, Vol. 7, No. 1, pp. 83–104.
   This article provides a good insight into the evolving struggle between regulators and creative accountants.
6. Mulford, C. and Comiskey, E. (2002) *The Financial Numbers Game. Detecting Creative Accounting Practices*. John Wiley and Sons Inc., New York.
   This book provides a wonderful insight into creative accounting in the US. Well researched and well written. It documents a large number of high-profile cases. It should be noted that this book predates both Enron and WorldCom.
7. Jones, M.J. (2010) *Creative Accounting, Fraud and International Accounting Scandals* (John Wiley & Sons Ltd).
   This book provides an original and interesting look at global business scandals. It investigates 54 accounting scandals from 12 countries: Australia, China, Germany, Greece, India, Italy, Japan, the Netherlands, Spain, Sweden, UK and the US. The author also writes on the background to creative accounting and fraud and draws some conclusions.
8. Beattie, V.A. and Jones, M.J. (2008). Corporate Reporting using Graphs: A Review and Synthesis, *Journal of Accounting Literature*, Vol. 27, pp. 71–110.
   This book provides an overview of 15 studies into graphs demonstrating widespread evidence of selectivity, measurement distortion and presentational enhancement.

Discussion Questions

Questions with numbers in blue have answers at the back of the book.

Q1 What is creative accounting? And why do you think that it might clash with the idea that the financial statements should give a 'true and fair view' of the accounts?

Q2 Does creative accounting represent the unacceptable face of accounting flexibility?

Q3 Why do you think that there are those strongly in favour and those strongly against creative accounting?

Q4 What incentives do managers have to indulge in creative accounting?

Q5 Will creative accounting ever be stopped?

Numerical Questions

Questions with numbers in blue have answers at the back of the book.

Q1 You are the financial accountant of Twister plc. The managing director has the following draft accounts. She is not happy.

Twister plc: Draft Income Statement Year Ended 30 June 2013

	Notes	£000	£000
Sales	1		750
Less: *Cost of Sales*			
Opening inventories		80	
Add Purchases		320	
		400	
Less Closing inventories	2	60	340
Gross Profit			410
Less *Expenses*			
Depreciation	3	60	
Interest payable	4	30	
Other expenses		332	422
Net Loss			(12)

Notes:

1. The company's policy is to record revenue prudently, one month after invoicing the customer so as to allow for any sales returns. If the company recognised revenue when invoiced, this would increase revenue by £150,000.
2. This is a prudent valuation, a more optimistic valuation gives £65,000.
3. Depreciation is currently charged on property, plant and equipment over ten years. This is a realistic expected life, but a competitor charges depreciation over 15 years.
4. Some of the interest payable relates to the borrowing of money to finance the construction of property, plant and equipment. It has been calculated that this ranges from 20% to 50%.

Required: Redraft the accounts using the notes above to present as flattering a profit as you can.

Go online to discover the extra features for this chapter at **www.wiley.com/college/jones**

Chapter 14

International accounting

'Whether we are ready or not, mankind now has a completely integrated financial and informational market place capable of moving money and ideas to any place on this planet in minutes.'

W. Wriston, *Risk and Other Four-letter Words,* p. 132, *The Executive's Book of Quotations* (1990), p. 150.

Learning Outcomes

After completing this chapter you should be able to:

- Explain and discuss the main divergent forces.
- Understand the macro and micro approaches to the classification of international accounting practices.
- Understand the accounting systems and environments in France, Germany, China, the UK and the US.
- Examine the convergent forces upon accounting, especially harmonisation in the European Union and standardisation through the International Accounting Standards Board.

Go online to discover the extra features for this chapter at **www.wiley.com/college/jones**

Chapter Summary

- Global trade and investment make national accounting very constrictive.
- Divergent forces are those factors that make accounting different in different countries.
- The main divergent forces are: objectives, users, sources of finance, regulation, taxation, the accounting profession, spheres of influence and culture.
- Countries can be classified into those with macro and micro accounting systems.
- France and Germany are macro countries with tight legal regulation, creditor orientation and weak accounting professions.
- The UK and the US are micro countries, guided by the idea of faithful presentation, with influential accounting standards, an investor-oriented approach and a strong accounting profession.
- Internationalisation causes pressure on countries to depart from national standards.
- The three main potential sources of convergence internationally are the European Union, the International Accounting Standards Board through International Financial Reporting Standards (IFRS) and US standards.

Introduction

Increasingly, we live in a global world where multinational companies dominate world trade. The world's stock exchanges are active day and night. Accounting is not immune from this globalisation. There is an increasing need to move away from a narrow national view of accounting and see accounting in an international context. The purpose of this chapter is to provide an insight into these wider aspects of accounting. In particular, we explore the factors that cause accounting to be different in different countries, such as objectives, users, regulation, taxation and the accounting profession. Accounting in some important countries (France, Germany, the UK and the US) is also explored. Finally, this chapter looks at the international pressures for convergence towards one universal world accounting system. In essence, therefore, the aim of this chapter is to provide a brief overview of the international dimension to accounting.

Context

Perhaps surprisingly, given the variety of peoples and cultures throughout the world, the fundamental techniques of accounting are fairly similar in most countries. In other words, in most countries businesses use double-entry bookkeeping, prepare a trial balance and then an income statement (profit and loss account) and statement of financial position (balance sheet). This system of accounting techniques was developed in Italy in the fifteenth century and spread around the world with trade.

However, the context of accounting in different countries is very different and causes trans-national differences in the measurement of profit, assets, liabilities and equity. The differences between countries are caused by so-called 'divergent forces', such as objectives, users, sources of finance, regulation, taxation, accounting profession, spheres of influence and culture. These divergent forces, which are examined in more detail in the next section, caused accounting in the UK to be different to that in, say, France or the US.

These international accounting differences caused few problems until the globalisation of international trade. However, with the rise of global trade and the erosion of national borders (see Soundbite 14.1), the variety of world accounting practices has been seen by many as a significant problem, particularly for multinational companies. There have been increasing pressures for the standardisation of accounting practices worldwide.

SOUNDBITE 14.1

National Boundaries

'National borders are no longer defensible against the invasion of knowledge, ideas, or financial data.'

Walter Wriston, *Risk and Other Four-Letter Words*, p. 133

Source: The Executive's Book of Quotations (1994), p. 202. Oxford University Press.

For large multinational companies, it is cheaper and easier to have just one set of world accounting standards. This is the aim of the International Accounting Standards Board (IASB). Meanwhile, within Europe there is pressure to harmonise accounting to create one set of Europe-wide standards. For European listed companies, the European Union (EU) has endorsed International Accounting Standards (IAS). These pressures for the harmonisation and standardisation of accounting are called 'convergent forces'. In essence, therefore, these divergent and convergent forces pull accounting internationally in different directions. Large global corporations, such as GSK, Microsoft, Nokia, Toyota and Volkswagen, dominate world trade. As Real-World View 14.1 shows, the revenue of many of these corporations is greater than the gross domestic product of many countries. For example, the revenue of Wal-Mart stores and Royal Dutch Shell were greater than the GDP of countries such as Thailand, Denmark, Colombia and Venezuela. In fact only 28 countries in the world exceeded the revenue of Wal-Mart stores.

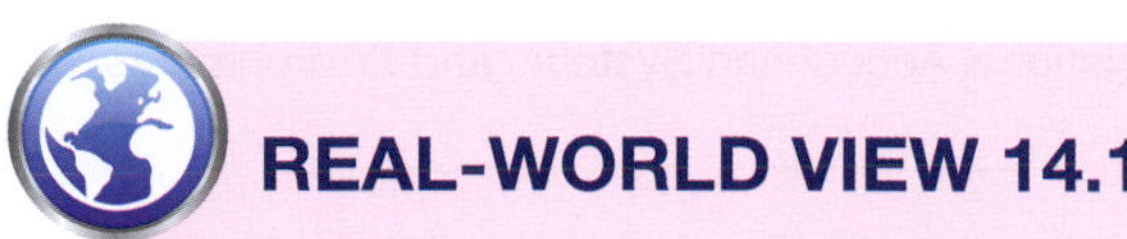

REAL-WORLD VIEW 14.1

The World's Top Economic Entities in 2011

Country/Company by GDP/Revenues		*Dollars (Bn)*
1.	United States	15,094
2.	China	7,298
3.	Japan	5,869
4.	Germany	3,577
5.	France	2,776
6.	Brazil	2,493
7.	United Kingdom	2,417
29.	Wal-Mart Stores	422
30.	Austria	419
31.	South Africa	408
32.	Royal Dutch Shell	378
33.	United Arab Emirates	360
34.	Exxon Mobil	355
35.	Thailand	346
36.	Denmark	333
37.	Colombia	328
38.	Venezuela	316
39.	BP	309
40.	Greece	303

Source: Wikipedia (2011), Countries by GDP from World Monetary Fund and Fortune, Global 2011 companies ranked by revenue.

Divergent Forces

Divergent forces are those factors that cause accounting to be different in different countries. These may be internal to a country (such as taxation system) or external (such as sphere of influence). There is much debate about the nature and identity of these divergent forces. For example, some writers exclude objectives and users. Each country has a distinct set of divergent forces and the relative importance of each divergent force varies between countries. These divergent forces are interrelated. The main divergent forces discussed in this chapter are shown in Figure 14.1. These divergent forces influence in particular a country's national practices.

(i) Objectives

The objectives of an accounting system are a key divergent force. There are two major objectives: economic reality, and planning and control. The basic idea behind economic reality is that accounts should provide a 'true and fair' view of the financial activities of the company. The UK holds this view. The US takes a similar view: 'present fairly . . . in accordance with generally

Figure 14.1 The Divergent Forces that Determine National Accounting Systems and Environments

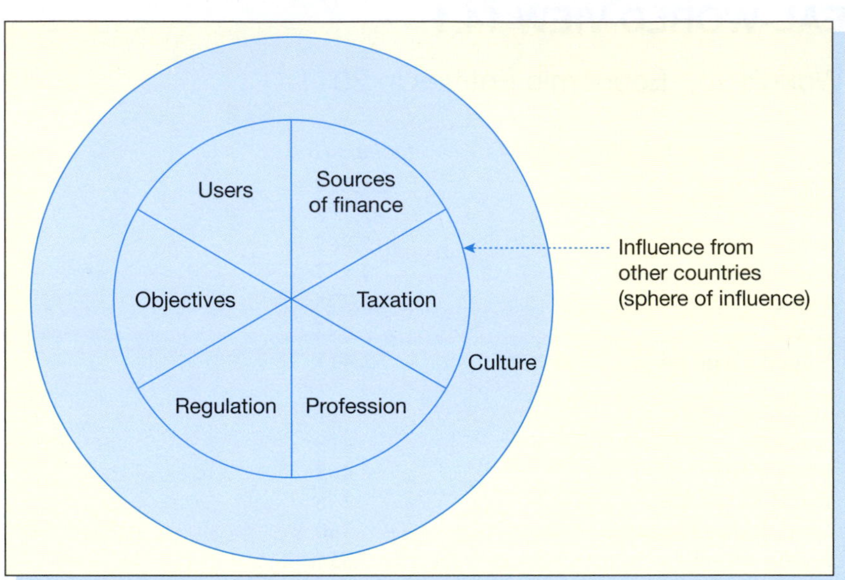

accepted accounting principles (GAAP)'. However, in the US there is a stronger presumption than in the UK that following GAAP will present a fair view of the company's activities. The UK's 'true and fair' concept is basically linked to the underlying idea that the purpose of accounting is to provide users with financial information so that they can make economic decisions.

In contrast to economic reality, planning and control place more emphasis on the provision of financial information to government. Accounting in countries such as China, France and Germany is more concerned with collecting statistical and regularised information for comparability and planning. For example, in France accounting has traditionally been seen as promoting national economic and fiscal planning. In France and Germany, the concept of a true and fair view is incorporated in national law. Unlike in the UK, this is more narrowly interpreted as compliance with the regulations.

(ii) Users

Users and objectives are closely interrelated. Users are also linked closely to another divergent force, sources of finance. In some countries, such as the UK and the US, shareholders are the main users of accounts. In the UK, institutional investors (such as insurance companies and pension firms) dominate, while in the US the role of the private individual is comparatively more important. When shareholders dominate, the accounting system focuses on profitability and the income statement becomes the main financial statement. However, recently standard setters have moved towards a statement of financial position approach.

In other countries, such as France and Germany, the power of the shareholder is less. In France, for example, the users of accounting are more diverse, ranging from the government for economic planning, to the tax authorities for fiscal planning, to the banks. In Germany, the main users are the tax authorities and the banks. In France and Germany, the users are generally relatively more concerned about liquidity and the statement of financial position than in the UK and the US. However, in both France and Germany, as more multinational companies are listed, the power of the shareholder is increasing. Both countries use IFRS for listed companies. In China, there is a range of users which includes investors, but, although the Chinese system is rapidly changing, investors are still not the main focus of the accounting system.

PAUSE FOR THOUGHT 14.1

Users

If the main users of accounts are banks rather than shareholders, how will that affect the items in the financial statements which they scrutinise?

Bankers essentially lend companies money and are concerned about two main things: loan security and loan repayments. They are, therefore, likely to focus on the statement of financial position, particularly on assets, gearing and liquidity. They will wish to make sure that any assets on which the loans are secured have not been sold or lost value. They will investigate the gearing ratios to see that the company has not taken on too many additional loans. In addition, they will scrutinise the amount of cash and the liquidity ratios to ensure that there is enough cash to pay the loan interest.

Shareholders invest their capital and look for a return. They will, therefore, principally be concerned with the income statement. In particular, they will look at earnings, earnings per share, dividends and dividend cover. They will wish to be assured that the company is profitable and will remain profitable.

(iii) Sources of Finance

A key question for any company is how to finance its operations. Apart from internally generated profits, there are two main sources: equity (or shareholder) finance and debt (or loan) finance. In some countries, such as the UK and the US, equity finance dominates. In other countries, for example, France and Germany, there is a much greater dependence on debt finance. The relative worldwide importance of the stock exchange (where equity is traded and raised) can be seen in Figure 14.2.

The presence of a strong equity stock market, such as in the US or the UK, leads countries to have an investor and an economic reality-orientated accounting system. There is a focus on profitability and the importance of auditing increases. By contrast, a strong debt market is historically associated with the increased importance of banks. Thus, Germany, whose economy is larger than that of the UK, has a much smaller stock market. As a consequence, much more of the funding for industry comes inevitably from loan finance.

(iv) Regulation

By regulation, we mean the rules that govern accounting. These rules are primarily set out by government as statutes or by the private sector as accounting standards (see Chapter 10 for more detail on the UK). The balance and interaction between statutory law and standards

Figure 14.2 Relative Strength of Selected Major Stock Exchanges as at January 2009

Country (Region)	Exchange	Domestic Companies	Market Capitalisation of Domestic Companies ($bn)
		No.	£bn
Europe	Euronext	1,013	1,863
Germany	Deutsche Börse	742	937
Spain	BME	3,517	871
United Kingdom	London	2,399	1,758
Canada	Toronto	3,747	998
United States:	NASDAQ	2,602	2,204
	New York	2,910	9,363
China:	Hong Kong	1,252	1,238
	Shanghai	864	1,557
India	Bombay	4,925	613
Japan	Tokyo	2,373	2,923
Australia	Australian	1,918	587

Source: Summarised from *Comparative International Accounting,* 12th edition, C. Nobes and R.H. Parker (2010, Table 1.5, p. 10) from data from The World Federation of Exchanges. Pearson Education.

within a particular country is often subtle. The regulatory burden is usually significantly greater for public listed companies than for smaller non-listed companies.

In the UK and the US, for example, accounting standards are very important. However, whereas in the UK there are Companies Acts applicable to all companies, in the US, the Securities Exchange Commission, an independent regulatory organisation with quasi-judicial powers, regulates the listed US companies. Other US companies are regulated by state legislation, which is often minimal.

In some countries, such as France and Germany, accounting standards are not so important. Indeed, France has no formal standard-setting body equivalent to the UK's Accounting Standards Board, while Germany only set up a standard-setting organisation in 1999. In France and Germany, accounting regulation originates from the government: in Germany, by way of a Commercial Code and in France, by way of a comprehensive government manual for accounting. However, French and German listed companies use IFRS and follow European Directives.

(v) Taxation

Strictly, the influence of taxation is part of a country's regulatory framework. However, as the relationship between accounting and taxation varies significantly between countries, it is discussed separately here. Essentially, national taxation systems may be classed as '*independent*' of, or '*dependent*' on, accounting. In independent countries, such as the UK, the taxation rules and regulations do not determine the accounting profit. There are, in effect, two profits (calculated quite legally!) – one for tax and the other for accounting. The US uses a broadly independent tax system. However, there is a curious anomaly. If US companies wish to lower their taxable profits, they can use the last-in-first-out (LIFO) method of inventory valuation (which usually values inventory lower than alternative inventory valuation methods, and thus lowers profits). However, these companies *must* also use this method in their shareholder accounts.

In France, Germany and China, however, for individual companies accounting profit is dependent upon taxable profit. In effect, the rules used for taxation determine the rules used for accounting. Accounting, therefore, becomes a process of minimising tax paid rather than showing a 'true and fair view' of the company's financial activities. However, group accounts in France and Germany can be prepared using international principles as tax is calculated on individual company, rather than group, accounts.

(vi) Accounting Profession

Accounting professions worldwide vary considerably in their size and influence. In the UK and US, accountants play an important interpretive and judgemental role. Although accounting standards are independently set, qualified accounting professionals generally constitute the majority of the members of the accounting standards boards.

Figure 14.3 shows the age and size of some professional accountancy bodies. In the UK and the US, the accounting profession is very strong and influential. In the US, for example, in 2008 there were about 339,000 Certified Public Accountants (CPA). By contrast, in Germany, there were only 13,000 *Wirtschaftsprüfer*, the German equivalent of the CPA. In China and India, both countries with huge populations, there were only 140,000 and 150,000 qualified accountants respectively. In those countries with comparatively big accounting professions, such as Australia, the UK and the US, accountants have traditionally played an important role in developing national accounting. However, in France and Germany, professionally qualified accountants have far less influence on accounting. In these countries, traditionally there has been less flexibility in the accounting rules and regulations and less need for judgement. However, given the use of IFRS by listed companies this is gradually changing.

(vii) Spheres of Influence

Accounting is not immune from the wider forces of economics and politics. Many countries' accounting systems have been heavily influenced by other countries. The UK, for example, imported double-entry bookkeeping from Italy in the fifteenth century. It then exported this to countries such as Hong Kong, India, Kenya, Malaysia, Nigeria and Singapore. These countries still follow a model inherited from the UK. The UK also originally exported its accounting system to the US. However, from the early 1900s, the US has influenced the UK rather than vice versa. Overall, it is perhaps possible to identify three broad spheres of influence: the UK, the US and the continental European. Currently, the UK is being influenced by both the US and the more prescriptive continental European model. China was originally influenced by the centrally planned Russian system, but nowadays it is increasingly influenced by the West.

Figure 14.3 Age and Size of Selected Professional Accountancy Bodies

Country	Body	Founding Date of Original Body	Approximate Membership (000) in 2008
Australia	CPA Australia (Institute of Chartered Accountants in Australia)	1952 (1886) 1928 (1885)	122 48
Canada	Canadian Institute of Chartered Accountants	1902 (1880)	74
China	Chinese Institute of Certified Public Accountants	1988	140+
France	Ordre des Experts Comptables	1942	19
Germany	Institut der Wirtschaftsprüfer	1932	13
India	Institute of Chartered Accountants in India	1949	150
Japan	Japanese Institute of Certified Public Accountants	1948 (1927)	18
Netherlands	Koninklijk Nederlands Instituut van Registeraccounants	1967 (1895)	14
New Zealand	Institute of Chartered Accountants of New Zealand	1909 (1894)	30
United Kingdom and Ireland	Institute of Chartered Accountants in England and Wales	1880 (1870)	132
	Institute of Chartered Accountants of Scotland	1951 (1854)	18
	Association of Chartered Certified Accountants	1939 (1891)	131
	Chartered Institute of Management Accountants	1919	71
	Chartered Accountants in Ireland	1888	18
United States	American Institute of Certified Public Accountants	1887	339

Note: Dates of earliest predecessor bodies in brackets.

Source: Abridged from C. Nobes and R. Parker, *Comparative International Accounting,* 12th edition, (2012, Table 1.12, p. 19). Pearson Education.

(viii) Culture

Culture is perhaps the most elusive of the divergent forces. Hofstede, in *Culture's Consequences* (Sage, 1980), defines culture as 'the collective programming of the mind which distinguishes the members of one human group from another'. Building on the work of Hofstede, accounting researchers have sought to establish whether culture influences accounting. For example, do the French or the British have a collective culture which influences accounting? Using such concepts as professionalism, uniformity, conservatism and secrecy, they have found some, if not overwhelming, support.

Classification

Accounting researchers have sought to classify national accounting systems using, for example, divergent forces, cultural characteristics, and accounting measurement and disclosure practices. A useful classification system is described by Nobes (1983). Broadly, his system classifies countries as either having macro or micro accounting systems. Figure 14.4 uses the divergent forces to summarise the major national characteristics of macro and micro countries. It can thus be seen that macro countries, such as France and Germany, are typified by governmentally orientated systems where the influence of tax is strong, but that of the accounting profession is weak. Meanwhile, micro countries, such as the UK and the US, are typified by investor-orientated systems where tax influence is weak, but the influence of the accounting profession is strong.

Figure 14.4 Main National Characteristics of the Macro and Micro Classification

Divergent Force	*Macro*	*Micro*
Objectives	Planning and control	Economic reality
Users	Government, banks, tax	Shareholders
Sources of finance	Banks	Stock exchange
Regulation	Government, relatively prescriptive	Private sector, relatively flexible
Taxation	Dominant, dependent system	Subordinate, independent system
Accounting profession	Weak, uninfluential	Strong, influential
Spheres of influence	Continental	UK, US
Examples	France, Germany	UK, US

Country Snapshots

Every country's accounting system and environment is a unique mixture of divergent forces. In this section, we look at the accounting systems and environments of five important developed and developing countries: France, Germany, China, the UK and the US. The aim is to provide a quick overview of the distinctive natural characteristics of each country's accounting systems.

France

The French accounting system is often cited as a good example of a standardised accounting system. It thus contrasts with the UK and US systems. Essentially, the French accounting system was introduced in order to provide the government with economic information for planning and controlling the French economy. The French system centres around *Le Plan Comptable Générale* (General Accounting Plan). This sets out a uniform system of accounting to be used throughout France. Of special interest is a chart of accounts where each item in the accounts is given a number. These numbers can then be used to aggregate items from different companies. Overall, *Le Plan Comptable Générale* resembles a comprehensive accounting manual which French companies follow.

In addition to *Le Plan Comptable Générale*, there are various detailed accounting and taxation laws. The role of taxation is particularly important. In essence, tax law drives accounting law. Standish (in Nobes and Parker, 2000, p. 205) states any company wanting to take advantage of various tax concessions needs to:

> *'. . . enter the relevant tax assessable income or tax deductible charges in its accounts as if valid for tax purposes, even if the effect is to generate assets or liabilities that do not conform to the accounting criteria for asset and liability recognition and measurement.'*

The accounting profession in France is much smaller than in the UK and US. There were 19,000 professional accountants in 2008 (Nobes and Parker, 2012, p. 19). Compared with other countries, the profession is not influential. There are, for example, no accounting standards in France comparable to those in the UK and US.

However, accounting in France has changed (see Soundbite 14.2) and is still changing rapidly. For many years, French companies have been permitted to use non-French accounting principles. Many large French groups, therefore, used US accounting principles or International Accounting Standards (IAS). Since 2005, French listed companies, like all EU listed companies, use IFRS in their group accounts. However, individual company accounts must still be prepared using French principles.

SOUNDBITE 14.2

France

'We're [France] somewhere between the United States and Germany on transparency, probably closer to US practices and certainly less able than German business to hide systematic abuses. We're going toward the US model, but it's going to take several years more.'

Alan Minc quoted in *International Herald Tribune* (October 10, 1996)

Source: The Wiley Book of Business Quotations (1998), p. 158.

Germany

Germany has traditionally had a relatively distinctive accounting system (see Real-World View 14.2). Essentially, it is very prescriptive, government controlled and creditor orientated. Currently, there is no comprehensive body of accounting standards. The main regulations are contained in the Companies Acts, Commercial Code and Publication Law. These laws set out very detailed regulations.

REAL-WORLD VIEW 14.2

German Accounting System

Traditionally, German accounting has followed a relatively distinct path. Germany, along with France, has always represented a continental accounting tradition based on a creditor rather than a shareholder approach. The Franco-German approach is in direct contrast to the Anglo-Saxon view of accounting. This latter view, typified by UK/US accounting, espouses an economic reality, user-based approach, with the main user being the shareholder.

Source: M.J. Jones, Germany: An Accounting System in Change, *Accountancy* (International edition), Vol. 124, No. 1272, August 1999, pp. 64–5. Copyright Wolters Kluwer, UK.

The measurement systems underpinning German accounting have traditionally been seen as very conservative. This is especially so when compared with UK accounting policies. For instance, in 1997 Rover, the UK car maker, would have made a profit of £147m under UK rules. Under German rules it reported a loss of £363m. Taxation law also dominates accounting; for example, expenses are only allowable for tax if they are deducted in the financial accounts of individual companies.

SOUNDBITE 14.3

Germany

'Accounting scandals are major drivers of the regulatory development. In response to accounting scandals, the legislative landscape in Germany has been changed fundamentally in the period between 1980 and 2006. For example, in 2005 the Financial Reporting Enforcement Panel, a new enforcement institution, was created responsible for the correctness of the financial statements.'

Source: Hansrudi Lenz (2010), Accounting Scandals in Germany, in Michael Jones, *Creative Accounting, Fraud and International Accounting Scandals,* p. 18. Reproduced by permission of John Wiley & Sons Ltd.

The German accounting profession is very small. In 2008, there were only 13,000 German professionally qualified accountants (Nobes and Parker, 2010, p. 20). There is, however, also a separate profession of tax specialists. Although small, the German profession is very well qualified. However, in Germany most accounting developments originate from the government rather than from the accounting profession.

By international standards, the German stock market is comparatively small. Its total market capitalisation is only about half that of the UK. German industry is financed principally by banks. The focus of German accounting, therefore, has traditionally been on assets rather than profit.

However, German accounting, like French accounting, has changed rapidly. Listed German companies, like listed French companies, use IFRS to prepare their group accounts. This internationalism of German accounting started in the 1990s. In 1990, no German companies were listed in the US. However, Daimler Benz caused a minor sensation in Germany by listing on the US exchange in 1993. Since then German companies have increasingly used US or International Accounting Standards. In Germany, in 2005, a German Financial Reporting Enforcement Panel was established to monitor the reporting standards of German companies.

China

China is modernising fast and its economy is growing rapidly. As a result, it has recently become the world's second biggest economy, overtaking Japan, but behind the US. China has had a long history of centralised government. This dictated its accounting system and up until the 1970s China's accounting was based on that of the Soviet Union. The Chinese economy was planned centrally and its accounting was a tool in that planned centralisation.

SOUNDBITE 14.4

China

'Since the introduction of economic reforms and "open door" policies in 1978, China has been in transition from a centrally planned to a market economy.'

Source: C.H. Chen, Y. Hu and J.Z. Xiao (2010), Corporate Accounting Scandals in China in Michael Jones, *Creative Accounting, Fraud and International Accounting Scandals*. Reproduced by permission of John Wiley & Sons Ltd.

However, from the 1970s the Chinese economy has modernised very fast, mainly towards a socialist market economic system. By 2003, China achieved a 73% marketisation (Chen et al., 2010). Although ownership of the business enterprises remains substantially with the government, management and ownership are now separated, making the concept of the business entity relevant (Nobes and Parker, 2010).

China's stock market has developed rapidly with nearly 2,000 listed firms (see www.scrc.gov.cn). The market capitalisation of Shanghai has now overtaken that of Hong Kong and by January 2009, China was approaching that of the UK in terms of domestic companies. However, the banking sector is still dominated by state-owned banks.

In terms of regulations, the government launched a major accounting reform in 1992. This resulted in several regulations including 'Accounting Regulations for Share Enterprises and Accounting Standards for Business Enterprises'. The main users in China were considered to be the government, banks, the public and an enterprise's own management rather than investors (Nobes and Parker, 2010). In addition, 'there is a high degree of conformity between tax and accounting figures, so that the calculation of taxable income is a major purpose of accounting' (Nobes and Parker, 2010, p. 321).

In October 1998, an Accounting Standards Committee was founded. In 2000, a new uniform accounting system was introduced to replace the existing industry-based standards. Moreover, China was also issuing accounting standards (Xiao, Weetman and Sun, 2004). Then, in February 2006, a new set of Accounting Standards was developed for Business Enterprises (ASBEs). These are required for listed companies from 2007 and are very similar to IFRS (Nobes and Parker, 2010). The imposition of these new laws so quickly and the rapid modernisation of the economy have meant that enforcement has lagged behind. There have, therefore, been many scandals in China (Chen et al., 2010).

There has, however, been a rapid growth in the audit profession. The Chinese Institute of Certified Public Accountants (CICPA) was founded in 1988. It has grown rapidly and in 2008 had approximately 140,000 members (Nobes and Parker, 2010). Although very small in terms of its population (e.g., the UK has 132,000 members of the ICAEW alone), it does reflect an important and developing body of professionals.

Overall, therefore, Chinese accounting has, like its economy, been transformed over the last generation. This is perhaps unsurprising as accounting is often called the handmaiden of economics. In other words, it serves to support and develop the economic infrastructure.

The UK

The UK is still an important player in accounting worldwide. However, it is no longer the world leader. The current UK system contains elements of US and continental European accounting. The generally recognised objective of accounting in the UK is to give a 'true and fair view' of a company's financial activities to the users, most notably the shareholders. There are two sources of regulation: company law and accounting standards. Company law, which now includes the European Fourth and Seventh Directives, sets out an increasingly prescriptive accounting framework. The financial reporting standards, now set by the Accounting Council, provide guidance on particular accounting issues. They are followed by UK non-listed companies, which constitute the vast bulk of UK companies. The UK has a Financial Reporting and Review Panel, which investigates companies suspected of non-compliance with the standards. The UK, therefore, has an unusual mix of regulations. UK listed companies now follow IFRS for their group accounts.

The UK's Accounting Standards Board is currently proposing a three-tier approach which will be operational in 2015. Under this, listed companies would continue to follow IFRS. Joining them would be some other publicly accountable companies such as those trading debt on public markets or holding deposits.

In the second tier, other non-listed companies would usually report under the ASB's proposed new accounting standard, FRS 102, based on IFRS for SMEs (FRSME). They can, however, choose to follow IFRS. This would be shorter and less complicated than current UK standards. Finally, the smallest companies will continue to use a simplified version of UK standards, known as FRSSE.

The accounting profession in the UK is very influential and accounting in the UK is a relatively high-status profession. It is also very fragmented, comprising the Institute of Chartered Accountants in England and Wales (ICAEW), the Institute of Chartered Accountants of Scotland, the Institute of Chartered Accountants in Ireland, the Association of Chartered

Certified Accountants, the Chartered Institute of Management Accountants and the Chartered Institute of Public Finance and Accountancy. The ICAEW has traditionally been the largest body numbering 132,000 professionally qualified accountants in 2008 (see Figure 14.3). However, the Association of Chartered Certified Accountants is growing rapidly with a particularly strong overseas presence and in 2008 had 131,000 members.

PAUSE FOR THOUGHT 14.2

Unique Features of UK Accounting System

Every country's accounting system and environment is unique. Can you think of three features of the UK's accounting and environment which contribute, in combination, to the uniqueness of the UK's accounting system?

There are many special features in the UK's system. Some of the main ones are listed below.

- Combination of a 'true and fair view' with Companies Acts, UK accounting standards and IFRS.
- The fragmentation of the accounting profession into six institutes.
- The dominance of the institutional investor in the stock market.
- The Financial Reporting Review Panel's role as guardian of good accounting practice.
- Non-listed companies are able to capitalise their goodwill and write it off to the income statement over five years when a reliable estimate cannot be made (from 1 January 2015).

The main users of accounts in the UK are the shareholders. In particular, in the UK, institutional investors dominate. The stock market is very active and its market capitalisation is very high. Unlike most other countries, there is a separation between accounting profit and taxable profit. In essence, there are two distinct bodies of law. Certainly, taxable profit does not determine accounting profit.

The US

The US is one of the most important forces in world accounting. Most important developments in accounting originate in the US. A particular feature of the US environment is the position of the Securities Exchange Commission (SEC). The SEC was set up in the 1930s after the Wall Street crash of 1929. It is an independent regulatory institution with quasi-judicial powers. Listed US companies have to file a detailed annual form, called the 10-K, with the SEC. The SEC also supervises the operation of the US standard-setting body, the Financial Accounting Standards Board (FASB). This body has been designated by the American Institute of Certified Public Accountants (AICPA) as the US's standard-setting body. At the time of writing this book, the FASB and the IASB are working on a project to converge US GAAP and IFRS.

FASB is the most active of the world's national standard-setting bodies. The members of FASB have to sever their prior business and professional links. FASB has published over

150 standards. It is supported by the Emerging Issues Task Force, which examines new and emerging accounting issues. The US accounting standard-setting model proved the blueprint for the current UK system. Unlike France, Germany and the UK, US listed companies follow their own national standards rather than IFRS.

US listed companies are thus well regulated. However, curiously for the mass of US companies, which are not listed, there may be very few accounting or auditing requirements. Company legislation is a state not a federal matter. Each state, therefore, sets its own laws.

The accounting profession in the US is both numerous and influential. There were 339,000 members of the AICPA in 2008 (see Figure 14.3). Most of the world's leading audit firms have their head offices in the US.

The objective of accounting in the US is generally recognised as being to provide users with information for decision making. Most of the finance for US industry is provided by shareholders. Unlike in the UK, the majority of shareholders in the US are still private shareholders. The market capitalisation of the US stock market is the greatest in the world. Many of the world's largest companies such as Microsoft or the General Electric Company are US-based. The high-quality financial information produced by US financial reporting standards is often argued to help the efficiency of the US stock market. However, in 2001 and 2002, a series of high-profile accounting scandals involving companies such as Enron, WorldCom and Xerox led to a questioning of the quality of US accounting and auditing standards.

Real-World View 14.3 shows the connection between US capital markets and financial reporting standards.

REAL-WORLD VIEW 14.3

US Financial Reporting

Financial Reporting and Capital Markets

There is a clear connection between the efficient and effective US capital markets and the high quality of US financial reporting standards. US reporting standards provide complete and transparent information to investors and creditors. The cost of capital is directly affected by the availability of credible and relevant information. The uncertainty associated with a lack of information creates an additional layer of cost that affects all companies not providing the information regardless of whether the information, if provided, would prove to be favorable or unfavorable to individual companies. More information always equates to less uncertainty, and it is clear that people pay more for better certainty.

Source: Edmund Jenkins, Global Reporting Standards, *IASC Insight*, June 1999, p. 11.

In the US, as the aim of the accounts is broadly to reflect economic reality, the tax and accounting systems are generally independent. There is, however, one curious exception: last-in-first-out (LIFO) inventory (stock) valuation. Many US companies adopt LIFO in their taxation accounts as it lowers their taxable profit. However, if they do so, federal tax laws state they must also use LIFO in their financial accounts. However, since LIFO inventory values are generally old and out of date, this fails to reflect economic reality.

Convergent Forces

Convergent forces are pressures upon countries to depart from their current national standards and adopt more internationally based standards. Convergent forces thus oppose divergent forces. The advantage of national standards is that they may reflect a particular country's circumstances. Unfortunately, the disadvantage is that they impair comparability between countries and are a potential barrier to international trade and investment.

PAUSE FOR THOUGHT 14.3

Pressures for Convergence

How might national accounting standards prove a barrier for a multinational company, such as Glaxo-Wellcome, or a large institutional investor, such as Aberdeen Asset Management?

The world of trade and investment is now global. Companies such as Glaxo-Wellcome will, therefore, trade all over the world and have subsidiaries in numerous countries. They will sometimes have to deal with accounting requirements in literally hundreds of countries. To do this takes time, effort and, more importantly, money. If there was one set of agreed international accounting standards, this would make the life of many multinationals easier and cheaper.

Large institutional investors will also be active in many countries. For them, there is a need to compare the financial statements of companies from different countries. For example, an institutional investor, such as Aberdeen Asset Management, may wish to achieve a balanced portfolio and invest funds in the motor car industry. It would wish to compare companies such as BMW in Germany, Fiat in Italy, General Motors in the US and Toyota in Japan. To do this effectively, there is a need for comparable information. A common set of international accounting standards would provide the comparable information.

There are three main potential sources for the convergence of accounting worldwide: the European Union (EU), the International Accounting Standards Board (IASB) and the United States. The process of convergence through the EU is normally termed *harmonisation*, while that through the IASB is called *standardisation*.

European Union (EU)

The European Union is concerned with harmonising the economic and social policies of its member states. Accounting represents part of the economic harmonisation within Europe. In countries such as France and Germany, accounting regulation has always been seen as a subset of a more general legal regulation. Differences in accounting between member states are seen as a barrier to the harmonisation of trade.

The main legal directives affecting accounts are the Fourth Directive and the Seventh Directive. The Fourth Directive is particularly important to the UK. It is based on the German Company Law of 1965. The Fourth Directive ended up as a compromise between the traditional UK and the Franco-German approaches to accounting. The UK approach was premised on flexibility and individual judgement. By contrast, the continental approach set out a prescriptive and detailed legal framework. In the end, the Fourth Directive married the two approaches.

The UK for the first time accepted a standardised format for presenting company accounts and much more detailed legal regulation. However, France and Germany agreed to incorporate into law the British concept of the presentation of a true and fair view.

At one time, the European Union appeared to be developing its own standards. However, it has now thrown its weight behind IFRS. These are now required to be used by the more than 9,000 European listed companies for their group accounts.

SOUNDBITE 14.5

Different Accounting Standards

'Different accounting standards are a drag on progress in much the same way as diverse languages are an inconvenience. Unlike creating a world language, creating one set of standards is achievable. Apart from the potential savings for companies with diverse international structures, complying with an internationally understood accounting paradigm opens up a wider investment audience.'

Source: Clem Chambers, Talking the Same Language, *Accountancy Age*, 3 February 2005, p. 6.

International Accounting Standards Board (IASB)

The International Accounting Standards Committee (IASC) was founded in 1973 by Sir Henry Benson to work for the improvement and harmonisation of accounting standards worldwide. Originally, there were nine members: Australia, Canada, France, Germany, Japan, Mexico, the Netherlands, the UK and Ireland, and the US. Member bodies were the national professional bodies of different countries. The IASC grew rapidly and, in 2001, 150 countries were members. The member bodies used their best endeavours to ensure that their countries followed International Accounting Standards (IAS). These were subsequently called International Financial Reporting Standards (IFRS). The IASC was reconstituted as the International Accounting Standards Board (IASB) in 2001 (to simplify matters we generally use IASB for both IASC and IASB throughout this book).

At first, the IASB merely codified the world's standards. After this initial step, the IASB began to work towards the improvement of standards. The IASB set out a restricted number of options within an accounting standard from which companies could then choose. Up until the mid-1990s, it is fair to say that the IASB made only limited progress. A threefold

PAUSE FOR THOUGHT 14.4

Are a set of global accounting standards a good thing?

Superficially, it might seem that the answer to this question is self-evident. If there was a set of global accounting standards, then it might seem that it would obviously be good as it would enable international users, such as international investment analysts, to compare the accounts of different international companies and thus make informed decisions. However, in practice, this may be potentially misleading. Different countries have very different accounting environments and if this is not taken into account then this will mean that false comparisons are made. For instance, in Japan, large companies often have a completely different organisational structure to Western companies; therefore, their levels of trade receivables and trade payables will be very different. German companies have, for example, a reputation of being very conservative in their accounting practices.

differentiation in the IASB's impact was possible: lesser developed countries, European countries and capital market countries. Lesser developed countries, such as Malaysia, Nigeria and Singapore, adopted IFRS because doing so was cheaper than developing their own standards. In continental Europe, the IFRS were seen both as a problem and a solution. They were a problem in that generally IFRS were seen to adopt a primarily investor-orientated approach to accounting which conflicted with the traditional continental European tax-driven, creditor-based model. They were a solution in that IFRS were preferable to US standards. Increasingly, in the early 1990s, French and German companies adopted US standards. Karel Van Hulle, Head of the EU's Accounting Unit, commented in 1995, 'It would be crazy for Europe to apply American standards, as it would be crazy for the Americans to apply European standards. We ought to develop those standards which we believe are the best for us or for our companies.' Finally, for capital market countries, such as the UK and the US, the IFRS were generally already similar to the national standards. Even so, there was a great reluctance, particularly by the US, to accept IFRS.

A breakthrough agreement came in 1995. IOSCO (The International Organisation of Securities Commissions), the body which represents the world's stock exchanges, agreed that when the IASB had developed a set of core standards, it would consider them for endorsement and would recommend them to national stock exchanges as an alternative to national standards. The advantage to IOSCO was that there would be a common currency of standards which could be used internationally. In particular, there was the hope that non-US companies could trade on the New York Stock Exchange without having to use US Generally Accepted Accounting Principles (GAAP) or provide a reconciliation to US GAAP. The IASB subsequently experienced severe problems compiling a set of core standards. However, by 2000 these were in place. The importance of the IASB is shown in Real-World View 14.4.

REAL-WORLD VIEW 14.4

Why IFRSs? Why Now?

The effective functioning of capital markets is essential to our economic well-being. In my view, a sound financial reporting infrastructure must be built on four pillars:

1. accounting standards that are consistent, comprehensive, and based on clear principles to enable financial reports to reflect underlying economic reality;
2. effective corporate governance practices, including a requirement for strong internal controls, that implement the accounting standards;
3. auditing practices that give confidence to the outside world that an entity is faithfully reflecting its economic performance and financial position; and
4. an enforcement or oversight mechanism that ensures that the principles as laid out by the accounting and auditing standards are followed.

As the world's capital markets integrate, the logic of a single set of accounting standards is evident. A single set of international standards will enhance comparability of financial information and should make the allocation of capital across borders more efficient. The development and acceptance of international standards should also reduce compliance costs for corporations and improve consistency in audit quality.

Sir David Tweedie, Chairman, International Accounting Standards Board
Testimony before the Committee of Banking, Housing and Urban Affairs of the United States Senate, Washington, 9 September 2004

Source: Deloitte, *IFRS in your pocket*, 2005, p. 2.

At the start of the new Millennium, three developments substantially enhanced the power of the IASB. First, in 2000 IOSCO allowed its members to use IFRS standards. Second, the IASC was reconstituted as the IASB in 2001 with a new chairman, Sir David Tweedie. The four main elements were: the IASC Foundation, the IASB, the Standards Advisory Council and the Standing Interpretations Committee. The IASC Foundation appoints the IASB, raises money and acts in a supervisory role. The main objectives of the IFRS foundation (IFRS, 2010) are 'to develop in the public interest, a single set of high-quality, understandable, enforceable and globally accepted financial reporting standards based upon clearly articulated principles'. To fulfil the required standards, financial statements and other reporting need to be of high quality, complete and transparent for investors and other users of financial information in the world's capital markets to make the right economic decisions. From July 2011, there is a new head of the IASB, Hans Hoogervorst, and as Real-World View 14.5 shows, the Board has a busy work programme.

REAL-WORLD VIEW 14.5

The IASB's Workload

One of the first tasks of the new board will be to set its work programme for the next five years. By the time it does this, several very significant projects (including revenue, leases, insurance contracts and financial assets and financial liabilities) should have been completed. China, Japan, India, Canada, Brazil and several other major jurisdictions should be well on their way to International Financial Reporting Standards adoption. The Securities and Exchange Commission should have decided whether US domestic issuers should be allowed or required to use IFRS in place of US GAAP. Ideally, all the standards issued by the old board should have proved acceptable to the EU and other jurisdictions that use IFRS and to G20 ministers.

Source: D. Cairns, Where next for the IASB? *Accountancy Magazine,* February 2011, pp. 30–1. Copyright Wolters Kluwer (UK) Ltd.

The IASB sets the IFRS. At the end of 2011, there were 14 members of the IASB board with each member having one vote. As at December 2012, there were eight IFRS and 29 International Accounting Standards (IAS) (i.e., developed by the IASC) in existence. The Standards Advisory Council gives general advice and guidance to the IASB. The Standing Interpretations Committee interprets current IFRS, but also issues guidance on other accounting matters. There is also a Monitoring Board that provides a formal link between the trustees and public authorities and an advisory council which provides a forum for organisations and individuals to participate in the IASB's work. The third important development was the decision in June 2000 by the European Union that all EU listed companies would follow IFRS from 2005.

These three developments considerably enhanced the power of the IASB. By 2013, 93 countries required the use of IFRS for all domestic listed companies and many of these countries also required their use by unlisted companies. The web addresses of some of these companies as well as the IASB website are given in Figure 14.5. The use of IFRS is also being encouraged by the International Federation of Accountants (IFAC), which is the global organisation for the accounting profession. They have worked with the World Bank to ensure the global adoption of accounting and auditing standards. In many cases, the World Bank has specified the adoption of IFRS before it would grant credit. This has encouraged governments in developing countries to adopt IFRS.

The IFRS are continually being revised. The standards in existence in 2012 are listed as an Appendix to this chapter. There are, in addition, many interpretations (guidance documents) as well as the IASB's *The Conceptual Framework,* which is in the process of being updated. This framework defines the objectives of financial statements, the qualitative characteristics of financial statements and the basic elements and concepts of financial statements. IFRS, like all standards, are ultimately political in nature; as Real-World View 14.6 shows, there has been much concern about the global rules on fair value accounting. Many critics have blamed fair value for the global financial crisis.

Figure 14.5 Some Useful Web Addresses for Companies using International Financial Reporting Standards

Company	*Nationality*	*Website*	*Sector*
Gucci	Dutch	Gucci.com	Leather, Fashion
Lufthansa	German	Lufthansa.com	Airlines
Nestle	Swiss	Nestle.com	Food and Drink
Nokia	Finnish	Nokia.com	Mobile Phones
Novartis	Swiss	Novartis.com	Drug Manufacturing
Puma	German	Puma.com	Sportswear
SAS	Danish	SASgroup.net	Airlines
Swatch	Swiss	Swatch.com	Watches
UBS	Swiss	UBS.com	Banking
Volkswagen	German	Volkswagen.com	Car Manufacturing

REAL-WORLD VIEW 14.6

A Pyrrhic Victory?

'IFRS is a good idea in principle, but the problem is the politics and whether the US gives up its sovereignty,' says Roger Barker, head of corporate governance at the Institute of Directors. 'And if too many global accounting rules are watered down in order to secure US support, IFRS will be a "pyrrhic victory",' Barker adds.

Jonathan Russell, a partner at Russell Phillips and Rees Russell and a former president of the UK 200 Group of chartered accountants and lawyers, says: 'For most small businesses, this is something that isn't even on their radar, so if and when the global accounting rules become compulsory, it will just be something else they expect their accountants to deal with.

At present at my firm I have about two clients who use international standards, which creates extra difficulties for us because we have to be familiar with UK and international GAAP.'

Big Four accounting firms appear more enthusiastic about IFRS. Pauline Wallace, UK head of public policy for PricewaterhouseCoopers, and an expert on IFRS, says that momentum towards global accounting standards appears unstoppable, and is not reliant on US support.

'The IASB has done a phenomenal job in getting its standards applied across the world,' she says. 'There is a real groundswell towards IFRS. If the US doesn't give its support for IFRS, it will be unfortunate, but it won't be a killer blow.'

Source: N. Huber, Rule the World, *Accountancy Magazine,* May 2010, p. 26. Copyright Wolters Kluwer (UK) Ltd.

A consistent problem for the IASB has been the attitude of the US. Traditionally, the US has been reluctant to adopt IFRS. Although, in principle, the US favours world standards, it has several concerns about IFRS. It feels they are not as rigorous as US standards and is also worried about their enforcement. However, the shortcomings of US accounting standards revealed by recent US accounting scandals have made the IAS potentially more attractive to US regulators. In October 2003, a joint convergence project was begun by the IASB and the FASB. The aim of this project is to eliminate differences between the standards set by the IASB and FASB. Short-term convergence projects were set to be completed by 2008 with a decision by the US on convergence to follow but no decision had been made when this book went to press. However, even if the US does replace US GAAP with IFRS, this is unlikely to be before 2015.

PAUSE FOR THOUGHT 14.5

US Acceptance of IAS Standards

Cynics argue that it is in the US's interests deliberately to delay accepting International Accounting Standards. Why do you think this might be?

US standards are probably the most advanced of any country in the world. The US is also the richest country in the world and a source of potential capital for companies from other countries. To gain access to US finance, many overseas companies list on the US Stock Exchange. However, to do this they must adopt US standards or provide reconciliations to US standards. As time passes, more foreign companies adopt US standards. Cynics, therefore, believe that the US may be playing a waiting game. The longer the US delays approving IAS, the more foreign companies will list on the US exchange. These cynics argue, therefore, that it is in the US's interests to delay accepting IAS.

From a UK perspective, the Accounting Standards Board, which sets standards for UK domestic non-listed companies, has accepted, in principle, the need for eventual international harmonisation. The current policy is to depart from an international consensus only when there are particular legal or tax difficulties or when the UK believes the international approach is wrong. Recently, the ASB has made important efforts to harmonise UK and IAS standards in key areas such as goodwill, taxation and pensions. The UK is also harmonising its accounting practices with those currently used in the US. The ASB has also agreed, in principle, that IFRS should be used for all publicly accountable entities.

US Standards

There is still the possibility that if the SEC refuses to endorse the IFRS, US standards will become a substitute for worldwide accounting standards. More and more companies worldwide are being listed in the US. The advantage of using US standards is that this enables non-US companies to list on the New York Stock Exchange. This is the world's largest stock exchange and a ready source of capital. Currently, these companies have to reconcile their earnings and net assets to US GAAP if they use IFRS or their own national standards.

Conclusion

Different countries have different accounting environments. These accounting environments are determined by divergent forces, such as objectives, users, sources of finance, regulation, taxation, the accounting profession, spheres of influence and culture. These divergent forces are interrelated and the mix of divergent forces is unique for each country. Countries can be classified as having macro or micro accounting systems. In macro countries, such as France or Germany, the emphasis is on tight legal regulation, with a creditor orientation and a weak accounting profession. By contrast, in micro countries such as the UK and the US, there is a focus on regulation via standards rather than the law and an overall investor-orientated approach with a strong accounting profession.

The great variety of accounting systems worldwide impedes the growth in world trade. Consequently, there are pressures for countries to depart from purely nationally based accounting. The pressures result from the growth in multinational companies and in cross-border trade and investment. These convergent forces thus counteract the divergent forces.

At the European level, the European Union works towards the harmonisation of accounting practices. On the global level, the International Accounting Standards Board sets International Financial Reporting Standards. Having made a slow start, the IASB is now gathering momentum.

There is now an agreement by the International Organisation of Securities Commission that its members are allowed to use IFRS when listing on individual exchanges. However, the US Securities and Exchange Commission still has reservations. In Europe, listed companies must now use IFRS.

Selected Reading

1. Books and Official Pronouncements

International Accounting is blessed with some very good, comprehensive books. As International Accounting is continually changing, it is always necessary to check that you have the latest edition.

Chen, C.H., Hu, Y. and Xiao, J.Z. (2010) Corporate Accounting Scandals in China, in Jones, M.J., *Creative Accounting, Fraud and International Accounting Scandals*.

Nobes, C.W. and R.H. Parker (2010) *Comparative International Accounting* (11th edition), (Pearson Education Limited: London).
This is the longest standing of the books. Nobes and Parker write some of the chapters themselves, but there are also useful chapters by other authors, especially Klaus Langer on Germany.

Roberts, C., Weetman, P. and Gordon, P. (2002) *International Financial Accounting: A Comparative Approach* (Financial Times Management: London).
This book provides a comprehensive coverage of the issues in this chapter.

Walton, P., Haller, A. and Raffournier, B. (1998) *International Accounting* (International Thompson Business Press: London).
Once more this is a useful book. Each chapter is written by a specialist.

These publications from the IASB will give readers an insight into the current developments of international accounting standards.

i. International Accounting Standards Board (IASB) (2011), 'Conceptual Framework', in *International Financial Reporting* (2011), paras 4.54–4.65.
ii. International Accounting Standards Board (IASB) (2013), *A Review of the Conceptual Framework for Financial Reporting*, IASB Discussion Paper, DP/2013/1.

2. Articles

Students may find the following three articles provide a reasonable coverage of the International Accounting Standards Board and Germany, respectively.

Jones, M.J. (1998) 'The IASB: Twenty-five years old this year', *Management Accounting*, May, pp. 30–32.

Jones, M.J. (1999) 'Germany: An accounting system in change', *Accountancy International*, August, pp. 64–65.

Nobes, C.W. (1997) 'German Accountancy Explained', *Financial Times Business Information*, London.

The key article on the micro–macro classification of accounting systems is listed below. Also there is a useful chapter in Nobes and Parker (2010).

Nobes, C.W. (1983) 'A Judgmental International Classification of Financial Reporting Practices', *Journal of Business Finance and Accounting*, Spring, pp. 1–19.

Xiao, Z., Weetman, P. and Sun, M.L. (2004) Political Influence and Co-existence of a Uniform Accounting System and Accounting Standards in China, *Abacus*, Vol. 40, No. 2, pp. 193–218.

Provides an overview of regulatory change in China.

Discussion Questions

Questions with numbers in blue have answers at the back of the book.

Q1 Why is the study of international accounting important?

Q2 What are the main divergent forces and which are the most important?

Q3 Compare and contrast the main features of the Anglo-American and continental European accounting systems.

Q4 Taking any one country, rank the divergent forces in order of importance.

Q5 Has the UK more in common with the US than with France?

Q6 Will the convergent forces outweigh the divergent forces?

Appendix 14.1: List of International Standards

IFRS as in Existence as at December 2012

IFRS 1	First-time Adoption of International Financial Reporting Standards
IFRS 2	Share-based Payment
IFRS 3	Business Combinations
IFRS 4	Insurance Contracts
IFRS 5	Non-current Assets Held for Sale and Discontinued Operations
IFRS 6	Exploration for and Evaluation of Mineral Resources
IFRS 7	Financial Instruments: Disclosures
IFRS 8	Operating Segments

International Accounting Standards (IASs)

IAS 1	Presentation of Financial Statements
IAS 2	Inventories
IAS 7	Statement of Cash Flows
IAS 8	Accounting Policies, Changes in Accounting Estimates and Errors
IAS 10	Events after the Reporting Period
IAS 11	Construction Contracts
IAS 12	Income Taxes
IAS 16	Property, Plant and Equipment
IAS 17	Leases
IAS 18	Revenue
IAS 19	Employee Benefits
IAS 20	Accounting for Government Grants and Disclosure of Government Assistance
IAS 21	The Effects of Changes in Foreign Exchange Rates
IAS 23	Borrowing Costs
IAS 24	Related Party Disclosures
IAS 26	Accounting and Reporting by Retirement Benefit Plans
IAS 27	Consolidated and Separate Financial Statements
IAS 28	Investments in Associates
IAS 29	Financial Reporting in Hyperinflationary Economies
IAS 31	Interests in Joint Ventures
IAS 32	Financial Instruments: Presentation
IAS 33	Earnings per Share
IAS 34	Interim Financial Reporting
IAS 36	Impairment of Assets
IAS 37	Provisions, Contingent Liabilities and Contingent Assets

IAS 38 Intangible Assets
IAS 39 Financial Instruments: Recognition and Measurement
IAS 40 Investment Property
IAS 41 Agriculture

As in existence at December 2012.

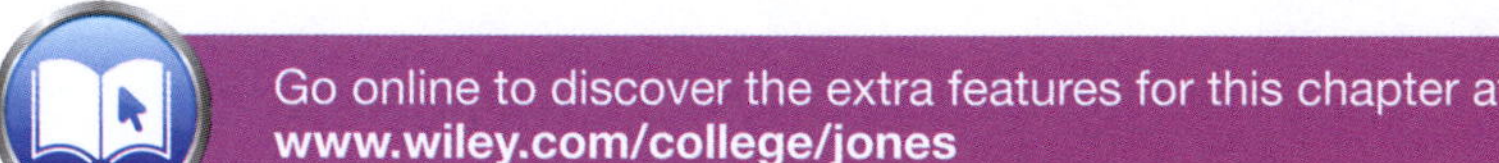

Glossary of Key Accounting Terms

This glossary contains most of the key accounting terms that students are likely to encounter. Words highlighted in bold are explained elsewhere in the glossary.

Acid test ratio

See **quick ratio.**

Accounting

The provision of information to managers and owners so they can make business decisions.

Accounting concept

A principle underpinning the preparation of accounting information.

Accounting Council

The Accounting Council took over from the **ASB** in 2012. It is the body which now sets UK accounting standards under the **Accounting Council**. The Accounting Council has taken over the role of the Urgent Issues Task Force (UITF).

Accounting equation

The basic premise that **assets** equal **liabilities**.

Accounting period

The time period for which the accounts are prepared. Audited financial statements are usually prepared for a year.

Accounting policies

The specific accounting methods selected and followed by a company in areas such as **revenue**, foreign currencies, inventories, goodwill and pensions.

Accounting standards

Accounting pronouncements which set out the disclosure and measurement rules businesses must follow to give a **true and fair view** when drawing up accounts.

Accounting Standards Board (ASB)

Until 2012, when it was replaced by the **Accounting Council**, this body set the UK's accounting standards.

Accruals

The amounts owed to the suppliers of services at the statement of financial position date, for expenses such as telephone or light and heat.

Accruals concept
See **matching concept.**

Accumulated depreciation
The total depreciation on **property, plant and equipment** including this year's and prior years' depreciation.

Annual report
A report produced annually by a **company** comprising both financial and non-financial information.

Appropriation account
The sharing out of partners' profit after net profit has been calculated in the **income statement.**

Asset turnover ratio
A ratio which compares **revenue** to total assets employed.

Assets
Essentially, items owned or leased by a business. Assets may be tangible or intangible, current or non-current. Assets bring economic benefits through either sale (for example, inventory) or use (for example, a car).

Associated company
A company in which 20–50% of the shares are owned by another company or in which another company has a significant influence.

Audit and Assurance Council
This body, created in 2012, advises the FRC board and the **Codes and Standards Committee** on audit and assurance matters.

Auditors
A team of professionally qualified accountants *independent* of a company. Appointed by the **shareholders** on the recommendation of the **directors**, the auditors check and report on the accounts prepared by the directors.

Auditors' report
A statement in a company's **annual report** which states whether the financial statements present a **'true and fair view'** of the company's activities over the previous financial year.

Authorised share capital
The amount of **share capital** that a company is *allowed* to issue to its shareholders.

Average cost (AVCO)
A method of inventory valuation where inventory is valued at the average purchase price (see also **first-in-first-out** and **last-in-first-out**).

Bad debts
Those debts that will definitely not be paid. They are an **expense** in the **income statement** and are written off **trade receivables** in the **statement of financial position.**

Balance off
In **double-entry bookkeeping**, the accounts are balanced off and the figures for **assets** and **liabilities** are carried forward to the next period. In effect, this signals the end of an **accounting period.**

Balance sheet – Alternative name for Statement of Financial Position
A financial statement which is a snapshot of a business at a particular point in time. It records the **assets, liabilities** and **equity** of a business. Assets less liabilities equals equity. Equity is the owners' interest in the business.

Bank overdraft
A business or individual owes the bank money.

Bank reconciliation
The process of reconciling a company's bank account to its bank statement to see if there are any errors.

Batch costing
A number of items of a similar nature are processed and costed together (e.g., baking bread).

Bookkeeping
The preparation of the basic accounts. Monetary transactions are entered into the books of account. A **trial balance** is then extracted, and an **income statement** and a **statement of financial position** are prepared.

Books of Prime Entry
Books such as the **Revenue Day Book** or **Purchases Day Book** where initial transactions are recorded.

Break-even analysis
Break-even analysis involves calculating the point at which a product or service makes neither a profit nor a loss. **Fixed costs** are divided by the contribution per unit giving the **break-even point.**

Break-even point
The point at which a firm makes neither a profit nor a loss. A firm's break-even point can be expressed as: **Revenue** − variable costs − fixed costs = 0.

Budget
A future plan which sets out a business's financial targets.

Called-up share capital
The amount of **issued share capital** that is fully paid up by **shareholders**. For example, a share may be issued for £1.50 and paid in three equal instalments. After two instalments the called-up share capital is £1.

Capital
An alternative to **equity** often used for sole traders, partnerships or private limited companies.

Capital expenditure
A payment to purchase an **asset** with a long life such as **property, plant and equipment**.

Capital expenditure and financial investment
In a **statement of cash flows** prepared under UK accounting standards, cash flows relating to the purchase and sale of **property, plant and equipment** and **investments**.

Capital maintenance concept
A way of determining whether the '**equity**' of a business has improved, deteriorated or stayed the same over a period of time. There is both **financial** and **physical capital maintenance**.

Capital reserves
Reserves not distributable to shareholders as dividends (e.g., the **share premium account** or **revaluation reserve**).

Carriage inwards
The cost of delivering raw materials. Refers to the days when goods were delivered by horse and carriage.

Carriage outwards
The cost of delivering the finished goods. Refers to the days when goods were delivered by horse and carriage.

Carrying costs
Costs such as insurance, obsolescence, interest on borrowed money or clerical/security costs incurred in holding inventory.

Cash and bank
The actual money held by the business either at the business as cash or at the bank.

Cash at bank
Money deposited with a bank.

Cash book
In large businesses, a separate book which records cash and cheque transactions.

Cash budget
This budget records the projected inflows and outflows of cash.

Cash and Cash Equivalent
This is cash at bank and cash held in short-term (say up to 30 days) deposit accounts.

Cash flow statement
Alternative name for the **statement of cash flows** used under UK GAAP. A financial statement which shows the cash inflows and outflows of a business.

Chairman's statement
A statement in a company's **annual report** which provides a personalised overview of the company's performance over the past year. It generally covers strategy, financial performance and future prospects.

Codes and Standards Committee
Established in 2012. It is responsible for advising the FRC board on monitoring an effective framework of UK codes and standards for corporate governance, stewardship, accounting, auditing and assurance and actuarial technical standards. This board is advised by the **Accounting Council**.

Companies Acts
Acts of Parliament which lay down the legal requirements for companies including accounting regulations.

Company
A business enterprise where the **shareholders** have **limited liability**.

Conceptual framework
A coherent and consistent set of accounting principles which underpin the preparation and presentation of financial statements.

Consistency concept
An accounting principle which states similar items should be treated similarly from year to year.

Control accounts
Accounts such as the **revenue control account** or the **purchases control account** that are used to reconcile the balances from the **revenue ledger** and **purchases ledger** to see if there are any errors.

Corporate governance
The system by which companies are directed and controlled. The financial aspects of corporate governance relate principally to internal control and the way in which the board of directors functions and reports to the shareholders on the activities and progress of the company.

Cost of capital
The interest rate at which a business raises funds.

Cost recovery
The process by which costs are recovered into a product or service to form the basis of pricing or inventory valuation.

Cost of sales
Essentially the cost of directly providing the **revenue**.

Costing
Recovering **costs** as a basis for pricing and inventory valuation.

Creative accounting
Using the flexibility within accounting to manage the measurement and presentation of the accounts so that they serve the interests of the preparers.

Credit
An entry on the right-hand side of a **'T' account**. Records principally increases in **liabilities, equity** or **income**. May also record decreases in **assets** or **expenses**.

Creditors
Alternative name for trade payables. Amounts owed to trade suppliers for goods supplied on credit, but not yet paid.

Creditors budget
An alternative name for the **trade payables budget**. This **budget** forecasts the level of future trade payables. It keeps a running balance of the **trade payables** by adding purchases and deducting cash payments.

Creditors collection period

An alternative term for the **trade payables** collection period (sometimes used for sole traders, partnerships and non-listed companies). Measures how long a business takes to pay its **trade payables** by relating the **trade payables** to cost of sales.

Current assets

Those **assets** (e.g., **inventories, trade receivables** and **cash**) that a company uses in its day-to-day operations.

Current liabilities

The liabilities that a business uses in its day-to-day operations (e.g., **trade payables**).

Current purchasing power

A **measurement system** where historical cost is adjusted by general changes in the purchasing power of money (e.g., inflation), often measured using the retail price index (RPI).

Current ratio

A short-term test of liquidity which determines whether short-term **assets** cover short-term **liabilities.**

Day Books

Books of Prime Entry where the initial transactions are recorded.

Debenture

Another name for a **long-term loan**. Debentures may be **secured** or **unsecured loans.**

Debit

An entry on the left-hand side of a **'T' account**. Records principally increases in either **assets** or **expenses.** May also record decreases in **liabilities, equity** or **income.**

Debtors

An alternative term for **trade receivables** sometimes used for sole traders, partnerships or non-listed companies. When there are credit sales, but the customers have not yet paid.

Debtors collection model

An alternative name for the **trade receivables** collection model (for sole traders, partnerships or non-listed companies). A technique for managing **working capital** which seeks to maintain the most efficient level of **trade receivables** for a company. It balances the extra revenue generated by increased **revenue** with the increased costs associated with extra **revenue** (e.g., credit control costs, bad debts and the delay in receiving money).

Debtors collection period
An alternative name for the trade receivables collection period. A ratio which measures how long customers take to pay their debts by relating trade receivables to **revenue**.

Decision-making objective of financial reporting
Providing users, especially shareholders, with financial information so that they can make decisions such as whether to buy or sell shares.

Depreciation
Depreciation attempts to match a proportion of the original cost of the **property, plant and equipment** to the **accounting period** in which the property, plant and equipment were used up as an annual expense.

Direct method of preparing the statement of cash flows
Classifies *operating* cash flows by function or type of activity (e.g., receipts from customers).

Directors
Those responsible for running the business. Accountable to the **shareholders** who, in theory, appoint and dismiss them.

Directors' remuneration report
A statement in an **annual report** in which companies include details of their directors' pay.

Directors' report
A narrative statement in an **annual report**. It supplements the financial information with information considered important for a full appreciation of a company's activities.

Discount allowed
A reduction in the selling price of a good or service allowed by the business to customers for prompt payment. Treated as an **expense**.

Discount received
A reduction in the purchase price of a good or service granted to a business from the supplier for paying promptly. Treated as an **income**.

Discounted cash flow
The future expected cash inflows and outflows of a potential project discounted back to their present value today to see whether or not proposed projects are viable.

Dividend cover
A ratio showing how many times profit available to pay ordinary dividends covers actual dividends.

Dividend yield
A ratio showing how much dividend ordinary shares earn as a proportion of market price.

Dividend
A cash payment to shareholders rewarding them for investing money in a company.

Double-entry bookkeeping
A way of systematically recording the financial transactions of a company so that each transaction is recorded twice.

Doubtful debts
Debts which may or may not be paid. Usually, businesses estimate a certain proportion of their debts as doubtful.

Drawings
Money which a **sole trader** or partner takes out of a business as living expenses. It is, in effect, the owner's salary and is really a withdrawal of capital.

Earnings per share (EPS)
A key ratio by which investors measure the performance of a company.

Efficiency ratios
Ratios which show how efficiently a business uses its assets.

Entity concept
A business has a distinct and separate identity from its owner. This is obvious in the case of a large limited company where **shareholders** own the company and managers manage the company. However, there is also a distinction between a **sole trader's** or **partnership's** personal and business assets.

Equity
Equity represents the owner's interest in the business. In effect, equity is a liability as it is owed by the business to the owner (e.g., **sole trader**, partner or **shareholder**). Equity is the assets of a business less its liabilities to third parties. Equity is accumulated wealth and is increased by profit, but reduced by losses.

Expenses
The day-to-day **costs** incurred in running a business; e.g., telephone, business rates and wages. Expenses are expenses even if goods and services are consumed, but not yet paid. Expenses are, therefore, different from cash paid.

Fair Value
The price that will be received when selling an asset or that is paid to transfer a liability in a market.

Financial accounting

The provision of financial information on a business's financial performance targeted at external users, such as shareholders. It includes not only **double-entry bookkeeping**, but also the preparation and interpretation of the financial accounts.

Financial capital maintenance concept

This concept is primarily concerned with **monetary measurement**, in particular the measurement of the net assets.

Financial Reporting Council (FRC)

The Financial Reporting Council is a supervisory body which ensures that the overall system is working. The FRC supervises a **Codes and Standards Committee**, an Executive Committee and a Conduct Committee. The main accounting functions come under the codes and standards committee in terms of the **Accounting Council** and **Audit and Assurance Council**. In addition, the **Financial Reporting Review Panel** comes under the monitoring committee. These are discussed more fully under the relevant entries.

Financial Reporting Review Panel (FRRP)

The FRRP investigates contentious departures from accounting standards and is part of the UK's standard-setting regime.

Finished goods inventory

The final inventory after the manufacturing process is completed; for example, finished tables. The cost includes materials and other manufacturing costs (e.g., labour and manufacturing overheads).

First-in-first-out (FIFO)

A method of inventory valuation where the inventory bought first is the first to be sold. See also **average cost** and **last-in-first-out**.

Fixed assets

The term for property, plant and equipment sometimes used in sole traders, partnerships and non-listed companies. Infrastructure assets used to run the business long-term and *not* used in day-to-day production. Includes **non-current assets** (e.g., motor vehicles, land and buildings, fixtures and fittings, plant and machinery) and **intangible fixed assets** (e.g., goodwill).

Free Cash Flow

Cash flow from operations after deducting interest, tax preference dividends and ongoing capital expenditure. This, however, excludes strategic capital expenditure and ordinary share dividends.

GAAP (Generally Accepted Accounting Practices)

The body of standards and accounting regulations that make up a complete set of accounting rules and regulations usually for a country. Often referred to as UK GAAP and US GAAP.

Gearing

The relationship between a company's ordinary shareholders' funds and the debt capital.

General reserve

A **revenue reserve** created to deal with general, unspecified contingencies such as inflation.

Going concern concept

The business will continue into the foreseeable future. **Assets, liabilities, incomes** and **expenses** are measured on this basis.

Goodwill

In takeovers, the purchase price less the amount paid for the net assets. It represents the value placed on the earning power of a business over and above its **net asset** value.

Gross profit

Revenue less **cost of sales.**

Gross profit ratio

This ratio relates the profit earned through trading to **revenue.**

Historical cost

A **measurement system** where monetary amounts are recorded at the date of original transaction.

Historical cost convention

The amount recorded in the accounts will be the *original* amount paid for a good or service.

Horizontal analysis

A form of ratio analysis which compares the figures in the accounts across time. It is used to investigate trends in the data.

Impression management

Managers try to influence the financial reporting process in their own favour. Includes both **creative accounting** and **narrative enhancement.**

Income

The revenue earned by a business; e.g., **revenue.** Income is income, even if goods and services have been delivered but customers have yet to pay. Income thus differs from cash received.

Income receivable
Receivable by the business from a third party; e.g., **dividends** receivable (from companies) or interest receivable (from the bank).

Income statement
A financial statement which records the **income** and **expenses** of a business over the **accounting period**, normally a year. **Income** less **expenses** equals **profit**. By contrast, where expenses are greater than income, losses will occur. The balance from the income statement is transferred annually to the **statement of financial position** where it becomes part of **revenue reserves**. The term **income statement** is used for a listed company.

Indirect costs
Those costs *not* directly identifiable *nor* attributable to a product or service; e.g., administrative, and selling and distribution costs. These costs are totalled and then recovered indirectly into the product or service. Also called **indirect overheads** or **period costs**.

Indirect method of preparing a statement of cash flows
Operating cash flow is derived from the **income statement** and **statement of financial position** and not classified directly by function (such as receipts from **revenue**).

Indirect overheads
See **indirect costs**.

Intangible assets
Non-current assets one cannot touch, unlike **tangible non-current assets** (such as land and buildings). Most common in **companies**.

Interest cover
A ratio showing the amount of profit available to cover the **interest payable** on long-term borrowings.

Interest payable
An expense related especially to bank loans. When paid becomes interest paid.

International Accounting Standards Board (IASB)
An international body founded in 1973 to work for the improvement and harmonisation of accounting standards worldwide. Originally called the International Accounting Standards Committee.

International Financial Reporting Standards (IFRS)
The accounting standards produced by the **International Accounting Standards Board**. The standards are now widely used for listed companies in, for example, Europe and Australia.

Interpretation of accounts
The evaluation of financial information, principally from the **income statement** and **statement of financial position**, so as to make judgements about profitability, efficiency, liquidity, gearing, cash flow, and the success of a financial investment. Sometimes called **ratio analysis.**

Inventory
Goods purchased and awaiting use (**raw materials**) or produced and awaiting sale (**finished goods**). Measures the time it takes for inventory to move through the business.

Inventory turnover ratio
An alternative to **stock turnover ratio** sometimes used for sole traders, partnerships and non-listed companies.

Investment centre
In **responsibility accounting**, where a manager is held responsible for the revenues, costs (i.e., profits) and investment.

Investment ratios
Measures the returns to the shareholder (**dividend yield, earnings per share** and **price/earnings ratio**) or the ability of a company to sustain its dividend or interest payments (**dividend cover** and **interest cover**).

Investments
Assets such as stocks and **shares.**

Issued share capital
The share capital *actually* issued by a **company.**

Last-in-first-out (LIFO)
A method of inventory valuation where the last inventory purchased is the first sold. See also **average cost** and **first-in-first-out.**

Leasing
Where the **assets** are owned by a third party which the business pays to use them.

Liabilities
Amounts the business owes (e.g., trade payables, bank loan). They can be short-term or long-term, third-party liabilities or equity (i.e., liability owed by the business to the owner).

Limited liability
Shareholders are only liable to lose the amount of money they initially invested.

Limiting factor
Where production is constrained by a particular shortage of a key element; e.g., a restricted number of labour hours.

Liquidity ratios
Ratios derived from the **statement of financial position** that measure how easily a firm can pay its debts.

Listed company
A **company** quoted on a stock exchange.

Loan capital
Money loaned to a company by third parties who do not own the company and are entitled to interest *not* dividends.

Loans
Amounts borrowed from third parties, such as a bank.

Long-term creditors
An alternative term for non-current liabilities sometimes used in sole traders, partnerships or non-listed companies accounts.

Long-term loan
A loan, such as a bank loan, not repayable within a year. Sometimes called a **debenture**.

Management accounting
The provision of both financial and non-financial information to managers for **cost accounting, planning, control and performance, and decision making**. It is thus concerned with the internal accounting of a business.

Market value
The value shares fetch on the open market; i.e., their trading value. This may differ significantly from their **nominal value**.

Matching concept
Recognises **income** and **expenses** when accrued (i.e., earned or incurred) rather than when money is received or paid. Income is matched with any associated expenses to determine the appropriate profit or loss. Also known as the accruals concept.

Measurement systems
The processes by which the monetary amounts of items in the financial statements are determined. Such systems are fundamental to the determination of **profit** and to the measurement

of **net assets**. There are six major measurement systems: **fair value, historical cost, current purchasing power, replacement cost, realisable value** and **present value.**

Monetary measurement convention
Only items measurable in financial terms (for example, pounds or dollars) are included in the accounts. Atmospheric pollution is thus excluded, as it has no measurable financial value.

Narrative enhancement
Managers use the narrative parts of the **annual report** to convey a more favourable impression of performance than is actually warranted; e.g., by omitting key data or stressing certain elements.

Net assets
Total assets less **non-current liabilities** and **current liabilities.**

Net book value
The cost of **tangible property, plant and equipment** less accumulated depreciation.

Net cash flow from operating activities
In a **statement of cash flows,** cash flows from the normal trading activities of a business when prepared using UK GAAP.

Net present value
A **capital investment appraisal** technique which discounts future expected cash flows to today's monetary values using an appropriate cost of capital.

Net profit
Revenue less **cost of sales** less **expenses.**

Net profit ratio
A ratio which relates **profit** after **expenses** (i.e., **net profit**) to **revenue.**

Net realisable value
See **Realisable value.**

Nominal value
The face value of the shares when originally issued.

Non-current assets
The term which covers both tangible and intangible long-term assets such as **property, plant and equipment** and **goodwill.**

Non-current liabilities
Amounts borrowed from third parties and repayable after a year. The most common are **long-term loans.**

Normal standards

In **standard costing**, standards which a business usually attains.

Note on historical cost profits and losses

A statement in the **annual report** which records any differences caused by departures from the **historical cost convention** (e.g., revaluation and subsequent depreciation of **property, plant** and **equipment**).

Notes to the accounts

In a company's **annual report**, they provide additional information about items in the accounts.

Objective of financial statements

To provide information about the financial position, performance and changes in financial position of an enterprise useful to a wide range of **users** in making decisions.

Operating and financial review

A statement in a company's **annual report**, originally developed by the United Kingdom's Accounting Standards Board, which enables companies to provide a formalised, structured and narrative explanation of financial performance. It has two parts. First, the operating review covers items such as a company's operating results, profit and dividends. Second, the financial review discusses items such as capital structure and treasury policy. It has been subject to much political controversy.

Operating cash flow

In a **statement of cash flows**, operating profit adjusted for movements in **working capital** and non-cash flow items such as **depreciation**.

Operating profit

Net profit before taxation adjusted for interest paid and interest received.

Ordinary (equity) share capital

Share capital issued to the **shareholders** who own the company and are entitled to ordinary **dividends**.

Overheads

See **indirect costs**.

Partnership

Business enterprises run by more than one person, whose liability is normally unlimited.

Partnership capital accounts

The long-term equity invested into a partnership by the individual partners.

Partnership current accounts
The partners' share of the profits of the business. The main elements are the opening balances, salaries, profit for year, drawings and closing balances.

Patents
An **intangible asset** resulting from expenditure to protect rights to an invention.

Periodicity convention
Accounts are prepared for a set period of time; i.e., an accounting period.

Physical capital maintenance concept
This concept is concerned with maintaining the physical productive capacity (i.e., operating capacity) of the business.

Preference share capital
Share capital issued to **shareholders** who are *not* owners of the company and who are entitled to fixed dividends.

Prepayment
The amount paid in advance to the suppliers of services; e.g., prepaid insurance.

Price/earnings ratio
A ratio which measures **earnings per share** against share price.

Prime cost
Direct materials, direct labour and direct expenses totalled.

Private limited company
A company where trading in shares is restricted.

Profit
Revenue less purchases and **expenses**.

Profit and loss account
A financial statement which records the **income** and **expenses** of a business over the **accounting period**, normally a year. **Income** less **expenses** equals **profit**. By contrast, where expenses are greater than income, losses will occur. The balance from the profit and loss account (income statement) is transferred annually to the **statement of financial position** where it becomes part of **revenue reserves**. The term **income statement** is used for a listed company, but profit and loss account is an alternative term for sole traders, partnerships and non-listed companies.

Profitability ratios
They establish how profitably a business is performing.

Property, plant and equipment
Infrastructure assets used to run the business long-term and *not* used in day-to-day production. Includes **tangible non-current assets** (e.g., motor vehicles, land and buildings, fixtures and fittings, plant and machinery) and **intangible assets** (e.g., **goodwill**).

Provision for doubtful debts
Those debts a business is dubious of collecting. Deducted from **trade receivables** in the **statement of financial position.** Only *increases* or *decreases* in the provision are entered in the **income statement.**

Prudence concept
Income and **profit** should only be recorded in the books when an inflow of cash is certain. By contrast, any **liabilities** should be provided as soon as they are recognised, even though the amount may be uncertain. Introduces an element of caution into accounting.

Public limited company
A **company** where shares are bought and sold by the general public.

Purchases day book
Accounts book where the purchases are initially entered.

Purchases ledger
A ledger account which records individual **trade payables** accounts.

Purchases ledger control account
Account where the balances from the **purchases ledger** are reconciled.

Quick ratio
Measures extreme short-term liquidity, i.e., **current assets** (excluding **inventory**) against **current liabilities.** Sometimes called the 'acid test ratio'.

Ratio analysis
See **interpretation of accounts.**

Raw material inventory
Inventory purchased and ready for use; e.g., a carpenter with wood awaiting manufacture into tables.

Realisable value
A **measurement system** where assets are valued at what they would fetch in an orderly sale. Also known as net realisable value.

Reconciliation of movements in shareholders' funds
A financial statement in the **annual report** which highlights major changes to the wealth of shareholders such as profit (or loss) for the year, annual dividends and new share capital.

Reducing balance method of depreciation
A set percentage of **depreciation** is written off the **net book value** of **property, plant and equipment** every year.

Regulatory framework
The set of rules and regulations which govern accounting practice, mainly prescribed by government and the accounting standard-setting bodies.

Relevance
Relevant information affects **users'** economic decisions. Relevance is a prerequisite of usefulness and, for example, helps to predict future events or to confirm or correct past events.

Reliability
Reliable information is free from material error and is unbiased.

Replacement cost
A **measurement system** where assets are valued at the amounts needed to replace them with an equivalent asset.

Reserves
The accumulated profits (**revenue reserves**) or capital gains (**capital reserves**) to shareholders.

Retained profits
The **profit** a company has not distributed via **dividends**. An alternative to external financing. In effect, the business finances itself from its past successes.

Return on capital employed
A ratio looking at how effectively a company uses its capital (**equity**). It compares **net profit** to capital employed. The most common definition measures **profit** before tax and **debenture** interest against long-term capital (i.e., **ordinary share capital** and **reserves, preference share capital** and **long-term loans**).

Return on investment
A ratio often used in **performance evaluation** which relates income to investment.

Return on sales
A ratio often used in **performance evaluation** which relates operating profit to **revenue**. Can be called 'Return on revenue'.

Returns on investments and servicing of finance
In a **cash flow statement prepared under UK GAAP**, cash received from investments or paid on loans.

Returns inwards book
Accounts book where the initial returns inwards transactions are initially recorded.

Returns outwards book
Accounts book where the initial returns outwards transactions are initially recorded.

Revaluation reserve
A **capital reserve** created when **property, plant and equipment** are revalued to more than the original amount for which they were purchased. The revaluation is a gain to the shareholders.

Revenue
Income earned from selling goods and other activities.

Revenue day book
Book accounts where the initial revenue transactions are initially entered.

Revenue control account
Accounts book where the balances from the revenue (sales) ledger are reconciled.

Revenue expenditure
Payments for a current year's good or service such as purchases for resale or telephone expenses.

Revenue reserves
Reserves potentially distributable to shareholders as **dividends**; e.g., the **retained earnings, general reserve.**

Review of operations
In a company's **annual report,** a narrative where the chief executive reviews the individual business operations.

Rights issue
Current **shareholders** are given the right to subscribe to new shares in proportion to their current holdings.

Sale and leaseback
Companies sell their **tangible non-current assets** to a third party and then lease them back.

Sales
Income earned from selling goods. Also known as **revenue.**

Sales control account
Alternative name for **revenue control account.**

Secured loans
Loans guaranteed (i.e., secured) by the **assets** of the company.

Securities Exchange Commission (SEC)
An independent regulatory institution in the US with quasi-judicial powers. US **listed companies** must file a detailed annual form, called the 10–K, with the SEC.

Share capital
The total capital of the business is divided into shares. Literally a 'share' in the capital of the business.

Share options
Directors or employees are allowed to buy shares at a set price. They can then sell them for a higher price at a future date if the share price rises.

Share premium account
A **capital reserve** created when new shares are issued for more than their **nominal value**. For example, for shares issued for £150,000 with a nominal value of £100,000, the share premium account is £50,000.

Shareholders
The owners of the company who provide share capital by way of shares.

Social and environmental accounting statement
A voluntary statement produced by companies in their **annual report** dealing with social and environmental issues such as sustainable development.

Sole trader
A business enterprise run by a sole owner whose liability is unlimited.

Statement of cash flows
A financial statement which shows the cash inflows and outflows of a business.

Statement of changes in equity
An alternative term to the **statement of total recognised gains and losses** and **reconciliation of movements in shareholders' funds** as produced by a listed company.

Statement of directors' responsibilities for the financial statements
A statement in a company's **annual report** where directors spell out their responsibilities including (i) keeping proper accounting records; (ii) preparing financial statements in accordance with the Companies Act 1985; (iii) applying appropriate accounting policies; and (iv) following all applicable accounting standards.

Statement of financial position
A financial statement which is a snapshot of a business at a particular point in time. It records the **assets, liabilities** and **equity** of a business. Assets less liabilities equals equity. **Equity** is the owners' interest in the business.

Statement of total recognised gains and losses (STRGL)
A financial statement in the **annual report** which attempts to highlight all shareholder gains and losses and not just those from trading. The STRGL begins with the **profit** from the **income statement** and then adjusts for *non-trading gains and losses*.

Stewardship
Making individuals accountable for **assets** and **liabilities**. Stewardship focuses on the physical monitoring of assets and the prevention of loss and fraud rather than evaluating how efficiently the assets are used.

Stock
An alternative to inventory often used for sole traders, partnerships or private limited companies. Goods purchased and awaiting use (**raw materials**) or produced and awaiting sale (**finished goods**).

Stock turnover ratio
An alternative to **inventory turnover ratio** sometimes used for sole traders, partnerships and non-listed companies. Measures the time taken for inventory to move through a business.

Straight line method of depreciation
The same amount of **depreciation** is written off the **tangible non-current assets** every year.

Subsidiary company
A **company** where more than half of the shares are owned by another company or which is effectively controlled by another company, or is a subsidiary of a subsidiary.

SWOT analysis
A strategic way of critically assessing a business's strengths and weaknesses, opportunities and threats.

'T' account (ledger account)
Each page of each book of account has a **debit** side (left-hand side) and a **credit** side (right-hand side). This division of the page is called a 'T' account.

'T' Account (ledger account)

Assets and expenses on the left-hand side DEBIT	Incomes, liabilities and equity on the right-hand side CREDIT

Tangible non-current assets
Non-current assets one can touch (e.g., land and buildings, plant and machinery, motor vehicles, fixtures and fittings). Tangible non-current assets are known as **property, plant and equipment** in **listed companies**.

Third-party liabilities
Amounts owing to third parties. They can be short-term (e.g., **trade payables**, bank overdraft) or long-term (e.g., a bank loan).

Total shareholders' funds
The **share capital** and **reserves** owned by both the ordinary and preference shareholders.

Trade payables
Amounts owed to trade suppliers for goods supplied on credit, but not yet paid.

Trade payables budget
An alternative term for creditors budget. This **budget** forecasts the level of future trade payables. It keeps a running balance of trade payables by adding purchases and deducting cash payments.

Trade payables collection period
An alternative term for creditors collection period. This budget forecasts the level of future trade payables

Trade receivables
An alternative term for debtors. When sales are made on credit, but the customers have not yet paid.

Trade receivables age schedule
An alternative name for debtors age schedule. A credit control technique which profiles the age of the debts and allow old debts to be quickly identified.

Trade receivables budget
An alternative name for debtors budget. This **budget** forecasts the level of future trade receivables. It keeps a running balance of trade receivables by adding **revenue** and deducting cash received.

Trade receivables collection model
A technique for managing **working capital** which seeks to maintain the most efficient level of **trade receivables** for a company. It balances the extra revenue generated by increased **revenue** with the increased costs associated with extra **revenue** (e.g., credit control costs, bad debts and the delay in receiving money).

Trade receivables collection period
A ratio which measures how long customers take to pay their debts by relating trade receivables to **revenue**.

Trading and profit and loss account
The formal name for the full income statement prepared by a **sole trader**.

Trading and profit and loss and appropriation account
The formal name for the income statement prepared by a **company** or a **partnership**.

Trial balance
A listing of debit and credit balances to check the correctness of the **double-entry bookkeeping** system.

True and fair view
Difficult to define but, essentially, a set of financial statements which faithfully, accurately and truly reflect the underlying economic transactions of the organisation.

Unsecured loans
Loans which are not guaranteed (i.e., secured) by a company's **assets**.

Urgent Issues Task Force (UITF)
The UITF is part of the UK's standard-setting process. It makes recommendations to curb undesirable interpretations of existing accounting standards or prevent accounting practices which the **Accounting Standards Council** considers undesirable.

Users
Those with an interest in using accounting information, such as shareholders, lenders, suppliers and other trade payables, customers, government, the public, management and employees.

Vertical analysis
In **ratio analysis**, vertical analysis is where key figures in the accounts (such as **revenue**, **statement of financial position** totals) are set to 100%.

Work-in-progress inventory
Partially completed inventory (sometimes called stock-in-process) which is neither **raw materials** nor **finished goods**.

Working capital
Current assets less **current liabilities** (in effect, the operating capital of a business).

Appendix: Answers

Chapter 1: Discussion *Answers*

The answers provide some outline points for discussion.

A1 Accounting is important because it is the language of business and provides a means of effective and understandable business communication. The general terminology of business is thus accounting-driven. Concepts such as profit and cash flow are accounting terms. In addition, accounting provides the backbone of a business's information system. It provides figures for performance measurement, for monitoring, planning and control and gives an infrastructure for decision making. It enables businesses to answer key questions about past business performance and future business policy.

A3 There are many differences. The six listed below will do for starters!

(a) Financial accounting is designed to provide information on a business's recent financial performance and is targeted at external users such as shareholders. However, the information is also often used by managers. By contrast, management accounting is much more internally focused and is used solely by managers.

(b) Financial accounting operates within a regulatory framework set out by accounting standards and the Companies Acts. There is no such framework for management accounting.

(c) The main work of financial accounting is preparing financial statements such as the statement of financial position and income statement. By contrast, management accounting uses a wider range of techniques for planning, control and performance, and for decision making.

(d) Financial accounting is based upon double-entry bookkeeping, while management accounting is not.

(e) Financial accounting looks backwards, while management accounting is forward looking.

(f) The end product of financial accounting is a standardised set of financial statements. By contrast, management accounting is very varied. Its output depends on the needs of its users.

Chapter 2: Discussion *Answers*

The answers provide some outline points for discussion.

A1 Financial accounting is essentially the provision of financial information to users for decision making. More formally:

> *'The objective of general purpose financial reporting is to provide financial information about the reporting entity that is useful to existing and potential investors, lenders and*

> ***other creditors in making decisions about providing resources to the entity. Those decisions involve buying, selling or holding equity and debt instruments, and providing or settling loans and other forms of credit.'***
>
> International Accounting Standards Board (2010), *The Conceptual Framework for Financial Reporting*.

In other words, financial accounting provides financial information (such as assets, liabilities, equity, expenses and income) to users (such as shareholders). This is useful because they can assess how well the managers run the company. On the basis of their assessment of the stewardship of management, they can make business decisions; for example, shareholders can decide whether or not to keep or sell their shares. Financial accounting is central to any understanding of business. It provides the basic language for assessing a business's performance. Unless we understand financial accounting, it is difficult to see how we can truly understand business. It would be like trying to drive a car without taking driving lessons. For non-specialists, a knowledge of financial accounting will help them to operate effectively in a business world.

A5 True or false?

(a) *True.* Assets show what a business owns, while liabilities show what a business owes.

(b) *False.* The profit and loss account does show income earned and expenses incurred. However, net assets are the assets less liabilities which are shown in the statement of financial position. Income less expenses equals profit.

(c) *False.* Stewardship used to be the main objective up until about the 1960s. However, now decision making is generally recognised as the main objective.

(d) *True.* This is because of the entity concept where the business is separate from the owner. Therefore, business assets, liabilities, income and expenses must be separated from private ones.

(e) *True.* This is because the matching concept seeks to match income and expenses to the accounting period in which they arise. There is thus accounting symmetry. By contrast, prudence dictates that although income should be matched to the year in which it is earned; any liabilities should be taken as soon as they are recognised. This means that if it is known that a liability would be incurred, say, in three years' time, it would be included in the current accounting period. There is thus accounting asymmetry. The two principles thus clash.

Chapter 2: Numerical *Answers*

A1 Sharon Taylor

Income Statement (Profit and Loss Account)

	£	£
Revenue		8,000
Less *Expenses*		
General expenses	4,000	
Trading expenses	3,000	7,000
Net Profit		1,000

A1 Sharon Taylor *(continued)*

Statement of Financial Position (Balance Sheet)

	£
Assets	15,000
Liabilities	(3,000)
Net Assets	12,000

EQUITY

	£
Opening equity	11,000
Add Profit	1,000
Closing equity	12,000

Statement of Cash Flows

	£
Cash inflows	10,000
Cash outflows	(12,000)
Net cash outflow	(2,000)

Chapter 3: Discussion *Answers*

The answers provide some outline points for discussion.

A1 Double-entry bookkeeping is the essential underpinning of accounting. It provides an efficient mechanism by which organisations can record their financial transactions. For instance, large companies, such as Tesco or British Petroleum, may have millions of transactions per year. Double-entry bookkeeping provides a useful way of consolidating these. In a sense, therefore, the double-entry process permits organisations to make order from chaos. Double-entry bookkeeping enables the preparation of a trial balance. This, in turn, permits the construction of the income statement and the statement of financial position.

A6 True or false?

(a) *True.*
(b) *False.* We credit the revenue account with revenue, but debit the purchases account with purchases.
(c) *True.*
(d) *True.*
(e) *False.* Revenue and equity are credits, but rent paid is a debit.

Chapter 3: Numerical *Answers*

A1 (i) Assets = Liabilities — £25,000 = £25,000

(ii) Assets = Liabilities + Equity — £25,000 = £15,000 + £10,000

(iii) Assets = Liabilities + Equity + Profit — £40,000 = £15,000 + £10,000 + £15,000

(iv) Assets = Liabilities + Equity + (Income − Expenses) — £40,000 = £15,000 + £10,000 + (£60,000 − £45,000)

(v) Assets + Expenses = Liabilities + Equity + Income — £40,000 + £45,000 = £15,000 + £10,000 + £60,000

(vi)

'T'Account	
Assets + Expenses	Liabilities + Equity + Income

'T'Account	
£40,000 + £45,000 = £85,000	£15,000 + £10,000 + £60,000 = £85,000

A2

	Account	*Debit*	*Account*	*Credit*
(a)	Wages	Increases an expense	Bank	Decreases an asset
(b)	Bank	Increases an asset	Equity	Increases equity
(c)	Hotel	Increases an asset	Bank	Decreases an asset
(d)	Electricity	Increases an expense	Bank	Decreases an asset
(e)	Bank	Increases an asset	Revenue	Increases income
(f)	Purchases	Increases an expense	A. Taylor (trade payable)	Increases a liability

A3 A. Bird

(i) Ledger accounts

Revenue

	£		£
		6 June Thrush	4,000
		6 June Raven	7,000
7 June Bal. c/f	17,000	6 June Starling	6,000
	17,000		17,000
		7 June Bal. b/f	17,000

Purchases

	£		£
1 June Robin	8,000		
1 June Falcon	6,000		
1 June Sparrow	5,000	*7 June Bal. c/f*	19,000
	19,000		19,000
7 June Bal. b/f	19,000		

Revenue returns

	£		£
7 June Starling	1,000	*7 June Bal. c/f*	1,000
	1,000		1,000
7 June Bal. b/f	1,000		

Purchases returns

	£		£
		4 June Robin	1,000
7 June Bal. c/f	3,000	4 June Falcon	2,000
	3,000		3,000
		7 June Bal. b/f	3,000

A3 A. Bird (*continued*)

Thrush trade receivable

	£		£
6 June Revenue	4,000	*7 June Bal. c/f*	*4,000*
	4,000		*4,000*
8 June Bal. b/f	*4,000*		

Raven trade receivable

	£		£
6 June Revenue	7,000	*7 June Bal. c/f*	*7,000*
	7,000		*7,000*
8 June Bal. b/f	*7,000*		

Starling trade receivable

	£		£
6 June Revenue	6,000	7 June Sales Rets.	1,000
		7 June Bal. c/f	*5,000*
	6,000		*6,000*
8 June Bal. b/f	*5,000*		

Robin trade receivable

	£		£
4 June Purchases Rets.	1,000	1 June Purchases	8,000
7 June Bal. c/f	*7,000*		
	8,000		*8,000*
		8 June Bal. b/f	*7,000*

Falcon trade payable

	£		£
4 June Purchases Rets.	2,000	1 June Purchases	6,000
7 June Bal. c/f	*4,000*		
	6,000		*6,000*
		8 June Bal. b/f	*4,000*

Sparrow trade payable

	£		£
7 June Bal. c/f	*5,000*	1 June Purchases	5,000
	5,000		*5,000*
		8 June Bal. b/f	*5,000*

Note. To aid understanding the balancing off process is italicised.

A6 Katherine Jones

(i) Ledger accounts

Equity

	£		£
7 July Bal. c/f	*195,000*	1 July Bank	195,000
	195,000		*195,000*
		8 July Bal. b/f	*195,000*

Bank

	£		£
1 July Equity	195,000	2 July Premises	75,000
7 July Edwards	5,000	2 July Office equipment	9,000
7 July Smith	4,500		
7 July Patel	3,500	2 July Purchases	7,000
		5 July Wages	4,000
		5 July Electricity	2,000
		5 July Telephone	1,000
		7 July Johnston	1,250
		7 July Singh	500
		7 July Bal. c/f	*108,250*
	208,000		*208,000*
8 July Bal. b/f	*108,250*		

Revenue

	£		£
		3 July Edwards	10,000
		3 July Smith	9,000
7 July Bal. c/f	*26,000*	3 July Patel	7,000
	26,000		*26,000*
		7 July Bal. b/f	*26,000*

Purchases

	£		£
2 July Bank	7,000		
2 July Johnston	3,000		
2 July Singh	1,000	*7 July Bal. c/f*	*11,000*
	11,000		*11,000*
7 July Bal. b/f	*11,000*		

A6 Katherine Jones (*continued*)

Telephone

	£		£
5 July Bank	1,000	*7 July Bal. c/f*	1,000
	1,000		1,000
7 July Bal. b/f	1,000		

Purchases returns

	£		£
7 July Bal. c/f	500	4 July Johnston	500
	500		500
		7 July Bal. b/f	500

Electricity

	£		£
5 July Bank	2,000	*7 July Bal. c/f*	2,000
	2,000		2,000
7 July Bal. b/f	2,000		

Wages

	£		£
5 July Bank	4,000	*7 July Bal. c/f*	4,000
	4,000		4,000
7 July Bal. b/f	4,000		

Premises

	£		£
2 July Bank	75,000	*7 July Bal. c/f*	75,000
	75,000		75,000
8 July Bal. b/f	75,000		

Office equipment

	£		£
2 July Bank	9,000	*7 July Bal. c/f*	9,000
	9,000		9,000
8 July Bal. b/f	9,000		

Edwards (trade receivable)

	£		£
3 July Revenue	10,000	7 July Bank	5,000
		7 July Bal. c/f	5,000
	10,000		10,000
8 July Bal. b/f	5,000		

Smith (trade receivable)

	£		£
3 July Revenue	9,000	7 July Bank	4,500
		7 July Bal. c/f	4,500
	9,000		9,000
8 July Bal. b/f	4,500		

Patel (trade receivable)

	£		£
3 July Revenue	7,000	7 July Bank	3,500
		7 July Bal. c/f	3,500
	7,000		7,000
8 July Bal. b/f	3,500		

Johnston (trade payable)

	£		£
4 July Purchases Rets.	500	2 July Purchases	3,000
7 July Bank	1,250		
7 July Bal. c/f	1,250		
	3,000		3,000
		8 July Bal. b/f	1,250

Singh (trade payable)

	£		£
7 July Bank	500	2 July Purchases	1,000
7 July Bal. c/f	500		
	1,000		1,000
		8 July Bal. b/f	500

A6 Katherine Jones *(continued)*

(ii) Trial balance

Katherine Jones
Trial Balance as at 7 July

	£	£
Equity		195,000
Bank	108,250	
Revenue		26,000
Purchases	11,000	
Purchases returns		500
Telephone	1,000	
Electricity	2,000	
Wages	4,000	
Premises	75,000	
Office equipment	9,000	
Edwards (trade receivable)	5,000	
Smith (trade receivable)	4,500	
Patel (trade receivable)	3,500	
Johnston (trade payable)		1,250
Singh (trade payable)		500
	223,250	223,250

A8 Jay Shah

Jay Shah
Trial Balance as at 31 December

	Debit £	Credit £	Type
Equity		45,300	Equity
Motor car	3,000		Asset
Building	70,000		Asset
Office furniture	400		Asset
A. Smith (trade receivable)	250		Asset
J. Andrews (trade payable)		350	Liability
T. Williams (trade payable)		550	Liability
G. Woolley (trade receivable)	150		Asset
Purchases returns		500	Income*
Bank	3,600		Asset
Electricity	1,400		Expense
Business rates	1,800		Expense
Rent	1,600		Expense
Wages	3,500		Expense
Long-term loan		9,000	Liability
Revenue		100,000	Income
Purchases	70,000		Expense
	155,700	155,700	

*An income because it reduces the expense of purchases.

A10 Rajiv Sharma

Rajiv Sharma
Trial Balance as at 31 December

	Debit	Credit
	£	£
Shop	55,000	
Machinery	45,000	
Car	10,000	
Revenue		135,000
Purchases	80,000	
Opening inventory	15,000	
Trade receivables	12,000	
Trade payables		8,000
Long-term loan		16,000
General expenses	300	
Telephone	400	
Light and heat	300	
Repairs	400	
Equity		59,400
	218,400	218,400

A13 Norton Limited

(a) Day books

Purchases Day Book

		£
May 1	Robin	4,000
May 1	Sparrow	6,000
May 1	Hare	10,000
May 31	To Purchases Account, General Ledger	20,000

Revenue Day Book

		£
May 10	Fox	5,000
May 10	Rabbit	6,000
May 10	Hare	7,000
May 31	To Revenue Account, General Ledger	18,000

Purchases Returns Day Book

		£
May 6	Robin	2,000
May 6	Sparrow	1,000
May 30	To Purchases Returns Account, General Ledger	3,000

Revenue Returns Day Book

		£
May 12	Fox	1,500
May 12	Rabbit	800
May 30	To Revenue Returns Account, General Ledger	2,300

A13 Norton Limited *(continued)*

(b) Ledgers

Purchases Ledger

Robin

		£		£
May 6	Purchases Returns Day Book	2,000	May 1 Purchases Day Book	4,000
May 18	Cash Book	1,500		
May 31	Bal c/f	500		
		4,000		4,000
			June 1 Bal b/f	500

Sparrow

		£		£
May 6	Purchases Returns Day Book	1,000	May 1 Purchases Day Book	6,000
May 18	Cash Book	2,500		
May 31	Bal c/f	2,500		
		6,000		6,000
			June 1 Bal b/f	2,500

Hare

		£		£
May 18	Cash Book	8,000	May 1 Purchases Day Book	10,000
May 31	Bal c/f	2,000		
		10,000		10,000
			June 1 Bal b/f	2,000

Revenue Ledger

Fox

		£		£
May 6	Revenue Day Book	5,000	May 12 Revenue Returns Day Book	1,500
			May 25 Cash Book	3,000
			May 31 Bal c/f	500
		5,000		5,000
June 1 Bal b/f		500		

Rabbit

		£		£
May 6	Revenue Day Book	6,000	May 12 Revenue Returns Day Book	800
			May 25 Cash Book	2,500
			May 31 Bal c/f	2,700
		6,000		6,000
June 1 Bal b/f		2,700		

A13 **Norton Limited** (*continued*)

Hare

		£		£
May 6	Revenue Day Book	7,000	May 25 Cash Book	6,000
			May 30 Bal c/f	1,000
		7,000		7,000
June 1 Bal b/f		1,000		

Balances from Purchases and Revenue Ledgers

Purchases Ledger	£	Revenue Ledger	£
Robin	500	Fox	500
Sparrow	2,500	Rabbit	2,700
Hare	2,000	Hare	1,000
	5,000 cr		4,200 dr

General Ledger Account

Purchases Account

	£		£
May 31 Purchases Day Book	20,000	May 31 Bal c/f	20,000
	20,000		20,000
June 1 Bal b/f	20,000		

Revenue Account

	£		£
May 31 Bal c/f	18,000	May 31 Revenue Day Book	18,000
	18,000		18,000
		June 1 Bal b/f	18,000

Revenue Returns Account

	£		£
May 31 Revenue Returns Day Book	2,300	May 31 Bal c/f	2,300
	2,300		2,300
June 1 Bal b/f	2,300		

Purchases Returns Account

	£		£
May 31 Bal c/f	3,000	May 31 Purchases Returns Day Book	3,000
	3,000		3,000
		June 1 Bal b/f	3,000

A13 Norton Limited (*continued*)

Cash Book

		£			£
May 25	Fox	3,000	May 18	Robin	1,500
May 25	Rabbit	2,500	May 18	Sparrow	2,500
May 25	Hare	6,000	May 18	Hare	8,000
May 31	Bal c/f	500			
		12,000			12,000
			June 1 Bal b/f		500

Norton Limited Trial Balance as at 31 May 2013

	£	£
Purchases Ledger (Trade payables)		5,000
Revenue Ledger (Trade receivables)	4,200	
Revenue Returns	2,300	
Purchases Returns		3,000
Purchases account	20,000	
Revenue account		18,000
Cash book		500
	26,500	26,500

A14 Delaware Ltd

Revenue Ledger Control Account

	£		£
Opening trade receivables	96,300	Revenue Returns	2,000
Revenue	70,700	Cash received	50,000
		Closing trade receivables	118,000
	167,000		170,000

Purchases Ledger Control Account

	£		£
Purchases Returns	1,500	Opening trade payables	71,600
Cash paid	40,500	Purchases	30,300
Closing trade payables	60,000		
	102,000		101,900

We can, therefore, see that neither the revenue ledger control account nor the purchases ledger control account balance. The revenue ledger control account is £3,000 out while the purchases ledger control account is only £100 out. Delaware needs to investigate and correct these errors.

Chapter 4: Discussion *Answers*

The answers provide some outline points for discussion.

A1 The income statement is used by a variety of users for a variety of purposes. Sole traders and partnerships use it to determine how well they are doing. They will want to know if the business is making a profit. This will enable them to make decisions such as how much they should take by way of salary (commonly called drawings). Similarly, the tax authorities will use the income statement as a starting point to calculate the tax that these businesses owe the government.

For the shareholders of a limited company, profit enables them to assess the performance of the company's management. Shareholders can then make decisions about their investments. Company directors, on the other hand, may use profits to work out the dividends payable to shareholders, or to calculate their own profit-related bonuses. In short, profit has multiple uses.

A5 True or false?

(a) *False*. Profit is income earned less expenses incurred.
(b) *True*.
(c) *False*. Revenue returns are returns by customers.
(d) *True*.
(e) *True*.

Chapter 4: Numerical *Answers*

A1 Joan Smith

Joan Smith
Income Statement for the Year Ended 31 December 2013

	£	£
Revenue		100,000
Less *Cost of Sales*		
Opening inventory	10,000	
Add Purchases	60,000	
	70,000	
Less Closing inventory	5,000	65,000
Gross Profit		35,000
Less *Expenses*		
General expenses	10,000	
Other expenses	8,000	18,000
Net Profit		17,000

A2 Dale Reynolds

Dale Reynolds
Trading Account Section of Income Statement for the Year Ended 31 December 2013

	£	£	£
Revenue			50,000
Less Sales returns			1,000
			49,000
Less *Cost of Sales*			
Opening inventory		5,000	
Add Purchases	25,000		
Less Purchases returns	2,000		
	23,000		
Add Carriage inwards	1,000	24,000	
		29,000	
Less Closing inventory		8,000	21,000
Gross Profit			28,000

A5 Good, Bad and Ugly

(i) Good

	Mark-up		Gross Margin
	%	£	%
Revenue	125	375,000	100
Cost of Sales	100	300,000	80
Gross Profit	25	75,000	20

(ii) Bad

	Mark-up		Gross Margin
	%	£	%
Revenue	142.8	600,000	100
Cost of Sales	100	420,000	70
Gross Profit	42.8	180,000	30

(iii) Ugly

	Mark-up		Gross Margin
	%	£	%
Revenue	140	280,000	100
Cost of Sales	100	200,000	71
Gross Profit	40	80,000	29

Chapter 5: Discussion *Answers*

The answers provide some outline points for discussion.

A1 The statement of financial position and income statement are indeed complementary. Both are prepared from a trial balance. The statement of financial position takes the assets, liabilities and equity, and arranges them into a position statement. By contrast, the income statement takes the income and expenses and arranges them into a performance statement. The statement of financial position represents a snapshot of the business at a certain point in time. The income statement represents a period, usually a month or a year. The statement of financial position deals with liquidity, while the income statement deals with performance. Both together, therefore, provide a complementary picture of an organisation both at a particular point in time and over a period.

A5 True or false?

(a) *True.*
(b) *False.* Inventory and bank are indeed current assets, but trade payables are current liabilities.
(c) *False.* Total net assets are non-current assets (i.e., intangible assets and property, plant and equipment) and current assets less current liabilities, and non-current liabilities.
(d) *True.*
(e) *False.* An accrual is an expense owing; for example, an unpaid telephone bill. An amount prepaid (for example, rent paid in advance) is a prepayment.

Chapter 5: Numerical *Answers*

A1 Jane Bricker

Jane Bricker
Capital Employed as at 31 December 2013

Equity	£
Opening equity	5,000
Add Profit	12,000
	17,000
Less Drawings	7,000
Closing equity	10,000

A2 Alpa Shah

Alpa Shah
Net Assets as at 30 June 2014

ASSETS	£
Non-current Liabilities	100,000
Current Assets	50,000
Total Assets	150,000
Total Liabilities	
Current Liabilities	(30,000)
Non-current Liabilities	(20,000)
Total Liabilities	(50,000)
Net Assets	100,000

Chapter 6: Discussion *Answer*

The answer provides some outline points for discussion.

A1 A sole trader is where only one person owns the business. For example, a retailer, such as a baker, might be a sole trader. It is important for sole traders to prepare accounts for several reasons. First, as a basis for assessing their own financial performance. This indicates whether they can take out more wages (known as drawings), whether they can expand or pay their workers more. Second, the tax authorities need to be assured that the profit figure, which is the basis for assessing tax, has been properly prepared. And third, if any money has been borrowed, for example, from the bank, then the bankers will be interested in assessing performance.

Chapter 6: Numerical *Answers*

A1 **M. Anet**

M. Anet
Income Statement for the Year Ended 31 December 2013

	£	£
Revenue		25,000
Less Cost of Sales		
Purchases		15,000
Gross Profit		10,000
Less Expenses		
Electricity	1,500	
Wages	2,500	4,000
Net Profit		6,000

M. Anet
Statement of Financial Position as at 31 December 2013

	£
ASSETS	
Non-current Assets	
Property, Plant and Equipment	
Hotel	40,000
Van	10,000
Total non-current assets	50,000
Current Assets	
Bank	8,000
A. Brush (trade receivable)	400
Total current assets	8,400
Total Assets	58,400

A1 M. Anet (*continued*)

	£
LIABILITIES	
Current Liabilities	
A. Painter (trade payable)	(500)
Non-current Liabilities	–
Total Liabilities	(500)
Net Assets	57,900

	£
EQUITY	
Opening equity	51,900
Add Net profit	6,000
Closing equity	57,900

A2 P. Icasso

P. Icasso
Income Statement for the Year Ended 31 March 2014

	£	£
Revenue		35,000
Less Revenue returns		3,000
		32,000
Less Cost of Sales		
Purchases	25,000	
Less Purchase returns	4,000	21,000
Gross Profit		11,000
Less Expenses		
Electricity	1,000	
Advertising	800	1,800
Net Profit		9,200

P. Icasso
Statement of Financial Position as at 31 March 2014

	£
ASSETS	
Non-current Assets	
Property, Plant and Equipment	
Hotel	50,000
Van	8,000
Total non-current assets	58,000
Current Assets	
Bank	9,000
Shah (trade receivable)	1,250
Chan (trade receivable)	2,250
Total current assets	12,500
Total Assets	70,500

A2 P. Icasso (*continued*)

	£
LIABILITIES	
Current Liabilities	
Jones (trade payable)	(1,250)
Non-current Liabilities	–
Total Liabilities	(1,250)
Net Assets	69,250
	£
EQUITY	
Opening equity	60,050
Add Net profit	9,200
Closing equity	69,250

A3 R. Ubens

R. Ubens
Income Statement for the Year Ended 31 December 2013

	£	£	£
Revenue			88,000
Less Revenue returns			800
			87,200
Less Cost of Sales			
Opening inventory		3,600	
Add Purchases	66,000		
Less Purchase returns	1,200	64,800	
		68,400	
Less Closing inventory		4,000	64,400
Gross Profit			22,800
Less Expenses			
Electricity		1,500	
Advertising		300	
Printing and stationery		50	
Telephone		650	
Rent and rates		1,200	
Postage		150	3,850
Net Profit			18,950

R. Ubens
Statement of Financial Position as at 31 December 2013

	£
ASSETS	
Non-current Assets	
Property, Plant and Equipment	
Building	20,400
Motor van	3,500
Total non-current assets	23,900

A3 R. Ubens (*continued*)

	£
Current Assets	
Inventory	4,000
Bank	4,400
Trade receivables	2,600
Total current assets	11,000
LIABILITIES	34,900
Current Liabilities	
Trade Payables	(3,800)
Non-current Liabilities	–
Total Liabilities	(3,800)
Net Assets	31,100
	£
EQUITY	
Opening equity	19,950
Add Net profit	18,950
	38,900
Less Drawings	7,800
Closing equity	31,100

A4 **C. Onstable**

Income Statement (extracts)

Expenses

Rent	£2,880 (i.e., 12 × £240)
Insurance	£360 (£480 – £120)

Statement of Financial Position (extracts)

Current assets

Prepayments £840*

*(Rent 3 × £240 = £720; Insurance £120)

A5 **V. Gogh**

V. Gogh
Income Statement for the Year Ended 31 December 2013

	£	£	£
Revenue			40,000
Less Revenue returns			500
			39,500
Less *Cost of Sales*			
Opening inventory		5,500	
Purchases	25,000		
Less Purchases returns	450	24,550	
		30,050	
Less Closing inventory		9,000	21,050
Gross Profit			18,450

A5 V. Gogh (*continued*)

	£	£
Less *Expenses*		
Business rates	1,000	
Rent	400	
Telephone	450	
Insurance	750	
General expenses	150	
Electricity	700	
Wages	10,500	13,950
Net Profit		4,500

	£
ASSETS	
Non-Current assets	
Property, Plant and Equipment	
Shop	9,000
Motor car	8,500
Total non-current assets	17,500
Current Assets	
Inventory	9,000
Bank	1,300
Trade receivables	3,500
Prepayments	200
Total current assets	14,000
Total Assets	31,500
LIABILITIES	
Current Liabilities	
Trade payables	(1,500)
Accruals	(350)
Total current liabilities	(1,850)
Non-current Liabilities	(3,700)
Total Liabilities	(5,550)
Net Assets	25,950

	£
EQUITY	
Opening equity	34,350
Add Net profit	4,500
	38,850
Less Drawings	12,900
Closing equity	25,950

A6 L. Da Vinci

L. Da Vinci
Income Statement for the Year Ended 30 September 2013

	£	£	£
Revenue			105,000
Less Revenue returns			8,000
			97,000
Less Cost of Sales			
Opening inventory		6,500	
Add Purchases	70,000		
Less Purchase returns	1,800		
	68,200		
Add Carriage inwards	250	68,450	
		74,950	
Less Closing inventory		7,000	67,950
Gross Profit			29,050
Less Expenses			
Discounts allowed		300	
Electricity		2,025	
Telephone		500	
Wages		32,500	
Insurance		200	
Rent		1,000	
Business rates		1,000	37,525
Net loss			(8,475)

L. Da Vinci
Statement of Financial Position as at 30 September 2013

	£
ASSETS	
Non-current Assets	
Property, Plant and Equipment	
Business premises	18,000
Motor van	7,500
Computer	1,500
Total non-current assets	27,000
Current Assets	
Inventory	7,000
Trade receivables	12,000
Bank	1,800
Prepayments	275
Total current assets	21,075
Total Assets	48,075

A6 L. Da Vinci (*continued*)

	£
LIABILITIES	
Current Liabilities	
Trade payables	(13,000)
Accruals	(1,375)
Total current liabilities	(14,375)
Non-current Liabilities	(6,600)
Total Liabilities	(20,975)
Net assets	27,100

	£
EQUITY	
Opening equity	44,075
Less Net loss	8,475
	35,600
Less Drawings	8,500
Closing equity	27,100

A7 H. Ogarth

Income Statement for the year ended 31 December 2013 (extracts)

Expenses	£
Depreciation on buildings	10,000
Depreciation on machinery	3,000
Depreciation on motor van	2000
	15,000

Statement of Financial Position (extracts)	£ *Cost*	£ *Accumulated depreciation*	£ *Net book value*
Property, Plant and Equipment			
Buildings	100,000	(10,000)	90,000
Machinery	50,000	(3,000)	47,000
Motor van	20,000	(2,000)	18,000
	170,000	(15,000)	155,000

A15 GasCo (Peter Piper)

GasCo Account

		£			£
30.4.2013	Cash Book	400	31.3.2013	Gas	400
31.7.2013	Cash Book	500	30.6.2013	Gas	500
31.10.2013	Cash Book	600	30.9.2013	Gas	600
31.12.2013	Bal c/f	700	30.12.2013	Gas	700
		2,200			2,200
			1.1.2014 Bal b/f		700

A15 GasCo (Peter Piper) (*continued*)

Gas

		£			£
31.3.2013	Gasco	400	31.12.2013	Income Statement	2,200
30.6.2013	Gasco	500			
30.9.2013	Gasco	600			
31.12.2013	Gasco	700			
		2,200			2,200

Cash Book (extracts)

	£			£
31.12.2013 Bal c/f	1,500	30.4.2013	GasCo	400
		31.7.2013	GasCo	500
		31.10.2013	GasCo	600
	1,500			1,500
		1.1.2014	Bal b/f	1,500

A16 Property Plc

Property Plc

	£			£
31.1.2013 Cash Book	2,000	3.1.2013	Rent	2,000
28.2.2013 Cash Book	2,000	28.2.2013	Rent	2,000
1.3.2013 Cash Book	12,000	1.3.2013 to		
1.9.2013 Cash Book	12,000	31.12.2013	Rent	20,000
	28,000	Bal c/f 31.12.2013		4,000
1.1.2014 Bal b/f	4,000			28,000

Cash Book (extracts)

	£			£
31.12.2013 Bal c/f	28,000	31.1.2013	Property Plc	2,000
		28.2.2013	Property Plc	2,000
		1.3.2013	Property Plc	12,000
		1.9.2013	Property Plc	12,000
	28,000			28,000
		1.1.2014 Bal b/f		28,000

Rent Account

		£			£
31.1.13	Rent	2,000	31.12.2013	Income Statement	24,000
29.2.13	Rent	2,000			
1.3.13 to					
31.12.13	Rent	20,000			
		24,000			24,000

A17 Delivery Co

(a) Accounts

Property, Plant and Equipment (at cost)

	£		£
1.1.2011 Van A cash	50,000	31.12.2011 Disposals	50,000
1.1.2011 Van B cash	50,000	31.12.2011 Bal c/f	110,000
1.7.2011 Van C cash	60,000		
	160,000		160,000
1.1.2012 Bal b/f	110,000	30.6.2012 Disposals	50,000
		31.12.2012 Bal c/f	60,000
	110,000		110,000
1.1.2013 Bal b/f	60,000	31.12.2013 Bal c/f	60,000
	60,000		60,000
1.1.2014 Bal c/f	60,000		

Depreciation Account

	£		£
31.12.2011 Prov for Dep Van A	10,000	31.12.2011 Income Statement	26,000
31.12.2011 Prof for Dep Van B	10,000		
31.12.2011 Prov for Dep Van C	6,000		
	26,000		26,000
31.12.2012 Prov for Dep Van B	5,000	31.12.2012 Income Statement	17,000
31.12.2012 Prov for Dep Van C	12,000		
	17,000		17,000
31.12.2013 Prov for Dep Van C	12,000	31.12.2013 Income Statement	12,000
	12,000		12,000

Provision for Depreciation Account

	£		£
31.12.2011 Disposals	10,000	31.12.2011 Dep A/C	26,000
31.12.2011 Bal c/f	16,000		
	26,000		26,000
30.6.2012 Disposals Van B	15,000	1.1.2011 Bal b/f	16,000
31.12.2012 Bal c/f	18,000	31.12.2012 Dep A/C	17,000
	33,000		33,000
31.12.2013 Bal c/f	30,000	1.1.2013 Bal b/f	18,000
		31.12.2013 Dep A/C	12,000
	30,000		30,000
		1.1.2014 Bal b/f	30,000

A17 Delivery Co (*continued*)

Disposals Account: Property, Plant and Equipment

	£		£
31.12.2011 PPE Account	50,000	31.12.2011 Prov for Dep A/C	10,000
		31.12.2011 Cash	35,000
		31.12.2011 Loss to IS	5,000
	50,000		50,000
30.6.2012 PPE Account	50,000	30.6.2012 Prov for Dep A/C	15,000
		30.6.2012 Cash	20,000
		31.12.2012 Loss to IS	15,000
	50,000		50,000

IS = Income Statement

(b) Extracts from the income statement and statement of financial position.

(i) Year 1

Income Statement Extracts Year ending 31 December 2011

	£
Depreciation	(26,000)
Loss on Disposal of PPE	(5,000)
	(31,000)

Statement of Financial Position Extracts as at 31.12.2011

	Cost	Accumulated Depreciation	Net Book Value
	£	£	£
PPE	110,000	(16,000)	94,000

In the first year, when we sell lorry A, there was a loss on disposal of £5,000. This is the cost £50,000 less allocated depreciation of £10,000. We thus might have expected to receive £40,000, but instead we received £35,000. It should be stressed that this is a book loss.

(ii) Year 2

Income Statement Extracts Year ending 31 December 2012

	£
Depreciation	(17,000)
Loss on Disposal of PPE	(15,000)
	(32,000)

Statement of Financial Position Extracts as at 31.12.2012

	Cost	Accumulated Depreciation	Net Book Value
	£	£	£
PPE	60,000	(18,000)	42,000

In the second year, when we sell van B, there is a book loss on disposal of £15,000. This is because the cost £50,000 less accumulated depreciation of £15,000 is worth £35,000. However, instead of receiving this, we only received £20,000.

A17 Delivery Co (*continued*)

(iii) Year 3

Income Statement Extracts
Year ending 31 December 2013

	£
Depreciation	(12,000)
	(12,000)

Statement of Financial Position Extracts as at 31.12.2013

	Cost	Accumulated Depreciation	Net Book Value
	£	£	£
PPE	60,000	(30,000)	30,000

In this year, we do not have a disposal. Cost £60,000 less accumulated depreciation of £30,000 gives a net book value of £30,000.

Chapter 7: Discussion *Answers*

The answers provide some outline points for discussion.

A1 These three forms of business enterprise fit various niches. The sole trader form is good for very small businesses, such as a window cleaner, carpenter or small shopkeeper. There is a limited amount of equity needed and the individual can do most of the work. The accounting records needed for this type of business are not extensive. Partnerships are useful where the business is a little more complicated. They are suitable for situations where more than one person works together. There is then a need to sort out each partner's share of equity and profits. Companies are useful where a lot of equity is needed. Thus, they are particularly suitable for medium-sized and large businesses. They are particularly appropriate when raising money externally because of the concept of limited liability. As shareholders are only liable for the amount of their initial investments, they will be keener to invest as their potential losses will be limited.

A5 True or false?

(a) *False*. Drawings are withdrawal of equity by the partners; they are found in the partners' current accounts.
(b) *True*.
(c) *False*. Nominal value is the face value of the shares, normally the amount the shares were originally issued at. Market value is their stock-market value.
(d) *False*. Unsecured loans are secured on the general assets of the business. It is secured loans which are attached to specific assets.
(e) *False*. Reserves are accumulated profits and cannot directly be spent. Only cash can be spent.

Chapter 7: Numerical *Answers*

A1 Tom and Thumb

Tom and Thumb
Income Statement for Year Ended 31 December 2013

		£	£
Net Profit before Appropriation			100,000
Less Salaries:			
Tom		10,000	
Thumb		30,000	40,000
			60,000
Profits:			
Tom	3	45,000	
Thumb	1	15,000	60,000

Tom and Thumb
Statement of Financial Position as at 31 December 2013

Equity	£	£	£
	Tom	Thumb	
Capital Accounts	8,000	6,000	14,000
Current Accounts			
Opening balances	3,000	(1,000)	
Add:			
Salaries	10,000	30,000	
Profit share	45,000	15,000	
	58,000	44,000	
Less Drawings	25,000	30,000	
Closing balances	33,000	14,000	47,000
Total Partners' Funds			61,000

A2 J.Waite and P. Watcher

J. Waite and P. Watcher
Income Statement for the Year Ended 30 November 2013

	£	£
Revenue		350,000
Less Cost of Sales		
Opening inventory	9,000	
Add Purchases	245,000	
	254,000	
Less Closing inventory	15,000	239,000
Gross Profit		111,000

A2 J.Waite and P. Watcher *(continued)*

Less Expenses			
Depreciation:			
Land and buildings		2,000	
Motor vehicles		3,000	
Electricity		3,406	
Wages		14,870	
Rent and business rates		6,960	
Telephone		1,350	
Interest on loan		2,800	
Other expenses		5,500	39,886
Net Profit before Appropriation			71,114
Less Salaries:			
Waite		18,000	
Watcher		16,000	34,000
			37,114
Profits:			
Waite	3	22,268	
Watcher	2	14,846	37,114

J. Waite and P. Watcher
Statement of Financial Position as at 30 November 2013

ASSETS	£	£	£
Non-Current Assets	*Cost*	*Accumulated depreciation*	*Net book value*
Property, Plant and Equipment			
Land and Buildings	166,313	(2,000)	164,313
Motor vehicles	65,000	(3,000)	62,000
	231,313	(5,000)	226,313
Current Assets			
Inventory			15,000
Trade receivables			12,000
Bank			6,501
Total current assets			33,501
Total Assets			259,814
LIABILITIES			
Current Liabilities			
Trade payables			(18,500)
Accruals			(300)
Total current liabilities			(18,800)
Non-current Liabilities			(28,000)
Total Liabilities			(46,800)
Net Assets			213,014

A2 J.Waite and P. Watcher (*continued*)

	Waite	Watcher	
EQUITY	£	£	£
Capital Accounts	88,000	64,000	152,000
Current Accounts			
Opening Balances	(2,500)	12,000	
Add:			
Salaries	18,000	16,000	
Profit share	22,268	14,846	
	37,768	42,846	
Less Drawings	13,300	6,300	
Closing balances	24,468	36,546	61,014
Total Partners' Funds			213,014

A5 Red Devils Ltd

Red Devils Ltd
Statement of Comprehensive Income and Retained Earnings for the Year Ended 30 November 2013 (unpublished)

	£	£
Revenue	[*As per Accounts of Sole*	
Less Cost of Sales	*Trader or Partnership*]	
Gross Profit		150,000
Less Expenses		
Debenture interest	14,000	
General expenses	22,100	
Directors' fees	19,200	
Auditors' fees	7,500	62,800
Profit before Taxation		87,200
Taxation		(17,440)
Profit after Taxation		69,760
Dividends on ordinary shares	(25,000)	
Dividends on preference shares	(9,000)	
Transfer to general reserve[1]	(3,500)	(37,500)
Retained Profit		32,260

A5 Red Devils Ltd *(continued)*

1. The transfer to general reserve could also be done in the statement of financial position.

Red Devils Ltd
Statement of Financial Position as at 30 November 2013

			£
ASSETS			
Non-current Assets			
Property, Plant and Equipment			680,900
Current Assets			
Inventories			105,000
Trade receivables			4,700
Bank			5,300
Total current assets			115,000
Total Assets			795,900
LIABILITIES			
Current Liabilities			
Trade payables			(46,200)
Taxation			(17,440)
Auditors' fees			(7,500)
Debenture interest			(14,000)
Total current liabilities			(85,140)
Non-current Liabilities			(200,000)
Total Liabilities			(285,140)
Net Assets			510,760
Share Capital and Reserves		Authorised	Issued
Share Capital		£	£
Ordinary share capital (£1 each)		400,000	250,000
6% preference shares		150,000	150,000
		550,000	400,000
Reserves			
Capital reserves			
Share premium account			55,000
Other reserves			
Opening general reserve	11,000		
Transfer for year	3,500		
Closing general reserve		14,500	
Opening retained earnings	9,000		
Retained earnings for year	32,260		
Closing retained earnings		41,260	55,760
Total equity			510,760

A6 Superprofit Ltd

Superprofit Ltd
Statement of Comprehensive Income and Retained Profits (Income Statement)
for the Year Ended 31 December 2013

	£000	£000	£000
Revenue			351
Less *Cost of Sales*			
Opening inventories		23	
Add Purchases		182	
		205	
Less Closing inventories		26	179
Gross Profit			172
Less *Expenses*			
Depreciation:			
Land and buildings		18	
Motor vehicles		7	
Auditors' fees		2	
Loan interest		4	
Electricity		12	
Insurance		3	
Wages		24	
Light and heat		8	
Telephone		5	
Other expenses		26	109
Profit before Taxation			63
Taxation			(13)
Net Profit after Taxation			50
Ordinary dividends		(9)	
Preference dividends		(3)	(12)
Retained Profit			38

Superprofit Ltd
Statement of Financial Position as at 31 December 2013

	£000	£000	£000
	Cost	*Accumulated depreciation*	*Net book value*
ASSETS			
Non-current Assets			
Intangible Assets			
Patents			12

A6 Superprofit Ltd *(continued)*

Property, Plant and Equipment			
Land and buildings	378	(18)	360
Motor vehicles	47	(7)	40
	425	(25)	400
Total non-current assets			412
Current Assets			
Inventories			26
Trade receivables			18
Bank			31
Total current assets			75
Total Assets			487
LIABILITIES			
Current Liabilities			
Trade payables			(45)
Taxation payable			(13)
Other accruals (see note below)			(6)
			(64)
Non-current Liabilities			(32)
Total Liabilities			(96)
Net Assets			391
Share Capital and Reserves			
Share Capital		Authorised	Issued
Ordinary share capital		250	210
Preference share capital		50	25
		300	235
Reserves			
Capital reserves			
Share premium account		40	
Other reserves			
Revaluation reserve		35	
General reserve		15	
Opening retained earnings	28		
Retained earnings for year	38		
Closing retained earnings		66	156
Total Equity			391

Note: Loan interest (£4) and auditors' fees (£2)

A9 Stock High plc

Stock High plc
Income Statement for the Year Ended 31 March 2014

	Notes	£000
Revenue		1,250
Cost of Sales		(400)
Gross Profit		850
Administrative expenses		(216)
Distribution expenses		(230)
Profit before Taxation		404
Taxation		(94)
Profit for year		310

Stock High plc
Statement of Financial Position as at 31 March 2014

	Notes	£000
ASSETS		
Non-current Assets		
Property, Plant and Equipment	1	814
Intangible Assets	2	50
Total non-current assets		864
Current Assets		
Inventories		20
Trade receivables		100
Bank		22
Total current assets		142
Total Assets		1,006
LIABILITIES		
Current Liabilities	3	(20)
Non-current Liabilities		(60)
Total Liabilities		(80)
Net Assets		926
EQUITY		£000
Capital and Reserves	4	750
Called-up share capital	5	550
Share premium account		25
Other reserves	6	55
Retained earnings		296
Total Equity		926

A9 Stock High plc (*continued*)

Stock High plc
Statement of Changes in Equity as at 31 March 2014

	£000
Balance as at 1 April 2013	36
Retained earnings for year	310
Less: Dividends	(50)
Balance as at 31 March 2014	296

Notes:

1. Property, Plant and Equipment

	£000 *Cost*	£000 *Accumulated depreciation*	£000 *Net book value*
Land and buildings	800	(156)	644
Motor vehicles	400	(230)	170
	1,200	(386)	814

2. Intangible Assets

Patents	50
	50

3. Current Liabilities

Trade payables	12
Taxation	8
	20

4. Authorised Share Capital

Ordinary share capital (£1)	600
Preference share capital (£1)	150
	750

5. Called-up Share Capital

Ordinary share capital	450
Preference share capital	100
	550

6. Other Reserves

Revaluation reserve	30
General reserve	25
	55

Chapter 8: Discussion *Answers*

The answers provide some outline points for discussion.

A1 Cash is king because it is central to the operations of a business. Unless you generate cash, you cannot pay employees, suppliers or expenses, or buy new property, plant and equipment. The end result of a lack of cash is the closure of a business. Cash is also objective. There is very little subjectivity involved in estimating cash. Either you have cash or you don't! With profits, however, there is much more subjectivity. Often one can alter the accounting policies of a business, for example, use a different rate of depreciation, and thus alter the amount of profit. It is not as easy to manipulate cash.

A5 True or false?

(a) *False.* It is true that both items are non-cash flow items and that depreciation is added back to operating profit. However, profit from the sale of property, plant and equipment is deducted from operating profit.
(b) *False.* Inventory and trade receivables are items of working capital. However, property, plant and equipment are not.
(c) *True.*
(d) *True.*
(e) *False.* It is much more commonly used than the direct method.

Chapter 8: Numerical *Answers*

A1 Bingo

Included in income statement	Included in statement of cash flows
(a) Not in full IFRS, but in IFRS for SMEs	No
(b) No	Yes, financing
(c) Yes	No
(d) Yes	Yes, Cash flows from operating activities
(e) No	Yes, Cash flows from investing activities
(f) No	Yes, Cash flows from investing activities
(g) No	Yes, Cash flows from investing activities
(h) Yes, part of charge for year	No
(i) No	Yes, Cash flows from financing activities
(j) Yes	Yes, Cash flows from investing activities

A2 Peter Piper

Peter Piper
Statement of Cash Flows for the Year Ended 31 December 2013

	£	£
Cash Flows From Operating Activities		
Receipts from customers	250,000	
Payments to suppliers	(175,000)	
Payments to employees	(55,000)	
Expenses	(10,000)	10,000
Cash Flows from Investing Activities		
Interest received	1,150	
Sale of property	25,000	
Purchase of office equipment	(15,000)	11,150
Cash Flows from Financing Activities		
Loan repaid	(25,000)	
Interest paid	(350)	(25,350)
Decrease in Cash		(4,200)

A4 D. Rink

D. Rink
Reconciliation of Operating Profit to Operating Cash Flow
Year Ended 31 December 2013

	£	£
Operating Profit		95,000
Add:		
Decrease in inventories	3,000	
Decrease in prepayments	1,500	
Increase in trade payables	300	
Increase in accruals	250	
Depreciation	8,000	13,050
Deduct:		
Increase in trade receivables	(1,150)	
Profit on sale of property, plant and equipment	(3,500)	(4,650)
Net Cash Inflow from Operating Activities		103,400

A6 Grow Hire Ltd

Grow Hire Ltd
Statement of Cash Flows for the Year Ended 31 December 2013

	£000	£000
Net Profit before Taxation		112,000
Add:		
Interest paid	6,500	
Decrease in inventories	2,000	
Decrease in trade receivables	7,000	
Increase in accruals	1,000	
Depreciation (£44,000 – £28,000)	16,000	32,500
Deduct:		
Taxation paid	(33,600)	
Decrease in trade payables	(25,000)	
Interest received	(13,000)	(71,600)
Cash Flows from Operating Activities		72,900
Cash Flows from Investing Activities		
Patents purchased	(34,200)	
Property, plant and equipment purchased	(20,000)	
Interest received	13,000	(41,200)
Cash Flows from Financing Activities		
Equity dividends paid	(35,800)	
Increase in non-current liabilities	12,000	
Increase in share capital	1,600	
Interest paid	(6,500)	(28,700)
Increase in Cash		3,000

	£000
Opening Cash	7,000
Increase in cash	3,000
Closing Cash	10,000

A8 Expenso plc

Expenso plc
Statement of Cash Flows for the Year Ended 30 September 2013

Cash Flows from Operating Activities	£000	£000
Net profit before Taxation		10,017
Add:		
Interest paid	85	
Increase in trade payables	400	
Depreciation	2,500	2,985
Deduct:		
Taxation paid	(4,005)	
Interest received	(868)	
Decrease in accruals	(50)	
Increase in inventories	(3,600)	
Increase in trade receivables	(1,300)	(9,823)
Cash Flows from Operating Activities		3,179
Cash Flows from Investing Activities		
Interest received	868	
Land and buildings purchased	(6,000)	
Plant and machinery purchased	(5,000)	
Patents purchased	(500)	(10,632)
Cash Flows from Financing Activities		
Equity dividends paid	(4,105)	
Increase in non-current liabilities	405	
Increase in share capital	3,938	
Interest paid	(85)	153
Decrease in Cash		(7,300)
		£000
Opening Cash		8,800
Decrease in cash		(7,300)
Closing Cash		1,500

Note: We needed to calculate taxation paid (in £000s).

	Opening accrual	+	Income statement	−	Amount paid	=	Closing accrual
Taxation	£4,200	+	£3,005	−	£4,005	=	£3,200

Or alternatively,

Taxation paid

	£		£
Paid	4,005	Bal. b/f	4,200
Bal. c/f	3,200	Income statement	3,005
	7,205		7,205

A9 Petrel

We need to reconcile our bank statement that shows £500 with the bank balance of £1,690.

(c) **Bank Reconciliation Statement for March**

	£	£
Bank statement closing balance		1,690
Add back:		
Items on bank statement, but not in bank account		
Direct debit	360	
Standing order	600	960
		2,650
Deduct:		
Items on bank account but not on bank statement		
Deduct Cheques not yet debited:	£	
28360 Baggott	600	
28361 Corden	750	
28350 Milligan	650	(2,000)
		650
Add Cheques not yet credited:		
Burke	200	
Howegate	650	850
Bank account closing balance		1,500

Chapter 9: Discussion *Answers*

The answers provide some outline points for discussion.

A1 Ratio analysis is simply the distillation of the figures in the accounts into certain key ratios so that a user can more easily interpret a company's performance. Ratio analysis is also known as financial statement analysis or the interpretation of accounts. There are traditionally thought to be six main types of ratios:

(a) *Profitability ratios*: Generally derived from the income statement, they seek to determine how profitable the business has been. Main ratios: return on capital employed, gross profit, net profit.
(b) *Efficiency ratios*: Compare the income statement to the statement of financial position figures. Try to work out how efficiently the company is utilising its assets and liabilities. Main ratios: trade receivables collection period, trade payables collection period, inventory turnover and asset turnover ratio.
(c) *Liquidity*: Assess the short-term cash position of the company. They are derived from the statement of financial position. Main ratios: current ratio and quick ratio.
(d) *Gearing*: Looks at the relationship between the owners' capital and the borrowed capital. This ratio is derived from the statement of financial position.
(e) *Cash flow*: This ratio seeks to measure how the company's cash inflows and cash outflows compare. The cash flow ratio, unlike the other ratios, is derived from the statement of cash flows.

(f) *Investment ratios*: These ratios are used by investors to determine how well their shares are performing. They generally compare share price with dividend or earnings information. The five main ratios are: dividend yield, dividend cover, earnings per share, price/earnings ratio and interest cover.

A5 True or false?

(a) *True.*

(b) *False*. More usually: Net profit $= \dfrac{\text{Net profit before taxation}}{\text{Revenue}}$

(c) *False*. Current ratio $= \dfrac{\text{Current assets}}{\text{Current liabilities}}$. The ratio given was the quick ratio.

(d) *True.*

(e) *False*. This is actually the property, plant and equipment turnover ratio.

Asset turnover ratio $= \dfrac{\text{Revenue}}{\text{Total assets}}$

(f) *False*. Dividend yield $= \dfrac{\text{Dividend per ordinary share}}{\text{Share price}}$

(g) *True.*

Chapter 9: Numerical *Answers*

A1 John Parry

The ratios below are calculated in £s.

(a) Return on capital employed $= \dfrac{\text{Net profit*}}{\text{Capital employed**}}$

$$= \frac{50{,}000}{(300{,}000 + 500{,}000) \div 2} = 12.5\%$$

*For sole traders, tax is not an issue.
**We take average for year.

(b) Gross profit ratio $= \dfrac{\text{Gross profit}}{\text{Revenue}} = \dfrac{80{,}000}{150{,}000} = 53.3\%$

(c) Net profit ratio $= \dfrac{\text{Net profit*}}{\text{Revenue}} = \dfrac{50{,}000}{150{,}000} = 33.3\%$

*For sole traders, tax is not an issue

(d) Trade receivables collection period $= \dfrac{\text{Average trade receivables}}{\text{Credit sales per day}}$

$$= \frac{(18{,}000 + 19{,}000) \div 2}{150{,}000 \div 365} = 45 \text{ days}$$

(e) Trade payables collection period $= \dfrac{\text{Average trade payables}}{\text{Credit purchases per day}}$

$$= \frac{(9{,}000 + 10{,}000) \div 2}{75{,}000 \div 365} = 46 \text{ days}$$

A1 John Parry (*continued*)

(f) Inventory turnover ratio $= \dfrac{\text{Cost of sales}}{\text{Average inventories}}$

$= \dfrac{70{,}000}{(25{,}000 + 30{,}000) \div 2} = 2.5 \text{ times}$

(g) Asset turnover ratio $= \dfrac{\text{Revenue}}{\text{Average total assets}}$

$= \dfrac{150{,}000}{(50{,}000 + 60{,}000) \div 2} = 2.7 \text{ times}$

A2 Henry Mellett

£

(a) Current ratio $= \dfrac{\text{Current assets}}{\text{Current liabilities}} = \dfrac{31{,}903}{14{,}836} = 2.2 \text{ times}$

(b) Quick ratio $= \dfrac{\text{Current assets–inventories}}{\text{Current liabilities}} = \dfrac{31{,}903 - 18{,}213}{14{,}836} = 0.9 \text{ times}$

(c) Gearing ratio $= \dfrac{\text{Long-term borrowings}}{\text{Total long-term capital*}} = \dfrac{30{,}000}{150{,}000 + 30{,}000} = 16.7\%$

*Remember, total net assets are equivalent to shareholders' funds.

A3 Jane Edwards Ltd

	Cash inflows	Cash outflows
	£	£
Customers	125,000	
Issue of shares	29,000	
Sale of property, plant and equipment	35,000	
Employees		18,300
Suppliers		9,250
Buy back loan		8,000
Dividends		8,000
Taxation		16,000
Purchase of property, plant and equipment		80,000
	189,000	139,550

Cash flow ratio $= \dfrac{\text{Total cash inflows}}{\text{Total cash outflows}} = \dfrac{£189{,}000}{£139{,}550} = 1.35$

A4 Clatworthy plc

£000*

(a) Dividend yield $= \dfrac{\text{Dividend per ordinary share}}{\text{Share price (in £s)}} = \dfrac{40 \div 500}{1.25} = 6.4\%$

(b) Dividend cover $= \dfrac{\text{Profit after tax and preference dividends}}{\text{Ordinary dividends}} = \dfrac{580}{40} = 14.5 \text{ times}$

(c) Earnings per share $= \dfrac{\text{Profit after tax and preference dividends}}{\text{Number of ordinary shares}} = \dfrac{580}{500} = £1.16$

A4 Clatworthy plc (*continued*)

(d) Price/earnings ratio $= \dfrac{\text{Share price}}{\text{Earnings per share}} = \dfrac{1.25}{1.16} = 1.08$

*Except for price/earnings ratio.

(e) Interest cover $= \dfrac{\text{Profit before tax and loan interest}}{\text{Loan interest}} = \dfrac{790}{40} = 19.8$ times

A7 Anteater plc

The ratios below are calculated from the accounts. There is insufficient information for the average return on capital employed and the efficiency ratios. The closing year figure is, therefore, taken from the balance sheet. This is indicated by a single asterisk. Except where indicated, calculations are in £000s.

	Ratio	*Calculations (£000s)*	
(a) Profitability ratios			
Return on capital employed	Net profit before tax and loan interest/ Average capital employed*	(100 + 3)/500* * = 300 + 20 + 10 + 70 + 100	= 20.6%
Gross profit ratio	Gross profit/Revenue	250/1,000	= 25%
Net profit ratio	Net profit before tax/Revenue	100/1,000	= 10%
(b) Efficiency ratios			
Trade receivables collection period	Average trade receivables*/ Credit sales per day	50/(1,000 ÷ 365)	= 18.3 days
Trade payables collection period	Average trade payables*/ Credit purchases per day (cost of sales taken)	40/(750 ÷ 365)	= 19.5 days
Inventory turnover ratio	Cost of sales/Average inventories*	750/40 = 18.8 times	
Asset turnover ratio	Revenue/Average total assets*	1,000/(420 + 120)	= 1.8 times
(c) Liquidity ratios			
Current ratio	Current assets/Current liabilities	120/40 = 3.0	
Quick ratio	Current assets − inventories/ Current liabilities	(120 − 40)/40	= 2.0
(d) Gearing ratio			
Gearing	Long-term borrowings/Total long-term capital	(100 + 20)/ (400 + 100)	= 24%
(e) Investment ratios			
Dividend yield	Dividend per ordinary share/ Share price (in £s)	(40 ÷ 300)/2.00	= 6.7%
Dividend cover	Profit after tax and preference dividends/Ordinary dividends	70/40	= 1.75
Earnings per share	Profit after tax and preference dividends/Number of ordinary shares	70/300	= 23.3p
Price/earnings ratio **Calculation in pence.	Share price/Earnings per share**	200/23.3	= 8.6
Interest cover	Profit before tax and loan interest/ Loan interest	103/3	= 34.3

Chapter 10: Discussion *Answers*

The answers provide some outline points for discussion.

A1 The role of the three is complementary.

(a) The directors run the business and prepare the accounts. They invest their labour and are rewarded, for example, by salaries and bonuses.

(b) The shareholders own the business and make decisions partly on the basis of the accounts they receive. They invest their equity and are rewarded, hopefully, by dividends and an increase in share price.

(c) The auditors check that the directors have prepared accounts that provide a 'true and fair' view of the company's performance over the year. They invest their labour and are rewarded by the auditors' fees. They are independent of the directors and, in theory, are responsible to the shareholders.

A2

> ***'The objective of general purpose financial reporting is to provide financial information about the reporting entity that is useful to existing and potential investors, lenders and other creditors in making decisions about providing resources to the entity. Those decisions involve buying, selling or holding equity and debt instruments, and providing or settling loans and other forms of credit.'***

International Accounting Standards Board (2010), *The Conceptual Framework for Financial Reporting*.

In other words, financial accounting provides financial information (such as assets, liabilities, equity, expenses and income) to users (such as shareholders). This is useful because they can assess how well the managers run the company. On the basis of their assessment of the stewardship of management, they can make business decisions; for example, shareholders can decide whether or not to keep or sell their shares. Financial accounting is central to any understanding of business. It provides the basic language for assessing a business's performance. Unless we understand financial accounting, it is difficult to see how we can truly understand business. It would be like trying to drive a car without taking driving lessons. For non-specialists, a knowledge of financial accounting will help them to operate effectively in a business world.

This appears reasonable as far as it goes. However, critics argue that the decision-making model has several flaws. First, it assumes that one set of financial statements is appropriate for all users. Second, what is appropriate for shareholders is assumed to be appropriate for all users. Third, the focus on decision making neglects other important aspects such as stewardship. And finally, and most radically, the decision-making model focuses on financial information, thus ignoring non-financial aspects such as the environment.

Chapter 11: Discussion *Answers*

The answers provide some outline points for discussion.

A1 An accounting measurement system is a method of determining the monetary amounts in the accounts. Different measurement systems will result in different valuations for net assets. This in turn will cause profit to be different. The measurement of assets and the determination of profit is key to the preparation of accounts. However, different accounting measurement systems can cause wide variation in both net assets and net profit. Thus, it is probably not unreasonable to call accounting measurement systems the skeleton that underpins the accounting body. The accounting measurement systems will determine the basic parameters of the accounting results.

A2 Historical cost is still widely used internationally. Indeed, it is certainly much more popular than the alternative measurement bases. However, historical cost has been widely criticised. In particular, there is concern that it fails to reflect changing asset values resulting from inflation or technological change. There has, therefore, been extensive debate over alternative measurement systems, most obviously by the Financial Accounting Standards Board in the US, the Accounting Standards Board in the UK and the International Accounting Standards Board. All these bodies have wrestled with alternative measurement systems, seeing them as essential to framing a successful conceptual theory for accounting.

So far, there has been little agreement on an alternative system. The first reason is that historical cost is widely used, easy to understand and objective. Users are, therefore, reluctant to abandon it. This is particularly true when the alternatives are often not easy to understand or use and are often subjective. In addition, the main incentive to change was the high level of inflation in the Western world, particularly in the UK and the US in the 1970s. However, more recently inflation rates have fallen and with them interest in alternatives to historical cost.

Chapter 12: Discussion *Answers*

The answers provide some outline points for discussion.

A1 The annual report plays a central role in corporate governance. Essentially, it is a key mechanism by which the directors report to the shareholders and other users on their stewardship of the company. The directors prepare the financial statements, which provide information on income and expenses, assets, liabilities and equity, so that shareholders can monitor the activities of the directors. This monitoring allows the shareholders to see that the managers are not abusing their position; for example, by paying themselves great salaries at the expense of the shareholders. In order to ensure that the accounts are true and fair, the auditors audit the financial statements. These financial statements will be included in an annual report along with other financial and non-financial information. The annual report itself is often prepared by design consultants.

A2 These three roles have the following functions:

(i) *Stewardship and accountability*
The directors provide information to the shareholders so that they can monitor the directors' activities. This has grown out of ideas of accountability (i.e., the control and safeguarding of corporate assets). The idea has been extended to corporate governance; in particular, the monitoring of directors' remuneration. The IASB takes the view that stewardship is a subset of decision making. However, other interested parties see it as an objective in its own right.

(ii) *Decision making*
The decision-making aim is 'to communicate economic measures of, and information about, the resources and performance of the reporting entity useful to those having reasonable rights to such information' (*The Corporate Report*, 1975). The aim, therefore, in essence, is to provide users, such as shareholders, with information so that they can make decisions, such as buying or selling shares.

(iii) *Public relations*
The public relations objective of the annual report is simply recognising the incentives that management has to use the annual report to show the results in a good light. It is often associated with the idea of the annual report as a marketing tool. The clash between these three objectives is that while the first two (accountability and decision making) are based on the idea of a true and fair view, public relations is not about truth and fairness. Public relations attempts to depart from truth and fairness to show the company in the best possible light.

Chapter 13: Discussion *Answers*

The answers provide some outline points for discussion.

A1 Creative accounting is using the flexibility within accounting to manage the measurement and presentation of the accounts so that they serve the interests of the managers. These interests may be to smooth profits, to increase profits or reduce gearing. The essential point of creative accounting is that it serves the interests of the preparers not the users. In particular, creative accounting may clash with the basic requirement that the financial statements should give a true and fair view of the company's financial position and financial performance. This is because creative accounting puts the interests of preparers first. The regulatory framework specifies that accounting should be unbiased and neutral and should faithfully represent the economic reality of the company. Accounting cannot do this if it is managed creatively for the benefit of the preparers.

A2 Creative accounting can exist, and indeed thrive, particularly in countries such as the UK where accounting is valued for its flexibility. The basic idea is that accounting professionals should be free to choose accounting policies which give a true and fair view. In other words, accounting should not be governed by a set of inflexible and constraining rules, as are found in some other countries, such as Germany.

However, the flexibility that allows accounting to present a 'true and fair view' is also the same flexibility that enables accounting to be used creatively. Indeed, it is all a matter of degree and intention. Creative accounting is when accounting policies are chosen to serve the managers' interests rather than to give a 'true and fair' view. However, in reality, it is extremely difficult for outsiders to distinguish between the two. This is especially true as there is generally more than one possible 'true and fair' view.

Chapter 14: Discussion *Answers*

The answers provide some outline points for discussion. However, they should not be taken as exhaustive or prescriptive. International accounting is a topic that is very fluid and open to interpretation.

A2 There are potentially eight divergent forces: objectives, users, sources of finance, regulation, taxation, the accounting profession, spheres of influence and culture. In their own way, they are all important. They are also interrelated. It is, therefore, very difficult to sort out the most important. Different individuals will legitimately have different views.

In my opinion, the most important divergent forces are the sources of finance, regulation, taxation and the accounting profession. This is because:

- Sources of finance provide the basic funding for industry (either debt or equity finance); they thus orientate the accounting system towards a statement of financial position or an income statement focus.
- Regulation determines the backbone of the accounting system, setting out the detailed rules and regulations.
- Taxation is one of the main drivers of financial accounting in some countries, such as Germany and France. Companies comply with taxation requirements which then dictate financial accounting practices.
- The accounting profession because qualified accountants provide the judgement and interpretation in countries such as the UK and US, which enable the achievement of a 'true and fair' view.

However, it must be stressed that this is just my opinion. Other viewpoints are equally justifiable.

A3 These two systems are distinguishable in many ways. However, globalisation and the introduction of IFRS for listed companies in many countries, including European countries, has considerably narrowed the differences in recent years. In essence, the Anglo-American system is followed by countries such as the US and the UK, and is often termed a 'micro' system. By contrast the continental accounting system is followed by countries such as France and Germany and is often termed a 'macro' system. The main differences are as follows:

- **Objectives.** The Anglo-American system favours the true and fair/present fairly objective of financial reporting designed to show economic reality. The continental system is more about planning and control.
- **Users.** In the Anglo-American model, these are primarily shareholders; in the continental model, they are the government, the banks and the tax authorities.

- **Sources of Finance.** In the Anglo-American model, shareholders provide risk capital; whereas in the continental model, banks provide loan capital.
- **Regulation.** In the Anglo-American model, standards are very important. In addition, in the UK, the Companies Acts provide detailed regulation, while in the US listed companies supply a detailed 10-K to the Securities Exchange Commission (an independent regulatory commission). In the continental model, detailed regulation generally comes from the government. In European countries, International Financial Reporting Standards are now increasingly important in the UK, France and Germany.
- **Taxation.** In the Anglo-American model, taxation is not an important driver of the financial accounts. In the continental model, taxation drives financial accounting.
- **Accounting Profession.** This is strong and influential in the Anglo-American model, comparatively weak and uninfluential in the continental model.

Index